The cliffs at Point Loma are a great place to watch the sunset. See chapter 7. © Richard Cummins/The Viesti Collection.

The 18th-century Mission Basilica San Diego de Alcala was the first in the chain of 21 missions established by Spanish missionary Junípero Serra. See chapter 7. *Photo above © David Olsen/Tony Stone Images; photo below © Robert Landau Photography.*

The Old Town section of San Diego is a reminder of the 19th-century days when the city was a Mexican outpost. See the walking tour in chapter 8. © Kelly/Mooney Photography.

Seaport Village is a waterfront shopping and dining complex designed to look like a small Cape Cod community. See chapter 9. © James Lemass/Folio, Inc.

The bullfights of Tijuana and the cantinas found in every town throughout Baja are two reasons to explore south of the border. Many appealing Mexican towns are within easy driving distance of San Diego. See chapter 11. *Photos above and below © Nik Wheeler Photography.*

After the spring rains, thousands of wildflowers burst into bloom in Anza-Borrego Desert State Park, 90 miles northeast of San Diego. See chapter 11. © Christopher Talbot Frank Photography.

A New Star-Rating System & Other Exciting News from Frommer's!

In our continuing effort to publish the savviest, most up-to-date, and most appealing travel guides available, we've added some great new features.

Frommer's guides now include a new **star-rating system.** Every hotel, restaurant, and attraction is rated from 0 to 3 stars to help you set priorities and organize your time.

We've also added **seven brand-new features** that point you to the great deals, in-the-know advice, and unique experiences that separate travelers from tourists. Throughout the guide, look for:

Finds	Special finds—those places only insiders know about
Fun Fact	Fun facts—details that make travelers more informed and their trips more fun
Kids	Best bets for kids—advice for the whole family
Moments	Special moments—those experiences that memories are made of
Overrated	Places or experiences not worth your time or money
Tips	Insider tips—some great ways to save time and money
Value	Great values—where to get the best deals

We've also added a **"What's New"** section in every guide—a timely crash course in what's hot and what's not in every destination we cover.

Here's what the critics say about Frommer's:

"Amazingly easy to use. Very portable, very complete."

—*Booklist*

"Detailed, accurate, and easy-to-read information for all price ranges."
—*Glamour Magazine*

"Hotel information is close to encyclopedic."
—*Des Moines Sunday Register*

"Frommer's Guides have a way of giving you a real feel for a place."
—*Knight Ridder Newspapers*

Other Great Guides for Your Trip:

Frommer's California
Frommer's California from $70 a Day
Frommer's Los Angeles
Frommer's Portable Disneyland
The Unofficial Guide to California with Kids
The Unofficial Guide to Disneyland

Frommer's®

San Diego

2003

by Stephanie Avnet Yates

Wiley Publishing, Inc.

About the Author

A native of Los Angeles and an avid traveler, antiques hound, and pop-history enthusiast, **Stephanie Avnet Yates** believes that California is best seen from behind the wheel of a little red convertible. In addition to contributing to travel websites and magazines, Stephanie writes and/or edits several regional guidebooks, cowrites *Frommer's California,* and is the author of *Frommer's Wonderful Weekends from Los Angeles.* She confesses to a special fondness for San Diego, having once attended UCSD. Online, Stephanie can be reached directly at *savvy_girl@hotmail.com.*

Published by:

Wiley Publishing, Inc.

909 Third Ave.
New York, NY 10022

ISBN 0-7645-6673-3
ISSN 1047-787X

Editor: Joel Enos
Production Editor: Suzanna R. Thompson
Photo Editor: Richard Fox
Cartographer: John Decamillis
Production by Wiley Indianapolis Composition Services

Front cover photo: Family walking past a lily pond in Balboa Park
Back cover photo: The Embarcadero marina

For information on our other products and services or to obtain technical support, please contact our Customer Care Department within the U.S. at 800-762-2974, outside the U.S. at 317-572-3993 or fax 317-572-4002.

Wiley also publishes its books in a variety of electronic formats. Some content that appears in print may not be available in electronic formats.

Manufactured in the United States of America

5 4 3 2 1

Contents

List of Maps   viii

What's New in San Diego   1

1 The Best of San Diego   4

1 Frommer's Favorite San Diego
Experiences 4

2 Best Hotel Bets 6

3 Best Dining Bets 8
*Site Seeing: San Diego
on the Web* 9

2 Planning Your Trip to San Diego   11

1 Visitor Information 11

2 Money 11
Red Alert Checklist 12
*What Things Cost in
San Diego* 13

3 When to Go 14
San Diego Calendar of Events ..14

4 Health & Insurance 20

5 Tips for Travelers with Special
Needs 22

6 Getting There 25
*What You Can Carry On—
And What You Can't* 27
Flying with Film & Video 29

7 Package Deals 30

8 Planning Your Trip Online 31
*Frommers.com: The Complete
Travel Resource* 32

9 Recommended Reading 34

3 For International Visitors   36

1 Preparing for Your Trip 36

2 Getting to the
United States 42

3 Getting Around the
United States 42
*Fast Facts: For the International
Traveler* 43

4 Getting to Know San Diego   48

1 Orientation 48
The Neighborhoods in Brief 51
*Off the Beaten Path:
Golden Hill* 55

2 Getting Around 55
Fast Facts: San Diego 62

5 Where to Stay   65

1 Downtown 67

2 Hillcrest/Uptown 73

3 Old Town & Mission Valley 76
*Family-Friendly
Accommodations* 78

4 Mission Bay & the Beaches 79
5 La Jolla 84
6 Coronado 89

*A Century of Intrigue: Scenes from
the Hotel del Coronado* 92
7 Near the Airport 93

6 Where to Dine   94

1 Restaurants by Cuisine 95
2 Downtown 97
3 Hillcrest/Uptown 102
4 Old Town 106
Family-Friendly Restaurants . . .109

5 Mission Bay & the Beaches . . .110
6 La Jolla 114
7 Coronado 120
8 Only in San Diego 123

7 What to See & Do   125

Suggested Itineraries 125
1 The Three Major Animal Parks .126
Panda-monium 129
2 San Diego's Beaches 131
*Beach Snack Staples: Quick
(& Cheap) Taco Stands* 134
3 Attractions in Balboa Park 135

4 More Attractions 141
5 Free of Charge & Full of Fun . .149
6 Especially for Kids 151
7 Special-Interest Sightseeing . . .152
8 Organized Tours 154
9 Outdoor Pursuits 157
10 Spectator Sports 165

8 City Strolls   168

*Walking Tour 1: The Gaslamp
Quarter* 168
*Walking Tour 2:
The Embarcadero* 174

Walking Tour 3: Old Town 177
Walking Tour 4: Balboa Park 181

9 Shopping   187

1 The Shopping Scene 187
2 The Top Shopping Streets
& Neighborhoods 187

3 Shopping A to Z 194

10 San Diego After Dark   200

1 The Performing Arts 200
2 The Club & Music Scene 202
3 The Bar & Coffeehouse Scene .204
*Pitcher This: San Diego's
Microbreweries* 205

4 Gay & Lesbian Nightlife 206
5 More Entertainment 207
6 Only in San Diego 208
7 Late-Night Bites 208

11 Side Trips from San Diego   209

1 North County Beach Towns:
  Spots to Surf & Sun 209
2 North County Inland:
  From Rancho Santa Fe
  to Palomar Mountain 221
3 Temecula: Touring the Wineries 225
4 Disneyland & Other Anaheim
  Area Attractions 231
5 Julian: Apple Pies & More 246
6 Anza-Borrego Desert
  State Park 252
7 Tijuana: Going South
  of the Border 257
8 Baja California: Exploring
  More of Mexico 267

Appendix: Useful Toll-Free Numbers & Websites   281

Index   284

General Index 284
Accommodations Index 297
Restaurant Index 298

List of Maps

San Diego Area at a Glance   5

San Diego Neighborhoods   52

San Diego Trolley System   60

Downtown San Diego
Accommodations   69

Hillcrest/Uptown
Accommodations   75

Accommodations in & Around
Old Town   77

Accommodations in Mission Bay
& the Beaches   81

La Jolla Accommodations   85

Coronado Accommodations   91

Downtown San Diego Dining   99

Hillcrest/Uptown Dining   103

Old Town Dining   107

Dining in Mission Bay
& the Beaches   111

La Jolla Dining   115

Coronado Dining   121

San Diego Area Attractions   127

San Diego Beaches   133

Balboa Park   137

Downtown San Diego
Attractions   143

Old Town Attractions   145

La Jolla Attractions   147

Outdoor Pursuits in the San Diego
Area   159

Walking Tour: The Gaslamp Quarter
169

Walking Tour: The Embarcadero
175

Walking Tour: Old Town   179

Walking Tour: Balboa Park   183

Downtown San Diego Shopping
188

Hillcrest/Uptown Shopping   190

Shopping in Mission Bay
& the Beaches   191

La Jolla Shopping   193

Northern San Diego County   211

Temecula   227

Getting Around the Disneyland
Resort   233

Tijuana   259

Upper Baja California   269

An Invitation to the Reader

In researching this book, we discovered many wonderful places—hotels, restaurants, shops, and more. We're sure you'll find others. Please tell us about them, so we can share the information with your fellow travelers in upcoming editions. If you were disappointed with a recommendation, we'd love to know that, too. Please write to:

Frommer's San Diego 2003
Wiley Publishing, Inc. • 909 Third Ave. • New York, NY 10022

An Additional Note

Please be advised that travel information is subject to change at any time—and this is especially true of prices. We therefore suggest that you write or call ahead for confirmation when making your travel plans. The authors, editors, and publisher cannot be held responsible for the experiences of readers while traveling. Your safety is important to us, however, so we encourage you to stay alert and be aware of your surroundings. Keep a close eye on cameras, purses, and wallets, all favorite targets of thieves and pickpockets.

New! Frommer's Star Ratings & Icons

Every hotel, restaurant, and attraction listing in this guide has been ranked for quality, value, service, amenities, and special features using a star-rating scale. In country, state, and regional guides, we also rate towns and regions to help you narrow down your choices and budget your time accordingly. Hotels and restaurants in the Very Expensive and Expensive categories are rated on a scale of one (highly recommended) to three stars (exceptional). Those in the Moderate and Inexpensive categories rate from zero (recommended) to two stars (very highly recommended). Attractions, towns, and regions are rated according to the following scale: zero stars (recommended), one star (highly recommended), two stars (very highly recommended), and three stars (must-see).

In addition to the rating system, we also use seven icons to highlight insider information, useful tips, special bargains, hidden gems, memorable experiences, kid-friendly venues, places to avoid, and other useful information:

(Finds   (Fun Fact   (Kids   (Moments   (Overrated   (Tips   (Value

The following abbreviations are used for credit cards:

AE	American Express	DISC	Discover	V	Visa
DC	Diners Club	MC	MasterCard		

Now that you have the guidebook to a great trip, visit our website at **www.frommers.com** for travel information on nearly 2,500 destinations. With features updated regularly, we give you instant access to the most current trip-planning information available. At Frommers.com, you'll also find the best prices on airfares, accommodations, and car rentals—and you can even book travel online through our travel booking partners. At Frommers.com, you'll also find the following:

- Online updates to our most popular guidebooks
- Vacation sweepstakes and contest giveaways
- Newsletter highlighting the hottest travel trends
- Online travel message boards with featured travel discussions

What's New in San Diego

If you've never been to San Diego or your last visit was more than a few years ago, this relaxed and scenic city will hold some surprises for you. It's grown up. San Diego is no longer just a laid-back navy town—avant-garde architecture, sophisticated dining options, and a booming tourist industry all point to its coming-of-age.

Although San Diegans generally prefer to keep things as they are—eagerly passing "no growth" legislation and vocalizing fears about the "Los Angeles-ization" of their metropolis—the city is still pleased when much-needed improvements are made, and quick to brag about the up-to-date attractions that residents enjoy as much as visitors. Here is a sampling of recent changes and additions.

PLANNING YOUR TRIP Sports fans, mark your calendars: **Super Bowl XXXVII** is coming to San Diego's Qualcomm Stadium on January 26, 2003. You might ask: What, again? That's right, San Diego is proving to be something of a favorite venue for this gridiron climax; the city hosted Super Bowls XXII (1988) and XXXII (1998). If history repeats itself, the event spawns a weeklong, star-studded celebration—plus an economic and publicity boom for the entire city.

WHERE TO STAY Hot on the heels of the Convention Center's high-profile expansion in 2001, new—and newly expanded—hotels are popping up all over downtown and beyond. Scheduled for completion in summer 2003, the **Manchester Grand Hyatt**

San Diego, 1 Market Pl. (© 619/232-1234), is hard at work on a new tower that will complement its new name (formerly the Hyatt Regency San Diego) and more than double meeting space and guest rooms.

Also kicking up dust at press time is the much-anticipated **W Hotel** at the corner of State and B streets (© 800/W-HOTELS), which promises the fashion-forward interiors and trendy dining that have become the W brand trademarks. It's slated to open in early 2003; for an up-to-date status report, call or log onto **www.whotels.com**.

Scheduled to open mere weeks after we went to press, the long awaited **Lodge at Torrey Pines,** 11480 N. Torrey Pines Rd. (© 858/453-4420; www.lodgeattorreypines.com), is a luxury resort meticulously designed in the craftsman style. With a stunning clifftop setting overlooking the Pacific and adjacent to Torrey Pines golf course, the Lodge was already booking up for picturesque weddings and classy golf getaways before even opening its doors!

In other news, more area hostelries are jumping on the pleasure bandwagon with full-service, pamper-heavy **spas.** Seems no hotel worth its bath salts these days can be caught without one. Sample an array of treatments at **Loews Coronado Bay Resort,** 4000 Coronado Bay Rd. (© 619/424-4000), whose 9,000-square-foot facility is set to open in late 2002. Or indulge in exotic Javanese treatments in the serenely tropical setting of **Paradise Point Resort & Spa,** 1404 Vacation Rd. (© 858/274-4630;

www.paradisepoint. com), where treatment rooms are just steps from the lagoon-style swimming pool. For the ultimate in privacy and personalized service, no one tops the 24-hour, in-room holistic health menu—from individual yoga to Thai massage, psychotherapy, and obscure Asian treatments—at **Hotel Parisi,** 1111 Prospect St. (© **858/454-1511;** www.hotel parisi.com), a La Jolla boutique hotel for the Zen-seeking jet-setter.

For more details, see chapter 5, "Where to Stay."

WHERE TO DINE La Jolla denizens and hotel guests welcomed the 2001 grand reopening of the **Grande Colonial**'s on-site restaurant **Nine-Ten,** 910 Prospect St. (© **858/ 964-5400**). After operating the distinctive Putman's Grill for as long as anyone can remember, the hotel recruited a culinary pinch-hitter in Michael Stebner, whose impressive credentials include time spent with überchef Thomas Keller at the acclaimed French Laundry, plus an impressive stint at San Diego's award-winning Azzura Point.

Meanwhile, downtown culture vultures and urban hipsters are flocking to be seen at **Chive,** 558 Fourth Ave. (© **619/232-4483**), a successful blending of chic moderne touches and artistically composed *delicious* food. Start with the alluring "Chive cocktail," an intoxicatingly green combination of sparkling wine and Midori liqueur in a sugar-rimmed Champagne flute.

We're also pleased to find the city's Mexican eateries rising to the border-adjacent challenge with Old Town's slightly hidden **El Agave Tequilaria,** 2304 San Diego Ave. (© **619/220-0692**), where an impressive selection of literally hundreds of boutique and artisan tequilas is surpassed only by the sometimes unfamiliar—but always delicious—authentically regional Mexican specialties.

See chapter 6, "Where to Dine."

EXPLORING SAN DIEGO No one visits San Diego without experiencing one of the city's fantastic animal parks, and each has some new residents to crow about. At Balboa Park's **San Diego Zoo,** 2920 Zoo Dr. (© **619/ 234-3153;** www.sandiegozoo. org), construction is underway to transform the outdated "monkey yard," one of the zoo's original enclosures, into the bioclimatically correct (and multi-species) Heart of the Zoo. By Memorial Day 2003, you can expect to see Borneo and Sumatran orangutans cavorting in their new home.

At the **San Diego Wild Animal Park,** 15500 San Pasqual Valley Rd., Escondido (© **760/747-8702;** www. wildanimalpark.org), they've been rescuing and breeding endangered California condors for years, and in 2001, for the first time, allowed visitors a peek. The condors continue to be a huge success story, as visitors flock to see these eerily impressive birds along the mountain trails of **Condor Ridge,** a habitat created for some of California's critically endangered species; along with condors, you'll see thick-billed parrots, black-footed ferrets, hawks, owls, and bighorn sheep.

Meanwhile, a hilarious new animal show awaits at **SeaWorld,** 500 Sea World Dr. (© **619/226-3901;** www. seaworld.com), which in 2002 welcomed *Pets Rule!,* whose remarkable cast of trained cats, dogs, and other domestic animals were all adopted from local shelters and given a new life in the SeaWorld spotlight. In addition to illustrating how the same techniques used to train killer whales and seals can teach your household pet to have perfect comic timing, the show provides some insight into the behavioral world of our favorite companions.

When it's time to see the rest of the city, how about climbing aboard the unique amphibious vehicles of **Sea and Land Adventure Tours (SEAL)**

(© **619/298-8687**)? The 90-minute excursions leave from Seaport Village and visit the Gaslamp Quarter, Old Town, Coronado, and Point Loma—with dips in San Diego and Mission bays in between. That's right, the bus/boat drives straight into the water! See chapter 7, "What to See & Do," for complete details.

SHOPPING Though San Diegans complain about the "Los Angeles-ization" of their city, Gaslamp Quarter hipsters have opened their arms to the chic sleaze of Larry Flynt's **Hustler Hollywood San Diego,** 929 Sixth Ave. (© **619/696-9007**). The 12,000-square-foot adult-oriented store mixes sophistication and erotica in a way that's generations ahead of the Gaslamp's notorious past (when it was called the Stingaree and filled with brothels and opium dens). Instead, this branch of the successful Sunset Strip boutique in L.A. features a coffee bar, *Hustler*-inspired lingerie and clothing, and a newsstand with mainstream as well as adult magazines. They're careful to display lotions, leather, erotic videos and DVDs, and adult "toys" far from the casual browser's view.

AFTER DARK Though San Diego's never had a reputation as a hard rockin' town, that may all change with the opening of the **Hard Rock Cafe.** Scheduled for completion by the end of 2002 in a 29,000-square-foot space at 1059 Fifth Avenue (near Broadway), the venue will follow the example of Hard Rocks around the country, with a state-of-the-art live music hall to accommodate 1,200 fans, logowear Company Store, and Southern-themed restaurant featuring down-home-style American food and the Hard Rock's award-winning "Sunday Gospel Brunch." For the latest, log onto **www.hob.com.**

SIDE TRIPS There are new operating hours at Carlsbad's kid-pleasing

LEGOLAND, 1 Lego Dr. (© **877/534-6526** or 760/918-LEGO; www.legoland.com), where off-season visitors may have to plan a little more carefully to include the park in their itinerary. Reduced tourism led to the changes, which leave the peak summer season (Memorial Day to Labor Day) hours unaffected. The rest of the year, LEGOLAND will only be open Thursday through Monday; for major holiday periods, though, they'll resume full operation. There's no indication how long this measure will last, so it's more important than ever to check the schedule when you're planning to be in town. (See listing on p. 214 for the complete new operating schedule.)

Meanwhile, families planning a Disneyland excursion in Anaheim should budget an extra day (or two) to experience the abundant new features of the renamed **Disneyland Resort** (© **714/781-4565;** www.disneyland.com). Next door to Disneyland you'll find **California Adventure,** which debuted its new live-action stage show **Blast!** in 2002. It's a high-concept, drum corps–style extravaganza (think halftime marching bands with rock-concert lighting and Broadway choreography).

If you're preparing to head across the border, you might notice that local phone numbers look a bit different. On February 16, 2002, a **new Mexican national phone numbering plan** was implemented, switching every number throughout the country from 8 to 10 digits. So while the new numbers look more like the area-code-plus-seven we're used to in the United States, pay close attention to the newly added digits, which are all included in our listings for the "Tijuana" and "Baja California" side trips.

See chapter 11, "Side Trips from San Diego" for more information.

1

The Best of San Diego

Approximately 1.3 million people live in San Diego, making it the seventh-largest city in the United States (after New York, Los Angeles, Chicago, Houston, Philadelphia, and Phoenix). Although the city's population keeps increasing, you'll find that San Diego hasn't lost its small-town ambience, and it retains a strong connection with its Hispanic heritage and culture.

1 Frommer's Favorite San Diego Experiences

- **Strolling Through the Gaslamp Quarter:** Victorian commercial buildings that fill a 16½-block area will make you think you've stepped back in time. The beautifully restored buildings, in the heart of downtown, house some of the city's most popular shops, restaurants, and nightspots. See "Walking Tour 1: The Gaslamp Quarter," in chapter 8.

- **Renting Bikes, Skates, or Kayaks in Mission Bay:** Landscaped shores, calm waters, paved paths, and friendly neighbors make Mission Bay an aquatic playground like no other. Explore on land or water, depending on your energy level, then grab a bite at funky Mission Cafe. See "Outdoor Pursuits," in chapter 7.

- **Listening to Free Sunday Organ Recitals in Balboa Park:** Even if you usually don't like organ music, you might enjoy these outdoor concerts and the crowds they draw—San Diegans with their parents, their children, and their dogs. The music, enhanced by the organist's commentary, runs the gamut from classical to contemporary. Concerts start at 2pm. See "Walking Tour 4: Balboa Park," in chapter 8.

- **Relaxing with Afternoon Tea:** A genteel tradition in San Diego, the custom of afternoon tea is dignified and old-fashioned at the U.S. Grant Hotel, cozy and Victorian at the Horton Grand, and elegantly charming at the grand Hotel Del Coronado. Take your pick. See chapter 5.

- **Taking the Ferry to Coronado:** The 15-minute ride gets you out into San Diego Harbor and provides some of the best views of the city. The ferry runs every hour from the Broadway Pier, so you can tour Coronado on foot, by bike, or by trolley, and return whenever you please. See "Getting Around," in chapter 4.

- **Driving Over the Bridge to Coronado:** The first time or the fiftieth, there's always an adrenaline rush as you follow this engineering marvel's dramatic curves and catch a glimpse of the panoramic view to either side. Driving west, you can easily pick out the distinctive Hotel Del in the distance long before you reach the "island." See "Orientation," in chapter 4.

- **Watching the Seals at Children's Pool Beach:** This tiny La Jolla cove was originally named for the

San Diego Area at a Glance

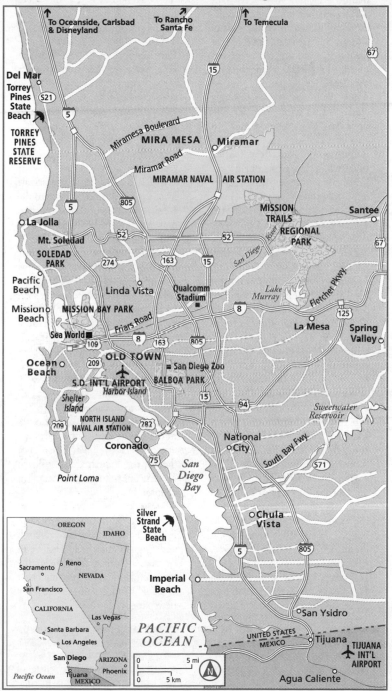

toddlers who could safely frolic behind a man-made seawall. These days, the sand is mostly off-limits to humans, who congregate along the seawall railing or onshore to admire the protected pinnipeds that sun themselves on the beach or on semisubmerged rocks. You can get surprisingly close, and it's a truly mesmerizing sight. See "San Diego Beaches," in chapter 7.

- **Riding on the San Diego Trolley to Mexico:** The trip from downtown costs a mere $2.50, takes only 40 minutes, and the clean, quick trolleys are fun in their own right. Once in Tijuana, load up on colorful souvenirs and authentic Mexican food. See "Getting Around," in chapter 4.
- **Listening to Jazz at Croce's:** Ideally located in the center of downtown in a historic Gaslamp Quarter building, Croce's celebrates the life of musician Jim Croce and showcases the city's jazz musicians. See "The Club & Music Scene," in chapter 10.
- **Watching the Sun Set Over the Ocean:** It's a free and memorable experience. Excellent sunset-watching spots include the Mission Beach and Pacific Beach boardwalks, as well as the beach in Coronado in front of the Hotel del Coronado. At La Jolla's Windansea Beach, wandering down to the water at dusk, wineglass in hand, is a nightly neighborhood event. See "San Diego Beaches," in chapter 7.
- **Drinking Coffee at a La Jolla Sidewalk Cafe:** San Diego offers a plethora of places to enjoy lattes,

espressos, and cappuccinos, but the coffeehouses in La Jolla serve them up with special panache. For some favorites, see the "Java Joints in La Jolla" box on p. 118.

- **Purchasing Just-Picked Produce at a Farmers' Market:** Markets throughout the area sell the bountiful harvest of San Diego County. For directions, see "Shopping A to Z," in chapter 9.
- **Walking Along the Water:** The city offers walkers several great places to stroll. One of our favorites, along the waterfront from the Convention Center to the Maritime Museum, affords views of aircraft carriers, tuna seiners, and sailboats. See "Walking Tour 2: The Embarcadero," in chapter 8.
- **Visiting the "Lobster Village" in Puerto Nuevo:** South of the border, they serve lobster with rice, beans, tortillas, and freshly made salsa; it's an affordable and deliciously filling meal. See "Baja California: Exploring More of Mexico," in chapter 11.
- **Floating Up, Up, and Away Over North County:** Hot-air balloons carry passengers over the golf courses and luxury homes north of the city. These rides are especially enjoyable at sunset. For details, see "North County Beach Towns: Spots to Surf & Sun," in chapter 11.
- **Watching the Grunion Run:** These tiny fish spawn on San Diego beaches between March and August, and the locals love to be there. To find the date of the next run, pick up a free tide chart at a surf shop or consult the daily newspaper.

2 Best Hotel Bets

- **Best Historic Hotel:** The **Hotel del Coronado,** 1500 Orange Ave. (© **800/HOTEL-DEL** or 619/435-8000), positively reeks of

history. Opened in 1888, this Victorian masterpiece had some of the earliest electric lights in existence, and legend has it that the course of history was changed when the Prince of Wales met Wallis Simpson here at a ball. Meticulous restoration has enhanced this glorious landmark, whose early days are well chronicled in displays throughout the hotel. See p. 90.

- **Best for Business Travelers:** The **San Diego Marriott Marina,** 333 W. Harbor Dr. (© 800/228- 9290 or 619/234-1500), screams "business traveler," with a full-service business center offering plenty of amenities for suits on the go. Its prime location offers excellent access to downtown. See p. 67.
- **Best for a Romantic Getaway:** The sense of seclusion at **Loews Coronado Bay Resort,** 4000 Coronado Bay Rd. (© 800/ 23-LOEWS or 619/424-4000), makes it a good choice for a tryst. You can snuggle under blankets on an authentic gondola ride or drink in the view from the elegant restaurant; large marble bathrooms and fine bed linens help frost the lovin' cake. See p. 91. (For a romantic getaway farther afield, see the listing for Rancho Valencia Resort on p. 222.)
- **Best for Families:** The **Paradise Point Resort & Spa,** 1404 W. Vacation Rd. (© 800/344-2626 or 858/274-4630), is a tropical playground offering enough activities to keep family members of all ages happy. In addition to a virtual Disneyland of on-site options, the aquatic playground of Mission Bay surrounds the hotel's private peninsula. See p. 80.
- **Best Moderately Priced Hotel:** The **Gaslamp Plaza Suites,** 520 E St. (© 619/232-9500), is an elegant landmark full of creature comforts that belie its super-friendly rates. You'll also be smack-dab in the heart of the trendy Gaslamp Quarter. See p. 71.

- **Best Budget Hotel:** In San Diego's Little Italy, **La Pensione Hotel,** 606 W. Date St. (© 800/ 232-4683 or 619/236- 8000), feels like a small European hotel and offers tidy lodgings at bargain prices. There's an abundance of great dining in the surrounding blocks, and you'll be perfectly situated to explore the rest of town by car. See p. 73.
- **Best Unusual Lodgings:** Fulfill the fantasies of your inner yachtsman with the **San Diego Yacht & Breakfast Company,** 1880 Harbor Island Dr., G-Dock (© 800/ YACHT-DO or 619/297-9484). It provides powerboats, sailboats, and houseboats docked in a Harbor Island marina. You can sleep on board, lulled by the gentle rocking of the hull, and then have breakfast ashore; complete the adventure with a skippered cruise later in the day. See p. 72.
- **Best B&B:** The picture-perfect **Heritage Park Bed & Breakfast Inn,** 2470 Heritage Park Row (© 800/995-2470 or 619/299-6832), has it all—an exquisitely maintained Victorian house, lively and gracious hosts who delight in creating a pampering and romantic ambience, and a location equally close to Old Town, Hillcrest, and Mission Bay. See p. 76.
- **Best for Bringing Your Pooch:** Check in with your dog at the **U.S. Grant Hotel,** 326 Broadway (© 800/237-5029 or 619/232-3121), and your pet just might be treated better than you. Pampering starts with gourmet dinners, chewy bones, sleeping pillows, and a nightly turndown biscuit. Walking service and special dog-walk maps (guide to local hydrants?) are available, and you'll be welcomed in all the hotel's public spaces. There's a grassy square across the street where you may even run

Impressions

Thanks be to God, I have arrived at this Port of San Diego. It is beautiful to behold and does not belie its reputation.

—Father Junípero Serra, 1769

I thought San Diego must be a Heaven on Earth . . . It seemed to me the best spot for building a city I ever saw.

—Alonzo Horton, who developed San Diego's first downtown

into Flapjack, the owner's Dalmatian, a full-time hotel resident. The best part? There's no extra charge. See p. 70.

- **Best Place to Stay on the Beach:** At **The La Jolla Beach & Tennis Club,** 2000 Spindrift Dr. (℅ **800/624-CLUB** or 858/454-7126), you can walk right onto the wide beach and frolic in the great waves. Lifeguards and the lack of undertow make this a popular choice for families. Though the rooms are plain, the country club staff will cater to your every whim. See p. 86.

- **Best for Travelers with Disabilities:** While many of San Diego's hotels make minimal concessions to wheelchair accessibility codes, downtown's **Manchester Grand Hyatt San Diego,** 1 Market Place (℅ **800/233-1234** or 619/232-1234), goes the distance. There are 23 rooms with roll-in showers and lowered closet racks and peepholes. Ramps are an integral part of all the public spaces, rather than an afterthought. The hotel's Braille labeling is also thorough. See p. 67.

- **Best Hotel Pool:** The genteel pool at **La Valencia,** 1132 Prospect St. (℅ **800/451-0772** or 858/454-0771), is oh-so-special, with its spectacular setting overlooking Scripps Park and the Pacific. See p. 84.

3 Best Dining Bets

- **Best Spot for a Business Lunch: Dakota Grill and Spirits,** 901 Fifth Ave., in the Gaslamp Quarter (℅ **619/234-5554**), has the three most important ingredients of a business lunch locale: great location, appropriate atmosphere, and excellent food. See p. 100.

- **Best View:** Many restaurants overlook the ocean, but only from **Brockton Villa,** 1235 Coast Blvd., La Jolla (℅ **858/454-7393**), can you see sublime La Jolla Cove. Diners with a window seat will feel as if they're looking out on a gigantic picture postcard. See p. 117.

- **Best Value:** The word *huge* barely begins to describe the portions at **Filippi's Pizza Grotto,** 1747 India St. (℅ **619/232-5095**), where a salad for one is enough for three, and an order of lasagna must weigh a pound. There's a kids' menu, and Filippi's has locations all over, including Pacific Beach, Mission Valley, and Escondido. See p. 101.

- **Best for Kids:** At the **Old Spaghetti Factory,** 275 Fifth Ave., in the Gaslamp Quarter (℅ **619/233-4323**), family dining is the name of the game—so if your kids are noisy, nobody will notice. See p. 101.

- **Best Chinese Cuisine: Panda Inn,** Horton Plaza (℅ **619/233-7800**), on the top floor of the megamall, is full of surprises. You wouldn't expect culinary greatness

Site Seeing: San Diego on the Web

You can find lots of information on San Diego on the Internet; here are a few of my favorite helpful planning and general information sites.

- **www.sandiego.org** is maintained by the San Diego Convention & Visitors Bureau and provides, among other things, up-to-date weather data and a calendar of events.
- **www.sandiego-online.com**, the *San Diego* magazine website, features abbreviated stories from the current month's issue, plus dining and events listings.
- **www.sdreader.com**, the site of the free weekly *San Diego Reader,* is a great source for club and show listings, plus edgy topical journalism. It has printable coupons you can really use, plus honest local dirt on eats and entertainment.
- **www.signonsandiego.com** is where CitySearch teams up with the *San Diego Union-Tribune,* catering as much to locals as to visitors. It offers plenty of helpful links, plus savvy reviews of restaurants, music, movies, performing arts, museums, outdoor recreation, beaches, and sports.
- **www.digitalcity.com/sandiego** is a lifestyle guide targeted at locals, and therefore is great for off-the-beaten-tourist-path recommendations. You'll find everything from personal ads to constantly changing restaurant spotlights and daily "Top Clicks."
- **www.gaslamp.org**, the site of the Gaslamp Quarter Association, is full of information about the Gaslamp's history and revival. Combining the cultural with the commercial, it has nice coverage of listings and links for restaurants, cafes, nightclubs, galleries, theaters, and shopping.
- **www.sandiegoinsider.com** is a well-rounded online guide containing bar, club, and movie reviews. The dining guide includes lengthy descriptions but few opinionated critiques. Suggestions abound for beach-going, hiking, and other outdoor excursions. Searching this site can be tedious, but the articles are generally rewarding.
- **www.coronadovisitors.com** is the Coronado Visitors Bureau's site, a colorful, comprehensive, and user-friendly virtual visit to the "island," with links to local businesses and enticing descriptions of beaches and attractions (including vital, practical info).

from a shopping mall, but this sleeper serves up artfully flavored Mandarin and Sichuan dishes in an elegant setting far removed from the consumer throngs just outside. See p. 100.

- **Best Italian Cuisine:** For gold card palates, **Fio's,** 801 Fifth Ave., in the Gaslamp Quarter (© 619/234-3467), offers fine northern Italian food in chic surroundings; see p. 99. But **Caffe Bella Italia,** 1525 Garnet Ave., Pacific Beach (© 858/273-1224), will make you wonder if you've stumbled across the Atlantic right into a friendly Milan neighborhood at mealtime. See p. 112.

- **Best Seafood:** Not only does **The Fish Market/Top of the Market,**

750 N. Harbor Dr. ((C) 619/232-FISH or 619/234-4TOP), offer the city's best fish, it also offers a memorable view across San Diego Bay. See p. 100.

• **Best American Cuisine:** The menu at **Croce's,** 802 Fifth Ave., in the Gaslamp Quarter ((C) 619/233-4355), cleverly fuses American and Southwestern with international touches. The results are delicious. See p. 98.

• **Best Mexican Cuisine:** Rather than the "combination plate" fare that's common on this side of the border, **El Agave Tequilaria,** 2304 San Diego Ave., Old Town ((C) 619/220-0692), offers a delightful combination of freshly prepared recipes from Veracruz, Chiapas, Puebla, and Mexico City—along with an impressive selection of boutique and artisan tequilas. See p. 108.

• **Best Vegetarian:** The **Vegetarian Zone,** 2949 Fifth Ave., Hillcrest ((C) 619/298-7302), offers tasty meat-free dishes influenced by a variety of ethnic cuisines. See p. 106.

• **Best Pizza:** For gourmet pizza from a wood-fired oven, head for **Sammy's California Woodfired Pizza,** a local institution with several locations, including 770 Fourth Ave., in the Gaslamp Quarter ((C) 619/230-8888). See p. 123. For the traditional Sicilian

variety, you'll have to visit **Filippi's Pizza Grotto** (see "Best Value," above, or p. 101).

• **Best Desserts:** You'll forget your diet at **Extraordinary Desserts,** 2929 Fifth Ave., Hillcrest ((C) 619/294-7001). Heck, it's so good you might forget your name! Proprietor Karen Krasne has a *Certificate de Patisserie* from Le Cordon Bleu in Paris, and makes everything fresh on the premises daily. See p. 105.

• **Best Late-Night Dining:** Open later than anyplace else downtown, **Café Lulu,** 419 F St. ((C) 619/238-0114), serves eclectic meat-free fare and inventive espresso drinks until 1am during the week, 3am on weekends. See p. 101.

• **Best Fast Food:** Fish tacos from **Rubio's,** 4504 E. Mission Bay Dr. ((C) 619/272-2801), and other locations, are legendary in San Diego. Taste one and you'll know why. See p. 124.

• **Best Picnic Fare:** Pack a humongous sandwich from the **Cheese Shop,** 627 Fourth Ave. ((C) 619/232-2303), for a picnic lunch, and you won't be hungry for dinner. See p. 124. In La Jolla, head to **Girard Gourmet,** 7837 Girard Ave. ((C) 858/454-3321), for sandwiches, prepared salads, imported cheeses, and baked goods. See p. 124.

2

Planning Your Trip to San Diego

This chapter contains all the practical information and logistical advice you need to make your travel arrangements a snap, from deciding when to go to finding the best airfare.

1 Visitor Information

You can do your homework by contacting the **International Visitor Information Center,** 11 Horton Plaza, San Diego, CA 92101 (© **619/ 236-1212;** fax 619/230-7084; www.sandiego.org). Ask for the *San Diego Visitors Planning Guide,* which includes information on accommodations, activities, and attractions, and has excellent maps. Also request the *Super Savings Coupon Book,* which is full of discount coupons. The center is open Monday through Saturday from 8:30am to 5pm year-round and Sunday from 11am to 5pm June through August; it's closed Thanksgiving, Christmas, and New Year's Day.

Some of the same materials are available from the **Mission Bay Visitor Information Center,** 2688 Mission Bay Dr., San Diego, CA 92109 (© **619/276-8200;** www.infosandiego.com), which is also helpful with recreational activities in the bay and beyond.

The **Coronado Visitors Center,** 1100 Orange Ave. (© **619/437-8788;** www.coronadohistory.org/visitorcenter), is a must for anyone visiting the "island." Located inside the

Coronado Museum, they have maps of the area, information-packed brochures and newsletters, and even the latest schedules. Open daily.

Information on businesses in La Jolla's "Village" is distributed by the **Promote La Jolla,** 1150 Silverado St., La Jolla, CA 92038 (© **858/454-5718;** www.lajollabythesea.com).

Additional visitor information is available from the **Balboa Park Visitors Center,** 1549 El Prado, San Diego, CA 92101 (© **619/239-0512**).

If you're thinking of attending the **theater** while you're in town, contact the **San Diego Performing Arts League** (© **619/238-0700;** www.sandiegoperforms.com) for a copy of *What's Playing?,* which contains information on upcoming performances.

The **San Diego North County Convention & Visitors Bureau,** 720 N. Broadway, Escondido, CA 92025 (© **800/848-3336** or 760/745-4741; www.sandiegonorth.com), can provide information on excursion areas in San Diego County, including Del Mar, Carlsbad, Escondido, Julian, and Anza-Borrego Desert State Park.

2 Money

If you're visiting from outside the United States, you can find more information on American currency and money exchange in chapter 3, "For International Visitors."

Red Alert Checklist

- Do any theater, restaurant, or travel reservations need to be booked in advance?
- Did you make sure your favorite attraction is open? Call ahead for opening and closing hours. Many scheduled tours, festivals, and special events are subject to cancellation. Call ahead for opening and closing hours.
- If you purchased traveler's checks, have you recorded the check numbers, and stored the documentation separately from the checks?
- Did you pack your camera and an extra set of camera batteries, and purchase enough film? If you packed film in your checked baggage, did you invest in protective pouches to shield film from airport X-rays?
- Do you have a safe, accessible place to store money?
- Did you bring your ID cards that could entitle you to discounts such as AAA and AARP cards, student IDs, etc.?
- Did you bring emergency drug prescriptions and extra glasses and/or contact lenses?
- Do you have your credit card personal identification numbers (PINs)?
- If you have an E-ticket, do you have documentation?
- Did you leave a copy of your itinerary with someone at home?

ATMS

One of California's most popular banks is Wells Fargo, a member of the Star, PLUS, Cirrus, and Global Access systems. It has hundreds of ATMs at branches and stores (including most Vons supermarkets) throughout San Diego County. To find the one nearest you, call ℂ 800/869-3557 or visit www.wellsfargo.com/findus. Other statewide banks include Bank of America (which accepts PLUS, Star, and Interlink cards), and First Interstate Bank (Cirrus).

To locate other ATMs in the Cirrus system, call ℂ 800/424-7787 or search www.mastercard.com; to find a PLUS ATM, call ℂ 800/843-7587 or visit www.visa.com. Be sure to check your bank's daily withdrawal limit before you depart.

TRAVELER'S CHECKS

Once the only safe method of guaranteeing ready cash, traveler's checks now seem anachronistic. Most cities (including San Diego) have plenty of 24-hour ATMs that allow you to withdraw small amounts of cash as needed.

But if you want to avoid the fees associated with ATM withdrawals, or feel more comfortable with checks that can be replaced if lost or stolen, you can get traveler's checks at almost any bank. American Express offers denominations of $10, $20, $50, $100, $500, and $1,000; you'll pay a service charge ranging from 1% to 4%. You can also get American Express traveler's checks over the phone by calling ℂ 800/221-7282; by using this number, Amex gold and platinum cardholders avoid the 1% fee. AAA members can obtain checks without a fee at most AAA offices.

What Things Cost in San Diego	U.S.$	U.K.£
Taxi from the airport to downtown	8.50	6.00
Bus from the airport to downtown	2.00	1.40
Local telephone call	25¢–35¢	17p–24p
Double at the Hotel del Coronado		
(very expensive)	250.00	175.00
Double at the Embassy Suites (expensive)	189.00	132.00
Double at the Ocean Park Inn (moderate)	124.00	86.75
Double at La Pensione Hotel (inexpensive)	60.00	42.00
Two-course lunch for one at		
Casa de Bandini (moderate)	16.00	11.00
Two-course lunch for one at the		
Vegetarian Zone (inexpensive)	12.00	8.50
Three-course dinner for one at		
Trattoria Acqua (expensive)	33.00	23.00
Three-course dinner for one at Mixx (moderate)	26.00	18.00
Three-course dinner for one at the		
Old Spaghetti Factory (inexpensive)	9.25	6.50
Bottle of beer	2.75	1.90
Coca-Cola	1.50	1.05
Cup of coffee	1.25	87p
Fuji Disposable Camera, 27 exposures w/flash	8.00	5.60
San Diego Zoo adult admission	19.50	13.5
San Diego Zoo children's admission	11.75	8.25
Theater ticket at Old Globe	36.00	25.00

Visa offers traveler's checks at Citibank locations nationwide, as well as several other banks. The service charge ranges from 1.5% to 2%; checks come in denominations of $20, $50, $100, $500, and $1,000. **MasterCard** also offers traveler's checks. Call ✆ **800/ 223-9920** for a location near you.

If you opt to carry traveler's checks, be sure to keep a record of their serial numbers—separate from the checks— so you're ensured a refund in an emergency.

CREDIT CARDS

San Diego's hotels, restaurants, and attractions accept most major credit cards; the most popular are **Visa, MasterCard, American Express,** and **Discover.** A handful of stores and restaurants accept only cash, however, so be sure to ask if you're not sure. The hotel and restaurant listings in chapters 5 and 6 list the credit cards each establishment accepts.

WHAT TO DO IF YOUR WALLET GETS STOLEN

Be sure to block charges against your account the minute you discover a card has been lost or stolen. Then be sure to file a police report.

Almost every credit-card company has an emergency toll-free number to call if your card is stolen. It may be able to wire you a cash advance off your credit card immediately, and in many places, it can deliver an emergency credit card in a day or two. **Visa's** 24-hour U.S. emergency number is ✆ **800/336-8472. American Express** cardholders and traveler's check holders should call ✆ **800/221-7282. MasterCard** holders should call ✆ **800/307-7309.** For other credit cards, call the toll-free number directory at © **800/555-1212.**

Odds are that, if your wallet is gone, the police won't be able to recover it for you. However, it's still worth informing the authorities. Your credit-card company or insurer may require a police report number or record of the theft.

If you choose to carry traveler's checks, be sure to keep a record of their serial numbers separate from your checks. You'll get a refund faster if you know the numbers.

If you need emergency cash, you can have money wired to you via **Western Union** (© **800/325-6000;** www.westernunion.com). You must present valid ID to pick up the cash at the Western Union office. However, in most places, you can pick up a money transfer even if you don't have valid identification, as long as you can answer a test question provided by the sender. Be sure to let the sender know in advance that you don't have ID. If you need to use a test question instead of ID, the sender must take cash to his or her local Western Union office, rather than transferring the money over the phone or online.

3 When to Go

San Diego is blessed with a mild climate, low humidity, good air quality, and welcoming blue skies. In fact, *Pleasant Weather Rankings,* published by Consumer Travel, ranked San Diego's weather number two in the world (behind Las Palmas, in the Canary Islands). Oceanside, the northernmost town in San Diego County, was number five.

Although the temperature can change 20° to 30°F between day and evening, it doesn't usually reach a point of extreme heat. San Diego receives very little precipitation (9½ in. of rainfall in an average year); what rain does fall comes primarily between late December and mid-April.

San Diego is most crowded between Memorial Day and Labor Day. The kids are out of school and *everyone* wants to be by the seashore; so if you visit in summer, you can expect fully booked hotels, crowded family attractions, and full parking lots at the beach. San Diego's popularity as a convention destination and its year-round pleasant weather keep the tourism business steady the rest of the year, as well. The only slow season is from Thanksgiving through mid-February. Hotels are less full, and the beaches are peaceful and uncrowded; the big family attractions are still busy, though, with residents taking advantage of holiday breaks.

Average Monthly Temperatures & Rainfall (in.)

	Jan	Feb	Mar	Apr	May	June	July	Aug	Sept	Oct	Nov	Dec
High (°F)	65	66	66	68	70	71	75	77	76	74	70	66
(°C)	18	19	19	20	21	21	24	25	25	23	21	19
Low (°F)	46	47	50	54	57	60	64	66	63	58	52	47
(°C)	7	9	10	12	14	15	17	19	17	15	10	8
Rainfall	1.88	1.48	1.55	0.81	0.15	0.05	0.01	0.07	0.13	0.34	1.25	1.73

SAN DIEGO CALENDAR OF EVENTS

You might want to plan your trip around one of these annual events in the San Diego area (including the destinations covered in chapter 11, "Side Trips from San Diego"). For even more up-to-date planning information, contact the **International Visitor**

Information Center (② 619/236-1212; www.sandiego.org).

January

Whale-Watching. Mid-December to mid-March is the eagerly anticipated whale-watching season. Scores of graceful yet gargantuan California gray whales make their annual migration to warm breeding lagoons in Baja, then return with their calves to springtime feeding grounds in Alaska. For information on vantage points and excursions that bring you closer to the largest mammals, see "Whale-Watching" in chapter 7.

San Diego Marathon. The course begins at Plaza Camino Real in Carlsbad and stretches 26¼ miles (42km), mainly along the coast. It's a gorgeous run, and spectators don't need tickets. For more information, call ② 858/792-2900. For an entry application, send a self-addressed stamped envelope to In Motion, 511 S. Cedros, Suite B, Solana Beach, CA 92075. Third Sunday in January.

Nations of San Diego International Dance Festival. Founded in 1993, this 10-day festival focuses on San Diego's numerous ethnic dance groups and companies. Performances are at the Lyceum Theatre, and free shows take place in public areas. Call ② 619/239-9255. Mid-January.

Super Bowl XXXVII. Plan now for the biggest event in football; if Super Bowls XXII and XXXII (also held in San Diego) are any indication, the city will swell with revelers the entire week leading up to the game, so book ahead for a room (or reschedule if you'd rather avoid the crowds). Call ② 619/641-3100; www.superbowl.com. January 26.

February

Wildflowers bloom in the desert, usually February through April at Anza-Borrego Desert State Park. The timing varies from year to year, depending on the winter rainfall (see chapter 11). For details, call ② 760/767-4684 or 760/767-4205 (park information).

Buick Invitational, Torrey Pines Golf Course, La Jolla. This PGA Tour men's tournament, an annual event since 1952, draws more than 100,000 spectators each year. It features 150 of the finest professionals in the world. For information, call ② 800/888-BUICK or 619/281-4653; fax 619/281-7947; or write Buick Invitational, 3333 Camino Del Rio S., Suite 100, San Diego, CA 92108. Early to mid-February.

Old Town Temecula Rod Run. It's a far cry from the clippity clop of the Butterfield Overland Stagecoach when the Old Town Temecula Rod Run roars down the Old West streets of Temecula. More than 1,200 street rods are on display during the 2-day event, including many vintage muscle cars. Admission is free to spectators;

Impressions

What a change in weather! It was sleeting when I left St. Louis. Here, on the 23rd of February, palm leaves flutter in warm wind and sun.

—Charles Lindbergh, 1927

If you stay here for any length of time, you develop a low tolerance to change in the weather: If it's over 80°, it's too hot, and if it's under 70°, it's too cold.

—Overheard in Horton Plaza

you'll also find food vendors, beer booths, and a lively Casino Night. For more information, call the **Temecula Town Association** (© 909/676-4718). See chapter 11 for information on Temecula. Mid-February.

March

Ocean Beach Kite Festival. The late-winter skies over the Ocean Beach Recreational Center get a brilliant shot of color. Learn to make and decorate a kite of your own, participate in an all-ages flying contest, take part in all types of food and entertainment, and finish up with the grand finale—a parade down to the beach. For more information, call © 619/224-0189. First weekend in March.

St. Patrick's Day Parade. A tradition since 1980, the parade starts at Sixth and Juniper and ends at Sixth and Laurel. An **Irish Festival** follows. For details, call © 619/299-7812. Sunday before March 17.

Flower Fields in Bloom at Carlsbad Ranch. One of the most spectacular sights in North County is the yearly blossoming of a gigantic sea of bright ranunculuses during March and April, creating a striped blanket that's visible from the freeway. Visitors are welcome to view and tour the fields, which are off Interstate 5 at the Palomar Airport Road exit. For more information, call © 760/431-0352.

April

Rosarito-Ensenada 50-Mile Fun Bicycle Ride, Mexico. About 8,000 participants cycle from the Rosarito Beach Hotel along the two-lane free road to Ensenada and the Finish Line Fiesta. There's another ride in September. For information, call © 619/583-3001 or visit **www. adventuresports.com/bike/ rosarito/welcome.htm**. Mid- to late April.

San Diego Crew Classic, Crown Point Shores, Mission Bay. Since 1973, it has drawn more than 2,000 athletes from collegiate teams in the United States and Canada. Call © 619/488-0700. First or second weekend in April.

Del Mar National Horse Show, Del Mar Fairgrounds. The first event in the Del Mar racing season takes place from late April into early May at the famous Del Mar Fairgrounds. The field at this show includes Olympic-caliber and national championship horse-and-rider teams; there are also Western fashion boutiques and artist displays and demonstrations. For more information, call © 858/792-4288 or 619/755-1161.

Day at the Docks, Harbor Drive and Scott Street, Point Loma. This sportfishing tournament and festival features food, entertainment, and free boat rides. It's usually the last weekend of April or the first weekend in May. Call © 800/994-FISH.

Newport-Ensenada Regatta, Ensenada, Mexico. Sailing aficionados might want to visit Ensenada in late April, when some 400 participants in the annual Newport-Ensenada Regatta turn the town into a nautical party. They sail from Newport Beach, California, on Friday at noon, and trickle into port until Sunday afternoon's trophy presentation. For this year's schedule, contact the Newport Ocean Sailing Association (© 949/435-9553).

Temecula Valley Balloon & Wine Festival. Colorful hot-air balloons dominate the sky over Lake Skinner during the 3-day festival, which also features wine tastings, good food, jazz music, and other entertainment. General admission is $15 ($12 in advance), and reservations for balloon rides ($100 and up) should be made in advance. The lake is about 10 miles northeast of Temecula. To find out about this year's festival or purchase advance tickets, call the event organizers (© 909/676-6713). See chapter 11 for information on Temecula. Late April.

May

Cinco de Mayo Celebration, Old Town. Uniformed troops march and guns blast to mark the 1862 triumph of Mexican soldiers over the French. Festivities include a battle reenactment with costumed actors, mariachi music, and margaritas galore. Free admission. For further details, call © 619/296-3161. Weekend closest to May 5.

June

Indian Fair, Museum of Man, Balboa Park. Native Americans from the southwestern United States gather to demonstrate tribal dances and sell arts and crafts. Call © 619/239-2001. Mid-June.

Twilight in the Park Concerts, Spreckels Organ Pavilion, Balboa Park. These free concerts have been held since 1979 and run from late June through late August. For information, call © 619/226-0819.

Del Mar Fair. This is the *other* event at the Del Mar Fairgrounds. All of San Diego County participates in this annual fair. Livestock competitions, thrill-a-minute rides, food and craft booths, carnival games, and home arts exhibits dominate the event, and concerts by top-name performers are free with admission. The fair usually lasts 3 weeks, from mid-June to early July. For details, call © 858/793-5555.

July

World Championship Over-the-Line Tournament, Mission Bay. This tournament is a San Diego

original. The beach softball event dates from 1953 and is renowned for boisterous, anything-goes behavior—it's a heap of fun for the open-minded, but a bit much for small kids. It takes place on two consecutive weekends in July, on Fiesta Island in Mission Bay, and the public is invited. Admission is free. For more details, call © 619/688-0817.

Festival of the Bells, Mission San Diego de Alcala. This fiesta commemorates the founding of California's first church. Music, dancing, food, and the blessing of the animals are included. For details, call © 619/281-8449. Mid-July.

Annual San Diego Lesbian and Gay Pride Parade, Rally, and Festival. This parade is one of San Diego's biggest draws. It begins at noon on Saturday, followed by a massive festival into the night. The festival continues Sunday afternoon and evening. The parade route is along University Avenue from Normal Street to Sixth Avenue. For more information, call © 619/297-7683. Third or fourth weekend in July.

Thoroughbred Racing Season. The "turf meets the surf" in Del Mar from July to September during the Thoroughbred racing season at the Del Mar Race Track. Post time is 2pm (4pm on the first four Fridays only), and the track is dark on Tuesdays. Hollywood stars continue to flock here, in the grand tradition begun by Bing Crosby, Betty Grable, and Jimmy Durante. For this year's schedule of events, call © 858/792-4242 or 858/755-1141.

August

Hillcrest Street Fair, Fifth Avenue, between Ivy Lane and University Avenue. Held since 1983, the street fair features arts and crafts, food booths, a beer garden, and live entertainment. Call ℂ 619/299-3330. The 1-day fair usually takes place at the beginning of August.

U.S. Open Sandcastle Competition, Imperial Beach Pier. Here's the quintessential beach event: There's a parade and children's sand castle contest on Saturday, followed by the main competition Sunday. Past years have seen creations of astounding complexity, and (weather permitting) the castles remain on view for some time after the event. For further details, call ℂ 619/424-6663.

Harvest Festival, Guadalupe Valley, Mexico. The fertile valleys of northern Baja produce most of Mexico's wine, and several vintners in the Guadalupe Valley near Ensenada join for a weeklong festival celebrating the first crush. Activities include the traditional blessing of the grapes, wine tastings, live music and dancing, riding exhibitions, and fireworks. Plenty of earlier vintages are for sale. For dates and locations, contact the **Baja California Information Office** (ℂ 800/522-1516 or 619/298-4105), or **Baja California Tours** (ℂ 619/454-7166), which organizes a special daylong excursion from San Diego. End of August.

Julian Weed Show, Julian. This is one event that's better than its name. Artwork and arrangements culled from the area's myriad wildflowers and indigenous plants (okay, weeds) are displayed and sold. The Julian Chamber of Commerce (ℂ 760/765-1857) has further details. Second half of August.

Surfing Competitions. Oceanside's world-famous surfing spots attract numerous competitions, including the **World Bodysurfing Championships** and **Longboard Surf Club Competition.** For information on the Bodysurfing Championships, held at the pier over a 3-day weekend in mid-August, call ℂ 760/966-4535. The Longboard Competition takes place the following weekend, also at the pier, and includes a trade show and gala awards presentation with music and dancers. For further details, call ℂ 760/439-5334.

September

Street Scene, Gaslamp Quarter. This 3-day extravaganza fills the historic streets of downtown's Gaslamp Quarter with music, food, dance, and international character. Twelve separate stages are erected to showcase jazz, blues, reggae, rock, and soul music all weekend. Saturday is usually all-ages day—attendees must be 21 or over the other 2 days. For ticket and show information, call ℂ 619/557-8487. Weekend after Labor Day.

La Jolla Rough-Water Swim, La Jolla Cove. The country's largest rough-water swimming competition began in 1916 and features masters men's and women's swims, a junior swim, and an amateur swim. All are 1-mile events except the junior swim and gator-man 3-mile championship. Spectators don't need tickets. To register or receive more information, call ℂ 858/456-2100. For an entry form, send a self-addressed stamped envelope to Entries Chairman, La Jolla Rough-Water Swim, P.O. Box 46, La Jolla, CA 92038. Sunday after Labor Day.

Art Festival in the Village of La Jolla, along Prospect and Girard streets. This free festival includes prize-winning artwork, live entertainment, gourmet food, and children's activities. For information, call ℂ 888/ART-FEST or 858/454-5718. Usually held the last weekend in September.

Julian's Arts and Crafts Show, Julian. Coinciding with the phenomenally popular apple harvest season, the town's arts-and-crafts show is held every weekend from mid-September through the end of November. Local artisans display their wares; there's also plenty of cider and apple pie, plus entertainment and brilliant fall foliage. For more information, contact the chamber of commerce (✆ 760/765-1857).

Rosarito-Ensenada 50-Mile Fun Bicycle Ride, Mexico. This race is held in September and April. See the April entry, above.

October

Zoo Founders Day. Admission to the San Diego Zoo is free for everyone on the first Monday in October, and children enter free all month. Call ✆ 619/234-3153.

Concours d'Elegance, Torrey Pines Golf Course, La Jolla. Classic car buffs won't want to pass this up. And we're not talking hot rods and jalopies here; the show features antique cars of the highest caliber, such as classic Jaguars, Rolls Royces, and Aston Martins. One year featured a salute to Ferrari, another to Alfa Romeo. For more information, call ✆ 619/283-4221. Mid-October.

Underwater Pumpkin Carving Contest, La Jolla. This event might never make it to the Olympics, but plenty of divers have turned out each year since 1981. The rules are relaxed, the panel of judges is serendipitous (one year it was the staff of a local dive shop, the next year five kids off the beach), and it's always a fun party. Spectators can hang out and wait for triumphant artists to break the surface with their creations. For details, call ✆ 858/565-6054. Weekend before Halloween.

November

Carlsbad Village Faire. Billed as the largest 1-day street fair in the United States, this festival features more than 800 vendors on 24 city blocks. Items for sale include ceramics, jewelry, clothing, glassware, and plants. Mexican, Italian, Japanese, Korean, Indonesian, and other edible fare is sold at booths along the way. Ground zero is the intersection of Grand Avenue and Jefferson Street. Call ✆ 760/931-8400 for dates.

New & Nouveau Wine & Food Tasting, Temecula. This is your chance to sample the newest wines of the harvest, complemented by international foods. After you pick up the official map and souvenir wineglass, you're on your own to visit the dozen or so participating wineries over the 2-day period, meeting winemakers and learning to taste young wine. Tickets ($45) usually sell out in advance. Contact the **Temecula Valley Vintners Association** (✆ 800/801-WINE or 909/699-3626; www.temecula wines.org). Third weekend of November.

December

Dr. Seuss Christmas Readings. The late Theodor Geisel's adopted home honors the author by celebrating the holidays with his best-loved characters. Beginning the weekend after Thanksgiving, the lobby of **Loews Coronado Bay Resort** is transformed into "Whoville," where the Cat in the Hat assembles an eager, young (and not-so-young) audience for regular readings of *How the Grinch Stole Christmas.* Punch and cookies are served, and carolers perform following each reading. The free event runs through Christmas Eve, with readings Saturday afternoons and Sunday through Tuesday evenings.

For more information, call ☎ 619/ 424-4000.

Coronado Christmas Celebration and Parade. Santa's arrival by ferry is followed by a small-town parade along Orange Avenue. Call ☎ 800/ 622-8300 or 619/437-8788. First Friday of December.

Christmas on the Prado, Balboa Park. Lovely Balboa Park is decked out in holiday splendor for a magical weekend of evening events. A candlelight procession, traditional caroling, and baroque music ensembles are just part of the entertainment. There are craft displays, ethnic food, traditional hot cider, and a grand Christmas tree and nativity scene in Spreckels Pavilion. The event is free and lasts from 5 to 9pm both days; the park's museums are free during those hours. For more information, call ☎ 619/ 239-0512. Early December.

Whale-Watching. The season starts in mid-December; see the January listing (earlier in this chapter).

Fall Flower Tours and the **Poinsettia Street Festival,** Encinitas. Like its close neighbor Carlsbad, Encinitas is a flower-growing center— 90% of the world's poinsettia plants get their start here. These two events celebrate the quintessential holiday plant and other late-flowering blooms. For information, call the Encinitas Visitors Center (☎ 800/953-6041 or 760/753-6041).

Mission Bay Boat Parade of Lights, from Quivira Basin in Mission Bay. Held on a Saturday, it concludes with the lighting of a 320-foot tower of Christmas lights at SeaWorld. Call ☎ 619/488-0501. Mid-December.

San Diego Harbor Parade of Lights, from Shelter Island to Harbor Island to Seaport Village. Decorated boats of all sizes and types participate, and spectators line the shore and cheer for their favorites. Held since 1971, it's on a Sunday in mid-December. Check the local newspapers for exact day and time.

4 Health & Insurance

HEALTH

If you worry about getting sick away from home, you may want to consider **travel medical insurance** (see below). In most cases, however, your existing health plan will provide all the coverage you need. Be sure to carry your identification card in your wallet.

If you suffer from a chronic illness, consult your doctor before your departure. For conditions like epilepsy, diabetes, or heart problems, wear a **Medic Alert Identification Tag** (☎ 800/825-3785; www.medicalert.org), which will immediately alert doctors to your condition and give them access to your records through Medic Alert's 24-hour hot line.

Pack prescription medications in your carry-on luggage. Carry written prescriptions in generic, not brandname, form, and dispense all prescription medications from their original labeled vials. Also bring along copies of your prescriptions in case you lose your pills or run out of them.

TRAVEL INSURANCE AT A GLANCE

Check your existing insurance policies before you buy travel insurance to cover trip cancellation, lost luggage, or medical expenses or car-rental insurance. You're likely to have partial or complete coverage. But if you need some, ask your travel agent about a comprehensive package. The cost of travel insurance varies widely, depending on the cost and length of your trip, your age and overall health, and the type of trip you're taking. Insurance for extreme sports or adventure travel, for example, will cost more than coverage for a cruise. Some insurers provide packages for specialty vacations, such as skiing or backpacking. More dangerous activities may be excluded from basic policies.

And keep in mind that in the aftermath of the September 11, 2001, terrorist attacks, a number of airlines, cruise lines, and tour operators are no longer covered by insurers. *The bottom line:* Always, always check the fine print before you sign on; more and more policies have built-in exclusions and restrictions that may leave you out in the cold if something does go awry.

For information, contact one of the following popular insurers:

- **Access America** (℃ 800/284-8300); www.accessamerica.com)
- **Travel Guard International** (℃ 800/826-1300; www.travelguard.com)
- **Travel Insured International** (℃ 800/243-3174; www.travelinsured.com)
- **Travelex Insurance Services** (℃ 800/228-9792; www.travelex-insurance.com)

TRIP-CANCELLATION INSURANCE (TCI)

There are three major types of trip-cancellation insurance—one, in the event that you pre-pay a cruise or tour that gets cancelled, and you can't get your money back; a second when you or someone in your family gets sick or dies, and you can't travel (but beware that you may not be covered for a pre-existing condition); and a third, when bad weather makes travel impossible. Some insurers provide coverage for events like jury duty; natural disasters close to home, like floods or fire; or even the loss of a job. A few have added provisions for cancellations due to terrorist activities. Always check the fine print before signing on, and don't

buy trip-cancellation insurance from the tour operator that may be responsible for the cancellation; buy it only from a reputable travel insurance agency. Don't overbuy. You won't be reimbursed for more than the cost of your trip.

MEDICAL INSURANCE

Most health-insurance policies cover you if you get sick away from home, but you should check, particularly if you're insured by an HMO. Members of **Blue Cross Blue Shield** can now use their cards at select hospitals in most major cities worldwide (℃ **800/ 810-BLUE** or www.bluecares.com for a list of hospitals).

LOST-LUGGAGE INSURANCE

On domestic flights, checked baggage is covered up to $2,500 per ticketed passenger. On international flights (including U.S. portions of international trips), baggage is limited to approximately $9.07 per pound, up to approximately $635 per checked bag. If you plan to check items more valuable than the standard liability, you may purchase "excess valuation" coverage from the airline, up to $5,000. Be sure to take any valuables or irreplaceable items with you in your carry-on luggage. If you file a lost luggage claim, be prepared to answer detailed questions about the contents of your baggage, and be sure to file a claim immediately, as most airlines enforce a 21-day deadline. Before you leave home, compile an inventory of all packed items and a rough estimate of the total value to ensure you're properly compensated if your luggage is lost. You will only be reimbursed for what you lose, no more. Once you've filed a complaint, persist in securing your reimbursement; there are no laws governing the length of time it takes for a carrier to reimburse you. If you arrive at a destination without your bags, ask the airline to forward them to your hotel or to your next destination; they will usually comply. If your bag is delayed or lost, the airline may reimburse you for reasonable expenses, such as a toothbrush or a set of clothes, but the airline is under no legal obligation to do so.

Lost luggage may also be covered by your homeowner's or renter's policy. Many platinum and gold credit cards cover you as well. If you choose to purchase additional lost-luggage insurance, be sure not to buy more than you need. Buy in advance from the insurer or a trusted agent (prices will be much higher at the airport).

CAR-RENTAL INSURANCE (LOSS/DAMAGE WAIVER OR COLLISION DAMAGE WAIVER)

If you hold a private auto-insurance policy, you probably are covered in the United States for loss or damage to a rental car and for liability in case a passenger is injured. The credit card you use to rent the car also may provide some coverage.

Car-rental insurance probably does not cover liability if you caused the accident. Check your own auto-insurance policy, the rental-company policy, and your credit-card coverage for the extent of coverage: Is your destination covered? Are other drivers covered? How much liability is covered if a passenger is injured? (If you rely on your credit card for coverage, you may want to bring a second credit card with you, as damages may be charged to your card, and you may find yourself stranded with no money.)

For information on car renter's insurance, see "Getting Around: By Car," in chapter 4.

5 Tips for Travelers with Special Needs

FOR TRAVELERS WITH DISABILITIES

The Accessible San Diego hot line (© 858/279-0704; fax 858/279-5118; www.accessandiego.com) helps travelers with disabilities find accessible hotels, tours, attractions, and transportation. If you call long distance and get the answering machine, leave a message, and the staff will call you back collect. Ask for the annual *Access in San Diego* pamphlet, a citywide guide with specifics on which establishments are accessible for those with visual, mobility, or hearing disabilities.

In the San Diego Convention & Visitors Bureau's **Dining and Accommodations** guide, a wheelchair symbol designates places that are accessible to persons with disabilities.

On buses and trolleys, riders with disabilities pay a fixed fare of 75¢. Many MTS buses and all trolleys are equipped with wheelchair lifts; priority seating is available on buses and trolleys. Stops served by accessible buses are marked with a wheelchair symbol. People with visual impairments benefit from the white reflecting ring that circles the bottom of the trolley door to increase its visibility.

Airport transportation for travelers with disabilities is available from **Cloud 9 Shuttle** (© 800/9-SHUTTLE or 858/9-SHUTTLE; www.cloud9shuttle.com). Other information sources to consider include the **Society for Accessible Travel and Hospitality,** 347 Fifth Ave., Suite 610, New York, NY 10016 (© 212/447-7284; fax 212/725-8253; www.sath.org). Membership costs $45 annually ($30 for seniors and students), and allows access to a vast network of connections in the travel industry. The society provides information sheets on travel destinations and referrals to tour operators that specialize in traveling with disabilities. The quarterly magazine, *Open World,* is full of good information and resources. A year's subscription is included with membership or costs $18 if purchased separately ($35 outside the U.S.).

Vision-impaired travelers should contact the **American Foundation for the Blind** (ⓒ 800/232-5463; www.afb.org) for information on traveling with Seeing Eye dogs.

Many of the major car-rental companies offer hand-controlled cars. **Avis** can provide a vehicle at any of its locations in the United States with 48-hour advance notice; **Hertz** requires 24 to 72 hours of advance reservation at most of its locations. **Wheelchair Getaways** (ⓒ 800/642-2402; www.wheelchair-getaways.com) rents specialized vans with wheelchair lifts and other features for travelers with disabilities in more than 100 cities across the United States.

FOR GAY & LESBIAN TRAVELERS

Gay and lesbian visitors might already know about Hillcrest, the stylish part of town near Balboa Park that's the city's most prominent gay community. Many gay-owned restaurants, boutiques, and nightspots cater to a gay and straight clientele, and the scene is lively most nights of the week.

The **Lesbian and Gay Men's Community Center** is located at 3916 Normal St. (ⓒ 619/692-2077; www.thecentersd.org). It's open Monday through Friday from 9am to 10pm and Saturday from 9am to 7pm. Community outreach and counseling are offered.

The **Annual San Diego Lesbian and Gay Pride Parade, Rally, and Festival** is held the third or fourth weekend in July. The parade begins at noon on Saturday at University Avenue and Normal Street, and proceeds west on University to Sixth Avenue. A festival follows on Saturday from 2 to 10pm and Sunday from noon to 10pm. For more information, call ⓒ 619/297-7683.

The free *San Diego Gay and Lesbian Times,* published every Thursday, is often available at **Obelisk** bookstore, 1029 University Ave., Hillcrest (ⓒ 619/297-4171). And check out the **San Diego Gay & Lesbian Chamber of Commerce** online at **www.gsdba.org,** where you can search the business directory and find a variety restaurants, cafes, hotels, and other businesses that welcome gay and lesbian clients.

The **International Gay & Lesbian Travel Association** (ⓒ 800/448-8550 or 954/776-2626; www.iglta.org) links travelers with the appropriate gay-friendly service organization or tour specialist. It has about 1,200 members and offers quarterly newsletters, marketing mailings, and a membership directory that's updated quarterly.

Out and About (ⓒ 800/929-2268 or 415/486-2591; www.outandabout.com) offers guidebooks and a monthly newsletter packed with good information on the global gay and lesbian scene. A year's subscription to the newsletter costs $49. *Gay Travel A to Z: The World of Gay & Lesbian Travel Options at Your Fingertips,* by Marianne Ferrari (Ferrari Publications), is a very good gay and lesbian guidebook series.

FOR SENIORS

Nearly every attraction in San Diego offers a senior discount; age requirements vary, and prices are discussed in chapter 7. Public transportation and movie theaters also have reduced rates. Don't be shy about asking for discounts, but always carry identification, such as a driver's license, that shows your date of birth. Also, mention the fact that you're a senior citizen when you first make your travel reservations. For example, both **Amtrak** (ⓒ 800/USA-RAIL; www.amtrak.com) and **Greyhound** (ⓒ 800/752-4841; www.greyhound.com) offer discounts to persons over 62, as do many airlines.

A delightful way to meet older San Diegans, many of whom are retired, is to join a free Saturday-morning stroll with **Downtown Sam,** a footloose retiree and guide with **Walkabout International** (see "Organized Tours" in chapter 7).

San Diego's special senior citizens referral and information line is ℂ **619/560-2500.**

Members of **AARP,** 601 E St. NW, Washington, DC 20049 (ℂ **800/424-3410** or 202/434-2277; www.aarp.org), get discounts not only on hotels but also on airfares and car rentals. AARP offers members a wide range of special benefits, including *Modern Maturity* magazine and a monthly newsletter. Anyone over 50 can join.

The Mature Traveler, a monthly 12-page newsletter on senior citizen travel, is a valuable resource. It is available by subscription ($30 a year) from GEM Publishing Group, Box 50400, Reno, NV 89513-0400. GEM also publishes *The Book of Deals,* a collection of more than 1,000 senior discounts on airlines, lodging, tours, and attractions around the country; it's available for $9.95 by calling ℂ **800/460-6676.** Another helpful publication is *101 Tips for the Mature Traveler,* available free from Grand Circle Travel (ℂ **800/221-2610** or 617/350-7500; www.gct.com). Also check your newsstand for the quarterly magazine *Travel 50 & Beyond.*

If you want something more than the average vacation or guided tour, try **Elderhostel** (ℂ **877/426-8056;** www.elderhostel.org). It organizes educational travel for people 55 and over (plus a spouse or companion of any age). On these escorted tours, the days are packed with seminars, lectures, and field trips, and academic experts lead the sightseeing. Most courses last about 3 weeks, and many include airfare, accommodations in student dormitories or modest inns,

meals, and tuition. There is an Elderhostel educational program in the San Diego area, at the Point Loma Youth Hostel.

FOR FAMILIES

Several books offer tips on traveling with kids. *Family Travel* (Lanier Publishing International) and *How to Take Great Trips with Your Kids* (The Harvard Common Press) are full of good general advice. *The Unofficial Guide to California with Kids* (Hungry Minds, Inc.) is an excellent resource that covers the entire state. It rates and ranks attractions for each age group, lists dozens of family friendly accommodations and restaurants, and suggests lots of beaches and activities that are fun for the whole clan.

Family Travel Times is published six times a year (ℂ **888/822-4388** or 212/477-5524; www.familytravel times.com), and includes a weekly call-in service for subscribers. Subscriptions are $39 a year.

Be sure to check out the "Family-Friendly" boxes in the hotel and restaurant chapters; they will point you to the most accommodating and fun establishments. The "Especially for Kids" section in chapter 7 offers tips about which San Diego sights and attractions have the most appeal for the little ones.

STUDENT TRAVEL

You'd be wise to arm yourself with an **international student ID card,** which offers substantial savings on hotel rooms, rail passes, plane tickets, and admission fees. It also provides you with basic health and life insurance and a 24-hour help line. The card is available for $22 from the **Council on International Educational Exchange**'s travel branch, **Council Travel** (ℂ **800/226-8624;** www.counciltravel.com), which is the biggest student travel agency in the world. If you're no longer a student but are still under 26, you can get a

GO 25 card from CIEE, which entitles you to insurance and some discounts.

STA Travel (© 800/781-4040; www.statravel.com) is another travel agency catering especially to young travelers, although their bargain-basement prices are available to people of all ages. In Canada, **Travel CUTS** (© 800/667-2887 or 416/614-2887; www.travelcuts.com), offers similar services.

TRAVELING WITH PETS

Many of us wouldn't dream of going on vacation without our pets. Under the right circumstances, it can be a memorable experience. And these days, more and more lodgings and restaurants are going the pet-friendly route. Many hotel and motel chains, such as Best Western, Motel 6, Holiday Inn, and Four Seasons–Regent Hotels, welcome pets. Policies vary, however, so call ahead to find out the rules.

An excellent resource is **www.pets welcome.com**, which dispenses medical tips, names of animal-friendly lodgings and campgrounds, and lists of kennels and veterinarians. Also check out *The Portable Petswelcome. com: The Complete Guide to Traveling with Your Pet* (Howell Book House), which features the best selection of pet travel information anywhere. Another resource is *Pets-R-Permitted Hotel, Motel & Kennel Directory: The Travel Resource for Pet Owners Who Travel* (Annenberg Communications).

If you plan to fly with your pet, the FAA has compiled a list of all requirements for transporting live animals at **www.dot.gov/airconsumer/animals. htm**. You may be able to carry your pet on board a plane if it's small enough to put inside a carrier that can slip under the seat. Pets usually count as one piece of carry-on luggage. Note that summer may not be the best time to fly with your pet: Many airlines will not check pets as baggage in the hot summer months. The ASPCA discourages travelers from checking pets as luggage at any time, as storage conditions on planes are loosely monitored, and fatal accidents are not unprecedented. Your other option is to ship your pet with a professional carrier, which can be expensive. Ask your veterinarian whether you should sedate your pet on a plane ride or give it anti-nausea medication. Never give your pet sedatives used by humans.

Keep in mind that dogs are prohibited on hiking trails and must be leashed at all times on federal lands administered by the National Park Service (national parks and monuments).

6 Getting There

BY PLANE

Flights arrive at San Diego International Airport/Lindbergh Field (named after aviation hero Charles Lindbergh), which is served by many national and regional air carriers as well as Aeroméxico and British Airways.

Terminal 1 airlines include: **Aeroméxico** (© 800/237-6639; www.aeromexico.com), **Alaska Airlines** (© 800/252-7522; www.alaska air.com), **Southwest Airlines** (© 800/435-9792; www.southwest.com), **United Airlines** (© 800/241-6522; www.united.com), and **US Airways** (© 800/428-4322; www.usairways. com).

Terminal 2 airlines include: **Air Canada** (© 888/247-2262; www.air canada.ca), **American Airlines** (© 800/433-7300; www.aa.com), **British Airways** (© 800/247-9297; www.british-airways.com), **Midwest Express** (© 800/452-2022; www. midwestexpress.com), and **Northwest Airlines** (© 800/225-2525; www. nwa.com).

The airlines in the Terminal 2 expansion are **America West** (© 800/ 235-9292; www.americawest. com), **Continental Airlines** (© 800/ 525-0280; www.continental.com), and **Delta Air Lines** (© 800/221-1212; www.delta.com).

The following airlines arrive at the Commuter Terminal: Alaska Commuter, American Eagle, Continental Connection, Delta Connection, Northwest AirLink, Skywest Airlines, United Express, and US Airways Express. For contact information on these regional carriers, refer to the appendix at the back of this book.

AIR TRAVEL SECURITY MEASURES

In the wake of the terrorist attacks of September 11, 2001, the airline industry implemented sweeping security measures in airports. Depending on the airline/airport, you might encounter a lengthy check-in process. You can expedite the process by taking the following steps:

- **Arrive early.** At press time airlines were advising passengers to arrive at the airport either 90 minutes (carry-on bags only) or 2 hours (to check luggage) before your scheduled flight. Call ahead for the latest guidelines.
- **Don't count on curbside check-in.** Some airlines and airports have stopped curbside check-in altogether, whereas others offer it on a limited basis. For up-to-date information on specific regulations and implementations, check with the individual airline.
- **Be sure to carry plenty of documentation.** A government-issued photo ID (federal, state, or local) is now required. You may need to show this at various checkpoints. With an E-ticket, you may be required to have with you printed confirmation of purchase, and perhaps even the credit card with

which you bought your ticket. This varies from airline to airline, so call ahead to make sure you have the proper documentation. And be sure that your ID is **up-to-date:** An expired driver's license, for example, may keep you from boarding the plane altogether.

- **Know what you can carry on— and what you can't.** Travelers in the United States are now limited to one carry-on bag, plus one personal bag (such as a purse or a briefcase). The TSA regularly updates its list of restricted carry-on items; see the box "What You Can Carry On—And What You Can't."
- **Prepare to be searched.** Expect spot-checks. Electronic items, such as a laptop or cellphone, should be readied for additional screening. Limit the metal items you wear on your person.
- **It's no joke.** When a check-in agent asks if someone other than you packed your bag, don't decide that this is the time to be funny. The agents will not hesitate to call an alarm.
- **No ticket, no gate access.** Only ticketed passengers will be allowed beyond the screener checkpoints, except for those people with specific medical or parental needs.

FLYING FOR LESS: TIPS FOR GETTING THE BEST AIRFARE

- Keep checking your newspaper for **sales.** You'll almost never see a sale during the peak summer vacation months of July and August, or during the Thanksgiving or Christmas holidays, but during slower times airlines may slash their fares dramatically.
- If your schedule is flexible, ask if you can secure a cheaper fare by staying an extra day, by staying over Saturday night, or by flying

---

Tips What You Can Carry On—And What You Can't

The Transportation Safety Administration (TSA) has devised new restrictions on carry-on baggage, not only to expedite the screening process but also to prevent potential weapons from passing through airport security. Passengers are now limited to bringing just one carry-on bag and one personal item onto the aircraft (previous regulations allowed two carry-on bags and one personal item, like a briefcase or a purse). For the latest list of restricted items, check the TSA's website at **www.tsa.gov**. The airline you fly may have additional restrictions on items you can and cannot carry on board. Call ahead to avoid problems.

Not permitted: knives and box cutters, corkscrews, straight razors, metal scissors, golf clubs, baseball bats, pool cues, hockey sticks, ski poles, ice picks.

Permitted: nail clippers, tweezers, eyelash curlers, safety razors (including disposable razors), syringes (with documented proof of medical need), walking canes and umbrellas (must be inspected first).

---

midweek. Many airlines won't volunteer this information, so ask them lots of questions.

- Formerly known as "bucket shops," *consolidators* (wholesalers who buy tickets in bulk at a discount) today are legitimate and offer some of the best deals around. You can get virtually any flight, on any airline, from them; sometimes their fare is identical to the airline's, but often it's discounted 15% to 50%. The tickets carry the same restrictions the airline imposes on advance and discount fares. Their ads usually run in the Sunday travel section, and many have followed the lead of the major airlines and travel agencies by setting up online reservations systems.

- There are lots of fly-by-night consolidators, though, and problems can range from disputing never-received tickets to finding you have no seat booked when you get to the airport. Play it safe by going with a reputable business. Here are some suggestions: **1-800-FLY-CHEAP** (www.flycheap.com); **Cheap Seats** (✆ 800/451-7200; www.cheapseatstravel.com); or my favorite, **Cheap Tickets** (✆ 800/377-1000; www.cheaptickets.com).

- **Search the Internet** for bargains. Great last-minute deals are available through free weekly e-mail services provided directly by the airlines. See "Planning Your Trip Online," below, for more information.

- Several major airlines offer a free e-mail service known as **E-Savers**, which allow them to send you their best bargain airfares on a regular basis. It's a service for the spontaneously inclined and travelers looking for a quick getaway. But the fares are cheap, so it's worth taking a look. Check directly with the individual airlines' websites (see above, or the appendix, "Useful Toll-Free Numbers & Websites").

Tips Packing for Your Trip

Bring a **sweater** or **light jacket,** even in summer. Because the ocean is close by, cold, damp breezes are common after the sun sets. But leave behind your heavy coats and cold-weather gear, no matter when you're coming. Pack **casual clothes.** Shorts, jeans, and T-shirts are common at all tourist attractions and many restaurants. Men who plan to try one of San Diego's nicer restaurants may want to bring a sports jacket, but this is really an informal town. Bring **good, comfortable walking shoes;** you can cover a lot of ground in this pleasant, outdoorsy city.

Don't forget **sunglasses,** an essential accessory (especially if you'll be on or near the water, which reflects and amplifies the sun's rays). If you have **binoculars,** bring them—they'll come in handy during whale-watching season. Regardless of the time of year, it's wise to pack a **bathing suit.** Most hotels have heated pools and whirlpools, and you might be surprised by a day warm enough for the beach.

HOW TO HAVE AN (ALMOST) FIRST-CLASS EXPERIENCE IN COACH

Anyone who has traveled in coach or economy class in recent years can attest to the frustrating reality of cramped seating. But with a little savvy and advance planning, you can make an otherwise unpleasant coach experience downright comfy.

Here are some tips for finding the right seat:

- For more legroom, check in early and ask for an aisle seat in an emergency-exit row or bulkhead.
- To have two seats for yourself, try for an aisle seat in a center section toward the back of coach.
- To sleep, avoid the last row or the row in front of the emergency exit, as these seats are the least likely to recline. You also may want to reserve a window seat so that you can rest your head and avoid being bumped in the aisle.
- If you're traveling with a companion, book an aisle and a window seat. Middle seats are usually booked last, so chances are good you'll end up with three seats to yourselves. And in the case that a third passenger is assigned the middle seat, they'll probably be more than happy to trade for a window or an aisle.
- Unless you love noise, avoid seats in the very back, or near toilets and pantries.

Here are some tips for making yourself comfortable during your flight:

- Wear comfortable, low-heeled shoes and dress in loose-fitting layers that you can remove as cabin temperature fluctuates. Don't underdress: Airline cabins can be notoriously chilly, and blankets may be unavailable. Wear breathable natural fabrics rather than synthetics.
- Hydrate before, during, and after your flight to combat the lack of humidity in airplane cabins— which can be as dry as the Sahara Desert. Bring a bottle of water on board.
- Pre-order a special meal. The airlines' vegetarian and kosher meals are usually fresher than standard plane fare. Or brown-bag your own meal.
- Get up and walk around whenever you can or perform stretching exercises in your seat to keep your blood flowing.

Flying with Film & Video

Never pack unprotected, undeveloped film in checked bags, which may be scanned. The film you carry with you can be damaged by scanners, too. X-ray damage is cumulative; the slower the film, and the more times you put it through a scanner, the more likely the damage. Film under 800 ASA is usually safe for up to five scans. If you're taking your film through additional scans, request a hand inspection. In U.S. airports, the Federal Aviation Administration guarantees hand inspections. In international airports, you're at the mercy of airport officials. On international flights, store your film in transparent baggies, so you can remove it easily before you go through scanners. Keep in mind that airports are not the only places where your camera may be scanned: Highly trafficked attractions are X-raying visitors' bags with increasing frequency.

Most photo-supply stores sell protective pouches designed to block damaging X-rays. The pouches fit both film and loaded cameras. They should protect your film in checked baggage, but they also may raise alarms and result in a hand inspection.

An organization called **Film Safety for Traveling on Planes** (℃ 888-301-2665; www.f-stop.org) can provide additional tips for traveling with film and equipment.

Carry-on scanners will not damage **videotape** in video camera, but the magnetic fields emitted by the walk-through security gateways and handheld inspection wands will. Always place your loaded camcorder on the screening conveyor belt or have it hand-inspected. Be sure your batteries are charged, as you will probably be required to turn the device on to ensure that it's what it appears to be.

• Bring a toothbrush and moisturizer to stay fresh.
• If you're flying with kids, don't forget a deck of cards, toys, extra bottles, pacifiers, diapers, and chewing gum to help them relieve ear pressure buildup during ascent and descent. Let each child pack his or her own backpack with favorite toys.
• If you're flying with a cold or chronic sinus problems, use a decongestant 10 minutes before ascent and descent, to minimize pressure buildup in the inner ear.
• Try to acclimate yourself to the local time as quickly as possible. Stay up as long as you can the first day, then try to wake up at a normal hour the next morning.

BY CAR
Visitors driving to San Diego from Los Angeles and points north do so via coastal route I-5. From points northeast, take I-15 (link up with I-8 West and Hwy. 163 South or Hwy. 94 West); from the east, use I-8 (link up with Hwy. 163 South). Entering the downtown area, Highway 163 turns into 10th Avenue, and Highway 94 turns into F Street. Try to avoid arriving during weekday rush hours, between 7 and 9am and 3 and 6pm. If you are heading to Coronado, take the Coronado Bridge from I-5. Maximum speed in the San Diego area is 65 mph (105kmph), and many areas are limited to 55 mph (80kmph).

> ### 📌 Tips American Automobile Association
>
> If you're planning a road trip, it's a good idea to be a member of the **American Automobile Association (AAA)**. Members who carry their cards with them not only receive free roadside assistance, but also have access to a wealth of free travel information (detailed maps and guidebooks). Also, many hotels and attractions throughout California offer discounts to AAA members—always inquire. Call 📞 **800/922-8228** or your local branch for membership information.

San Diego is 130 miles (209km; 2 hr.) from **Los Angeles;** 149 miles (240km) from **Palm Springs,** a 2½-hour trip; and 532 miles (857km), or 8 hours, from **San Francisco.**

BY TRAIN

Trains from all points in the United States and Canada will take you to Los Angeles, where you'll need to change trains for the 3-hour journey to San Diego. You'll arrive at the striking, mission-style Santa Fe Station, built in 1914 and located downtown at Broadway and Kettner Boulevard. For price and schedule information, call **Amtrak** (📞 **800/USA-RAIL;** www. amtrak.com).

7 Package Deals

PACKAGE TOURS FOR INDEPENDENT TRAVELERS

Package tours are not the same thing as escorted tours. With a package tour, you travel independently but pay a group rate. Packages usually include airfare, a choice of hotels, and car rentals, and packagers often offers several options at different prices. In many cases, a package that includes airfare, hotel, and transportation to and from the airport will cost you less than just the hotel alone would have, had you booked it yourself. That's because packages are sold in bulk to tour operators—who resell them to the public at a cost that drastically undercuts standard rates.

THE PROS & CONS OF PACKAGE TOURS

Packages can save you money because they are sold in bulk to tour operators, who resell them to the public. They offer group prices but allow for independent travel. The disadvantages are that you're usually required to make a large payment upfront; you may end up on a charter flight; and you have to deal with your own luggage and with transfers between your hotel and the airport, if transfers are not included in the package price. Packages often don't allow for complete flexibility or a wide range of choices. For instance, you may prefer a quiet inn but have to settle for a popular chain hotel instead. Your choice of travel days may be limited as well.

RECOMMENDED PACKAGE TOUR OPERATORS

For information on independent fly-drive packages, contact **American Airlines Vacations** (📞 800/321-2121; www.aavacations.com), **Continental Airlines Vacations** (📞 800/301-3800; www.coolvacations.com), **Delta Vacations** (📞 800/654-6559; www.deltavacations.com), **Southwest Airlines Vacations** (📞 800/423-5683; www.swavacations.com), or **United Vacations** (📞 888/854-3899; www.unitedvacations.com).

Online Vacation Mall (📞 800/839-9851; www.onlinevacationmall.com) allows you to search for and book packages offered by a number of tour operators and airlines. The **United States Tour Operators Association**'s website (www.ustoa.com) has a search engine that allows you to look for operators that offer packages to a specific destination. Travel packages are also listed in the travel section of your local Sunday newspaper. **Liberty Travel** (✆ 888/271-1584; www.libertytravel.com), one of the biggest packagers in the Northeast, often runs full-page ads in Sunday papers.

Availability of all packages varies widely based upon season and demand, but it always pays to investigate what the major air carriers are offering. The packages are best suited to travelers who can be flexible in the following ways:

- Understand that not every hotel in the city will be an option. That's not to say packages force you to stay in dumps—quite the contrary. They often include the city's top choices, but you'll have a limited selection. Pinpoint roughly where you'd like to stay, and ask if there's a participating hotel there.

(The biggest hotel chains and resorts also offer package deals. If you already know where you want to stay, call the resort and ask if it offers land-air packages.)

- Avoid scheduling your departure and arrival on the weekend, if you can; airfares will usually be at least $25 to $50 lower per person. And it goes without saying that the popular season (summer in San Diego) is the most restrictive season. Package deals will still save you some money over booking separately, though.

- Always ask the reservationist questions, and mention the activities you're considering for your visit. All the companies have access to various goodies they can hitch to your package for far less than you'd pay separately. Examples include tickets to SeaWorld, the San Diego Zoo, or the Wild Animal Park; passes for city tours, harbor cruises, and other excursions; tickets for theater events; rental-car upgrades; and, other specials.

8 Planning Your Trip Online

Researching and booking your trip online can save time and money. Then again, it may not. It is simply not true that you always get the best deal online. Most booking engines do not include schedules and prices for budget airlines, and from time to time you'll get a better last-minute price by calling the airline directly, so it's best to call the airline to see if you can do better before booking online.

On the plus side, Internet users today can tap into the same travel-planning databases that were once accessible only to travel agents—and do it at the same speed. Sites such as **Frommers.com, Travelocity.com, Expedia.com,** and **Orbitz.com** allow consumers to comparison shop for airfares, access special bargains, book

flights, and reserve hotel rooms and rental cars.

But don't fire your travel agent just yet. Although online booking sites offer tips and hard data to help you bargain shop, they cannot endow you with the hard-earned experience that makes a seasoned, reliable travel agent an invaluable resource, even in the Internet age. And for consumers with a complex itinerary, using a trusty travel agent is still the best way to arrange the most direct flights to and from the best airports.

Still, there's no denying the Internet's emergence as a powerful tool in researching and plotting travel time. The benefits of researching your trip online can be well worth the effort:

- **Last-minute specials,** known as **E-Savers,** such as weekend deals or Internet-only fares, are offered by airlines to fill empty seats. Most of these are announced on Tuesday or Wednesday and must be purchased online. They are only valid for travel that weekend, but some can be booked weeks or months in advance. Sign up for weekly e-mail alerts at airline websites (see Appendix B) or check megasites that compile comprehensive lists of E-savers, such as **Smarter Living** (www.smarterliving.com) or **WebFlyer** (www.webflyer.com).
- Some sites will send you **e-mail notification** when a cheap fare to your favorite destination becomes available. Some will also tell you when fares to a particular destination are lowest.
- The best of the travel-planning sites are now **highly personalized;** they track your frequent-flier miles, and store your seating and meal preferences, tentative itineraries, and credit-card information, letting you plan trips or check agendas quickly.
- All major airlines offer **incentives**—bonus frequent-flier miles,

Internet-only discounts, sometimes even free cellphone rentals—when you purchase online or buy an E-ticket.

- Advances in mobile technology provide business travelers and other frequent travelers with **the ability to check flight status, change plans, or get specific directions** from hand-held computing devices, mobile phones, and pagers. Some sites will e-mail or page you if a flight is delayed.

TRAVEL PLANNING & BOOKING SITES

Keep in mind that because several airlines are no longer willing to pay commissions on tickets sold by online travel agencies, these agencies may either add a $10 surcharge to your bill if you book on that carrier—or neglect to offer those carriers' schedules.

The list of sites below is selective, not comprehensive. Some sites will have evolved or disappeared by the time you read this.

- **Travelocity** (www.travelocity.com or www.frommers.travelocity.com) and **Expedia** (www.expedia.com) are among the most popular sites, each offering an excellent range of

---

 Frommers.com: The Complete Travel Resource

For an excellent travel planning resource, we highly recommend **Frommers.com** (www.frommers.com). We're a little biased, of course, but we think you'll find the travel tips, reviews, monthly vacation giveaways, and online-booking capabilities thoroughly indispensable. Among the special features are our popular **Message Boards,** where Frommer's readers post queries and share advice (sometimes even our authors show up to answer questions); **Frommers.com Newsletter,** for the latest travel bargains and inside travel secrets; and Frommer's **Destinations Section,** where you'll get expert travel tips, hotel and dining recommendations, and advice on the sights to see for more than 2,500 destinations around the globe. When your research is done, the **Online Reservation System** (www.frommers.com/booktravelnow) takes you to Frommer's favorite sites for booking your vacation at affordable prices.

options. Travelers search by destination, dates, and cost.

- **Orbitz** (www.orbitz.com) is a popular site launched by United, Delta, Northwest, American, and Continental airlines. (Stay tuned: At press time, travel-agency associations were waging an antitrust battle against this site.)
- **Qixo** (www.qixo.com) is another powerful search engine that allows you to search for flights and accommodations from some 20 airline and travel-planning sites (such as Travelocity) at once. Qixo sorts results by price.
- **Priceline** (www.priceline.com) lets you "name your price" for airline tickets, hotel rooms, and rental cars. For airline tickets, you can't say what time you want to fly—you have to accept any flight between 6am and 10pm on the dates you've selected, and you may have to make one or more stopovers. Tickets are nonrefundable, and no frequent-flyer miles are awarded.

SMART E-SHOPPING

The savvy traveler is armed with insider information. Here are a few tips to help you navigate the Internet successfully and safely.

- **Know when sales start.** Last-minute deals may vanish in minutes. If you have a favorite booking site or airline, find out when last-minute deals are released to the public. (For example, Southwest's specials are posted every Tues at 12:01am central time.)
- **Shop around.** If you're looking for bargains, compare prices on different sites and airlines—and against a travel agent's best fare. Try a range of times and alternative airports before you make a purchase.
- **Stay secure.** Book only through secure sites (some airline sites are

not secure). Look for a key icon (Netscape) or a padlock (Internet Explorer) at the bottom of your Web browser before you enter credit card information or other personal data.

- **Avoid online auctions.** Sites that auction airline tickets and frequent-flier miles are the number-one perpetrators of Internet fraud, according to the National Consumers League.
- **Maintain a paper trail.** If you book an E-ticket, print out a confirmation, or write down your confirmation number, and keep it safe and accessible—or your trip could be a virtual one!

ONLINE TRAVELER'S TOOLBOX

Veteran travelers usually carry some essential items to make their trips easier. Following is a selection of online tools to bookmark and use.

- **Visa ATM Locator** (www.visa.com), for locations of PLUS ATMs worldwide, or **MasterCard ATM Locator** (www.mastercard.com), for locations of Cirrus ATMs worldwide.
- **Intellicast** (www.intellicast.com) and **Weather.com** (www.weather.com). Gives weather forecasts for all 50 states and for cities around the world.
- **Mapquest** (www.mapquest.com). This best of the mapping sites lets you choose a specific address or destination, and in seconds, it will return a map and detailed directions.
- **Cybercafes.com** (www.cybercafes.com) or **Net Café Guide** (www.netcafeguide.com/mapindex.htm). Locate Internet cafes at hundreds of locations around the globe. Catch up on your e-mail and log on to the Web for a few dollars per hour.

9 Recommended Reading

While New York and San Francisco may be more well known for their cosmopolitan literary mentions, San Diego is no slouch when it comes to colorful characters, bigger-than-life biographies, hard-core history, and famous fiction.

Philip Marlowe, Raymond Chandler's classic detective, spent most of his time in the literary Los Angeles of the 1940s. But the last Marlowe mystery, *Playback* (Vintage Books, 1988), includes a beautiful woman who hides out in "Esmeralda," a coastal town north of downtown San Diego that's actually La Jolla, where Chandler spent the last 13 years of his life.

The 1980 film starring Christopher Reeve and Jane Seymour may have moved the story from the Hotel del Coronado to a turn-of-the-century hotel in Mackinac Island, Michigan, but *Somewhere in Time* (St. Martin's Press, 1999), penned by master thriller novelist Richard Matheson—also known for *A Stir of Echoes* (Tor Books, 1999) and *What Dreams May Come* (Tor Books, 1998)—is one of the most famous stories set in San Diego to date. Originally published in 1975 under the title *Bid Time Return* (Buccaneer Books, 1995), this science fiction slanted romantic fantasy works not only as a love story but a vivid travelogue of Southern California and the Coronado.

Coronado also figures largely in L. Frank Baum's *Oz* books, including *The Wizard of Oz* (Tor Books, 1995). The author, who lived in Coronado, based his description of the Emerald City on it. Another San Diego local, Theodore Geisel (aka Dr. Seuss), wrote many of his much-loved fantasy books while living in La Jolla.

Best-selling cop novelist Joseph Wambaugh has also placed two of his recent novels in his adopted hometown. *Finnegan's Week* (Bantam Books, 1996) depicts a week in the life of an aging detective juggling his midlife crisis with citywide crimes and hijinks. And *Floaters* (Bantam Books, 1997) is a mystery revolving around an impending America's Cup sailing race.

The Pump House Gang (Bantam Doubleday Dell, 1999), a psychedelic collection of 1960s essays by Tom Wolfe, is named for the often-crazy coterie of expert surfers that hung out at La Jolla's Windansea beach; the eponymous short story vividly captures a sense of place and of an entire generation.

Generally recognized as the most accurate depiction of sea life at the time, Richard Henry Dana's *Two Years Before the Mast* (Signet, 2000) is an autobiographical account of Dana's voyage along the coast of California in the 1840s. Much of the book features Dana's experiences in ports in San Diego and Orange County.

Thomas S. Hines's gorgeous coffee-table book, *Irving Gill and the Architecture of Reform: A Study in Modernist Architectural Culture* (Monacelli, 2000), features photographs and text that showcases the artist's early-20th-century modern style. Architectural buffs will enjoy Gill's designs that, while lesser known than those of his contemporaries like Wright, Frey, Neutra, and Schindler, are local landmarks. Much of Gill's work is in La Jolla.

Mission San Luis Rey in northern San Diego County inspired the setting in Helen Hunt Jackson's 1884 novel, *Ramona: A Story* (New American Library, 1988). A love story that holds up even with today's jaded audiences, Jackson's tale incorporates a changing California (the fading Spanish order, the decline of Native American tribes, the arrival of white settlers) into its enduring drama. The Estudillo House in Old Town is sometimes called

"Ramona's House" because it so closely resembles the vivid description in the book.

Local sports hero Greg Louganis (a San Diego native) is best known for his gold medal–winning diving performances at the 1984 and 1988 Olympics, but *Breaking the Surface* (Plume, 1996), his emotional and inspiring autobiography, paints a portrait not just of physical accomplishment, but of a sensitive athlete who struggled with self-doubt before coming out as an HIV-positive gay man. An avid animal lover and breeder, Louganis is also the author of *For the Life of Your Dog: A Complete Guide to Having a Dog in Your Life* (Pocket Books, 1999).

Published by the San Diego Historical Society, Elizabeth C. MacPhail's *The Story of New San Diego and of its Founder, Alonzo E. Horton* (San Diego Historical Society, 1989) is packed with facts about Horton's tireless belief that San Diego could be a major port city, and reasons why his "New" San Diego—the genesis of today's bustling downtown—succeeded where two previous attempts to relocate from "Old Town" had failed. Even just flipping through the many archival photos is eye-opening.

The brother-and-sister team of E. W. and Ellen Browning were responsible for, among other things, the establishment of the Scripps Institute of Oceanography, early funding of the San Diego Zoo, creating Torrey Pines State Park, and leaving a permanent imprint on the community of La Jolla. In *Edward Willis and Ellen Browning Scripps: An Unmatched Pair* (Image Books, 1990), Charles Preece offers the best biography of these two pillars of San Diego's philanthropic Scripps family.

Another local luminary, Dr. Harry M. Wegeforth, was the energetic founder of the San Diego Zoo and is the subject of *It Began With a Roar* (Zoological Society of San Diego, 1990), written by Wegeforth and San Diego newspaperman Neil Morgan. This thin, fun volume relates the adventures of the zoo's early days from Wegeforth's own memoirs.

3

For International Visitors

Whether it's your first visit or your tenth, a trip to the United States may require an additional degree of planning. This chapter will provide you with essential information, helpful tips, and advice for the more common problems that some visitors encounter.

1 Preparing for Your Trip

ENTRY REQUIREMENTS

Check at any U.S. embassy or consulate for current information and requirements. You can also obtain a visa application and other information online from the **U.S. State Department**'s website at **http://travel.state. gov.**

VISAS The U.S. State Department has a **Visa Waiver Program** allowing citizens of certain countries to enter the United States without a visa for stays of up to 90 days. At press time these included Andorra, Australia, Austria, Belgium, Brunei, Denmark, Finland, France, Germany, Iceland, Ireland, Italy, Japan, Liechtenstein, Luxembourg, Monaco, the Netherlands, New Zealand, Norway, Portugal, San Marino, Singapore, Slovenia, Spain, Sweden, Switzerland, the United Kingdom, and Uruguay. Citizens of these countries need only a valid passport and a round-trip air or cruise ticket in their possession upon arrival. If they first enter the United States, they may also visit Mexico, Canada, Bermuda, and/or the Caribbean islands and return to the United States without a visa. Further information is available from any U.S. embassy or consulate. Canadian citizens may enter the United States without visas; they need only proof of residence.

Citizens of all other countries must have (1) a valid passport that expires at least 6 months later than the scheduled end of their visit to the United States, and (2) a tourist visa, which may be obtained without charge from any U.S. consulate.

British subjects can obtain up-to-date passport and visa information by calling the American Embassy London's **Visa Information Line** (© 09055/444-546) or by visiting the U.S. Embassy website (www. usembassy.org.uk).

Irish citizens can obtain up-to-date passport and visa information through the **Embassy of USA Dublin** (© 353/1-668-8777) or checking the visa website at www.usembassy.ie.

Australian citizens can obtain up-to-date passport and visa information by calling the **U.S. Embassy Canberra** (© 02/6214-5600) or by checking the website's visa page (www. usis-australia.gov).

Citizens of **New Zealand** can obtain up-to-date passport and visa information by calling the **U.S. Embassy New Zealand** (© 644/472-2068) or get the information directly from the website (http://usembassy. org.nz).

MEDICAL REQUIREMENTS

Unless you're arriving from an area

known to be suffering from an **epidemic** (particularly cholera or yellow fever), inoculations or vaccinations are not required for entry into the United States. If you have a medical condition that requires **syringe-administered medications,** carry a valid signed prescription from your physician—the Federal Aviation Administration (FAA) no longer allows airline passengers to pack syringes in their carry-on baggage without documented proof of medical need. If you have a disease that requires treatment with **narcotics,** you should also carry documented proof with you—smuggling narcotics aboard a plane is a serious offense that carries severe penalties in the United States.

For **HIV-positive visitors,** requirements for entering the United States are somewhat vague and change frequently. According to the latest publication of *HIV and Immigrants: A Manual for AIDS Service Providers,* the Immigration and Naturalization Service (INS) doesn't require a medical exam for entry into the United States, but INS officials may stop individuals because they look sick or because they are carrying AIDS/HIV medicine.

If an HIV-positive noncitizen applies for a nonimmigrant visa, the question on the application regarding communicable diseases is tricky no matter which way it's answered. If the applicant checks "no," INS may deny the visa on the grounds that the applicant committed fraud. If the applicant checks "yes" or if INS suspects the person is HIV-positive, it will deny the visa unless the applicant asks for a special waiver for visitors. This waiver is for people visiting the United States for a short time, to attend a conference, for instance, to visit close relatives, or to receive medical treatment. It can be a confusing situation. For further up-to-the-minute information, contact the Centers for Disease Control's **National Center for HIV** (© 404/332-4559; www.hivatis.org) or the **Gay Men's Health Crisis** (© 212/367-1000; www.gmhc.org).

DRIVER'S LICENSES Foreign driver's licenses are mostly recognized in the United States, although you may want to get an international driver's license if your home license is not written in English.

PASSPORT INFORMATION

Safeguard your passport in an inconspicuous, inaccessible place like a money belt. Make a copy of the critical pages, including the passport number, and store it in a safe place, separate from the passport itself. If you lose your passport, visit the nearest consulate of your native country as soon as possible for a replacement. Passport applications are downloadable from the Internet sites listed below.

Note that the International Civil Aviation Organization (ICAO) has recommended a policy requiring that *every* individual who travels by air have his or her own passport. In response, many countries are now requiring that children must be issued their own passport to travel internationally, where before those under 16 or so may have been allowed to travel on a parent or guardian's passport.

IN CANADA You can pick up a passport application at one of 28 regional passport offices or most travel agencies. As of December 11, 2001, Canadian children who travel will need their own passport. However, if you hold a valid Canadian passport issued before December 11, 2001, that bears the name of your child, the passport remains valid for you and your child until it expires. Applications are available at travel agencies throughout Canada or from the central **Passport Office,** Department of Foreign Affairs and International Trade, Ottawa K1A 0G3 (© 800/567-6868; www.dfait-maeci.gc.ca/passport). Processing takes 5 to 10 days if you apply in person, or about 3 weeks by mail.

IN THE UNITED KINGDOM To pick up an application for a standard 10-year passport (5-year passport for children under 16), visit the nearest passport office, major post office, or travel agency. You can also contact the **United Kingdom Passport Service** at ℂ 0870/571-0410 or visit its website at www.passport.gov.uk. Passports are £30 for adults and £16 for children under 16, with an additional £15 fee if you apply in person at a passport office. Processing takes about 2 weeks.

IN IRELAND You can apply for a 10-year passport, costing 57€, at the main **Passport Office,** Setanta Centre, Molesworth Street, Dublin 2 (ℂ 01/671-1633; www.gov.ie/iveagh/services/passports/passportforms.htm). You can also apply at 1A South Mall, Cork (ℂ 021/272-525), or over the counter at most main post offices. Travelers under 18 and over 65 must apply for a 3-year passport, which costs 12€.

IN AUSTRALIA You can pick up an application from your local post office or any **Australian State Passport Office,** but you must schedule an interview at a passport office to present your application materials. Call the passport office information service at ℂ 131-232 or visit the government website at www.passports.gov.au for complete details. Passports for adults are A$136 and for those under 18 A$68.

IN NEW ZEALAND You can pick up a passport application at any New Zealand Passports Office or download it from their website. Contact the **Passport Office** at ℂ 0800/225-050 in New Zealand or 04/474-8100, or log on to www.passports.govt.nz. Passports for adults are NZ$80 and for children under 16 NZ$40.

CUSTOMS
WHAT YOU CAN BRING IN
Every visitor more than 21 years of age may bring in, free of duty, the following: (1) 1 liter of wine or hard liquor; (2) 200 cigarettes, 100 cigars (but not from Cuba), or 3 pounds of smoking tobacco; and (3) $100 worth of gifts. These exemptions are offered to travelers who spend at least 72 hours in the United States and who have not claimed them within the preceding 6 months. It is altogether forbidden to bring into the country foodstuffs (particularly fruit, cooked meats, and canned goods) and plants (vegetables, seeds, tropical plants, and the like). Foreign tourists may bring in or take out up to $10,000 in U.S. or foreign currency with no formalities; larger sums must be declared to U.S. Customs on entering or leaving, which includes filing form CM 4790. For more specific information regarding U.S. Customs, call your nearest U.S. embassy or consulate, or the **U.S. Customs** office at ℂ 202/927-1770 or www.customs.gov.

WHAT YOU CAN TAKE HOME
FOR CANADIAN CITIZENS If you've been out of the country for over 48 hours, you may bring back C$200 worth of goods, and if you've been gone for 7 consecutive days or more, not counting your departure, the limit is C$750. The limit for alcohol is up to 1.5 liters of wine or 1.14 liters of liquor, or 24 12-ounce cans or bottles of beer; and up to 200 cigarettes, 50 cigars, or 200 grams of tobacco. You may not ship tobacco or alcohol, and you must be of legal age for your province to bring these items through Customs. For the helpful booklet *I Declare,* call the **Canada Customs and Review Agency** at ℂ 800/461-9999 in Canada, or 204/983-3500, or visit its website at www.ccra-adrc.gc.ca.

FOR U.K. CITIZENS U.K. citizens returning from a non-EU country have an allowance of 200 cigarettes; 50 cigars; 250 grams of smoking tobacco; 2 liters of still table wine; 1 liter of spirits or strong liqueurs (over 22% volume); 2 liters of fortified wine, sparkling wine or other liqueurs; 60cc (ml) perfume; 250cc (ml) of toilet water; and £145 worth of all other goods, including gifts and souvenirs. People under 17 cannot have the tobacco or alcohol allowance. For more information, call the **HM Customs & Excise** at *(C)* **0845/ 010-9000,** or log on to www.hmce. gov.uk.

FOR AUSTRALIAN CITIZENS
The duty-free allowance in Australia is A$400 or, for those under 18, A$200. Citizens can bring in 250 cigarettes or 250 grams of loose tobacco, and 1,125ml of alcohol. If you're returning with valuables you already own, such as foreign-made cameras, you should file form B263. A helpful brochure available from Australian consulates or Customs offices is *Know Before You Go.* For more information, call the **Australian Customs Service** at *(C)* **1300/363-263,** or log on to www. customs.gov.au.

FOR NEW ZEALAND CITIZENS
The duty-free allowance for New Zealand is NZ$700. Citizens over 17 can bring in 200 cigarettes, 50 cigars, or 250 grams of tobacco (or a mixture of all three if their combined weight doesn't exceed 250g); plus 4.5 liters of wine and beer, or 1.125 liters of liquor. New Zealand currency does not carry import or export restrictions. Fill out a certificate of export, listing the valuables you are taking out of the country; that way, you can bring them back without paying duty. Most questions are answered in a free pamphlet available at New Zealand consulates and Customs offices: *New Zealand Customs Guide for Travellers, Notice no. 4.* For more information,

contact **New Zealand Customs,** The Customhouse, 17–21 Whitmore St., Box 2218, Wellington (*(C)* **0800/428- 786** or 04/473-6099; www.customs. govt.nz).

HEALTH INSURANCE

Although it's not required of travelers, health insurance is highly recommended. Unlike many European countries, the United States does not usually offer free or low-cost medical care to its citizens or visitors. Doctors and hospitals are expensive, and in most cases will require advance payment or proof of coverage before they render their services. Policies can cover everything from the loss or theft of your baggage and trip cancellation to the guarantee of bail in case you're arrested. Good policies will also cover the costs of an accident, repatriation, or death. See "Health & Insurance" in chapter 2 for more information. Automobile clubs and travel agencies sell packages such as **Europ Assistance** in Europe at attractive rates. **Worldwide Assistance Services, Inc.** (*(C)* **800/ 821-2828;** www.worldwideassistance. com), is the agent for Europ Assistance in the United States.

Though lack of health insurance may prevent you from being admitted to a hospital in nonemergencies, don't worry about being left on a street corner to die: the American way is to fix you now and bill the heck out of you later.

INSURANCE FOR BRITISH TRAVELERS Most big travel agents offer their own insurance, and will probably try to sell you their package when you book a holiday. Think before you sign. **Britain's Consumers' Association** recommends that you insist on seeing the policy and reading the fine print before buying travel insurance. **The Association of British Insurers** (*(C)* **020/7600- 3333;** www.abi.org.uk) gives advice by phone and publishes *Holiday*

Insurance, a free guide to policy provisions and prices. You might also shop around for better deals: Try **Columbus Direct** (© 020/7375-0011; www.columbusdirect.net) or, for students, **Campus Travel** (© 020/7730-2101).

INSURANCE FOR CANADIAN TRAVELERS Canadians should check with their provincial health plan offices or call **Health Canada** (© 613/957-2991) to find out the extent of their coverage and what documentation and receipts they must take home in case they are treated in the United States.

MONEY

CURRENCY The U.S. monetary system is very simple: The most common **bills** are the $1 (colloquially, a "buck"), $5, $10, and $20 denominations. There are also $2 bills (seldom encountered), $50 bills, and $100 bills (the last two are usually not welcome as payment for small purchases). All the paper money was recently redesigned, making the famous faces adorning them disproportionately large. The old-style bills are still legal tender.

There are seven denominations of coins: 1¢ (1 cent, or a penny); 5¢ (5 cents, or a nickel); 10¢ (10 cents, or a dime); 25¢ (25 cents, or a quarter); 50¢ (50 cents, or a half dollar); the new gold "Sacagawea" coin worth $1; and, prized by collectors, the rare, older silver dollar.

Note: The "foreign-exchange bureaus" so common in Europe are rare even at airports in the United States, and nonexistent outside major cities. It's best not to change foreign money (or traveler's checks denominated in a currency other than U.S. dollars) at a small-town bank, or even a branch in a big city; in fact, leave any currency other than U.S. dollars at home—it may prove a greater nuisance to you than it's worth.

TRAVELER'S CHECKS Though traveler's checks are widely accepted, make sure that they're denominated in U.S. dollars, as foreign-currency checks are often difficult to exchange. The three traveler's checks that are most widely recognized—and least likely to be denied—are **Visa, American Express,** and **Thomas Cook.** Be sure to record the numbers of the checks, and keep that information in a separate place in case they get lost or stolen. Most businesses are pretty good about taking traveler's checks, but you're better off cashing them in at a bank (in small amounts, of course) and paying in cash. Remember: You'll need identification, such as a driver's license or passport, to change a traveler's check.

CREDIT CARDS & ATMS Credit cards are the most widely used form of payment in the United States: **Visa** (BarclayCard in Britain), **MasterCard** (EuroCard in Europe, Access in Britain, Chargex in Canada), **American Express, Diners Club,** and **Discover.** There are, however, a handful of stores and restaurants that do not take credit cards, so be sure to ask in advance. Most businesses display a sticker near their entrance to let you know which cards they accept. (*Note:* Businesses may require a minimum purchase, usually around $10, to use a credit card.)

It is strongly recommended that you bring at least one major credit card. You must have a credit or charge card to rent a car. Hotels and airlines usually require a credit-card imprint as a deposit against expenses, and in an emergency a credit card can be priceless.

You'll find **automated-teller machines (ATMs)** on just about every block—at least in almost every town—across the country. Some ATMs will allow you to draw U.S. currency against your bank and credit cards. Check with your bank before

Travel Tip

Be sure to keep a copy of all your travel papers separate from your wallet or purse, and leave a copy with someone at home should you need it faxed in an emergency.

leaving home, and remember that you will need your personal identification number (PIN) to do so. Most accept Visa, MasterCard, and American Express, as well as ATM cards from other U.S. banks. Expect to be charged up to $3 per transaction, however, if you're not using your own bank's ATM.

One way around these fees is to ask for cash back at grocery stores that accept ATM cards and don't charge usage fees. Of course, you'll have to purchase something first.

SAFETY

GENERAL SAFETY SUGGES-TIONS Although tourist areas are generally safe, U.S. urban areas tend to be less safe than those in Europe or Japan. You should always stay alert. This is particularly true of large American cities. If you're in doubt about which neighborhoods are safe, don't hesitate to make inquiries with the hotel front desk staff or the local tourist office.

Avoid deserted areas, especially at night, and don't go into public parks after dark unless there's a concert or similar occasion that will attract a crowd. In **Balboa Park,** stay on designated walkways and away from secluded areas, day and night. In the **Gaslamp Quarter,** don't stray east of Fifth Avenue.

Avoid carrying valuables with you on the street, and keep expensive cameras or electronic equipment bagged up or covered when not in use. If you're using a map, try to consult it inconspicuously—or better yet, study it before you leave your room. Hold onto your pocketbook, and place your billfold in an inside pocket. In theaters, restaurants, and other public places, keep your possessions in sight.

Always lock your room door—don't assume that once you're inside the hotel you are automatically safe and no longer need to be aware of your surroundings. Hotels are open to the public, and in a large hotel, security may not be able to screen everyone who enters.

DRIVING SAFETY Driving safety is important too, and carjacking is not unprecedented. Question your rental agency about personal safety and ask for a traveler-safety brochure when you pick up your car. Obtain written directions—or a map with the route clearly marked—from the agency showing how to get to your destination. (Many agencies now offer the option of renting a cellular phone for the duration of your car rental; check with the rental agent when you pick up the car.) And, if possible, arrive and depart during daylight hours.

If you drive off a highway and end up in a dodgy-looking neighborhood, leave the area as quickly as possible. If you have an accident, even on the highway, stay in your car with the doors locked until you assess the situation or until the police arrive. If you're bumped from behind on the street or are involved in a minor accident with no injuries, and the situation appears to be suspicious, motion to the other driver to follow you. Never get out of your car in such situations. Go directly to the nearest police precinct, well-lit service station, or 24-hour store. You may want to look into renting a cellphone on a short-term basis. One recommended wireless rental company is **InTouch**

USA (© 800/872-7626; www.in touchusa.com).

Whenever possible, always park in well-lit and well-traveled areas. Always keep your car doors locked, whether the vehicle is attended or unattended.

Never leave any packages or valuables in sight. If someone attempts to rob you or steal your car, don't try to resist the thief/carjacker. Report the incident to the police department immediately by calling © 911.

2 Getting to the United States

The only direct international flights to San Diego are from Mexico and England. Other overseas travelers bound for San Diego will need to change planes at another U.S. gateway. If your port of entry is Los Angeles, you can fly to San Diego or take a train or bus. Unfortunately, the Los Angeles train and bus stations are a long way from Los Angeles International Airport (LAX), so it isn't convenient to use these modes of transportation to get to San Diego. However, if you're flying into Los Angeles and staying there a few days, taking the train or bus to San Diego makes a lot of sense.

In addition to the domestic U.S. airlines listed in chapter 2, many international carriers serve LAX and other U.S. gateways. These include **Aer Lingus** (© 01/705-3333 in Dublin, or 800/IRISH-AIR in the U.S.; www. aerlingus.ie); **Air Canada** (© 888/247-2262 in Canada, or 800/776-3000 in the U.S.; www.aircanada. com); **Air New Zealand** (© 0800/737-000 in Auckland, or 800/262-1234 in the U.S.; www.airnz.com); **British Airways** (© 0345/222-111 in London, or 800/247-9297 in the U.S.;

www.british-airways.com); **Japan Airlines** (© 0354/89-1111 in Tokyo, or 800/JAL-FONE in the U.S.; www.jal. co.jp); and **Qantas** (© 13-13-13 in Australia, or 800/227-4500 in the U.S.; www.qantas.com.au).

AIRLINE DISCOUNTS The smart traveler can find numerable ways to reduce the price of a plane ticket simply by taking time to shop around. For example, overseas visitors can take advantage of the APEX (Advance Purchase Excursion) reductions offered by all major U.S. and European carriers. For more money-saving airline advice, see "Getting There," in chapter 2. For the best rates, compare fares and be flexible with the dates and times of travel.

IMMIGRATION & CUSTOMS CLEARANCE Visitors arriving by air, no matter what the port of entry, should cultivate patience and resignation before setting foot on U.S. soil. Getting through immigration control can take as long as 2 hours on some days, especially on summer weekends, so be sure to carry this guidebook or something else to read.

3 Getting Around the United States

BY PLANE

Some large airlines (for example, Northwest and Delta) offer travelers on their transatlantic or transpacific flights special discount tickets under the name **Visit USA,** allowing mostly one-way travel from one U.S. destination to another at very low prices. These discount tickets are not on sale

in the United States and must be purchased abroad in conjunction with your international ticket. This system is the best, easiest, and fastest way to see the United States at low cost. You should obtain information well in advance from your travel agent or the office of the airline concerned, since the conditions attached to these discount tickets can be changed without advance notice.

BY TRAIN

International visitors (excluding Canada) can also buy a **USA Railpass,** good for 15 or 30 days of unlimited travel on Amtrak (© **800/USA-RAIL;** www.amtrak.com). The pass is available through many foreign travel agents. Prices at press time for a 15-day pass were $295 off-peak, $440 peak; a 30-day pass costs $385 off-peak, $550 peak. With a foreign passport, you can also buy passes at some Amtrak offices in the United States, including locations in San Francisco, Los Angeles, Chicago, New York, Miami, Boston, and Washington, D.C. Reservations are generally required and should be made for each part of your trip as early as possible. Regional rail passes are also available.

BY BUS

Although bus travel is often the most economical form of public transit for short hops between U.S. cities, it can also be slow and uncomfortable—certainly not an option for everyone (particularly when Amtrak, which is far more luxurious, offers similar rates).

Greyhound/Trailways (© **800/231-2222**), the sole nationwide bus line, offers an **International Ameripass** that must be purchased before coming to the United States, or by phone through the Greyhound International Office at the Port Authority Bus Terminal in New York City (© **212/ 971-0492**). The pass can be obtained from foreign travel agents and costs less than the domestic version. Passes cost as follows: 7 days ($185), 10 days ($239), 15 days ($285), 21 days ($335), 30 days ($385), 45 days ($419), or 60 days ($509). You can get more info on the pass at www.greyhound.com, or by calling © **800/231-2222** in the United States, or **402/330-8552.** In addition, special rates are available for senior citizens and students.

BY CAR

The most cost-effective, convenient, and comfortable way to travel around the United States—especially California—is by car. For detailed information on automobile rentals in San Diego, see "Getting Around: By Car," in chapter 4. A comprehensive list of rental car agencies, complete with websites and toll-free U.S. phone numbers, can be found in the appendix at the end of this book.

 FAST FACTS: For the International Traveler

Automobile Organizations Auto clubs will supply maps, suggested routes, guidebooks, accident and bail-bond insurance, and emergency road service. The **American Automobile Association (AAA)** is the major auto club in the United States. If you belong to an auto club in your home country, inquire about AAA reciprocity before you leave. You may be able to join AAA even if you're not a member of a reciprocal club; to inquire, call AAA (© **800/222-4357;** www.aaa-calif.com).

Business Hours Banks and offices are usually open weekdays from 9am to 5pm. Stores, especially in shopping complexes, tend to stay open until about 9pm on weekdays and 6pm on weekends.

Currency Exchange See "Entry Requirements" and "Money" under "Preparing for Your Trip," earlier in this chapter.

Drinking Laws The legal age for purchase and consumption of alcoholic beverages is 21; proof of age is required and often requested at bars, nightclubs, and restaurants, so it's always a good idea to bring ID when you go out. Beer and wine often can be purchased in supermarkets, but liquor laws vary from state to state.

Do not carry open containers of alcohol in your car or any public area that isn't zoned for alcohol consumption. The police can fine you on the spot. And nothing will ruin your trip faster than getting a citation for DUI ("driving under the influence"), so don't even think about driving while intoxicated.

Electricity Like Canada, the United States uses 110 to 120 volts AC (60 cycles), compared to 220 to 240 volts AC (50 cycles) in most of Europe, Australia, and New Zealand. If your small appliances use 220 to 240 volts, you'll need a 110-volt transformer and a plug adapter with two flat parallel pins to operate them here. Downward converters that change 220-240 volts to 110-120 volts are difficult to find in the United States, so bring one with you.

Embassies & Consulates All embassies are located in the nation's capital, Washington, D.C. Some consulates are located in major U.S. cities, and most nations have a mission to the United Nations in New York City. If your country isn't listed below, call for directory information in Washington, D.C. (© 202/555-1212), for the number of your national embassy.

The embassy of **Australia** is at 1601 Massachusetts Ave. NW, Washington, DC 20036 (© 202/797-3000; www.austemb.org). There are consulates in New York, Honolulu, Houston, Los Angeles, and San Francisco.

The embassy of **Canada** is at 501 Pennsylvania Ave. NW, Washington, DC 20001 (© 202/682-1740; www.cdnemb-washdc.org). Other Canadian consulates are in Buffalo (New York), Detroit, Los Angeles, New York, and Seattle.

The embassy of **Ireland** is at 2234 Massachusetts Ave. NW, Washington, DC 20008 (© 202/462-3939; www.irelandemb.org/contact.html). Irish consulates are in Boston, Chicago, New York, and San Francisco.

The embassy of **Japan** is at 2520 Massachusetts Ave. NW, Washington, DC 20008 (© 202/238-6700; www.embjapan.org). Japanese consulates are located in Atlanta, Kansas City, San Francisco, and Washington, D.C.

The embassy of **New Zealand** is at 37 Observatory Circle NW, Washington, DC 20008 (© 202/328-4800; www.emb.com/nzemb). New Zealand consulates are in Los Angeles, Salt Lake City, San Francisco, and Seattle.

The embassy of the **United Kingdom** is at 3100 Massachusetts Ave. NW, Washington, DC 20008 (© 202/462-1340; www.britainusa.com/consular/embassy/). Other British consulates are in Atlanta, Boston, Chicago, Cleveland, Houston, Los Angeles, New York, San Francisco, and Seattle.

Emergencies Call © 911 to report a fire, call the police, or get an ambulance anywhere in the United States. This is a toll-free call (meaning that no coins are required at public telephones).

If you encounter serious problems, contact the San Diego chapter of **Traveler's Aid Society** (© 619/231-7361; www.travelersaid.org) to help direct you to a local branch. This nationwide, nonprofit, social-service organization geared to helping travelers in difficult straits offers services that might include reuniting families separated while traveling, providing food and/or shelter to people stranded without cash, or even emotional counseling. If you're in trouble, seek them out.

Gasoline (Petrol) Petrol is known as gasoline (or simply "gas") in the United States, and petrol stations are known as both gas stations and service stations. Gasoline costs about half as much here as it does in Europe (about $1.45 per gal. at press time), and taxes are already included in the printed price. One U.S. gallon equals 3.8 liters or .85 imperial gallons.

Holidays Banks, government offices, post offices, and many stores, restaurants, and museums are closed on the following legal national holidays: January 1 (New Year's Day), the third Monday in January (Martin Luther King, Jr., Day), the third Monday in February (Presidents' Day, Washington's Birthday), the last Monday in May (Memorial Day), July 4 (Independence Day), the first Monday in September (Labor Day), the second Monday in October (Columbus Day), November 11 (Veterans' Day/Armistice Day), the fourth Thursday in November (Thanksgiving Day), and December 25 (Christmas). Also, the Tuesday following the first Monday in November is Election Day and is a federal government holiday in presidential-election years (held every 4 years, and next in 2004).

Legal Aid If you are "pulled over" for a minor infraction (such as speeding), never attempt to pay the fine directly to a police officer; this could be construed as attempted bribery, a much more serious crime. Pay fines by mail, or directly into the hands of the clerk of the court. If accused of a more serious offense, say and do nothing before consulting a lawyer. Here the burden is on the state to prove a person's guilt beyond a reasonable doubt, and everyone has the right to remain silent, whether he or she is suspected of a crime or actually arrested. Once arrested, a person can make one telephone call to a party of his or her choice. Call your embassy or consulate.

Mail If you aren't sure what your address will be in the United States, mail can be sent to you, in your name, c/o General Delivery, San Diego Post Office, 2535 Midway Dr., San Diego, CA 92138 U.S.A. (Call © 800/ 275-8777 for more information, or log onto www.usps.gov) The addressee must pick up mail in person and must produce proof of identity (driver's license, passport, and so on). Most post offices will hold your mail for up to one month, and are open Monday to Friday from 8am to 5pm, and Saturday from 9am to 3pm.

Generally found at intersections, mailboxes are blue with a red-and-white stripe and carry the inscription U.S. MAIL. If your mail is addressed to a U.S. destination, don't forget to add the five-digit postal code (or ZIP code), after the two-letter abbreviation of the state to which the mail is addressed. This is essential to prompt delivery.

At press time, domestic postage rates were 23¢ for a postcard and 37¢ for a letter. For international mail, a first-class letter of up to a half ounce costs 60¢ (46¢ to Canada and 40¢ to Mexico); a first-class postcard costs 50¢ (including Canada and Mexico); and a preprinted postal aerogramme costs 50¢.

Taxes The United States has no value-added tax (VAT) or other indirect tax at the national level. Every state, county, and city has the right to levy its own local tax on all purchases, including hotel and restaurant checks, airline tickets, and so on. These taxes are not included in the price you'll see on merchandise, and are not refundable for foreign visitors. Sales tax in San Diego is 7.5%; tax on hotel rooms is 10.5%.

Telephone & Fax The telephone system in the United States is run by private corporations, so rates, especially for long-distance service and operator-assisted calls, can vary widely. Generally, hotel surcharges on long-distance and local calls are astronomical, so you're usually better off using a **public pay telephone**, which you'll find clearly marked in most public buildings and private establishments as well as on the street. Convenience grocery stores and gas stations always have them. Many convenience groceries and packaging services sell **prepaid calling cards** in denominations up to $50; these can be the least expensive way to call home. Many public phones at airports now accept American Express, MasterCard, and Visa credit cards. **Local calls** made from public pay phones in most locales cost either 25¢ or 35¢. Pay phones do not accept pennies, and few will take anything larger than a quarter.

Most long-distance and international calls can be dialed directly from any phone. **For calls within the United States and to Canada,** dial 1 followed by the area code and the seven-digit number. **For other international calls,** dial 011 followed by the country code, city code, and the telephone number of the person you are calling.

Calls to area codes **800, 888,** and **877** are toll-free. However, calls to numbers in area codes **700** and **900** (chat lines, bulletin boards, "dating" services, and so on) can be very expensive—usually a charge of 95¢ to $3 or more per minute, and they sometimes have minimum charges that can run as high as $15 or more.

For **reversed-charge or collect calls,** and for person-to-person calls, dial 0 (zero, not the letter O) followed by the area code and number you want; an operator will then come on the line, and you should specify that you are calling collect, or person-to-person, or both. If your operator-assisted call is international, ask for the overseas operator.

For **directory assistance** ("information"), dial 411 for both local and long distance numbers.

Most hotels have **fax machines** available for guest use (be sure to ask about the charge to use it). Many hotel rooms are even wired for guests' fax machines. A less expensive way to send and receive faxes may be at stores such as Mail Boxes Etc., a national chain of packing service shops. (Look in the Yellow Pages directory under "Packing Services.")

Time The continental United States is divided into **four time zones:** eastern standard time (EST), central standard time (CST), mountain standard time (MST), and Pacific standard time (PST). Alaska and Hawaii have their own zones. For example, noon in New York City (EST) is 11am in Chicago (CST), 10am in Denver (MST), 9am in Los Angeles (PST), 8am in Anchorage (AST), and 7am in Honolulu (HST).

Daylight saving time is in effect from 1am on the first Sunday in April through 1am on the last Sunday in October, except in Arizona, Hawaii, part of Indiana, and Puerto Rico. Daylight saving time moves the clock 1 hour ahead of standard time.

Tipping Tipping is so ingrained in the American way of life that the annual income tax of tip-earning service personnel is based on how much they should have received in light of their employers' gross revenues. Accordingly, they may have to pay tax on a tip you didn't actually give them.

Here are some rules of thumb:

In hotels, tip **bellhops** at least $1 per bag ($2–$3 if you have a lot of luggage) and tip the **chamber staff** $1 to $2 per day (more if you've left a disaster area for him or her to clean up, or if you're traveling with kids and/or pets). Tip the **doorman** or **concierge** only if he or she has provided you with some specific service (for example, calling a cab for you or obtaining difficult-to-get theater tickets). Tip the **valet-parking attendant** $1 every time you get your car.

In restaurants, bars, and nightclubs, tip **service staff** 15% to 20% of the check, tip **bartenders** 10% to 15%, and tip **valet-parking attendants** $1 per vehicle. Tip the **doorman** only if he has provided you with some specific service (such as calling a cab for you). Tipping is not expected in cafeterias and fast-food restaurants.

Tip **cab drivers** 15% of the fare.

As for other service personnel, tip **skycaps** at airports at least $1 per bag ($2–$3 if you have a lot of luggage) and tip **hairdressers** and **barbers** 15% to 20%.

Tipping ushers at movies and theaters, and gas-station attendants, is not expected.

Toilets You won't find public toilets or "restrooms" on the streets in most U.S. cities, but they can be found in hotel lobbies, bars, restaurants, museums, department stores, railway and bus stations, and service stations. Large hotels, shopping malls, and fast-food restaurants are probably the best bet for good, clean facilities. If possible, avoid the toilets at parks and beaches, which tend to be dirty, some may be unsafe. Restaurants and bars may reserve their restrooms for patrons. Some establishments display a notice indicating this. You can ignore this sign or, better yet, avoid arguments by paying for a cup of coffee or a soft drink, which will qualify you as a patron.

4

Getting to Know San Diego

San Diego is laid out in an easy-to-decipher manner, so learning the lay of the land is neither confusing nor daunting. Most San Diegans welcome visitors and are eager to answer questions and provide assistance; you'll feel like a local before you know it.

1 Orientation

ARRIVING

BY PLANE

San Diego International Airport (© 619/231-2100; www.portofsandiego. org/sandiego-airport/index.html), also known as **Lindbergh Field,** lies just north of downtown. The landing approach is right over the central business district, creating the familiar sight of planes threading through high-rise buildings on their way to the airport. A curfew (11:30pm–6:30am) cuts down on noise in the surrounding residential areas. Planes may land during the curfew period, but they can't take off.

In 1998, the Port of San Diego completed a sorely needed 300,000-square-foot expansion of Lindbergh Field, so return visitors will be in for a surprise. The practical changes include an elevated pedestrian walkway between Terminal 2 and the parking area, and the renaming of the former East and West Terminals as 1 and 2. The addition onto the former West Terminal is known as the Terminal 2 Addition. Besides adding much-needed space to an airport that's grown awkwardly since the 1920s, the renovation brought dramatic pieces of local artwork, which are displayed in public spaces; there's even a slick, colorful brochure describing the art. The **Commuter Terminal,** a half mile away, remains unchanged; the "red bus" provides free service from the main airport to the Commuter Terminal.

General **information desks** with visitor materials, maps, and other services are in **Terminal 1,** near the United Airlines ticket counter, and in **Terminal 2** in the baggage-claim area and near the American Airlines ticket counter. You can **exchange foreign currency** at Travelex America (© 619/295-1501; www.travelexusa.com), in Terminal 1 across from the United Airlines ticket counter. **Hotel reservation phones** and **car-rental courtesy phones** are located in the baggage-claim areas of Terminals 1 and 2.

Getting into Town from the Airport

BY BUS The **Metropolitan Transit System (MTS)** (© 619/233-3004; www.sdcommute.com/sdmts), bus route no. 992, provides service between the airport and downtown San Diego. Bus stops are located at each of Lindbergh Field's three terminals. The one-way fare is $2.25, and exact change is required. Request a transfer if you're connecting to another bus or San Diego Trolley route downtown. Downtown, route 992 stops on Broadway. The ride takes about 15 minutes; buses come at 10- to 15-minute intervals.

⎛Tips Need a Lift into Town?

When you're thinking about transportation from Lindbergh Field, remember to ask your **hotel** whether it has an **airport shuttle**. It's common for San Diego hotels to offer this service—usually free, sometimes for a nominal charge—and some also offer complimentary shuttles from the hotel to popular shopping and/or dining areas around town. Make sure the hotel knows when you're arriving, and get precise directions on where it'll pick you up.

Web-surfers who'd like to investigate airport transportation options beforehand should visit **QuickAid's Guide to the San Diego Airport** (www.quickaid.com/airports/san/), a low-tech site with excellent resources including ground transportation options, terminal maps, airline lists, and nearby hotels.

At the **Transit Store,** 102 Broadway, at First Avenue (℃ **619/234-1060**), you can get information about greater San Diego's mass transit system (bus, rail, and ferry) and pick up free brochures, route maps, and timetables.

BY TAXI Taxis line up outside both terminals and charge around $8 (before tip) for the trip to a downtown location, usually a 5- to 10-minute ride.

BY SHUTTLE Several airport shuttles run regularly from the airport to downtown hotels; you'll see designated areas outside each terminal. The fare is $5 to $9 per person. The shuttles are a good deal for single travelers; two or more people traveling together might as well take a taxi. Companies that serve the whole county include **Cloud 9 Shuttle** (℃ **800/9-SHUTTLE** or 858/9-SHUTTLE; www.cloud9shuttle.com), **Coronado Livery** (℃ **619/435-6310**), and **Peerless Shuttle** (℃ **619/554-1700**). Coronado Livery is the least expensive to Coronado, and Cloud 9 is the cheapest to downtown.

BY CAR If you're driving to downtown from the airport, take Harbor Drive south to Broadway, the main east-west thoroughfare, and turn left. To reach Hillcrest or Balboa Park, exit the airport toward I-5, and follow the signs for Laurel Street. To reach Mission Bay (home of SeaWorld), take I-5 north to I-8 west. To reach La Jolla, take I-5 north to the Ardath Road exit, turning left onto Torrey Pines Road. For complete information on rental cars in San Diego, see "Getting Around," later in this chapter.

BY CAR

Three main interstates lead into San Diego. I-5 is the popular route from Los Angeles and coastal points north; it runs straight through downtown and is the main local freeway. I-15 leads from inland destinations and the deserts to the north; as you enter San Diego, take I-8 west to reach the main parts of the city. I-8 cuts across California from points east like Phoenix, crossing I-5 and ending at Mission Bay.

BY TRAIN

San Diego's **Santa Fe Station** is centrally located downtown, on Broadway between Front Street and First Avenue, within walking distance of many downtown hotels and the Embarcadero. Taxis line up outside the main door, the trolley station is across the street, and a dozen local bus routes stop on Broadway or Pacific Highway, 1 block away.

VISITOR INFORMATION

There are staffed information booths at airport terminals, the train station, and the cruise-ship terminal.

In downtown San Diego, the Convention & Visitors Bureau's **International Visitor Information Center** (© **619/236-1212;** fax 619/230-7084; www.sandiego.org) is on First Avenue at F Street, street level at Horton Plaza. The glossy *San Diego Visitors Planning Guide* includes information on accommodations, dining, activities, attractions, tours, and transportation. Ask for the *Super Savings Coupon Book,* which is full of money-saving coupons. The center is open Monday through Saturday from 8:30am to 5pm year-round and Sunday from 11am to 5pm, June through August; it is closed January 1, Thanksgiving, and December 25.

Some of the same materials are available at the **Mission Bay Visitor Information Center,** 2688 Mission Bay Dr. (© **619/276-8200;** www.infosandiego. com). You can also get pointers on recreational activities in the bay and beyond. From I-5, take the Clairemont Drive exit west to the end. There's plenty of parking; stop in between 9am and dusk.

The **Coronado Visitors Center,** 1100 Orange Ave. (© **619/437-8788;** www.coronadohistory.com/visitorcenter), dispenses maps, newsletters, and information-packed brochures. Located inside the Coronado Museum, they're open Monday through Friday from 9am to 5pm, Saturday 10am to 5pm, and Sunday 11am to 4pm.

Information on La Jolla is distributed by **Promote La Jolla,** 1150 Silverado St. (© **858/454-5718;** www.lajollabythesea.com). The office is open Monday through Friday from 9am to 5pm.

Additional visitor information is available from the **Balboa Park Visitors Center,** 1549 El Prado (© **619/239-0512**).

For the latest on San Diego nightlife and entertainment, pick up the *Reader,* a free newspaper that comes out on Thursday and is available all over the city. Also check "Night and Day," the Thursday supplement in the *San Diego Union-Tribune.* For addresses of websites with plenty of up-to-the-minute information, see "Site Seeing: San Diego on the Web," in chapter 1.

CITY LAYOUT
MAIN ARTERIES & STREETS

It's not hard to find your way around downtown San Diego. Most streets run one way. First through Twelfth avenues alternate running north and south (Fifth Avenue is two way in the Gaslamp Quarter only); A through K streets alternate running east and west. Broadway, the equivalent of D Street, is a two-way street, as are Market Street and Harbor Drive. East-west streets (north of A St.) bear the names of trees, in alphabetical order: Ash, Beech, Cedar, Date, and so on. Harbor Drive runs past the airport and along the waterfront, which is known as the Embarcadero. Ash Street and Broadway are the downtown arteries that connect with Harbor Drive. The Coronado Bay Bridge leading to Coronado is accessible from I-5, and I-5 north leads to Old Town, Mission Bay, La Jolla, and North County.

Balboa Park (home of the San Diego Zoo), Hillcrest, and uptown areas lie northeast of downtown San Diego. The park and zoo are easily reached by way of Twelfth Avenue, which becomes Park Boulevard and leads to the parking lots. Fifth Avenue leads to Hillcrest and uptown (turn right onto University Ave. to get to the latter).

CORONADO   The main streets are Orange Avenue, where most of the hotels and restaurants are clustered, and Ocean Drive, which follows Coronado Beach.

DOWNTOWN   The major thoroughfares are Broadway (a major bus artery), Fourth and Fifth avenues (which run south and north, respectively), C Street (the trolley line), and Harbor Drive, which hugs the waterfront and passes the Maritime Museum, Seaport Village, and the Convention Center.

HILLCREST   In this area near Balboa Park, the main streets are University Avenue and Washington Street (both two way, running east and west), and Fourth and Fifth avenues.

LA JOLLA   The main avenues are Prospect and Girard, which are perpendicular to each other.

PACIFIC BEACH   Mission Boulevard is the main drag, and perpendicular to it are Grand and Garnet avenues and Pacific Beach Drive. East and West Mission Bay drives and Ingraham Street enable you to zip around the periphery of the bay or bisect it.

STREET MAPS
The **International Visitor Information Center,** at First Avenue and F Street (© **619/236-1212**), provides the *San Diego Visitors Planning Guide,* which includes five free, easy-to-read maps.

The **Automobile Club of Southern California** has several locations, including 815 Date St. (© **619/233-1000**). It distributes great maps, which are free to its members and to members of international auto clubs. The **Transit Store,** 102 Broadway, at First Avenue (© **619/233-3004**), is a storehouse of bus and trolley maps, with a friendly staff on duty to answer specific questions.

Hotels often provide complimentary maps of the downtown area. You can buy maps of the city and vicinity at **Le Travel Store** at 745 Fourth Ave. If you're moving to San Diego or plan to spend a long time here, I suggest you buy the *Thomas Bros. Guide,* available at bookstores, drugstores, and large supermarkets. This all-encompassing book of maps deciphers San Diego street by street.

THE NEIGHBORHOODS IN BRIEF
In this guidebook, San Diego is divided into six areas, each with its own hotel and restaurant listings (see chapters 5 and 6).

Downtown   The business, shopping, dining, and entertainment heart of the city, the downtown area encompasses Horton Plaza, the Gaslamp Quarter, the Embarcadero (waterfront), and the Convention Center. The Maritime Museum, the downtown branch of the Museum of Contemporary Art, and the Children's Museum are also here. Visitors with business in the city center would be wise to stay downtown. This is also the best area for those attending meetings at the Convention Center. The **Gaslamp Quarter** is the center of a massive redevelopment kicked off in the mid-1980s with the opening of Horton Plaza; now, the once-seedy area is filled with trendy boutiques, restaurants, and nightspots. **Little Italy,** a small neighborhood along India Street between Cedar and Fir at the northern edge of downtown, is the best place to find gelato, espresso, pizza, and pasta.

Hillcrest/Uptown   At the turn of the 20th century, the neighborhoods north of downtown were home to San Diego's white-collar elite (hence such sobriquets as

San Diego Neighborhoods

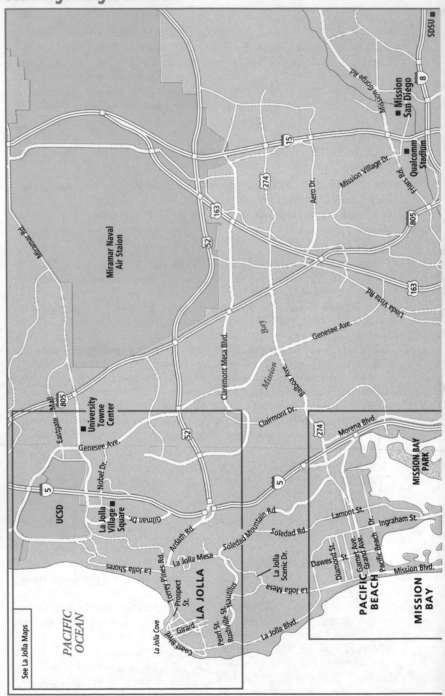

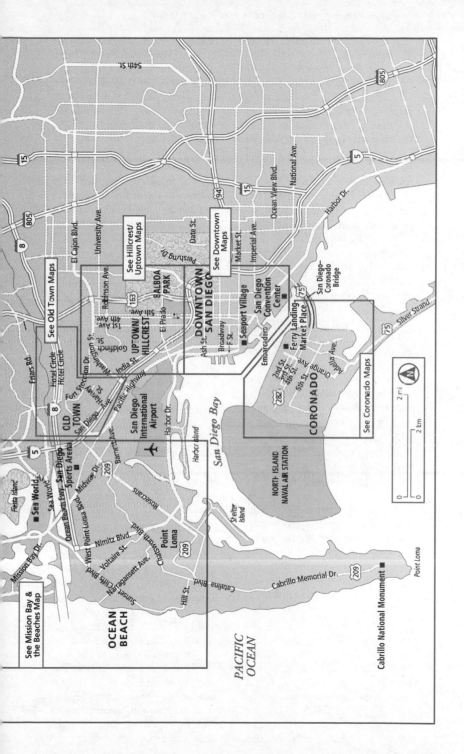

See Old Town Maps

See Hillcrest/
Uptown Maps

See Downtown Maps

See Coronado Maps

See Mission Bay &
the Beaches Map

54th St.

805

15

805

8

15

94

15

5

El Cajon Blvd.

University Ave.

Robinson Ave.

Date St.

Market St.

Imperial Ave.

Ocean View Blvd.

National Ave.

Harbor Dr.

163

1st Ave.

4th Ave.

5th Ave.

El Prado

BALBOA
PARK

Pershing Dr.

UPTOWN/
HILLCREST

Goldfinch
St.

Washington St.

India St.

Fort Stockton Dr.

Friars Rd.

Hotel Circle

Hotel Circle

OLD
TOWN

Harney
St.

San Diego Ave.

Pacific Highway

San Diego
International
Airport

Harbor Dr.

Harbor Island

Ash St.

Broadway

F St.

DOWNTOWN
SAN DIEGO

Seaport Village

San Diego
Convention
Center

Embarcadero

Ferry Landing
Market Place

San Diego–
Coronado
Bridge

75

75

Silver Strand

San Diego Bay

2nd St.

3rd St.

4th St.

5th St.

Orange Ave.

Adella Ave.

282

CORONADO

NORTH ISLAND
NAVAL AIR STATION

Shelter
Island

5

209

8

Sea World

See World

San Diego
Sports Arena

Ocean Beach Fwy.

Midway Dr.

Barnett Ave.

Rosecrans

West Point Loma Blvd.

Nimitz Blvd.

Voltaire St.

Narragansett Ave.

Sunset Cliffs Blvd.

Chatsworth Blvd.

Point
Loma

209

Hill St.

Catalina Blvd.

Cabrillo Memorial Dr.

209

Cabrillo National Monument

Point Loma

PACIFIC
OCEAN

OCEAN
BEACH

Fiesta Island

Mission Bay Dr.

N

0

0

2 mi

2 km

53

Bankers Hill and Pill Hill, named for the area's many doctors). Hillcrest was the city's first self-contained suburb in the 1920s. Despite the cachet of being next to Balboa Park (home of the San Diego Zoo and numerous museums, including the Museum of Art, the Museum of Photographic Arts, and the Reuben H. Fleet Science Center), the area fell into neglect in the 1960s and '70s. However, since the turn of the 20th century, legions of preservation-minded residents—including an active and fashionable gay community—have restored Hillcrest's charms. I'd say Hillcrest is the local equivalent of L.A.'s West Hollywood or New York's SoHo. Centrally located and packed with the latest in stylish restaurants and avant-garde boutiques, Hillcrest also offers less expensive and more personalized accommodations than any other area in the city. Other uptown neighborhoods of interest are **North Park** and **Kensington.**

Old Town & Mission Valley This area encompasses the Old Town State Historic Park, Presidio Park, Heritage Park, and numerous museums that recall the turn of the century and the city's beginnings. There's shopping and dining here, too—all aimed at tourists. Not far from Old Town lies the vast suburban sprawl of Mission Valley, home to San Diego's gigantic shopping centers. Between them is Hotel Circle, adjacent to I-8, where a string of moderately priced and budget hotels offer an alternative to the ritzier neighborhoods.

Mission Bay & the Beaches Here's where they took the picture on the postcard you'll send home. Mission Bay is a watery playground perfect for water-skiing, sailing, and windsurfing. The adjacent communities of Ocean Beach, Mission

Beach, and Pacific Beach are known for their wide stretches of sand, active nightlife, and casual dining. Many single San Diegans live here, and once you've visited you'll understand why. The boardwalk, which runs from South Mission Beach through North Mission Beach to Pacific Beach, is a popular place for in-line skating, bike riding, and watching sunsets. This is the place to stay if you are traveling with beach-loving children or want to walk barefoot on the beach.

La Jolla With an atmosphere that's a cross between Rodeo Drive and a Mediterranean village, this seaside community is home to an inordinate number of wealthy folks who could live anywhere. They choose La Jolla, surrounded by the beach, the University of California, San Diego, outstanding restaurants, pricey and traditional shops, and some of the world's best medical facilities. The wise tourist beds down here, taking advantage of the community's attributes without having to buy its high-priced real estate. The name is a compromise between Spanish and American Indian, as is the pronunciation (la-*hoy*-ya); it has come to mean "the jewel."

Coronado You may be tempted to think of Coronado as an island. It does have an isolated, resort ambience and is accessible only by ferry or bridge, but the city of Coronado is actually on a bulbous peninsula connected to the mainland by a narrow sand spit, the Silver Strand. The northern portion of the peninsula is home to the massive U.S. Naval Air Station. The southern sector has a rich history as an elite playground and a reputation as a charming community of suburbs. Quaint shops line the main street, Orange Avenue, and

Off the Beaten Path: Golden Hill

You don't think the trendy Gaslamp Quarter will be the last San Diego neighborhood to be rediscovered and gentrified, do you? If you like to explore, check out another old neighborhood that's quietly attracting history-minded fans . . . will it be the preservationists' next stop?

When the downtown area we now call the Gaslamp Quarter was enjoying its turn-of-the-century heyday as the city's commercial center, the most convenient suburb was Golden Hill. Directly east of downtown, Golden Hill had the added advantage of being next to Balboa Park—it "wraps" around the southeast corner of the park. Homes here also enjoyed a sweeping view south to the bay, now mostly blocked by development. For a drive-by look at some oldies but goodies, visit Broadway, where finely preserved Victorians now serve as legal and medical offices; 28th Street along the park; and any other side street that catches your eye.

Some of the neighborhood's best Victorians and bungalows already show the caring touch of deep-pocketed architecture buffs, though plenty have fallen victim to the wrecking ball. Sandwiched between a natural arroyo (now the pathway of the 94 freeway) and vast Balboa Park, Golden Hill is an area where you're likely to see coyotes, opossums, and even red foxes trotting down quiet streets. You'll find (tie-) dyed-in-the-wool hippies shacking up in unrestored shanties and hanging out at Santos Coffeehouse, whose bohemian style is reminiscent of San Francisco's Haight-Ashbury.

Small stretches of retail interest lie at the intersection of Beech and 30th streets (Santos Coffeehouse, grass-roots art galleries, and funky antique stores), and along 25th Street north of Broadway, home to several Mexican restaurants and the retro grill-your-own Turf Supper Club.

you'll find plenty of ritzy hotels and resorts, including the landmark **Hotel del Coronado.** Coronado has a lovely duned beach (one of the area's most popular), fine restaurants, and a downtown area that's reminiscent of a small Midwestern town; it's also home to more retired admirals than any other community in the country.

2 Getting Around

San Diego has many walkable neighborhoods, from the historic downtown area, to Hillcrest and nearby Balboa Park, to the Embarcadero, to Mission Bay Park. You get there by car, bus, or trolley, and your feet do the rest. For inspiration, turn to chapter 8, "City Strolls."

BY CAR

San Diegans complain of increasing traffic, but the city is still easy to navigate by car. Most downtown streets run one way, which may frustrate you until you learn your way around. Finding a parking space can be tricky, but some reasonably priced lots are fairly centrally located.

RENTALS

If you don't drive to San Diego with your own car, you'll want to rent one. While it's possible to get around by public transportation, having your own wheels is a big advantage.

All the major firms have offices at the airport and in the larger hotels. See the appendix in the back of the book for telephone numbers. **Avis** (© **800/ 331-1212**), like several other companies, will allow its cars into Mexico as far as Ensenada. Beyond Ensenada, the roads aren't as well maintained, and it's more difficult to get to the car should there be a breakdown or other problems (see "Tijuana: Going South of the Border," in chapter 11).

Saving Money on a Rental Car

Car-rental rates vary even more than airline fares. Prices depend on the size of the car, where and when you pick it up and drop it off, the length of the rental period, where and how far you drive it, whether you buy insurance, and a host of other factors. A few key questions could save you hundreds of dollars:

- Are weekend rates lower than weekday rates? Ask if the rate is the same for pickup Friday morning, for instance, as it is for Thursday night. Reservations agents won't volunteer this information, so don't be shy about asking lots of questions.
- Does the agency assess a drop-off charge if you don't return the car to the same location where you picked it up?
- Are special promotional rates available? If you see an advertised price in your local newspaper, be sure to ask for that specific rate; otherwise you may be charged the standard cost. Terms change constantly.
- Are discounts available for members of AARP, AAA, frequent-flyer programs, or trade unions? If you belong to any of these organizations, you may be entitled to discounts of up to 30%.
- How much tax will be added to the rental bill? Local tax? State use tax?
- How much does the rental company charge to refill your gas tank if you return with the tank less than full? Though most rental companies claim these prices are competitive, fuel is almost always cheaper in town. Try to allow enough time to refuel the car yourself before returning it.

Some companies offer "refueling packages," in which you pay for an entire tank of gas up front. The cost is usually fairly competitive with local prices, but you don't get credit for any gas remaining in the tank. If a stop at a gas station on the way to the airport will make you miss your plane, then by all means take advantage of the fuel-purchase option. Otherwise, skip it.

Impressions

People in other places work hard to get somewhere, but in San Diego you're already there.

—Neil Morgan, associate editor, *San Diego Union-Tribune*

My first impulse was to get out in the street at high noon and shout four-letter words.

—Author Raymond Chandler, upon arriving in the genteel village of La Jolla, circa 1949

Demystifying Renter's Insurance

Before you drive off in a rental car, be sure you're insured. Hasty assumptions about your personal auto insurance or a rental agency's additional coverage could end up costing you tens of thousands of dollars, even if you are involved in an accident that was clearly the fault of another driver.

If you already hold a **private auto insurance** policy, you are most likely covered in the United States for loss of or damage to a rental car and liability in case of injury to any other party involved in an accident. Be sure to find out whether you are covered in the area you are visiting, whether your policy extends to everyone who will be driving the car, how much liability is covered in case an outside party is injured in an accident, and whether the type of vehicle you are renting is included under your contract. (Rental trucks, sport-utility vehicles, and luxury vehicles or sports cars may not be covered.)

Most **major credit cards** (especially gold and platinum cards) provide some degree of coverage as well, provided they're used to pay for the rental. Terms vary widely, however, so be sure to call your credit card company directly before you rent.

If you are **uninsured,** your credit card will probably provide primary coverage as long as you decline the rental agency's insurance and as long as you rent with that card. This means that the credit card will cover damage or theft of a rental car for the full cost of the vehicle. (In a few states, however, theft is not covered; ask specifically about state law where you will be renting and driving.) If you already have insurance, your credit card will provide secondary coverage, which basically covers your deductible.

Note: Though they may cover damage to your rental car, *credit cards will not cover liability,* or the cost of injury to an outside party, damage to an outside party's vehicle, or both. If you do not hold an insurance policy, you may seriously want to consider purchasing additional liability insurance from your rental company, even if you decline collision coverage. Be sure to check the terms, however. Some rental agencies cover liability only if the renter is not at fault; even then, the rental company's obligation varies from state to state.

The basic insurance coverage offered by most car-rental companies, known as the **Loss/Damage Waiver (LDW)** or **Collision Damage Waiver (CDW),** can cost as much as $20 a day. It usually covers the full value of the vehicle with no deductible if an outside party causes an accident or other damage to the rental car. In all states but California, you will probably be covered in case of theft as well. Liability coverage varies according to the company policy and state law, but the minimum is usually at least $15,000. If you are at fault in an accident, you will be covered for the full replacement value of the car, but not for liability. Some states allow you to buy additional liability coverage for such cases. Most rental companies will require a police report to process any claims you file, but your private insurer will not be notified of the accident.

PARKING

The **garage at Horton Plaza,** at G Street and Fourth Avenue, is free to shoppers for the first 3 hours. (A merchant must validate the parking ticket, or you must show your cinema or theater stub from Horton Plaza.) After the first 3 hours, it's $1 per half hour. A quick way to zip into Horton Plaza and avoid the ever-upward spiral is to enter the back way, off Third Avenue. The fenced-in lot adjacent to the Embarcadero, **Allright Parking,** 900 Broadway, at Harbor Drive (© **619/298-6944**), charges $3 to park between 5:30am and midnight. More convenient to downtown shopping and the Children's Museum is the **open-air lot on Market Street** between Front and First streets, where you can park all day on weekdays for $3, and weekends for $2.

Parking meters are plentiful in most areas: downtown and the Gaslamp Quarter, Hillcrest, and the beach communities. Posted signs indicate operating hours—generally 8am to 6pm, even on weekends. Be prepared with several dollars in quarters—most meters take no other coin, and 25¢ rarely buys more than 15 minutes, even on a 2-hour meter. Most unmetered areas have signs restricting street parking to 1 or 2 hours; count on vigilant chalking and ticketing during the regulated hours. Three-hour meters line Harbor Drive opposite the ticket offices for harbor tours; even on weekends, you have to feed them.

DRIVING RULES

California has a seat-belt law for both drivers and passengers, so buckle up before you venture out. You may turn right at a red light after stopping unless a sign says otherwise. Likewise, you can turn left on a red light from a one-way street onto another one-way street after coming to a full stop. Keep in mind when driving in San Diego that pedestrians have the right of way at all times, so stop for pedestrians who have stepped off the curb.

BY PUBLIC TRANSPORTATION
BY BUS

San Diego has an adequate bus system that will get you to where you're going—eventually. Most drivers are friendly and helpful. The system encompasses more than 100 routes in the greater San Diego area. The **Transit Store,** 102 Broadway, at First Avenue (✆ **619/234-1060**), dispenses passes, tokens, timetables, maps, brochures, and lost-and-found information. It issues ID cards for seniors 60 and older, and for travelers with disabilities, all of whom pay $1 per ride. Request a copy of the useful brochure *Your Open Door to San Diego,* which details the city's most popular tourist attractions and the buses that will take you to them. You may also call the number above and say where you are and where you want to go; the Transit Store staff will tell you the nearest bus stop and what time the next couple of buses will pass by. The office is open Monday through Friday from 8:30am to 5:30pm, Saturday and Sunday noon to 4pm. If you know your route and just need schedule information—or automated answers to FAQs—call ✆ **619/685-4900** from any touch-tone phone. You can call 24 hours a day. The line is often busy; the best times to call are from noon to 3pm and on weekends.

Bus stops are marked by rectangular blue signs every other block or so on local routes, farther apart on express routes. More than 20 bus routes pass through the downtown area. Most **bus fares** range from $1.50 to $2.50, depending on distance and type of service (local or express). Buses accept dollar bills, but the driver can't give change.

Tips **Money-Saving Bus & Trolley Passes**

The **Day Tripper pass** allows unlimited rides on MTS (bus) and trolley routes. Passes are good for 1, 2, 3, and 4 consecutive days, and cost $5, $8, $10, and $12, respectively. Day Trippers are for sale at the Transit Store and all trolley station automatic ticket vending machines; call ✆ **619/ 685-4900** for more information.

You can request a free transfer as long as you continue on a bus or trolley with an equal or lower fare (if it's higher, you pay the difference). Transfers must be used within 2 hours, and you can return to where you started.

Some of the most popular tourist attractions served by bus and rail routes are Balboa Park (Routes 1, 3, 7, 7A, 7B, and 25); the San Diego Zoo (Routes 7, 7A, and 7B); the Children's Museum, Convention Center, and Gaslamp Quarter (San Diego Trolley's Orange Line); Coronado (Route 901); Horton Plaza (most downtown bus routes and the San Diego Trolley's Blue and Orange Lines); Old Town (San Diego Trolley's Blue Line); Cabrillo National Monument (Rte. 26 from Old Town Transit Center); Seaport Village (Rte. 7 and the San Diego Trolley's Orange Line); SeaWorld (Rte. 9 from the Old Town Transit Center); Qualcomm Stadium (San Diego Trolley's Blue Line); and, Tijuana (San Diego Trolley's Blue Line to San Ysidro).

The Coronado Shuttle, bus Route 904, runs between the Coronado Island Marriott Hotel and the Old Ferry Landing, and then continues along Orange Avenue to the Hotel del Coronado, Glorietta Bay, Loews, and back again. It costs $1 per person. Route 901 goes all the way to Coronado from San Diego and costs $2 for adults and $1 for seniors and children. Call ✆ **619/233-3004** for more information about this and other bus routes. You can also view timetables, maps, and fares online—and learn how the public transit system accommodates travelers with disabilities—at **www.sdcommute.com/sdmts**.

When planning your route, note that schedules vary and most buses do not run all night. Some stop at 6pm, while other lines continue to 9pm, midnight, and 2am—ask your bus driver for more specific information. On Saturdays some routes run all night.

BY TROLLEY

The San Diego Trolley routes serve downtown, the Mexican border (a 40-min. trip from downtown), Old Town, and the city of Santee, to the east. The recently completed Mission Valley extension carries sports fans to Qualcomm Stadium, major hotels, and shopping centers. Downtown, trolleys run along C Street (1 block north of Broadway) and stop at Broadway and Kettner (America Plaza), Third Avenue (Civic Center), Fifth Avenue, and 12th Avenue (City College). Trolleys also circle around downtown's Bayside (parallel to Harbor Dr.), with stops serving the Gaslamp Quarter, the Convention Center, Seaport Village, and the Santa Fe Depot.

Trolleys operate on a self-service fare-collection system; riders buy tickets from machines in stations before boarding. The machines list fares for each destination ($1.25–$2.50) and dispense change. Tickets are valid for 3 hours from the time of purchase, in any direction. Fare inspectors board trains at random to check tickets. The bright-red trains run every 15 minutes during the day (every 10 min. on the Blue Line, between Old Town and the border during weekday rush hours) and every 30 minutes at night. Trolleys stop at each station for only 30 seconds. To open the door for boarding, push the lighted green button; to open the door to exit the trolley, push the lighted white button.

For recorded transit information, call ✆ **619/685-4900.** To speak with a customer service representative, call ✆ **619/233-3004** (TTY/TDD 619/234-5005) daily from 5:30am to 8:30pm. The trolley generally operates daily from 5am to about 12:30am; the Blue Line, which goes to the border, runs 24 hours on Saturday.

San Diego Trolley System

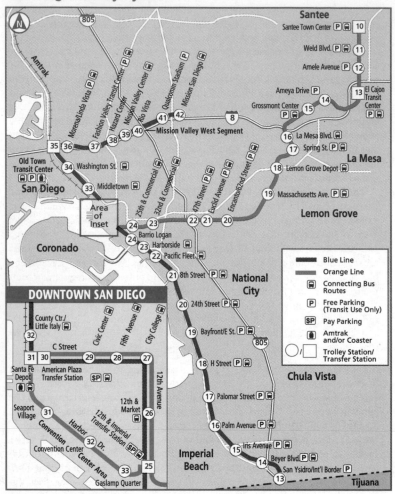

Privately owned **Old Town Trolley Tours** (☎ 619/298-TOUR; www.trolley tours.com) offers an alternative way to tour the city by trolley. If you'd like to hit the tourist high points in a short visit, without having to drive, it is a worthwhile option. The narrated tours cover a 30-mile route, including the highlights of areas such as Old Town, Downtown, Coronado, and Balboa Park. You can board and reboard the trolley at more than a dozen stops every half hour. The fare is $24 for adults, $12 for children 4 to 12, free for children under 4 (who must sit on an adult's lap).

BY TAXI

Half a dozen taxi companies serve the San Diego area. They do not charge standard rates, except from the airport into downtown, which costs around $8.50 with tip. Taxis don't cruise the streets as they do in other cities, so you have to call ahead for quick pickup. If you are at a hotel or restaurant, the front-desk attendant or maitre d' will call one for you. Among the local companies are

Orange Cab (© 619/291-3333), San Diego Cab (© 619/226-TAXI), and Yellow Cab (© 619/234-6161). The Coronado Cab Company (© 935/435-6211) serves Coronado. In La Jolla, use La Jolla Cab (© 858/453-4222).

BY TRAIN

San Diego's express rail commuter service, the **Coaster,** travels between the downtown Santa Fe Depot station and the Oceanside Transit Center, with stops at Old Town, Sorrento Valley, Solana Beach, Encinitas, and Carlsbad. Fares range from $3 to $3.75 each way, depending on how far you go. Eligible seniors and riders with disabilities pay half price. The trip between Oceanside and downtown San Diego takes just under an hour. Trains run Monday through Saturday; call © **800/COASTER** for the current schedule, or log onto **www.sdcommute.sdmts/coasterpage.htm**.

Amtrak (© **800/USA-RAIL;** www.amtrakwest) trains run daily between San Diego and Los Angeles. Trains to Los Angeles depart from the Santa Fe Depot and stop at Solana Beach and Oceanside. Some trains stop at San Juan Capistrano. A round-trip ticket to Solana Beach is $10, to Oceanside $15, to San Juan Capistrano $24, and to Los Angeles $40. The train also serves the Disneyland Resort in Anaheim; see chapter 11.

BY FERRY, WATER TAXI, OR BOAT

BY FERRY   There's regularly scheduled ferry service between San Diego and Coronado (© **619/234-4111** for information). Ferries leave from the Broadway Pier on the hour from 9am to 9pm Sunday through Thursday and from 9am to 10pm Friday and Saturday. They return from the Old Ferry Landing in Coronado to the Broadway Pier every hour on the 42-minute mark from 9:42am to 9:42pm Sunday through Thursday and from 9:42am to 10:42pm Friday and Saturday. The ride takes 15 minutes. Ferries also run from the Fifth Avenue Landing near the Convention Center to the Old Ferry Landing every hour on the half hour from 9:30am to 9:30pm Sunday through Thursday and from 9:30am to 10:30pm Friday and Saturday. The trip from Coronado to the Fifth Avenue Landing is every hour at the 18-minute mark from 9:18am to 9:18pm Sunday through Thursday and from 9:18am to 10:18pm Friday and Saturday. The fare is $2 for each leg of the journey (50¢ extra if you bring your bike). You can buy tickets in advance at the Harbor Excursion kiosk on Broadway Pier, the Fifth Avenue Landing in San Diego, or the Old Ferry Landing in Coronado.

BY WATER TAXI   Water taxis (© **619/235-TAXI**) will take you around most of San Diego Bay for $5, and operate daily between 10am and 10pm.

You can call a taxi to pick you up from any landing in the bay, or go to the Harbor Excursion Dock at the foot of Broadway Pier, where taxis wait for passengers.

BY BOAT   Boat tours provide a great way to explore San Diego from one of its many bays, including Mission Bay and San Diego Bay. For complete information, see "Bay Excursions," in chapter 7.

BY BICYCLE

San Diego is flat enough for easy exploration by bicycle, and many roads have designated bike lanes. The San Diego Ridelink publishes a comprehensive map of the county detailing bike *paths* (separate rights-of-way for bicyclists), bike *lanes* (alongside motor vehicle ways), and bike *routes* (shared ways designated only by bike-symbol signs). The **San Diego Region Bike Map** is available at visitor centers; to receive a copy in advance, call © **619/231-BIKE.**

Bikes are available for rent in most areas; see "Biking" in chapter 7 for suggestions. If you want to take your two-wheeler on a city bus, look for bike-route signs at the bus stop. The signs mean that the buses that stop here have bike racks. Let the driver know you want to stow your bike on the back of the bus, then board and pay the regular fare. With this service, you can bus the bike to an area you'd like to explore, do your biking there, then return by bus. Not all routes are served by buses with bike racks; call ✆ **619/233-3004** for information.

The San Diego Trolley has a **Bike-N-Ride** program that lets you bring your bike on the trolley for free. You'll need a bike permit before you board. Permits for bikers age 16 and older cost $4 and are issued through the **Transit Store,** 102 Broadway, at First Avenue (✆ **619/234-1060**). Bikers must board at the back of the trolley car, where the bike-storage area is located; cars carry two bikes except during weekday rush hours, when the limit is one bike per car. Several trolley stops connect with routes for buses with bike racks. For more information, call the **Transit Information Line** (✆ **619/233-3004**).

Bikes are permitted on the ferry connecting San Diego and Coronado, which has 15 miles (24km) of dedicated bike paths.

 FAST FACTS: San Diego

Airport   See "Getting There," in chapter 2.

American Express   A full-service office is located downtown at 258 Broadway, at Third Avenue (✆ **619/234-4455**).

Area Codes   In the past couple of years, San Diego County's area code layout has become more complicated—much like the rest of California! The main area code, **619,** is now used primarily by the core city, including downtown, uptown, Mission Valley, and Point Loma. Northern and coastal areas, including Mission Beach, Pacific Beach, La Jolla, Del Mar, Rancho Sante Fe, and Rancho Bernardo, received the new area code **858** during 1999. At the start of 2000, the vast southeastern portion of the city, primarily bedroom communities like El Cajon, La Mesa, National City, and Chula Vista, began using **935.** Use **760** to reach the remainder of San Diego County, including Encinitas, Carlsbad, Oceanside, Escondido, Ramona, Julian, and Anza-Borrego.

Babysitters   **Marion's Childcare** (✆ **619/582-5029**) has bonded babysitters available to come to your hotel room.

Business Hours   Banks are open weekdays from 9am to 4pm or later, and sometimes Saturday morning. Shops in shopping malls tend to stay open until about 9pm weekdays and until 6pm weekends.

Camera Repair   Both **George's Camera & Video,** 3827 30th St. (✆ **619/297-3544**), and **Professional Photographic Repair,** 7910 Raytheon Rd. (✆ **619/277-3700**), provide cameras and repair services. In La Jolla, try **Bob Davis' Camera Shop,** 7720 Fay St. (✆ **858/459-7355**). Other good choices are **Nelson Photo Supply,** 1909 India St., at Fir Street (✆ **619/234-6621**; fax 619/232-6153), and **Point Loma Camera Store,** 1310 Rosecrans St. (✆ **619/224-2719**).

Car Rentals   See "Getting Around," earlier this chapter.

Climate See "When to Go," in chapter 2.

Dentists For dental referrals, contact the **San Diego County Dental Society** at ✆ **800/201-0244**, or call ✆ 800/DENTIST.

Doctors **Hotel Docs** (✆ **800/468-3537** or 619/275-2663) is a 24-hour network of physicians, dentists, and chiropractors who claim they'll come to your hotel room within 35 minutes of your call. They accept credit cards, and their services are covered by most insurance policies. In a life-threatening situation, dial ✆ **911.**

Driving Rules See "Getting Around," earlier in this chapter.

Drugstores See "Pharmacies," below.

Embassies & Consulates See chapter 3, "For International Visitors."

Emergencies Call ✆ **911** for fire, police, and ambulance. The main police station is at 1401 Broadway, at 14th Street (✆ **619/531-2000**, or 619/531-2065 for the hearing impaired).

Eyeglass Repair **Optometric Expressions,** 55 Horton Plaza (✆ **619/544-9000),** is at street level near the Westin Hotel; it's open Monday, Wednesday, and Friday from 8am to 6pm and Tuesday, Thursday, and Saturday from 9:30am to 6pm. **Optometry on the Plaza,** 287 Horton Plaza (✆ **619/ 239-1716),** is open Monday through Friday from 10am to 9pm and Saturday from 10am to 7pm. Both can fill eyeglass prescriptions, repair glasses, and replace contact lenses.

Hospitals In Hillcrest, near downtown San Diego, **UCSD Medical Center-Hillcrest,** 200 W. Arbor Dr. (✆ **619/543-6400),** has the most convenient emergency room. In La Jolla, **Thornton Hospital,** 9300 Campus Point Dr. (✆ **858/657-7600),** has a good emergency room, and you'll find another in Coronado, at **Coronado Hospital,** 250 Prospect Place, opposite the Marriott Resort (✆ **619/435-6251).**

Hot Lines HIV Hot Line: ✆ 619/236-2352. Alcoholics Anonymous: ✆ 619/ **265 8762.** Debtors Anonymous: ✆ 619/525-3065. Mental Health Access & Crisis Line: ✆ **800/479-3339.** Traveler's Aid Society: ✆ **619/231-7361.**

Information See "Visitor Information," in chapter 2. For telephone directory assistance, dial ✆ **411.**

Liquor Laws The drinking age in California is 21. Beer, wine, and hard liquor are sold daily from 6am to 2am and are available in grocery stores.

Maps See "City Layout," earlier in this chapter.

Newspapers & Magazines The *San Diego Union-Tribune* is published daily, and its informative entertainment section, "Night & Day," is in the Thursday edition. The free alternative, *Reader,* published weekly (on Thurs), is available at many shops, restaurants, theaters, and public hot spots; it's the best source for up-to-the-minute club and show listings. *San Diego* magazine is filled with entertainment and dining listings for an elite audience (which explains all the ads for face-lifts and tummy tucks). *San Diego Home-Garden Lifestyles* magazine highlights the city's homes and gardens, and includes a monthly calendar of events and some savvy articles about the restaurant scene. Both magazines are published monthly and sold at newsstands.

Pharmacies Long's, Rite-Aid, and Sav-On sell pharmaceuticals and non-prescription products. Look in the phone book to find the one nearest you. If you need a pharmacy after normal business hours, the following branches are open 24 hours: **Sav-On Drugs,** 8831 Villa La Jolla Dr., La Jolla (© **858/457-4390**), and 3151 University Ave., North Park; **Rite-Aid,** 535 Robinson Ave., Hillcrest (© **619/291-3703**); and **Long's Drug Store,** 5685 Balboa Ave., Clairemont (© **619/279-2753**). Local hospitals also sell prescription drugs.

Police The downtown police station is at 1401 Broadway (© **619/531-2000**). Call © **911** in an emergency.

Post Office Post offices are located downtown, at 815 E St. and at 51 Horton Plaza, beside the Westin Hotel. They are generally open Monday through Friday during regular business hours, plus Saturday morning; for specific branch information, call © **800/ASK-USPS** or log on to **www.usps.gov.** Also see "Mail," under "Fast Facts: For the International Traveler," in chapter 3.

Restrooms Horton Plaza and Seaport Village downtown, Balboa Park, Old Town State Historic Park in Old Town, and the Ferry Landing Marketplace in Coronado all have well-marked public restrooms. In general, you won't have a problem finding one.

Safety For suggestions on personal safety and driving safety tips, see "Safety" in chapter 3.

Smoking Smoking is prohibited in nearly all indoor public places, including theaters, hotel lobbies, and enclosed shopping malls. In 1998, California enacted legislation prohibiting smoking in all restaurants and bars, except those with outdoor seating. Opponents immediately began preparing to appeal the law, so things may have changed by the time you visit; be sure to inquire before you light up, or if you're determined to avoid those who do.

Taxes Sales tax in restaurants and shops is 7.5%. Hotel tax is 10.5%.

Taxis See "Getting Around," earlier this chapter.

Time Zone San Diego, like the rest of the West Coast, is in the Pacific standard time zone, which is 8 hours behind Greenwich (mean) time. Daylight saving time is observed. To check the time, call © **619/853-1212.**

Transit Information Call © **619/233-3004** (TTY/TDD 619/234-5005). If you know your route and just need schedule information, call © **619/685-4900.**

Useful Telephone Numbers For the latest San Diego arts and entertainment information, call © **619/238-0700;** for half-price day-of-performance tickets, call © **619/497-5000;** for a beach and surf report, call © **619/221-8824.**

Weather Call © **619/289-1212.**

Where to Stay

Where would you prefer to sleep? Over the water? On the beach? In historic surroundings? Facing the bay? With ocean views? Whatever your fancy, San Diego offers a variety of places to stay that range from pricey high-rise hostelries to inexpensive low-rise motels and some out-of-the-ordinary B&Bs.

In this chapter, I'll take you through all the options. For a list of my favorites in all kinds of categories, see "Best Hotel Bets" in chapter 1.

A note on air-conditioning: Unless you have a particular sensitivity to even mild heat, A/C is more a convenience than a necessity. In San Diego's temperate climate, ocean breezes cool the air year-round.

TIPS FOR SAVING ON YOUR HOTEL ROOM

A hotel's rack rate is the official published rate—we list these prices to help readers make a fair comparison. The truth is, hardly anybody pays these prices, and you can nearly always do better. Here's how we've organized our price categories: **Very Expensive** = Rooms average over $250 (high-season, weekend rates with no discounts applied); **Expensive** = $180 to $249; **Moderate** = $110 to $179; **Inexpensive** = under $110. *Our tip for you:* Remember to peruse the price category *above* your target—you might just find the perfect match, especially if you follow the advice below.

- **Don't be afraid to bargain.** Get in the habit of asking for a lower price than the first one quoted. Most rack rates include commissions of 10% to 25% or more for travel agents, which many hotels will cut if you make your own reservations and haggle a bit. Always ask politely whether a less expensive room is available, or whether any special rates apply to you. You may qualify for corporate, student, military, senior citizen, or other discounts. Be sure to mention membership in AAA, AARP, frequent-flyer and traveler programs, or trade unions, which may entitle you to special deals as well.
- **Remember the law of supply and demand.** Coastal and resort hotels are most crowded and therefore most expensive on weekends, so discounts are often available for midweek stays. Downtown and business hotels are busiest during the week; expect discounts over the weekend. Avoid high-season stays whenever you can: Planning your vacation just a week before or after official peak season can mean big savings.
- **Rely on a qualified professional.** Certain hotels give travel agents discounts in exchange for steering business their way, so if you're shy about bargaining, an agent may be better equipped to negotiate discounts for you.
- **Dial direct.** When booking a room in a chain hotel, call the hotel's local line and the toll-free number, and see where you get the best deal. A hotel makes nothing on a room that stays empty. The clerk who runs the place is more

likely to know about vacancies and will often grant deep discounts in order to fill up.

- **Look into group or long-stay discounts.** If you come as part of a large group, you should be able to negotiate a bargain, because the hotel can guarantee occupancy in a number of rooms. Likewise, when you're planning a long stay (usually 5 days to a week), you'll qualify for a discount. As a rule, you will receive 1 night free after a 7-night stay.
- **Avoid excess charges.** When you book a room, ask whether the hotel charges for parking. Most hotels have free spaces, but many urban or beachfront hotels don't. Also, find out before you dial whether your hotel imposes a surcharge on local or long-distance calls. A pay phone, however inconvenient, may save you money.
- **Consider a suite.** If you are traveling with your family or another couple, you can pack more people into a suite (which often comes with a sofa bed), and reduce your per-person rate. Remember that some places charge for extra guests, some don't.
- **Book an efficiency.** A room with a kitchenette allows you to grocery shop and eat some meals in. Especially during long stays with families, you're bound to save money on food this way.
- **Investigate reservation services.** These outfits usually work as consolidators, buying up or reserving rooms in bulk, and then dealing them out to customers at a profit. They do garner deals that range from 10% to 50% off, but remember, the discounts apply to rack rates—inflated prices that people rarely end up paying. You're probably better off dealing directly with a hotel, but if you don't like bargaining, this is certainly a viable option. Most of them offer online reservation services as well. Here are a few of the more reputable providers: **San Diego Hotel Reservations** (© 800/SAVE-CASH; www.san diegohotelres.com); **Hotel Locators** (© 800/576-0003; www. hotellocators.com); **Accommodations Express** (© 800/950-4685; www.accommodationsexpress.com); **Hotel Discounts** (© 800/ 715-7666; www.hoteldiscount. com); and **Quikbook** (© 800/ 789-9887, includes fax-on-demand service; www.quikbook. com).

Note: Rates given in this chapter do not include the hotel tax, which is an additional 10.5%. Also, some listings mention a free airport shuttle. This is common in San Diego hotels, so before you take a taxi from the airport, check to see what your hotel offers.

LANDING THE BEST ROOM

Somebody has to get the best room in the house. It might as well be you.

Always ask for a corner room. They're usually larger, quieter, and closer to the elevator. They often have more windows and light than standard rooms, and they don't always cost more.

When you make your reservation, ask if the hotel is being renovated; if it is, request a room away from the renovation work. Many hotels now offer rooms for nonsmokers; if smoke bothers you, by all means ask for one. Inquire, too, about the location of restaurants, bars, and nightclubs in the hotel—these could all be sources of irritating noise. If you aren't happy with your room when you arrive, talk to the front desk staff. If they have another room, they should be happy to accommodate you, within reason.

Tips **Chains on the Web**

For the website addresses of the hotel chains mentioned in this chapter, see the appendix at the end of the book.

BED & BREAKFASTS

Travelers who seek bed-and-breakfast accommodations will be pleasantly surprised by the variety and affordability of San Diego B&Bs (especially compared to the rest of California). The trend was late in coming to San Diego, but new establishments are popping up all the time. Many are traditional, strongly reflecting the personality of an on-site innkeeper and offering as few as two guest rooms; others accommodate more guests in a slickly professional way. More than a dozen are part of the close-knit **San Diego Bed & Breakfast Guild** (*©* **619/523-1300;** www.bandbguildsandiego.org), whose members work actively at keeping prices reasonable; many outstanding B&Bs remain near $100 a night.

1 Downtown

Visitors with business in the city center—including the Convention Center—will find the downtown area convenient. Keep in mind that our "downtown" heading includes hotels in the stylish Gaslamp Quarter, as well as properties conveniently located near the harbor and other leisure attractions.

VERY EXPENSIVE

Manchester Grand Hyatt San Diego ⋩⋩   The 40-story Grand Hyatt is generally the first choice of business travelers and convention groups, so the rack rates can be deceptively high—but don't let them scare you off if you want to stay in downtown's best modern high rise. Weekend rates in particular can be a great deal.

While a behemoth with nearly 900 rooms can't offer very personalized service, you'll definitely enjoy all the amenities those with expense accounts are used to. All the public spaces and guest rooms are light and airy, and boast stunning views over the city or sea. Built in 1992, the hotel (the tallest waterfront lodging on the West Coast) sports a limestone-and-marble neoclassical theme; guest rooms are quiet and furnished with high-quality but standard Hyatt-issue furnishings. Bathrooms have ample counter space, and the Hyatt gets kudos for superior service for travelers with disabilities (see "Best Hotel Bets," in chapter 1). A major expansion project had already started kicking up dust at press time; by summer of 2003, a second tower will more than double the hotel's meeting space and guest rooms.

1 Market Place (at Harbor Dr.), San Diego, CA 92101. *©* **800/233-1234** or 619/232-1234. Fax 619/239-5678. 875 units. $275–$345 double; from $500 suite. Extra person $25. Children under 12 stay free in parents' room. Packages and weekend rates available. AE, DC, DISC, MC, V. Valet parking $16; self-parking $12. Trolley: Seaport Village. **Amenities:** 3 restaurants; 2 bars; 3rd-story bay-view outdoor pool; 6 outdoor tennis courts (4 lit for night play); health club and spa; whirlpool; watersports-equipment rentals; bike rental; concierge; car-rental desk; courtesy car; business center; salon; 24-hr. room service; in-room massage; babysitting; laundry service; dry cleaning. *In room:* A/C, TV w/pay movies, dataport, minibar, coffeemaker, hair dryer, iron.

San Diego Marriott Marina ⋩⋩   In the prosperous late 1980s, long before San Diego's Convention Center was even a blueprint, this mirrored tower arose. Heck, with more than 1,400 rooms and multiple banquet and ballrooms, the

Marriott *was* a convention center. Today it merely stands next door, garnering a large share of convention attendees. They're drawn by the scenic 446-slip marina, lush grounds, waterfall pool, and breathtaking bay-and-beyond views. The Marriott competes with the much newer Grand Hyatt, and guests benefit from constantly improved facilities and decor. Leisure travelers can also take advantage of greatly reduced weekend rates. Because the Marriott tends to focus on public features and business services, guest quarters are well maintained but plain, and standard rooms are on the small side. Hallway noise can sometimes be disturbing.

333 W. Harbor Dr. (at Front St.), San Diego, CA 92101-7700. © 800/228-9290 or 619/234-1500. Fax 619/234-8678. 1,408 units. $265–$300 double; from $500 suite. Children under 18 stay free in parents' room. Weekend rates, AARP discount; honeymoon and other packages available. Pets accepted. AE, DC, DISC, MC, V. Valet parking $18; self-parking $13. Bus: 7. Trolley: Convention Center. **Amenities:** 3 restaurants (1 with lounge); 2 lagoonlike outdoor pools; 6 night-lit tennis courts; fitness center; 2 whirlpools; sauna; boat rentals; bike rentals; game room; concierge, tour desk; car-rental desk; business center with secretarial services; salon; 24-hr. room service; laundry service; coin-op laundry; dry cleaning. *In room:* A/C, TV w/pay movies, dataport, minibar, coffeemaker, hair dryer, iron.

The Westgate Hotel 🎭🎭🎭 It's hard not to compare the lavish Westgate with its equally elegant neighbor, the U.S. Grant. But whereas the latter came by its formality during an era when royal treatment was expected, the Westgate might be considered nouveau riche. It was built in 1970 by a wealthy financier whose wife toured Europe collecting the antiques that fill each guest room. Ultimately, the hotel became a money pit for C. Arnholt Smith, but not before it established a standard of luxury—including fruit baskets and deferential service—that today appeals mainly to European and Latin American travelers and dignitaries.

The lobby appears straight out of 18th-century France; it's a precise recreation of a Versailles anteroom, featuring brocade upholstery, tapestries, luxurious Baccarat crystal chandeliers, and Persian rugs. If you're downtown for a night at the theater or symphony, the Westgate fills the bill, but casual tourists may find the formality a bit stifling.

1055 Second Ave. (between Broadway and C St.), San Diego, CA 92101. © 800/221-3802 or 619/238-1818. Fax 619/557-3604. www.westgatehotel.com. 223 units. $259–$339 double; from $440 suite. Extra person $10. Children 18 and under stay free in parents' room. Weekend rates and packages available. AE, DC, DISC, MC, V. Underground valet parking $12. Bus: 2. Trolley: Civic Center (C St. and Third Ave.). **Amenities:** 3 restaurants (formal, casual, and deli); lounge; fitness center; concierge; courtesy car; business center; barbershop; 24-hr. room service; laundry/dry-cleaning service. *In room:* A/C, TV w/pay movies, dataport, minibar, hair dryer, safe.

EXPENSIVE

Embassy Suites 🎭🎭 What might seem like an impersonal business hotel is actually one of the better deals in town. It provides modern accommodations with lots of room for families or claustrophobes. Built in 1988, this neoclassical high-rise is topped with a distinctive neon bull's-eye that's visible from far away. Every room is a suite, with sofa beds in the living/dining areas and convenient touches like microwaves in the kitchenette. All rooms open onto a 12-story atrium filled with palm trees, koi ponds, and a bubbling fountain; each also has a city or bay view. One block from Seaport Village and 5 blocks from downtown, the Embassy Suites is the second choice of Convention Center groups (after the pricier Manchester Grand Hyatt) and consequently can be fully booked at unexpected times.

601 Pacific Hwy. (at N. Harbor Dr.), San Diego, CA 92101. © 800/EMBASSY or 619/239-2400. Fax 619/239-1520. 337 suites. $189–$300 suite. Rates include full breakfast and afternoon cocktail. Children under 18 stay free in parents' room. AE, DC, DISC, MC, V. Valet parking $14; indoor self-parking $11. Bus: 7.

Downtown San Diego Accommodations

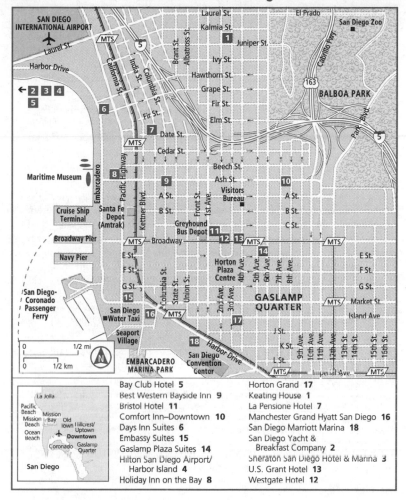

Bay Club Hotel **5**	Horton Grand **17**
Best Western Bayside Inn **9**	Keating House **1**
Bristol Hotel **11**	La Pensione Hotel **7**
Comfort Inn–Downtown **10**	Manchester Grand Hyatt San Diego **16**
Days Inn Suites **6**	San Diego Marriott Marina **18**
Embassy Suites **15**	San Diego Yacht &
Gaslamp Plaza Suites **14**	Breakfast Company **2**
Hilton San Diego Airport/	Sheraton San Diego Hotel & Marina **3**
Harbor Island **4**	U.S. Grant Hotel **13**
Holiday Inn on the Bay **8**	Westgate Hotel **12**

Trolley: Seaport Village. **Amenities:** 2 restaurants; indoor pool; tennis court; exercise room; whirlpool, concierge; car-rental desk; babysitting; laundry service; self-service laundry; VIP rooms. *In room:* A/C, TV w/pay movies, dataport, kitchenette, fridge, coffeemaker, hair dryer, iron.

Holiday Inn on the Bay ⚘⚘ (Kids)   This better-than-average Holiday Inn is reliable and nearly always offers great deals. The multibuilding high-rise complex is located on the Embarcadero across from the harbor and the Maritime Museum—this scenic spot is only 1½ miles (2.5km) from the airport (you can watch planes landing and taking off), and 2 blocks from the train station and trolley. Rooms, while basic, always seem to sport clean new furnishings and plenty of thoughtful comforts. Choose your room carefully; while the bay views are astounding, city views can be depressing (you're looking at utilitarian older office buildings). In either case, request the highest floor possible.

1355 N. Harbor Dr. (at Ash St.), San Diego, CA 92101-3385. ☎ **800/HOLIDAY** or 619/232-3861. Fax 619/232-4924. 600 units. $189–$209 double; from $400 suite. Children under 18 stay free in parents' room. Terrific packages are available, as well as AARP and AAA rates as low as $99–$139. Pets accepted with $25

⟨Tips Accommodations Farther Afield

If you're interested in staying in nearby Del Mar or Carlsbad—only 20 to 40 minutes from downtown San Diego—see "North County Beach Towns: Spots to Surf & Sun" in chapter 11.

---

fee and $75 deposit. AE, DC, MC, V. Self-parking $13 or valet parking $18. Bus: 22, 23, 992. **Amenities:** 4 restaurants; lounge; outdoor heated pool; exercise room; concierge; business center; room service (6–11am and 5–11pm); babysitting; laundry service; self-service laundry. *In room:* A/C, TV w/pay movies, dataport, coffeemaker, hair dryer, iron.

U.S. Grant Hotel ⭐⭐⭐   In 1910, Ulysses S. Grant Jr. opened this stately hotel, now on the National Register of Historic Places, in honor of his famous father. Former guests have included Albert Einstein, Charles Lindbergh, FDR, and JFK. Resembling an Italianate palace, the hotel is of a style more often found on the East Coast. An elegant atmosphere prevails, with age-smoothed marble, wood paneling, crystal chandeliers, and formal room decor that verges on stuffy. Guest rooms are quite spacious, as are the richly outfitted bathrooms. Extras in the suites make them worth the splurge; each has a fireplace and whirlpool tub, and suite rates include continental breakfast and afternoon cocktails and hors d'oeuvres. Afternoon tea is served in the lobby Tuesday through Saturday with soft piano music as a backdrop. While the hotel has preserved a nostalgic formality, the surrounding neighborhood has become a hodgepodge of chic bistros, wandering panhandlers, and the visually loud Horton Plaza shopping center (which looms large right across the street). Plus, pets are not only welcomed, but also pampered with gourmet dinners, nightly treats, special doggie beds, and a walking service.

326 Broadway (between Third and Fourth aves.), San Diego, CA 92101. ℂ **800/237-5029** or 619/232-3121. Fax 619/232-3626. www.grandheritage.com. 340 units. $195–$215 double; from $275 suite. AAA, off-season, and weekend rates ($139–$179 double) available; off-season packages available. Children under 12 stay free in parents' room. AE, DC, MC, V. Parking $17. Bus: 2. Trolley: Civic Center (C St. and Third Ave.). Pets welcome. **Amenities:** Restaurant; jazz lounge; 24-hr. fitness center; in-room exercise bike/rowing machine rental; concierge; courtesy airport shuttle; business center; 24-hr. room service; babysitting; laundry and dry-cleaning service. *In room:* A/C, TV w/pay movies, dataport, minibar, hair dryer.

MODERATE

Best Western Bayside Inn ⭐   Though noisy downtown is just outside, this high-rise representative of reliable Best Western offers quiet lodgings. The hotel has an accommodating staff, and stunning city and harbor views. A mecca for business travelers, it's also close to more touristy downtown sites. It's an easy walk to the Embarcadero ("Bayview" would be a more accurate name for the hotel than "Bayside"), a bit farther to Horton Plaza, 4 blocks to the trolley stop, and 5 blocks to the train station. Rooms and bathrooms are basic chain-hotel issue, but are well maintained and feature brand-new bedding, towels, and draperies; all have balconies overlooking the bay or downtown (ask for the higher floors).

555 W. Ash St. (at Columbia St.), San Diego, CA 92101. ℂ **800/341-1818** or 619/233-7500. Fax 619/239-8060. www.baysideinn.com. 122 units. $119–$219 double. Children under 12 stay free in parents' room. Rates include continental breakfast. Packages and fall, winter, spring weekend rates available. AE, DC, DISC, MC, V. Free covered parking. Trolley: C St. and Kettner. **Amenities:** Restaurant; outdoor pool; whirlpool; laundry/dry-cleaning service. *In room:* A/C, TV w/pay movies, dataport, coffeemaker, hair dryer, iron.

Bristol Hotel ⚔ (Value   If you're looking for a basic business hotel with a sunny splash of style, you can do no better than the economical Bristol, which boasts a boxy, IKEA-esque geometric decor accented by energetic primary colors and an admirable collection of late-20th-century pop art from personalities as varied as Warhol, Kandinsky, Lichtenstein, and Haring. Everything still feels crisply new from the 2001 makeover that rendered this formerly baroque boutique property almost unrecognizable. Though it doesn't offer many on-site amenities to keep you around during the day, these brightly modern rooms are fun to come home to. Each morning a very nice breakfast spread is laid out in the downstairs Daisies Bistro, which offers all-day dining and a cozy, after-work bar.

1055 First Ave. (between Broadway & C St.), San Diego, CA 92101. ℂ 800/662-4477 or 619/232-6141. Fax 619/232-1948. www.bristolhotelsandiego.com. 102 units. $129–$199 double. Children under 17 stay free in parents' room. Rates include continental breakfast. Seasonal discounts and Internet rates available (as low as $79). AE, DC, DISC, MC, V. Valet parking $12. Bus: 2. Trolley: Civic Center. **Amenities:** Restaurant; lounge; concierge; laundry/dry-cleaning service. *In room:* A/C, TV w/pay movies, dataport, minibar, coffeemaker, hair dryer, iron.

Gaslamp Plaza Suites ⚔⚔ (Value   You can't get closer to the center of the vibrant Gaslamp Quarter than this impeccably restored late Victorian. At 11 stories, it was San Diego's first skyscraper in 1913. Built (at great expense) of Australian gumwood, marble, brass, and exquisite etched glass, this splendid building originally housed San Diego Trust & Savings. Various other businesses (jewelers, lawyers, doctors, photographers) set up shop here until 1988, when the elegant structure was placed on the National Register of Historic Places and reopened as a boutique hotel.

You'll be surprised at the timeless elegance, from the dramatic lobby and wide corridors to guest rooms furnished with European flair. Each bears the name of a writer (Emerson, Swift, Zola, Shelley, Fitzgerald, and so on). Most rooms are spacious and offer luxuries rare in this price range, like pillow-top mattresses and premium toiletries; microwave ovens and dinnerware; and, impressive luxury bathrooms. Beware of the few cheapest rooms, however; they are uncomfortably small (although they do have regular-size bathrooms). The higher floors boast stunning city and bay views, as do the patio, whirlpool, and breakfast room on the rooftop.

Despite the welcome recent addition of new, noise-muffling windows, don't be surprised to hear a hum from the street below, especially when the Quarter gets rockin' on the weekends.

520 E St. (corner of 5th Ave.), San Diego, CA 92101. ℂ 619/232-9500. Fax 619/238-9945. www.gaslamp plaza.com. 64 units. $89–$159 double; $179–$259 suite. Rates include continental breakfast. AE, DC, DISC, MC, V. Valet parking $18. Bus: 1, 3, 25. Trolley: Fifth Ave. **Amenities:** Restaurant; access to nearby health club; rooftop whirlpool. *In room:* A/C, TV w/VCR, dataport, fridge, coffeemaker, hair dryer, iron, safe.

Horton Grand ⚔⚔   A cross between an elegant hotel and a charming inn, the Horton Grand combines two hotels that date from 1886—the Horton Grand (once an infamous red-light establishment) and the Brooklyn Hotel (which for a time was the Kahle Saddlery Shop). Both were saved from demolition, moved to this spot, and connected by an airy atrium lobby filled with white wicker. The facade, with its graceful bay windows, is original.

Each room is utterly unique—all were renovated in 2000 with vintage furnishings, gas fireplaces, and business-savvy features—and bathrooms are resplendent with reproduction floor tiles, fine brass fixtures, and genteel appointments. Rooms overlook either the city or the fig tree-filled courtyard;

they're divided between the clubby and darker "saddlery" side and the pastel-toned and Victorian "brothel" side. The suites (really just large studio-style rooms) are located in a newer wing; choosing one means sacrificing historic character for a sitting area/sofa bed and minibar with microwave oven. With all these offerings, there's a room that's right for everyone, so query your reservationist on the different features.

The Palace Bar serves afternoon tea Tuesday through Saturday from 2:30 to 5pm; there's live music Thursday through Saturday evenings and Sunday afternoons.

311 Island Ave. (at Fourth Ave.), San Diego, CA 92101. © 800/542-1886 or 619/544-1886. Fax 619/544-0058. www.hortongrand.com. 132 units. $139–$199 double; $259 suite. Packages available. Children under 18 stay free in parents' room. AE, DC, MC, V. Valet parking $15. Bus: 1. **Amenities:** Restaurant; lounge. *In room:* A/C, TV, dataport, hair dryer.

San Diego Yacht & Breakfast Company 🅠🅠 *Finds* Here's an unusual opportunity to sleep on the water in your own power yacht, sailboat, or floating villa. You fall asleep to the gentle lapping of waves and awaken to the call of seagulls. The vessels are docked in a recreational marina on Harbor Island, near the airport and close to downtown; for an additional charge ($75–$200 an hr.) you can even charter a private cruise aboard your "room" (power and sailboats only).

The floating villas are 650 square feet and feel like modern condos, with their own laundry facilities, comfortable furnishings, multiple TVs, a stereo, and many other comforts. The well-kept power yachts have two staterooms, two heads, a full galley, and stereo system. Serious sailors may prefer to sleep on a sailboat. They range in length from 25 feet to 45 feet (7.5m–14m) and accommodate two to four people, but are best suited for one couple. If showering on board any of the boats is too cramped for you, guests have the use of full restrooms at the marina headquarters, as well as the swimming pool there.

Marina Cortez, 1880 Harbor Island Dr., G-Dock, San Diego, CA 92101. © 800/YACHT-DO or 619/297-9484. Fax 619/298-6625. www.yachtdo.com. 12 vessels. $150–$325 double May 15–Oct 15 and Dec 15–Jan 5; $125–$295 off-season. Extra person $25–$50. Midweek, multinight, and other discounts available. Rates include full breakfast ashore. AE, DISC, MC, V. Free parking. **Amenities:** Casual restaurant; outdoor pool; access to nearby health club; watersports-equipment rentals; bike rental. *In room:* TV w/VCR, kitchen, coffeemaker, hair dryer, iron.

INEXPENSIVE

Inexpensive motels line Pacific Highway between the airport and downtown. The **Days Inn Suites,** 1919 Pacific Hwy. at Grape Street (© **800/325-2525** or 619/232-1077), is within walking distance of the Embarcadero, the Maritime Museum, and the Harbor Excursion. Rates range from $49 to $69.

Comfort Inn–Downtown In the northern corner of downtown, this terrific value is popular with business travelers without expense accounts, and vacationers who just need reliable, safe accommodations. This humble chain motel must be surprised to find itself in a quickly regentrifying part of town: the landmark El Cortez Hotel across the street has been transformed into upscale condos and shops, and new residential construction hums on the surrounding blocks. The Comfort Inn is smartly designed so rooms open onto exterior walkways surrounding the drive-in entry courtyard, lending an insular feel in this once-dicey corner of town. There are few frills here, but coffee is always brewing in the lobby. The hotel operates a free shuttle to the airport and the train and bus stations.

719 Ash St. (at Seventh Ave.), San Diego, CA 92101. © 800/228-5150 or 619/232-2525. Fax 619/687-3024. www.comfortinnsandiego.com. 67 units. $79–$84 double. Extra person $15. Children under 18 stay free in

parents' room. AARP and AAA discounts and off-season rates available. Rates include continental breakfast. AE, DISC, MC, V. Free parking. **Amenities:** Whirlpool; laundry service. *In room:* A/C, TV, dataport, coffeemaker.

Keating House 🏛️🏛️ *(Finds*   This grand Bankers Hill mansion, between downtown and stylish Hillcrest, is being meticulously restored by two energetic new innkeepers with a solid background in architectural preservation. Doug Scott and Ben Baltic not only know old houses, but are also neighborhood devotees filled with historical knowledge and savvy area recommendations. At press time, they had completed installing/upgrading private bathrooms for every room— featuring reproduction fixtures and authentic period design—and were turning to the already sumptuous gardens that bloom on four sides of this local landmark. The house contains a comfortable hodgepodge of antique furnishings and appointments; three additional rooms are in the restored carriage house opening onto an exotic garden patio. The downstairs entry, parlor, and dining room all have cozy fireplaces; breakfast (special dietary needs are cheerfully considered) is served in a sunny, friendly setting. In contrast to many B&Bs in Victorian-era homes, this one eschews dollhouse frills for a classy, sophisticated approach.

2331 Second Ave. (between Juniper and Kalmia sts.), San Diego, CA 92101. ℂ **800/995-8644** or 619/239-8585. Fax 619/239-5774. www.keatinghouse.com. 9 units. $90–$155 double. Rates include full breakfast. AE, DISC, MC, V. Bus: 11. From the airport, take Harbor Dr. toward downtown; turn left on Laurel St., then right on Second Ave. *In room:* Hair dryer, no phone.

La Pensione Hotel 🏛️ *(Value*   This place has a lot going for it: modern amenities, remarkable value, a convenient location within walking distance of the central business district, a friendly staff, and parking (a premium for small hotels in San Diego). The three-story La Pensione is built around a courtyard and feels like a small European hotel; in fact, it's the number one choice of foreign students attending the downtown **Language Institute.** The decor throughout is modern and streamlined, with plenty of sleek black and metallic surfaces, crisp white walls, and minimal furniture. Guest rooms, while not overly large, make the most of their space and leave you with room to move around. Each room offers a tub-shower combination, ceiling fan, and microwave oven; try for a bay or city view rather than the concrete courtyard view. La Pensione is in San Diego's Little Italy and within walking distance of eateries (mostly Italian) and nightspots; there are two restaurants directly downstairs.

606 W. Date St. (at India St.), San Diego, CA 92101. ℂ **800/232-4683** or 619/236-8000. Fax 619/236-8088. www.lapensionehotel.com. 80 units. $60–$80 double. AE, DC, DISC, MC, V. Limited free underground parking. Trolley: County Center/Little Italy. **Amenities:** Access to nearby health club; bike rental; self-service laundry. *In room:* TV, dataport, fridge.

2 Hillcrest/Uptown

Although they're certainly no longer a secret, the gentrified historic neighborhoods north of downtown are still something of a bargain. They're convenient to Balboa Park and offer easy access to the rest of town. Filled with chic casual restaurants, eclectic shops, movie theaters, and sizzling nightlife, the area is also easy to navigate.

MODERATE

Balboa Park Inn 🏛️   Insiders looking for unusual, well-located accommodations head straight for this small pink inn at the northern edge of Balboa Park. It's a cluster of four Spanish Colonial–style former apartment buildings in a mostly residential neighborhood close to the trendy Hillcrest area. The hotel caters to a straight clientele as well as gay travelers drawn to Hillcrest's hip restaurants and clubs. All the rooms and suites are tastefully decorated; the specialty suites, however, are over-the-top. There's the "Tara Suite," as in *Gone With the Wind;* the "Nouveau Ritz," which employs every Art Deco cliché, including mirrors and Hollywood lighting; and the "Greystoke" suite, a jumble of jungle, safari, and tropical themes with a completely mirrored bathroom and whirlpool tub. From here, you're close enough to walk to Balboa Park attractions.

3402 Park Blvd. (at Upas St.), San Diego, CA 92103. © 800/938-8181 or 619/298-0823. Fax 619/294-8070. www.balboaparkinn.com. 26 units. $89–$99 double; $119–$149 suite; $149–$200 specialty suite. Extra person $10. Children under 11 stay free in parent's room. Rates include continental breakfast. AE, DC, DISC, MC, V. Parking available on street. From I-5, take Washington St. east, follow signs to University Ave. E. Turn right at Park Blvd. Bus: 7, 7A/B. *In room:* TV, fridge, coffeemaker.

Crone's Cobblestone Cottage Bed & Breakfast *Finds* After just one night at this magnificently restored Craftsman bungalow, you'll feel like an honored guest rather than a paying customer. Artist Joan Crone lives in the architectural award-winning addition to her 1913 home, which is a designated historical landmark. Guests have the run of the entire house, including a book-filled, wood-paneled den and antique-filled living room. Both cozy guest rooms have antique beds, goose-down pillows and comforters, and eclectic bedside reading. They share a full bathroom; the Eaton Room also has a private half bathroom. Bookmaker and illustrator Crone lends a calm and literary aesthetic to the surroundings, aided by Sam the cat, who peers in from his side of the house. The quiet, historic Mission Hills neighborhood, just blocks from Hillcrest and Old Town, is one of San Diego's best-kept secrets.

1302 Washington Place (2½ blocks west of Washington St. at Ingalls St.), San Diego, CA 92103. © 619/295-4765. 2 units. $125 double. Rates include continental breakfast. Minimum 2 nights. No credit cards; checks accepted. From I-5, take Washington St. exit east uphill. Make a U-turn at Goldfinch, then keep right at Y intersection onto Washington Place. Bus: 3. *In room:* No phone.

Park Manor Suites *Value* Popular with actors appearing at the Old Globe Theatre in neighboring Balboa Park, this eight-floor Italianate masterpiece was built as a full-service luxury hotel in 1926 on a prime corner overlooking the park. One of the original investors was the family of child actor Jackie Coogan. The Hollywood connection continued—the hotel became a popular stopping-off point for celebrities headed for Mexican vacations in the 1920s and '30s. Guest rooms are spacious and comfortable, featuring full kitchens, dining rooms, living rooms, and bedrooms with a separate dressing area. A few have glassed-in terraces; request one when you book. The overall feeling is that of a prewar East Coast apartment building, complete with steam heat and lavish moldings. Park Manor Suites does have its weaknesses: Bathrooms have mostly original fixtures and could use some renovation; and the rooftop banquet room, where a simple continental breakfast buffet is served, suffers from bad 1980s decor (though the view is spectacular). But prices are quite reasonable for Hillcrest; there's a darkly old-world restaurant (aptly named Inn at the Park) on the ground floor, and laundry service is also available.

525 Spruce St. (between Fifth and Sixth aves.), San Diego, CA 92103. © 800/874-2649 or 619/291-0999. Fax 619/291-8844. www.parkmanorsuites.com. 74 units. $99–$129 studio; $139–$179 1-bedroom suite; $199–$239 2-bedroom suite. Extra person $15. Children under 12 stay free in parents' room. Rates include continental breakfast. Weekly rates available. AE, DC, DISC, MC, V. Free parking. Bus: 1, 3, 25. **Amenities:** Restaurant/bar; access to nearby health club; bike rental; laundry/dry-cleaning service; self-service laundry. *In room:* TV, dataport, kitchen, coffeemaker, hair dryer, iron.

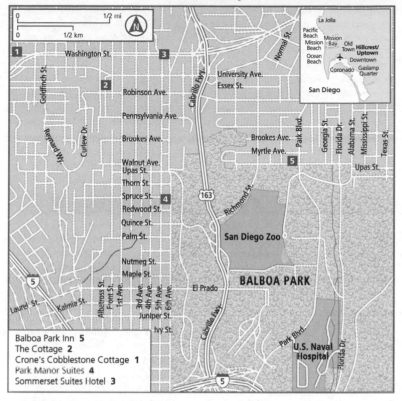

Balboa Park Inn **5**
The Cottage **2**
Crone's Cobblestone Cottage **1**
Park Manor Suites **4**
Sommerset Suites Hotel **3**

Sommerset Suites Hotel ★★ This all-suite hotel on a busy street was originally built as apartment housing for interns at the hospital nearby. It retains a residential ambience and unexpected amenities such as huge closets, medicine cabinets, and fully equipped kitchens in all rooms (executive suites even have dishwashers). Poolside barbecue facilities encourage warm-weather mingling. The hotel has a personal, welcoming feel, from the friendly, helpful staff to the snacks, soda, beer, and wine served each afternoon. You'll even get a welcome basket with cookies and microwave popcorn. Rooms are comfortably furnished, and each has a private balcony. Be prepared for noise from the busy thoroughfare below, though. Several blocks of Hillcrest's restaurants and shops (plus a movie multiplex) are within easy walking distance. Guest services include a courtesy van to the airport, SeaWorld, the zoo, and other attractions within a 5-mile (8km) radius.

606 Washington St. (at Fifth Ave.), San Diego, CA 92103. ✆ **800/962-9665** or 619/692-5200. Fax 619/692-5299. www.sommersetsuites.com. 80 units. $109–$195 double. Children under 12 stay free in parents' room. Rates include continental breakfast and afternoon refreshments. AE, DC, DISC, MC, V. Free covered parking. Take Washington St. exit off I-5. Bus: 16 or 25. **Amenities:** Outdoor pool; whirlpool; coin-op laundry. *In room:* A/C, TV, dataport, coffeemaker, hair dryer, iron.

INEXPENSIVE

The Cottage Built in 1913, the two-room Cottage sits in a secret garden, a private hideaway tucked behind a homestead-style house, at the end of a residential cul-de-sac. There's an herb garden out front, birdbaths, and a flower-lined walkway. The cottage has a king-size bed, a living room with a wood-burning stove and a queen-size sofa bed, and a charming kitchen with a coffeemaker. The guest room in the main house features a king-size bed. Both accommodations are filled with fresh flowers and antiques put to clever uses, and each has a private entrance. Owner Carol Emerick (she used to run an antique store—and it shows!) serves a scrumptious breakfast, complete with the morning paper. Guests are welcome to use the dining room and parlor in the main house, where they sometimes light a fire and rev up the 19th-century player piano. The Cottage is close to the cafes of Mission Hills and Hillcrest, and a short drive from Balboa Park.

3829 Albatross St. (off Robinson Ave.), San Diego, CA 92103. © 619/299-1564. Fax 619/299-6213. www.sandiegobandb.com/cottage.htm. 2 units. $75 double; $99 cottage. Extra person in cottage $10. Rates include continental breakfast. AE, DISC, MC, V. *In room:* TV, fridge, hair dryer.

3 Old Town & Mission Valley

Old Town is a popular area for families because of its proximity to Old Town State Historic Park and other attractions that are within walking distance. **Hotel Circle,** on the way to Mission Valley, offers easy freeway access. Its many hotels cater to convention groups, sports fans heading to Qualcomm Stadium, families visiting the University of San Diego or San Diego State University, and leisure travelers drawn by the lower prices and competitive facilities.

MODERATE

Heritage Park Bed & Breakfast Inn ∂∂   This exquisite 1889 Queen Anne mansion is set in a Victorian park—an artfully arranged cobblestone cul-de-sac lined with historic buildings saved from the wrecking ball and assembled here, near Old Town, as a tourist attraction. Most of the Inn's rooms are in the main house, with a handful of equally appealing choices in an adjacent 1887 Italianate companion. Owner Nancy Helsper is an amiable and energetic innkeeper with an eye for every necessary detail; she's always eager to share tales of these homes' fascinating history and how they crossed paths with Nancy and her husband, Charles. A stay here is about surrendering to the pampering of afternoon tea, candlelight breakfast, and a number of romantic extras (champagne and chocolates, private in-room dinner) available for special celebrations. Like the gracious parlors and porches, each room is outfitted with meticulous period antiques and luxurious fabrics; the practiced staff provides turndown service and virtually anything else you might require. Although the fireplaces are all ornamental, some rooms have whirlpool baths. In the evenings, vintage films are shown in the Victorian parlor.

2470 Heritage Park Row, San Diego, CA 92110. © 800/995-2470 or 619/299-6832. Fax 619/299-9465. www.heritageparkinn.com. 12 units. $120–$250 double. Extra person $20. Rates include full breakfast and afternoon tea. AE, DC, DISC, MC, V. Free parking. Take I-5 to Old Town Ave., turn left onto San Diego Ave., then turn right onto Harney St. *In room:* A/C, hair dryer, iron.

Red Lion Hanalei Hotel ∂   Our favorite hotel on Hotel Circle has a Polynesian theme and comfort-conscious sophistication that sets it apart from the rest of the pack. Rooms are split between two high-rise towers, set far away from the freeway and cleverly positioned so that the balconies open onto the tropically landscaped pool courtyard or the luxurious links of a formerly private golf club on the Mission Valley floor. The heated outdoor pool is large enough for any luau, as is the oversized whirlpool beside it. The hotel boasts an unmistakable 1960s vibe and Hawaiian ambience—the restaurant and bar have

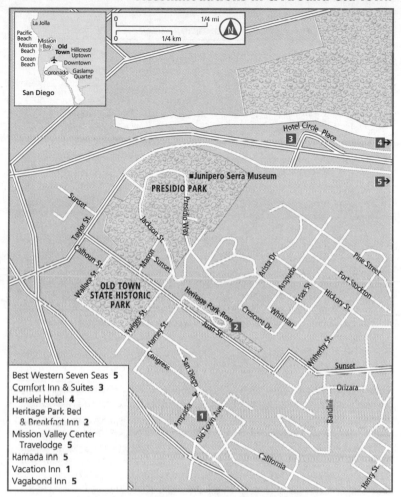

Best Western Seven Seas **5**
Comfort Inn & Suites **3**
Hanalei Hotel **4**
Heritage Park Bed
& Breakfast Inn **2**
Mission Valley Center
Travelodge **5**
Ramada Inn **5**
Vacation Inn **1**
Vagabond Inn **5**

over-the-top kitschy decor, with waterfalls, outrigger canoes, and more. But guest rooms are outfitted with contemporary furnishings and conveniences; some have microwaves and refrigerators. Services include a free shuttle to Old Town and other attractions, plus meeting facilities.

2270 Hotel Circle North, San Diego, CA 92108. Ⓒ **800/RED-LION** or 619/297-1101. Fax 619/297-6049. www.redlion.com. 416 units. $109–$159 double; $275–$375 suite. Extra person $10. Off-season, AARP, and AAA discounts and golf packages available. Pets accepted with $25 fee. AE, DISC, MC, V. Parking $8. From I-8, take Hotel Circle exit, follow signs for Hotel Circle N. Bus: 6. **Amenities:** 2 restaurants; lounge; outdoor pool; nearby golf course; fitness center; whirlpool; game room; activities desk; 24-hr. business center; room service (6am–10pm); laundry/dry-cleaning service; self-service laundry. *In room:* A/C, TV w/pay movies, dataport, coffeemaker, hair dryer, iron.

Vacation Inn Ⓕ Just a couple of easy walking blocks from the heart of Old Town, the Vacation Inn has a Colonial Spanish exterior that suits the neighborhood's theme. Inside you'll find better-than-they-have-to-be contemporary furnishings and surprising small touches that make this hotel an affordable

Kids Family-Friendly Accommodations

Holiday Inn on the Bay (p. 69)   Kids under 18 stay free, so the hotel is well priced for strained family budgets, and even offers babysitting services for strained parents.

Catamaran Resort Hotel (p. 79)   Numerous sports facilities and a safe swimming beach make this resort an ideal place for families. Accommodations are comfortable, but not so posh that Mom and Dad need to worry.

Paradise Point Resort & Spa (p. 80)   This self-contained property in the middle of Mission Bay has plenty of space for kids to safely explore, and is just up the street from SeaWorld.

The Beach Cottages (p. 80)   Kids enjoy the informal atmosphere and the close proximity to the beach.

The Sea Lodge (p. 87)   Right smack on the beach, kids can choose between the pool and the ocean. They can even eat in their swimsuits on the patio.

Loews Coronado Bay Resort (p. 91)   In the summer, the Commodore Kids Club, for children ages 4 to 12, provides supervised indoor and outdoor activities during the day and some evenings, too. Programs for older kids keep them out of harm's way without making them feel babysat.

option favored by business travelers and families alike. There's nothing scenic on the adjacent streets, so the hotel is smartly oriented toward the inside; request a room whose patio or balcony opens onto the pleasant courtyard. Rooms are thoughtfully and practically appointed, with extras like microwave ovens and writing tables. The lobby, surrounded by French doors, features a large fireplace, several sitting areas, and a TV. The hotel entrance, on Jefferson Street, is hard to find but definitely worth the search.

3900 Old Town Ave., San Diego, CA 92110. © 800/451-9846 or 619/299-7400. Fax 619/299-1619. 124 units. $119–$129 double, $130–$175 suite June–Sept; $89–$109 double, $99–$165 suite Oct–May. Extra person $10. Children under 18 stay free in parents' room. Rates include continental breakfast and afternoon refreshments. AE, DC, DISC, MC, V. Free parking. Bus: 5, 5A. **Amenities:** Outdoor pool; whirlpool; laundry/dry-cleaning service. *In room:* A/C, TV, fridge, coffeemaker.

INEXPENSIVE

Room rates at properties on Hotel Circle are significantly cheaper than those in many other parts of the city. You'll find a cluster of inexpensive chain hotels and motels, including **Best Western Seven Seas** (© 800/421-6662 or 619/291-1300), **Mission Valley Center Travelodge** (© 800/255-3050 or 619/297-2271), **Ramada Inn** (© 800/532-4241 or 619/291-6500), and **Vagabond Inn** (© 800/522-1555 or 619/297-1691).

Comfort Inn & Suites   This well-priced, modern, four-story motel sits at the western, or Old Town, end of Hotel Circle. Rooms and suites are sparingly but adequately outfitted, with standard hotel-issue furnishings; bathrooms are small but well equipped. Suites are the way to go here; all have sleeper sofas in the living room, two TVs, a microwave, refrigerator, and separate vanity area. Stay away from the loud freeway side, and ask instead for a room looking toward the newly refurbished 18-hole public golf course across the street. The hotel doesn't have a restaurant, but offers room service at dinner from the steakhouse next door.

2485 Hotel Circle Place, San Diego, CA 92108. © **800/647-1903** or 619/291-7700. Fax 619/297-6179. 200 units. $89–$129 double high season. Extra person $10. Children under 18 stay free in parents' room. Rates include continental breakfast. Off-season discounts available. AE, DC, DISC, MC, V. Free parking. From I-8, take Hotel Circle exit, follow signs for Hotel Circle north. Bus: 6. **Amenities:** Outdoor pool; whirlpool; game room; car-rental desk; coin-op laundry. *In room:* A/C, TV, coffeemaker, hair dryer.

4 Mission Bay & the Beaches

If you plan to enjoy the beach and aquatic activities, this part of town is the right spot. Some hotels are right on Mission Bay, San Diego's water playground; they're always good choices for families, especially those planning to visit SeaWorld. Ocean Beach, Mission Beach, and Pacific Beach provide a taste of the laid-back surfer lifestyle, but can be unpredictable and raucous at times. Don't worry about missing out on the rest of San Diego; even though the beach communities are far removed in atmosphere, downtown is only a 10-minute drive away.

VERY EXPENSIVE

Pacific Terrace Hotel ✻✻ The best modern hotel on the boardwalk recently emerged from a multimillion-dollar renovation with a soothing South Seas ambience—rattan fans caress the lobby and hint at the sunny Indonesian-inspired decor in guest rooms. Hands-on owners kicked the luxury factor (and prices) up a notch, resulting in an upscale atmosphere and relaxed ambience that stand apart from the casual beach pads in the area.

Large, comfortable guest rooms each come with balconies or terraces and fancy wall safes; bathrooms—newly redesigned with warm-toned marble and natural woods—have a separate sink/vanity area. About half the rooms have kitchenettes, and top-floor rooms in this three-story hotel enjoy particularly nice views—you'll find yourself mesmerized by the rhythmic waves and determined surfers below. Management keeps popcorn, coffee, and lemonade at the ready throughout the day; the lushly landscaped pool and hot tub face a relatively quiet stretch of beach with fire rings for bonfires or barbecues. Several local restaurants allow meals to be billed to the hotel but there's no restaurant on the premises.

610 Diamond St., San Diego, CA 92109. © **800/344-3370** or 858/581-3500. Fax 858/274-3341. www.pacific terrace.com. 75 units. $269 standard, $369 oceanfront double; from $395 suite. 10% AAA discount June 15–Sept 15 (25% Sept 16–June 14). Rates include continental breakfast. AE, DC, DISC, MC, V. Parking $5. Take I-5 to Grand/Garnet exit and follow Grand or Garnet west to Mission Blvd., turn right (north), then left (west) onto Diamond; hotel is at the end of the street on the right. Bus: 34 or 34A. **Amenities:** Oceanview outdoor pool; access to nearby health club; whirlpool; bike rental nearby; activities desk; room service (7am–midnight); in-room massage; laundry/dry-cleaning service; coin-op laundry. *In room:* A/C, TV w/pay movies, dataport, minibar, coffeemaker, hair dryer, iron.

EXPENSIVE

Catamaran Resort Hotel ✻✻ *Kids* Ideally situated right on Mission Bay, the Catamaran has its own bay and ocean beaches, complete with watersports facilities. Built in the 1950s, the hotel has been fully renovated to modern standards without losing its trademark Polynesian theme; the atrium lobby holds a 15-foot (4.5m) waterfall and full-size dugout canoe, and koi-filled lagoons meander through the property. After dark, torches blaze throughout the grounds, with numerous varieties of bamboo and palm sprouting; during the day, the resident tropical birds chirp away. Guest rooms—in a 13-story building or one of the six two-story buildings—have subdued South Pacific decor, and each has a balcony or patio. Tower rooms have commanding views of the bay, the San Diego skyline, La Jolla, and Point Loma. Studios and suites have the added convenience of kitchenettes. The Catamaran is within walking distance of Pacific Beach's restaurant and nightlife. It's also steps away from the bay's exceptional jogging and biking path; runners with tots-in-tow can rent jogging strollers at the hotel.

3999 Mission Blvd. (4 blocks south of Grand Ave.), San Diego, CA 92109. © 800/422-8386 or 858/488-1081. Fax 858/488-1619. www.catamaranresort.com. 313 units. $195–$265 double; from $400 suite. Children under 12 stay free in parents' room. Off-season discounts and packages available. AE, DC, DISC, MC, V. Valet parking $10, self-parking $8. Take Grand/Garnet exit off I-5 and go west on Grand Ave., then south on Mission Blvd. Bus: 34, 34A/B. **Amenities:** Restaurant; nightclub; piano bar; outdoor pool; tennis courts; health club; whirlpool; watersports-equipment rentals; bike rental; children's programs; concierge; activities desk; car-rental desk; room service (5am–11pm); in-room massage; babysitting; laundry/dry-cleaning service. *In room:* A/C, TV w/pay movies, dataport, fridge, coffeemaker, hair dryer, iron.

Paradise Point Resort & Spa 🏖️🏖️🏖️ *Kids*   Smack dab in the middle of Mission Bay, this hotel complex is almost as much a theme park as its closest neighbor, SeaWorld (a 3-min. drive). Single-story accommodations are spread across 44 acres of duck-filled lagoons, tropical gardens, and swim-friendly beaches; all have private lanais (patios) and plenty of thoughtful conveniences. Recently updated to keep its low-tech 1960s charm but lose tacky holdovers—for example, rooms now have a refreshingly colorful beach cottage decor. And despite daunting high-season rack rates, there's usually a deal to be had here. In 2000, the resort unveiled its upscale waterfront Baleen restaurant (excellent fine dining in a contemporary, fun space), followed in 2001 by a stunning Indonesian-inspired spa that offers cool serenity and aroma-tinged Asian treatments—this spa is a vacation in itself!

1404 W. Vacation Rd. (off Ingraham St.), San Diego, CA 92109. © 800/344-2626 or 858/274-4630. Fax 858/581-5977. www.paradisepoint.com. 462 units. $220–$350 double, from $325 suite Memorial Day to Labor Day; $175–$325 double, from $300 suite off-season. Extra person $20. Children 17 and under stay free in parents' room. Discounts and packages frequently available. AE, DC, DISC, MC, V. Free parking. Follow I-8 west to Mission Bay Dr. exit; take Ingraham St. north to Vacation Rd. **Amenities:** 3 restaurants; lounge; pool bar; 6 outdoor pools; 18-hole putting course; tennis courts; croquet; sand volleyball; fitness center; full-service spa; whirlpool; bike rental; shuttle to area shopping; room service (7am–10pm); laundry/dry-cleaning service. *In room:* A/C, TV w/pay movies, dataport, fridge, coffeemaker, hair dryer, iron.

MODERATE

The Beach Cottages *Kids*   This family owned operation has a variety of guest quarters (most geared to the long-term visitor), but the cute little detached cottages steps from the sand give it real appeal. Most other units are perfectly adequate, especially for budget-minded families who want to log major hours on the beach, but stay away from the plain motel rooms—they're just dingy. All accommodations except the motel rooms have fully equipped kitchens. The Beach Cottages are within walking distance of shops and restaurants—look both ways for speeding cyclists before crossing the boardwalk—and enjoy shared barbecue grills, shuffleboard courts, and table tennis. The cottages themselves aren't pristine, but have a rustic charm that makes them popular with young honeymooners and those nostalgic for the golden age of laid-back California beach culture. With one or two bedrooms, each cottage sleeps up to six; each has a patio with tables and chairs.

To make a reservation, call between 9am and 9pm, when the office is open. Reserve the most popular cottages well in advance.

4255 Ocean Blvd. (1 block south of Grand Ave.), San Diego, CA 92109-3995. © 858/483-7440. Fax 858/273-9365. www.beachcottages.com. 61 units, 17 cottages. July 1 to Labor Day $95–$120 double; $135

Accommodations in Mission Bay & the Beaches

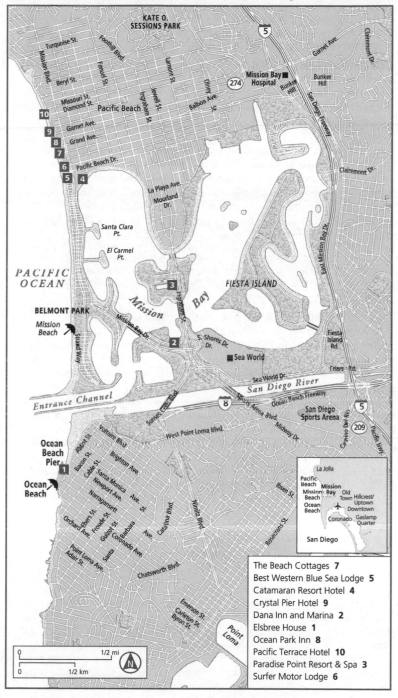

The Beach Cottages **7**
Best Western Blue Sea Lodge **5**
Catamaran Resort Hotel **4**
Crystal Pier Hotel **9**
Dana Inn and Marina **2**
Elsbree House **1**
Ocean Park Inn **8**
Pacific Terrace Hotel **10**
Paradise Point Resort & Spa **3**
Surfer Motor Lodge **6**

studio for up to 4; $160–$170 apt or cottage for up to 4; $185–$210 apt or cottage for up to 6; $230–$250 2-bedroom suite for up to 6. Off-season discounts and off-season weekly rates available. AE, DC, DISC, MC, V. Free parking. Take I-5 to Grand/Garnet exit, go west on Grand Ave. and left on Mission Blvd. Bus: 34 or 34A. **Amenities:** Self-service laundry. *In room:* TV, fridge, coffeemaker.

Best Western Blue Sea Lodge   The three-story Blue Sea Lodge is a reliable choice in a prime location. While I'd like to see more meticulous maintenance and decor upgrades, Best Western keeps up with the other bargain properties in the chain. And, despite the rates listed, this is a bargain. There are many ways to get a discount—including just asking. Aesthetically, these rooms are a dreary snore, but nevertheless boast a balcony or patio and a handful of necessary comforts. Rooms with full ocean views overlook the sand and have more privacy than those on the street, but the Pacific Beach boardwalk has never been known for quiet or solitude. Casual beach cafes and grills are nearby, along with several raucous Pacific Beach bars. The lobby offers coffee, tea, and a microwave for guests, and its heated pool and whirlpool are steps from the beach.

707 Pacific Beach Dr., San Diego, CA 92109-5094. (C) **800/BLUE-SEA** or 858/488-4700. Fax 858/488-7276. www.bestwestern-bluesea.com. 100 units. $149–$199 double, up to $319 suite Memorial Day–Sept; $109–$179 double, up to $229 suite off-season. Children under 18 stay free in parents' room. AAA and AARP discounts available. AE, DC, DISC, MC, V. Underground and outdoor parking $7. Take I-5 to Grand/Garnet exit, follow Grand Ave. to Mission Blvd. and turn left, then turn right onto Pacific Beach Dr. Bus: 34. **Amenities:** Outdoor pool; whirlpool; coin-op laundry. *In room:* A/C, TV w/pay movies, dataport, coffeemaker, hair dryer, iron, safe.

Crystal Pier Hotel *Finds*   When historic charm is higher on your wish list than hotel-style service, head to this utterly unique cluster of cottages sitting literally over the surf on the vintage Crystal Pier. Like renting your own self-contained hideaway, you'll get a separate living room and bedroom, fully equipped kitchen, and private patio with breathtaking ocean views—all within the white-washed walls of blue-shuttered cottages that date from 1936 but have been meticulously renovated. The sound of waves is soothing, but the boardwalk action is only a few steps (and worlds) away, and the pier is a great place for watching sunsets and surfers. Guests drive right out and park beside their cottages, a real boon on crowded weekends. There are vending machines and movie rentals; Boogie Boards, fishing poles, beach chairs, and umbrellas are also available, but it's strictly BYOBT (beach towels!). The office is open daily from 8am to 8pm. These accommodations book up fast, especially with long-term repeat guests, so reserve for summer at least 4 months in advance.

4500 Ocean Blvd. (at Garnet Ave.), San Diego, CA 92109. (C) **800/748-5894** or 858/483-6983. Fax 858/483-6811. www.crystalpier.com. 26 units. Cottages for 2–6 people $135–$335 mid-June to mid-Sept; $105–$275 mid-Sept to mid-June. 3-night minimum in summer. DISC, MC, V. Free parking. Take I-5 to Grand/Garnet exit; follow Garnet to the pier. Bus: 34 or 34A. **Amenities:** Beach equipment rental. *In room:* TV, kitchen.

Elsbree House   Katie and Phil Elsbree have turned this recently constructed Cape Cod–style building into an immaculate, exceedingly comfortable B&B half a block from the water's edge in Ocean Beach. One condo unit rents only by the week; the Elsbrees occupy another. Each of the six guest rooms has a patio or balcony. Guests share the cozy living room (with a fireplace and TV), breakfast room, and kitchen. Although other buildings on this tightly packed street block the ocean view, sounds of the surf and fresh sea breezes waft in open windows, and a beautifully landscaped garden—complete with trickling fountain—runs the length of the house. This Ocean Beach neighborhood is eclectic, occupied by ocean-loving couples, dedicated surf bums, and a sometimes-disturbing contingent of punk skater kids who congregate near the pier. Its strengths are proximity to the beach, a limited but pleasing selection of eateries that attract mostly locals, and some of the best antiquing in the city (along Newport Avenue).

5054 Narragansett Ave., San Diego, CA 92107. ⓒ **619/226-4133**. www.oceanbeach-online.com/b&b. 7 units. $110–$135 double; $1,450–$1,600 per week 3-bedroom condo. Room rates include continental breakfast. MC, V. Bus: 35 or 23 to Narragansett Ave. and Cable St., 1½ blocks away. From airport, take Harbor Dr. west to Nimitz Blvd. to Lowell St., which becomes Narragansett Ave. Bus: 23, 35. *In room:* Hair dryer, iron, no phone.

Ocean Park Inn ☆   This modern oceanfront motor hotel offers attractive, spacious rooms with well-coordinated contemporary furnishings. Although the inn has a level of sophistication uncommon in this casual, surfer-populated area, you won't find solitude and quiet. The cool marble lobby and plushly carpeted hallways will help you feel a little insulated from the raucous scene outside, though. You can't beat the location (directly on the beach) and the view (ditto). Rates vary according to view, but most rooms have at least a partial ocean view; all have a private balcony or patio. Units in front are most desirable, but it can get noisy directly above the boardwalk; try for the second or third floor. The Ocean Park Inn doesn't have its own restaurant, but the casual High Tide Cafe (see chapter 6 for full review) is outside the front door.

710 Grand Ave., San Diego, CA 92109. ⓒ **800/231-7735** or 858/483-5858. Fax 858/274-0823. www.ocean parkinn.com. 73 units. $104–$239 double, $169–$304 suite mid-May to mid-Sept; $89–$214 double, $124–$274 suite off-season. Rates include continental breakfast. AE, DC, DISC, MC, V. Free indoor parking. Take Grand/Garnet exit off I-5; follow Grand Ave. to ocean. Bus: 34, 34A/B. **Amenities:** Outdoor pool; whirlpool; laundry/dry-cleaning service. *In room:* A/C, TV, dataport, fridge, coffeemaker, hair dryer.

INEXPENSIVE

Beach Haven Inn ☆   A great spot for beach lovers, this motel is about half a block from the sand. Rooms face an inner courtyard, where guests enjoy a secluded ambience for relaxing by the pool. On the street side it looks kind of marginal, but once on the property we found all quarters well maintained and sporting clean modern furnishings—nearly all units have eat-in kitchens. The friendly staff provides free coffee in the lobby and rents VCRs and movies.

4740 Mission Blvd. (at Missouri St.), San Diego (Pacific Beach), CA 92109. ⓒ **800/831-6323** or 858/272-3812. Fax 858/272-3532. www.beachhaveninn.com. 23 units. $105–$165 double summer (June to mid-Sept); $69–$145 double off-season. Extra person $5. Children under 12 stay free in parents' room. Rates include continental breakfast. AE, DC, DISC, MC, V. Free parking. Bus: 30 or 34. **Amenities:** Outdoor pool; whirlpool. *In room:* A/C, TV, kitchenette (most units).

Dana Inn and Marina   Advertising itself as the closest lodging to SeaWorld (with a complimentary shuttle to and from the park), this friendly, low-tech hotel features several low-rise buildings with vaguely nautical blue-and-white exteriors. Some overlook bobbing sailboats in the recreational marina, others face onto the sunny kidney-shaped pool whose surrounding tiki torch–lit gardens offer shuffleboard and Ping-Pong. You'll pay a premium for bay and marina views; if view doesn't matter, save your money—every room is the same size, with rather plain but well-maintained furnishings. Convenient meals and room service (including poolside food and cocktail service) are available at the casual Red Hen Country Kitchen next door.

1710 W. Mission Bay Dr., San Diego, CA 92109. ⓒ **800/345-9995** or 619/222-6440. Fax 619/222-5916. 196 units. $131–$177 room for up to 5 Memorial Day weekend–Oct; $116–$154 room for up to 5 off-season. AE, DC, DISC, MC, V. Free parking. Follow I-8 west to Mission Bay Dr. exit. **Amenities:** Outdoor heated pool and whirlpool; tennis court; shuffleboard and Ping-Pong courts; bike and watersports rentals; room service (7am–9pm); laundry/dry-cleaning service; coin-op laundry. *In room:* A/C, TV, dataport, fridge, coffeemaker, iron, hair dryer.

5 La Jolla

The name "La Jolla" is often translated from the Spanish as "the jewel," a fitting comparison for this section of the city with a beautiful coastline, as well as a compact downtown village that makes for delightful strolling. You'll have a hard time finding bargain accommodations in this upscale, conservative community. But remember, most hotels—even those in our "Very Expensive" category—have occupancy-driven rates, meaning you can score surprising discounts during the off-season or when the hotel isn't very full. Here at Frommer's, we can't say it often enough: It always pays to ask.

Most of our choices are downtown, with two below the cliffs right on the beach. Chain hotels farther afield include a **Hyatt Regency,** 3777 La Jolla Village Dr. (© **800/233-1234** or 858/552-1234). It's a glitzy, business-oriented place with several acclaimed restaurants on-site. The **Marriott Residence Inn,** 8901 Gilman Dr. (© **800/331-3131** or 858/587-1770), is a good choice for those who want a fully equipped kitchen and more space. Both are near the University of California, San Diego.

A note on driving directions: To reach the places listed here, use the Ardath Road exit from **I-5 north** or the La Jolla Village Drive west exit from **I-5 south,** then follow individual directions.

VERY EXPENSIVE

Hotel Parisi 𝘈𝘈𝘈 *Finds* Nestled among the "Village's" fashionable boutiques, and across the street from grande dame La Valencia, the 3-year-old Hotel Parisi caters to the city-savvy traveler seeking inner peace for both entertainment and relaxation. Named for Del Mar's Parisi design firm, the small, second-story boutique hotel features their northern-Italy-meets-Zen composition, as well as signature modern-yet-comfy furnishings. Parisi's nurturing, wellness-inspired intimacy first becomes evident in the lobby, where elements of earth, wind, fire, water, and metal are blended according to classic feng shui principles. In the oversized rooms (the hotel calls them "suites"), ergonomic desks, dimmable lighting, goose-down superluxe bedding, and creamy neutral decor continue the calming effect. Each darkly cool marble bathroom boasts twin shower heads, contoured backrests in tubs, and smoothly sculpted fixtures. Parisi's personal service stops at nothing; there's a menu of 24-hour in-room holistic health services (from individual yoga to Thai massage, psychotherapy, and obscure Asian treatments), and you can even arrange a special session at Deepak Chopra's world-famous center down the street. Room service (dinner only) features the international flavors of nearby Tamarindo restaurant (same owners).

1111 Prospect St. (at Herschel Ave.), La Jolla, CA 92037. © **877-4-PARISI** or 858/454-1511. Fax 858/454-1531. www.hotelparisi.com. 20 units. $275–$485 double. Rates include continental breakfast. Unique packages and seasonal discounts available. AE, DC, DISC, MC, V. Free covered parking. Take Torrey Pines Rd. to Prospect Place and turn right. Prospect Place becomes Prospect St., turn left on Herschel. **Amenities:** 24-hr. in-room spa treatments; room service (5–10pm); laundry/dry-cleaning service. *In room:* A/C, TV w/VCR, dataport, minibar w/complimentary beverages, coffeemaker, hair dryer, iron, safe.

La Valencia Hotel 𝘈𝘈𝘈 Within its bougainvillea-draped walls and wrought-iron garden gates, this gracious bastion of gentility does a fine job of resurrecting its golden-age elegance, when celebrities like Greta Garbo and Charlie Chaplin vacationed alongside the world's moneyed elite. The clifftop hotel has been the centerpiece of La Jolla since opening in 1926. Today, brides pose in front of the lobby's picture window (against a backdrop of La Jolla Cove and the Pacific), well-coiffed ladies lunch in the dappled shade of the garden

La Jolla Accommodations

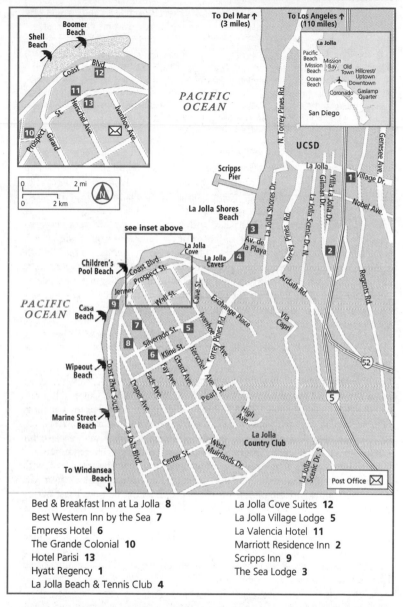

Bed & Breakfast Inn at La Jolla **8**
Best Western Inn by the Sea **7**
Empress Hotel **6**
The Grande Colonial **10**
Hotel Parisi **13**
Hyatt Regency **1**
La Jolla Beach & Tennis Club **4**

La Jolla Cove Suites **12**
La Jolla Village Lodge **5**
La Valencia Hotel **11**
Marriott Residence Inn **2**
Scripps Inn **9**
The Sea Lodge **3**

patio, and neighborhood cronies quaff libations in the clubby Whaling Bar, once a western Algonquin for literary inebriates. One chooses La Valencia for its history and unbeatably scenic location, but you won't be disappointed by the old-world standards of service and style. Rooms are comfortably and traditionally furnished, each boasting an individual decor, lavish appointments, and all-marble bathrooms with signature toiletries. Because rates vary wildly according to view, our advice is to get a cheaper room and enjoy the view from one of the many cozy lounges, serene garden terraces, or the amazing genteel pool, which offers views of the Pacific and nearby Scripp's Park. Room decor and layouts vary wildly too—a few extra minutes spent with the reservationist will ensure a custom match for you.

1132 Prospect St. (at Herschel Ave.), La Jolla, CA 92037. 📞 800/451-0772 or 858/454-0771. Fax 858/456-3921. www.lavalencia.com. 118 units. $250–$500 double; from $550 suite. Extra person $15. AE, DC, DISC, MC, V. Valet parking $15. Take Torrey Pines Rd. to Prospect Place and turn right. Prospect Place becomes Prospect St. **Amenities:** 3 restaurants; bar; outdoor pool; exercise room w/spa treatments; whirlpool; sauna; concierge; secretarial services; 24-hr. room service; babysitting; laundry/dry-cleaning service. *In room:* A/C, TV w/VCR, dataport, minibar, coffeemaker, hair dryer, iron, safe.

EXPENSIVE

The Bed & Breakfast Inn at La Jolla ⋒⋒⋒   A 1913 Cubist house designed by prominent local architect Irving Gill—and once occupied by John Philip Sousa and his family—is the setting for this genteel and elegant B&B. Reconfigured for this purpose, the house has lost none of its charm, and appropriately unfrilly period furnishings add to the sense of history. The inn also features lovely enclosed gardens and a cozy library and sitting room. Sherry and fresh-cut flowers await in every room, some of which feature a fireplace or ocean view. Each room has a private bathroom, most of which are on the compact size. The furnishings are tasteful and cottage-style, with plenty of historic photos of La Jolla. Gourmet breakfast is served wherever you desire—dining room, patio, sun deck, or in your room. Picnic baskets (extra charge) are available with a day's notice.

7753 Draper Ave. (near Prospect), La Jolla, CA 92037. 📞 800/582-2466 or 858/456-2066. Fax 858/456-1510. www.InnLaJolla.com. 15 units. $159–$339 double; $379. suite. Extra person $25. Rates include full breakfast and afternoon wine and cheese. AE, DISC, MC, V. Take Torrey Pines Rd. to Prospect Place and turn right. Prospect Place becomes Prospect St.; proceed to Draper Ave. and turn left. *In room:* A/C, iron, hair dryer.

The Grande Colonial ⋒⋒   Possessed of an old-world European flair that's more London or Georgetown than seaside La Jolla, the Grande Colonial has garnered accolades for the complete restoration of its polished mahogany paneling, brass fittings, and genteel library and lounge. A large spray of fresh flowers is the focal point in the lounge, where guests gather in front of the fireplace for drinks—often before enjoying a fine dinner at attached Nine-Ten restaurant (see chapter 6 for a full review). Guest rooms are quiet and elegantly appointed, with beautiful draperies and traditional furnishings. The hotel is 1 block from the ocean. Numerous historic photos on the walls illustrate the hotel's fascinating history; the reception desk has a printed sheet with more details of its beginnings as a full-service apartment hotel in 1913. Relics from the early days include oversized closets, meticulously tiled bathrooms, and heavy fireproof doors suspended in the corridors. The guest rooms have newly installed air-conditioning and thoughtful amenities; terry robes are available on request. Walking tours of La Jolla depart from the hotel (see chapter 7).

910 Prospect St. (between Fay and Girard), La Jolla, CA 92037. 📞 800/826-1278 or 858/454-2181. Fax 858/454-5679. www.thegrandecolonial.com. 75 units. $239–$349 double summer (mid-June to Labor Day); $189–$269 double off-season. From $429 suite. Rates include continental breakfast. AE, DC, DISC, MC, V. Valet parking $14. Take Torrey Pines Rd. to Prospect Place and turn right. Prospect Place becomes Prospect St. **Amenities:** Restaurant; outdoor pool; access to nearby health club; nearby bike rental; courtesy car; room service (6am–10pm); laundry/dry-cleaning service. *In room:* A/C, TV w/pay movies, dataport, hair dryer, iron, safe.

La Jolla Beach & Tennis Club ⋒⋒   Pack your best tennis whites for a stay at La Jolla's private "B&T" (as it's locally known), where CEOs and MDs come to relax and recreate. Surprisingly, rates for the club's overnight accommodations aren't that much higher than at the sister hotel next door, the Sea Lodge, but the

exclusive atmosphere and extensive amenities are far superior. Guest rooms are unexpectedly plain and frill-free, though they are equipped with the basic amenities you'll need. Most have well-stocked full kitchens that are ideal for families or longer stays. This historic property was founded in the 1920s, when original plans included constructing a private yacht harbor. Today it's known primarily for tennis. The beach is popular here; the staff sets up comfy sand chairs and umbrellas, and races to supply club members and guests with fluffy towels, beverages, and snacks. Kayaks and watersports equipment can be rented; there's even a sand croquet court. Surprisingly, there's no room service; besides the on-site dining options, several cozy neighborhood trattorias are 2 blocks away. Take a peek into the hotel's distinctive Marine Room restaurant, where waves literally smash against the windows inches away from well-coifed diners. The menu is pricey, but for the price of a cocktail you can enjoy the same astounding view.

2000 Spindrift Dr., La Jolla, CA 92037. (©) **800/624-CLUB** or 858/454-7126. Fax 858/456-3805. www.ljbtc.com. 90 units. $170–$349 double June–Sept, from $275 suite; $139–$239 double, from $215 suite off-season. Extra person $20. Children under 12 stay free in parents' room. AE, DC, MC, V. Take La Jolla Shores Dr., turn left on Paseo Dorado, and follow to Spindrift Dr. **Amenities:** 2 restaurants; seasonal beach hut; elegant Olympic-size pool; 12 championship tennis courts and a tennis shop; 9-hole pitch-and-putt course; fitness room; watersports equipment rental; playground; massage, babysitting, laundry/dry-cleaning service; coin-op laundry. *In room:* TV w/pay movies, dataport, coffeemaker, hair dryer, iron.

Scripps Inn ★★
It's not easy to find this meticulously maintained inn, tucked away behind the Museum of Contemporary Art, but you're rewarded with seclusion even though the attractions of La Jolla are just a short walk away. Only a small, grassy park comes between the inn and the beach, cliffs, and tide pools; the view from the second-story deck seems to hypnotize guests, who gaze out to sea indefinitely. Rates vary depending on ocean view (all have one, but some are better than others); rooms have a pleasant pale cream/sand palette, and are furnished in "early-American comfortable," with new bathroom fixtures and appointments. All rooms have sofa beds and refrigerators; two have wood-burning fireplaces, and four have kitchenettes. The inn supplies beach towels, firewood, and French pastries each morning. Repeat guests keep their favorite rooms for up to a month each year, so book ahead for the best choice.

555 Coast Blvd. S. (at Cuvier), La Jolla, CA 92037. (©) **858/454-3391.** Fax 858/456-0389. 14 units. $225 double, $255–$415 suite mid-June to mid-Oct and holidays; $165 double, $195–$315 suite off-season. Extra person $10. Children under 5 stay free in parents' room. Rates include continental breakfast. AE, DC, DISC, MC, V. Free parking. Take Torrey Pines Rd., turn right on Prospect Place; past the museum, turn right onto Cuvier. *In room:* TV, fridge, coffeemaker, hair dryer, iron, safe.

The Sea Lodge ★ *Kids*
This three-story, 1960s hotel in a mainly residential enclave is under the same management as the La Jolla Beach & Tennis Club next door. It has an identical on-the-sand location, minus the country club ambience—there are no reciprocal privileges. Most rooms have some view of the ocean, and the rest look out on the pool or a tiled courtyard. From the Sea Lodge's beach you can gaze toward the top of the cliffs, where La Jolla's village hums with activity (and relentless traffic). The rooms are pretty basic, priced by view and size. Bathrooms feature separate dressing areas with large closets; balconies or patios are standard, and some rooms have fully equipped kitchenettes. Like the "B&T," the Sea Lodge is popular with families but also attracts business travelers looking to balance meetings with time on the beach or the tennis court.

8110 Camino del Oro (at Avenida de la Playa), La Jolla, CA 92037. (©) **800/237-5211** or 858/459-8271. Fax 858/456-9346. 128 units. $239–$599 double, $699 suite mid-June to mid-Sept; $179–$399 double, $479 suite off-season. Extra person $20. Children under 12 stay free in parents' room. AE, DC, DISC, MC, V. Free covered parking. Take La Jolla Shores Dr., turn left onto Avenida de la Playa, turn right on Camino del Oro. **Amenities:** Restaurant; 2 outdoor pools (1 for kids); 2 night-lit tennis courts; fitness room; whirlpool; laundry/dry-cleaning service; babysitting. *In room:* A/C, TV, dataport, fridge, coffeemaker, hair dryer, iron.

MODERATE

Best Western Inn by the Sea ⊕   Occupying an enviable location at the heart of La Jolla's charming village, this independently managed property puts guests just a short walk from the cliffs and beach. The low-rise tops out at five stories, with the upper floors enjoying ocean views (and the highest room rates). The Best Western (and the more formal Empress, a block away), offer a terrific alternative to pricier digs nearby. Rooms here are Best Western standard issue— freshly maintained, but nothing special. All rooms do have balconies, though, and refrigerators are available at no extra charge; the hotel offers plenty of welcome amenities.

7830 Fay Ave. (between Prospect and Silverado sts.), La Jolla, CA 92037. © **800/462-9732,** 800/526-4545 in California and Canada, or 858/459-4461. Fax 858/456-2578. 132 units. $129–$229. double; $350–$475 suite. Off-season discounts available. Rates include continental breakfast. AE, DC, DISC, MC, V. Parking $7. Take Torrey Pines Rd. to Prospect Place and turn right. Prospect Place becomes Prospect St.; proceed to Fay Ave. and turn left. **Amenities:** Outdoor heated pool; car-rental desk; laundry/dry-cleaning service; room service (7am–9pm). *In room:* A/C, TV w/pay movies, dataport, coffeemaker, hair dryer, iron.

Empress Hotel of La Jolla ⊕⊕   The Empress Hotel offers spacious quarters with traditional furnishings a block or two from La Jolla's main drag and the ocean. It's quieter here than at the premium clifftop properties, and you'll sacrifice little other than direct ocean views. (Many rooms on the top floors afford a partial view.) If you're planning to explore La Jolla on foot, the Empress is a good base, and it exudes a classiness many comparably priced chains lack. Rooms are tastefully decorated (and frequently renovated), and well equipped. Bathrooms are of average size but exceptionally well appointed, and four "Empress" rooms have sitting areas with full-size sleeper sofas. On nice days, breakfast is set up on a serene sundeck.

7766 Fay Ave. (at Silverado), La Jolla, CA 92037. © **888/369-9900** or 858/454-3001. Fax 858/454-6387. www.empress-hotel.com. 73 units. $149–$229 double; $349 suite. Extra person $10. Children under 18 stay free in parents' room. Rates include continental breakfast. Off-season and long-stay discounts available. AE, DC, DISC, MC, V. Valet parking $8. Take Torrey Pines Rd. to Girard Ave., turn right, then left on Silverado St. **Amenities:** Fitness room and spa; room service (11:30am–9pm). *In room:* A/C, TV, dataport, fridge, coffeemaker, hair dryer, iron.

La Jolla Cove Suites *(Value*   Tucked in beside prime oceanview condos across from Ellen Browning Scripps Park, this family run 1950s-era complex actually sits closer to the ocean than pricey uphill neighbors La Valencia and the Grande Colonial. The to-die-for ocean view is completely unobstructed, and La Jolla Cove—one of California's prettiest swimming spots—is steps away from the hotel. The property is peaceful at night, but Village dining and shopping are only a short walk away. You'll pay more depending on the quality of your view; about 80% of guest quarters gaze upon the ocean. On the plus side, rooms are wonderfully spacious, each featuring a fully equipped kitchen, plus private balcony or patio. On the minus side, their functional but almost institutional furnishings could use a touch of Martha Stewart. An oceanview rooftop deck offers lounge chairs and cafe tables; breakfast is served up here each morning, indoors or outdoors depending on the weather.

1155 Coast Blvd. (across from the cove), La Jolla, CA 92037. © **888/LA-JOLLA** or 858/459-2621. Fax 858/551-3405. www.lajollacove.com. 90 units. $135–$175 double, $190–$280 suite summer (Memorial

Day–Labor Day); $110–$135 double, $145–$225 suite off-season. Extra person $15. Midweek, AAA, and weekly discounts available. Rates include continental breakfast. AE, DC, DISC, MC, V. Free parking. Take Torrey Pines Rd. to Prospect Place and turn right. When the road forks, veer right (downhill) onto Coast Blvd. **Amenities:** Outdoor (nonview) pool; whirlpool; car-rental desk; coin-op laundry. *In room:* TV, kitchen, safe.

INEXPENSIVE

Wealthy, image-conscious La Jolla is *really* not the best place for deep bargains, but if you're determined to stay here as cheaply as possible, you won't do better than the **La Jolla Village Lodge,** 1141 Silverado St., at Herschel Ave. (© **858/ 551-2001**). This 30-room motel is standard Americana, arranged around a small parking lot with cinder-block construction and small, basic rooms. The surrounding La Jolla glamour—and bargain rates as low as $80 including breakfast—make it an acceptable option.

6 Coronado

The "island" (really a peninsula) of Coronado is a great escape. It offers quiet, architecturally rich streets, a small-town, navy-oriented atmosphere, and laid-back vacationing on one of the state's most beautiful and welcoming beaches. Choose a hotel on the ocean side for a view of Point Loma and the Pacific, or stay facing the city for a spectacular skyline vista (especially at night). You may feel pleasantly isolated here, so it isn't your best choice if you're planning to spend lots of time in more central parts of the city.

A note on driving directions: To reach the places listed here, take I-5 to the Coronado Bridge, then follow individual directions. If you have two or more passengers in a car, stay in the far right lanes to avoid paying the bridge toll.

EXPENSIVE

Coronado Island Marriott Resort ☞ Once expected to give competitor Loews a run for its money in the leisure market, this high-end Marriott seems content with the substantial group business it gets from the Convention Center across the bay. Elegance and luxury here are understated—without a lot of flash, guests just seem to get whatever they need, be it a lift downtown (by water taxi from the private dock), a tee time at the neighboring golf course, or a prime appointment at the property's spa.

Despite its all-business attitude, this hotel offers many enticements: a prime waterfront location; view of the San Diego skyline (but within easy distance of Coronado shopping and dining); casual, airy architecture; lushly planted grounds filled with preening exotic birds; and, a wealth of sporting and recreational activities. Guest rooms are generously sized and attractively furnished—actually decorated—in colorful French country style, and all feature balconies or patios. The superbly designed bathrooms hold an array of fine toiletries.

2000 Second St. (at Glorietta Blvd.), Coronado, CA 92118. © **800/228-9290** or 619/435-3000. Fax 619/435-3032. http://marriotthotels.com/SANCI. 300 units. $150–$300 double; from $300 suite; from $495 villa. Children under 12 stay free in parents' room. Packages available. AE, DC, MC, V. Valet parking $18; self-parking $14. From Coronado Bridge, turn right onto Glorietta Blvd., take first right to hotel. Bus: 901. Ferry: from Broadway Pier. **Amenities:** 2 restaurants; lounge; 3 outdoor pools; 6 night-lit tennis courts; fitness center; spa; 2 whirlpools; watersports equipment rental; bike rental; concierge; courtesy shuttle to Horton Plaza; business center; salon; 24-hr. room service; babysitting; laundry/dry-cleaning service. *In room:* A/C, TV w/pay movies, dataport, minibar, coffeemaker, hair dryer, iron, safe.

Glorietta Bay Inn ☞ Right across the street and somewhat in the (figurative) shadow of the Hotel del Coronado, this pretty white hotel consists of the charmingly historic John D. Spreckels mansion (1908) and several younger, motel-style buildings. Only 11 rooms are in the mansion, which boasts original fixtures, a grand staircase, and old-fashioned wicker furniture; the guest rooms are also decked out in antiques, and have a romantic and nostalgic ambience.

Rooms and suites in the modern annexes are much less expensive but were recently upgraded from motel-plain to match the main house's classy ambience (though lacking the mansion's superluxe featherbeds); some have kitchenettes and marina views. Wherever your room is, you'll enjoy the inn's trademark personalized service including extra-helpful staffers who remember your name and happily offer dining and sightseeing recommendations or arrange tee times; special attention to return guests and families with toddlers; and a friendly continental breakfast. In addition to offering rental bikes and boat rentals on Glorietta Bay across the street, the hotel is within easy walking distance of the beach, golf, tennis, watersports, shopping, and dining. Rooms in the mansion get booked early, but are worth the extra effort and expense.

1630 Glorietta Blvd. (near Orange Ave.), Coronado, CA 92118. ℭ 800/283-9383 or 619/435-3101. Fax 619/435-6182. www.gloriettabayinn.com. 100 units. Double $255–$275 mansion; $150–$275 annex. Suite $305–$585 mansion; from $255 annex. Extra person $10. Children under 18 stay free in parents' room. Rates include continental breakfast and afternoon refreshment. AE, DC, DISC, MC, V. Self-parking $7. From Coronado Bridge, turn left on Orange Ave. After 2 miles (3km), turn left onto Glorietta Blvd.; the inn is across the street from the Hotel del Coronado. **Amenities:** Outdoor pool; whirlpool; in-room massage; babysitting; laundry/dry-cleaning service; coin-op laundry. *In room:* A/C, TV w/pay movies, dataport, fridge, coffeemaker, hair dryer.

Hotel del Coronado 🏵🏵🏵   Opened in 1888 and designated a National Historic Landmark in 1977, the "Hotel Del," as it's affectionately known, is the last of California's grand old seaside hotels. Legend has it that the duke of Windsor met his American duchess here, and Marilyn Monroe frolicked around the hotel in *Some Like It Hot.* This monument to Victorian grandeur boasts tall cupolas, red turrets, and gingerbread trim, all spread out over 26 acres. Rooms run the gamut from compact to extravagant, and all are packed with antique charm; most have custom-made furnishings. The best rooms have balconies fronting the ocean and large windows that take in one of the city's finest white-sand beaches. If you're a stickler for detail, ask to stay in the original building rather than in the contemporary tower additions.

In 2000, the hotel completed a painstaking, multimillion-dollar, 3-year restoration. Purists will rejoice to hear that historical accuracy was paramount, resulting in this priceless grande dame being returned to its turn-of-the-19th-century splendor. Even if you don't stay here, don't miss a stroll through the grand, wood-paneled lobby or along the pristine wide beach. Accolades have been awarded to the Prince of Wales Grill, recently remodeled from a dark, clubby room to an airy, elegant salon with oceanfront dining; cocktails and afternoon tea are served in the wood-paneled lobby and adjoining conservatory lounge.

1500 Orange Ave., Coronado, CA 92118. ℭ 800/468-3533 or 619/435-8000. Fax 619/522-8238. www.hoteldel.com. 700 units. Double $215–$340 garden or city view; $360–$640 ocean view. Suite from $700. Sport, spa, and romance packages available. Children under 18 stay free in parents' room. AE, DC, DISC, MC, V. Valet parking $16, self-parking $12. From Coronado Bridge, turn left onto Orange Ave. Bus: 901. Ferry: from Broadway Pier. **Amenities:** 9 restaurants/lounges; 2 outdoor pools; 3 tennis courts; health club and spa; 2 whirlpools; bike rental; children's activities; concierge; car-rental desk; shopping arcade; 24-hr. room service; babysitting; laundry/dry-cleaning service. *In room:* A/C, TV w/pay movies, dataport, minibar, hair dryer, iron, safe.

MODERATE

El Cordova Hotel 🏵   This Spanish hacienda across the street from the Hotel del Coronado began life as a private mansion in 1902. By the 1930s it had

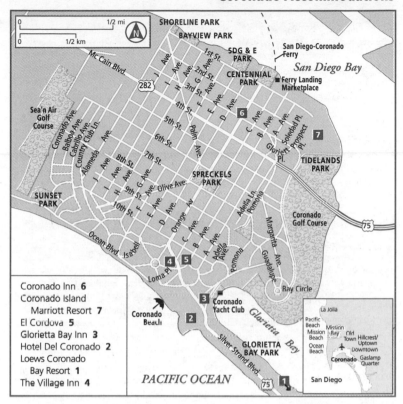

Coronado Inn **6**
Coronado Island
   Marriott Resort **7**
El Cordova **5**
Glorietta Bay Inn **3**
Hotel Del Coronado **2**
Loews Coronado
   Bay Resort **1**
The Village Inn **4**

become a hotel; the original building augmented by a series of attachments housing retail shops along the ground-floor arcade. Shaped like a baseball diamond and surrounding a courtyard with meandering tiled pathways, flowering shrubs, a swimming pool, and patio seating for Miguel's Cocina Mexican restaurant, El Cordova hums pleasantly with activity.

Each room is a little different from the next—some sport a Mexican colonial ambience, while others evoke a comfy beach cottage. All feature ceiling fans and brightly tiled bathrooms, but lack the frills that would command exorbitant rates. El Cordova has a particularly inviting aura, and its prime location makes it a popular option; We advise reserving several months in advance, especially for the summer. Facilities include a barbecue area with picnic table.

1351 Orange Ave. (at Adella Ave.), Coronado, CA 92118. ℂ **800/229-2032** or 619/435-4131. Fax 619/435-0632. www.elcordovahotel.com. 40 units. $119–$167 double, $203–$306 suite mid-Apr to Sept; $114–$155 double, $179–$246 suite off-season. Children under 12 stay free in parents' room. Weekly and monthly rates available in winter. AE, DC, DISC, MC, V. No off-street parking. From Coronado Bridge, turn left onto Orange Ave. Parking available on street. **Amenities:** Restaurant; outdoor pool; shopping arcade; coin-op laundry. *In room:* A/C, TV.

Loews Coronado Bay Resort 🦀🦀 (Kids)   This luxury resort opened in 1991 on a secluded 15-acre peninsula, slightly removed from downtown Coronado and San Diego. It's perfect for those who prefer a self-contained resort in a getaway-from-it-all location, and is surprisingly successful in appealing to business travelers, convention groups, vacationing families, and romantically inclined

Fun Fact **A Century of Intrigue: Scenes from the Hotel del Coronado**

San Diego's romantic Hotel del Coronado is an unmistakable landmark, filled with enchanting and colorful memories.

Several familiar names helped shape the hotel. In 1887, it was among the first buildings with Thomas Edison's new invention, electric light; the building had its own electrical power plant, which supplied the entire city of Coronado until 1922. Author L. Frank Baum, a frequent guest, designed the Crown Dining Room's elegant crown-shaped chandeliers. Baum wrote several of the books in his beloved *Wizard of Oz* series in Coronado, and many believe he modeled the Emerald City's geometric spires after the Del's conical turrets.

The hotel has played host to royalty and celebrities as well. The first visiting monarch was Kalakaua, Hawaii's last king, who spent Christmas here in 1890. But the best-known royal guest was Edward, Prince of Wales (later Edward VIII, then duke of Windsor). He came to the hotel in April 1920, the first British royal to visit California. Of the many lavish social affairs held during his stay, at least two were attended by Wallis Simpson (then navy-wife Wallis Warfield), 15 years before her official introduction to the prince in London. Speculation continues about whether their love affair, which culminated in his abdication of the throne, might have begun right here.

America's own "royalty" often visited the hotel. In 1927, San Diego's beloved son Charles Lindbergh was honored here following his historic 33½-hour solo flight across the Atlantic. Hollywood stars including Mary Pickford, Greta Garbo, Charlie Chaplin, and Esther Williams have flocked to the Del. Director Billy Wilder filmed *Some Like It Hot* at the hotel; longtime staffers remember seeing stars Marilyn Monroe, Tony Curtis, and Jack Lemmon romping on the beach. The hotel has also hosted 10 U.S. presidents. And some guests have never left: The ghost of Kate Morgan, whose body was found in 1892 where the tennis courts are today, supposedly still roams the halls.

Visitors and guests intrigued by the hotel's past can stroll through the lower-level History Gallery, a minimuseum of hotel memorabilia.

couples. All units offer terraces that look onto the hotel's private 80-ship marina, the Coronado Bay Bridge, or San Diego Bay. A private pedestrian underpass leads to nearby Silver Strand Beach. Rooms boast finely appointed marble bathrooms; VCRs come standard in suites, and are available free upon request to any room. Video rentals are available. A highlight here is the **Gondola Company** (© 619/429-6317), which offers romantic and fun gondola cruises through the canals of tony Coronado Cays. The seasonal Commodore Kids Club, for children ages 4 to 12, offers supervised half-day, full-day, and evening programs with meals.

4000 Coronado Bay Rd., Coronado, CA 92118. © 800/81-LOEWS or 619/424-4000. Fax 619/424-4400. 438 units. $145–$265 double; from $450 suite. Children under 18 stay free in parents' room. Packages available. AE, DC, DISC, MC, V. Valet parking $16, covered self-parking $13. From Coronado Bridge, go left onto Orange Ave, continue 8 miles (13km) down Silver Strand Hwy. Turn left at Coronado Bay Rd., entrance to the resort.

Pets welcomed. **Amenities:** 3 restaurants (including acclaimed Azzura Point); lounge; 3 outdoor pools; tennis courts; fitness center; spa; whirlpool; watersports-equipment rentals; bike and skate rental; children's programs; concierge; car-rental desk; business center; salon; 24-hr. room service; in-room massage; babysitting; laundry/dry-cleaning service. *In room:* A/C, TV, dataport, minibar, coffeemaker, hair dryer, iron.

INEXPENSIVE

Coronado Inn 🐾 Well located and terrifically priced, this renovated 1940s courtyard motel has such a friendly ambience; it's like staying with old friends. Iced tea, lemonade, and fresh fruit are even provided poolside on summer days. It's still a motel, though—albeit with brand-new paint and fresh tropical floral decor—so rooms are pretty basic. The six rooms with bathtubs also have small kitchens; microwaves are available for the rest, along with hair dryers and irons (just ask upfront). Rooms close to the street are noisiest, so ask for one toward the back. The Coronado shuttle stops a block away; it serves the shopping areas and Hotel Del.

266 Orange Ave. (corner of 3rd St.), Coronado, CA 92118. ℂ 800/598-6624 or 619/435-4121. www. coronadoinn.com. 30 units (most with shower only). $110–$175 double for up to 4 people Memorial Day–Labor Day; $90–$120 off-season. Rates include continental breakfast. Discounts available. AE, DISC, MC, V. Free parking. From Coronado Bridge, stay on 3rd St. Pets accepted with $10 nightly fee. **Amenities:** Outdoor pool; coin-op laundry. *In room:* A/C, TV, dataport, fridge.

The Village Inn *Value* Its location a block or two from Coronado's main sights—the Hotel Del, the beach, shopping, and cafes—is this inn's most appealing feature. Historic charm runs a close second; a plaque outside identifies the three-story brick-and-stucco hotel as the once-chic Blue Lantern Inn, built in 1926. The charming vintage lobby sets the mood in this European-style hostelry; each simple but well-maintained room holds antique dressers and armoires, plus lovely Battenberg lace bedcovers and shams. Front rooms enjoy the best view, and coffee and tea are available all day in the kitchen where breakfast is served. The appealing inn's only Achilles' heel is tiny, tiny bathrooms, so cramped that you almost have to stand on the toilet to use the small-scale sinks. Surprisingly, some bathrooms have been updated with whirlpool tubs.

1017 Park Place (at Orange Ave.), Coronado, CA 92118. ℂ 619/435-9318. 14 units. $90–$95 double summer. Winter and weekly rates available. Rates include continental breakfast. AE, MC, V. Parking available on street. From Coronado Bridge, turn left onto Orange Ave., then right on Park Place. *In room:* No phone.

7 Near the Airport

San Diego's airport has the unusual distinction of being virtually in downtown. While locals grouse about the noise and decreased property values, it's good news for travelers: Most of the accommodations in the "Downtown," "Hillcrest," and "Old Town" (including Hotel Circle) neighborhoods are only 5 to 10 minutes from the airport.

For those who must stay as close as possible to the airport, there are two good choices literally across the street. The 1,045-room **Sheraton San Diego Hotel and Marina,** 1380 Harbor Island Dr. (ℂ **800/325-3535** or 619/291-2900), offers rooms from $150 to $280. At the 208-room **Hilton San Diego Airport/Harbor Island,** 1960 Harbor Island Dr. (ℂ **800/774-1500** or 619/291-6700), rooms go for $149 to $219. Both hotels offer a marina view, a pool, and proximity to downtown San Diego. We also recommend the nearby **Bay Club Hotel,** 2131 Shelter Island Dr. (ℂ **800/672-0800** or 619/224-8888; www.bayclubhotel.com), a pretty marina-front low-rise offering a vacation ambience even for business travelers; rates range from $129 to $199, including breakfast.

6

Where to Dine

The city's dining scene, once a bastion of rich Continental and heavy American cuisine, has come into its own during the past decade. The explosion of a transplant population and the diversification of San Diego neighborhoods have sparked a new spirit of experimentation and style. An improved economy helped out too, motivating folks to step out and exercise their palates. The restaurant scene races to keep up with current trends and desires. One positive sign is that the culinary bible, the *Zagat Survey*, now publishes an annual edition exclusively for San Diego and its environs.

As you can imagine, San Diego offers terrific seafood: Whether at unembellished market-style restaurants that let freshness take center stage or at upscale restaurants that feature extravagant presentations, the ocean's bounty is everywhere.

Those traditional mainstays, American and Continental cuisine, are (metaphorically speaking) still carrying their share of the weight in San Diego. But, with increasing regularity, they're mating with lighter, more contemporary, often ethnic styles. The movement is akin to the eclectic fusion cuisine that burst onto the scene in the early 1990s. That's not to say traditionalists will be disappointed—San Diego still has plenty of clubby steak-and-potatoes stalwarts on the West Coast.

If you love Italian food, you're also in luck. Not only does San Diego boast a strong contingent of old-fashioned Sicilian-style choices, but also these days you can't turn a corner without running into a trattoria. The Gaslamp Quarter corners the market with upscale northern Italian bistros on virtually every block. Hillcrest, La Jolla, and other neighborhoods also boast their fair share. They cater mostly to locals (which is usually a good thing) and their menus most always include gourmet pizzas baked in wood-fired ovens, a trend that shows no signs of slowing down (see "Only in San Diego," at the end of this chapter).

Ethnic foods are still rising in popularity. Number one on everyone's list of favorites is Mexican—a logical choice given the city's history and location. You'll find lots of highly Americanized fare along with a few hidden jewels, like El Agave and Berta's, that serve true south-of-the-border cuisine. The most authentic Mexican food may be the humble fish taco (see "Only in San Diego," at the end of this chapter). This Baja import, faithfully re-created by Rubio's, has become San Diego's favorite fast food. Asian cuisine runs a close second, with Thai and Vietnamese restaurants starting to catch up with Chinese and Japanese. Many intrepid chefs fuse Asian ingredients and preparations with more familiar Mediterranean or French menus, and sushi bars are on the rise.

In this chapter, restaurants are indexed by cuisine as well as by location and price category. *Note:* For a list of our favorites in all kinds of categories, see "Best Dining Bets" in chapter 1.

For diners on a budget, the more expensive San Diego restaurants are accommodating if you want to order a few appetizers instead of a main course, and many offer more reasonably priced lunch menus. In keeping with beach culture, even in the more pricey places, dress tends to be casual; some notable exceptions are La Jolla's more expensive restaurants and the hotels on Coronado, where jeans are a no-no and gentlemen ought to wear dinner jackets.

A note on parking: Unless a listing specifies otherwise, drivers can expect to park within 2 or 3 blocks of the restaurants listed here. If you can't find a free or metered space on the street, you can seek out a garage or lot (see "Getting Around," in chapter 4).

1 Restaurants by Cuisine

AMERICAN

Bay Beach Cafe (Coronado, $$, p. 122)

The Chart House ⋒ (Coronado, La Jolla, $$$, p. 120)

Chive ⋒⋒⋒ (Downtown, $$$, p. 98)

Clayton's Coffee Shop (Coronado, $, p. 122)

Corvette Diner ⋒ (Hillcrest/Uptown, $, p. 105)

Croce's Restaurant & Nightclubs ⋒⋒⋒ (Downtown, $$$, p. 98)

Dakota Grill and Spirits ⋒⋒ (Downtown, $$, p. 100)

The Green Flash ⋒ (Pacific Beach, $$, p. 113)

High Tide Cafe (Pacific Beach, $, p. 113)

Hob Nob Hill ⋒ (Hillcrest/Uptown, $$, p. 104)

Kansas City Barbecue (Downtown, $, p. 101)

Karl Strauss Brewery & Grill ⋒ (Downtown, La Jolla, $$, p. 100)

Rhinoceros Cafe & Grill ⋒ (Coronado, $$, p. 122)

San Diego Chicken Pie Shop ⋒ (Hillcrest/Uptown, $, p. 106)

BREAKFAST

Brockton Villa ⋒⋒ (La Jolla, $$, p. 117)

Café Lulu ⋒ (Downtown, $, p. 101)

Clayton's Coffee Shop (Coronado, $, p. 122)

The Cottage ⋒ (La Jolla, $, p. 120)

Hob Nob Hill ⋒ (Hillcrest/Uptown, $$, p. 104)

The Mission (Mission Beach, $, p. 113)

Primavera Pastry Caffé ⋒ (Coronado, $, p. 123)

CALIFORNIAN

Azzura Point (Coronado, $$$$, p. 120)

Baleen ⋒⋒⋒ (Mission Bay, $$$$, p. 110)

Brockton Villa ⋒⋒ (La Jolla, $$, p. 117)

Cafe Pacifica ⋒⋒ (Old Town, $$$, p. 108)

California Cuisine ⋒⋒ (Hillcrest/ Uptown, $$$, p. 102)

The Cottage ⋒ (La Jolla, $, p. 120)

George's at the Cove ⋒⋒⋒ (La Jolla, $$$$, p. 114)

George's Ocean Terrace and Cafe/Bar ⋒⋒ (La Jolla, $$, p. 118)

Mixx ⋒⋒ (Hillcrest/Uptown, $$, p. 104)

Nine-Ten ⋒⋒⋒ (La Jolla, $$$, p. 117)

Prince of Wales (Coronado, $$$$, p. 120)

Qwiig's 🐸🐸 (Ocean Beach, $$$, p. 110)

Wolfgang Puck Cafe (Mission Valley, $$, p. 123)

CHINESE

Panda Inn 🐸🐸 (Downtown, $$, p. 100)

COFFEE & TEA

Brockton Villa 🐸🐸 (La Jolla, $$, p. 117)

Café Lulu 🐸 (Downtown, $, p. 101)

The Living Room ($, p. 118)

The Mission (Mission Beach, $, p. 113)

Pannikin ($, p. 118)

CONTINENTAL

Thee Bungalow 🐸🐸 (Ocean Beach, $$$, p. 112)

Top O' the Cove 🐸🐸🐸 (La Jolla, $$$$, p. 115)

DESSERTS

Extraordinary Desserts 🐸🐸🐸 (Hillcrest/Uptown, $, p. 105)

ECLECTIC

Chive 🐸🐸🐸 (Downtown, $$$, p. 98)

Croce's Restaurant & Nightclubs 🐸🐸🐸 (Downtown, $$$, p. 98)

Parallel 33 🐸🐸 (Hillcrest/Uptown, $$, p. 104)

Roppongi 🐸 (La Jolla, $$$, p. 116)

ENGLISH

Princess Pub & Grille (Downtown, $, p. 102)

FRENCH

Chez Loma 🐸🐸 (Coronado, $$$, p. 121)

Laurel 🐸🐸🐸 (Hillcrest/ Uptown, $$$, p. 103)

Liaison 🐸🐸 (Hillcrest/Uptown, $$, p. 104)

Thee Bungalow 🐸🐸 (Ocean Beach, $$$, p. 112)

INTERNATIONAL

The Mission (Mission Beach, $, p. 113)

Mixx 🐸🐸 (Hillcrest/Uptown, $$, p. 104)

Parallel 33 🐸🐸 (Hillcrest/Uptown, $$, p. 104)

ITALIAN

Caffe Bella Italia 🐸🐸 (Pacific Beach, $$, p. 112)

Filippi's Pizza Grotto 🐸🐸 (Downtown, Pacific Beach, and other locations, $, p. 101)

Fio's 🐸🐸🐸 (Downtown, $$$, p. 99)

Old Spaghetti Factory (Downtown, $, p. 101)

Trattoria Acqua 🐸🐸 (La Jolla, $$$, p. 117)

JAPANESE/SUSHI

Cafe Japengo 🐸🐸 (La Jolla, $$$, p. 116)

Sushi Ota 🐸 (Mission Bay, $$, p. 113)

LATIN AMERICAN

Berta's Latin American Restaurant 🐸🐸 (Old Town, $$, p. 108)

LIGHT FARE

Bread & Cie. Bakery and Cafe 🐸🐸 (Hillcrest/Uptown, $, p. 105)

Brockton Villa 🐸🐸 (La Jolla, $$, p. 117)

Primavera Pastry Caffé 🐸 (Coronado, $, p. 123)

MEDITERRANEAN

Azzura Point (Coronado, $$$$, p. 120)

Bread & Cie. Bakery and Cafe
☆☆ (Hillcrest/Uptown, $,
p. 105)

Laurel ☆☆☆ (Hillcrest/Uptown,
$$$, p. 103)

Nine-Ten ☆☆☆ (La Jolla, $$$,
p. 117)

Trattoria Acqua ☆☆ (La Jolla, $$$,
p. 117)

MEXICAN

Casa de Bandini ☆ (Old Town,
$$, p. 109)

Casa de Pico (Old Town, $$,
p. 109)

El Agave Tequilaria ☆☆ (Old
Town, $$$, p. 108)

Old Town Mexican Cafe ☆ (Old
Town, $, p. 109)

Miguel's Cocina (Coronado, $$,
p. 120)

PACIFIC RIM/
ASIAN FUSION

Cafe Japengo ☆☆ (La Jolla, $$$,
p. 116)

Peohe's ☆ (Coronado, $$$,
p. 122)

Roppongi ☆ (La Jolla, $$$,
p. 116)

SEAFOOD

Baleen ☆☆☆ (Mission Bay, $$$$,
p. 110)

Bay Beach Cafe (Coronado, $$,
p. 122)

Brigantine Seafood Grill ☆
(Old Town, Coronado, $$$,
p. 107)

Cafe Pacifica ☆☆ (Old Town, $$$,
p. 108)

The Fish Market/Top of the
Market ☆☆ (Downtown, $$$,
p. 100)

Peohe's ☆ (Coronado, $$$, p. 122)

Star of the Sea ☆☆☆ (Downtown,
$$$$ p. 97)

SOUTHWESTERN

Dakota Grill and Spirits ☆☆
(Downtown, $$, p. 100)

THAI

Spice & Rice Thai Kitchen ☆
(La Jolla, $$, p. 119)

VEGETARIAN

Café Lulu ☆ (Downtown, $,
p. 101)

The Vegetarian Zone ☆☆
(Hillcrest/Uptown, $, p. 106)

2 Downtown

Downtown dining tends to be more formal than elsewhere, because of the business clientele and evening theater- and operagoers. Once the domain of high-priced and highfalutin Continental and American restaurants, downtown was turned on its ear when chic spots began filling the Gaslamp Quarter's restored Victorian buildings. If you stroll down Fifth Avenue between E and Market streets, you'll find a month's worth of restaurants, all packed with a fashionable, mainly local crowd. The Embarcadero, a stretch of waterfront along the bay, is also home to several great eating spots, all of which capitalize on their bay views.

VERY EXPENSIVE

Star of the Sea ☆☆☆ SEAFOOD   After being an Embarcadero fine dining institution since 1966, the former Anthony's Star of the Sea Room had been taking a lot of flack for being stuffy and outmoded. Presto chango! After an extensive makeover in 1999, this seafood restaurant reopened sporting a new look, new chef, and new name—to differentiate from the casual waterfront fish houses in the Anthony's restaurant family. Gone are the dated dress code and off-putting formality, replaced by a comfortable ambience and modern decor matched to the still-stunning harbor view. The focus here is on the finest of food, though—new executive chef Brian Johnston imbues the menu with sophisticated touches that show he's in touch with today's gourmand audience. The menu is seasonally composed; representative dishes include seared scallops with fragrant herbs de Provence over a pillow of roasted garlic potatoes, oven-roasted Norwegian salmon in a crunchy artichoke crust and rich Cabernet sauce, or an irresistible appetizer of foie gras paired with crisp Asian pears and enhanced with ginger. There's a very reasonably priced wine list here, and a welcoming bar with its own abbreviated menu.

1380 N. Harbor Dr. (at Ash St.) ℂ 619/232-7408. www.starofthesea.com. Reservations recommended. Main courses $22–$36. AE, DC, DISC, MC, V. Daily 5:30–10:30pm. Closed major holidays. Valet parking $4. Bus: 2. Trolley: America Plaza or Seaport Village.

EXPENSIVE

Chive 𝒜𝒜𝒜 AMERICAN/ECLECTIC   If we could award an extra half-star for class and aplomb, this big-city-style Gaslamp newcomer would deserve it. Chive balances the chic ambience of its angular, wide space and fashionably composed menu with cozy lighting, warm fabrics, and a pervasive sense of relaxed fun. For example, steaming edamame (fresh soybeans) served instead of bread subtly reinforces the green of the restaurant's namesake herb, which also garnishes many dishes—and whose hue reappears in the "Chive cocktail," a sugar-rimmed elixir of champagne and Midori liqueur. Gentle jazz and table conversation hum together, while a legion of practiced servers help decipher such unfamiliar menu ingredients as *nairagi* (an ahilike Hawaiian fish) and *picholine* (a tiny French olive). The most popular dishes include braised veal cheeks accented with Mediterranean couscous and preserved lemon; Asian-tinged sea bass in a chili-garlic crust atop black-bean sauce; a nightly ravioli of the chef's whim; and salads that balance crispy greens with pungent, creamy cheeses, and sweet fruit accents. An international wine list offers many intriguing selections by "cork" or "stem," and includes postmeal sipping tequilas, ports, and Scotch.

558 Fourth Ave. (at Market St.) ℂ 619/232-4483. www.chiverestaurant.com. Reservations recommended. Main courses $20–$28. AE, DC, DISC, MC, V. Daily 5pm–midnight. Valet parking $7. Bus: 3, 5, 16, or 25. Trolley: Convention Center.

Croce's Restaurant & Nightclubs 𝒜𝒜𝒜 AMERICAN/ECLECTIC   Ingrid Croce, widow of singer-songwriter Jim, was instrumental in the resurgence of the once-decayed Gaslamp Quarter, and her establishment has expanded to fill every corner of this 1890 Romanesque building. Croce's features a menu that fuses Southern soul food and Southwestern spice with Asian flavors and Continental standards. Add the raucous Top Hat Bar & Grille and the intimate Jazz Bar, and the complex is the hottest ticket in town, with crowds lining up for dinner tables and nightclub shows.

An evening in the Gaslamp Quarter isn't complete without at least strolling by the Croce's corner; expect a festive good time any night of the week. Those who dine in either of the restaurant's side-by-side seating areas can enter the two nightspots (see chapter 10 for a full listing) without paying the cover charge.

802 Fifth Ave. (at F St.) ℂ 619/233-4355. www.croces.com. Reservations not accepted; call for same-day "priority seating" (before walk-ins). Main courses $14–$23. AE, DC, DISC, MC, V. Daily 5pm–midnight. Valet parking $7 with validation. Bus: 3, 5, 16, or 25. Trolley: Gaslamp Quarter.

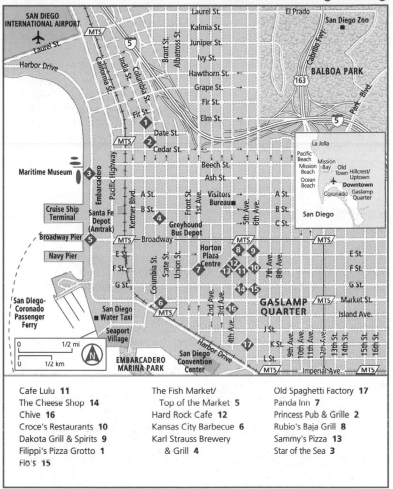

Cafe Lulu **11**
The Cheese Shop **14**
Chive **16**
Croce's Restaurants **10**
Dakota Grill & Spirits **9**
Filippi's Pizza Grotto **1**
Fio's **15**

The Fish Market/
   Top of the Market **5**
Hard Rock Cafe **12**
Kansas City Barbecue **6**
Karl Strauss Brewery
   & Grill **4**

Old Spaghetti Factory **17**
Panda Inn **7**
Princess Pub & Grille **2**
Rubio's Baja Grill **8**
Sammy's Pizza **13**
Star of the Sea **3**

Fio's ★★★ ITALIAN Fio's has been *the* spot to see and be seen in the Gaslamp Quarter since it opened, and it's the granddaddy of the new wave of trendy Italian restaurants. Set in an 1881 Italianate Victorian that once housed chic Marston's department store, Fio's has a sophisticated ambience and is *always* crowded. Once cutting-edge, the upscale trattoria menu is now practiced and consistently superior. It features jet-black linguini tossed with the freshest seafood, delicate angel hair pasta perfectly balanced with basil and pine nuts, and gourmet pizzas served at regular tables and the special pizza bar. The menu pleases both light eaters (with antipasti and pastas) and heartier palates—the impressive list of meat entrees includes mustard-rosemary rack of lamb, veal shank on saffron risotto, and delicately sweet hazelnut-crusted pork loin with Frangelico and peaches. If you stop by without a reservation, you can sit at the elegant cocktail bar and order from the complete menu.

801 Fifth Ave. (at F St.). ✆ **619/234-3467.** www.fioscucina.com. Reservations recommended. Main courses $11–$25. AE, DC, DISC, MC, V. Mon–Thurs 5–10:30pm; Fri–Sat 5–11pm; Sun 5–10pm. Valet parking $6 with validation. Bus: 3, 5, 16, or 25. Trolley: Gaslamp Quarter.

The Fish Market/Top of the Market 🌂🌂 SEAFOOD   Ask any San Diegan where to go for the biggest selection of the freshest fish, and they'll send you to the bustling Fish Market on the end of the G Street Pier on the Embarcadero. Chalkboards announce the day's catches—be it Mississippi catfish, Maine lobster, Canadian salmon, or Mexican yellowtail—which are sold by the pound or available in a number of classic, simple preparations in the casual restaurant. Upstairs, the related Top of the Market offers similar fare at jacked-up prices; we recommend having a cocktail in Top's posh clubby atmosphere with stupendous panoramic bay views—then head downstairs for affordable fare and/or treats from the sushi and oyster bars.

There is another Fish Market Restaurant in **Del Mar** at 640 Via de la Valle (© **858/755-2277**).

750 N. Harbor Dr. © 619/232-FISH. www.thefishmarket.com. Reservations not accepted. Main courses $9–$25. AE, DC, DISC, MC, V. Daily 11am–10pm. Valet parking $4. Bus: 7/7B. Trolley: Seaport Village.

MODERATE

Dakota Grill and Spirits 🌂🌂 AMERICAN/SOUTHWESTERN   This downtown business lunch favorite is always busy and noisy; the Southwestern cowboy kitsch matches the cuisine but can be a little too themey for some. Little pistols on the menu indicate the most popular items, which include shrimp tasso (sautéed with Cajun ham and sweet peas in ancho chili cream), spit-roasted chicken with orange chipotle glaze or Dakota barbecue sauce, and mixed grill served with roasted garlic and grilled red potatoes. When the kitchen is on, Dakota's innovation makes it one of San Diego's best, but an occasional dud results from the overzealous combination of too many disparate ingredients. Still, it's not losing any ground as one of the Gaslamp Quarter's star eateries, and the raucous, casual atmosphere fits the lively cuisine. A pianist plays weekend nights.

901 Fifth Ave. (at E St.). © 619/234-5554. Reservations recommended. Main courses $10–$20. AE, DC, DISC, MC, V. Mon–Fri 11:30am–2:30pm; Mon–Thurs 5–10pm; Fri–Sat 5–11pm; Sun 5–9pm. Valet parking (after 5pm) $5; self-parking in the area $7. Bus: 3, 5, 16, or 25. Trolley: Gaslamp Quarter.

Karl Strauss Downtown Brewery & Grill 🌂 AMERICAN   Brew master Karl Strauss put San Diego on the microbrewery map with this unpretentious factory setting. The smell of hops and malt wafts throughout, and the stainless steel tanks are visible from the bar. Brews, all on tap, range from pale ale to amber lager. Five-ounce samplers are $1 each; if you like what you taste, 12-ounce glasses, pints, and hefty schooners stand chilled and ready. There's also nonalcoholic beer and wine by the glass. Accompaniments include Cajun fries, hamburgers, German sausage with sauerkraut, fish and chips, and other greasy bar food, but that's secondary to the stylish suds. Beer-related memorabilia and brewery tours are available. (For more information, see "Pitcher This: San Diego's Microbreweries," in chapter 10.)

1157 Columbia St. (between B and C sts.). © 619/234-BREW (2739). Main courses $7–$15. MC, V. Sun–Wed 11:30am–10pm (beer and wine until 11pm); Thurs–Sat 11:30am–midnight (beer and wine until 1am). Bus: 5. Trolley: America Plaza.

Panda Inn 🌂🌂 CHINESE   Circuslike Horton Plaza holds many restaurants, but this stylish, upscale choice is on the opposite end of the spectrum from your average Hot Dog on a Stick. Its elegant interior—decorated with modern art and Chinese pottery—matches the gourmet selection of Mandarin and Sichuan dishes. Standouts include lemon scallops, honey-walnut shrimp, and enoki-mushroom chicken. The dining room has a view of the city skyline, and the lounge area has a full bar. Some will find the location convenient for shopping and moviegoing, while others will be irritated at dealing with parking and the crowded shopping mall maze. However, Panda Inn really is one of San Diego's best and well worth the effort.

506 Horton Plaza (top floor). ℂ 619/233-7800. Reservations recommended. Main courses $8–$18. AE, DC, DISC, MC, V. Sun–Thurs 11am–10pm; Fri–Sat 11am–10:30pm. Trolley: American Plaza.

INEXPENSIVE

Café Lulu ✦ BREAKFAST/COFFEE & TEA/VEGETARIAN   Smack-dab in the heart of the Gaslamp Quarter, Café Lulu aims for a hip, bohemian mood despite its location half a block from commercial Horton Plaza. Ostensibly a coffee bar, the cafe makes a terrific choice for casual dining; if the stylishly metallic interior is too harsh for you, watch the street action from a sidewalk table. The food is health conscious, prepared with organic ingredients and no meat. Soups, salads, cheese melts, and veggie lasagna are on the menu; breads come from the incomparable Bread & Cie. uptown (see review, below). Eggs, granola, and waffles are served in the morning, but anytime is the right time to try one of the inventive coffee drinks, like cafe Bohème (mocha with almond syrup) or cafe L'amour (iced latte with a hazelnut tinge). Beer and wine are also served.

419 F St. (near Fourth Ave.). ℂ 619/238-0114. Main courses $3–$7. No credit cards. Sun–Thurs 10am–1am; Fri–Sat 9:30am–3am. Bus: 3, 5, 16, or 25. Trolley: Gaslamp Quarter.

Filippi's Pizza Grotto ✦✦ *Kids* *Value* ITALIAN   Think Little Italy, and this is the picture that comes to mind. To get to the dining area, decorated with Chianti bottles and red-checked tablecloths, you walk through an Italian grocery store and deli strewn with cheeses, pastas, wines, bottles of olive oil, and salamis. You might even end up eating behind shelves of canned olives, but don't feel bad—this has been a tradition since 1950. The intoxicating smell of pizza wafts into the street; Filippi's has more than 15 varieties (including vegetarian), plus old-world spaghetti, lasagna, and other pasta. Children's portions are available, and kids will feel right at home.

The original of a dozen branches, this Filippi's has free parking; other locations include 962 Garnet Ave., **Pacific Beach** (ℂ 858/483-6222); Kearny Mesa; East Mission Valley; and Escondido.

1747 India St. (between Date and Fir sts.), Little Italy. ℂ 619/232-5095. Main courses $5–$13. AE, DC, DISC, MC, V. Sun–Thurs 11am–10pm; Fri–Sat 11am–11pm. Free parking. Bus: 5. Trolley: County Center/Little Italy.

Kansas City Barbecue AMERICAN   Kansas City Barbecue's honky-tonk mystique was fueled by its appearance as the fly-boy hangout in the movie *Top Gun*. Posters from the film share wall space with county-fair memorabilia, old Kansas car tags, and a photograph of official "bar wench" Carry Nation. This homey dive is right next to the railroad tracks and across from the tony Hyatt Regency. The spicy barbecue ribs, chicken, and hot links are slow-cooked over an open fire and served with sliced white bread and your choice of coleslaw, beans, fries, onion rings, potato salad, or corn on the cob. The food is okay, but the atmosphere is the real draw.

610 W. Market St. ℂ 619/231-9680. Reservations accepted only for parties of 8 or more. Main courses $9–$12. MC, V. Daily 11am–1am. Trolley: Seaport Village.

Old Spaghetti Factory *Kids* ITALIAN   It's lively, it's family friendly, and it's a great deal—no wonder folks are always waiting for tables. The menu is basic spaghetti-and-meatball fare; for the price of a main course, you also get salad, sourdough bread, ice cream, and coffee or tea (with refills). Table wines are available by the glass or decanter. Part of a chain that always has creative settings; the restaurant is in a former printing factory, with some tables enclosed in a 1917 trolley car. The decor is lavish early bordello—fun for adults and stimulating for kids, who can frolic in the small play area.

275 Fifth Ave. (at K St.). ✆ 619/233-4323. Main courses $5–$10. DISC, MC, V. Mon–Fri 11:30am–2pm and 5–10pm; Sat–Sun noon–10pm. Bus: 1. Trolley: Gaslamp Quarter.

Princess Pub & Grille ENGLISH   This local haunt is great for Anglophiles and others hungry for a ploughman's plate, Cornish pastry, steak-and-kidney pie, fish and chips, or bangers in hefty portions. Formerly known as the Princess of Wales, the bar still has photos and commemorative plates of Princess Diana hanging everywhere, along with flags from England, a well-worn dartboard, and a photo of the Queen Mother downing a pint. You can usually find a copy of the *Union Jack* (the newspaper published in the United States for British expats), too. Among the English beers available are Bass, Fuller's, and Watney's. For a taste of Ireland, order a Guinness; the Princess also serves hard Devon cider. Friday and Saturday nights are particularly busy, as patrons fill sidewalk tables and observe neighborhood goings-on.

1665 India St. (at Date St.). ✆ 619/702-3021. www.princesspub.com. Reservations not accepted. Main courses $6–$14. DISC, MC, V. Daily 11am–1am. Bus: 5. Trolley: Little Italy.

3 Hillcrest/Uptown

Hillcrest and the other fashionable uptown neighborhoods are jam-packed with great food for any palate (and any wallet). Some are old standbys filled nightly with loyal regulars; others are cutting-edge experiments that might be gone next year. Ethnic food, French food, health-conscious bistro fare, retro comfort food, specialty cafes and bakeries, and California cuisine (as in the restaurant of the same name)—they're all done with the panache you'd expect in the trendiest part of town.

If none of the listings below appeals to you, here are more: **Cafe W,** 3680 Sixth Ave. (✆ 619/291-0200), is the latest venture of Chris Walsh, who created a following at California Cuisine. This time he does flavorful international tapas-style small plates in a revived Hillcrest cottage; the combination was an instant success. Nearby, **Hash House a Go Go,** 3628 Fifth Ave. (✆ 619/298-4646), is another quirky old bungalow with an equally eclectic pun-filled menu. They serve three meals a day, but breakfast is the locals' choice; better be hungry, because portions are mountainous.

EXPENSIVE

California Cuisine ✰✰ CALIFORNIAN   While this excellent restaurant's name is no longer as cutting-edge as when it opened in the early 1980s, the always-creative menu keeps up with contemporary trends. A quiet, understated dining room and delightfully romantic patio set the stage as the smoothly professional and respectful staff proffers fine dining at reasonable prices to a casual crowd.

The menu changes daily and contains mouth-watering appetizers like sesame-seared ahi with hot-and-sour raspberry sauce, or caramelized onion and Gruyère tart on balsamic baby greens. Main courses are, more often than not, stacked in trendy towers, and their flavors are composed with equal care: Blackened beef tenderloin sits atop sun-dried mashed potatoes surrounded by bright tomato

Bread & Cie **6**
Cafe W **8**
California Cuisine **2**
Corvette Diner **4**
Extraordinary Desserts **12**
Hash House a Go Go **10**
Hob Nob Hill **14**
Laurel **13**
Liaison **15**
Mixx **9**
Parallel 33 **7**
Pizza Nova **3**
Rubio's Baja Grill **5**
San Diego
  Chicken Pie Shop **1**
Vegetarian Zone **11**

puree, and Chilean sea bass is poached in saffron broth with tangy capers and buttery Yukon gold potatoes. Parking can be scarce along this busy stretch of University. You'll spot the light-strewn bushes in front of the restaurant.

1027 University Ave. (east of 10th St.). © 619/543-0790. www.californiacuisine.com. Reservations recommended for dinner. Main courses $15–$23. AE, DISC, MC, V. Tues–Fri 11am–10pm; Sat–Sun 5–10pm. Bus: 8, 11, 16, or 25.

Laurel ☆☆☆ FRENCH/MEDITERRANEAN Given its sophisticated decor, pedigreed chefs, prime Balboa Park location, and well-composed menu of country French dishes with a Mediterranean accent, it's no wonder this relatively new restaurant was an instant success. It's also popular with theatergoers, offering shuttle service to the Old Globe. Live piano music adds to the glamour of dining in this swank room on the ground floor of a new office building. Start by choosing from an extensive selection of tantalizing appetizers, including saffron-tinged red pepper-and-shellfish soup, veal sweetbreads with portobello mushrooms and grainy mustard sauce, and warm caramelized onion and Roquefort tart. Main courses include crisp Muscovy duck confit, roasted salmon with tangy red-beet vinaigrette, and venison in a rich shallot-port wine sauce. One of the most stylish choices near often-funky Hillcrest, Laurel has an almost New York ambience coupled with reasonable prices.

505 Laurel St. (at Fifth Ave.). © 619/239-2222. www.laurelrestaurant.com. Reservations recommended. Main courses $15–$26. AE, DC, DISC, MC, V. Sun–Thurs 5–10pm; Fri–Sat 5–11pm. Valet parking $6. Bus: 1, 3, or 25.

MODERATE

Hob Nob Hill ℱ AMERICAN/BREAKFAST   This homey coffee shop and deli began as a 14-stool lunch counter in 1944, and has grown into one of the most popular neighborhood hangouts in the city. At any given time it's a sure bet no patron lives farther than 5 miles (8km) away; this is no destination restaurant. You'll find comfort food at its best, priced reasonably enough for many regulars to dine here more often than in their own homes. The career waitresses are accustomed to plenty of hobnobbing professionals conducting power breakfasts over beef hash, oatmeal with pecans, or fried eggs with thick, hickory-smoked bacon. Stick-to-your-ribs meals appear at lunch and dinner—old favorites like chicken and dumplings, roast turkey, prime rib, or liver grilled with onions. It's a great place to bring the kids, especially on Sunday, when many local families come to observe a multigenerational dinner tradition.

2271 First Ave. (at Juniper St.). ℂ **619/239-8176.** Reservations recommended for dinner. Breakfast and lunch menu items $3.25–$8.55; dinner main courses $8–$14. AE, DC, DISC, MC, V. Daily 7am–9pm. Bus: 1, 3, or 25.

Liaison ℱℱ FRENCH   The cuisine and decor at this cozy, inviting cafe evoke a Gallic farmhouse kitchen. It has stone walls, blue-and-white tablecloths, candlelit tables, and copper pots hanging from the rafters. Conveniently located for Balboa Park theatergoers, this fave has a hearty French country menu that includes lamb curry, medallions of pork or beef, coquilles St. Jacques, roast duckling à l'orange, salmon with crayfish butter, and more. The nightly fixed price dinner—paté, soup, salad, main course, dessert, and wine for two—is a great deal. The house specialty dessert costs extra: a Grand Marnier chocolate or amaretto soufflé for two, at $6 per person. Ooh la la!

2202 Fourth Ave. (at Ivy St.). ℂ **619/234-5540.** Main courses $10.75–$19.75; fixed-price dinner $46 per couple. AE, DC, DISC, MC, V. Tues–Sun 5–10:30pm. Bus: 1, 3, or 25.

Mixx ℱℱ *Finds* CALIFORNIAN/INTERNATIONAL   Aptly named for its subtle global fusion fare, Mixx embodies everything good about Hillcrest dining: an attractive, relaxing room; a sophisticated crowd; thoughtfully composed dinners; and polished, friendly service. It's easy to see why hip locals gravitate to Mixx's wood-paneled, street-level cocktail lounge and the often-jovial dining room above. Menu standouts include a starter of pepper-seared ahi over ginger-jicama slaw, duck and wild mushroom ravioli, and pepper filet mignon on truffle mashed potatoes with an armagnac, cream, and port wine reduction. Even carnivores should check out chef Josh McGinnis's surprisingly inventive nightly vegetarian special. Prepared and presented with finesse, one meal here will quickly convince you that Mixx cares about style, substance, *and* value. Allow time to search for that elusive Hillcrest parking space!

3671 Fifth Ave. (at Pennsylvania Ave.). ℂ **619/299-6499.** Reservations recommended, especially on weekends. Main courses $14–$24. AE, DC, DISC, MC, V. Sun–Thurs 5–10pm; Fri–Sat 5–11pm. Bus: 1, 3, or 25.

Parallel 33 ℱℱ ECLECTIC/INTERNATIONAL   Inspired by a theory that all locales along the 33rd parallel of the globe might share the rich culinary traditions of the Tigris-Euphrates valley (birthplace of civilization), chef Amiko Gubbins presents a cuisine that beautifully combines flavors from Morocco, Lebanon, India, China, and Japan. Even if you find the concept befuddling, you're sure to savor the creativity displayed in a menu that leaps happily from fragrant Moroccan chicken *b'stilla* to soft shell crab crusted with *panko* (wispy Japanese bread crumbs) and black sesame seeds, and then enthusiastically back to grilled duck with fiery Chinese five-spice sauce alongside crisp spring rolls.

The ahi poke appetizer fuses a Hawaiian mainstay with sweet mango and Japanese wasabi—it's a winner! The restaurant is nice but not fancy, just an upscale neighborhood joint (in the most stylish section of town). A multiethnic Indian/African/Asian decor throws soft shadows throughout, inviting conversation and leisurely dining. This place was instantly popular after opening in 1999, and devout fans show no signs of waning—so reserve a table in advance.

741 W. Washington St. (at Falcon), Mission Hills. (C) **619/260-0033.** Reservations recommended. Main courses $17–$28. AE, DISC, MC, V. Mon–Thurs 5:30–10pm; Fri–Sat 5:30–11pm. Bus: 3, 8 or 16.

INEXPENSIVE

Bread & Cie. Bakery and Cafe ☆☆ LIGHT FARE/MEDITERRANEAN
Delicious aromas permeate this cavernous Hillcrest bakery, where the city's most unusually flavored breads are baked before your eyes all day long. The traditions of European artisan bread-making and attention to the fine points of texture and crust quickly catapulted Bread & Cie. to local stardom. Mouthwatering favorites include anise and fig, black olive, *panella dell'uva* (grape bread), and rye currant (weekends only). Even the relatively plain sourdough *batard* is tart, chewy perfection. Ask for a free sample, or order one of the many Mediterranean-inspired sandwiches on the bread of your choice. Try tuna niçoise on potato dill; mozzarella, roasted peppers, and olive tapenade on rosemary olive oil; or roast turkey with hot pepper cheese on jalapeño. The specialty coffee drinks make a perfect accompaniment to a light breakfast of fresh scones, muffins, and fruit turnovers. Seating is at bistro-style metal tables in full view of the busy ovens.

350 University Ave. (between Third and Fourth sts.). (C) **619/683-9322.** Sandwiches and light meals $3–$6. No credit cards. Mon–Fri 7am–7pm; Sat 7am–6pm; Sun 8am–6pm. Bus: 8, 11, or 16.

Corvette Diner ☆ *Kids* AMERICAN   Time travel back into the rockin' 1950s at this theme diner, where the jukebox is loud, the gum-snapping waitresses slide into your booth to take your order, and the decor is vintage Corvette to the highest power. Equal parts *Happy Days* hangout and Jackrabbit Slim's (from *Pulp Fiction*), the Corvette Diner is a comfy time warp in the midst of trendy Hillcrest, and the eats ain't bad, either. Burgers, sandwiches, appetizer munchies, blue-plate specials, and salads share the menu with a *very* full page of fountain favorites. Beer and wine are served, and there's a large bar in the center of the cavernous dining room. The party jumps a notch at night, with DJs and even a magician providing more entertainment (on top of the already entertaining atmosphere).

3946 Fifth Ave. (between Washington St. and University Ave.). (C) **619/542-1001.** Reservations not accepted. Main courses $5–$10. AE, DC, DISC, MC, V. Sun–Thurs 11am–10pm; Fri–Sat 11am–midnight. Free weekday valet parking; evening and weekend valet $4. Bus: 1 or 3.

Extraordinary Desserts ☆☆☆ DESSERTS   If you're a lover of sweets—heck, if you've ever eaten a dessert at all—you owe it to yourself to visit this unique cafe. Chef and proprietor Karen Krasne's name features prominently on the sign, as well it should: Krasne's talent surpasses the promise of her impressive pedigree, which includes a *Certificate de Patisserie* from Le Cordon Bleu in Paris. Dozens of divine creations are available daily, and even the humble carrot cake is savory enough to wow naysayers. Others include a raspberry Linzer torte layered with white-chocolate butter cream; Grand Marnier chocolate cheesecake on a brownie crust, sealed with bittersweet ganache; and, 24-karat chocolate praline dacquoise—crunchy chocolate praline mousse balanced by Frangelico-soaked hazelnut meringues and coated with dark chocolate and gold leaf.

Originally educated in Hawaii, Krasne likes to incorporate island touches like macadamia nuts, ultrafresh coconut, passion fruit, and pure Kona coffee. Her Parisian experience is also represented; the shop sells tea and accouterments from the fine salon Mariage Frères. If you're trying to moderate your diet, eat at the Vegetarian Zone next door (see review below)—it helps justify dessert!

2929 Fifth Ave. (between Palm and Quince sts.). © **619/294-7001**. www.extraordinarydesserts.com. Desserts $2–$9. MC, V. Mon–Thurs and Sun 8:30am–11pm; Fri 8:30am–midnight; Sat 11am–midnight. Bus: 1, 3, or 25.

San Diego Chicken Pie Shop ℛ (*Value* AMERICAN   Visitors might think this throwback diner is hidden away in a nondescript neighborhood northeast of Balboa Park, but residents and regulars know it well. Whether you're looking for a quick-but-hearty lunch, need a square meal on a Skid Row budget, desire a freezer-full of easy-bake dinners, or simply want to experience a genuine 1940s moment, this humble institution fits the bill. Decorated with 60+ years' worth of chicken (and turkey) tchotchkes sent by grateful patrons, the dining room is welcoming enough for solo diners, and casual enough for the kids' soccer team. The eponymous pies (fresh-from-the-oven) are so good, we've never even wanted to try the baked ham, roast sirloin, chicken-fried steak, or sautéed chicken livers on the dinner menu. But, they're there for dissenters, and a full dinner—including soup, potatoes, vegetable, cole slaw, bread, and dessert—clocks in at under $6! Order a $2 pie a la carte and you can still get a slice of apple pie for just 85¢. Ridiculous, huh? At lunchtime, sandwiches round out the menu.

2633 El Cajon Blvd. (at Oregon), North Park. © **619/295-0156**. Most menu items under $5. No credit cards. Daily 10am–8pm. Bus: 1.

The Vegetarian Zone ℛℛ VEGETARIAN   San Diego's only strictly vegetarian restaurant is a real treat, and word has gotten around—it's nearly always crowded, and everyone knows about it. Even if you're wary of tempeh, tofu, and meat substitutes, there are plenty of veggie ethnic selections on the menu. Greek spinach-and-feta pie has crispy edges and buttery phyllo layers; Indian turnovers are sweet and savory, flavored with pumpkin and curry; and, the Mediterranean roasted-vegetable sandwich is accented with smoky mozzarella cheese. If you're ordering salad, don't miss the tangy miso-ginger dressing. In business since 1975, the Vegetarian Zone has opened a deli next door. There's seating indoors and on a casual patio; soothing music creates a pleasant ambience enjoyed by trendy Hillcrest types, business lunchers, and the health-conscious from all walks of life. Wine is served by the glass. In case you feel deserving of a treat after such a healthful meal, the heavenly Extraordinary Desserts (see above) is next door.

2949 Fifth Ave. (between Palm and Quince sts.). © **619/298-7302**, or 619/298-9232 for deli and takeout. Reservations accepted only for parties of 6 or more. Main courses $5–$10. AE, DC, DISC, MC, V. Mon–Thurs 11:30am–9pm; Fri 11:30am–10pm; Sat 10:30am–10pm; Sun 10:30am–9pm. Free parking. Bus: 1, 3, or 25.

4 Old Town

Visitors usually have at least one meal in the Old Town area. San Diego's oldest historic district is also its most touristy, and most restaurants here follow suit—Mexican food and bathtub-size margaritas are the big draw, as are mariachi music and colorful decor. For a change of pace, try Cafe Pacifica, Berta's, or El Agave.

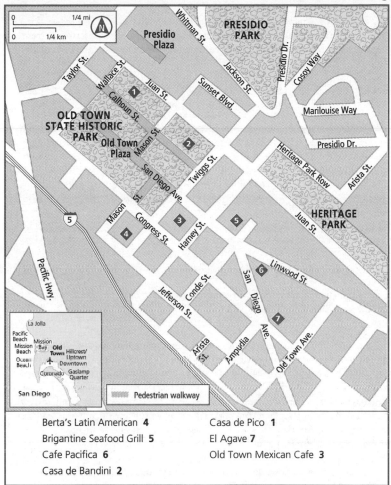

Berta's Latin American **4**   Casa de Pico **1**

Brigantine Seafood Grill **5**   El Agave **7**

Cafe Pacifica **6**   Old Town Mexican Cafe **3**

Casa de Bandini **2**

EXPENSIVE

Brigantine Seafood Grill ✧ SEAFOOD   The Brigantine is best known for its oyster-bar happy hour from 4 to 7pm (until 9:30pm on Mon). Beer, margaritas, and food are heavily discounted, and you can expect standing room only. Early bird dinners include seafood, steak, or chicken served with several side dishes and bread. The food is good but not great; it's above average for a chain, but the congenial atmosphere seems the primary draw. Inside, the decor is upscale and nautical; outside, there's a pleasant patio with a fireplace to take the chill off the night air. At lunch, you can get everything from crab cakes or fish and chips to fresh fish or pasta. Lunch specials come with sourdough bread and two side dishes. The bar and oyster bar are open daily until midnight.

There's also a Brigantine Seafood Grill in **Coronado,** at 1333 Orange Ave. (© **619/435-4166**).

2444 San Diego Ave. ℂ **619/298-9840.** Reservations recommended on weekends. Main courses $8–$30; early bird special (Sun–Thurs 5–7pm) $10–$14. AE, DC, MC, V. Mon–Thurs 11am–10:30pm; Fri–Sat 11am–11pm; Sun 10am–10:30pm. Bus: 5/5A. Trolley: Old Town.

Cafe Pacifica ★★ CALIFORNIAN/SEAFOOD   You can't tell a book by its cover: Inside this cozy Old Town *casita*, the decor is cleanly contemporary (but still romantic) and the food anything but Mexican. Established in 1980 by the now revered duo of Kipp Downing and Deacon Brown, Cafe Pacifica serves upscale, imaginative seafood and produces kitchen alumni who go on to enjoy local fame. Among the temptations on the menu are crab-stuffed portobello mushroom topped with grilled asparagus, anise-scented bouillabaisse, and daily fresh-fish selections served grilled with your choice of five sauces. Signature items include Hawaiian ahi with shiitake mushrooms and ginger butter, griddled mustard catfish, and the "Pomerita," a pomegranate margarita. Patrons tend to dress up, though it's not required. To avoid the crowds, arrive in the early evening.

2414 San Diego Ave. ℂ **619/291-6666.** www.cafepacifica.com. Reservations recommended. Main courses $12–$22. AE, DC, DISC, MC, V. Mon–Sat 5:30–10pm; Sun 5–9:30pm. Valet parking $4. Bus: 5/5A. Trolley: Old Town.

El Agave Tequilaria ★★ MEXICAN   Don't be misled by this restaurant's less-than-impressive location—above a liquor store on the outskirts of Old Town. This warm, bustling eaterie continues to draw local gourmands for the regional Mexican cuisine and rustic elegance that leave the touristy fajitas-and-cerveza joints of Old Town far behind. El Agave is named for the agave plant from which tequilas are derived, and they boast more than 600 boutique and artisan tequilas from throughout the Latin world—bottles of every size, shape, and jewel-like hue fill shelves and cases throughout the dining room. But even teetotalers will enjoy the restaurant's authentically flavored *mole* sauces (from Chiapas, rich with peanuts; tangy tomatillo from Oaxaca; the more familiar dark mole flavored with chocolate and sesame), along with giant shrimp and sea bass prepared in a dozen variations, or El Agave's signature beef filet with goat cheese and dark tequila sauce.

2304 San Diego Ave. ℂ **619/220-0692.** www.elagaverestaurant.com. Reservations recommended. Main courses $12–$22. AE, MC, V. Daily 11am–10pm. Street parking. Bus: 5/5A. Trolley: Old Town.

MODERATE

Berta's Latin American Restaurant ★★ *Finds* LATIN AMERICAN   Berta's is a welcome change from the nacho-and-fajita joints that dominate Old Town dining, though it can attract as large a crowd on weekends. Housed in a charming, basic cottage tucked away on a side street, Berta's faithfully re-creates the sunny flavors of Central America, where slow cooking mellows the heat of chilies and other spices. Everyone starts with a basket of fresh flour tortillas and mild salsa verde, which usually vanishes before you're done contemplating such mouthwatering dishes as Guatemalan *chilimal,* a rich pork-and-vegetable casserole with chilies, tomatoes, cornmeal *masa,* cilantro, and cloves. Try the Salvadoran *pupusas* (at lunch only)—dense corn-mash turnovers with melted cheese and black beans, their texture perfectly offset with crunchy cabbage salad and one of Berta's special salsas. Or opt for a table full of Spanish-style tapas, grazing alternately on crispy *empanadas* (filled turnovers), strong Spanish olives, or *Pincho Moruno,* skewered lamb and onion redolent of spices and red saffron.

3928 Twiggs St. (at Congress St.). ℂ **619/295-2343.** Main courses $5–$7 at lunch, $11–$13 at dinner. AE, MC, V. Tues–Sun 11am–10pm (lunch menu until 3pm). Bus: 5/5A. Trolley: Old Town.

Family-Friendly Restaurants

Casa de Bandini (below)   With the ambient noise of fountains and mariachis, fidgety children won't feel like they have to be on best behavior at this casual Mexican eatery—there's also plenty for them to wander and look at.

Corvette Diner (p. 105)   Resembling a 1950s diner, this place appeals to teens and preteens. Parents will have fun reminiscing, and kids will enjoy the burgers and fries or other short-order fare, served in sock-hop surroundings.

Filippi's Pizza Grotto (p. 101)   Children's portions are available, and kids will feel right at home at this red-checked-vinyl-tablecloth joint. The pizzas are among the best in town.

Old Spaghetti Factory (p. 101)   Kids get special attention here, and even their own toys. There's a play area, too.

Casa de Bandini ✿ *Kids* MEXICAN   As much an Old Town tradition as the mariachi music that's played here on weekends, Casa de Bandini is the most picturesque of several Mexican restaurants with predictable food and birdbath-size margaritas. It fills the nooks and crannies of an adobe hacienda built in 1823 for Juan Bandini, a local merchant and politician. The superbly renovated enclosed patio has iron gates, flowers blooming around a bubbling fountain, and umbrella-shaded tables for year-round alfresco dining. Some of the dishes are gourmet Mexican, others simple south-of-the-border fare. The crowd consists mainly of out-of-towners, but the ambience and towering tostada salads draw a lunchtime crowd. The setting makes this restaurant extra-special, and makes the less-than-remarkable meal worthwhile.

2754 Calhoun St. (opposite Old Town Plaza). ✆ 619/297-8211. www.casadebandini.com. Reservations not accepted. Main courses $6–$16. AE, DC, DISC, MC, V. Daily 11am–9pm (until 10pm in summer). Free parking. Bus: 5/5A. Trolley: Old Town.

Casa de Pico MEXICAN   The heartbeat of Bazaar del Mundo, Casa de Pico has a carnival atmosphere and a colorful courtyard complete with a fountain, flags, umbrellas, and mariachis who will serenade your table on request. The restaurant sits on the original site of the home of General Pío Pico, the last governor of Mexican California. Diagrammed explanations of Mexican dishes on the menu are a tip-off to the touristy element, but plenty of visitors are eager to dine at the heart of Old Town's historic center. A selection of bodacious margaritas helps keep things lively. The menu holds no surprises to anyone familiar with enchiladas, tacos, and burritos; a popular selection is the Mexican sampler, "La Especial de Juan," with chimichangas, enchiladas, and fajitas. To avoid standing in line for a table, try coming here before 5pm or after 8pm Sunday through Thursday.

2754 Calhoun St. ✆ 619/296-3267. www.casadepico.com. Reservations not accepted. Main courses $5–$14. AE, DC, MC, V. Sun–Thurs 10am–9pm; Fri–Sat 10am–9:30pm. Free parking. Bus: 5/5A. Trolley: Old Town.

INEXPENSIVE
Old Town Mexican Cafe ✿ MEXICAN   This place is so popular that it's become an Old Town tourist attraction in its own right. It keeps expanding into

additional colorful dining rooms and outdoor patios, but the wait for a table is still often 30 to 60 minutes. Pass the time gazing in from the sidewalk as tortillas are hand-patted the old-fashioned way, soon to be a hot-off-the-grill treat accompanying every meal. Once inside, order what some consider the best margarita in town, followed by one of the cafe's two specialties: *carnitas,* the traditional Mexican dish of deep-fried pork served with tortillas, guacamole, sour cream, beans, and rice; or rotisserie chicken with the same trimmings. It's loud and crowded and the *cerveza* flows like, well, beer . . . but this Old Town mainstay is the best in the city for traditional Mexican.

2489 San Diego Ave. ℂ 619/297-4330. Reservations accepted only for parties of 10 or more. Main courses $7.50–$11.50. AE, DISC, MC, V. Sun–Thurs 7am–11pm; Fri–Sat 7am–midnight; bar service until 2am. Bus: 5/5A. Trolley: Old Town.

5 Mission Bay & the Beaches

Generally speaking, restaurants at the beach exist primarily to provide an excuse for sitting and gazing at the water. Because this activity is most commonly accompanied by steady drinking, it stands to reason that the food isn't often remarkable. We've tried to balance the most scenic of these typical hangouts with places actually known for outstanding food—with a little effort, they can be found.

Noteworthy beach spots include **Kono's Surf Club Cafe,** 704 Garnet Ave., Pacific Beach (ℂ **858/483-1669**), a Hawaiian-themed boardwalk breakfast shack that's cheap and delicious. A plump Kono's breakfast burrito provides enough fuel for a day of surfing or sightseeing, while a side order of savory "Kono Potatoes" is a meal in itself.

VERY EXPENSIVE

Baleen ✫✫✫ SEAFOOD/CALIFORNIAN   Crowning the multimillion-dollar transformation of the former Vacation Village into the contemporary playground Paradise Point Resort, this fine waterfront eatery is exactly the touch of class planners hoped for when they lured celebrity restaurateur Robbin Haas (creator of Baleens in Coconut Grove and Naples, Fla.). With a spectacular bay-front view (and dining deck for pleasant weather), it's easy to miss the design details indoors—from a monkey motif that includes simians hanging off chandeliers, to specialized serving platters for many of Baleen's artistically arranged dishes. Start with chilled lobster in a martini glass, a warm salad of roasted mushrooms and asparagus, or fresh oysters delivered in a small cart and shucked table side. Then savor a selection of seafood simply grilled, wood-roasted, or sautéed with hummus crust, honey wasabi glaze, or ginger sauce. Wood-roasted meats include Roquefort-crusted filet mignon and veal T-bone marinated in olive oil, rosemary, and roasted garlic. Should you have appetite—and credit—left over, indulge in an intricately rich dessert like chocolate fondue, or the quartet of fruit-infused custards.

In Paradise Point Resort, 1404 Vacation Rd., Mission Bay. ℂ 858/490-6363. www.paradisepoint.com. Reservations recommended. Main courses $10–$21 lunch, $18–$30 dinner. AE, DC, DISC, MC, V. Sun–Thurs 7am–9pm; Fri–Sat 7am–11pm. Follow I-8 west to Mission Bay Dr. exit; take Ingraham St. north to Vacation Rd.

EXPENSIVE

Qwiig's ✫✫ CALIFORNIAN   It's taken more than a sunset view overlooking the Ocean Beach Pier to keep this upscale bar and grill going since 1985; the restaurant owes its consistent popularity to first-rate food served without

Dining in Mission Bay & the Beaches

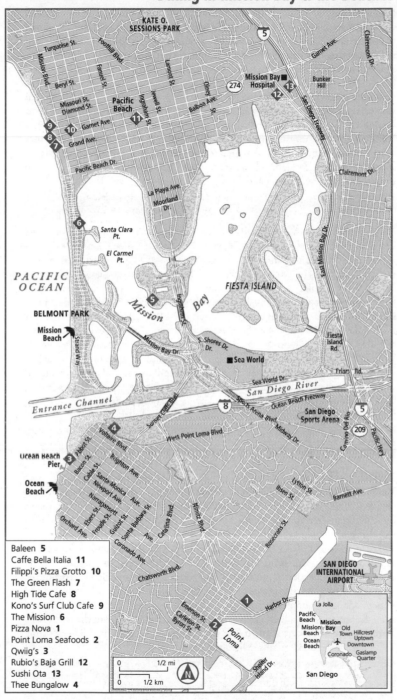

Baleen **5**
Caffe Bella Italia **11**
Filippi's Pizza Grotto **10**
The Green Flash **7**
High Tide Cafe **8**
Kono's Surf Club Cafe **9**
The Mission **6**
Pizza Nova **1**
Point Loma Seafoods **2**
Qwiig's **3**
Rubio's Baja Grill **12**
Sushi Ota **13**
Thee Bungalow **4**

pretense. Every table faces the sea, but the best view is from slightly elevated crescent-shaped booths (ask for one when reserving). Even the after-work crowd that gathers at the bar to munch on fried calamari, artichokes, and oysters can see to the pier; only sushi bar patrons in the corner miss out on the view.

Large and welcoming, Qwiig's hums pleasantly with conversation and serves food that's better than any other view-intense oceanfront spot in this area. The fresh-fish specials are most popular; choices often include rare ahi with braised spinach and sesame-sherry sauce, and Chilean sea bass with lime, tequila, and roasted garlic. Several seafood pastas are offered. Meat and poultry dishes include prime rib, an outstanding half-pound burger, and nightly specials that always shine. Wines are well matched to the cuisine, and there are imaginative, special cocktails each night. The restaurant got its strange name from a group of Ocean Beach surfers nicknamed "qwiigs."

5083 Santa Monica St. (at Abbott St.), Ocean Beach. © 619/222-1101. Reservations recommended. Main courses $12–$24. AE, MC, V. Mon–Fri 11:30am–9pm; Sat 5–10pm; Sun 5–9pm. Bus: 23 or 35.

Thee Bungalow 🍴🍴 FRENCH/CONTINENTAL This small cottage stands alone at the edge of Robb Field near the Ocean Beach channel, a romantic hideaway beckoning diners for consistently good Continental cuisine augmented by a well-chosen, well-priced wine list. By far the fanciest restaurant in laid-back Ocean Beach, Thee Bungalow endears itself to the local crowd with daily early bird specials ($12–$16). The house specialty is crispy roast duck, served with your choice of sauce (the best are black cherry or spiced pepper rum), ideally followed by one of the decadent, made-to-order dessert soufflés for two (chocolate or Grand Marnier). Another menu standout is *osso buco*–style lamb shank adorned with shallot-red-wine puree. Equally appealing first courses include brie and asparagus baked in puff pastry, and warm chicken salad (stuffed with sun-dried tomatoes and basil, and then presented with feta cheese and fruit, it also doubles as a light meal). There's always a sampler plate featuring house-made patés with Dijon, cornichons, capers, and little toasts.

4996 W. Point Loma Blvd. (at Bacon St.), Ocean Beach. © 619/224-2884. www.theebungalow.com. Reservations recommended. Main courses $16–$27; early bird specials $12–$16. AE, MC, V. Mon–Thurs 5:30–9:30pm; Fri–Sat 5–10pm; Sun 5–9pm. Free parking. Bus: 26 or 34B.

MODERATE

Caffe Bella Italia 🍴🍴 ITALIAN You'd think passersby might flock to this excellent family run Garnet Avenue newcomer, but most just look . . . and keep on walking or driving. They're discouraged by Bella Italia's—the kindest word I can think of is *underwhelming*—street presence, housed in a former plain-Jane stucco dry cleaner. Trust me on this one: It's lovely inside, and the food will knock your socks off. Romantic lighting, sheer draperies, and warmly earthy walls create an unexpected ambience, assisted by the lilting Milan accents of the staff. Every item on the menu bears the unmistakable flavor of freshness and homemade care—even the simplest curled-edge ravioli stuffed with ricotta, spinach, and pine nuts is elevated to culinary nirvana. Indulge in the traditional *tartufo* ice cream dessert (bathed in a shot of espresso), and you'll leave wishing you could be adopted by this delicious family.

1525 Garnet Ave. (between Ingraham and Haines), Pacific Beach. © 858/273-1224. www.caffebellaitalia.com. Reservations suggested for dinner. Lunch $7–$11; dinner $9–21. AE, MC, V. Tues–Thurs 11:30am–2:30pm and 5–10pm; Fri–Sat 11:30am–2:30pm and 5–11pm; Sun 5–10pm. Free parking lot. Bus: 27.

The Green Flash ☆ AMERICAN   Known throughout Pacific Beach for its location and hip, local clientele, the Green Flash serves reasonably good (and typically beachy) food at decent prices. The menu includes plenty of grilled and deep-fried seafood, straightforward steaks, and giant main-course salads. You'll also find platters of shellfish (oysters, clams, shrimp) and ethnic appetizers. On the glassed-in patio, locals congregate every evening to catch a glimpse of the optical phenomenon for which this boardwalk hangout is named. It has something to do with the color spectrum at the moment the sun disappears below the horizon, but the scientific explanation becomes less important—and the decibel level rises—with every round of drinks.

701 Thomas Ave. (at Mission Blvd.), Pacific Beach. ☎ 858/270-7715. Reservations not accepted. Main courses $10–$20; sunset specials Sun–Thurs 4:30–6pm. AE, DC, DISC, MC, V. Daily 8am–10pm (bar until 2am). Bus: 34/34A.

Sushi Ota ☆ JAPANESE   If you like statistics, you should know that chef-owner Yukito Ota's masterful sushi garnered a nearly perfect food rating in the San Diego *Zagat Survey.* This sophisticated, traditional restaurant (no Asian fusion here) is a minimalist bento box with stark white walls and black furniture, softened by indirect lighting. The sushi menu is short, because savvy regulars look first to the 8 to 10 daily specials posted behind the counter. The city's most experienced chefs, armed with nimble fingers and very sharp knives, turn the day's fresh catch into artful little bundles accented with mounds of wasabi and ginger. The rest of the varied menu features seafood, teriyaki-glazed meats, feather-light tempura, and a variety of small appetizers perfect to accompany a large sushi order.

This restaurant is difficult to find, mainly because it's hard to believe that such outstanding dining would hide behind a Laundromat and convenience store in the rear of a mini-mall that's perpendicular to the street. It's also in a nondescript part of Pacific Beach, nearer to I-5 than the ocean, but none of that should discourage you from seeking it out.

4529 Mission Bay Dr. (at Bunker Hill), Mission Bay. ☎ 858/270-5670. Reservations recommended on weekends. Main courses $8–$15; sushi $2.50–$8. AE, MC, V. Tues–Fri 11am–2pm; daily 5:30–10:30pm.

INEXPENSIVE

High Tide Cafe AMERICAN   Ceiling fans stir the air in this cheerful, comfortably crowded place, and there's pleasant rooftop dining with an ocean view if you're lucky enough to snag a seat. Just off the Pacific Beach boardwalk, the cafe sees a lot of foot traffic and socializing locals. Those in the know go for great breakfasts—choices include Mexican-style eggs and breakfast burritos, French toast, and omelets. During happy hour (4–6pm), you'll find bargain prices on drinks and finger-lickin' appetizers. The rest of the menu is adequate, running the gamut from fish tacos to Tex-Mex fajitas to lasagna and all-American burgers.

722 Grand Ave., Pacific Beach. ☎ 858/272-1999. Reservations recommended on weekends. Main courses $6–$13. AE, DISC, MC, V. Sun–Thurs 7am–9pm; Fri–Sat 7am–10pm. Free parking. Bus: 34/34A.

The Mission *(Value* BREAKFAST/COFFEE & TEA   Located alongside the funky surf shops, bikini boutiques, and alternative galleries of bohemian Mission Beach, the Mission is this neighborhood's central meeting place. But it's good enough to attract more than just locals, and now has an upscale sister location east of Hillcrest that serves dinner. At the beach, the menu features all-day breakfasts (from traditional pancakes to nouvelle egg dishes and Latin-flavored burritos and quesadillas), plus light lunch sandwiches and salads. Standouts include tamales and eggs with tomatillo sauce, chicken-apple sausage with eggs and a mound of rosemary potatoes, and cinnamon French toast with blackberry puree. Seating is casual, comfy, and conducive to lingering (tons of students, writers, and diarists hang out here), if only with a soup bowl–size latte.

The other location is in **North Park,** at 2801 University Ave. (© 619/ 220-8992).

3795 Mission Blvd. (at San Jose), Mission Beach. © 858/488-9060. Menu items $4.50–$8. AE, MC, V. Daily 7am–3pm. Bus: 27, 34, 34A, or 34B.

6 La Jolla

As befits an upscale community with time (and money) on its hands, La Jolla seems to have more than its fair share of good restaurants. Happily, they are mostly affordable, and more ethnically diverse than you might expect in a community that still supports a haberdashery called The Ascot Shop. While many restaurants are clustered in the village, on Prospect Street and the few blocks directly east, you can also cruise down La Jolla Boulevard or up by the La Jolla Beach & Tennis Club for additional choices.

Branches of establishments described elsewhere in this chapter include the reliable **Chart House,** 1270 Prospect St. (© 858/459-8201).

La Jolla restaurants don't serve very late. If you get hungry after the traditional dinner hour, head for **Karl Strauss Brewery & Grill,** 1044 Wall St. (© 858/ 551-BREW), where the kitchen stays open until 9pm Monday through Wednesday, 10pm on Thursday and Sunday, and 11pm on Friday and Saturday (see "Pitcher This: San Diego's Microbreweries" in chapter 10 for more information).

VERY EXPENSIVE

George's at the Cove ✿✿✿ CALIFORNIAN   You'll find host and namesake George Hauer at his restaurant's door most nights; he greets loyal regulars by name, and his confidence assures newcomers that they'll leave impressed with this beloved La Jolla tradition. Voted most popular in the *Zagat Survey,* George's wins consistent praise for impeccable service, gorgeous views of the cove, and outstanding California cuisine.

The menu, in typical San Diego fashion, presents many inventive seafood options, filtered through the myriad influences of chef Trey Foshee. Classical culinary training, Hawaiian ingenuity, and a stint at Robert Redford's Utah Sundance resort are among his many accomplishments. Dishes combine many flavors with practiced artistry, ranging from the Asian-tinged grilled swordfish atop gingered vegetables accented with Thai coconut sauce, to a Provençal-inspired rack of lamb in aromatic spices with Foshee's version of ratatouille. George's signature smoked chicken, broccoli, and black-bean soup is still a mainstay; they'll even give out the recipe for this local legend. As an alternative to dinner's pricey main courses, try the tasting menu, which offers a seasonally composed five-course sampling for around $50 per person; or, try the more reasonably priced lunch menu. The informal Ocean Terrace Cafe (see review later in this section) is upstairs.

1250 Prospect St. © 858/454-4244. www.georgesatthecove.com. Reservations recommended. Lunch $13–$17; dinner $25–$35. AE, DC, DISC, MC, V. Mon–Fri 11:30am–2:30pm; Sat–Sun 11:30am–3pm; Mon–Thurs 5:30–10pm; Fri–Sat 5–10:30pm; Sun 5–10pm. Valet parking $5–$6.

La Jolla Dining

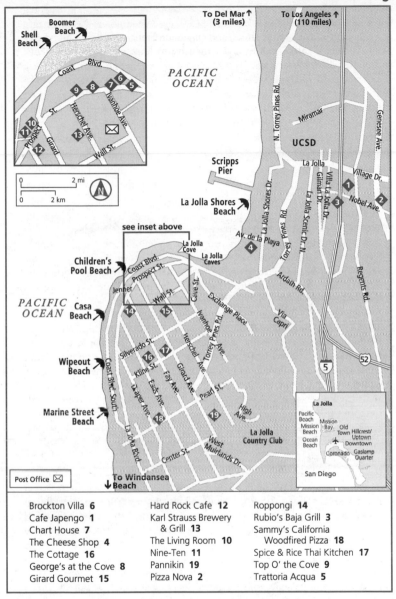

Brockton Villa **6**	Hard Rock Cafe **12**	Roppongi **14**
Cafe Japengo **1**	Karl Strauss Brewery	Rubio's Baja Grill **3**
Chart House **7**	& Grill **13**	Sammy's California
The Cheese Shop **4**	The Living Room **10**	Woodfired Pizza **18**
The Cottage **16**	Nine-Ten **11**	Spice & Rice Thai Kitchen **17**
George's at the Cove **8**	Pannikin **19**	Top O' the Cove **9**
Girard Gourmet **15**	Pizza Nova **2**	Trattoria Acqua **5**

Top O' the Cove ♦♦♦ CONTINENTAL   Always voted "most romantic" in annual diner surveys, Top O' the Cove is traditionally where San Diegans go for special occasions—first dates, marriage proposals, anniversaries. They're banking that its timeless elegance will enhance the evening's mood, and they're rarely disappointed. The finely proportioned historic cottage is one of the last remaining along Prospect Street, and it's shaded by 100-year-old Australian fig trees. Fireplaces glow on chilly evenings, and a gazebo and patio make the perfect setting for balmy summer dining or Sunday brunch.

The menu is peppered with French names and classic preparations with just a few welcome contemporary accents. Standouts include bacon-wrapped filet mignon in a Cabernet sauce, duck breast dressed with tamarind glaze and a mild five-spice kick, a Mediterranean-style crusted lamb loin, and lobster ravioli in a warm mushroom broth. Sorbet is served between courses. Lunch is lighter; salads, sandwiches, and pasta bring a sunny Mediterranean flavor. The dessert specialty is a bittersweet-chocolate box filled with cream and fruit in a raspberry sauce—try it with a liqueur-laced house coffee. Aficionados will thrill to the extensive wine list, but its steep markup threatens to spoil the mood.

1216 Prospect St. © 858/454-7779. www.topofthecove.com. Reservations recommended. Jackets suggested for men at dinner. Lunch $10–$22; dinner $25–$38. AE, MC, V. Daily 11:30am–11:30pm. Valet parking $6.

EXPENSIVE

Cafe Japengo 🐾🐾 JAPANESE/SUSHI/PACIFIC RIM/ASIAN FUSION

Despite being contrived and self-conscious, Cafe Japengo is worth a trip for the food alone. With subdued lighting and a highly stylized Asian atmosphere, this restaurant is the best of several attached to the Golden Triangle's behemoth Hyatt Regency Hotel. The beautiful people know they look even more so among the warm woods and leafy shadows here, so there's lots of posing and people-watching. It's always packed; patrons come from all over the county for Japengo's Pacific Rim fusion cuisine, which incorporates South American and even European touches.

Some offerings, like the pot stickers in tangy cilantro-mint sauce or lemon-grass-marinated swordfish, are superb; others, like the seared ahi "napoleon," suffer from extra ingredients that just make the dish fussy. Sushi here is the same way; Japengo features the finest and freshest fish, but churns out enormously popular specialty rolls (combinations wrapped in even more ingredients, often drenched in sauce and garnished even further). The dramatic, colorfully presented inventions are enormously popular, but sushi purists will be happiest sticking to the basics.

At the Hyatt Regency La Jolla, 8960 University Center Lane. © 858/450-3355. Reservations recommended. Main courses $14–$28. AE, DC, DISC, MC, V. Mon–Fri 11:30am–2:30pm; Sun–Thurs 5–10pm; Fri–Sat 5–10:30pm. Sushi bar open until 11pm Mon–Thurs, midnight Fri–Sat. Valet parking $3, validated self-parking free. From I-5, take La Jolla Village Dr. E.

Roppongi 🐾 PACIFIC RIM/ASIAN FUSION/ECLECTIC

Restaurateur Sami Ladeki (Sammy's California Woodfired Pizza) proves once again he knows his audience with this always-crowded media darling where the cuisines of Japan, Thailand, China, Vietnam, Korea, and India collide in a creative explosion of flavors. You might not get past the first menu page, a long list of small tapas dishes designed for sharing—each table is even preset with a tall stack of plates that quietly encourage a communal meal of successive appetizers. It takes an adventuresome palate to hip-hop from Thai satay to Chinese pot stickers to a Mongolian duck quesadilla—then back to Indonesian spicy shrimp—without missing a beat. Traditionally sized main courses feature seafood, meat, and game all colorfully prepared, and the weekend brunch menu is also a real eye-opener. Although the restaurant claims to utilize the Chinese discipline of feng shui to enhance contentment among diners, I couldn't shake the suspicion this bamboo-and-booth interior was like a Bangkok version of Denny's. That's alright, because day or night the outdoor patio is always preferable, anchored by a leaping fire pit and accented with ponds and torches.

875 Prospect St. (at Fay Ave.) © 858/551-5252. www.roppongiusa.com. Reservations recommended. Tapas $7–$16, main courses $15–$24. AE, DISC, MC, V. Sun–Thurs 11:30am–10pm; Fri–Sat 11:30am–11pm.

Nine-Ten 𝕽𝕽𝕽 CALIFORNIAN/MEDITERRANEAN   The anticipation was almost too much to bear as eager La Jollans awaited this overhaul of venerable Putnam's, and the arrival of pedigreed chef Michael Stebner. We're happy to report, though, there are no signs of overhype or spotlight jitters here; Stebner delivers on a superbly crafted and executed menu in a warmly stylish and understated space. Window-side and sidewalk tables enjoy a street scene of La Jolla's beautiful people, who in turn gaze in at mouthwatering seasonal presentations like chestnut agnolotti with fennel and sweet squash, rich veal tenderloin with rosemary and olives atop creamy polenta, and scallops braised in a rich mushroom broth. A favorite Stebner wouldn't dare take off the menu is the delicious porcini risotto topped with lobster and aromatic white truffle oil. We particularly appreciate the multitude of "tasting portions," a boon to smaller appetites or creative types who want to compose their own multicourse "sampling" meal. It also helps leave room for never-too-heavy desserts like spicy carrot-parsnip cake, persimmon panna cotta, or refreshing honey-rosemary ice cream. When you're looking for a classy fine-dining experience—with none of the old guard "fancy" attitude—this hotel eatery stands alone on the culinary scene.

910 Prospect St. (between Fay and Girard aves.). © 858/964-5400. www.thegrandecolonial.com. Reservations recommended. Lunch main courses $8–$12; dinner $18–$32. AE, DC, DISC, MC, V. Daily 6:30–11am, 11:30am–2:30pm, and 6–10:30pm.

Trattoria Acqua 𝕽𝕽 ITALIAN/MEDITERRANEAN   Nestled on tiled terraces close enough to catch ocean breezes, this excellent northern Italian spot has a more relaxed ambience than similarly sophisticated Gaslamp Quarter trattorias. Rustic walls and outdoor seating shaded by flowering vines evoke a romantic Tuscan villa. A mixed crowd of suits and well-heeled couples gather to enjoy expertly prepared seasonal dishes; every table starts with bread served with an indescribably pungent Mediterranean spread. Acqua's pastas (all available as appetizers or main courses) are as good as it gets—rich, heady flavor combinations like spinach, chard, and four-cheese gnocchi, or veal-and-mortadella tortellini in fennel cream sauce. Other specialties include *saltimbocca con funghi* (veal scaloppini with sage, prosciutto, and forest mushroom sauce), *cassoulet* (traditional Toulouse-style duck confit, sausage, and braised lamb baked with white beans, tomato, and fresh thyme), and *salmone al pepe* (roasted peppercorn-crusted Atlantic salmon served over lentils with sherry-and-shallot vinaigrette). The well-chosen wine list has received *Wine Spectator* accolades several years in a row.

1298 Prospect St. (on Coast Walk). © 858/454-0709. www.trattoriaacqua.com. Reservations recommended. Main courses $13–$27. AE, MC, V. Daily 11:30am–2:30pm; Sun–Thurs 5–9:30pm; Fri–Sat 5–10:30pm. Validated self-parking.

MODERATE

Brockton Villa 𝕽𝕽 *Finds* BREAKFAST/CALIFORNIAN/COFFEE & TEA/LIGHT FARE   In a restored 1894 beach bungalow, this charming cafe has a history as intriguing as its varied, eclectic menu. Named for an early resident's hometown (Brockton, Mass.), the cottage is imbued with the spirit of artistic souls drawn to this breathtaking perch overlooking La Jolla Cove. Rescued by the trailblazing Pannikin Coffee Company in the 1960s, the restaurant is now independently run by a Pannikin alum.

Finds Java Joints in La Jolla

While cafes specializing in espresso, latte, and cappuccino have sprung up all over San Diego, no other area caters to java hounds the way La Jolla does. Here are two area coffeehouses that serve up caffeine as well as charm. (They appear on the "La Jolla Dining" map on p. 115.)

When it opened in 1968, the **Pannikin,** 7467 Girard Ave., near Pearl Street (**©** **858/454-5453**), was La Jolla's first coffeehouse, and, in some ways, it still seems frozen in 1968. Long-haired men ponder chess moves on the porch, and the notice board touts meditation seminars. This is a favored hangout of UCSD students and faculty. Inside the old house, the fireplace and communal seating are conducive to impromptu intellectual discussions. Some customers wander next door to the D. G. Wills bookstore. The Pannikin's retail store across the street draws loyal locals.

At the **Living Room,** 1010 Prospect St., at Girard Ave. (**©** **858/459-1187;** www.livingroomcafe.com), you're liable to hear the foreign buzz of conversations from students on break from the International Language School across the street. Grab a sidewalk table and enjoy some splendid people-watching and/or breakfast, lunch, or light dinner fare from the extensive cafe menu. This local minichain (four other San Diego locations) is also known for temptingly good pastries and desserts. The Living Room is a good choice for early risers and insomniacs alike: They're open daily from 6am to midnight.

And we always recommend **Brockton Villa** (see full review on p. 117), where a blissful view of La Jolla Cove can keep you transfixed for hours—as long as you're drinking decaf, that is!

No matter where you enjoy your java, mind the time limit for your parking spot. La Jolla doesn't have meters, but street parking in the village is restricted to 1 or 2 hours, and zealous parking-enforcement officers dole out tickets with regularity.

The biggest buzz is at breakfast, when you can enjoy inventive dishes such as soufflélike "Coast Toast" (the house take on French toast) and Greek "steamers" (eggs scrambled with an espresso steamer, then mixed with feta cheese, tomato, and basil). The dozens of coffee drinks include the "Keith Richards"—four shots of espresso topped with Mexican hot chocolate (Mother's Little Helper indeed!). Lunch stars include homemade soups and salads, plus unusual sandwiches like turkey meat loaf on toasted sourdough bread with spicy tomato-mint chutney. The constantly expanding dinner menu includes salmon *en croûte* (wrapped in prosciutto, Gruyère, and sage, with a grainy mustard sauce), plus pastas, stews, and grilled meats. Steep stairs from the street limit access for wheelchair users.

1235 Coast Blvd. (across from La Jolla Cove). **©** **858/454-7393.** Reservations recommended (call by Thurs for Sun brunch). Breakfast $4–$8; dinner main courses $12–$21. AE, DISC, MC, V. Mon 8am–5pm; Tues–Sun 8am–9pm.

George's Ocean Terrace and Cafe/Bar ☆☆ CALIFORNIAN The legendary main dining room at George's at the Cove has won numerous awards for its haute cuisine. But George's also accommodates those seeking good food and a spectacular setting with a more reasonable price tag—the upstairs Ocean Terrace and Cafe prepares similar dishes as well as new creations in the same kitchen

Booked seat 6A, open return.

Rented red 4-wheel drive.

Reserved cabin, no running water.

Discovered space.

With over 700 airlines, 50,000 hotels, 50 rental car companies and 5,000 cruise and vacation packages, you can create the perfect get-away for you. Choose the car, the room, even the ground you walk on.

Travelocity.com
A Sabre Company
Go Virtually Anywhere.

Book your air, hotel, and transportation all in one place.

Hotel or hostel? Cruise or canoe? Car?
Plane? Camel? Wherever you're going,
visit Yahoo! Travel and get total control
over your arrangements. Even choose
your seat assignment. So. One hump
or two? travel.yahoo.com

powered by
COMPAQ

YAHOO!
Travel

as the high-priced fare. The two areas offer indoor and outdoor seating over-looking La Jolla Cove, and the same great service as the main dining room. For dinner, you can choose from several seafood or pasta dishes, or have something out of the ordinary like George's meatloaf served with mushroom-and-corn mashed potatoes. The award-winning smoked chicken, broccoli, and black-bean soup appears on both menus.

1250 Prospect St. © 858/454-4244. www.georgesatthecove.com. Reservations not accepted. Lunch $10–$15; dinner $9.50–$14.95. AE, DC, DISC, MC, V. Sun–Thurs 11am–10pm; Fri–Sat 11am–10:30pm. Valet parking $6.

Spice & Rice Thai Kitchen ⋆ THAI   This stylish Thai restaurant is a couple of blocks from the village's tourist crush—far enough to ensure effortless parking. The lunch crowd consists of shoppers and curious tourists, while dinner is quieter; all the local businesses have shut down and many diners are going to the old-fashioned Cove movie theater next door. The food is excellent, with polished presentations and expert renditions of the classics like pad Thai, satay, curry, and glazed duck. The starters often sound as good as the entrees—consider making a grazing meal of house specialties like "gold bags" (minced pork, vegetables, and herbs wrapped in crispy rice paper and served with earthy plum sauce) or minced roast duck spiced with chilies and lime juice; spicy calamari is flavored with ginger, cilantro, lime, and chili sauce. The romantically lit covered front patio has a secluded garden feel, and inside tables also have indirect lighting. Despite the passage of time, this all-around satisfier remains something of an insider's secret.

7734 Girard Ave. © 858/456-0466. Reservations recommended. Main courses $8–$13. AE, MC, V. Mon–Thurs 11am–3pm and 5–10pm; Fri–Sat 11am–3pm and 5–11pm; Sun 5–10pm.

Moments To See . . . Perchance to Eat

Incredible ocean views, a sweeping skyline, and sailboats fluttering along the shore—it's the classic backdrop for a memorable meal. So where can you find the best views?

Downtown, the **Fish Market** and its pricier cousin **Top of the Market** overlook San Diego Bay, and the management even provides binoculars for getting a good look at aircraft carriers and other vessels. Across the harbor in Coronado, the **Bay Beach Cafe** and **Peohe's** offer panoramic views of the San Diego skyline, and the tony **Azzura Point** at Loews Coronado Bay Resort looks out across the bay. In Pacific Beach, the **Green Flash** is just steps from the sand, and the **High Tide Cafe**'s lofty deck provides another perspective of the same scene. Nearby, the **Atoll** (© 619/539-8635), in the Catamaran Resort Hotel, has a romantic patio facing tranquil Mission Bay. In La Jolla, **George's at the Cove** and **Top O' the Cove** are near the water (and offer panoramic elevated views), but **Brockton Villa** actually offers the La Jolla Cove as advertised on every postcard stand in town.

If you want to get up close and personal, grab your gold card and head to the **Marine Room** (© 858/539-8635), where SeaWorld technology (yes, SeaWorld) helped build the windows that withstand the crashing tide each day. It's at the La Jolla Beach & Tennis Club.

INEXPENSIVE

The Cottage ⚜ BREAKFAST/CALIFORNIAN   La Jolla's best—and friendliest—breakfast is served at this turn-of-the-century bungalow on a sunny village corner. Newly modernized, the cottage is light and airy, but most diners opt for tables outside, where a charming white picket fence encloses the trellis-shaded brick patio. Omelets and egg dishes feature Mediterranean, Asian, or classic American touches; my favorite has creamy mashed potatoes, bacon, and melted cheese folded inside. The Cottage bakes its own muffins, breakfast breads, and—you can quote me on this—the best brownies in San Diego. While breakfast dishes are served all day, toward lunch the kitchen begins turning out freshly made, healthful soups, light meals, and sandwiches. Summer dinners (never heavy, always tasty) are a delight, particularly when you're seated before dark on a balmy seaside night.

7702 Fay Ave. (at Kline St.). ℭ **858/454-8409.** www.cottagelajolla.com. Reservations accepted for dinner only. Breakfast and lunch $5–$12; dinner $8–$18. AE, DISC, MC, V. Daily year-round 7:30am–3pm; May 15–Sept 30 Tues–Sat 5–9:30pm.

7 Coronado

Rather like the conservative, old-school navy aura that pervades the entire "island," Coronado's dining options are reliable and often quite good, but the restaurants aren't breaking new culinary ground.

Some notable exceptions are the resort dining rooms, which seem to be waging a little rivalry over who can attract the most prestigious, multiple-award-winning executive chef. If you're in the mood for a special-occasion meal that'll knock your socks off, consider **Azzura Point** (ℭ **619/424-4000**), in Loews Coronado Bay Resort. With its plushly upholstered, gilded, and view-endowed setting, this stylish dining room wins continual raves from deep-pocketed San Diego foodies willing to cross the bay for inventive and artistic California-Mediterranean creations. The Hotel Del's fancy **Prince of Wales** (ℭ **619/522-8496**) is equally scenic, gazing at the beach across the hotel's regal Windsor Lawn; the eclectic California menu always showcases the best of seasonally fresh ingredients.

But if you seek ethnic or funky food, better head back across the bridge. Mexican fare (gringo-style, but well practiced) is served on the island at popular **Miguel's Cocina,** inside El Cordova hotel (ℭ **619/437-4237**). A branch of the **Brigantine Seafood Grill** (see "Old Town," earlier in this chapter) is at 1333 Orange Ave. (ℭ **619/435-4166**).

EXPENSIVE

The Chart House ⚜ AMERICAN   Perched at the edge of Glorietta Bay, this restaurant resembles a cupola that must have escaped from the Hotel del Coronado, up the hill. It has been here, in the Del's former boathouse, since 1968. The upscale Chart House chain is known for restoration of historic structures, and this project is a beauty; it holds 38 antique tables and the largest collection of Tiffany lamps in Southern California (about 20 at last count). Enjoy dinner on the deck in the summer or in the upstairs lounge; the mahogany, teak, and stained-glass bar came from Atlanta and dates from 1880.

The fare is straightforward—seafood and steaks, with plenty of fresh-fish specials daily. Tourist-oriented and overpriced by local standards, the Chart House still guarantees the best prime rib or Australian lobster tail you'll find. The view

0   5 mi

0   5 km

SHORELINE PARK
BAYVIEW PARK
SDG & E PARK
CENTENNIAL PARK
San Diego-Coronado Ferry
San Diego Bay
Mc Cain Blvd.
1st St.
2nd St.
3rd St.
4th St.
5th St.
6th St.
7th St.
8th St.
9th St.
10th St.
Sea'n Air Golf Course
Coronado Ave.
Balboa Ave.
Cabrillo Ave.
Country Club Ln.
Alameda Ave.
Palm Ave.
Orange Ave.
Olive Ave.
Ocean Blvd.
Isabella
Loma Pl.
A Ave.
B Ave.
C Ave.
D Ave.
E Ave.
F Ave.
G Ave.
H Ave.
I Ave.
J Ave.
Ferry Landing Marketplace
Glorietta Pl.
Soledad Pl.
Prospect Pl.
TIDELANDS PARK
SPRECKELS PARK
Adella Ln.
Adella Ave.
Pomona
Margarita Ave.
Guadalupe
Coronado Golf Course
SUNSET PARK
Coronado Beach
Coronado Yacht Club
Bay Circle
Glorietta Bay
Silver Strand Blvd.
GLORIETTA BAY PARK
PACIFIC OCEAN
282
75

Azzura Point **1**
Bay Beach Cafe **11**
The Brigantine **7**
Chart House **2**
Chez Loma **5**
Clayton's Coffee Shop **8**
Miguel's Cocina **4**
Peohe's **10**
Primavera Pastry Caffé **9**
Prince of Wales **3**
Rhinoceros Cafe & Grill **6**

La Jolla
Pacific Beach
Mission Beach
Mission Bay
Old Town
Hillcrest/Uptown
Ocean Beach
Downtown
Coronado
Gaslamp Quarter
San Diego

from the restaurant encompasses Glorietta Bay, the Coronado Yacht Club, and the Coronado Bay Bridge.

There's also a branch in **La Jolla,** at 1270 Prospect St. (C **858/459-8201**).

1701 Strand Way. C 619/435-0155. Reservations recommended. Main courses $11–$26. AE, DC, DISC, MC, V. Daily 5–10pm. Free parking. Bus: 901.

Chez Loma ★★ FRENCH   You'd be hard-pressed to find a more romantic dining spot than this intimate Victorian cottage filled with antiques and subdued candlelight. The house dates from 1889, the French-Continental restaurant from 1975. Tables are scattered throughout the house and on the enclosed garden terrace; an upstairs wine salon, reminiscent of a Victorian parlor, is a cozy spot for coffee or conversation.

Among the creative entrees are salmon with smoked-tomato vinaigrette, and roast duckling with green-peppercorn sauce. All main courses are served with soup or salad, rice or potatoes, and fresh vegetables. California wines and American microbrews are available. Follow dinner with a creamy crème caramel or Kahlúa crème brûlée. Chez Loma's service is attentive, the herb rolls addictive, and early birds enjoy specially priced meals.

1132 Loma (off Orange Ave.). C **619/435-0661**. www.chezloma.com. Reservations recommended. Main courses $17–$25. AE, DC, MC, V. Daily 5–10pm; Sun 10am–2pm. Bus: 901.

Peohe's 𝄐 PACIFIC RIM/ASIAN FUSION/SEAFOOD With over-the-top Polynesian decor of which Disneyland would be proud, Peohe's is definitely touristy and definitely overpriced—but there's no denying the awesome view across the bay or the excellent Hawaiian-style seafood and Pacific Rim–accented cuisine. Every table in the giant, light- and plant-filled atrium has a view; there are even better tables on the wooden deck at the water's edge. Dinner main courses include acclaimed crunchy coconut shrimp; island-style halibut sautéed with banana, macadamia nuts, and Frangelico liqueur; and rack of New Zealand lamb with Hunan barbecue sauce. Lunchtime options include more casual sandwiches and salads, and the tropical fantasy desserts are delectably rich. For those who love theme restaurants and Polynesian kitsch, Peohe's is a worthwhile splurge.

1201 First St. (Ferry Landing Marketplace). 𝄐 **619/437-4474.** www.peohes.com. Reservations recommended. Lunch $9–$16; dinner $19–$30. AE, DC, DISC, MC, V. Daily 11:30am–2:30pm; Mon–Thurs 5:30–9pm; Fri 5:30–10pm; Sat 5–10pm; Sun 4:30–9pm. Bus: 901 or 904.

MODERATE

Bay Beach Cafe AMERICAN/SEAFOOD This loud, friendly gathering place isn't on the beach at all, but enjoys a prime perch on San Diego Bay. Seated indoors or on a glassed-in patio, diners gaze endlessly at the city skyline, which is dramatic by day and breathtaking at night. The cafe is quite popular at happy hour, when the setting sun glimmers on downtown's mirrored high-rises. The ferry docks at a wooden pier a few steps away, discharging passengers into the complex of gift shops and restaurants with a New England fishing-village theme. At the Bay Beach Cafe, the food takes a back seat to the view, but the pub menu of burgers, sandwiches, salads, and appetizers is inexpensive and satisfying. Dinner entrees aren't quite good enough for the price.

1201 First St. (Ferry Landing Marketplace). 𝄐 **619/435-4900.** Reservations recommended for dinner on weekends. Main courses $9–$18; pub menu $6–$10. DISC, MC, V. Mon–Fri 7–10:30am and 11am–4pm; Sat–Sun 7–11:30am and noon–4pm; daily 5–10:30pm. Free parking. Bus: 901 or 904.

Rhinoceros Cafe & Grill 𝄐 AMERICAN With its quirky name and something-for-everyone menu, this light, bright bistro is a welcome addition to the Coronado dining scene. It's more casual than it looks from the street and offers large portions, though the kitchen is a little heavy-handed with sauces and spices. At lunch, every other patron seems to be enjoying the popular penne à la vodka in creamy tomato sauce; favorite dinner specials are monkfish cioppino over spaghettini, Southwestern-style meatloaf, and simple herb-roasted chicken. Plenty of crispy fresh salads balance out the menu. There's a good wine list, or you might decide to try Rhino Chaser's American Ale.

1166 Orange Ave. 𝄐 **619/435-2121.** Main courses $9–$18. AE, DISC, MC, V. Daily 11am–2:45pm and 5–9pm. Bus: 901.

INEXPENSIVE

Clayton's Coffee Shop AMERICAN/BREAKFAST The Hotel Del isn't the only relic of a bygone era in Coronado—just wait until you see this humble neighborhood favorite. Clayton's has occupied this corner spot seemingly forever, at least since a time when *everyone's* menus were full of plain American good eatin' in the $1 to $5 range. Now their horseshoe counter, chrome barstools, and well-worn pleather-lined booths are "retro," but the burgers, fries, and chicken noodle soup just as good—plus you can still play three oldies for a quarter on the table-side jukebox. Behind the restaurant, Clayton's Mexican takeout kitchen does a brisk business in homemade tamales.

959 Orange Ave. © **619/437-8811.** Menu items under $10. No credit cards. Mon–Sat 6am–8pm; Sun 6am–2pm. Bus: 901 or 904.

Primavera Pastry Caffé ⚛ *Value* BREAKFAST/LIGHT FARE If the name sounds familiar, it's because this fantastic little cafe—the best of its kind on the island—is part of the family that includes Primavera Ristorante, up the street. In addition to fresh-roasted coffee and espresso drinks, it serves omelets and other breakfast treats (until 1:30pm), burgers and deli sandwiches on the delicious house bread, and a daily fresh soup. It's the kind of spot where half the customers are greeted by name. Locals rave about the "Yacht Club" sandwich, a croissant filled with yellowfin tuna, and the breakfast croissant, topped with scrambled ham and eggs and cheddar cheese. I can't resist Primavera's fat, gooey cinnamon buns.

956 Orange Ave. © **619/435-4191.** Main courses $4–$6. MC, V. Daily 6:30am–5pm (closes at 6pm in summer). Bus: 901.

8 Only in San Diego
WOOD-FIRED PIZZA

It all started with Wolfgang Puck, that crafty Austrian chef who dazzled Hollywood restaurant-goers at Spago and went on to build a dynasty of California cuisine. By now, everyone is familiar with the building block of that empire; heck, you can even get it in the frozen-food section. We're talking about pizza, of course. Not the marinara-and-pepperoni variety found in other pizza meccas like New York and Chicago—for a whole generation of Californians, pizza will always mean barbecued chicken, tomato basil, or goat cheese and sun-dried tomato. Gourmet pizzas appear to have overtaken the traditional variety in popularity, and kitchens all over San Diego stoke their wood-fired ovens to keep up with the demand.

Most of the Italian restaurants in this chapter feature at least a handful of individual-size pizzas. Always tops in San Diego polls is **Sammy's California Wood-fired Pizza,** at 770 Fourth Ave., at F Street, in the Gaslamp Quarter (© **619/230-8888**); 702 Pearl St., at Draper Street, La Jolla (© **858/456-8018**); and 12925 El Camino Real, at Del Mar Heights Road, Del Mar (© **858/259-6600**). Conveniently located and always frustratingly crowded, Sammy's serves creations like duck sausage, potato garlic, or Jamaican jerk shrimp atop 10-inch rounds. It also excels at enormous salads, making it easy to share a meal and save a bundle.

A similar menu is available at **Pizza Nova,** a similarly stylish minichain with a similarly vibrant atmosphere. Despite being alike, each chain thrives by covering the neighborhoods the other doesn't. You'll find Pizza Nova at 3955 Fifth Ave., north of University Avenue, Hillcrest (© **619/296-6682**); 5120 N. Harbor Dr., west of Nimitz Boulevard, Point Loma (© **619/226-0268**); and 8650 Genesee Ave., at Nobel Drive, in La Jolla's Golden Triangle (© **858/458-9525**).

If you're a purist, or unfamiliar with this trend's granddaddy, head to Mission Valley and San Diego's branch of **Wolfgang Puck Cafe,** 1640 Camino del Rio N., in Mission Valley Center (© **619/295-9653**). Like its cousins throughout Southern California, the casual cafe has dizzying decor, loud music, and an army of fresh-faced staffers ferrying much more than pizza. (Another of Puck's excellent signature dishes is bacon-wrapped meatloaf served on a bed of mashed potatoes.)

BAJA FISH TACOS

One of San Diego's culinary ironies is that, although the city is conscious of its Hispanic roots—not to mention within visual range of the Mexican border—it's hard to find anything other than gringo-ized combo plates in most local Mexican restaurants.

Perhaps the most authentic recipes are those found inside humble **Rubio's Baja Grill.** Actually, it's not so humble anymore, since proprietor Ralph Rubio began branching out into every corner of Southern California with his enormously successful yet deceptively simple fare; you can now find Rubio's in Phoenix, Las Vegas, Los Angeles, and even edging out hot dogs in the stands at San Diego's own Qualcomm Stadium. But, back in 1983, it was an achievement for local surfer Rubio to open a tiny walk-up taco stand on busy Mission Bay Drive. After years of scarfing down cheap beers and fish tacos in the Mexican fishing village of San Felipe, Ralph secured the "secret" recipe for this quintessentially Baja treat; batter-dipped, deep-fried fish fillets folded in corn tortillas and garnished with shredded cabbage, salsa, and tangy *crema* sauce. You'll find them dispensed from thatched-roof shacks along Baja's beach roads, and in the past decade they've taken this side of the border by storm. Rubio's has since expanded its menu to include other Mexican specialties, all accented by the distinctively Baja flavors of fresh lime and tangy cilantro. And unlike your average McDrive-through, at Rubio's you can wash it all down with an icy-cold beer. Because many of the newer locations have a homogenous fast-food look to them, it's fun to stop by the original stand, at 4504 E. Mission Bay Dr., at Bunker Hill Street (© **858/272-2801**), if you're in the neighborhood.

Rubio's also has locations in the **Gaslamp Quarter,** 901 Fourth St., at E Street (© **619/231-7731**); **Hillcrest,** 3900 Fifth Ave., at University Avenue (© **619/299-8873**); **La Jolla,** 8855 Villa La Jolla Dr., at Nobel Drive (© **858/546-9377**); **Pacific Beach,** 910 Grand Ave. (© **858/270-4800**); and **Point Loma,** 3555 Rosecrans St., at Midway Drive (© **619/223-2631**).

PICNIC FARE

San Diego's benign climate lends itself to dining alfresco. An excellent spot to pick up sandwiches is the **Cheese Shop,** a gourmet deli with locations downtown at 627 4th Ave. (© **619/232-2303**) and in La Jolla Shores at 2165 Avenida de la Playa (© **858/459-3921**). Other places to buy picnic fare include **Girard Gourmet,** 7837 Girard Ave., La Jolla (© **858/454-3321**); **Boudin Sourdough Bakery and Cafe** (© **619/234-1849**) and the **Farmer's Market,** both in Horton Plaza; and **Old Town Liquor and Deli,** 2304 San Diego Ave. (© **619/291-4888**).

Another spot that's very popular with San Diegans is **Point Loma Seafoods,** on the water's edge in front of the Municipal Sportfishing Pier, at 2805 Emerson near Scott Street, south of Rosecrans and west of Harbor Drive (© **619/223-1109**). There's a fish market here, and you can pick up seafood sandwiches, fresh sushi, and salads to go. If you decide to make your own sandwiches, the best bread in the county comes from **Bread & Cie. Bakery and Cafe,** 350 University Ave., Hillcrest (© **619/683-9322**), and **Primavera Pastry Caffé,** 956 Orange Ave., Coronado (© **619/435-4191**).

7

What to See & Do

You won't run out of things to see and do in San Diego. The San Diego Zoo, SeaWorld, and the Wild Animal Park are the three top drawing cards, but many other activities—lots of them free!—also await.

SUGGESTED ITINERARIES

If You Have 1 Day

With only 1 day in San Diego, you'll have to choose between two major draws: the zoo and Sea-World. Get there when the gates open to maximize your time, and make sure to allow time to enjoy lunch at an ocean view restaurant in Ocean Beach, Pacific Beach, or La Jolla. In the afternoon, shoppers will want to do a little antiquing in Ocean Beach or Hillcrest, or stroll the boutiques of La Jolla if that was the chosen lunch spot. If shopping isn't your style, spend some time walking along the boardwalk or the Embarcadero, perhaps stopping to tour the vessels that make up the Maritime Museum. Either way, finish the day in the Gaslamp Quarter, which always promises a lively evening street scene. Choose from dozens of excellent restaurants, and stick around for some live music after dinner—if you have the energy!

If You Have 2 Days

With 2 full days in the city, you can devote each one to a separate major attraction. In addition to the zoo and SeaWorld, consider spending several hours strolling through the rest of Balboa Park, enjoying the great architecture and peeking into a couple of its fantastic museums. Some, such as the

Automotive Museum, the Model Railroad Museum, the Mingei International Museum, the Museum of Man, and the Museum of San Diego History, won't take more than 30 to 60 minutes. Or, if the weather is too perfect to believe, forego an organized attraction, rent some recreational gear (bikes, in-line skates, kayaks—they're all available), and spend several hours soaking up the sun on beautiful Mission Bay.

If You Have 3 Days

Plan the first 2 days as above, reserving the third for an excursion to the Wild Animal Park in the morning. When you return to the city, ride the ferry to Coronado for a tour of the majestic Hotel del Coronado and dinner on the island. Take a sunset walk along the beach before or after dinner.

If You Have 4 Days or More

On your fourth day, visit the Cabrillo National Monument in the morning. Spend the rest of the day enjoying the outdoors San Diego is famous for—assemble a picnic for the beach, or, if you haven't visited Balboa Park's Prado, take your picnic there and then catch an exciting OMNIMAX movie at the Fleet Science Center. Another option for day 4 would be to take the trolley into Tijuana, and spend the day shopping there and

sampling south-of-the-border flavors. With an extended stay comes
the opportunity to indulge your
own passion. For example, play one
of San Diego's challenging golf
courses; take kayak lessons on a
North County beach; treat the kids
to a day at LEGOLAND in Carlsbad; or poke around a historic
house museum (like the Marston
House, Villa Montezuma, or the
William Heath Davis House).

1 The Three Major Animal Parks

Looking for wild times? San Diego supplies them as no other city can. Its world-
famous zoo is home to more than 4,000 animals, many of them rare and exotic.
A sister attraction, the San Diego Wild Animal Park, offers another 3,200 creatures representing 275 species in an au naturel setting. And, Shamu and his
friends form a veritable chorus line at SeaWorld—waving their flippers, wad-
dling across an ersatz Antarctica, and blowing killer-whale kisses—in more than
a dozen shows a day.

San Diego Zoo 🌟🌟🌟 *(Kids* More than 4,000 animals reside at this world-
famous zoo, which was founded in 1916 with a handful of animals originally
brought here for the 1915–16 Panama-California International Exposition.
Many of the buildings you see in surrounding Balboa Park were built for the
exposition. The zoo's founder, Dr. Harry Wegeforth, a local physician and life-
long animal lover, once braved the fury of an injured tiger to toss medicine into
its roaring mouth.

In the early days of the zoo, "Dr. Harry" traveled around the world and
bartered native Southwestern animals such as rattlesnakes and sea lions for more
exotic species. The loan of two giant pandas from the People's Republic of China
was a twist on the long-standing tradition—instead of exchanging exotic species,
the San Diego Zoo agreed to pay $1 million for each year that the pandas are
here, to aid the conservation effort in China. The lovable pandas, which arrived
in 1996, were an instant hit with zoo-goers, but their keepers' behind-the-scenes
mission was to scientifically encourage the breeding of this near-extinct animal.
In August 1999, their efforts were rewarded with the birth of Hua Mei, a healthy
and perfect female cub—see the feature "Panda-monium" in this chapter for full
details on the panda family.

The zoo is also an accredited botanical garden, representing more than 6,000
species of flora from many climate zones, all installed to help simulate the
animals' native environments.

The giant pandas may be the big attention-getters, but the zoo has many
other rare and exotic species: cuddly koalas from Australia, long-billed kiwis
from New Zealand, wild Przewalski horses from Mongolia, lowland gorillas
from Africa, and giant tortoises from the Galapagos. Of course, the zoo's regulars—lions, elephants, giraffes, tigers, and bears—prowl around as well, and the

---

(*Tips* **Looking For LEGOLAND?**

In 1999, San Diego's "Big Three" family attractions were joined by the
instantly popular LEGOLAND, which is located about 30 miles (48km) away
in the seaside San Diego County community of Carlsbad. You'll find full
information on visiting the park on p. 214.

San Diego Area Attractions

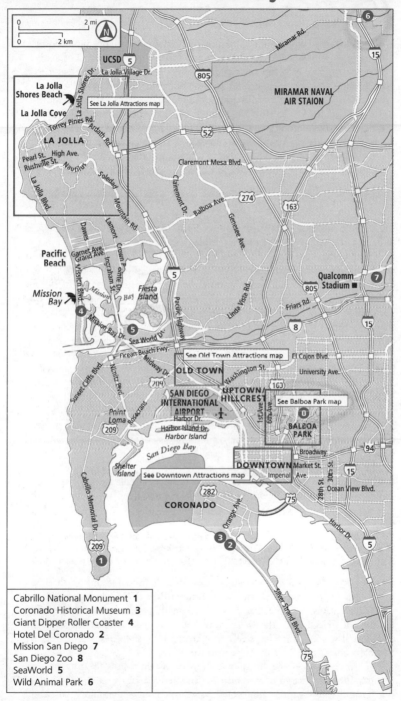

0	2 mi
0	2 km

UCSD 5
La Jolla Village Dr.

La Jolla
Shores Beach

La Jolla Cove

See La Jolla Attractions map

Torrey Pines Rd.

LA JOLLA

Pearl St. High Ave.
Rushville St.
Nautilus

La Jolla Blvd

Soledad

Mountain Rd.

MIRAMAR NAVAL
AIR STAION

Miramar Rd.

Claremont Mesa Blvd.

Claremont Dr.

Balboa Ave.

Genesee Ave.

Pacific
Beach

Garnet Ave.
Grand Ave.
Ingraham St.

Mission
Bay

Fiesta
Island

Crown Pointe Dr.

Linda Vista Rd.

Qualcomm
Stadium

Friars Rd.

Mission Bay Dr.

Sea World Dr.

Ocean Beach Fwy.

Midway Dr.

See Old Town Attractions map

OLD TOWN

Washington St.

El Cajon Blvd.

University Ave.

Sunset Cliffs Blvd.

Nimitz Blvd.

Rosecrans

Point
Loma

SAN DIEGO
INTERNATIONAL
AIRPORT

Harbor Dr.

Harbor Island Dr.
Harbor Island

UPTOWN/
HILLCREST

See Balboa Park map

BALBOA
PARK

San Diego Bay

Shelter
Island

See Downtown Attractions map

DOWNTOWN

Broadway

Market St.
Imperial Ave.

Ocean View Blvd.

Cabrillo Memorial Dr.

CORONADO

Orange Ave.

Silver Strand Blvd.

Harbor Dr.

Cabrillo National Monument **1**
Coronado Historical Museum **3**
Giant Dipper Roller Coaster **4**
Hotel Del Coronado **2**
Mission San Diego **7**
San Diego Zoo **8**
SeaWorld **5**
Wild Animal Park **6**

(Value) Now That's What I Call a Deal!

Always aware of what side their tourism bread is buttered on, San Diego's three main family attractions have joined forces with combo ticket deals that reward you with big savings for visitors with recreational stamina. Here's how it works: If you plan to visit both the zoo and Wild Animal Park, a two-park ticket (deluxe zoo package, Wild Animal Park admission) is $46.80 adults, $27.85 children 3 to 11. You get one visit to each attraction, to be used within 5 days of purchase.

If SeaWorld is foremost in your plans, how about an almost twofer? For just $4 more than the regular 1-day admission price ($42.95 for adults, $32.95 for kids 3–11), you can trade up for a 2-day ticket in order to see it all without missing a beat.

---

zoo is home to a great number of tropical birds. Most of the animals are housed in barless, moated enclosures that resemble their natural habitats.

The zoo offers two types of bus tours. Both provide a narrated overview and allow you to see 75% of the park. On the **35-minute guided bus tour,** you get on the bus and complete a circuit around the zoo. It costs $4 for adults, $3 for children 3 to 11, and is included in the deluxe package. The **Kangaroo Bus Tour** allows you to get on and off the bus as many times as you want at any of the eight stops—you can even go around more than once. It costs $8 for adults and $5 for children. In general, it's better to take the tour early in the morning or later in the afternoon, when the animals are more active. Call the **Bus Tour Hot Line** (© 619/685-3264) for information about these tours, as well as Spanish-language tours, a comedy tour, and signed tours for the hearing impaired.

You can also get an aerial perspective from the **Skyfari,** which costs $1 per person each way. The ride lasts about 5 minutes—but, because it doesn't get particularly close to the animals, it's better for a bird's-eye view of Balboa Park and a survey of the zoo.

The **Children's Zoo** is scaled to a youngster's viewpoint. There's a nursery with baby animals and a petting area where kids can cuddle up to sheep, goats, and the like. The resident wombat is a special favorite here.

2920 Zoo Dr., Balboa Park. © 619/234-3153. www.sandiegozoo.org. Admission $19.50 adults, $11.75 children 3–11, military in uniform free. Deluxe package (admission, guided bus tour, round-trip Skyfari aerial tram) $32 adults, $19.75 children. Combination Zoo and Wild Animal Park package (deluxe zoo package, Wild Animal Park admission) $46.80 adults, $27.85 children; valid for 5 days from date of purchase. DISC, MC, V. Daily year-round 9am–4pm (grounds close at 5pm); summer 9am–9pm (grounds close at 10pm). Bus: 7, 7A/B.

San Diego Wild Animal Park ★★★ (Kids)   Just 30 miles (48km) north of San Diego, outside of Escondido, the Wild Animal Park (WAP) transports you to the African plains and other landscapes. Originally begun as a breeding facility for the San Diego Zoo, the WAP now holds around 3,200 animals—many endangered species—roaming freely over the park's 1,800 acres. Approximately 650 baby animals are born every year in the park.

The simplest way to see the animals is by riding the 5-mile (8km) **monorail** (included in the price of admission); for the best views, sit on the right-hand side. During the 50-minute ride, you'll pass through areas resembling Africa and Asia, past water holes and swaying grasses. Trains leave every 20 minutes from

Fun Fact **Panda-monium**

Two giant pandas from China, Shi Shi (a 13-year-old male) and Bai Yun (a 3-year-old female), arrived at the San Diego Zoo in late 1996 after 3 years of intense negotiation with the U.S. Department of the Interior, the Wolong Giant Panda Conservation Centre, and the Chinese government. Along with Tian Tian and Mei Xiang, who arrived in December 2000 at the Smithsonian National Zoo in Washington, D.C., they are the only giant pandas in the United States; only about 15 giant pandas live in zoos outside China and North Korea.

Giant pandas are among the rarest mammals in the world—fewer than 1,000 remain in the wild, where they live in dense bamboo and coniferous forests at altitudes of 5,000 to 10,000 feet (1,500m–3,000m). Their numbers have dwindled due to the destruction of their natural habitat and poaching. As part of the agreement to get the pandas here, the San Diego Zoo agreed to contribute $1 million each year to wild-panda habitat protection projects in China.

Shi Shi, who weighs 230 pounds, was born in the wild and taken to the Wolong Giant Panda Conservation Centre after he was found critically wounded—probably from a fight with another male panda. Bai Yun was born at the Wolong center on September 7, 1991, and was raised by her mother, Dong Dong. The pandas came to the United States primarily for reproductive research: They have an unusual set of mating rituals and requirements, and the alteration of their wilderness environments has contributed to a decrease in new births. Zoo researchers—and all of San Diego—were elated when, on August 21, 1999, Bai Yun gave birth to a healthy baby girl. She was named Hua Mei (pronounced "hwa may"), meaning "China USA," and will ultimately return to China with her parents. Successful breeding in captivity is also scarce—before Hua Mei's birth, the last panda birth in the Western Hemisphere was to Hsing-Hsing and Ling-Ling, the previous giant pandas at the National Zoo. Of the five babies born to them between 1983 and 1989, the longest surviving cub lived only 4 days.

Giant pandas are related to both bears and raccoons. They are bearlike in shape, with striking black-and-white markings, and have unique front paws that enable them to grasp stalks of bamboo. Bamboo makes up about 95% of their diet, and they eat 20 to 40 pounds of food every day. This takes them 10 to 16 hours, so there's a pretty good chance that you'll see them eating.

Because of the exhibit's enormous popularity and the fact that the pandas are not always on display, the zoo provides a panda-viewing hot line (© 888/MY-PANDA). Call before you go.

the station in Nairobi Village, the commercial hub of the park with more traditional animal exhibits, souvenir stores, and refreshment vendors. (It may sound persnickety, but the food inside the park is mediocre and overpriced . . . think about smuggling in your own snacks!)

Nairobi Village isn't much more than a small zoo whose best feature is the nursery area, where irresistible young 'uns can be seen frolicking, being bottle-fed, and sleeping. If you want to experience the vast landscape and large animals that make the Wild Animal Park unique, you can take one of two self-guided walking trails: the 1¾-mile (2.8km) **Kilimanjaro safari walk,** which visits the Australian rain forest and East Africa, or the **Heart of Africa,** a three-quarter mile (1km) trail that winds through dense forest, flourishing wetlands, sprawling savannas, and open plains.

The surest way to get up-close-and-personal, though, is to take a **photo caravan tour** ($65–$95 per person, park admission included). In our experience, the photos are secondary to the enjoyment. (How many of us point-and-shoot shutterbugs can really hope to top the professional shots gracing the official souvenir postcards, anyway?) What matters is crossing the fence to meet the rhinos, ostriches, zebras, deer, and giraffes on their home turf, even feeding giraffes along the way.

15500 San Pasqual Valley Rd., Escondido. ℂ 760/747-8702. www.wildanimalpark.org. Admission $26.50 adults, $23.85 seniors 60 and over, $19.50 children 3–11, free for children under 3 and military in uniform. Combination Zoo and Wild Animal Park package (includes deluxe zoo package) $46.80 adults, $27.85 children; valid for 5 days from date of purchase. DISC, MC, V. Daily 9am–4pm (grounds close at 5pm); extended hours during summer and Festival of Lights in Dec. Parking $6 per car. Take I-15 to Via Rancho Pkwy.; follow signs for about 3 miles (5km).

SeaWorld ★★★ *Kids*   One of the best-promoted attractions in California, SeaWorld may be your main reason for coming to San Diego. The 165-acre, multimillion-dollar aquatic playground is a showplace for marine life, made politically correct with a nominally educational atmosphere. Several successive 4-ton black-and-white killer whales have functioned as the park's mascot, Shamu. At its heart, SeaWorld is a family entertainment center where the performers are dolphins, otters, sea lions, walruses, and seals. Shows run continuously throughout the day, while visitors can rotate through the various theaters.

The 2-acre hands-on area called **Shamu's Happy Harbor** encourages kids to handle things—and features everything from a pretend pirate ship, with plenty of netted towers, to tube crawls, slides, and chances to get wet. The newest attraction is **Shipwreck Rapids,** a wet adventure ride on raftlike inner tubes through caverns, waterfalls, and wild rivers. Other draws include **Wild Arctic,** a virtual-reality trip to the frozen North, complete with polar bears, beluga whales, walruses, harbor seals, and the 4-D interactive movie *Pirates,* a comic

---

(*Fun Fact*   **Things that Go Bump in the Night**

The **Roar and Snore** program, which runs from May through September, lets you camp out in the park compound and observe the nocturnal movements of rhinos, tigers, and other animals. The park provides all the equipment, including cookout dinner (and pancake breakfast). After dinner, sit around the campfire listening to tales of animal behavior punctuated by the extraordinary animal calls emanating from dark corners of the park. After breakfast in the morning (sorry, no showers), spend the day enjoying the rest of the park. The weekend-only 1-night camp-overs are $87.50 for adults, $67.50 for kids 8 to 11; children under 8 are not permitted. To request Roar and Snore information by mail, call ℂ 760/738-5049; make reservations by calling ℂ 800/934-CAMP.

adventure written by *Monty Python*'s Eric Idle and starring the deadpan Leslie Nielsen.

The **Dolphin Interaction Program** creates an opportunity for people to meet bottlenose dolphins. Although the program stops short of allowing you to swim with the dolphins, it does offer the opportunity to wade waist-deep, and plenty of time to stroke the mammals and try giving training commands. This 1-hour program includes some classroom time before you wriggle into a wet suit and climb into the water; it costs $125 per person, excluding admission to the rest of the adventure park. Space is limited, so advance reservations are required (© **877/4-DOLPHIN**). Participants must be 6 or older.

Although SeaWorld is best known as Shamu's home, the facility also plays an important role in rescuing and rehabilitating beached animals found along the West Coast—including more than 300 seals, sea lions, marine birds, and dolphins in an average year. Following the successful rescue and 1998 release of a young California gray whale, SeaWorld turned its attention to the manatee, an unusual aquatic mammal rarely seen outside Florida's tropical waters—several permanent residents are on display in the **Manatee Rescue** exhibit area.

500 Sea World Dr., Mission Bay. © **619/226-3901.** www.seaworld.com. Admission $39 adults, $35 seniors 55 and over, $30 children 3–11, free for children under 3. AE, DISC, MC, V. Parking $7. Guided 90-min. walking tours, $8 adults, $7 children. Memorial Day–Labor Day daily 9am–11pm or midnight; Sept–May daily 10am–5pm. Bus: 9. By car from I-5, take Sea World Dr. exit; from I-8, take W. Mission Bay Dr. exit to Sea World Dr.

2 San Diego's Beaches

San Diego County is blessed with 70 miles (113km) of sandy coastline and more than 30 beaches that attract surfers, snorkelers, swimmers, and sunbathers. In summer, the beaches teem with locals and visitors alike. The rest of the year, when the water is cooler, they are popular places to walk and jog, and surfers don wet suits to pursue their passion.

Here's a list of San Diego's most accessible beaches, each with its own personality and devotees. They are listed geographically from south to north. If you are interested in others, *The California Coastal Access Handbook*, published by the California Coastal Commission, is helpful; it's available at most area bookstores for $17.95, or you can order it through your local bookseller. All California beaches are public to the mean high-tide line, and this publication tells you how to get to each one.

Exploring tide pools—areas that retain water after the tide has gone out, providing homes for a plethora of sea creatures—can be a lot of fun. You can get a tide chart free or for a nominal charge from many surf and diving shops, including **Emerald City Surf & Sport,** 1118 Orange Ave., Coronado, and **San Diego Divers Supply,** 5701 La Jolla Blvd., La Jolla.

Note: All beaches are good for swimming unless otherwise indicated.

IMPERIAL BEACH

Half an hour south of San Diego by car or trolley, and only a few minutes from the Mexican border, lies Imperial Beach. It's popular with surfers and local youth, who can be somewhat territorial about "their" sands in summer. The beach boasts 3 miles (5km) of surf breaks plus a guarded "swimmers only" stretch; check with lifeguards before getting wet, though, since sewage from nearby Mexico can sometimes foul the water. Imperial also plays host to the annual U.S. Open Sandcastle Competition each August, with world-class sand creations ranging from sea scenes to dragons to dinosaurs.

CORONADO BEACH

Lovely, wide, and sparkling white, this beach is conducive to strolling and lingering, especially in the late afternoon. The southeastern end fronts Ocean Boulevard and is especially pretty in front of the Hotel del Coronado; toward the north, you can watch fighter jets in formation flying from the Naval Air Station. Waves are gentle here, so the beach draws many Coronado families—and their dogs, which are allowed off-leash at the most northwesterly end. The islands visible from here, "Los Coronados," are 18 miles (29km) away and belong to Mexico.

OCEAN BEACH

The northern end of Ocean Beach Park is officially known as "Dog Beach," and is one of only two in San Diego where your pooch can roam freely on the sand (and frolic with several dozen other people's pets). Surfers generally congregate around the Ocean Beach Pier, mostly in the water but often at the snack shack on the end. Rip currents are strong here and discourage most swimmers from venturing beyond waist depth. Facilities at the beach include rest rooms, showers, picnic tables, volleyball courts, and plenty of metered parking lots. To reach the beach, take West Point Loma Boulevard all the way to the end.

MISSION BAY PARK

In this 4,600-acre aquatic playground, you'll find 27 miles (43km) of bay-front, picnic areas, children's playgrounds, and paths for biking, in-line skating, and jogging. The bay lends itself to windsurfing, sailing, riding personal watercraft, water-skiing, and fishing. There are dozens of access points; one of the most popular is off I-5 at Clairemont Drive, where there's a visitor information center.

BONITA COVE/MARINER'S POINT & MISSION POINT

Enclosed in Mission Bay Park (facing the bay, not the ocean) this pretty and protected cove's calm waters, grassy picnic areas, and playground equipment make it perfect for families—or as a paddling destination if you've rented kayaks elsewhere in the bay. Get there from Mission Blvd. in south Mission Beach.

MISSION BEACH

While Mission Bay Park is a body of saltwater surrounded by land and bridges, Mission Beach is actually a beach on the Pacific Ocean. Surfing is popular year-round here, but the sands and wide cement "boardwalk" sizzle with activity and great people-watching in summer. The long beach and boardwalk extend from Pacific Beach Drive south to Belmont Park and beyond to the jetty; parking is often tough, with your best bets being the public lots at Belmont Park or at the foot of West Mission Bay Drive.

PACIFIC BEACH

There's always some action at Mission Beach, particularly along **Ocean Front Walk,** a paved promenade featuring a human parade akin to that at L.A.'s Venice Beach boardwalk. It runs along Ocean Boulevard (just west of Mission Blvd.), north of Pacific Beach Drive. The beach is well staffed with lifeguards, but you're on your own to find street parking. Pacific Beach is also the home of **Tourmaline Surfing Park,** where the sport's old guard gathers to surf waters where swimmers are prohibited.

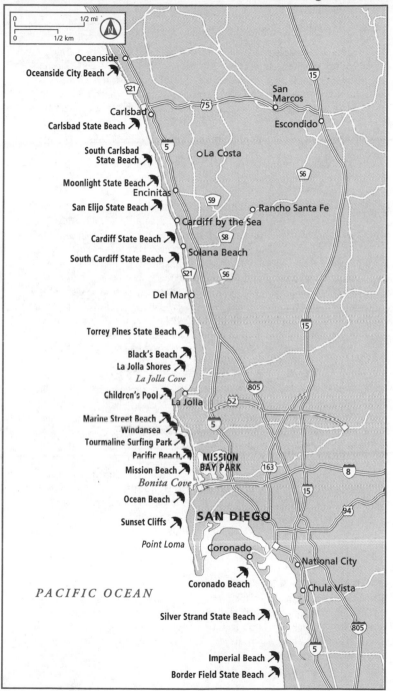

San Diego Beaches

0 _____ **1/2 mi**
0 _____ **1/2 km**

Oceanside ○
Oceanside City Beach

S21

San Marcos
15

Carlsbad ○
Carlsbad State Beach

75
Escondido ○

5
○ La Costa

South Carlsbad State Beach

S6

Moonlight State Beach
Encinitas ○

San Elijo State Beach

S9

○ Rancho Santa Fe

○ Cardiff by the Sea

Cardiff State Beach

S8

South Cardiff State Beach

Solana Beach ○

S21

S6

Del Mar ○

15

Torrey Pines State Beach

Black's Beach
La Jolla Shores
La Jolla Cove

805

Children's Pool
La Jolla ○

52

Marine Street Beach
Windansea
Tourmaline Surfing Park
Pacific Beach
Mission Beach
Bonita Cove

5

MISSION BAY PARK

163

8

15

Ocean Beach

Sunset Cliffs

SAN DIEGO

94

Point Loma

Coronado ○

○ National City

Coronado Beach

○ Chula Vista

PACIFIC OCEAN

Silver Strand State Beach

805

Imperial Beach

5

Border Field State Beach

133

Beach Snack Staples: Quick (& Cheap) Taco Stands

Looking for some sustenance after a day cavorting on San Diego's beautiful beaches? Someplace that's tasty, affordable—and doesn't enforce that pesky shirt-and-shoes policy? Then follow the example of serious surfers and beach bums, who always know where the nearest taco stand can be found. Tacos—and accompanying Mexican favorites like burritos and tamales—are ubiquitous in Southern California, as common as burger stands in the heartland (or hot dog carts in New York City). And like those other famously utensil-less foods, tacos are easy to eat out-of-hand—perfect for a quickie meal before heading back to catch some more waves or rays. Here are a few of our favorites in San Diego's beach communities (from south to north):

A block from the pier—and across the street from Belmont Park—**Roberto's Taco Shop**, 3202 Mission Blvd., Mission Beach (✆ **858/488-1610**), is an institution on this corner, feeding beach-goers and amusement park revelers alike. Step inside the historic corner building for a full menu of family recipe Mexican favorites.

Paquito's Mexican Food, 3852 Mission Blvd., Mission Beach (✆ **858/488-9212**), sits in the heart of Mission Beach's best people-watching, and is a happy-hour favorite with locals who stop by in sandy flip-flops straight from the sand. Sit on their sidewalk patio to enjoy a bottle of Mexican beer and the daily special; Thursday is 99¢ fish taco day.

When time is of the essence, roll through the 24-hour drive-through window at **Ramiro's**, 4525 Mission Blvd., Pacific Beach (✆ **858/273-5227**), for some truly tasty burritos and tacos at rock-bottom prices. There's also a walk-up window and a few outdoor tables.

The name says it all at **Taco Surf**, 4657 Mission Blvd., Pacific Beach (✆ **858/272-3877**), the most "formal" of the bunch—for the laid-back surfing crowd, that means table service. They've got a fine selection of beers to accompany platters of Baja-style fish tacos, along with a full Mexican menu.

As you make your way toward La Jolla, join the throngs of beach-goers and lunch-breakers at tiny **Los Dos Pedros #1**, 723 Turquoise St., Pacific Beach (✆ **858/488-3102**); surfers from Windansea fuel their day at **Los Dos Pedros #2**, 6986 La Jolla Blvd., La Jolla (✆ **858/456-2692**), a welcome sight on a stretch lacking many fast-food options.

WINDANSEA BEACH

The fabled locale of Tom Wolfe's *Pump House Gang*, Windansea is legendary to this day among California's surf elite. Reached by way of Bonair Street (at Neptune Place), Windansea has no facilities, and street parking is first-come, first-served. Come to surf, watch surfers, or soak in the camaraderie and party atmosphere.

CHILDREN'S POOL

A man-made seawall protects this crescent of sand, originally intended as a safe swimming spot for children. Today, much of the beach is cordoned off for the resident sea lion population; curious shutterbugs and families taking advantage of the same calm conditions that keep the sea lions around inhabit the rest. The beach is at Coast Boulevard and Jenner Street; there's limited free street parking. *Our advice:* Come here to admire the regal sea lions, but do your swimming elsewhere.

LA JOLLA COVE

The protected, calm waters—praised as the clearest along the coast—attract snorkelers and scuba divers, along with a fair share of families. The stunning setting offers a small sandy beach, as well as, on the cliffs above, the **Ellen Browning Scripps Park.** The cove's "look but don't touch" policy protects the colorful Garibaldi, California's state fish, plus other marine life, including abalone, octopus, and lobster. The unique Underwater Park stretches from here to the northern end of Torrey Pines State Reserve and incorporates kelp forests, artificial reefs, two deep submarine canyons, and tidal pools. La Jolla Cove is accessible from Coast Boulevard.

LA JOLLA SHORES BEACH

The wide, flat mile of sand at La Jolla Shores is popular with joggers, swimmers, and beginning body- and board surfers, as well as families. It looks like a picture postcard, with powdery sand under blue skies, kissed by gentle waves. Weekend crowds can be enormous, though, quickly occupying both the sand and the metered parking spaces in the lot. There are rest rooms, showers, and picnic areas here, as well the grassy, palm-lined Kellogg Park across the street.

BLACK'S BEACH

The area's unofficial (and illegal) nude beach, it lies between La Jolla Shores Beach and Torrey Pines State Beach. Located below some steep cliffs, it is out of the way and not easy to reach, but draws scores with its secluded beauty—and the colorful spectacle of hang-gliders launching from the cliffs above. To get here, take North Torrey Pines Road, park at the Glider Port, and walk from there. To avoid the cliff descent, you can walk to Black's from beaches north or south, but check the tides first, since the route is often obstructed at high tide. *Note:* Although the water is shallow and pleasant for wading, this area is known for its rip currents.

DEL MAR

After a visit to the famous fairgrounds that are home to the Del Mar Thoroughbred Club, you may want to make tracks for the beach, a long stretch of sand backed by grassy cliffs and a playground area. Del Mar is about 15 miles (24km) from downtown San Diego (see chapter 11).

NORTHERN SAN DIEGO COUNTY

Those inclined to venture farther north in San Diego County won't be disappointed. Pacific Coast Highway leads to some inviting beaches, such as these in Encinitas: peaceful **Boneyards Beach, Swami's Beach** for surfing, and **Moonlight Beach,** popular with families and volleyball buffs. Farthest north is **Oceanside,** which has one of the West Coast's longest wooden piers, wide sandy beaches, and several popular surfing areas.

3 Attractions in Balboa Park

Balboa Park's 1,174 acres encompass walkways, gardens, historic buildings, restaurants, an ornate pavilion with the world's largest outdoor organ, a high-spouting

---

Tips   Balboa Park Money-Savers

Many Balboa Park attractions are open free of charge one Tuesday each month; there's a rotating schedule so three or more participate each Tuesday (see "Free of Charge & Full of Fun," later in this chapter). If you plan to visit more than three of the park's museums, buy the **Passport to Balboa Park,** a coupon booklet that allows entrance to one of 13 museums (the rest are always free) and is valid for 1 week. The $30 passport can be purchased at any participating museum or the Visitors Center.

---

fountain, an OMNIMAX theater, a nationally acclaimed theater, and the world-famous zoo (see "The Three Major Animal Parks," earlier in this chapter, for a complete review). The park's most distinctive features are the architectural beauty of the Spanish-Moorish buildings lining El Prado, its main street, and the outstanding and diverse museums contained within it.

Free **tram** transportation within the park runs Monday through Friday from 8am to 5pm and Saturday and Sunday from 11am to 4pm. Stop in the **Balboa Park Visitor Center,** located in the House of Hospitality (© **619/239-0512;** www.balboapark.org) to learn about free walking and museum **tours.** We've also mapped out a **walking tour** in chapter 8.

Botanical Building and Lily Pond   Within a serene park, ivy, ferns, orchids, impatiens, begonias, and other plants—about 1,200 tropical and flowering varieties—are sheltered beneath the domed lath house. The building, part of the 1915 Panama-California Exposition, measures 250 feet (75m) long by 75 feet (23m) wide by 60 feet (18m) high, and is one of the world's largest wood lath structures, and emerged from a complete renovation in 2002. The lily pond out front attracts sun worshipers and street entertainers.

El Prado. Free admission. Fri–Wed 10am–4pm. Bus: 7, 7A/B, 25.

Hall of Champions   One of the country's few multisport museums, Hall of Champions has been popular with sports fans since 1961. The museum highlights more than 40 professional and amateur sports. More than 25 exhibits surround a centerpiece statue, the *Discus Thrower.* One particularly interesting exhibit is devoted to athletes with disabilities.

2131 Pan American Plaza. © 619/234-2544. www.sandiegosports.org. Admission $5 adults, $3 seniors 65 and older and military, $1 children 6–17, free for children under 6. Free 2nd Tues of each month. Daily 10am–4:30pm. Bus: 7/7B.

House of Pacific Relations International Cottages   This cluster of one- and two-room cottages disseminates information about the culture, traditions, and history of 31 countries. Light refreshments are served, and outdoor lawn programs are presented March through October.

Adjacent to Pan American Plaza. © 619/234-0739. Free admission; donations welcome. Sun 12:30–4:30pm; 4th Tues of each month 11:30am–3pm. Bus: 7, 7A/B.

Japanese Friendship Garden (*Finds*)   Of the 11½ acres designated for the garden, only 1 acre—a beautiful, peaceful one—has been developed. The garden's Information Center shows a model of the future installation, San-Kei-En (Three-Scenery Garden). It will eventually include a shallow lake with a shoreline of Japanese irises; a pastoral scene, such as a meadow abloom with springtime trees; and, a rushing mountain waterfall and a stream filled with colorful

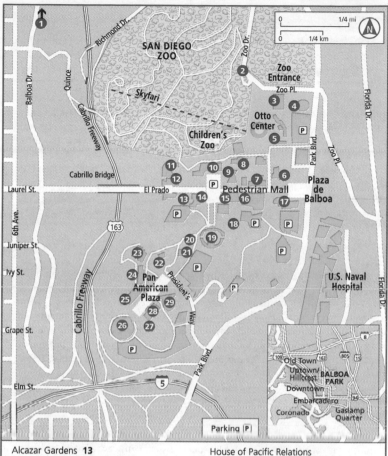

Alcazar Gardens **13**
Balboa Park Club **23**
Botanical Building **8**
Carousel **4**
Casa de Balboa **16**
  Hall of Champions Sports Museum
  Model Railroad Museum
  Museum of Photographic Arts
  San Diego Historical Society Museum
Casa del Prado **7**
Federal Building **29**
The Globe Theaters **11**
Hall of Nations **20**
House of Charm **14**
  Mingei International Museum
  San Diego Art Institute
House of Hospitality **15**
  Balboa Park Visitors Center
  Prado Restaurant

House of Pacific Relations
  International Cottages **22**
Japanese Friendship Garden **18**
Marston House Museum **1**
Municipal Museum **28**
Museum of Art **10**
Museum of Man **12**
Natural History Museum **6**
Palisades Building **24**
  Marie Hitchcock Puppet Theater
Reuben H. Fleet Science Center **17**
San Diego Aerospace Museum **26**
San Diego Automotive Museum **25**
San Diego Miniature Railroad **3**
San Diego Zoo **2**
Spanish Village Art Center **5**
Spreckels Organ Pavilion **19**
Starlight Bowl **27**
Timken Museum of Art **9**
United Nations Building **21**

> **Tips Activities Farther Afield**
>
> To find information on attractions in nearby Del Mar, Carlsbad, Encinitas, and Oceanside—only 20 to 40 minutes from downtown San Diego—turn to "North County Beach Towns," in chapter 11.

koi. A self-guided tour is available at the main gate. From the gate, a crooked path (to confound evil spirits, who move only in a straight line) threads its way to the information center in a Zen-style house; here you can view the most ancient kind of garden, the *sekitei*, made only of sand and stone. Refreshments are served on a Japanese-style deck to the left of the entrance. Japanese holidays are celebrated here, and the public is invited.

2125 Park Blvd., adjacent to the Organ Pavilion. ✆ 619/232-2721. www.niwa.org. Admission $3 adults, $2 students and military, free to kids 6 and under. Free 3rd Tues of each month. Tues–Sun 10am–4pm. Bus: 7, 7A/B, 25.

Marston House Museum   The noted San Diego architect Irving Gill designed this house in 1905 for George Marston, a local businessman and philanthropist. Now managed by the San Diego Historical Society, the house is a classic example of Craftsman-style architecture, reminiscent of the work of Frank Lloyd Wright. Some of its interesting features are wide hallways, brick fireplaces, and redwood paneling. Opened to the public in 1991, it contains few original pieces, but does exhibit Roycroft, Stickley, and Lampert furniture and is slowly being furnished with Craftsman-era pieces or copies as funds become available. Tours take about 45 minutes. Enter at the left. There's a small bookstore and gift shop.

3525 Seventh Ave. (northwest corner of Balboa Park at Balboa Dr. and Upas St.). ✆ 619/298-3142. Guided tour $5 adults, $2 kids 6–17, free for children 5 and under. Fri–Sun 10am–4:30pm (last tour at 3:45pm). Bus: 1, 3, or 25.

Mingei International Museum 🅖   This museum (pronounced "*min*-gay," meaning "art of the people" in Japanese), offers changing exhibitions generally describable as folk art. Artists from countries across the globe have works here; displays include textiles, costumes, jewelry, toys, pottery, paintings, and sculpture. Martha Longenecker, a potter and professor emeritus of art at San Diego State University, founded the museum in 1977. It is one of only two major museums in the United States devoted to folk crafts on a worldwide scale (the other is in Santa Fe, N.M.).

1439 El Prado, in the House of Charm. ✆ 619/239-0003. www.mingei.org. Admission $5 adults, $2 children 6–17 and students with ID, free for children under 6. AE, MC, V. Free 3rd Tues of each month. Tues–Sun 10am–4pm. Bus: 7, 7A/B, 25.

Model Railroad Museum 🅖 *Kids*   Okay, so it's not high culture as we know it, but this museum is cool and cute, and worth 30 to 60 minutes of your time. Six permanent, scale-model railroads depict Southern California's transportation history and terrain with an astounding attention to miniature details. Children will enjoy the hands-on Lionel trains, and train buffs of all ages will appreciate the interactive multimedia displays.

1649 El Prado (Casa de Balboa). ✆ 619/696-0199. www.sdmodelrailroadm.com. Admission $4 adults, free for children under 15. Senior, student, and military (with ID) discounts. Free 1st Tues of each month. Tues–Fri 11am–4pm; Sat–Sun 11am–5pm. Bus: 7, 7A/B, 25.

Museum of Man In a landmark building just inside the park entrance at the Cabrillo Bridge, this museum is devoted to anthropology, with an emphasis on the peoples of North and South America. Favorite exhibits include life-size replicas of a dozen varieties of Homo sapiens, from Cro-Magnon and Neanderthal to Peking Man. Don't overlook the annex across the street, which houses more exhibits. The museum's annual **Indian Fair**, held in June, features American Indians from the Southwest demonstrating tribal dances and selling ethnic food, arts, and crafts.

1350 El Prado. © 619/239-2001. www.museumofman.org. Admission $6 adults, $5 seniors, $3 children 6–17, free for children under 6. Free 3rd Tues of the month. Daily 10am–4:30pm. Bus: 25.

Museum of Photographic Arts If the names Ansel Adams, Margaret Bourke-White, Imogen Cunningham, Edward Weston, and Henri Cartier-Bresson stimulate your interest, then don't miss the 3,600-plus image collection of this museum—one of few in the United States devoted exclusively to the photographic arts. A 1999 expansion allowed the museum to display *even more* of the permanent collection, still leaving room for the provocative traveling exhibits that change every few months.

1649 El Prado. © 619/238-7559. www.mopa.org. Admission $6 adults, $4 seniors and students, free for children under 12 with adult. Free 2nd Tues of each month. Daily 10am–5pm (Thurs until 9pm). Bus: 7, 7A/B, 25.

Reuben H. Fleet Science Center 🌟🌟 *Kids* A must-see for kids of any age—as well as for plenty of grown-up kids—is this tantalizing collection of interactive exhibits and rides designed to provoke the imagination and teach scientific principles. The newest feature is **SciTours**, a simulator ride that lurches you into virtual space on a vaguely suspenseful, but ultimately fun scientific mission. The Fleet also houses a 76-foot (23m) domed OMNIMAX theater that shows IMAX films so realistic that ocean footage can actually give you motion sickness! And in 2001, the Fleet proudly unveiled a spiffy new planetarium simulator powered by computer graphics. Planetarium shows are the first Wednesday of each month ($5 adults, $3 kids).

On your way out, don't miss the gift shop, an inspired collection of toys, gadgets, and clever souvenirs.

1875 El Prado. © 619/238-1233. www.rhfleet.org. Admission (includes IMAX film, SciTours ride, and exhibit galleries) $11.50 adults, $9.50 seniors 65 and over, $8.50 children 3–12. Free 1st Tues of each month (exhibit galleries only). MC, V. Sun–Tues and Thurs 9:30am–6pm; Wed 9:30am–9pm; Fri–Sat 9:30am–10pm. Bus: 7, 7A/B, 25.

San Diego Aerospace Museum 🌟🌟 *Kids* Probably the number two kid-pleaser of the museums (after the Fleet Science Center, below), this enormously popular facility provides an overview of the nation's air-and-space history, from the days of hot-air balloons to the space age, with plenty of biplanes and military fighters in between. It emphasizes local aviation history, particularly the construction here of the *Spirit of St. Louis*. The museum is housed in a stunning cylindrical hall built by the Ford Motor Company in 1935 (for another International Exposition), and has an imaginative gift shop with items like old-fashioned leather flight hoods and new-fashioned freeze-dried astronaut ice cream.

2001 Pan American Plaza. © 619/234-8291. www.aerospacemuseum.org. Admission $8 adults, $3 children 6–17, free for active military with ID and children under 6. Free 4th Tues of each month. Sept–May daily 10am–4:30pm; June–Aug daily 10am–5:30pm (last admission ½ hr. before closing). Closed Thanksgiving, Christmas. Bus: 7, 7A/B.

San Diego Automotive Museum 🛝   Even if you don't know a distributor from a dipstick, you're bound to ooh-and-aah over the classic, antique, and exotic cars here. Every one is so pristine you'd swear it just rolled off the line, from an 1886 Benz to a 1931 Rolls Royce Phaeton to the 1981 DeLorean. Some days you can take a peek at the ongoing restoration program, and the museum sponsors many outdoor car rallies and other events.

2080 Pan American Plaza. ℭ 619/231-2886. www.sdautomuseum.org. Admission $7 adults, $6 seniors and active military, $3 children 6–15, free for children under 6. Free 4th Tues of each month. MC, V. Daily 10am–5pm (last admission 4:30pm). Closed Thanksgiving, Christmas, and January 1. Bus: 7, 7A/B.

San Diego Historical Society Museum   A good place to start if you are a newcomer to San Diego, the recently remodeled museum offers permanent and changing exhibits on topics related to the history of the region, from pioneer outposts in the 1800s to the present day. Many of the museum's photographs depict Balboa Park and the growth of the city. Docent tours are available; call ℭ **619/232-6203,** ext. 117, for information and reservations. Books about San Diego's history are available in the gift shop.

1649 El Prado, in Casa del Balboa. ℭ 619/232-6203. www.sandiegohisotry.org. Admission $5 adults, $4 seniors and military with ID, $4 for groups of 10 or more, $2 children 6–12, free for children 5 and under. Free 2nd Tues of each month. Tues–Sun 10am–4:30pm. Bus: 7, 7A/B, or 25.

San Diego Museum of Art 🛝   With one of the grandest entrances along El Prado—the rotunda at the head of dramatic stairs features striking Spanish tile work—the museum is known in the art world for outstanding collections of Italian Renaissance and Dutch and Spanish baroque art, along with an impressive collection of Toulouse-Lautrec. Prestigious traveling exhibits are often shown here, and the museum's high-tech touch is an interactive computer image system that allows visitors to locate museum highlights and custom-design a tour. In 2003, look for a rare exhibition of Edgar Degas's bronze sculptures (June 28–Sept 28).

1450 El Prado. ℭ 619/232-7931. www.sdmart.org. Admission $8 adults 25 and older, $6 seniors 65 and over, military, and youths 18–24, $3 children 6–17, free for children under 6. Admission to traveling exhibits varies. Free 3rd Tues of each month. Tues–Sun 10am–6pm (Thurs until 9pm). Bus: 7, 7A/B, 25.

San Diego Natural History Museum   The museum focuses on the flora, fauna, and mineralogy of the Southwest. Kids marvel at the animals they find here and enjoy exploring the Desert Lab, home to live snakes and tarantulas. Call or check the museum's website for a current schedule of special visiting exhibits.

1788 El Prado. ℭ 619/232-3821. www.sdnhm.org. Admission $7 adults, $6 seniors and active-duty military, $5 children 3–17, free for children under 3. Free 1st Tues of each month. Daily 9:30am–4:30pm; open later in summer. Bus: 7, 7A/B, 25.

Spreckels Organ Pavilion   Given to San Diego citizens in 1914 by brothers John D. and Adolph Spreckels, the ornate, curved pavilion houses a magnificent organ with 4,445 individual pipes. They range in length from less than a half inch to more than 32 feet (9.5m). With only brief interruptions, the organ has been in continuous use in the park, and today visitors can enjoy free hour-long concerts on Sundays at 2pm. There's seating for 2,400.

South of El Prado. ℭ 619/226-0819. Free 1-hr. concerts Sun year-round; free Summer Festival concerts July–Aug Mon 8pm and Tues–Thurs 6:15pm. Bus: 7, 7A/B, or 25.

Timken Museum of Art   Called the "Jewel of the Park," this museum houses the Putnam Foundation's collection of 19th-century American paintings and works by European old masters, as well as an outstanding display of Russian icons.

1500 El Prado. © 619/239-5548. www.timkenmuseum.org. Free admission. Tues–Sat 10am–4:30pm; Sun 1:30–4:30pm. Closed Sept. Bus: 7, 7A/B, or 25.

4 More Attractions
DOWNTOWN & BEYOND

In downtown San Diego, you can wander in the **Gaslamp Quarter** (see "Walking Tour 1: The Gaslamp Quarter," in chapter 8) or the **Horton Plaza** shopping center. You can shop for hours, stroll, snack or dine, enjoy free entertainment, see a movie, and people-watch—all within a unique and colorful architectural framework. The Gaslamp Quarter, San Diego's trendiest area, consists of 16 or so blocks of restored historic buildings. It gets its name from the old-fashioned street lamps that line the sidewalks.

Seaport Village is a shopping and dining complex on the waterfront. It was designed to look like a New England seaport community. The views across the water are terrific.

Cabrillo National Monument 🎈   Breathtaking views mingle with the early history of San Diego, which began when Juan Rodríguez Cabrillo arrived in 1542. His statue dominates the tip of Point Loma, which is also a vantage point for watching migrating gray whales en route from the Arctic Ocean to Baja California from December through March. The restored lighthouse (1855) allows a glimpse of what life was like here in the past century. National Park Service rangers lead walks at the monument, and there are tide pools that beg for exploration. Free 30-minute films on Cabrillo, tide pools, and California gray whales are shown on the hour daily from 10am to 4pm. The drive from downtown is about a half hour; Gray Line tours also offers an excursion to the monument (see p. 155 for details).

1800 Cabrillo Memorial Dr., Point Loma. © 619/557-5450. www.nps.gov/cabr. Admission $5 per vehicle, $2 for walk-ins, free for children under 17 and seniors 62 and over (with a National Parks Service Golden Age Passport). Daily 9am–5:15pm. Take I-5 or I-8 to Hwy. 209/Rosecrans St. and follow signs. Bus: 26.

Children's Museum of San Diego *(Kids)*   This interactive attraction, which encourages participation, is a home away from home for kids. It provides ongoing supervised activities, as well as a monthly special celebration, recognizing important issues such as earth awareness or African American history. The indoor-outdoor art studio is a big draw for kids aged 2 to 10. There is also a theater with costumes for budding actors to don, plus an observation walk above the exhibits that kids climb on and exit by way of a spiral slide. The museum shop is filled with toys, games, crafts, and books. School groups come in the morning, so you might want to schedule your visit for the afternoon.

200 W. Island Ave. © 619/233-KIDS. www.sdchildrensmuseum.org. Admission $6 adults and children, $3 seniors, free for children under 3. Tues–Sat 10am–4pm. Trolley: Convention Center; museum is a block away. All-day parking (across the street) about $3.

Firehouse Museum   Appropriately housed in San Diego's oldest firehouse, the museum features shiny fire engines, including hand-drawn and horse-drawn models, a 1903 steam pumper, and memorabilia such as antique alarms, fire hats, and foundry molds for fire hydrants. There's also a small gift shop.

1572 Columbia St. (at Cedar St.). © 619/232-FIRE. www.globalinfo.com/noncom/firehouse/Firehouse.html. Admission $2 adults, $1 seniors and military in uniform, $1 youths 13–17, free for children under 13. Thurs–Fri 10am–2pm; Sat–Sun 10am–4pm. Bus: 5, 16, or 105.

Maritime Museum ⛵⛵ *(Kids)*   This unique museum consists of a trio of fine ships: the full-rigged merchant vessel *Star of India* (1863), whose impressive masts are an integral part of the San Diego cityscape; the gleaming white San Francisco–Oakland steam-powered ferry *Berkeley* (1898), which worked round-the-clock to carry people to safety following the 1906 San Francisco earthquake; and the sleek *Medea* (1904), one of the world's few remaining large steam yachts. You can board and explore each vessel, and from April through October you can watch movies on deck (see chapter 10).

1306 N. Harbor Dr. ⓒ **619/234-9153.** www.sdmaritime.com. Admission $6 adults, $4 seniors over 62 and youths 13–17, $2 children 6–12, free for children under 6. Daily 9am–8pm. Bus: 2. Trolley: America Plaza.

Museum of Contemporary Art, Downtown (MCA)   MCA Downtown is the second location of the Museum of Contemporary Art, San Diego (the first is in La Jolla). Two large and two smaller galleries present changing exhibitions of nationally and internationally distinguished contemporary artists. Lectures and tours for adults and children are also offered. There's a gift shop and bookstore on the premises.

1001 Kettner Blvd. (at Broadway). ⓒ **619/234-1001.** www.mcasandiego.org. Free admission. Thurs–Tues 11am–5pm. Parking $2 with validation at America Plaza Complex. Trolley: America Plaza.

Villa Montezuma ⛵ *(Finds)*   This stunning mansion just east of downtown was built in 1887 for internationally acclaimed musician and author Jesse Shepard. Lush with Victoriana, it features more stained glass than most churches have; windows depict Mozart, Beethoven, Sappho, Rubens, St. Cecilia (patron saint of musicians), and other notables. The striking ceilings are of Lincrusta Walton—pressed canvas coated with linseed oil, a forerunner of linoleum, which never looked this good. Shepard lived here with his life companion, Lawrence Tonner, for only 2 years, and died in obscurity in Los Angeles in 1927. The San Diego Historical Society painstakingly restored the house, which is on the National Register of Historic Places, and furnished it with period pieces. Unfortunately, the neighborhood is not as fashionable as the building, but it's safe to park your car in the daytime. If you love Victorian houses, don't miss this one for its quirkiness.

1925 K St. (at 20th Ave.). ⓒ **619/239-2211.** Admission $5 adults, $4 seniors and students, $2 kids 6–17, 5 and under free. Fri–Sun 10am–4:30pm. Bus: 3, 3A, 4, 5, 16, or 105 to Market and Imperial sts. By car, follow K St.

William Heath Davis House Museum   Shipped by boat to San Diego in 1850 from Portland, Maine, this is the oldest structure in the Gaslamp Quarter. It is a well-preserved example of a prefabricated "saltbox" family home, and has remained structurally unchanged for more than 120 years. A museum, on the first and second floors, is open to the public, as is the small park adjacent to the house. The house is also home to the Gaslamp Quarter Historical Foundation, which sponsors walking tours of the quarter for about $8 (the fee includes museum admission). At least one tour is conducted each day, including a Saturday morning tour at 11am; call ahead for the specific schedule.

410 Island Ave. (at Fourth Ave.). ⓒ **619/233-4692.** www.gaslampquarter.org. Suggested donation $3. Tues–Sun 11am–3pm. Call ahead to verify hours. Bus: 1, 3, or 3A. Trolley: Gaslamp Quarter/Convention Center W.

OLD TOWN

The birthplace of San Diego—indeed, of California—Old Town takes you back to the Mexican California, which existed here until the mid-1800s.

Downtown San Diego Attractions

Children's Museum
of San Diego **6**
Convention Center **7**
Firehouse Museum **2**
Horton Plaza **9**
Maritime Museum **3**

Museum of Contemporary Art,
Downtown **4**
San Diego Zoo **1**
Seaport Village **5**
Villa Montezuma **10**
William Heath Davis House **8**

"Walking Tour 3" in chapter 8 goes through Old Town. In addition, free walking tours leave daily at 10:30am and 2pm from **Seeley Stables Visitor Center (© 619/220-5422)**, at the head of the pedestrian walkway that is the continuation of San Diego Avenue.

Seven of the park's 20 structures are original; the rest are reconstructed. Admission to all museums, open daily from 10am to 5pm, is free, although donations are welcome. They're accepted at the McCoy Interpretive Center; La Casa de Estudillo, which depicts the living conditions of a wealthy family in 1872; and Seeley Stables, named after A. L. Seeley, who ran the stagecoach and mail service in these parts from 1867 to 1871. The stables have two floors of wagons, carriages, stagecoaches, and other memorabilia, including washboards, slot machines, and hand-worked saddles, as well as a 17-minute slide show.

On weekdays during the school year, Old Town buzzes with fourth-graders.

Heritage Park   This 7.8-acre county park contains seven original 19th-century houses moved here from other places and given new uses. Among them are a bed-and-breakfast, a doll shop, and a gift shop. The most recent addition is the small synagogue, placed near the park's entrance in 1989. A glorious coral tree crowns the top of the hill.

2450 Heritage Park Row (corner of Juan and Harney sts.). (C) **858/694-3049.** Free admission. Daily 9:30am–3pm. Bus: 4 or 5/105.

Mission Basilica San Diego de Alcala 𝕲   Established in 1769, this was the first link in a chain of 21 missions founded by Spanish missionary Junípero Serra. In 1774, the mission was moved to its present site for agricultural reasons, and to separate Native American converts from the fortress that included the original building. A few bricks belonging to the original mission can be seen in Presidio Park in Old Town. Mass is said daily in this active Catholic parish. Other missions in the San Diego area include Mission San Luis Rey de Francia in Oceanside, Mission San Antonia de Pala near Mount Palomar, and Mission Santa Ysabel near Julian.

10818 San Diego Mission Rd., Mission Valley. (C) **619/281-8449.** Admission $3 adults, $2 seniors and students, $1 children under 13. Free Sun and for daily masses. Daily 9am–5pm; mass daily 7am and 5:30pm. Take I-8 to Mission Gorge Rd. to Twain Ave. Bus: 6, 16, 25, 43, or 81.

Serra Museum   Perched on a hill above Old Town, the stately mission-style building overlooks the hillside where, in 1769, the first mission and first non-native settlement on the west coast of the United States and Canada were founded. The museum's exhibits introduce visitors to the Native American, Spanish, and Mexican people who first called this place home. On display are their belongings, from cannons to cookware; a Spanish furniture collection; and, one of the first paintings brought to California, which survived being damaged in an Indian attack. The mission remained San Diego's only settlement until the 1820s, when families began to move down the hill into what is now Old Town. You can also watch an ongoing archaeological dig uncovering more of the items used by early settlers. From the 70-foot (21m) tower, visitors can compare the spectacular view with historic photos to see how this land has changed over time.

The museum is in Presidio Park and is called the "Plymouth Rock of the Pacific." The large cross in the park was made of floor tile from the Presidio ruins. Sculptor Arthur Putnam made the statues of Father Serra, founder of the missions in California. Climb up to **Inspiration Point,** as many have done for marriage ceremonies, for a sweeping view of the area.

2727 Presidio Dr., Presidio Park. (C) **619/297-3258.** www.sandiegohistory.org. Admission $5 adults, $4 seniors and students, $2 children 6–17, free for children under 6. Fri–Sun 10am–4:30pm. Take I-8 to the Taylor St. exit. Turn right on Taylor, then left on Presidio Dr.

Whaley House   In 1856, this striking two-story brick house (the first one in these parts) 1 block from Old Town State Historic Park was built for Thomas Whaley and his family. Whaley was a New Yorker who arrived via San Francisco, where he had been lured by the gold rush. The house is one of only two authenticated haunted houses in California, and 10,000 schoolchildren visit each year to see for themselves. Apparently, four spirits haunt the house, and other paranormal phenomena have taken place. Exhibits include a life mask of Abraham Lincoln, one of only six made; the spinet piano used in the movie *Gone With the Wind;* and the concert piano that accompanied Swedish soprano Jenny Lind on her final U.S. tour in 1852. Director June Reading will make you feel at home, in spite of the ghosts.

2482 San Diego Ave. (C) **619/297-7511.** Admission $5 adults, $4 seniors over 60, $3 children 3–12. Wed–Mon 10am–4:30pm. Closed Christmas and Jan 1.

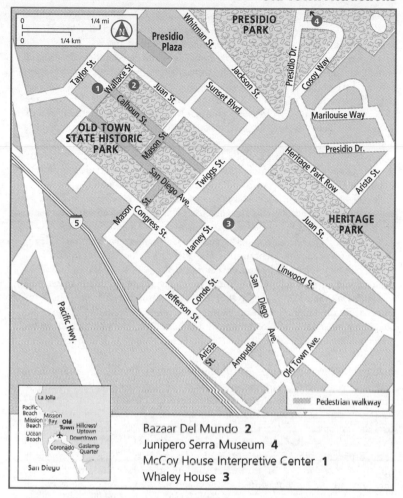

Bazaar Del Mundo **2**
Junipero Serra Museum **4**
McCoy House Interpretive Center **1**
Whaley House **3**

MISSION BAY & THE BEACHES

This is a great area for walking, jogging, in-line skating, biking, and boating. See the appropriate headings in "Outdoor Pursuits," later in this chapter.

Giant Dipper Roller Coaster   A local landmark for 70 years, the Giant Dipper is one of two surviving fixtures from the original Belmont Amusement Park (the other is the Plunge swimming pool). After sitting dormant for 15 years, the vintage wooden roller coaster, with more than 2,600 feet (780m) of track and 13 hills, underwent extensive restoration and reopened in 1991. If you're in the neighborhood (especially with older kids), it's worth a stop. You must be 50 inches tall to ride the roller coaster. You can also ride on the Giant Dipper's neighbor, the Liberty Carousel ($1).

3190 Mission Blvd. ℂ 858/488-1549. www.giantdipper.com. Ride on the Giant Dipper $3.50. MC, V. Sun–Thurs 11am–10pm; Fri–Sat 11am–11pm. Take I-5 to the SeaWorld exit, and follow W. Mission Bay Dr. to Belmont Park.

LA JOLLA

The area's most scenic spot—star of postcards for more than 100 years—is **La Jolla Cove** and **Ellen Browning Scripps Park** on the cliff above it. Both are on Coast Boulevard. The park is a boat-free zone, with protected undersea flora and fauna that draw many scuba divers and other visitors. Swimming, sunning, picnicking, barbecuing, reading, and strolling along the oceanfront walkway are all ongoing activities. The unique 6,000-acre **San Diego–La Jolla Underwater Park,** established in 1970, stretches from La Jolla Cove to the northern end of Torrey Pines State Reserve. It can be reached from La Jolla Cove or La Jolla Shores.

For a scenic drive, follow La Jolla Boulevard to Nautilus Street and turn east to get to **Mount Soledad,** which offers a 360° view of the area. The cross on top, erected in 1954, is 43 feet (13m) high and 12 feet (3.5m) wide.

Highlights in town include **Mary Star of the Sea,** 7727 Girard (at Kline), a beautiful Roman Catholic church; and, the **La Valencia Hotel,** 1132 Prospect St., a fine example of Spanish Colonial structure. The **La Jolla Woman's Club,** 7791 Draper Ave.; the adjacent **Museum of Contemporary Art, San Diego;** the **La Jolla Recreation Center;** and **The Bishop's School** are all examples of village buildings designed by architect Irving Gill.

At La Jolla's north end, you'll find the 1,200-acre, 15,000-student **University of California, San Diego** (UCSD), which was established in 1960. The campus features the Stuart Collection of public sculpture and the Birch Aquarium at Scripps Institution of Oceanography (see individual listings, below). Louis Kahn designed the **Salk Institute for Biological Studies,** 10010 N. Torrey Pines Rd.

Birch Aquarium at Scripps 𝒶𝒶 This beautiful facility is both an aquarium and a museum, operated by the world-famous Scripps Institute of Oceanography. To make the most of the self-guided experience, be sure to pick up a visitor guide from the information booth just inside the entrance, and take time to read the text on each of the exhibits. The aquarium affords close-up views of the Pacific Northwest, the California coast, Mexico's Sea of Cortez, and the tropical seas, all presented in 33 marine-life tanks. The giant kelp forest is particularly impressive (keep an eye out for a tiger shark or an eel swimming through). Be sure to notice the fanciful white anemones and the ethereal moon jellies (which look like parachutes). The rooftop demonstration tide pool not only shows

---

Finds Insiders' Suggestions

While droves of folks stroll the sidewalks adjacent to the San Diego–La Jolla Underwater Park and La Jolla Cove, only a few know about **Coast Walk.** Starting behind the **Cave Store,** 1325 Coast Blvd. (© **858/459-0746**), it meanders along the wooded cliffs and affords a wonderful view of the beach and beyond. The shop also serves as entry for **Sunny Jim Cave,** a large and naturally occurring sea cave reached by a steep and narrow staircase through the rock. The tunnel was hand-carved in 1903—it lets out on a wood-plank observation deck from which you can gaze out at the sea. It's a cool treat, particularly on a hot summer day, and costs only $2 per person ($1 for kids). Hold the handrail and your little ones' hands tightly.

La Jolla Attractions

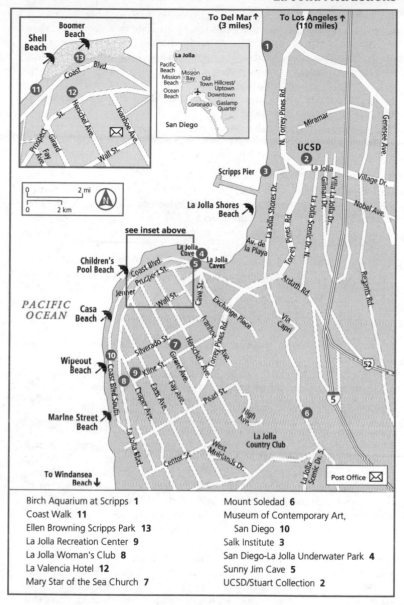

Birch Aquarium at Scripps **1**
Coast Walk **11**
Ellen Browning Scripps Park **13**
La Jolla Recreation Center **9**
La Jolla Woman's Club **8**
La Valencia Hotel **12**
Mary Star of the Sea Church **7**

Mount Soledad **6**
Museum of Contemporary Art, San Diego **10**
Salk Institute **3**
San Diego-La Jolla Underwater Park **4**
Sunny Jim Cave **5**
UCSD/Stuart Collection **2**

visitors marine coastal life but also offers an amazing view of Scripps Pier, La Jolla Shores Beach, the village of La Jolla, and the ocean. Free tide-pool talks are offered on weekends, which is also when the aquarium is most crowded.

The museum section has numerous interpretive exhibits on current and historic research at the Scripps Institution, which was established in 1903 and became part of the university system in 1912. You'll learn what fog is and why salt melts snow; the number of supermarket products with ingredients that come from the sea (toothpaste, ice cream, and matches, to name a few) might surprise you; and you can feel what an earthquake is like and experience a 12-minute simulated submarine ride. The bookstore is well stocked with textbooks, science books, educational toys, gifts, and T-shirts.

A series of **"Seaside Explorations,"** such as the La Jolla Coast Walk, Tide-pooling Adventures, and Running with Grunion, are offered. Call ⓒ **858/543-6691** for information and prices.

2300 Expedition Way. ⓒ **858/534-FISH**. www.aquarium.ucsd.edu. Admission $8.50 adults, $7.50 seniors, $5 children 3–17, free for children under 3. Parking $3. AE, MC, V. Daily 9am–5pm. Take I-5 to La Jolla Village Dr. exit, go west 1 mile (1.5km), and turn left at Expedition Way. Bus: 34.

Museum of Contemporary Art (MCA), San Diego ⭑⭑

Focusing primarily on work produced since 1950, the museum is known internationally for its permanent collection and thought-provoking exhibitions. The MCA's collection of contemporary art comprises more than 3,000 works of painting, sculpture, drawings, prints, photography, video, and multimedia works. The holdings include every major art movement of the past half-century, with a strong representation by California artists. You'll see particularly noteworthy examples of minimalism, light and space work, conceptualism, installation, and site-specific art—the outside sculptures were designed specifically for this site. The museum is perched on a cliff overlooking the Pacific Ocean, and the views from the galleries are gorgeous. The original building on the site was the residence of the legendary Ellen Browning Scripps, designed by Irving Gill in 1916. It became an art museum in 1941, and the original Gill building facade was recently uncovered and restored.

700 Prospect St. ⓒ **858/454-3541**. www.mcasandiego.org. Admission $4 adults, $2 students and seniors, free for children under 12; free 3rd Tues and 1st Sun of each month. Summer (Memorial Day–Labor Day) Thurs–Fri and Mon–Tues 11am–8pm, Sat–Sun 11am–5pm; rest of year Fri–Tues 11am–5pm, Thurs 11am–8pm. Take the Ardath Rd. exit off I-5 north or the La Jolla Village Dr. west exit off I-5 south. Take Torrey Pines Rd. to Prospect Place and turn right. Prospect Place becomes Prospect St.

Stuart Collection

Consider the Stuart Collection a work in progress on a large scale. Through a 1982 agreement between the Stuart Foundation and UCSD, the still-growing collection consists of site-related sculptures by leading contemporary artists throughout the 1,200 acres of the campus. Among the 12 diverse sculptures on view are Niki de Saint-Phalle's *Sun God,* a jubilant 14-foot-high (4m) fiberglass bird on a 15-foot (4.5m) concrete base. Nicknamed "Big Bird," it's been made an unofficial mascot by the students, who use it as the centerpiece of their annual celebration, the Sun God Festival. Also in the collection are Alexis Smith's *Snake Path,* a 560-foot-long (168m) slate-tile pathway that winds up the hill from the Engineering Mall to the east terrace of the University Library; and Terry Allen's *Trees,* three eucalyptus trees encased in lead. One tree emits songs, and another poems and stories, while the third stands silent in a grove of trees the students call "The Enchanted Forest." Pick up a brochure and map with marked sculpture locations from the information booth at the Northview Drive or Gilman Drive entrance to the campus. Guides, parking permits, and general information are also available.

University of California, San Diego (UCSD). ⓒ **858/534-2117**. www.stuartcollection.ucsd.edu. Free admission. From La Jolla, take Torrey Pines Rd. to La Jolla Village Dr., turn right, go 2 blocks to Gilman Dr. and turn left into the campus; in about a block the information booth will be visible on the right.

Impressions

Let Coronado wear her crown
As Empress of the Sea;
Nor need she fear her earthly peer
Will e'er discovered be.

—L. Frank Baum, 1905

CORONADO

It's hard to miss one of Coronado's most famous landmarks: the **Coronado Bay Bridge.** Completed in 1969, this five-lane bridge spans 2 miles (3km) across the bay, linking San Diego and Coronado. When it opened, it put the commuter ferries out of business, although in 1986 passenger ferry service restarted. Crossing the bridge by car or bus is a thrill because you can see Mexico, the San Diego skyline, Coronado, the naval station, and San Diego Bay. The bridge's middle section floats, so that if it's destroyed in wartime, naval ships will still have access to the harbor and sea beyond. In 2002, the bridge toll was abolished, so passage is free in both directions. Bus 901 from downtown will also take you over the bridge.

Coronado Historical Museum   Formerly located in a historic 1898 house, this museum's spacious new facility allows the display of more archival materials about the development of Coronado. Exhibits range from photographs of the Hotel Del in its infancy; the old ferries; and Tent City, a seaside campground for middle-income vacationers from 1900 to 1939 and notable residents and visitors. Other memorabilia include army uniforms, old postcards, and even recorded music. You'll also learn about the island's military aviation history during World Wars I and II.

1100 Orange Ave. (C) 619/435-7242. www.coronadohistory.org. $4 adults, $3 seniors and military, $2 youths 9–18, free to kids 8 and under. Mon, Tues, Thurs–Sat 10am–4pm, Sun noon–4pm.

Hotel del Coronado ❀❀   Built in 1888, this turreted Victorian seaside resort remains an enduring, endearing national treasure. Whether you stay here, dine here, dance here, or simply wander through to tour its grounds and photo gallery, prepare to be enchanted. See "A Century of Intrigue: Scenes from the Hotel del Coronado" in chapter 5 for more details.

1500 Orange Ave., Coronado. (C) **619/435-6611.** Free admission. Bus: 901. Ferry: Broadway Pier. Then ½-hr. walk, or take a bus or the Coronado trolley, or rent a bike.

5 Free of Charge & Full of Fun

It's easy to get charged up on vacation—$10 here, $5 there, and pretty soon your credit-card balance looks like the national debt. To keep that from happening, we offer this list of free San Diego activities. In addition, scan the lists of "Outdoor Pursuits," "Spectator Sports," and "Special-Interest Sightseeing," later in this chapter, and the "San Diego Calendar of Events" in chapter 2. Many events listed in these sections, such as the U.S. Open Sandcastle Competition, are free. San Diego also has numerous parades, such as the Holiday Bowl Parade and the Parade of Lights, both in December.

DOWNTOWN & BEYOND

It doesn't cost a penny to stroll around the Gaslamp Quarter, which is full of restaurants, shops, and historic buildings, or along the Embarcadero (waterfront), and around the shops at Seaport Village or Horton Plaza. And don't forget: Walk-about International offers free guided walking tours (described later in this chapter), and Centre City Redevelopment Corporation's Downtown Information Center gives bus tours.

If you'd rather drive around, ask for the map of the **52-mile San Diego Scenic Drive** when you're at the International Visitor Information Center.

The downtown branch of the Museum of Contemporary Art, San Diego, is always free to the public. And you can fish free of charge from any municipal pier. The **Children's Park,** across the street from the Children's Museum of San Diego, is free, as are all parks in San Diego.

BALBOA PARK

Although it's a local best-kept secret, the **San Diego Zoo** is free to all on the first Monday of October (Founders Day), and children under 12 enter free every day during October.

All the **museums** in Balboa Park are open to the public without charge 1 day a month. Here's a list of the free days:

1st Tuesday of each month: Natural History Museum, Reuben H. Fleet Science Center, Model Railroad Museum.

2nd Tuesday: Museum of Photographic Arts, Hall of Champions Sports Museum, Historical Society Museum.

3rd Tuesday: Museum of Art, Museum of Man, Mingei International Museum, Japanese Friendship Garden, Art Institute.

4th Tuesday: Aerospace Museum, Automotive Museum.

These Balboa Park attractions are always free: The Botanical Building and Lily Pond, House of Pacific Relations International Cottages, and Timken Museum of Art.

Free 1-hour Sunday concerts and free Summer Festival concerts are given at the Spreckels Organ Pavilion.

OLD TOWN & BEYOND

Explore **Heritage Park, Presidio Park,** or **Old Town State Historic Park.** There's free entertainment (mariachis and folk dancers) at the **Bazaar del Mundo,** 2754 Calhoun (© **619/296-3161**), on Saturdays and Sundays. **Mission Trails Regional Park,** which offers hiking trails and an interpretive center, is at the east end of Highway 52.

MISSION BAY, PACIFIC BEACH & BEYOND

Walk along the beach or around the bay—it's free, fun, and good for you. (See "Hiking/Walking" in "Outdoor Pursuits," later in this chapter.)

LA JOLLA

Enjoy free outdoor **concerts** at Scripps Park on Sundays from 2 to 4pm, mid-June through mid-September (© **858/525-3160**).

Anytime is a good time to walk around the La Jolla Cove, Ellen Browning Scripps Park, and Torrey Pines State Reserve, or watch the harbor-seal colony at Seal Rock or the Children's Pool.

It's also fun to meander around the campus of the University of California, San Diego (UCSD), and view the Stuart Collection of Outdoor Sculpture. The excellent La Jolla branch of the Museum of Contemporary Art, San Diego, is free the first Tuesday of each month.

For the best vista, follow the "Scenic Drive" signs to Mount Soledad and a 360° view of the area.

CORONADO

Drive across the Coronado Bay Bridge (free to all after the abolishment of the toll in 2002) and take a self-guided tour of the Hotel del Coronado's grounds and photo gallery. A walk on beautiful Coronado beach costs nothing—so does a lookie-loo tour of the neighborhood's restored Victorian and Craftsman homes.

FARTHER AFIELD: ARCO TRAINING CENTER

Free tours of the ARCO Training Center in Chula Vista are given year-round. This is the country's first warm-weather, year-round, multisport Olympic training complex. It's on the western shore of Lower Otay Reservoir in Chula Vista, and is one of three United States Olympic Committee training centers. (The others are in Colorado Springs, Colo., and Lake Placid, N.Y.) Visitors see a 6-minute film about the Olympic movement, followed by a narrated tour (1½-mile/2.5km walk) of the 150-acre campus. The hour-long tours are available Monday through Saturday from 9am to 4pm, Sunday 11am to 4pm. Call ℭ **619/482-6222** for more information and to make reservations.

To get here, take I-805 south to Telegraph Canyon Road, then go east about 7 miles (11km) until you reach a sign directing you to turn right; follow this road to the visitor center.

6 Especially for Kids

If you didn't know better, you would think that San Diego was designed by parents planning a long summer vacation. Activities abound for toddlers to teens. Dozens of public parks, 70 miles (113km) of beaches, and myriad museums are just part of what awaits kids and families. For up-to-the-minute information about activities for children, pick up a free copy of the monthly *San Diego Family Press;* its calendar of events is geared toward family activities and kids' interests. The **International Visitor Information Center,** at First Avenue and F Street (ℭ **619/236-1212**), is always a great resource.

THE TOP ATTRACTIONS

- **Balboa Park** (p. 135) has street entertainers and clowns that always rate high with kids. They can usually be found around El Prado on weekends. The Natural History Museum, the Aerospace Museum, and the Reuben H. Fleet Science Center—with its hands-on exhibits and IMAX theater—draw kids like magnets.
- **The San Diego Zoo** (p. 126) appeals to children of all ages, and the double-decker bus tours bring all the animals into easy view of even the smallest visitors.
- **SeaWorld** (p. 130), on Mission Bay, entertains everyone with killer whales, pettable dolphins, and plenty of penguins—the park's penguin exhibit is home to more penguins than are in all other zoos combined. Try out the new family adventure land, "Shamu's Happy Harbor," where everyone is encouraged to explore, crawl, climb, jump, and get wet in more than 20 interactive areas; or, brave a raging river in Shipwreck Rapids.
- **The Wild Animal Park** (p. 128) brings geography classes to life when kids find themselves gliding through the wilds of Africa and Asia in a monorail.

OTHER ATTRACTIONS

- **Children's Museum of San Diego** (p. 141) provides a wonderful interactive and imagination-probing experience.
- **Children's Park** (p. 150) is across the street from the Children's Museum. The park holds grassy knolls, trees, lighted pathways, and a 200-foot-diameter (60m) pond with a spray fountain. Children's Park is a 1996 addition to Martin Luther King, Jr. Promenade—a 12-acre park that faces Harbor Drive and includes a walkway with landscaping and benches. Fifteen inscribed granite segments along the walkway focus on Dr. King's philosophy.
- **Seaport Village** (p. 141) has an old-fashioned carousel for children to enjoy.
- **Old Town State Historic Park** (p. 150) has a one-room schoolhouse that rates high with kids. They'll also enjoy the freedom of running around the safe, park-like compound to "discover" their own fun.
- **Birch Aquarium at Scripps** (p. 146), in La Jolla, is an aquarium that lets kids explore the realms of the deep and learn about life in the sea.
- **LEGOLAND** (p. 214), in Carlsbad, is a brand-new theme park primarily for children; kids can see impressive models built entirely with LEGO blocks. There are also rides, refreshments, and LEGO and DUPLO building contests. The park advertises itself as a "country just for kids" . . . need we say more?

THAT'S ENTERTAINMENT

San Diego Junior Theatre is in Balboa Park's Casa del Prado Theatre (© **619/ 239-8355;** www.juniortheatre.com). The productions—shows like *Peter Pan* and *Little Women*—are acted and managed by kids 8 to 18; ticket prices are generally under $10 for both kids and adults.

Sunday afternoon is a great time for kids in **Balboa Park.** They can visit both the outdoor Spreckels Organ Pavilion for a free concert (the mix of music isn't too highbrow for a young audience) and the House of Pacific Relations to watch folk dancing on the lawn and experience food from many nations. Or, get a taste of Punch and Judy at **Marie Hitchcock Puppet Theatre,** in Balboa Park's Palisades Building (© **619/685-5045**). Shows are given Wednesday through Friday at 10 and 11:30am and Saturday and Sunday at 11am, 1, and 2:30pm. The shows cost $2 for adults, $1.50 for children over 2, and they're free for children under 2.

7 Special-Interest Sightseeing

FOR ARCHITECTURE BUFFS

Lovers of period houses will enjoy walking through the Victorian **Villa Montezuma** and the Craftsman-style **Marston House Museum** (both described earlier in this chapter). The **Gaslamp Quarter** walking tour (see chapter 8) will lead you past the area's restored Victorian commercial buildings.

Downtown high-rises of particular interest include the **Manchester Grand Hyatt San Diego,** the **Emerald-Shapery Center** at 400 W. Broadway, and **One America Plaza** at 600 W. Broadway. This last building is 498 feet (149m) high, which is 24 inches under the maximum height allowed by the FAA. Some people say San Diego's new skyline resembles the contents of a toolbox: a straight screwdriver, a Phillips screwdriver, and a cluster of Allen wrenches. Take a look and see what you think.

While you're in the central business district, the 12-by-12-foot (3.5m-by-3.5m) **scale model** of the city at the Centre City Development Corporation's

Downtown Information Center, 225 Broadway (© **619/235-2200**), might be of interest.

Students of architecture will also want to see the Louis Kahn–designed **Salk Institute** and the classic buildings created by **Irving Gill** (see "La Jolla" in "More Attractions," earlier in this chapter). La Jolla's **Brockton Villa** (described in chapter 6, "Dining") has won architectural awards for excellence.

In contrast, the Hyatt Regency San Diego received a Major Raw Onion (an award given for architectural flops)—the same year the Salk Institute was lambasted for adding an extension that compromised Louis Kahn's design. Not far from the Salk Institute, the Michael Graves–designed **Hyatt Regency La Jolla** has also garnered an Onion. For further information on San Diego architecture, phone the **AIA** (© **619/232-0109**).

FOR GARDENERS

San Diego is a gardener's paradise, thanks in part to the efforts and inspiration of Kate Sessions. In Balboa Park, visit the Japanese Friendship Garden, the Botanical Building and Lily Pond, and the rose and desert gardens (across the road from Plaza de Balboa). And when you're at the San Diego Zoo and Wild Animal Park, you'll notice that both are outstanding botanical gardens. Many visitors who admire the landscaping at the zoo don't realize that the plantings have been carefully developed over the years. The 100 acres were once scrub-covered hillsides with few trees. Today, towering eucalyptus and graceful palms, birds-of-paradise, and hibiscus are just a few of the 6,500 botanical species from all over the world that flourish here, providing a beautiful garden setting as well as dinner for some animals. In fact, the plant collection is worth more than the zoo's animals.

In North County, garden enthusiasts will want to visit the 30-acre **Quail Botanical Gardens** (see chapter 11). If you'd like to take plants home with you, visit some of the area's nurseries, including the one started in 1910 by Kate Sessions, **Mission Hills Nursery**, 1525 Fort Stockton Dr., San Diego (© **619/ 295-2808**). **Walter Andersen's Nursery**, 3642 Enterprise St., San Diego (© **619/224-8271**), is also a local favorite. See chapter 11 for information on nurseries in North County. Flower growing is big business in this area, and plant enthusiasts could spend a week just visiting the retail and wholesale purveyors of everything from pansies to palm trees. The **San Diego Floral Association,** in the Casa del Prado in Balboa Park (© **619/232-5762**), may also be able to provide information.

FOR MILITARY BUFFS

The public is welcome to attend a recruit parade at the Marine Corps Recruit Depot (MCRD), off Pacific Coast Highway, most Fridays at 10am (© **619/ 524-1765**). Old Town Trolley Tours (© **619/298-TOUR**) is the only company allowed on San Diego military bases. On its Friday morning tour to North Island Naval Air Station, passengers get a close-up look at any aircraft carriers that are in port. The tour lasts 2 to 3 hours and allows an opportunity to purchase military memorabilia.

FOR WINE LOVERS

Visit **Orfila Vineyards** (© **760/738-6500;** www.orfila.com), near the Wild Animal Park in Escondido. Italian-born wine-maker Leon Santoro is a veteran of Napa Valley (Louis Martini and Stag's Leap). Besides producing excellent

chardonnay and Merlot, the winery also makes several Rhone and Italian varietals, including sangiovese. Tours and tastings are offered daily from 10am to
6pm. The property includes a parklike picnic area and a shop.

If you have time to go farther afield, the wineries along Rancho California
Road in **Temecula,** just across the San Diego County line, are open for tours
and tastings. For details, see chapter 11.

8 Organized Tours

It's almost impossible to get a handle on the diversity of San Diego in a short
visit, but one way to maximize your time is to take an organized tour that introduces you to the city. Many are creative, not as touristy as you might fear, and
allow you a great deal of versatility in planning your day.

Centre City Development Corporation's Downtown Information Center
((C) **619/235-2222**) offers free downtown bus tours Saturdays at 10am and
noon. The tours require reservations and start at 225 Broadway, Suite 160. Go
inside to see models of the Gaslamp Quarter and the downtown area. The office
is open Monday through Saturday from 9am to 5pm.

BAY EXCURSIONS

Bahia Belle   Cruise Mission Bay and dance under the moonlight aboard this
festive stern-wheeler. It picks up passengers at the dock of the Bahia Hotel, 998
W. Mission Bay Dr., on the half hour from 7:30pm (6:30pm in summer) to
12:30am, and at the Catamaran Resort Hotels, 3999 Mission Blvd., on the hour
from 8pm (7pm in summer) to midnight.

998 W. Mission Bay Dr. (C) **858/539-7779** (recorded information) or 858/539-7720. www.stern
wheelers.com. Tickets $6 adults, $3 children under 12. June and Sept Wed–Sat 6:30pm–12:30am; July–Aug
Wed–Sun 6:30pm–12:30am; Oct 1–Nov 30 and Jan 1–May 31 Fri–Sat 7:30pm–12:30am. Children accompanied by an adult allowed until 9pm; after 9pm, 21 or over only (with valid ID).

The Gondola Company   This unique business operates from Loews Coronado Bay Resort, plying the calm waters between pleasure-boat docks in gon-
dolas crafted according to centuries-old designs from Venice. It features all the
trimmings, right down to the striped-shirt-clad gondolier with ribbons waving
from his (or her) straw hat. Mediterranean music plays while you and up to
three friends recline with snuggly blankets, and the company will even provide
antipasto appetizers (or chocolate-dipped strawberries) and chilled wineglasses
and ice for the beverage of your choice (BYOB). A 1-hour cruise for two is $60,
and expanded packages are available. The hours of operation are 11am to midnight daily, year-round. Reservations are necessary.

4000 Coronado Bay Rd., Coronado. (C) **619/429-6317**. Tickets $60 per couple, $17 for each additional
passenger.

Hornblower Cruises & Events   This company offers 1- and 2-hour narrated
tours of San Diego Bay. Nightly dinner cruises with music and dancing run
from 7 to 9pm, Sunday brunch cruises from 11am to 1pm. Whale-watching
trips are offered in the winter.

1066 N. Harbor Dr. (C) **800/ON-THE-BAY** or 619/686-8715. www.hornblower.com. Tickets start at $51 for
dinner cruise, $35 for brunch cruise; half price for children. Harbor tours $13–$18.

San Diego Harbor Excursion   The company offers daily 1- and 2-hour narrated tours of the bay, plus dinner cruises. In the winter, it runs whale-watching
excursions. The narrators have been with the company for at least 5 years. Times
and frequency vary seasonally.

Tips **See San Diego by Land & Sea—at the Same Time**

If you can't decide between a bus tour of San Diego's most popular neighborhoods and a cruise of the city's prettiest waterways, then opt for an
amphibious tour from **Sea and Land Adventures (SEAL)**. Their 90-minute
tours depart from Seaport Village hourly every day starting at 10am; each
specially built boat holds 50 passengers. After cruising the streets of the
Gaslamp Quarter, Old Town, and Coronado—and garnering the curious
stares of passersby—you'll take a dip into San Diego and Mission bays to
experience the rich maritime and military history of San Diego from the
right perspective. The trips cost $24 for adults and $12 for kids 4 to 12. For
information and tickets, call ✆ **619/298-8687,** or visit www.historic
tours.com.

1050 N. Harbor Dr. (foot of Broadway). ✆ **800/442-7847** or 619/234-4111. www.sdhe.com. Tickets $13 for
1 hr., $18 for 2 hr.; half price for children.

BUS TOURS

Note: Both of these bus companies pick up passengers at most area hotels.

Contact Tours (✆ **800/235-5393** or 619/477-8687; www.contactours.com)
offers city sightseeing tours, including a "Grand Tour" that covers San Diego,
Tijuana, and a 1-hour harbor cruise. It also runs trips to the San Diego Zoo, Sea-
World, Disneyland, Universal Studios, Tijuana, Rosarito Beach, and Ensenada.
Prices range from $26 to $62 for adults, $14 to $44 for children under 12, and
include admissions. Multiple tours can be combined for discounted rates.

Gray Line San Diego (✆ **800/331-5077** or 619/491-0011; www.grayline
sandiego.com) offers city sightseeing, including tours of Cabrillo National Monument, SeaWorld, and La Jolla. Other trips go farther afield, to the Wild Animal
Park, wine country, and Tijuana and Ensenada, Mexico. Prices range from $24
to $56 for adults and $10 to $35 for children.

TROLLEY TOURS

Not to be confused with the public transit trolley, the narrated **Old Town Trolley** (✆ **619/298-TOUR**) is a perennial favorite. You can get a comprehensive
look at the city—or just the parts that interest you—along the trolley's 30-mile
(48km) circular route. Hop off at any one of a dozen stops, explore at leisure,
and reboard when you please (the bus/trolley runs every half hour). You can
begin wherever you want; stops include the Embarcadero, downtown area, Horton Plaza, Gaslamp Quarter, Coronado, San Diego Zoo, Balboa Park, and Heritage Park. The tour costs $24 for adults ($12 for kids 4–12, kids 3 and under
free) for one complete loop, no matter how many times you hop on and off; the
route by itself takes about 90 minutes.

WHALE-WATCHING

As it is everywhere along the coast, whale-watching is an eagerly anticipated win-
tertime activity in San Diego. If you've ever been lucky enough to spot one of
these gentle behemoths swimming gracefully and purposefully through the
ocean, you'll understand the thrill. When they pass the San Diego shores, California gray whales are more than three-quarters of the way from Alaska to their
breeding grounds at the southern tip of Baja—or just beginning the trip home
to their rich Alaskan feeding grounds (with calves in tow). Mid-December to

mid-March is the best time to see the migration, and there are several ways to view the spectacular parade.

The easiest is to grab a pair of binoculars and head to a good land-bound vantage point. **Cabrillo National Monument,** on Point Loma peninsula, offers a glassed-in observatory and educational whale exhibits. Each January the rangers conduct a special "Watch Weekend" featuring presentations by whale experts, programs for children, and entertainment. The monument is open daily 10am to 5pm, and admission is $5 per car; call ☎ **619/557-5450** for more information.

In La Jolla, the **Birch Aquarium at Scripps Institution of Oceanography** celebrates the gray whale season with "WhaleFest" throughout January and February. A variety of educational activities and whale exhibits are planned, and the aquarium's outdoor plaza offers an excellent vantage point for spotting the mammals from shore. Aquarium admission is $8.50 for adults, $7.50 for seniors, and $5 for children 3 to 17. Daily hours are 9am to 5pm; call ☎ **858/534-3474** for further information.

If you want to get a closer look, head out to sea on one of the excursions that locate and follow gray whales, taking care not to disturb their journey. **Classic Sailing Adventures** (☎ **800/659-0141** or 619/224-0800) offers two trips per day (8:30am and 1pm); each lasts 4 hours and carries a maximum of six passengers. Sailing is less distracting to the whales, but more expensive; tickets are $50 per person, including beverages and snacks.

Companies that offer traditional, engine-driven expeditions include **Hornblower Cruises** and **San Diego Harbor Excursions** (see "Bay Excursions," above). Excursions are generally 3 hours, and fares run around $19 for adults, with discounts for kids.

The **San Diego Natural History Museum** begins offering naturalist-led, half-day whale-watching trips in January aboard the 88-passenger *Pacific Queen.* Your guide will discuss whale behavior and biology, as well as seabirds, harbor seals, sea lions, and other coastal life. Passengers must be 12 years or older, and fares are $49 to $66 for non–museum members. For an excursion schedule and preregistration, call ☎ **619/232-3821,** ext. 203.

WALKING TOURS

Walkabout International, 835 Fifth Ave., Room 407 (☎ **619/231-7463**), sponsors more than 100 free walking tours every month that are led by local volunteers. A lively guide known as Downtown Sam, who retired from the Air Force in 1972, leads downtown tours that are particularly popular with retired San Diegans eager for exercise and camaraderie. He's easy to spot, in walking shorts and a cap with a button proclaiming "No thanks, I'd rather walk." Sam's Saturday-morning tours draw 20 to 40 people, and they end with a stop for coffee or a meal. Sam also leads a 1½-hour downtown theme tour at 11am on Tuesday, focusing on bookstores, shopping, pubs, thrift shops, bank lobbies—you name it.

Coronado Touring, 1110 Isabella Ave., Coronado (☎ **619/435-5993**), provides upbeat, informative 90-minute walking tours of Coronado, including the Hotel del Coronado. Enthusiastic guide Nancy Cobb has been doing this since 1980, so she knows her subject well. Tours leave at 11am on Tuesday, Thursday, and Saturday from the Glorietta Bay Inn, 1630 Glorietta Blvd. (near Orange Ave.). The price is $8.

At the **Cabrillo National Monument** on the tip of Point Loma, rangers often lead free walking tours (see "More Attractions," earlier in this chapter). The

Gaslamp Quarter Historical Foundation offers tours of the quarter Tuesday through Saturday. Tours depart from the William Heath Davis House Museum, 410 Island Ave., and cost around $8, which includes admission to the museum. For specific schedules, contact the foundation directly (© **619/233-4692;** www.gaslampquarter.org).

Docents at **Torrey Pines State Reserve** in La Jolla lead guided nature walks on weekends (see "Hiking & Walking" in "Outdoor Pursuits," later in this chapter).

You can explore La Jolla by taking walking and shopping tours conducted by **La Jolla Walking Tours** (© **619/291-2222**). These leave from the Grande Colonial hotel, 910 Prospect St., on Saturday at 10am and cost $10. Reservations are required, and other departure times can be scheduled as long as there are 4 or more in your group.

Volunteers from the **Natural History Museum** (© **619/232-3821,** ext. 203) lead nature walks throughout San Diego County.

9 Outdoor Pursuits

See section 2 of this chapter for a complete rundown of San Diego's beaches, and section 8 for details on whale-watching excursions.

BALLOONING

For a balloon's-eye glimpse of the area at sunrise or sunset, followed by champagne and hors d'oeuvres, contact **Skysurfer Balloon Company** (© **800/ 660-6809** or 858/481-6800) or **California Dreamin'** (© **800/373-3359** or 760/438-3344; www.californiadreamin.com). The balloon rides provide sweeping vistas of the Southern California coast, rambling estates, and golf courses. They cost between $120 and $150 per person, depending on the day of the week and seasonal specials. You may also be interested in the **Temecula Balloon and Wine Festival** held in late April. Call © **909/676-4713** for information.

BIKING

Most major thoroughfares offer bike lanes. To receive a great map of San Diego County's bike lanes and routes, call **Ride Link Bicycle Information** (© **619/ 231-BIKE**). You might also want to talk to the **City of San Diego Bicycle Coordinator** (© **619/533-3110**) or the **San Diego Bicycle Coalition** (© **619/ 685-7742**). For more practical information on biking on city streets, turn to "Getting Around: By Bicycle," in chapter 4. Always remember to wear a helmet; it's the law.

The Mission Bay and Coronado areas, in particular, are good for leisurely bike rides. The boardwalk in Pacific Beach and Mission Beach can get very crowded, especially on weekends. Coronado has a 16-mile (26km) round-trip bike trail that starts at the Ferry Landing Marketplace and follows a well-marked route around Coronado to Imperial Beach.

RENTALS, ORGANIZED BIKE TOURS & OTHER TWO-WHEEL ADVENTURES

Downtown, call **Bike Tours San Diego,** 509 Fifth Ave. (© **619/238-2444**), which offers free delivery. In Mission Bay there's **Hamel's Action Sports Center,** 704 Ventura Place, off Mission Boulevard at Ocean Front Walk (© **619/ 488-8889**), and **Hilton San Diego Resort,** 1775 E. Mission Bay Dr. (© **619/ 276-4010**). In La Jolla, try **La Jolla Sports and Photo,** 2199 Avenida de la

Playa (© **858/459-1114**). In Coronado, check out **Bikes and Beyond,** 1201 First St. at the Ferry Landing Marketplace (© **619/435-7180**), which also offers surrey and skate rentals. Expect to pay $6 an hour for bicycles, $15 an hour for surreys (pedal-powered carriages).

Adventure Bike Tours, 333 W. Harbor Dr., in the San Diego Marriott Marina (© **619/234-1500,** ext. 6514), conducts bicycle tours from San Diego to Coronado. The cost of about $40 includes ferry fare and equipment. The company offers a guided tour around the bay (the Bayside Glide) for $22 per person and rents bikes for $8 an hour, $18 for half a day, or $25 for a full day. In-line skates are also available for hire.

For a downhill thrill of a lifetime, take the **Palomar Plunge.** From the top of Palomar Mountain to its base is a 5,000-foot (1,500m) vertical drop, stretched over 16 miles (26km). Or try the **Desert Descent,** a 12-mile (19km), 3,700-foot (1,110m) descent down the Montezuma Valley Grade to the desert floor, followed by a tour of the Visitor Center and a delicious lunch. For about $80 per person, **Gravity Activated Sports** (© **800/985-4427** or 760/742-2294; www.gasports.com) supplies the mountain bike, helmet, gloves, souvenir photo, and T-shirt. The company also offers a bike tour through the Temecula wine region.

Adventurous cyclists might like to participate in the **Rosarito-Ensenada 50-Mile Fun Bicycle Ride,** held every April and September just across the border in Mexico. This event attracts more than 8,000 riders of all ages and abilities. It starts at the Rosarito Beach Hotel and finishes in Ensenada. For information, contact **Bicycling West, Inc.** (© **619/583-3001;** www.adventuresports.com/bike/rosarito/welcome.htm).

BOATING

Club Nautico, a concession at the San Diego Marriott Marina, 333 W. Harbor Dr. (© **619/233-9311**), provides guests and nonguests with an exhilarating way to see the bay. It rents 20- to 27-foot (6m–8m) offshore powerboats by the hour, half day, or full day. Rentals start at $89 an hour. The company allows boats to be taken into the ocean, and also offers diving, water-skiing, and fishing packages.

Seaforth Boat Rental, 1641 Quivira Rd., Mission Bay (© **888/834-2628** or 619/223-1681; www.seaforth-boat-rental.com/seaforth), has a wide variety of boats for bay and ocean. It rents 15- to 135-horsepower powerboats for $55 to $95 an hour, 14- to 30-foot (4m–9m) sailboats for $20 to $45 an hour, and ski boats and personal watercraft for $65 to $75 an hour. Half- and full-day rates are available. Canoes, pedal boats, and rowboats are available for those who prefer a slower pace.

Mission Bay Sportcenter, 1010 Santa Clara Place (© **858/488-1004;** www.missionbaysports.com), rents sailboats, catamarans, sailboards, kayaks, personal watercraft, and motorboats. Prices range from $12 to $72 an hour, with discounts for 4-hour and full-day rentals. Instruction is available.

San Diego Yacht & Breakfast Club, 1880 Harbor Island Dr. (© **619/298-6623**), rents kayaks for $20 an hour, 3-horsepower dinghies for $15 an hour, Windriders for $40 an hour, and Waverunners for $65 an hour. Half- and full-day rentals are available. **The San Diego Sailing Club,** at the same address and phone number, rents yachts and offers sailing lessons.

Coronado Boat Rental, 1715 Strand Way, Coronado (© **619/437-1514**), rents powerboats with 90- and 110-horsepower motors for $55 to $90 an hour,

Outdoor Pursuits in the San Diego Area

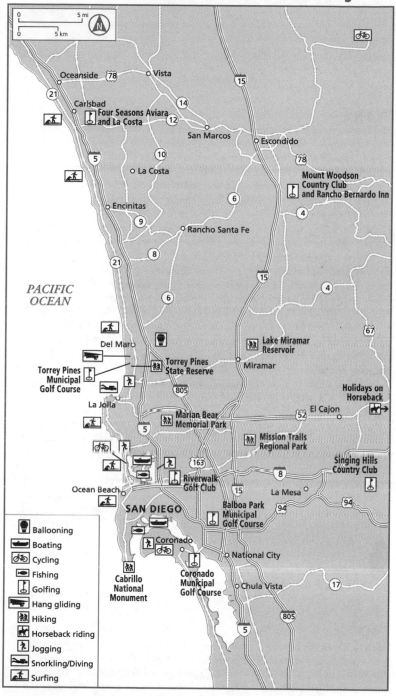

Oceanside
Vista
Carlsbad
Four Seasons Aviara and La Costa
San Marcos
Escondido
La Costa
Mount Woodson Country Club and Rancho Bernardo Inn
Encinitas
Rancho Santa Fe

PACIFIC OCEAN

Del Mar
Torrey Pines State Reserve
Torrey Pines Municipal Golf Course
Miramar
Lake Miramar Reservoir
Holidays on Horseback
La Jolla
Marian Bear Memorial Park
El Cajon
Mission Trails Regional Park
Singing Hills Country Club
Riverwalk Golf Club
Ocean Beach
La Mesa
SAN DIEGO
Balboa Park Municipal Golf Course
Coronado
National City
Cabrillo National Monument
Coronado Municipal Golf Course
Chula Vista

0   5 mi
0   5 km
N
PACIFIC

Ballooning
Boating
Cycling
Fishing
Golfing
Hang gliding
Hiking
Horseback riding
Jogging
Snorkling/Diving
Surfing

with half- and full-day rates, and 14- to 30-foot (4m–9m) sailboats for $25 to $45 an hour. It also rents personal watercraft, ski boats, canoes, pedal boats, fishing skiffs, and charter boats.

Sail USA (© 619/298-6822) offers custom-tailored skippered cruises on a 34-foot (10m) Catalina sloop. A half-day bay cruise costs $275 for six passengers. Full-day and overnight trips are also available, as are trips to Ensenada and to Catalina.

FISHING

For information on fishing, call the **City Fish Line** (© 619/465-3474). Anglers of any age can fish free of charge without a license off any municipal pier in California. Public fishing piers are on Shelter Island (where there's a statue dedicated to anglers), Ocean Beach, and Imperial Beach.

Fishing charters depart from Harbor and Shelter Islands, Point Loma, the Imperial Beach pier, and Quivira Basin in Mission Bay (near the Hyatt Islandia Hotel). Participants over 16 need a California fishing license.

For sportfishing, you can go out on a large boat for about $25 for half a day or $35 to $85 for three-quarters to a full day. To charter a boat for up to six people, the rates run about $550 for half a day and $850 for an entire day, more in summer. Call around and compare prices. Summer and fall are excellent times for excursions. Locally, the waters around Point Loma are filled with bass, bonito, and barracuda; the Coronado Islands, which belong to Mexico but are only about 18 miles (29km) from San Diego, are popular for abalone, yellowtail, yellowfin, and big-eyed tuna. Some outfitters will take you farther into Baja California waters. The following outfitters offer short or extended outings with daily departures: **H & M Landing,** 2803 Emerson (© 619/222-1144); **Islandia Sportfishing,** 1551 W. Mission Bay Rd. (© 858/222-1164); **Lee Palm Sportfishers** (© 619/224-3857); **Point Loma Sportfishing,** 1403 Scott St. (© 619/223-1627); and **Seaforth Boat Rentals,** 1641 Quivira Rd. (© 619/233-1681).

For freshwater fishing, San Diego's lakes and rivers are home to bass, channel and bullhead catfish, bluegill, trout, crappie, and sunfish. Most lakes have rental facilities for boats, tackle, and bait, and they also provide picnic and (usually) camping areas.

Lake Cuyamaca, 45 minutes from San Diego near Julian, is 5,000 feet (1,500m) above sea level, set in the midst of pines and cedars, and filled with trout year-round. It's open daily from sunrise to sunset; there are motorboat and rowboat rentals and a small charge for fishing (© 877/581-9904 or 760/765-0515; www.lakecuyamaca.org).

For more information on fishing in California, contact the **California Department of Fish and Game** (© 858/467-4200; www.dfg.ca.gov).

For fishing in Mexican waters, including the area off the Coronado Islands, angling permits are required. Contact the **Mexican Department of Fisheries,** 2550 Fifth Ave., Suite 101, San Diego, CA 92103-6622 (© 619/233-6956).

GOLF

With nearly 80 courses, 50 of them open to the public, San Diego County offers golf enthusiasts innumerable opportunities to play their game. Courses are diverse—some have vistas of the Pacific, others views of country hillsides or desert landscapes. I've listed my favorites below; for a full listing of area courses, including fees, stats, and complete scorecards, visit **www.golfsd.com.**

San Diego Golf Reservations (© 800/905-0230; www.sandiegogolf reservations.com) can arrange tee times for you at most golf courses. And when you just want to practice your swing, head to **Stadium Golf Center,** 2990 Murphy Canyon Rd., in Mission Valley (© 858/277-6667; www.stadiumgolf center. com), They're open from 7am to 10pm daily, with 72 artificial turf and natural grass hitting stations, plus greens and bunkers to practice your short game. A complete pro shop offers club rentals at $1 each; a bucket of balls costs $6 to $10; and golf instruction and clinics are also available.

Balboa Park Municipal Golf Course 🏌 Everybody has a humble municipal course like this at home, with a bare-bones 1940s clubhouse where old guys hold down lunch counter stools for hours after the game—and players take a few more mulligans than they would elsewhere. Surrounded by the beauty of Balboa Park, this 18-hole course features mature, full trees; fairways sprinkled with eucalyptus leaves; and distractingly nice views of the San Diego skyline. It's so convenient and affordable that it's the perfect choice for visitors who want to work some golf into their vacation rather than the other way around. The course even rents clubs. Nonresident greens fees are $32 weekdays, $37 weekends; cart rental is $20, pull carts $5. Reservations are suggested at least a week in advance.
2600 Golf Course Dr. (off Pershing Dr. or 26th St. in southeast corner of the park), San Diego. © 619/239-1660.

Coronado Municipal Golf Course This is the first sight that welcomes you as you cross the Coronado Bay Bridge (the course is to the left). It is an 18-hole, par-72 course overlooking Glorietta Bay, and there's a coffee shop, pro shop, and driving range. Two-day prior reservations are strongly recommended; call anytime after 7am. Greens fees are $20 to walk and $34 to ride for 18 holes; $10 to walk and $18 to ride after 4pm. Club rental is $15, and pull-cart rental is $4.
2000 Visalia Row, Coronado. © 619/435-3121.

Four Seasons Resort Aviara Golf Club 🏌🏌 Uniquely landscaped to incorporate natural elements compatible with the protected Batiquitos Lagoon nearby, Aviara doesn't infringe on the wetlands bird habitat. The course is 7,007 yards from the championship tees, laid out over rolling hillsides with plenty of bunker and water challenges. Casual duffers may be frustrated here. Greens fees are $175 (including mandatory cart) during the week, and $195 Friday, Saturday, and Sunday; there are practice areas for putting, chipping, sand play, and driving. The pro shop is fully equipped, as is the clubhouse. Golf packages are available for guests of the Four Seasons.
7447 Batiquitos Dr., Carlsbad. © 760/603-6900. From I-5 northbound, take the Aviara Pkwy. exit east to Batiquitos Dr. Turn right and continue 2 miles (3km) to the clubhouse.

Mount Woodson Country Club 🏌 One of San Diego County's dramatic golf courses, Mount Woodson is a par-70, 6,180-yard course on 150 beautiful acres. The award-winning 18-hole course, which opened in 1991, meanders up and down hills, across bridges, and around granite boulders. Elevated tees provide striking views of Ramona and Mount Palomar, and on a clear day you can see for almost 100 miles (161km). It's easy to combine a game of golf with a weekend getaway to Julian (see chapter 11). Greens fees for 18 holes (including mandatory cart) are $49 Monday through Thursday, $75 Friday, $80 on Saturday and Sunday. Lower twilight rates are available. Mount Woodson is about 40 minutes north of San Diego.

16422 N. Woodson Dr., Ramona. ℂ 760/788-3555. Take I-15 north to Poway Rd. exit; at the end of Poway Rd., turn left (north) onto Rte. 67 and drive 3¾ miles (6km) to Archie Moore Rd.; turn left. Entrance is on the left.

Rancho Bernardo Inn ★★ Home to Ken Blanchard's Golf University of San Diego since 1992, Rancho Bernardo has a mature 18-hole, 72-par championship course with different terrains, water hazards, sand traps, lakes, and waterfalls. Lessons or 1-hour clinics with a pro, 2- to 4-day schools through the Golf University with meals and lodging included, and a standard golf package are available. Greens fees are $85 during the week and $105 Saturday through Sunday, including a cart. Twilight rates (after 2pm) are $39 weekdays and $54 weekends.

17550 Bernardo Oaks Dr., Rancho Bernardo. ℂ 800/426-0966 or 858/485-8880; www.golfuniversity.com. From I-15 north, exit at Rancho Bernardo Rd. Head east to Bernardo Oaks Dr., turn left, and continue to the resort entrance.

Riverwalk Golf Club Designed by Ted Robinson and Ted Robinson, Jr., these links wander along the Mission Valley floor. Replacing the private Stardust Golf Club, the course reopened in 1998, sporting a slick, upscale new clubhouse, four lakes with waterfalls (in play on 13 of the 27 holes), open, undulating fairways, and one peculiar feature—trolley tracks! The bright red trolley speeds through now and then, but doesn't prove too distracting. Nonresident greens fees, including cart, are $75 Monday through Thursday, $85 Friday and Sunday, and $95 Saturday (fees for residents are $30 less).

1150 Fashion Valley Rd., Mission Valley. ℂ 619/296-4653. http://riverwalk.americangolf.com. Take I-8 to Hotel Circle south, turn on Fashion Valley Rd.

Singing Hills Resort ★ The only resort in Southern California offering 54 holes of golf (two championship courses and a par-54 executive course), Singing Hills has taken advantage of the area's natural terrain. Mountains, natural rock outcroppings, and aged oaks and sycamores add character to individual holes. In 1997, this course made the *Golf for Women* magazine's Top Fairways list as one of the courses that "best meet women golfers' needs." Singing Hills is the home of the 19-year-old School of Golf for Women. The golf courses are part of the Singing Hills Resort, but nonguests are welcome. Greens fees are $37 Monday through Thursday, $45 Friday through Sunday for the two par-72 courses, and $15 on the shorter course. Cart rental costs $22. The resort offers a variety of good-value packages.

3007 Dehesa Rd., El Cajon. ℂ 800/457-5568 or 619/442-3425. www.singinghills.com. Take Calif. 94 to the Willow Glen exit. Turn right and continue to the entrance.

Torrey Pines Golf Course ★★ Two gorgeous 18-hole championship courses are on the coast between La Jolla and Del Mar, only 15 minutes from downtown San Diego. Home of the Buick Invitational Tournament, these municipal courses are very popular. Both overlook the ocean; the north course is more picturesque, the south course more challenging.

Tee times are taken by computer, starting at 5am, up to 7 days in advance by telephone only. Confirmation numbers are issued, and you must have the number and photo identification with you when you check in with the starter 15 minutes ahead of time. If you're late, your time may be forfeited.

Insider's tip: Single golfers stand a good chance of getting on the course if they just turn up and wait for a threesome. The locals also sometimes circumvent the reservation system by spending the night in a camper in the parking lot. The starter lets these diehards on before the reservations made by the computer go into effect at 7:30am.

Golf professionals are available for lessons, and the pro shop rents clubs. Greens fees for out-of-towners are $55 during the week and $60 Saturday, Sunday, and holidays for 18 holes; $30 for 9 holes. After 4pm April through October and after 3pm November through March, the 18-hole fee is only $30. Cart rental is $30. San Diego city and county residents pay much less.

11480 Torrey Pines Rd., La Jolla. ℂ 800/985-4653 or 858/452-3226; www.torreypinesgolfcourse.com.

HIKING & WALKING

San Diego's mild climate makes it a great place to walk or hike most of the year, and the options are diverse. Walking along the water is particularly popular. The best **beaches** for walking are La Jolla Shores, Mission Beach, and Coronado, but pretty much any shore is a good choice. You can also walk around Mission Bay on a series of connected footpaths. If a four-legged friend is your walking companion, head for Dog Beach in Ocean Beach or Fiesta Island in Mission Bay—two of the few areas where dogs can legally go unleashed. Coast Walk in La Jolla offers supreme surf-line views (see "La Jolla" under "More Attractions," earlier in this chapter).

The **Sierra Club** sponsors regular hikes in the San Diego area, and nonmembers are welcome to participate. There's always a Wednesday mountain hike, usually in the Cuyamaca Mountains, sometimes in the Lagunas; there are evening and day hikes as well. Most are free. For a recorded message about upcoming hikes, call ℂ **619/299-1744,** or call the office (ℂ **619/299-1743**) weekdays from noon to 5pm or Saturday from 10am to 4pm.

Torrey Pines State Reserve in La Jolla (ℂ **858/755-2063**) offers hiking trails with wonderful ocean views and a chance to see the rare Torrey pine. To reach it, use North Torrey Pines Road. Trail access is free; parking costs $4 per car, $3 for seniors. Guided nature walks are available on weekends.

The **Bayside Trail** near Cabrillo National Monument also affords great views. Drive to the monument and follow signs to the trail.

Mission Trails Regional Park, 8 miles (13km) northeast of downtown, offers a glimpse of what San Diego looked like before development. Located between Highway 52 and I-8 and east of I-15, rugged hills, valleys, and open areas provide a quick escape from the urban bustle. A visitor and interpretive center (ℂ **619/668-3275**) is open daily from 9am to 5pm. Access is by way of Mission Gorge Road.

Marian Bear Memorial Park, also known as San Clemente Canyon (ℂ **619/581-9952** for park ranger), is a 10-mile (16km), round-trip trail that runs directly underneath Highway 52. Most of the trail is flat, hard-packed dirt, but some areas are rocky. There are benches and places to sit and have a quiet picnic. From Highway 52 west, take the Genesee South exit; at the light, make a U-turn and an immediate right into the parking lot. From Highway 52 east, exit at Genesee and make a right at the light, then an immediate right into the parking lot.

Lake Miramar Reservoir has a 5-mile (8km), paved, looped trail with a wonderful view of the lake and mountains. Take I-15 north and exit on Mira Mesa Boulevard. Turn right on Scripps Ranch Boulevard, then left on Scripps Lake Drive, and make a left at the Lake Miramar sign. Parking is free, but the lot closes at 6:30pm. There's also a wonderful walkway around **Lake Murray.** Take the Lake Murray Boulevard exit off I-8 and follow the signs.

Volunteers from the **Natural History Museum** (ℂ **619/232-3821**) lead nature walks throughout San Diego County.

HORSEBACK RIDING

Jim and Suzanne Miller of **Holidays on Horseback** (© **619/445-3997;** fax 619/659-6097; www.holidaysonhorseback.com), 40 miles (64km) east of San Diego in Descanso, offer trail rides in the mountains of the Cuyamaca Rancho State Park, which has 135 miles (217km) of wilderness trails. Excursions take 1½ to 4 hours. Riders pass through beautiful scenery that includes native chaparral, live oak, and manzanita. The horses are all experienced, gentle trail horses suitable for every riding level. Rides are limited to 10 people, and children must be 7 or older. A 4-hour ride with a picnic lunch in the forest costs $100; a 1½-hour trail ride is $35.

JOGGING & RUNNING

An invigorating route downtown is along the wide sidewalks of the Embarcadero, stretching around the bay. A locals-favorite place to jog is the sidewalk that follows the east side of Mission Bay. Start at the Visitor Information Center and head south past the Hilton to Fiesta Island. A good spot for a short run is La Jolla Shores Beach, where there's hard-packed sand even when it isn't low tide. The beach at Coronado is also a good place for jogging, as is the shore at Pacific Beach and Mission Beach—just watch your tide chart to make sure you won't be there at high tide.

Safety note: Avoid secluded areas of Balboa Park, even in broad daylight.

SCUBA DIVING & SNORKELING

San Diego Divers Supply, 4004 Sports Arena Blvd. (© **619/224-3439**) and 5701 La Jolla Blvd. (© **858/459-2691**), will set you up with scuba and snorkeling equipment. The **San Diego–La Jolla Underwater Park,** especially the La Jolla Cove, is the best spot for scuba diving and snorkeling. For more information, see "San Diego's Beaches," earlier in this chapter. The Underwater Pumpkin Carving Contest, held at Halloween, is a fun local event. For information, call © **858/565-6054.**

SKATING

Gliding around San Diego, especially the Mission Bay area, on in-line skates is the quintessential Southern California experience. In Mission Beach, rent a pair of regular or in-line skates from **Skates Plus,** 3830 Mission Blvd. (© **858/488-PLUS**), or **Hamel's Action Sports Center,** 704 Ventura Place, off Mission Boulevard at Ocean Front Walk (© **858/488-8889**). In Pacific Beach, try **Pacific Beach Sun and Sea,** 4539 Ocean Blvd. (© **858/483-6613**). In Coronado, go to **Mike's Bikes,** 1343 Orange Ave. (© **619/435-7744**), or **Bikes and Beyond,** 1201 First St. and at the Ferry Landing (© **619/435-7180**). Be sure to ask for protective gear.

If you'd rather ice skate, try the **Ice Capades Chalet** at University Towne Center, La Jolla Village Drive at Genesee Street (© **858/452-9110**).

SURFING

With its miles of beaches, San Diego is a popular surf destination. Some of the best spots include Windansea, La Jolla Shores, Pacific Beach, Mission Beach, Ocean Beach, and Imperial Beach. In North County, you might consider Carlsbad State Beach and Oceanside.

If you didn't bring your own board, they are available for rent at stands at many popular beaches. Many local surf shops also rent equipment; they include

La Jolla Surf Systems, 2132 Avenida de la Playa, La Jolla Shores (© 858/456-2777), and **Emerald Surf & Sport,** 1118 Orange Ave., Coronado (© 619/435-6677).

For surfing lessons, with all equipment provided, check with **Kahuna Bob's Surf School** (© 800/KAHUNAS or 760/721-7700; www.kahunabob.com) or **San Diego Surfing Academy** (© 800-447-SURF or 858/565-6892; www.surfSDSA.com).

SWIMMING

Most San Diego hotels have pools, and there are plenty of other options for the visitor. Downtown, head to the **YMCA,** 500 W. Broadway, between Columbia and India Streets (© 619/232-7451). There's a $10 day-use fee for non-YMCA members; towels are supplied. It's open Monday through Friday from 5:45am to 9pm, Saturday from 8am to 5pm. In Balboa Park, you can swim in the **Kearns Memorial Swimming Pool,** 2229 Morley Field Dr. (© 619/692-4920). The fee for using the public pool is $2 for adults; call for seasonal hours and laps-only restrictions. In Mission Bay, you'll find the famous indoor **Plunge,** 3115 Oceanfront Walk, (© 858/488-3110), part of Belmont Park since 1925. Pool capacity is 525, and there are 10 lap lanes and a viewing area inside. It's open to the public Monday through Friday from 6 to 8am, noon to 1pm, and 2:30 to 8pm, and Saturday and Sunday from 8am to 4pm. Admission is $2.50 for adults, $2.25 for children.

In La Jolla you can swim at the **Jewish Community Center,** 4126 Executive Dr. (© 858/457-3161). It has an ozone pool (kept clean by an ozone generator), instead of the typical chlorinated pool. It is open to the public Monday through Thursday from 6:30am to 7:30pm, Friday from 6:30am to 6pm, Saturday from 11am to 6pm, and Sunday from 10am to 6pm. Admission is $5 for adults, $3 for children under 17.

Swimmers may want to compete in (or watch) a rough-water swim. These include the **Oceanside Rough Water Swim** (© 760/941-0946) and the **La Jolla Rough Water Swim** (© 858/456-2100), both held in early September.

TENNIS

There are 1,200 public and private tennis courts in San Diego. Public courts include the **La Jolla Tennis Club,** 7632 Draper, at Prospect (© 858/454-4434), which is free and open daily from dawn until the lights go off at 9pm. At the **Balboa Tennis Club,** 2221 Morley Field Dr., in Balboa Park (© 619/295-9278), court use is free, but reservations are required. The courts are open Monday through Friday from 10am to 8pm, Saturday and Sunday 8am to 6pm. The ultra-modern **Barnes Tennis Center,** 4490 W. Point Loma Blvd., near Ocean Beach and SeaWorld (© 619/221-9000; www.tennissandiego.com) has 20 lighted hard courts and four clay courts; they're open every day from 8am to 9pm. Court rental is $5 to $10 an hour, instruction an additional $12 to $14 per hour.

10 Spectator Sports

AUTO RACING

The **Score Baja 500,** held in June, is an annual off-road car, motorcycle, and truck loop race that starts and ends in Ensenada. The **Score Baja 1,000** takes place in November. For information, call © 818/583-8068.

BASEBALL

The **San Diego Padres** (www.padres.com), led to the National League championship in 1998 by stars Tony Gwynn and Trevor Hoffman, play from April through October at **Qualcomm Stadium,** 9449 Friars Rd., in Mission Valley (✆ **619/283-4494** for schedules and information; 619/29-PADRES for tickets). The **Padres Express** bus (✆ **619/685-4900** for information) costs $5 round-trip and picks up fans at several locations throughout the city, beginning 2 hours before the game. The bus operates only for home games on Friday, Saturday, and Sunday. Tickets are readily available.

BOATING

San Diego has probably played host to the America's Cup for the last time, but several other boating events of interest are held here. They include the **America's Schooner Cup,** held every March or April (✆ **619/223-3138**), and the **Annual San Diego Crew Classic,** held on Mission Bay every April (✆ **619/488-0700**). The Crew Classic rowing competition draws teams from throughout the United States and Canada. The **Wooden Boat Festival** is held on Shelter Island every May (✆ **619/574-8020**). Approximately 90 boats participate in the festival, which features nautical displays, food, music, and crafts.

FISHING TOURNAMENTS

Enthusiasts will want to attend the **Day at the Docks** event, held at the San Diego Sportfishing Landing, Harbor Drive and Scott Street, in Point Loma, every April. For information, call ✆ **619/294-7912.**

FOOTBALL

San Diego's professional football team, the **San Diego Chargers** (www.chargers. com), plays at **Qualcomm Stadium** ("The Q"), 9449 Friars Rd., Mission Valley (✆ **619/280-2111**). The season runs from August through December. The Chargers Express bus (✆ **619/685-4900** for information) costs $5 round-trip and picks up passengers at several locations throughout the city, beginning 2 hours before the game. The bus operates for all home games.

The collegiate **Holiday Bowl,** held at Qualcomm Stadium every December, pits the Western Athletic Conference champion against a team from the Big 10. For information, call ✆ **619/283-5808.**

GOLF

San Diego is the site of some of the country's most important golf tournaments, including the **Buick Invitational,** held in February at Torrey Pines Golf Course in La Jolla (✆ **800/888-BUICK** or 619/281-4653). The **HGH Pro-Am Golf Classic** takes place at Carlton Oaks Country Club in September (✆ **619/448-8500**).

HORSE RACING

Live Thoroughbred racing takes place at the **Del Mar Race Track** (✆ **858/755-1141** for information; 619/792-4242 for the ticket office; www.dmtc.com) from late July through mid-September. Post time for the nine-race program is 2pm (except the first four Fridays of the meet, when it's 4pm); there is no racing on Tuesdays. Admission to the clubhouse is $6; to the grandstand, $3. Bing Crosby and Pat O'Brien founded the track in 1937, and it has entertained stars such as Lucille Ball and Desi Arnaz, Dorothy Lamour, Red Skelton, Paulette Goddard, Jimmy Durante, and Ava Gardner. Del Mar's 1993 season marked the opening of a new $80 million grandstand, built in the Spanish mission style of the original structure. The new grandstand features more seats, better race viewing, and a centrally located scenic paddock. The **$1 million Pacific Classic,** featuring the top horses in the country, is held the second weekend in August (see chapter 11).

HORSE SHOWS

The **Del Mar National Horse Show** takes place at the Del Mar Fairgrounds from late April to mid-May. Olympic-caliber and national championship riders participate. For information, call ℂ **858/792-4288** or 858/755-1161.

ICE HOCKEY

The **San Diego Gulls** of the West Coast Hockey League skate at the San Diego Sports Arena from late October into March. For schedules, tickets, and information, call ℂ **619/224-4625** or 619/224-4171.

MARATHONS & TRIATHLONS

San Diego is a wonderful place to run or watch a marathon because the weather is usually mild. The **San Diego Marathon** takes place in January. It's actually in Carlsbad, 35 miles (56km) north of San Diego, and stretches mostly along the coastline. For more information, contact the **San Diego Track Club** (ℂ **858/452-7382**) or **In Motion** (ℂ **619/792-2900**).

Another popular event is the **La Jolla Half Marathon,** held in April. It begins at the Del Mar Fairgrounds and finishes at La Jolla Cove. For information, call ℂ **858/454-1262.**

The **America's Finest City Half Marathon** is held in August every year. The race begins at Cabrillo National Monument, winds through downtown, and ends in Balboa Park. For information, call ℂ **619/297-3901.**

The **San Diego International Triathlon,** held in the middle of June, includes a 1,000m (3,280 ft.) swim, 30km (19-mile) bike ride, and 10km (6-mile) run. It starts at Spanish Landing on Harbor Island. For information, call ℂ **619/627-9111** or 619/687-1000.

POLO

The public is invited to watch polo matches on Sundays from June through October at the **Rancho Santa Fe Polo Club,** 14555 El Camino Real, Rancho Santa Fe (ℂ **858/481-9217**). Admission is $5.

SOCCER

The **San Diego Sockers,** popular members of the Continental Indoor Soccer League, play from June through September at the San Diego Sports Arena, 3500 Sports Arena Blvd. (ℂ **619/224-GOAL**). Admission is $5 to $12.50.

SOFTBALL

The highlight of many San Diegans' summer is the softball event known as the **World Championship Over-the-Line Tournament,** held on Fiesta Island in Mission Bay on the second and third weekends of July. For more information, see the "San Diego Calendar of Events," in chapter 2.

TENNIS

San Diego plays host to some major tennis tournaments, including the **Toshiba Tennis Classic,** held at the La Costa Resort and Spa in Carlsbad. The tournament is usually held between late July and early August. For tickets, call ℂ **619/438-LOVE;** for information, ℂ **619/436-3551.**

City Strolls

Wandering a city's streets and parks gives you insights that are hard to come by any other way—and the exercise can't be beat, especially under the warm (but usually not unbearably hot) Southern California sun. From the history-heavy Gaslamp Quarter to the ultra-busy Embarcadero, San Diego easily lends itself to the long, leisurely stroll. The four walking tours in this chapter will give you a special sense of the city, as well as a look at some of its most unique and appealing sights and structures.

WALKING TOUR 1 THE GASLAMP QUARTER

Start:	Fourth Avenue and E Street, at Horton Plaza.
Finish:	Fourth Avenue and F Street.
Time:	Approximately 1½ hours, not including shopping and dining.
Best Times:	During the day.
Worst Times:	Evenings, when the area's popular restaurants and nightspots attract big crowds.

A National Historic District covering 16½ city blocks, the Gaslamp Quarter contains many Victorian-style commercial buildings built between the Civil War and World War I. The quarter—set off by electric versions of old gas lamps—lies between Fourth Avenue to the west, Sixth Avenue to the east, Broadway to the north, and L Street and the waterfront to the south. The blocks are noticeably short; developer Alonzo Horton knew corner lots were desirable to buyers, so he created more of them. This tour hits some highlights of buildings along Fourth and Fifth avenues. If it whets your appetite for more, the **Gaslamp Quarter Historic Foundation,** 410 Island Ave. (© **619/233-4692;** www.gaslampquarter.org), offers 2-hour walking tours (about $5, which includes museum admission) from Tuesday through Saturday. Call them for specific tour schedule. The book *San Diego's Historic Gaslamp Quarter: Then and Now,* by Susan H. Carrico and Kathleen Flanagan, makes an excellent, lightweight walking companion. It has photos, illustrations, and a map.

The tour begins at:
❶ Horton Plaza
It's a colorful conglomeration of shops, eateries, and architecture—and a tourist attraction. Ernest W. Hahn, who planned and implemented the redevelopment and revitalization of downtown San Diego, built the plaza in 1985. This core project, which covers 11½ acres and 6½ blocks in the heart of downtown, represents the successful integration of public and private funding.

The ground floor at Horton Plaza is home to the 1906 Jessop Street Clock. The timepiece has 20 dials, 12 of

Walking Tour: The Gaslamp Quarter

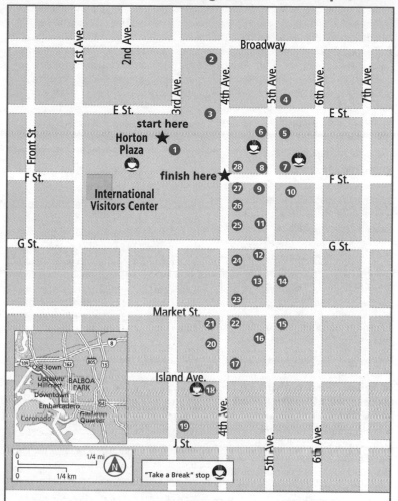

1 Horton Plaza	**10** William Penn Hotel	**20** Royal Pie Bakery Building
2 Horton Plaza Park	**11** Llewelyn Building	**21** Frey Block Building
3 Balboa Theatre	**12** Old City Hall	**22** Hotel Lester
4 Watts-Robinson Building	**13** Backesto Building	**23** Brokers Building
5 Louis Bank of Commerce	**14** Yuma Building	**24** Carriage Works
6 F.W. Woolworth Building	**15** Metropolitan Hotel	**25** Las Flores Hotel
7 Marston Building	**16** Lincoln Hotel	**26** Whitney Building
8 Keating Building	**17** William Heath Davis House	**27** Minear Building
9 Spencer-Ogden Building	**18** Horton Grand Hotel	**28** Ingle Building
	19 Former Home of Ah Quinn	

which tell the time in places throughout the world. Designed by Joseph Jessop, Sr., and built primarily by Claude D. Ledger, the clock stood outside Jessop's Jewelry Store on Fifth Avenue from 1927 until being moved to Horton Plaza in 1985. In 1935, when Mr. Ledger died, the clock stopped; it was restarted, but it stopped again 3 days later—the day of his funeral.

In front of Horton Plaza is:

② Horton Plaza Park

Its centerpiece is a fountain designed by well-known local architect Irving Gill and modeled after the choragic monument of Lysicrates in Athens. Dedicated October 15, 1910, it was the first successful attempt to combine colored lights with flowing water. On the fountain's base are bronze medallions of Juan Rodríguez Cabrillo, Father Junípero Serra, and Alonzo Horton, three men who were important to San Diego's development.

Walk along Horton Plaza, down Fourth Avenue, to the:

③ Balboa Theatre, at the southwest corner of Fourth Avenue and E Street

Constructed in 1924, the Spanish Renaissance–style building has a distinctive tile dome, striking tile work in the entry, and two 20-foot-high (6m) ornamental waterfalls inside. In the past, the waterfalls ran at full power during intermission; however, when turned off, they would drip and irritate the audience. The ship mosaic at Fourth and E depicts Balboa discovering the Pacific Ocean in 1513. In the theater's heyday, plays and vaudeville took top billing. It's currently closed, awaiting renovation.

Cross Fourth Avenue and proceed along E Street to Fifth Avenue. The tall, striking building to your left is the:

④ Watts-Robinson Building

Built in 1913, it was one of San Diego's first skyscrapers. It once

housed 70 jewelers and is now a stellar boutique hotel (for complete information, see the review for Gaslamp Plaza Suites in chapter 5). Take a minute to look inside at the marble wainscoting, tile floors, ornate ceiling, and brass ornamentation.

Return to the southwest corner of Fifth Avenue. To your right, at 837 Fifth Ave., is the unmistakable "grand old lady of the Gaslamp," the twin-towered baroque revival:

⑤ Louis Bank of Commerce

You can admire the next few buildings from the west side of the street and then continue south from here. Built in 1888, this proud building was the first in San Diego made of granite. It once housed a 24-hour ice-cream parlor for which streetcars made unscheduled stops; an oyster bar frequented by Wyatt Earp; and, a number of upstairs rooms inhabited by ladies of the night. After a fire in 1903, the original towers of the building, with eagles perched atop them, were removed.

On the west side of Fifth Avenue, at no. 840, near E Street, you'll find the:

⑥ F. W. Woolworth Building

Built in 1910, it has housed **San Diego Hardware** since 1922. The original tin ceiling, wooden floors, and storefront windows remain, and the store deserves a quick browse.

Across the street, at 801 Fifth Ave., stands the two-story:

⑦ Marston Building

This Italianate Victorian-style building dates from 1881 and housed humanitarian George W. Marston's department store for 15 years. In 1885, San Diego Federal Savings' first office was here, and the Prohibition Temperance Union held its meetings here in the late 1880s. After a fire in 1903, the building was remodeled extensively.

The red brick Romanesque revival on the northwest corner of Fifth Avenue and F Street is the:

⑧ Keating Building

A San Diego landmark dating from 1890, Mrs. Keating built it as a tribute to her late husband, George, whose name can still be seen in the top cornice. Originally heralded as one of the city's most prestigious office buildings, it featured conveniences such as steam heat and a wire-cage elevator. Note the architecturally distinctive rounded corner and windows.

TAKE A BREAK
Housed in the Keating Building, the **Croce's** (📞 619/ 233-4355) cluster of dining and entertainment possibilities serves up generous portions of good food and drink, live jazz, national acts, and inviting ambiance. Owner Ingrid Croce has created a memorial to the life and music of her late husband, musician Jim Croce, with photos, guitars, and other memorabilia. Across the street is the perennially popular **Fio's** (📞 619/234-3467), an Italian restaurant.

Continuing south on Fifth Avenue, cross F Street and stand in front of the:

⑨ Spencer-Ogden Building

It's located on the southwest corner at 770 Fifth Avenue. Built in 1874, it was purchased by business partners Spencer and Ogden in 1881 and has been owned by the same families ever since. *San Diego's Historic Gaslamp Quarter: Then and Now* notes that a number of druggists leased space in the building over the years, including the notorious one "who tried to make firecrackers on the second floor [and] ended up blowing away part of the building." Other tenants included realtors, an import business, a home-furnishing business, and dentists, one of whom called himself "Painless Parker."

Directly across the street stands the:

⑩ William Penn Hotel

Built in 1913, in the building's former life it was the elegant Oxford Hotel,

and touted itself as "no rooming house but an up-to-the-minute, first-class, downtown hotel;" a double room with private bathroom and toilet cost $1.50. It reopened in 1992 as a hotel with mostly suites—and substantially higher prices.

On the west side of the street, at 726 Fifth Ave., you'll find the:

⑪ Llewelyn Building

Built in 1887 by William Llewelyn, the family shoe store was here until 1906. Over the years, it has been home to hotels of various names with unsavory reputations. Of architectural note are its arched windows, molding, and cornices.

On the southwest corner of Fifth Avenue and G Street is the:

⑫ Old City Hall

Dating from 1874, when it was a bank, this Florentine Italianate building features 16-foot (5m) ceilings, 12-foot (3.5m) windows framed with brick arches, antique columns, and a wrought-iron cage elevator. Notice that the windows on each floor are different. (The top two stories were added in 1887, when it became the city's public library.) The entire city government filled this building in 1900, with the police department on the first floor and the council chambers on the fourth.

Continue down Fifth Avenue toward Market Street, and you'll notice the three-story:

⑬ Backesto Building

Built in 1873, it fills most of the block. Originally a one-story structure on the corner, the classical revival and Victorian-style building expanded to its present size and height over its first 15 years.

Across the street in the middle of the block, at 631–633 Fifth Ave., is the:

⑭ Yuma Building

Built in 1882, it later expanded upward two floors to feature inviting bay windows. It was one of the first brick buildings downtown.

Across Market Street, on the east side of the street, is the former:

⑮ Metropolitan Hotel

The building had bay windows when it was built in 1886. To the casual observer it looks decidedly contemporary, until you spot the rugged 19th-century columns still visible on the street level. The Metropolitan also features arrestingly realistic *trompe l'oeil* effects painted on the facade by artists Nonni McKinnoon and Kitty Anderson.

In the middle of the block, at 536 Fifth Ave., is the small but distinctive:

⑯ Lincoln Hotel

It dates from 1913—the date cast in a grand concrete pediment two stories up. An equally grand stone lion's head once reigned atop the parapet, but tumbled to the street during an earthquake in 1986 and was quickly snatched by a passerby. The building's unusual green-and-white ceramic tile facade is thankfully intact.

Proceed to Island Avenue and turn right. The saltbox house at the corner of Fourth Avenue is the:

⑰ William Heath Davis House

This 140-year-old New England prefabricated lumber home was shipped to San Diego around Cape Horn in 1850 and is the oldest surviving structure from Alonzo Horton's "New Town." Horton lived here in 1867. The first floor and the small park next to it are open to the public; the Gaslamp Quarter Association and Gaslamp Quarter Historical Foundation have their headquarters on the second floor. Organized tours of the Gaslamp Quarter leave from here.

At the southwest corner of Island and Fourth avenues you'll see the bay windows of a building that's sure to steal your heart, the:

⑱ Horton Grand Hotel

It is two 1886 hotels that were moved here—very gently—from other sites, and then renovated and connected by an atrium; the original Horton Grand is to your left, the Brooklyn Hotel to your right. The life-size papier-mâché horse (Sunshine), in the lobby near the reception area, stood in front of the Brooklyn Hotel when it was a saddlery. The reception desk is a recycled pew from a choir loft, and old post-office boxes now hold guests' keys. By the concierge desk, to your right, is an old photo of the original and much less elegant Horton Grand Hotel. In its small museum hangs a portrait of Ida Bailey, a local madam whose establishment, the Canary Cottage, once stood on this spot. Artist Pamela Russ had been asked to retouch the somewhat austere face of her subject, but Russ's husband murdered her before she could get around to it.

Around the corner from the Horton Grand, at 429–431 Third Ave., stands the:

⑲ Former home of Ah Quinn

The first Chinese resident of San Diego, Ah Quinn arrived in 1879 at the age of 27 and became known as the "Mayor of Chinatown" (an area bound by Island Ave., J St., and Third and Fourth aves.). Ah Quinn helped hundreds of Chinese immigrants find work on the railroad and owned a successful general merchandise store on Fifth Avenue. He was a respected father (of 12 children), leader, and spokesperson for the city's Chinese population. When he died in 1914—he was hit by a motorcycle—his wealth included farmland, a mine, and other real estate. The modest house is not open to the public.

TAKE A BREAK
The Palace Bar (✆ 619/544-1886) in the Horton Grand Hotel is the perfect place to relax for teatime. The bar is part of the same choir-loft pew that has been turned into the reception desk.

When you leave the Horton Grand, head north on Fourth Avenue; in the middle of the block on the west side you will come to the:

⑳ Royal Pie Bakery Building

Erected in 1911, this bakery, preceded by others, has been here since 1920; the second floor used to house the Anchor Hotel, run by "Madam Cora."

At the southwest corner of Fourth Avenue and Market Street stands the:

㉑ Frey Block Building

Built in 1911, a plaque reads "Home of the Crossroads, the oldest live jazz club in San Diego."

Across the street on the southeast corner, at 401–417 Market St., is the:

㉒ Hotel Lester

This hotel dates from 1906. It housed a saloon, pool hall, and hotel of ill repute when this was a red-light district. Unbelievably, it's still a scruffy hotel (not for long, if urban renewal has its way!), while a welcoming tearoom and espresso bar operate at street level.

On the northeast corner of Fourth Avenue and Market Street, at 402 Market St., stands the:

㉓ Brokers Building

Constructed in 1889, it has 16-foot (5m) wood-beam ceilings and cast-iron columns. It's been recently converted to artists' lofts with retail space below.

At the north end of this block, you will find the:

㉔ Carriage Works

Established in 1890, it once served as storage for wagons and carriages. It now houses restaurants and clubs catering to Gaslamp Quarter's Bohemian residents and energetic nightlife.

Cross G Street and walk to the middle of the block to the:

㉕ Las Flores Hotel

The gray building with blue-and-red trim at 725–733 Fourth Ave. was built in 1912. It is the only Gaslamp Quarter structure completely designed by architect Irving Gill, whose work can be seen throughout San Diego and in La Jolla.

Next door, at 739–745 Fourth Ave., is the:

㉖ Whitney Building

Dating from 1906, it has striking arched windows on the second floor. While you're studying details, take a look at the trim on the top of the:

㉗ Minear Building

Built in 1910, it's located at the end of the block, on the southeast corner of Fourth Avenue and F Street.

Across the street is the:

㉘ Ingle Building

It dates from 1907 and now holds the Hard Rock Cafe. The mural on the F Street side of the building depicts a group of deceased rock stars (including Hendrix and Joplin, of course) lounging at *trompe l'oeil* sidewalk tables. Original stained-glass windows from the original Golden Lion Tavern (1907–32) front Fourth Avenue. Inside, the restaurant's stained-glass ceiling was taken from the Elks Club in Stockton, California, and much of the floor is original.

WINDING DOWN
Walk to **Café Lulu**, 419 F St. (© 619/238-0114), near Fourth Avenue, for casual coffeehouse fare; or try **Horton Plaza**, where you can choose from many kinds of cuisine, from California to Chinese, along with good old American fast food.

WALKING TOUR 2   THE EMBARCADERO

Start: The Maritime Museum, Harbor Drive and Ash Street.
Finish: The Convention Center, Harbor Drive and Fifth Avenue.
Time: 1½ hours, not including museum and shopping stops.
Best Times: Weekday mornings (when it's less crowded and easier to park.)
Worst Times: Weekends, especially in the afternoon, when the Maritime Museum and
                  Seaport Village are crowded; also when cruise ships are in port (days vary).

San Diego's colorful Embarcadero, or waterfront, cradles a bevy of seagoing vessels—frigates, ferries, paddle-wheelers, yachts, cruise ships, and even a merchant vessel. You'll also find equally colorful Seaport Village, a shopping and dining center with a nautical theme.

Start at the:

① Maritime Museum

It's located at Harbor Drive at Ash Street (see listing in chapter 7). Making up part of the floating museum is the magnificent *Star of India,* the world's oldest merchant ship still afloat, built in 1863 as the *Euterpe.* The ship, whose billowing sails are a familiar sight along Harbor Drive, once carried cargo to India and immigrants to New Zealand, and it braved the Arctic ice in Alaska to work in the salmon industry. Another component of the Maritime Museum is the ferry *Berkeley,* built in 1898 to operate between San Francisco and Oakland. In service through 1958, it carried survivors to safety 24 hours a day for 4 days after the 1906 San Francisco earthquake. The *Medea,* the third and smallest display in the floating museum, is a steam yacht. One ticket gets you onto all three boats.

From this vantage point, you get a fine view of the:

② County Administration Center

This building was built in 1936 with funds from the Works Progress Administration, and was dedicated in 1938 by President Franklin D. Roosevelt. The 23-foot-high (7m) granite sculpture in front, *Guardian of Water,* was completed by Donal Hord in 1939. It represents a pioneer woman shouldering a water

jug. The building is even more impressive from the other side because of the carefully tended gardens; it's well worth the effort and extra few minutes to walk around to Pacific Highway for a look. On weekdays the building is open from 8am to 5pm; there are restrooms and a cafeteria inside.

TAKE A BREAK
The cafeteria on the fourth floor of the **County Administration Center** has lovely harbor views; it's open weekdays until 3:35pm. If you can't pass up the chance to have some seafood, return to the waterfront to **Anthony's Fishette** (② 619/232-5105), the simplest entity in the Anthony's group of seafood houses, which serves fish and chips, shrimp, and other snacks alfresco. Next door is the **Star of the Sea** restaurant (② 619/232-7408), one of the city's finest seafood restaurants, where the views are stunning and reservations are a must; it's open for dinner only.

Continue south along the Embarcadero. The large carnival-colored building on your right is the:

③ San Diego Cruise-Ship Terminal

Located on the B Street Pier, it has a large nautical clock at the entrance. Totally renovated in 1985, the flag-decorated terminal's interior is light

Walking Tour: The Embarcadero

1. Maritime Museum
2. County Administration Center
3. San Diego Cruise Ship Terminal
4. Harbor Cruises
5. Coronado Ferry
6. Santa Fe Railroad Station
7. Waterfront Park
8. U.S. Air Carrier Memorial
9. Tuna Harbor
10. Seaport Village
11. San Diego Marriott Marina
12. Convention Center

and airy. Inside, you'll also find a snack bar and gift shop. Farther along is the location for the:

❹ Harbor cruises

They depart from sunup to sundown on tours of San Diego's harbor; ticket booths are right on the water.

A little farther south, near the Broadway Pier, is the:

❺ Coronado Ferry

It makes frequent trips between San Diego and Coronado. See "Getting Around: By Ferry" in chapter 4 for more information. Buy tickets from the Harbor Excursion booth.

To your left as you look up Broadway, you'll see the two gold mission-style towers of the:

❻ Santa Fe Railroad Station

It was built in 1915. It's only 1½ blocks away, so walk up and look inside at the vaulted ceiling, wooden benches, and walls covered in striking green-and-gold tiles.

Continuing south on Harbor Drive, you'll stroll through a small tree- and bench-lined:

❼ Waterfront park

South of that, at Pier 11, is the:

❽ U.S. Air Carrier Memorial

Erected in 1993, it's a compact black granite obelisk that honors the nation's carriers and crews. It stands on the site of the old navy fleet landing, where thousands of servicemen boarded ships over the years.

Continue along the walkway to:

❾ Tuna Harbor

This is where the commercial fishing boats congregate. San Diego's tuna fleet, with about 100 boats, is one of the world's largest (and perhaps smelliest).

Keep walking south, where you can meander along the winding pathways of:

❿ Seaport Village

It contains myriad shops and restaurants. The Broadway Flying Horses

TAKE A BREAK
The red building to your right houses the **Fish Market** (© 619/232-FISH), a market and casual restaurant, and its elegant upstairs counterpart, **Top of the Market** (© 619/234-4TOP). You can be assured that a meal here is fresh off the boat. Both serve lunch and dinner, and the Fish Market has a children's menu and an oyster and sushi bar. It's acceptable to drop in just for a drink and to savor the view, which is mighty. Prices are moderate to expensive. If you prefer something quick and cheap, save yourself a walk and stop in at casual **Anthony's Fishette** (© 619/232-5105). A cousin of the one you passed earlier, it's just outside Seaport Village. For dessert or coffee, go inside Seaport Village to **Upstart Crow** (© 619/232-4855), a bookstore and coffeehouse, and sip cappuccino in the company of your favorite authors.

Carousel is pure nostalgia. Charles Looff, of Coney Island, carved the animals out of poplar in 1890. The merry-go-round was originally installed at Coney Island and later moved to Salisbury, Massachusetts. Seaport Village bought it in the 1970s and spent more than 2 years restoring it to its original splendor—the horses even have real horsehair tails. If you decide to take a twirl, pick your mount from the 40 horses, 3 goats, and 3 Saint Bernard dogs. This carousel comes complete with the elusive brass ring.

As you stroll farther, you will no doubt notice the official symbol of Seaport Village. The 45-foot-high (14m) detailed replica of the famous turn-of-the-century Mukilteo Lighthouse of Everett, Washington, towers above the other buildings.

From Seaport Village, continue your waterfront walk south to the:

⑪ San Diego Marriott Marina

Adjacent to Embarcadero Marina Park, which is well used by San Diegans for strolling and jogging, it provides a terrific view of the Coronado Bridge. A concession at the marina office rents boats by the hour at reasonable rates and arranges diving, water-skiing, and fishing outings. The impressive hotel resembles an ocean liner.

The waterfront walkway continues to the:

⑫ Convention Center

This building is another striking piece of architecture on the city's waterfront. When it was first completed in late 1989, its presence on the waterfront was a major factor in the revitalization of downtown San Diego. Recently, it was enlarged to an even more imposing size.

WINDING DOWN
The Marriott's waterfront bar, the **Yacht Club** (© 619/234-1500), looks out onto the marina and the bay beyond. It's a choice spot for watching the sunset. (You might want to plan your walking tour so the end coincides with it.) You can get drinks, appetizers, and light fare here, and if you linger into the evening, there's likely to be live music and dancing. Across from the Convention Center, at the water's edge, is the **Chart House** (© 619/435-0155). Housed in the historic 1899 San Diego Rowing Club, it's a more upscale candidate for a drink or a bite to eat.

WALKING TOUR 3   OLD TOWN

Start:	Old Town State Historic Park headquarters.
Finish:	Heritage Park.
Time:	Approximately 2 hours, not including shopping or dining.
Best Times:	Weekends (except the first one in May—Cinco de Mayo) and any day before 2pm or after 3pm. The free park tour runs from 2pm to 3pm.
Worst Times:	Weekdays, when numerous school groups are touring (although it's fun to watch on-site education in action). On Cinco de Mayo weekend, the first weekend in May, Old Town is a madhouse. The holiday celebrates Mexico's defeat of the French on May 5, 1862, in the Battle of Puebla.

Old Town is the Williamsburg of the West. When you visit, you go back to a time of one-room schoolhouses and village greens, when many of the people who lived, worked, and played here spoke Spanish. Even today, life moves more slowly in this part of the city, where the buildings are old or built to look that way. The stillness is palpable, especially at night, when you can stroll the streets and look up at the stars. You don't have to look hard or very far to see yesterday.

Begin at the park headquarters, at the eastern end of this historic district, which preserves the essence of the small Mexican and fledgling American communities that existed here from 1821 to 1872. The center of Old Town is a 6-block area with no vehicular traffic.

The headquarters are near the intersection of Wallace and Calhoun, the location of the:

① McCoy House

This interpretive center and main entryway was completed in 2001, and is an historically accurate replication of the home of James McCoy, San Diego's larger-than-life lawman/legislator who lived on this site until the devastating fire of 1872. The house contains exhibits, artifacts, and visitor information. After checking in here and getting your bearings, head to the neighboring:

❷ Robinson-Rose House

Built in 1853 as a family home, it has also served as a newspaper and railroad office; until the McCoy addition, it was also the visitor center for the Park. Here you will see a large model of Old Town the way it looked prior to 1872, the year a large fire broke out (or was set). It destroyed much of the town and initiated the population exodus to New Town, now downtown San Diego. Old Town State Historic Park contains seven original buildings, including the Robinson-Rose House, and replicas of other buildings that once stood here.

From here, turn left and stroll into the colorful world of Mexican California called:

❸ Bazaar del Mundo

Located at 2754 Calhoun St., it's where international shops and restaurants spill into a flower-filled courtyard. Designer Diane Powers created the unique setting from the dilapidated Casa de Pico motel, constructed in 1936. On Saturday and Sunday afternoons, Mexican dancers perform free at the bazaar. While you're here, be sure to visit the **Guatemala Shop,** the **Design Center,** and **Libros** bookstore.

TAKE A BREAK
This is a terrific opportunity to sample the Mexican food in Bazaar del Mundo. Try **Rancho El Nopal** (© 619/295-0584), **Casa de Pico** (© 619/296-3267), or, a block away, **Casa de Bandini** (© 619/297-8211). All offer indoor and outdoor dining, a lively ambience, and steaming platters of enchiladas, burritos, and other familiar fare. Historic Casa de Bandini, completed in 1829, was the home of Peruvian-born Juan Bandini, who became a Mexican citizen; in 1869, the building, with a second story added, became the Cosmopolitan Hotel. Within the park, restaurants are open from 10am to 9pm and stores from 10am to 8pm (9pm in Bazaar del Mundo).

From Bazaar del Mundo, stroll into the grassy plaza, where you'll see a:

❹ Large rock monument

This commemorates the first U.S. flag flown in Southern California (on July 29, 1846). In the plaza's center stands a flagpole that resembles a ship's mast. There's a reason: The original flag hung from the mast of an abandoned ship.

Straight ahead, at the plaza's eastern edge, is:

❺ La Casa de Estudillo

An original adobe building dating from 1827, the U-shaped house has covered walkways and an open central patio. The patio covering is made of corraza cane, the seeds for which were brought by Father Serra in 1769. The walls are 3 to 5 feet thick (1m–1.5m), holding up the heavy beams and tiles, and they work as terrific insulators against summer heat. In those days, the thicker the walls, the wealthier the family. The furnishings in the "upper-class" house are representative of the 19th century (don't overlook the beautiful four-poster beds); the original furniture came from the East Coast and from as far away as Asia. The Estudillo family, which then numbered 12, lived in the house until 1887; today family members still live in San Diego.

After you exit La Casa de Estudillo, turn left. In front of you is the reconstruction of the three-story:

❻ Colorado House

Built in 1851, it was destroyed by fire in 1872—as were most buildings on this side of the park. Today it's the home of the **Wells Fargo Historical Museum,** but the original housed San Diego's first two-story hotel. The museum features an original Wells Fargo stagecoach, numerous displays of the overland-express business, and a video show. Next door to the Wells Fargo museum, and kitty-corner to La Casa de Estudillo, is the small, red-brick

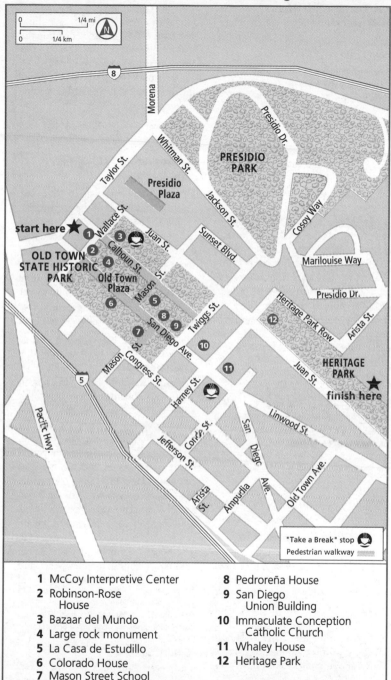

1   McCoy Interpretive Center
2   Robinson-Rose
      House
3   Bazaar del Mundo
4   Large rock monument
5   La Casa de Estudillo
6   Colorado House
7   Mason Street School
8   Pedroreña House
9   San Diego
      Union Building
10 Immaculate Conception
      Catholic Church
11 Whaley House
12 Heritage Park

San Diego Court House and City Hall. (A reconstruction of the three-story Franklin House is planned to the right of the Colorado House.)

From here, continue along the pedestrian walkway one short block, turn right, and walk another short block to a reddish-brown building on your right. This is the one-room:

⑦ Mason Street School

An original building dating from 1865, it was commissioned by Joshua Bean, uncle to the notorious "hanging judge" Roy Bean; Joshua Bean was also San Diego's first mayor and California's first governor. If you look inside, you'll notice that the boards that make up the walls don't match; they were leftovers from the construction of San Diego homes. Mary Chase Walker, the first teacher, ventured here from the East when she was 38 years old. She enjoyed the larger salary but hated the fleas, mosquitoes, and truancy; after a year, she resigned to marry the president of the school board.

When you leave the schoolhouse, retrace your steps to the walkway (which is the extension of San Diego Ave.) and turn right. On your left, you will see two buildings with brown shingle roofs. The first is the:

⑧ Pedroreña House

No. 2616 is an original Old Town house built in 1869, with stained glass over the doorway. The owner, Miguel Pedroreña, also owned the house next door, which became the:

⑨ San Diego Union Building

The newspaper was first published in 1868. This house arrived in Old Town after being prefabricated in Maine in 1851 and shipped around the Horn. Inside you'll see the original hand press used to print the paper, which merged with the *San Diego Tribune* in 1992. The offices are now in Mission Valley, about 3 miles (5km) from here.

At the end of the pedestrian part of San Diego Avenue stands a railing; beyond it is Twiggs Street, dividing the historic park from the rest of Old Town, which is more commercial. In this part of town, you'll find interesting shops and galleries and outstanding restaurants.

At the corner of Twiggs Street and San Diego Avenue stands the Spanish mission–style:

⑩ Immaculate Conception Catholic Church

The cornerstone was laid in 1868, but with the movement of the community to New Town in 1872, it lost its parishioners and was not dedicated until 1919. Today the church serves about 300 families in the Old Town area. (Visitors sometimes see the little church and on a whim decide to get married here, but arrangements have to be made 9 months in advance.)

Continue along San Diego Avenue 1 block to Harney Street. On your left is the restored:

⑪ Whaley House

The first two-story brick structure in Southern California, it was built from 1855 to 1857. The house is said to be haunted by the ghost of a man who was executed (by hanging) out back. It's beautifully furnished with period pieces and features the life mask of Abraham Lincoln, the spinet piano used in the film *Gone With the Wind,* and the concert piano that accompanied Swedish soprano Jenny Lind on her final U.S. concert tour in 1852. The house's north room served as the county courthouse for a few years, and the courtroom looks now as it did then.

From the Whaley House, walk uphill 1½ blocks along Harney Street to a Victorian jewel called:

⑫ Heritage Park

The seven buildings on this grassy knoll were moved here from other parts of the city and are now used in a variety of ways. Among them are a winsome bed-and-breakfast inn (in the Queen Anne shingle-style Christian House, built in 1889), a doll shop, an antique store, and offices. Toward the bottom of the hill is the classic revival Temple Beth Israel, dating from 1889. On Sunday, local art is often exhibited in the park. If you've brought picnic supplies, enjoy them under the sheltering coral tree at the top of the hill.

WINDING DOWN
At the end of your walk, wend your way back down Harney Street, and turn left at San Diego Avenue. Just ahead on the right you'll be able to stop outside the **Old Town Mexican Cafe**, 2489 San Diego Ave. (© **619/297-4330**) and watch corn and flour tortillas being hand-patted the old-fashioned way. Even if you thought you'd had your fill of Mexican food, this fresh spectacle—or the hungry looks from fellow patrons—might convince you to stop in for a refreshing margarita, *cerveza*, or fresh-squeezed lemonade along with a basket of warm tortillas and salsa.

WALKING TOUR 4 | BALBOA PARK

Start:	Cabrillo Bridge, entry at Laurel Street and Sixth Avenue.
Finish:	San Diego Zoo.
Time:	2 hours, not including museum or zoo stops. If you get tired, hop on the free park tram.
Best Times:	Anytime. If you want to get especially good photographs, come in the afternoon, when the sun lends a glow to the already photogenic buildings. Most museums are open until 4:30pm. The zoo closes at 5pm in the summer, 4pm other times of the year.
Worst Times:	More people (especially families) visit the park on weekends. But there is a festive, rather than overcrowded spirit even then—particularly on Sunday afternoons, when you can catch a free organ concert at the outdoor Spreckels Organ Pavilion at 2pm.

Balboa Park is the second-oldest city park in the United States, after New York's Central Park (built in the late 1800s). Much of its striking architecture was the product of the Panama-California Exposition in 1915 to 1916 and the California Pacific International Exposition in 1935 to 1936. The structures now house outstanding museums and contribute to the park's uniqueness and beauty. The park, previously called "City Park," was renamed in 1910 when Mrs. Harriet Phillips won a name contest. "Balboa Park" honors the Spanish explorer who, in 1513, was the first European to see the Pacific Ocean.

Take bus no. 1 or 3 along Fifth Avenue or bus no. 25 along Sixth Avenue to Laurel Street, which leads into Balboa Park through its most dramatic entrance, the:

① Cabrillo Bridge

It has striking views of downtown San Diego and scenic, sycamore-lined Highway 163. Built in 1915 for the Panama-California Exposition and patterned after a bridge in Ronda, Spain, the dramatic cantilever-style bridge has seven pseudo-arches. As you cross the bridge, to your left you'll see the yellow cars of the zoo's Skyfari and, directly ahead, the distinctive California Tower of the Museum of Man. The delightful sounds of the 100-bell Symphonic Carillon can be

Impressions

This is the most beautiful highway I've ever seen.
—John F. Kennedy (speaking about Hwy. 163,
which winds through Balboa Park), 1963

heard every quarter hour. Sitting atop this San Diego landmark is a weather-vane shaped like the ship in which Cabrillo sailed to California in 1542. The city skyline lies to your right.

Once you've crossed the bridge, go through the:

❷ Arch

The two figures represent the Atlantic and Pacific oceans and lead into the park, where you'll find a treasure of nature and culture. For now, just view the museums from the outside (you can read more about them in chapter 7). You have entered the park's major thoroughfare, El Prado—if you're driving a car, this is as far as you can proceed, so find a parking space (the map on p. 183 shows all public lots) and return to the:

❸ Museum of Man

An anthropological museum, it focuses on the peoples of North and South America. Architect Bertram Goodhue designed this structure, originally known as the California Building, in 1915. Goodhue, considered the world's foremost authority on Spanish-colonial architecture, was the master architect for the 1915 to 1916 exposition.

Just beyond and up the steps to the left is the nationally acclaimed:

❹ Old Globe Theatre

The original theater is part of the Globe Theatres performing arts complex. The Globe, as the locals refer to it, was built for the 1935 exposition. The replica of Shakespeare's Old Globe Theatre was meant to be demolished after the exposition but survived. In 1978, an arsonist destroyed the theater, which was

rebuilt into what you see today. It's California's oldest professional theater. If you have the opportunity to go inside, you can see the bronze bust of Shakespeare that miraculously survived the fire with minor damage.

Beside the theater is the:

❺ Sculpture Garden of the Museum of Art

Across the street, to your right as you stroll along the Prado, is the:

❻ Alcazar Garden

It was designed in 1935 by Richard Requa. He patterned it after the gardens surrounding the Alcazar Castle in Seville, Spain. The garden is formally laid out and trimmed with low clipped hedges; in the center walkway are two star-shaped yellow-and-blue tile fountains.

Exit to your left at the opposite end of the garden, and you'll be back on El Prado. Proceed to the corner; on your right is the:

❼ House of Charm

This is the site of the San Diego Art Institute Gallery and the Mingei International Museum of World Folk Art. The gallery is a nonprofit space that primarily exhibits works of local artists; the museum offers changing exhibitions that celebrate human creativity expressed in textiles, costumes, jewelry, toys, pottery, paintings, and sculpture.

To your left is the imposing:

❽ Museum of Art

This is a must for anyone who fancies fine art. The latticework building you see beyond it is the:

❾ Botanical Building

An open-air conservatory, it's filled with colorful flowers and plants shaded within.

Walking Tour: Balboa Park

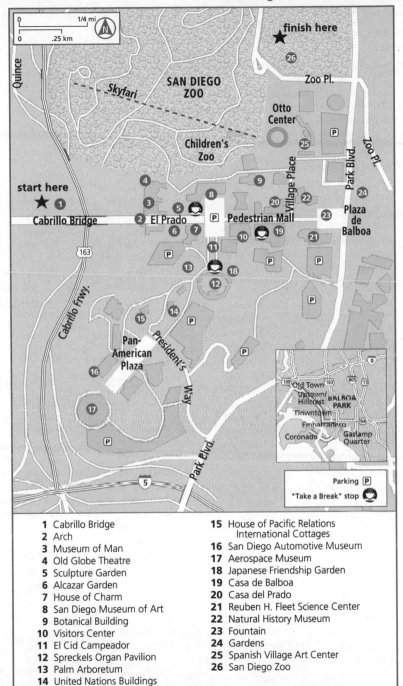

1 Cabrillo Bridge
2 Arch
3 Museum of Man
4 Old Globe Theatre
5 Sculpture Garden
6 Alcazar Garden
7 House of Charm
8 San Diego Museum of Art
9 Botanical Building
10 Visitors Center
11 El Cid Campeador
12 Spreckels Organ Pavilion
13 Palm Arboretum
14 United Nations Buildings

15 House of Pacific Relations
   International Cottages
16 San Diego Automotive Museum
17 Aerospace Museum
18 Japanese Friendship Garden
19 Casa de Balboa
20 Casa del Prado
21 Reuben H. Fleet Science Center
22 Natural History Museum
23 Fountain
24 Gardens
25 Spanish Village Art Center
26 San Diego Zoo

Directly in front of you are the newly renovated House of Hospitality and the park's:

⑩ Visitor Center

Pick up maps, souvenirs, and a discount ticket to some of the museums here. In the courtyard behind is the attractive **Prado** restaurant (see the "Winding Down" box, at the end of this tour).

Turn right toward the statue of the mounted:

⑪ El Cid Campeador

Created by Anna Hyatt Huntington and dedicated in 1930, this sculpture of the 11th-century Spanish hero was made from a mold of the original statue in the court of the Hispanic Society of America in New York. A third one is in Seville, Spain.

Walk downhill to the ornate:

⑫ Spreckels Organ Pavilion

Donated to San Diego by brothers John D. and Adolph B. Spreckels, famed contralto Ernestine Schumann-Heink sang at the December 31, 1914, dedication. A brass plaque honors her charity and patriotism. Free, lively recitals featuring the largest outdoor organ in the world (its vast structure contains 4,428 pipes) are given Sunday at 2pm, with additional concerts and events scheduled during summertime.

Exit to your right, cross the two-lane road, and follow the sidewalk down the hill. The pathway leading into the ravine to your right will take you to the:

⑬ Palm Arboretum

Getting to this site requires some climbing. It's secluded, and may not always be as safe as the main roads, but you can get a good sense of its beauty by venturing only a short distance along the path. As you walk down the hill, you'll see the Hall of Nations on your left, and beside it, the:

⑭ United Nations Building

This building also houses the United Nations International Gift Shop, a favorite for its diverse merchandise, much of it handmade around the world. You'll recognize the shop by the United States and United Nations flags out front. Check the bulletin board, or ask inside, for the park's calendar of events. If you need to rest, there's a pleasant spot with a few benches opposite the gift shop.

You will notice a cluster of small houses with red-tile roofs. They are the:

⑮ House of Pacific Relations International Cottages

These cottages promote ethnic and cultural awareness and are open to the public on Sunday afternoons year-round. From March through October, there are lawn programs with folk dancing. Take a quick peek into some of the cottages, then continue on the road to the bottom of the hill to see more of the park's museums; to your right, the notable:

⑯ San Diego Automotive Museum

It's filled with exquisite and exotic cars, and the cylindrical:

⑰ Aerospace Museum

The museums in this part of the park operate in structures built for the 1935 exposition.

It is not necessary to walk all the way to the bottom of the hill, unless you plan to tour one or two of the museums now. Instead, cross the road and go back up the hill past a parking lot and the Organ Pavilion. Take a shortcut through the pavilion, exit directly opposite the stage, and follow the sidewalk to your right, leading back to El Prado.

Almost immediately, you come to the:

⑱ Japanese Friendship Garden

This 11½-acre canyon is being carefully developed to include traditional Japanese elements. At the entrance is an attractive teahouse whose deck overlooks the entire ravine, with a small meditation garden beside.

TAKE A BREAK
Now is your chance to have a bite to eat, sip a cool drink, and review the tourist literature you picked up at the Visitor Center. The **Tea Pavilion** (© 619/232-2721) at the Japanese Garden serves fresh sushi, Japanese noodle soups, and Asian salads—they also carry quirky imported Japanese candies and beverages (plus Pokemon!) in addition to some familiar American snacks.

Returning to El Prado, which is strictly a pedestrian mall from this point, set your sights on the fountain at the end of the street and head toward it. On weekends you'll probably pass street musicians, artists, and clowns. One of their favorite haunts is in front of the Botanical Building; it takes only a few minutes to wander through, and is a delightful detour. Stroll down the middle of the street to get the full benefit of the lovely buildings on either side.

On your right, you'll see the:

⑲ Casa de Balboa Building

Inside you'll find the Hall of Champions Sports Museum, the Museum of Photographic Arts, the Model Railroad Museum, and the Museum of San Diego History, with engaging exhibits that interpret past events in the city and relate them to the present. Be sure to view the realistic-looking bare-breasted figures atop the Casa de Balboa.

On the other side of El Prado, on your left, note the ornate work on the:

⑳ Casa del Prado

While it doesn't house a museum, it's one of the best—and most ornate—of the El Prado buildings, featuring almost rococo Spanish-Moorish ornamentation.

At the end of El Prado are two museums particularly popular with children; the first is the:

㉑ Reuben H. Fleet Science Center

See p. 139 for a complete listing on this popular attraction. To the left is the:

㉒ Natural History Museum

You're likely to find kids climbing on the whale statue outside. Look for the sundial that is inscribed "Presented by Joseph Jessop; December 1908; "I stand amid ye sommere flowers To tell ye passage of ye houres." This sundial, which is accurate to the second, was originally presented to the San Diego Public Library, and moved here in the mid-1950s when the library relocated.

In the center of the Plaza de Balboa is a high-spouting:

㉓ Fountain

This seemingly ordinary installation, built in 1972, holds 25,000 gallons of water and spouts 50 to 60 feet (15m–18m) into the air. The unique feature is on top of the Natural History Museum, where a wind regulator is located. As the wind increases, the fountain's water pressure is lowered so that the water doesn't spray over the edges. The fountain fascinates children, who giggle when it sprays them and marvel at the rainbows it creates.

From here, cross the road to visit the nearly secret:

㉔ Gardens

They are tucked away on the other side of the highway: to your left, a garden for cacti and other plants at home in an arid landscape; to your right, formal rose gardens. After you've enjoyed the flowers and plants, return to El Prado.

A block from El Prado on Village Place is a voluptuous Moreton Bay Fig tree, planted in 1915 for the exposition; now it's more than 62 feet (19m) tall, with a canopy 100 feet (30m) in diameter.

Farther on is the sleepy:

㉕ Spanish Village Art Center

Artists are at work here daily from 11am to 4pm. They create jewelry, paintings, and sculptures in tile-roofed studios around a courtyard. There are restrooms here, too.

Impressions

Wouldn't it be splendid if San Diego had a zoo!
　　　　　　　　　—Dr. Harry Wegeforth, San Diego Zoo founder, 1916

Exit at the back of the Spanish Village Art Center and take the paved, palm-lined sidewalk to the left. Then turn right onto the palm-lined path that will take you to the world-famous:

㉖ San Diego Zoo

You can also retrace your steps and visit some of the tempting museums you just passed, saving the zoo for another day.

Bus tip: From here, you can walk out to Park Boulevard through the zoo parking lot to the bus stop (a brown-shingled kiosk), on your right. The no. 7 bus will take you back to downtown San Diego.

WINDING DOWN
Back on El Prado (in the House of Hospitality), the **Prado Restaurant** (☏ 619/557-9441) has a stunning view of the sloping park from oversize windows. Far from your average park concession, the Prado is run by the restaurant group responsible for some of San Diego's trendiest eateries, and boasts a zesty menu with colorful ethnic influences—plus inventive margaritas and Latin cocktails. They begin serving lunch at 11am, and switch to a festive dinner menu at 5pm (reservations advisable). In between, a long list of *tapas* (appetizers) will satisfy any hunger pangs.

9

Shopping

Whether you're looking for a souvenir, a gift, or a quick replacement for an item inadvertently left at home, you'll find no shortage of stores in San Diego. This is, after all, Southern California, where looking good is a high priority and shopping is a way of life.

1 The Shopping Scene

All-American San Diego has embraced the suburban shopping mall with vigor. Many residents do the bulk of their shopping at several massive complexes in Mission Valley where every possible need is represented. The city has even adapted the mall concept, with typically California examples like whimsical Horton Plaza and historic Old Town Plaza.

Local neighborhoods, on the other hand, offer specialty shopping that meets the needs—and mirrors the personality—of that part of town. For example, trendy Hillcrest is the place to go for cutting-edge boutiques, while conservative La Jolla offers many upscale traditional shops, especially jewelers. And don't forget that Mexico is only half an hour away; *tiendas* (stores) in Tijuana, Rosarito Beach, and Ensenada stock colorful crafts perfectly suited to the California lifestyle. San Diegans head across the border en masse each weekend in search of bargains.

Shops tend to stay open late, particularly in malls like Horton Plaza and Fashion Valley, tourist destinations like Bazaar del Mundo and Seaport Village, and areas like the Gaslamp Quarter and Hillcrest that see a lot of evening foot traffic. Places like these keep the welcome mat out until 9pm on weeknights and 6pm on Saturdays and Sundays. Individual stores elsewhere generally close by 5 or 6pm.

Sales tax in San Diego is 7.5%, and savvy out-of-state shoppers have larger items shipped directly home at the point of purchase, avoiding the tax.

2 The Top Shopping Streets & Neighborhoods

DOWNTOWN & THE GASLAMP QUARTER

Space is at a premium in the constantly improving Gaslamp Quarter, and rents are rising. While a few intrepid shops—mostly women's boutiques and vintage clothing shops—are scattered among the area's multitudinous eateries, shopping is primarily concentrated in the destination malls listed below.

Horton Plaza *Kids* The Disneyland of shopping malls, Horton Plaza is in the heart of San Diego; in fact, it is the heart of the revitalized city center, bounded by Broadway, First and Fourth Avenues, and G Street. Covering 7½ city blocks, the multilevel shopping center has 140 specialty shops, including art galleries, clothing and shoe stores, several fun shops for kids, and bookstores. There's a 14-screen cinema, three major department stores, and a variety of restaurants and short-order eateries. It's almost as much an attraction as SeaWorld or the San

Downtown San Diego Shopping

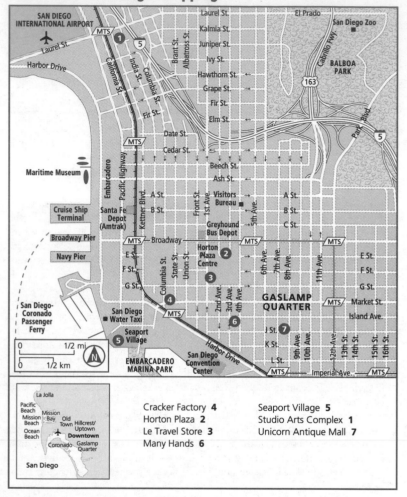

Cracker Factory **4**
Horton Plaza **2**
Le Travel Store **3**
Many Hands **6**

Seaport Village **5**
Studio Arts Complex **1**
Unicorn Antique Mall **7**

Diego Zoo, transcending its genre with a conglomeration of rambling paths, bridges, towers, piazzas, sculptures, fountains, and live greenery. Performers provide background entertainment throughout the year. Supposedly inspired by European shopping streets and districts like Athens's Plaka and London's Portobello Road, Horton Plaza opened in 1985 to rave reviews and has steadily grown in popularity.

Parking is free with validation for the first 3 hours (4 hr. at the movie theater and the Lyceum Theatre), $1 per half-hour thereafter. The parking levels are confusing, and temporarily losing your car is part of the Horton Plaza experience. 324 Horton Plaza. © 619/238-1596. www.hortonplaza.shoppingtown.com. Mon–Fri 10am–9pm; Sat 10am–6pm; Sun 11am–6pm, with extended summer and holiday hours. Bus: 2, 7, 9, 29, 34, or 35. Trolley: City Center.

Seaport Village   This ersatz 14-acre village snuggled alongside San Diego Bay was built to resemble a small Cape Cod community, but the 75 shops are very much the Southern California cutesy variety. Favorites include the **Tile**

Shop; the **Seasick Giraffe** for resort wear; and the **Upstart Crow bookshop and coffeehouse,** with the Crow's Nest children's bookstore inside. Be sure to see the 1890 carousel imported from Coney Island, New York. 849 W. Harbor Dr. (at Kettner Blvd.). © 619/235-4014, or 619/235-4013 for events information. Sept–May daily 10am–9pm; June–Aug daily 10am–10pm. Bus: 7. Trolley: Seaport Village.

HILLCREST/UPTOWN

Compact Hillcrest is an ideal shopping destination. You can browse the unique and often wacky shops and check out the area's vintage clothing stores, memorabilia shops, chain stores, bakeries, and cafes. Start at the neighborhood's hub, the intersection of University and Fifth avenues. Street parking is available; most meters run 2 hours and devour quarters at a rate of one every 15 minutes, so be armed with plenty of change. You can also park in a lot—rates vary, but you'll come out ahead if you're planning to stroll for several hours.

If you're looking for postcards or provocative gifts, step into wacky **Babette Schwartz,** 421 University Ave. (© **619/220-7048**), a pop-culture emporium named for a local drag queen. You'll find books, clothing, and accessories that follow current kitsch trends. A couple of doors away, **Cathedral,** 435 University Ave. (© **619/296-4046**), is dark and heady, filled with candles of all scents and shapes, plus unusual holders.

Around the corner, **Circa a.d.,** 3867 Fourth Ave. (© **619/293-3328**), is a floral design shop with splendid gift items; at holiday time it has the most extravagant Christmas ornaments in the area. Head gear from straw hats to knit caps to classy fedoras fills the **Village Hat Shop,** 3821 Fourth Ave. (© **619/683-5533;** www.villagehatshop.com), whose best feature may be its minimuseum of stylishly displayed vintage hats.

Lovers of rare and used books will want to poke around the used bookstores on Fifth Avenue between University and Robinson avenues. This block is also home to **Off the Record,** 3865 Fifth Ave. (© **619/298-4755**), a new and used music store known for an alternative bent and the city's best vinyl selection. For a comprehensive choice of brand-new CDs and tapes, you're better off at **Blockbuster Music,** 3965 Fifth Ave. (© **619/683-3293**), where you can preview any disk before committing to the purchase.

San Diego's self-proclaimed **Antique Row** is north of Balboa Park, along Park Boulevard (beginning at University Ave. in Hillcrest) and Adams Avenue (extending to around 40th St. in Normal Heights). Antique and collectible stores, vintage-clothing boutiques, coffeehouses and pubs, funky restaurants, and dusty used book and record stores line this L-shaped district, providing many hours of happy browsing and treasure hunting. For more information and an area brochure with a map, contact the **Adams Avenue Business Association** (© **619/282-7329;** www.GoThere.com/AdamsAve).

Lovers of vintage clothing—both female and male—won't want to miss **Wear It Again Sam,** 3823 Fifth Ave., south of Robinson (© **619/299-0185;** www.wearitagainsamvintage.com). It's a classy step back in time, with only the most pristine examples of styles from the 1920s to the '50s. After occupying an off-the-beaten-path corner for nearly 20 years, they recently relocated to this prime Hillcrest avenue.

OLD TOWN & MISSION VALLEY

Old Town Historic Park is a restoration of some of San Diego's historic sites and adobe structures, a number of which now house shops that cater to tourists. Many have a "general store" theme, and carry gourmet treats and inexpensive

Hillcrest/Uptown Shopping

Babette Schwartz **5**
Blockbuster Music **4**
Cathedral **5**
Circa a.d. **6**
Hillcrest Farmers' Market **2**
John's Fifth Avenue Luggage **6**
Obelisk Bookstore **3**
Off the Record **7**
Park/Adams "Antique Row" **1**
Taboo Studio **9**
Village Hat Shop **6**
Wear it Again Sam **8**

Mexican crafts alongside the obligatory T-shirts, baseball caps, snow domes, and other souvenirs. A reconstruction of San Diego's first tobacco shop carries cigars and smoking paraphernalia; more shops are concentrated in colorful Bazaar del Mundo (see below).

Mission Valley is ground zero of San Diego's suburban mall explosion. There are several sprawling shopping centers here, all discussed in detail (see "Malls," later in this chapter).

Bazaar del Mundo Take a stroll down Mexico way—and points south—through the arched passageways of this colorful corner of Old Town. Always festive, its central courtyard vibrates with folkloric music, mariachis, and a splashing fountain. Shops feature one-of-a-kind folk art, home furnishings, clothing, and textiles from Mexico and South America. You'll also find a top-notch bookstore, **Libros,** with a large kids' selection. Don't miss the **Design Center** and the **Guatemala Store.** You won't find any bargains here—it's clearly tourist central—but there isn't a more colorful place to browse in San Diego. 2754 Calhoun St., Old Town State Historic Park. ✆ **619/296-3161.** www.bazaardelmundo.com. Daily 10am–9pm. Bus: 4 or 5/105.

MISSION BAY & THE BEACHES
The beach communities offer laid-back shopping in typical California fashion, with plenty of surf shops, recreational gear, casual garb, and youth-oriented music stores.

Shopping in Mission Bay & the Beaches

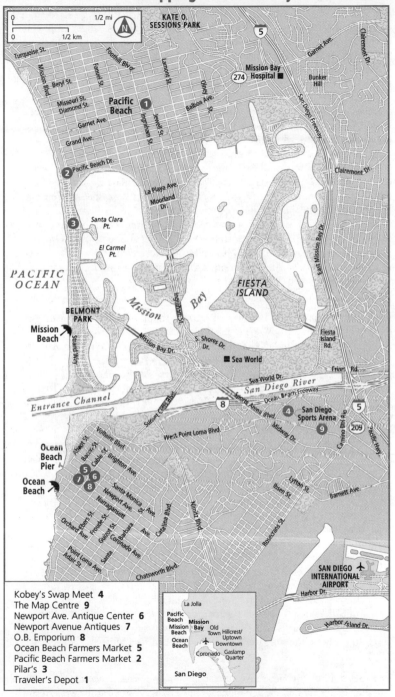

0   1/2 mi
0   1/2 km

KATE O.
SESSIONS PARK

5

Turquoise St.

Mission Blvd

Beryl St.

Missouri St.
Diamond St.

Garnet Ave.

Grand Ave.

Foothill Blvd.

Fanuel St.

Lamont St.

**Pacific
Beach** ①

Jewell St.

Ingraham St.

Balboa Ave.

Olney St.

Garnet Ave.

Mission Bay
Hospital ■

274

Bunker
Hill

Clairemont Dr.

② Pacific Beach Dr.

La Playa Ave.

Moorland
Dr.

San Diego Freeway

East Mission Bay Dr.

Clairemont Dr.

③ Santa Clara
Pt.

El Carmel
Pt.

**PACIFIC
OCEAN**

Mission   Bay

FIESTA
ISLAND

Ingraham St.

**BELMONT
PARK**

**Mission
Beach** ➚

Strand Way

Mission Bay Dr.

S. Shores Dr.
Dr.

■ Sea World

Fiesta
Island
Rd.

Friars Rd.

Sea World Dr.

San Diego River

Entrance Channel

Sunset Cliffs Blvd.

Ocean Beach Freeway

8

Sports Arena Blvd.

④ **San Diego
Sports Arena**

209

5

Pacific Hwy.

Camino Del Rio

⑨

West Point Loma Blvd.

Midway Dr.

**Ocean
Beach
Pier** ➙

Voltaire Blvd.

Abbott St.

Bacon St.

Cable St.

Brighton Ave.

**Ocean
Beach** ➚

⑤ ⑥
⑦
⑧

Santa Monica Ave.
Newport Ave.
Narragansett
Ave.

Catalina Blvd.

Nimitz Blvd.

Lytton St.

Ibsen St.

Barnett Ave.

Orchard Ave.

Ebers St.

Froude St.

Guizot St.

Santa Barbara
Ave.
Coronado Ave.

Rosecrans St.

Point Loma Ave.

Adair St.

Santa

Chatsworth Blvd.

**SAN DIEGO
INTERNATIONAL
AIRPORT** ✈

Harbor Dr.

Harbor Island Dr.

Kobey's Swap Meet **4**
The Map Centre **9**
Newport Ave. Antique Center **6**
Newport Avenue Antiques **7**
O.B. Emporium **8**
Ocean Beach Farmers Market **5**
Pacific Beach Farmers Market **2**
Pilar's **3**
Traveler's Depot **1**

La Jolla

Pacific
Beach
Mission
Beach
Ocean
Beach

**Mission
Bay**

Old
Town

Hillcrest/
Uptown
Downtown

Coronado

Gaslamp
Quarter

San Diego

If you're in need of a new bikini, the best selection is at **Pilar's,** 3745 Mission Blvd., Pacific Beach (© **619/488-3056**), where choices range from chic designer suits to hot trends like suits inspired by surf- and skate-wear. There's a smaller selection of one-piece suits, too. It's open daily.

Some of the area's best **antiquing** can be found in Ocean Beach, along a single block of **Newport Avenue,** the town's main drag. The selection is high quality enough to make it interesting, without pricey, centuries-old European antiques. Most of the stores are mall-style, featuring multiple dealers under one roof. Highlights include **Newport Avenue Antiques,** 4836 Newport Ave. (© **619/224-1994**), which offers the most diversity. Its wares range from Native American crafts to Victorian furniture and delicate accessories, from Mighty Mouse collectibles to carved Asian furniture. **O.B. Emporium,** 4847 Newport Ave. (© **619/523-1262**), has a more elegant setting and glass display cases filled with superb collectible pottery and china. Names like Roseville, McCoy, and Royal Copenhagen abound, and there's a fine selection of quality majolica and Japanese tea sets. The **Newport Ave. Antique Center,** 4864 Newport Ave. (© **619/222-8686**), is the largest store, and has a small espresso bar. One corner is a haven for collectors of 1940s and '50s kitchenware (Fire King, Bauer, melamine); there's also a fine selection of vintage linens. Most antique stores in Ocean Beach are open daily from 10am to 6pm.

LA JOLLA

It's clear from the look of La Jolla's village that shopping is a major pastime in this upscale community. Women's clothing boutiques tend to be conservative and costly, like those lining Girard and Prospect Streets (**Ann Taylor, Armani Exchange, Polo Ralph Lauren, Talbots,** and **Sigi's Boutique**).

Recommended stores include **Island Hoppers,** 7844 Girard Ave. (© **858/ 459-6055**), for colorful Hawaiian-print clothing from makers like Tommy Bahama; the venerable **Ascot Shop,** 7750 Girard Ave. (© **858/454-4222**), for conservative men's apparel and accessories; and **La Jolla Shoe Gallery,** 7852 Girard Ave. (© **858/551-9985**), for an outstanding selection of Clark's, Birkenstock, Mephisto, Josef Siebel, and other shoes built for walking.

Even if you're not in the market for furnishings and accessories, La Jolla's many home-decor boutiques make for great window shopping, as do its ubiquitous jewelers: Swiss watches, tennis bracelets, precious gems, and pearl necklaces sparkle in windows along every street.

No visit to La Jolla is complete without seeing **John Cole's Book Shop,** a local icon discussed later in this chapter under "Books."

Another unique experience awaits at the **Cave Store,** 1325 Coast Blvd., just off Prospect Street (© **858/459-0746**). This clifftop shop is equal parts art gallery and antique store, but the main attraction is **Sunny Jim Cave,** a large and naturally occurring sea cave reached by a steep and narrow staircase through the rock. At press time the Cave Store was reestablishing the **Crescent Cafe,** a local institution that stood on this site decades ago. Black-and-white photo enlargements line the walls, depicting this quirky corner of La Jolla through the years, and making the store well worth a stop for history buffs and collectors.

CORONADO

This rather insular, conservative navy community doesn't have a great many shopping opportunities; the best of the lot line Orange Avenue at the western end of the island. You'll find some scattered housewares and home-decor boutiques, several small women's boutiques, and the gift shops at Coronado's major resorts.

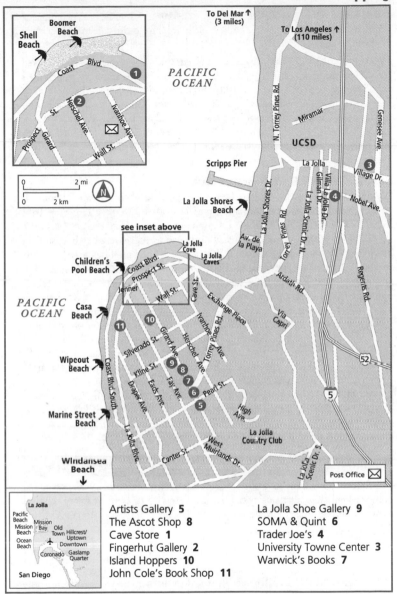

La Jolla Shopping

To Del Mar ↑
(3 miles)

To Los Angeles ↑
(110 miles)

Shell Beach

Boomer Beach

PACIFIC OCEAN

Coast Blvd.

Prospect St.

Girard

Herschel Ave.

Ivanhoe Ave.

Wall St.

0   2 mi
0   2 km

Miramar

UCSD

Scripps Pier

La Jolla Shores Beach

La Jolla

Village Dr.

Nobel Ave.

N. Torrey Pines Rd.

Villa La Jolla Dr.

Gilman Dr.

La Jolla Scenic Dr. N.

La Jolla Shores Dr.

Genesee Ave.

see inset above

La Jolla Cove

La Jolla Caves

Av. de la Playa

Children's Pool Beach

Coast Blvd.

Prospect St.

Jenner

Wall St.

Cave St.

Exchange Place

Ardath Rd.

Via Capri

PACIFIC OCEAN

Casa Beach

Silverado St.

Girard Ave.

Herschel Ave.

Torrey Pines Rd.

Ivanhoe Ave.

Wipcout Beach

Kline St.

Eads Ave.

Fay Ave.

Pearl St.

Coast Blvd. South

Draper Ave.

High Ave.

Marine Street Beach

La Jolla Blvd.

La Jolla Country Club

Regents Rd.

52

5

Windansea Beach ↓

Center St.

West Muirlands Dr.

La Jolla Scenic Dr. S.

Post Office ✉

La Jolla

Pacific Beach
Mission Beach
Ocean Beach

Mission Bay

Old Town

Hillcrest/Uptown

Downtown

Coronado

Gaslamp Quarter

San Diego

Artists Gallery **5**
The Ascot Shop **8**
Cave Store **1**
Fingerhut Gallery **2**
Island Hoppers **10**
John Cole's Book Shop **11**

La Jolla Shoe Gallery **9**
SOMA & Quint **6**
Trader Joe's **4**
University Towne Center **3**
Warwick's Books **7**

Coronado has an excellent independent bookshop, **Bay Books,** 1029 Orange Ave. (© **619/435-0700**). It carries a nice selection in many categories, plus volumes of local historical interest, and books on tape available for rent. **La Provençale,** 1122 Orange Ave. (© **619/437-8881**), is a little shop stocked with textiles, pottery, and gourmet items from the French countryside; nearby **In Good Taste,** 1146 Orange Ave. (© **619/435-8356**), has a staggering selection of gourmet and food gift items—in addition to a tempting display of luscious truffles and sweets. And, if you're in pursuit of swimwear, poke your head into

Dale's Swim Shop, 1150 Orange Ave. (✆ 619/435-7301), a tiny boutique jam-packed with suits to fit all bodies, including rare European makers seldom available in this country.

The Ferry Landing Marketplace The entrance is impressive—turreted red rooftops with jaunty blue flags that draw closer to you as the ferry pulls in. As you stroll up the pier, you'll find yourself in the midst of shops filled with gifts, imported and designer fashions, jewelry, and crafts. You can get a quick bite to eat or have a leisurely dinner with a view, wander along landscaped walkways, or laze on a beach or grassy bank. 1201 First St. (at B Ave.), Coronado. ✆ 619/435-8895. Daily 10am–9pm. Take I-5 to Coronado Bay Bridge, to B Ave., and turn right. Bus: 901. Ferry: From Broadway Pier.

ELSEWHERE IN SAN DIEGO COUNTY

If you're looking for San Diego's best outlet mall, head to Carlsbad, about 40 minutes north (for more information on Carlsbad, see chapter 11, "Side Trips from San Diego"). The **Carlsbad Company Stores,** 5620 Paseo del Norte (✆ 760/804-9000), include the usual outlets and upscale retailers like Barneys New York, Donna Karan, and Polo Ralph Lauren. The mall has several unique specialty shops, like **Thousand Mile Outdoor Wear** (✆ 760/804-1764), which sells outerwear manufactured from recycled products, and makes the swimsuits worn by Southern California lifeguards. To get there, take the Palomar Airport Road exit off I-5.

Garden fanciers will find North County the best hunting grounds for bulbs, seeds, and starter cuttings. **North County nurseries** are known throughout the state for rare and hard-to-find plants, notably begonias, orchids, bromeliads, succulents, ranunculus, and unusual herbs. For more information on the area's largest growers, **Carlsbad Ranch** and **Weidners' Gardens,** turn to chapter 11.

One off-the-beaten-path treasure in Carlsbad is **Charles B. Ledgerwood Seeds,** 3862 Carlsbad Blvd., between Redwood and Tamarack (✆ 760/729-3282). Open Monday through Saturday, the 65-year-old shop has a mind-boggling selection that includes heirloom vegetables and rare herbs.

3 Shopping A to Z

Large stores and shops in malls tend to stay open until about 9pm weekdays, 6pm weekends. Smaller businesses usually close at 5 or 6pm or may keep odd hours. When in doubt, call ahead.

ANTIQUES

See also "Hillcrest/Uptown" and "Mission Bay & the Beaches," earlier in this chapter.

The Cracker Factory Antiques Shopping Center Prepare to spend some time here, exploring three floors of individually owned and operated shops filled with antiques and collectibles. It's across the street from the Hyatt Regency San Diego, a block north of Seaport Village. 448 W. Market St. (at Columbia St.). ✆ 619/233-1669. Bus: 7. Trolley: Seaport Village.

Unicorn Antique Mall Antiques and collectibles fill three floors of this 30,000-square-foot building. You'll see a wide selection of American oak and European furniture. Free off-street parking is available. 704 J St. (at Seventh Ave.). ✆ 619/232-1696.

ART

The San Diego area stages numerous arts-and-crafts fairs, such as the **La Jolla Arts Festival,** which is held every September (℃ 858/454-5718).

The Artists Gallery   This gallery features 20 regional artists in a variety of media, including paintings, sculpture, and three-dimensional paper wall sculptures. 7420 Girard Ave., La Jolla. ℃ 858/459-5844.

Fingerhut Gallery   Fingerhut is a Southern California minichain offering fine quality lithographs and etchings from masters like Picasso, Chagall, and Matisse. This branch, however, is notable for the art of La Jolla's own Theodor Geisel, whose whimsical-yet-provocative works explode with the same color and exuberance of illustrations from his famous Dr. Seuss books. 1205 Prospect St., La Jolla. ℃ 800/774-2278 or 858/456-9912.

Many Hands   This cooperative gallery, in existence since 1972, has 35 members who engage in a variety of crafts, including toys, jewelry, posters, pottery, baskets, and wearable art. 302 Island Ave., Suite 101, Gaslamp Quarter. ℃ 619/557-8303.

SOMA and Quint   These galleries, in a grand space once occupied by I. Magnin, specialize in contemporary art. 7661 Girard Ave., La Jolla. SOMA ℃ 858/551-5821; Quint ℃ 858/454-3409.

Studio Arts Complex *(Finds*   Little Italy has been steadily gaining a reputation as San Diego's cutting-edge art and design district, and several local artists maintain studios in this industrial-style complex at the heart of the area's transformation. Some—especially the street-level galleries—maintain regular open hours. For the smaller studio/galleries upstairs, you can either call ahead for an appointment (don't be shy, the artists are eager to share their work) or take your chances with whoever is on site working when you visit. Some recommended highlights include the **David Zapf Gallery** (#104, ℃ 619/232-5004), which can feature painting, sculpture, drawings, or furniture. They also distribute the *Arts Down Town* guide. Photographer **Steve McClelland** (#213, ℃ 619/582-9812) divides his time between traveling (his images bring the colors, textures, and emotions of the world vividly to life) and commissioned architectural photography in color and black-and-white. Artist **Charlotte Bird** (#224, ℃ 619/239-9353) works in fiber arts, producing fine quilts, dolls, and one-of-a-kind women's clothing. The **Pratt Gallery** (℃ 619/236-0211), has a changing display space, often featuring innovative paintings, photography, or other highly individual work. 2400 Kettner Blvd. (at Kalmia St.), Little Italy.

Taboo Studio   This impressive shop exhibits and sells the work of jewelry designers from throughout the United States. The jewelry is made of silver, gold, and inlaid stones, in one-of-a-kind pieces, limited editions, or custom work. The gallery represents 65 artists. 1615½ W. Lewis St., Mission Hills. ℃ 619/692-0099.

BOOKS

Barnes & Noble   The San Diego branch of this book discounter sits among Mission Valley's megamalls. Besides a wide selection of paperback and hardcover titles, it offers a comprehensive periodicals rack. 7610 Hazard Center Dr., Mission Valley. ℃ 619/220-0175. Daily 9am–11pm.

Borders Books & Music   This full-service book and CD store in Mission Valley's main shopping region offers discounts on many titles. Borders also stocks a stylish line of greeting cards and encourages browsing; there's an adjoining coffee lounge. 1072 Camino del Rio N., Mission Valley. ℃ 619/295-2201. Mon–Thurs 9am–11pm; Fri–Sat 9am–midnight; Sun 9am–10pm.

John Cole's Book Shop *(Finds)* Cole's, a favorite of many locals, is in a turn-of-the-century wisteria-covered cottage, the former guesthouse of philanthropist Ellen Browning Scripps. John and Barbara Cole founded the shop in 1946 and moved it into the cottage 20 years later. Barbara and her children continue to run it today. Visitors will find cookbooks in the old kitchen, paperbacks in a former classroom, and CDs and harmonicas in Zach's music corner. The children's section bulges with a diverse selection, and there are plenty of books about La Jolla and San Diego. Sitting and reading in the patio garden is acceptable, and even encouraged. 780 Prospect St., La Jolla. © 858/454-4766. Mon–Sat 9:30am–5:30pm.

Obelisk Bookstore This bookstore, which caters to gay men and lesbians, is where Greg Louganis signed copies of his book *Breaking the Surface.* 1029 University Ave., Hillcrest. © 619/297-4171. www.obeliskbooks.com. Mon–Sat 10am–11pm; Sun 10am–9pm.

Traveler's Depot This bookstore offers an extensive selection of travel books and maps, plus a great array of travel gear and accessories, with discounts on backpacks and luggage. The well-traveled owners, Ward and Lisl Hampton, are happy to give advice about restaurants in a given city while pointing you to the right shelf for the appropriate book or map. 1655 Garnet Ave., Pacific Beach. © 858/483-1421. Mon–Fri 10am–6pm (until 8pm in summer); Sat 10am–5pm; Sun noon–5pm.

Warwick's Books This popular family run bookstore is a browser's delight, with more than 40,000 titles, a large travel section, gifts, cards, and stationery. The well-read Warwick family has been in the book and stationery business for almost 100 years, and the current owners are the third generation involved with the store. 7812 Girard Ave., La Jolla. © 858/454-0347. www.warwicks.com. Mon–Sat 9am–6pm; Sun 11am–5pm.

DEPARTMENT STORES

Macy's There are several branches of this comprehensive store, which carries clothing for women, men, and children, as well as housewares, electronics, and luggage. Macy's also has stores in Fashion Valley (clothing only), Mission Valley (housewares only), University Towne Center, and North County Fair. Horton Plaza. © 619/231-4747. Mon–Fri 10am–9pm; Sat 10am–8pm; Sun 11am–7pm. Bus: 2, 7, 9, 29, 34, or 35.

Nordstrom An all-time San Diego favorite, Nordstrom is best known for its outstanding customer service and fine selection of shoes. It features a variety of stylish fashions and accessories for women, men, and children. Tailoring is done on the premises. There's a full-service restaurant on the top floor, where coffee and tea cost only 25¢. Nordstrom also has stores in Fashion Valley, University Towne Center, and North County Fair. Horton Plaza. © 619/239-1700. Mon–Fri 10am–9:30pm; Sat 10am–7pm; Sun 11am–6pm. Bus: 2, 7, 9, 29, 34, or 35.

(*Fun Fact* **Know Your Guacamole: Avocado Trivia**

1. What is the avocado's nickname?
2. In which U.S. city are the most avocados eaten?
3. What is the best way to ripen an avocado?

For answers, see the next page.

FARMERS' MARKETS

San Diegans love their open-air markets. Throughout the county there are no fewer than two dozen regularly scheduled street fests stocked with the freshest fruits and vegetables from Southern California farms, augmented by crafts, fresh-cooked ethnic foods, flower stands, and other surprises. San Diego County produces more than $1 billion worth of fruits, flowers, and other crops each year. Avocados, known locally as "green gold," are the most profitable crop and have been grown here for more than 100 years. Citrus fruit follows close behind, and flowers are the area's third most important crop; ranunculus bulbs from here are sent all over the world, as are the famous Ecke poinsettias.

Here's a schedule of farmers' markets in the area:

In **Hillcrest,** the market runs Sundays from 9am to noon at the corner of Normal Street and Lincoln Avenue, several blocks north of Balboa Park. The atmosphere is festive, and exotic culinary delights reflect the eclectic neighborhood. For more information, call the **Hillcrest Association** (② **619/299-3330**).

In **Ocean Beach,** there's a fun-filled market Wednesday evenings between 4 and 8pm (until 7pm in fall and winter) in the 4900 block of Newport Avenue. In addition to fresh-cut flowers, produce, and exotic fruits and foods laid out for sampling, the market features llama rides and other entertainment. For more information, call the **Ocean Beach Business Improvement District** (② **619/224-4906**).

Head to **Pacific Beach** on Saturday from 8am to noon, when Mission Boulevard between Reed Avenue and Pacific Beach Drive is transformed into a bustling marketplace.

In **Coronado,** every Tuesday afternoon the Ferry Landing Marketplace (corner of First and B sts.) hosts a produce and crafts market from 2:30 to 6pm.

FLEA MARKETS

Kobey's Swap Meet (Value   Since 1980, this gigantic open-air market has been a bargain-hunter's dream-come-true. Approximately 3,000 vendors fill row after row with new and used clothing, jewelry, electronics, hardware, appliances, furniture, collectibles, crafts, antiques, auto accessories, toys, and books. There's produce, too, along with food stalls and restrooms.

Insider's tip: Although the market is open Thursday through Sunday from 7am to 3pm, skip weekdays. Saturday and Sunday are when the good stuff is out—and it goes quickly, so arrive early. Sports Arena Parking Lot (west end), 3500 Sports Arena Blvd. ② 619/226-0650 for information. Admission Thurs–Fri 50¢; Sat–Sun $1; children under 12 free. Take I-8 to Sports Arena Blvd. turnoff or I-5 to Rosecrans St. and turn right on Sports Arena Blvd.

Know Your Guacamole: Avocado Answers

1. Alligator pear.
2. Los Angeles.
3. Place it in an ordinary paper bag and store at room temperature. (To accelerate the process, include an apple in the bag.)

MALLS

See "Downtown & the Gaslamp Quarter" for details on **Horton Plaza.** See "Elsewhere in San Diego County," earlier in this chapter, for information on the **Carlsbad Company Stores Factory Outlet Center.**

Fashion Valley Center   The Mission Valley—Hotel Circle area, northeast of downtown along I-8, contains San Diego's major shopping centers. Fashion Valley is the most attractive and most upscale, with anchor stores like **Neiman Marcus, Nordstrom** (which keeps longer hours), **Saks Fifth Avenue,** and **Macy's,** plus 140 specialty shops and a quadruplex movie theater. Particularly interesting specialty shops include **Williams-Sonoma, Smith & Hawken,** and **Bang & Olufsen.** 352 Fashion Valley Rd. ℂ 619/297-3381. Mon–Fri 10am–9pm; Sat 10am–6pm; Sun 11am–6pm. Hwy. 163 to Friars Rd. W. Bus: 6, 16, 25, 43, or 81.

Mission Valley Center   This old-fashioned outdoor mall predates sleek Fashion Valley, and has found a niche with budget-minded stores like **Loehmann's, Nordstrom Rack,** and **Michael's** (arts and crafts). There's a 20-screen movie theater and about 150 other stores and places to eat. 1640 Camino del Rio N. ℂ 619/ 296-6375. Mon–Fri 10am–9pm, Sat 10am–6pm, Sun 11am–6pm. I-8 to Mission Center Rd. Bus: 6, 16, 25, 43, or 81.

San Diego Factory Outlet Center *(Value)*   This strip of 35 factory outlets saves you money because you buy directly from the manufacturers. Some familiar names include Mikasa, Levi's, Calvin Klein, Guess?, Maidenform, Van Heusen, Bass, Nike, Carter's, OshKosh B'Gosh, Ray-Ban, and Jockey. 4498 Camino de la Plaza, San Ysidro. ℂ 935/690-2999. Mon–Fri 10am–8pm; Sat 10am–7pm; Sun 10am–6pm. I-5 or I-805 south to Camino de la Plaza exit (last exit in U.S.). Turn right and continue 1 block; center is on right. Trolley: Southbound to last stop (San Ysidro). Walk back (north) 1 block and turn left on Camino de la Plaza; it's a ½-mile walk or a short taxi ride.

University Towne Center (UTC)   This outdoor shopping complex has a landscaped plaza and 160 stores, including some big ones like **Nordstrom, Sears,** and **Macy's.** It is also home to a year-round ice-skating rink, the popular Hops Bistro and Brewery, and a six-screen cinema. 4545 La Jolla Village Dr. ℂ 858/ 546-8858. Mon–Fri 10am–9pm; Sat 10am–7pm; Sun 11am–6pm. I-5 to La Jolla Village Dr. and go east, or I-805 to La Jolla Village Dr. and go west. Bus: 50 express, 34, or 34A.

TOYS

Freddy's Teddies & Toys   With shelves stacked literally from floor to ceiling, this Coronado shop's comprehensive inventory defies its cozy size and truly has something to interest anyone who steps inside. From vintage and antique treasures that great-granddad might remember to Hotwheels and Matchbox collections, Freddy's even has mechanized gadgets for the modern child. 930 Orange Ave. ℂ 619/437-0130. www.freddys-toys.com. Daily 10am–5pm.

TRAVEL ACCESSORIES

Along with the stores listed below, try **Eddie Bauer** in Horton Plaza (ℂ 619/ 233-0814) or **Traveler's Depot** (see "Books," above) for travel gear.

John's Fifth Avenue Luggage   This San Diego institution carries just about everything you can imagine in the way of luggage, travel accessories, business cases, pens, and gifts. The on-premises luggage-repair center is an authorized airline repair facility. There is also a store in Fashion Valley. 3833 Fourth Ave. ℂ 619/ 298-0993 or 619/298-0995. Mon–Fri 9am–5:30pm; Sat 9am–4pm.

Le Travel Store   In business since 1976, Le Travel Store has a good selection of soft-sided luggage, travel books, language tapes, maps, and lots of travel accessories. The cafe serves beverages and snacks. The long hours and central location make this spot extra handy. 745 Fourth Ave. (between F and G sts.). ℂ **619/544-0005.** Fax 619/544-0312. www.letravelstore.com. Mon–Sat 10am–10pm; Sun noon–6pm. Bus: 2, 7, 9, 29, 34, or 35. Trolley: Gaslamp.

The Map Centre   This shop, recently relocated to this shopping plaza across I-5 from Old Town, has the whole world covered—in maps, that is. From topographical maps and nautical charts to GPS global positioning toys, the Map Centre makes for terrific browsing. Any local needs are easily met as well, with San Diego and California maps galore. 3191 Sports Arena Blvd. (west of Rosecrans). ℂ **619/291-3830.** www.mapcentre.com. Mon–Fri 10am–5:30pm; Sat 10am–5pm.

10

San Diego After Dark

San Diego's rich and varied cultural scene includes classical and contemporary plays at more than a dozen theaters throughout the year, performances by the San Diego Opera, and rock and pop concerts. Among the numerous movie houses and multiscreen complexes are several that feature foreign and avant-garde films. Not all of the city streets pulsate with nightlife, but there are growing areas of late-night activity.

Half-price tickets to theater, music, and dance events are available at the **ARTS TIX** booth, in Horton Plaza Park, at Broadway and Third Avenue. Pull into in the Horton Plaza garage (where you can validate your parking) or, if there's room, just pause at the curb. The kiosk is open Tuesday through Saturday from 10am to 7pm. Half-price tickets are available only the day of the show except for Sunday and Monday performances, sold on Saturday. Only cash is accepted. For a

daily listing of offerings, call © **619/ 497-5000.** Full-price advance tickets are also sold; the kiosk doubles as a Ticketmaster outlet, selling tickets to concerts throughout California.

For a rundown of the latest performances, gallery openings, and other events, check the listings in "Night and Day," the Thursday entertainment section of the *San Diego Union-Tribune* (www.uniontrib.com), or the *Reader* (www.sdreader.com), San Diego's free alternative newspaper, published weekly on Thursday. For what's happening at the gay clubs, get the weekly *San Diego Gay and Lesbian Times. What's Playing?* is a performing arts guide that the **San Diego Performing Arts League** produces every 2 months. You can pick one up at the ARTS TIX booth or write to 701 B St., Suite 225, San Diego, CA 92101-8101 (© **619/238-0700;** www.sandiegoperforms.com).

1 The Performing Arts

These listings focus on the best known of San Diego's many talented theater companies. Don't hesitate to try a less prominent venue if the show appeals to you. Also, keep in mind that the **California Center for the Performing Arts** in Escondido has its own productions (see chapter 11), as does the **East County Performing Arts Center,** 210 E. Main St., El Cajon (© **800/696-1929** or 935/588-0206).

The **San Diego Repertory Theatre** mounts plays and musicals at the Lyceum Theatre, 79 Broadway Circle, in Horton Plaza (© **619/544-1000;** www.sandiegorep.com). The theaters—the 550-seat Lyceum Stage and the 250-seat Lyceum Space—present dance and musical programs, as well as other events. Situated at the entrance to Horton Plaza, the two-level subterranean theaters are tucked behind a tile obelisk. Ticket prices are $21 to $32.

Founded in 1948, the **San Diego Junior Theatre,** at Balboa Park's Casa del Prado Theatre (© **619/239-8355;** fax 619/239-5048; www.juniortheatre.com), is one of the country's oldest continuously producing children's theaters. It provides training and performance opportunities for children and young adults. Students make up the cast and technical crew of six main-stage shows each year. Tickets cost $5 to $9.

In Coronado, **Lamb's Players Theatre,** 1142 Orange Ave. (© 619/437-0600; www.lambsplayers.org), is a professional repertory company whose season runs from February through December. Shows take place in the 340-seat theater in Coronado's historic Spreckels Building, where no seat is more than seven rows from the stage. Tickets cost $18 to $40. Recent productions include *My Fair Lady,* the Dorothy L. Sayers mystery *Busman's Honeymoon,* and a macabre adaptation of Bram Stoker's *Dracula.*

MAJOR THEATER COMPANIES

The Globe Theatres This complex of three performance venues sits just inside Balboa Park, behind the Museum of Man; though best known for the 581-seat Old Globe—fashioned after Shakespeare's—it also includes the 245-seat Cassius Carter Centre Stage and the 620-seat open-air Lowell Davies Festival Theatre. Between them, they mount 14 plays a year between January and October, from world premieres of such Broadway hits as *Into the Woods,* or the live production of *The Full Monty,* to the excellent Shakespeare San Diegans have come to expect from "their" Globe. Leading performers regularly grace the stage, including Marsha Mason, John Goodman, Hal Holbrook, Jon Voight, and Christopher Walken. Tours are offered Saturday and Sunday at 11am and cost $3 for adults, $1 for students, seniors, and military. The box office is open Tuesday through Sunday from noon to 8:30pm. Balboa Park. © 619/239-2255 or 619/23-GLOBE (24-hr. hot line). Fax 619/231-5879. www.theglobetheatres.org. Tickets $23–$39. Senior and student discounts. Bus: 7 or 25. Free parking.

La Jolla Playhouse Boasting a Hollywood pedigree (founded in 1947 by Gregory Peck, Dorothy McGuire, and Mel Ferrer), and a 1993 Tony Award for outstanding American regional theater, the Playhouse stages six productions each year (Apr or May–Nov) at two fine theaters on the UCSD campus. It seems like each one has something outstanding to recommend it, a nationally acclaimed director, for example, or highly touted revival (such as when Matthew Broderick starred in *How to Succeed in Business Without Really Trying* before it went on to Broadway). The box office is open daily from noon to 6pm. For each show, one Saturday matinee is a "pay what you can" performance. Each night, any unsold tickets are available for $10 each in a "public rush" sale 10 minutes before curtain. 2910 La Jolla Village Dr. (at Torrey Pines Rd.). © 858/550-1010. Fax 858/550-1025. www.lajollaplayhouse.com. Tickets $21–$52. Bus: 30, 34, or 34A.

OPERA

San Diego Opera The opera season runs from January through May, with seasonal offerings ranging from familiar classics (like Mozart's *Don Giovanni*) performed by local singers and guest performers, to special recitals that feature heavy-hitters like the Three Tenors (separately) or Marilyn Horne performing a variety of excerpts and songs.

The box office is outside Golden Hall, adjacent to the Civic Theatre. It's open Monday through Friday from 9am to 5:30pm; hours vary on weekends and on the day of performance. Civic Theatre, 202 C St. © 619/570-1100 (box office) or 619/232-7636. Fax 619/231-6915. www.sdopera.com. Tickets $31–$112. Standing room, student and senior discounts available. Bus: 2, 7, 9, 29, 34, or 35. Trolley: Civic Center.

DANCE

San Diego–based dance companies include the **California Ballet** (© 858/ 560-5676; www.californiaballet.org), a traditional ballet company, plus other minor companies. San Diego's **International Dance Festival,** held annually in January, spotlights the city's ethnic dance groups and emerging artists. Most performances are at the **Lyceum Theatre,** 2 Broadway Circle, in Horton Plaza (© **619/235-8025** or 619/231-3586), and there are free performances in public areas. Dance companies generally perform in San Diego from September through June. For specific information or a monthly calendar of events, call the **San Diego Area Dance Alliance Calendar** (© **619/239-9255**).

2 The Club & Music Scene

ROCK, POP, FOLK, JAZZ & BLUES

Belly Up Tavern *Finds* This club in Solana Beach, a 20-minute drive from downtown, has played host to critically acclaimed and international artists of all genres. The eclectic mix ranges from John Mayall to Ladysmith Black Mambazo to Erykah Badu to Lucinda Williams. A funky setting in recycled Quonset huts underscores the venue's uniqueness. Look into advance tickets, if possible. 143 S. Cedros Ave., Solana Beach. © **760/481-9022.** www.bellyup.com.

The Casbah It may have a total dive ambience (and bathrooms grimy enough to make you clench muscles you didn't even *know* you had), but this blaring downtown club has a well-earned rep for showcasing alternative and rock bands that either are, were, or will be famous. Past headliners have included Jon Spencer Blues Explosion, Alanis Morissette, Royal Crown Revue, and local act Rocket From the Crypt. Look into advance tickets if possible. 2501 Kettner Blvd., near the airport. © **619/232-4355.** www.casbahmusic.com.

Croce's Nightclubs Croce's is the cornerstone of Gaslamp Quarter nightlife; a loud, crowded, and mainstream gathering place around the corner from Horton Plaza. Two separate clubs a couple doors apart offer traditional jazz (Croce's Jazz Bar) and rhythm and blues (Croce's Top Hat) 7 nights a week; the music blares onto the street, making it easy to decide whether to go in or not. The clubs are named for the late Jim Croce and are owned by his widow, Ingrid. Their son, A. J., an accomplished musician, often performs. The cover charge is waived if you eat at the restaurant (see chapter 6). 802 Fifth Ave. (at F St.). © **619/ 233-4355.** www.croces.com. Cover $5–$10.

4th & B Located in a former bank building downtown, 4th & B is a no-frills music venue made comfortable with haphazardly placed seating (balcony theater seats, cabaret tables on the main floor) and a handful of bar/lounge niches—one actually inside the old vault. Its genre is no genre; everyone from B. B. King to Dokken to Joan Baez to local-girl-made-good Jewel has shown up here, along

---

Tips **A Note on Smoking**

In January 1998, California enacted controversial legislation that banned smoking in all restaurants and bars. Despite repeated efforts by opponents to repeal the law—and willful disregard on the part of some proprietors—it's more widely enforced every year; if you're looking to light up in clubs, lounges, and other nightspots, better check around to see what the locals are doing first.

with regular bookings of the San Diego Chamber Orchestra. Look into advance tickets, if possible. 345 B St., downtown. ℰ **619/231-4343.** www.4thandB.com.

LARGER LIVE VENUES

San Diego has become a popular destination for many major recording artists. In fact, there is a concert just about every week. The *Reader* is the best source of concert information; check its website (www.sdreader.com) for an advance look. Tickets typically go on sale at least 6 weeks before the event. Depending on the popularity of a particular artist or group, last-minute seats are often available through the box office or **Ticketmaster** (ℰ **619/220-8497**). You can also go through an agency like **Advance Tickets** (ℰ **619/581-1080**) and pay a higher price for prime tickets at the last minute.

Main concert venues include the **San Diego Sports Arena** (ℰ **619/225-9813;** www.sandiegoarena.com), on Point Loma, west of Old Town. The 15,000- to 18,000-seat indoor venue doesn't have the best acoustics, but a majority of concerts are held here because of the seating capacity and availability of paid parking. **Qualcomm Stadium** (ℰ **619/641-3131**), in Mission Valley, is a 71,000-seat outdoor stadium. It has acceptable acoustics and is used only for concerts by major bands like the Who and the Rolling Stones. **SDSU Open Air Amphitheater** (ℰ **619/594-6947**), on the San Diego State campus, northeast of downtown along I-8, is a 4,000-seat outdoor amphitheater. It has great acoustics—if you can't get a ticket, you can stand outside and hear the entire show. **Embarcadero Marina Park,** on San Diego Bay adjacent to downtown, is a 4,400-seat outdoor setting with great acoustics.

Humphrey's, 2241 Shelter Island Dr. (ℰ **619/523-1010;** www.humphreys concerts.com), is a 1,300-seat outdoor venue on the water. It has great acoustics, and its seasonal lineup covers the spectrum of entertainment—rock and jazz to comedy, blues, folk, and international music. Concerts are held from mid-May through October only. Parking is $5.

COMEDY CLUBS

The Comedy Store   Yes, it's a branch of the famous Sunset Strip club in Los Angeles, and yes, plenty of L.A. comics make the trek to headline Friday and Saturday shows here. Less prominent professional comedians perform live Tuesday through Thursday, and Sunday's open-mike night can be hilarious, horrendous—or maybe both. 916 Pearl St., La Jolla. ℰ **858/454-9176.** Cover $6–$10 (plus 2-drink minimum).

DANCE CLUBS & CABARETS

The following clubs impose cover charges that vary with the night of the week and the entertainment.

Harmony on Fifth   With a healthy dose of nostalgia—coupled with a truly modern high-tech sound system and fashionable Pacific Rim cuisine—this Gaslamp Quarter cabaret is a raging success. Old-fashioned oval booths flank the room so diners can enjoy the stage and dance floor; nightly live performers range from swing bands to jazz crooners to blues ensembles. Many patrons dress the part in vintage swing skirts or sleek dancing duds, and there's usually a high-energy, join-the-party atmosphere. Reservations are recommended to guarantee a table. 322 Fifth Ave., downtown. ℰ **619/702-8848.**

Olé Madrid   Loud and energetic, this dance club features a changing lineup of celebrated DJs spinning house, funk, techno, and hip-hop. The adjoining restaurant has terrific *tapas* (appetizers) and sangria. 751 Fifth Ave., Gaslamp Quarter. ℂ 619/557-0146. Cover $10 after 9:30pm.

Sevilla   Most nights of the week you can salsa and meringue to Brazilian dance music; sometimes the club features Spanish-language rock. Sevilla also has a *tapas* (appetizer) bar. 555 Fourth Ave., Gaslamp Quarter. ℂ **619/233-5979.**

CRUISES WITH ENTERTAINMENT

Hornblower Cruises   Aboard the 151-foot (45m) antique-style yacht *Lord Hornblower,* you'll be entertained—and encouraged to dance—by a DJ playing a variety of recorded music. The three-course meal is standard-issue banquet style, but the scenery is marvelous. Boarding is at 6:30pm, and the cruise runs from 7 to 9:30pm. 1066 N. Harbor Dr. (at Broadway Pier). ℂ 619/725-8888. www.hornblower.com/sandiego. Tickets Sun–Fri $49; Sat $55 adults and children. Price does not include alcoholic beverages. Bus: 2. Trolley: Embarcadero.

San Diego Harbor Excursion   This company offers dinner on board the 150-foot (45m), three-deck *Spirit of San Diego,* with two main courses, dessert, and cocktails. A DJ plays dance music during the 2½-hour cruise. Sometimes there's also a country-western band or even a karaoke singalong. Boarding is at 7pm, and the cruise lasts from 7:30 to 10pm. Cruises run Thursday through Monday only. 1050 N. Harbor Dr. (at Broadway Pier). ℂ 800/44-CRUISE or 619/234-4111. www.harborexcursion.com. Tickets $50 adults ($69 adult price with alcoholic beverages), $30 children 3–12, children under 3 free. Bus: 2. Trolley: Embarcadero.

3 The Bar & Coffeehouse Scene

BARS & COCKTAIL LOUNGES

The Bitter End   With three floors, this conceited Gaslamp Quarter hot spot manages to be a sophisticated martini bar, after-hours dance club, and relaxing cocktail lounge all in one. Weekends subject to velvet rope/dress code nonsense. 770 Fifth Ave., Gaslamp Quarter. ℂ 619/338-9300. www.thebitterend.com. Cover charge (Fri–Sat only) $7.

Cannibal Bar   Attached to the lobby of the Polynesian-themed Catamaran hotel, the Cannibal Bar thumps to the beat of a different drum machine— though you *can* get a mean mai tai at the bar. Party central at the beach for thundering DJ-driven music, the Cannibal also books some very admirable bands now and then. 3999 Mission Blvd. ℂ 858/539-8650.

Martini Ranch   The Gaslamp Quarter's newest crowd-pleaser is this split-level bar boasting 30 kinds of martinis (or martini-inspired concoctions). Downstairs resembles an upscale sports bar playing videos, cartoons, and sports simultaneously across the room. If the sensory overload addles your brain, traipse upstairs to relax in scattered couches, love seats, and conversation pits. 528 F St., Gaslamp Quarter. ℂ 619/235-6100.

Ould Sod   Irish through and through, this little gem sits in a quiet neighborhood of antique shops northeast of Hillcrest. Occasionally the tavern hosts low-key folk or world-music performances. 3373 Adams Ave., Normal Heights. ℂ 619/284-6594.

Palace Bar   A class act inside the frilly Victorian Horton Grand, this cocktail lounge is close to the Gaslamp Quarter action, but nowhere near as frenetic. In the Horton Grand Hotel, 311 Island Ave., downtown. ℂ 619/544-1886.

Pitcher This: San Diego's Microbreweries

A microbrewery revolution? Not exactly, but San Diego suds have come a long way in the last few years. It started in 1989 when Karl Strauss, a Bavarian brew master with 44 years of experience working for Pabst in Milwaukee, came to town. He opened Old Columbia Brewery, the first local brewery in more than 50 years. He named his brews after local attractions—Gaslamp Gold Ale, Red Trolley Ale, Black's Beach Extra Dark, Star of India Pale Ale—but used recipes from the old world. They adhere to the Bavarian Purity Laws of 1516.

Karl's crew continues to make 23 beers a year, on a rotational basis, with 8 available at any time. Want to try them all and still be able to walk? At any of the Karl Strauss breweries around town, you can order a Taster Series—4 ounces each of eight brews. Free brewery tours are conducted Saturday and Sunday at 1 and 2pm at the downtown branch (see below). An in-depth tour, which includes a comparative tasting of Karl Strauss beers with America's best-selling beers, is available both days at 3pm. The cost of $25 per person includes a T-shirt, appetizers, and Karl's Taster Series, plus a pilsner of your choice. **Karl Strauss Brewery & Grill, Downtown** (formerly Old Columbia), 1157 Columbia St. (© 619/234-BREW; www.karlstrauss.com), serves American fare along with beer (see listing in chapter 6). Happy hours run from 4 to 6pm Monday through Friday, and 10pm to 1am Thursday through Saturday. Other Karl Strauss locations include **Karl Strauss Brewery & Grill, La Jolla,** 1044 Wall St. (© 858/551-BREW), and **Karl Strauss Brewery Gardens,** 9675 Scranton Rd., Sorrento Mesa (© 619/587-BREW).

In contrast to the polished atmosphere of the Karl Strauss breweries, the **La Jolla Brewing Company,** 7536 Fay Ave. (© 858/456-BREW), feels like a neighborhood pub. The wood floor is appropriately worn, and you can play pool and darts in the back room. The brew master is John Atwater, a graduate of La Jolla High, class of 1976. During his years at UC Santa Barbara (where he earned a Ph.D. in biochemistry), John home-brewed in 5-gallon bottles. He makes his handcrafted beers from his own recipes and names them after local spots: Windansea Wheat (American-style wheat beer), Sea Lane Amber (similar to California steam beer), Red Roost Ale (red ale), and Pump House Porter (dark, slightly sweet ale balanced with a bitter finish). There's a decent bar menu, and happy hour is 4 to 7pm Monday through Friday. If you're trying to decide between the two La Jolla brewpubs, La Jolla Brewing Company has better beer, Karl Strauss Brewery & Grill, better food.

Princess Pub & Grille   A local haunt for Anglophiles and others thirsting for a pint o' Bass, Fuller's, Watney's, or Guinness, this slice of Britain (in Little Italy . . . go figure) also serves up bangers 'n' mash, steak-and-kidney pie, and other hearty pub grub. 1665 India St., Little Italy. © 619/702-3021. www.princesspub.com.

Tips **Your Link to Home: Internet Cafes**

If you're looking to send e-mail or surf the Web, it's easy to do. In Hillcrest, the popular coffeehouse and study hall **Euphoria,** 1045 University Ave. (© 619/295-1769), has two Internet terminals. Resembling video games, they take dollar bills ($1 = 10 min.). It's open daily from 6am to 1 or 2am.

In La Jolla's Golden Triangle, next to Von's supermarket, you'll find **Espresso Net,** 7770 Regents Rd., at Arriba Street (© 858/453-5896; www.espressonet.com). It's a comfy, welcoming hangout with tempting desserts. The state-of-the-art computer terminals have ergonomic keyboards; online time is $6 an hour, or $1.50 for 15 minutes. It's open weekdays 7am to 10pm, weekends 8am to 10pm.

Near the Gaslamp Quarter, **Internet Coffee,** 800 Broadway, at Eighth Avenue (© 619/702-2233), has an institutional feel and isn't much on atmosphere. Still, the up-to-date computer stations will do the job. Open daily from 11am to midnight.

Top O' The Cove   At this intimate piano bar in one of La Jolla's most scenic restaurants, the vibe is mellow and relaxing. On nice evenings, the music—mainly standards and show tunes—is piped into the outdoor patio. 1216 Prospect Ave., La Jolla. © 858/454-7779.

Turf Supper Club *(Finds*   Hidden in one of San Diego's old, obscure, and newly hip neighborhoods (about 10 min. east of downtown), this retro steakhouse's gimmick is "grill your own" dinners. The decor and piano bar are pure 1950s, and wildly popular with the cocktail crowd. 1116 25th Ave., Golden Hills. © 619/234-6363.

COFFEEHOUSES WITH PERFORMANCES

Java Joe's   A popular hangout for Ocean Beach locals, this friendly coffeehouse has entertainment most nights—from acoustic folk acts to open mike to occasional poetry readings. 4994 Newport Ave., Ocean Beach. © 619/523-0356.

Twiggs Tea and Coffee Co *(Finds*   Tucked away in a peaceful neighborhood, this popular coffeehouse has adjoining room for poetry readings. It often books performances by artists like Cindy Lee Berryhill. 4590 Park Blvd. (south of Adams Ave.), University Heights. © 619/296-0616. www.twiggs.org.

4 Gay & Lesbian Nightlife

Bourbon Street   With an elegant piano bar and outdoor patio meant to evoke jazzy New Orleans, this relaxing spot draws mainly smartly dressed, dignified men—and an occasional guest singer like Sam Harris or Nell Carter. 4612 Park Blvd., University Heights. © 619/291-4043. www.bourbonstreetbar.com.

The Brass Rail   San Diego's oldest (since the 1960s) gay bar, this Hillcrest institution is loud and proud, with energetic dancing every night, go-go boys, bright lights, and a come-as-you-are attitude. 3796 Fifth Ave., Hillcrest. © 619/298-2233.

Club Bombay   Mellower than the Flame (see below), this casual lesbian gathering place north of Little Italy has a small dance floor, occasional live entertainment, and popular Sunday barbecues. 3175 India St. (at Spruce St.). © 619/296-6789.

Club Montage   This state-of-the-art dance club has all the bells and whistles: laser-and-light show, 12-screen video bar, pool tables, and arcade games. 2028 Hancock St. © **619/294-9590.** Fax 619/294-9592. www.clubmontage.com.

The Flame   The city's top lesbian hangout has a large dance floor and two bars. It's packed on Saturdays. A mixed crowd attends Friday's drag show, and gender reversal takes place for Tuesday's "Boys Night Out." 3780 Park Blvd. © **619/ 295-4163.** Cover Sun–Fri $2; Sat $3. Bus: 7 or 7B.

Kickers   This country-western dance hall next to Hamburger Mary's restaurant attracts an equally male-female crowd for two-stepping and line-dancing. There are free lessons on weekdays. 308 University Ave. (at Third Ave.), Hillcrest. © **619/ 491-0400.**

Rich's   High-energy and popular with the see-and-be-seen set, Rich's has nightly revues, plenty of dancing to house music, and a small video bar. Thursday is Club Hedonism, with compelling tribal rhythms. 1051 University Ave. (between 10th and Vermont). © **619/497-4588.** www.richs-sandiego.com.

5 More Entertainment

MOVIES

Many multiscreen complexes around the city show first-run films. More avantgarde and artistic current releases play at **Hillcrest Cinema,** 3965 Fifth Ave., Hillcrest, which offers 3 hours of free parking (© **619/299-2100**); the **Ken Cinema,** 4061 Adams Ave., Kensington near Hillcrest (© **619/283-5909**); and, the **Cove,** 7730 Girard Ave., La Jolla (© **858/459-5404**). The irrepressible *Rocky Horror Picture Show* is resurrected every Friday and Saturday at midnight at the Ken. The **OMNIMAX** theater at the Reuben H. Fleet Science Center (© **619/238-1233**), in Balboa Park, features movies and three-dimensional laser shows projected onto the 76-foot (23m) tilted dome screen.

CASINOS

Native American tribes operate three **casinos** in east county. **Barona Casino** is at 1000 Wildcat Canyon Rd., Lakeside (© **888/7-BARONA** or 619/443-2300; www.barona.com). Take I-8 east to Calif. 67 north. At Willow Road, turn right and continue to Wildcat Canyon Road; turn left, and continue 5½ miles (9km) to the Barona Reservation. Allow 40 minutes from downtown. **Sycuan Gaming Center** is in El Cajon, at 5469 Dehesa Rd. (© **800/2-SYCUAN** or 619/445-6002; www.sycuan.com). Follow I-8 east for 10 miles (16km) to the El Cajon Blvd. exit. Take El Cajon to Washington Avenue, turning right and continuing on Washington as it turns into Dehesa Road; signs will direct you to the casino, about 7 miles (11km) from the freeway. Allow 25 minutes from downtown. **Viejas Casino and Turf Club** is at 5000 Willows Rd., in Alpine (© **800/ YELL-BINGO** or 619/445-5400; www.viejas.com). To get there, take I-8 east 25 miles (40km) to Willows Rd. exit; turn left to casino. Allow 35 to 40 minutes from downtown. All three offer Las Vegas–style casino gambling, off-track betting, and bingo.

To bet on the ponies, go to the **Del Mar** racetrack during the local racing season (July–Sept). At any time of the year, you can bet on races being run far and wide at **Del Mar Satellite Wagering,** at the Del Mar fairgrounds (© **858/ 755-1167**). To place a wager on **greyhound racing** or **jai alai,** you have to cross the international border to Tijuana. It's a 40-minute ride by car or trolley from San Diego; from the border you'll need a cab to get to the racetrack or jai alai palace (see "Tijuana: Going South of the Border," in chapter 11). Bookmaker offices, where you can place a bet on just about any sport, are located throughout Tijuana.

6 Only in San Diego

San Diego's top three attractions—the San Diego Zoo, Wild Animal Park, and SeaWorld—keep extended summer hours. SeaWorld caps its **Summer Nights** off at 9pm with a free **fireworks** display. You can catch them from SeaWorld or anywhere around Mission Bay.

Free concerts are offered on Sunday at 2pm year-round at the Spreckels Organ Pavilion in Balboa Park. In the summer, concerts are also held on Monday, Tuesday, and Wednesday nights (Tues and Wed showcase bands, dance, and vocal groups instead of the organ) as part of **Twilight in the Park** (© 619/235-1105). **Starlight Theater** presents Broadway musicals in the Starlight Bowl in Balboa Park in July and August (© 619/544-STAR). This venue is in the flight path to Lindbergh Field, and when planes pass overhead, singers stop in mid-note and wait for the roar to cease. The **Festival Stage** (© 619/239-2255) in Balboa Park is a popular outdoor summer theater venue.

Another Balboa Park event, **Christmas on the Prado,** has been a San Diego tradition since 1977. The weekend of evening events is held the first Friday and Saturday in December. The park's museums and walkways are decked out in holiday finery, and the museums are free and open late, from 5 to 9pm. There is entertainment galore, from bell choruses to Renaissance and baroque music to barbershop quartets. Crafts (including unusual Christmas ornaments), ethnic nibbles, hot cider, and sweets are for sale. A Christmas tree and nativity scene are displayed at the Spreckels Organ Pavilion.

Unique movie venues include **Movies Before the Mast** (© 619/234-9153), aboard the *Star of India* at the Maritime Museum. Movies of the nautical genre (such as *Captain Blood, Hook,* or *The Muppets' Treasure Island*) are shown on a special "screensail" from approximately March through October.

7 Late-Night Bites

See chapter 6, "Where to Dine," for complete listings on the following restaurants. We haven't included other parts of the city because, frankly, late-night meals aren't a big part of San Diego life outside downtown and the immediate area. In La Jolla, your best bet might be the **Hard Rock Cafe,** open till midnight on Friday and Saturday only.

DOWNTOWN   The kitchen at **Croce's** stays open till midnight all week. You can order inexpensive appetizers from the eclectic menu, or opt for a full meal. The stylish coffeehouse **Café Lulu,** a block from Horton Plaza, stays open till 2am Sunday through Thursday and 4am Friday and Saturday. It serves health-conscious, vegetarian light meals, and bread from Bread & Cie. Or go for traditional British pub food at the **Princess Pub & Grille** in Little Italy. You can get Cornish pasties, steak-and-kidney pie, or fish and chips till 1am nightly.

HILLCREST/UPTOWN   These two places stay open until midnight on Friday and Saturday. The relentlessly 1950s-themed **Corvette Diner** serves up terrific coffee shop–style food—and a page-long menu of fountain favorites. Or satisfy your sweet tooth with a sublime creation from **Extraordinary Desserts,** which also serves imported teas and coffees along with not-so-sweet scones and tea cakes.

11

Side Trips from San Diego

If you have time for a day trip, popular destinations include the beaches and inland towns of **"North County"** (as locals call the northern part of San Diego County), as well as our south-of-the-border neighbor, Tijuana. All are no more than an hour away.

If you have time for a longer trip, you can explore some distinct areas, all within an hour or two of the city. They include the wine country of **Temecula,** due north of San Diego; **Disneyland,** a little farther north; the

gold-mining town of **Julian,** to the northeast, now known for its apple pies; and the vast **Anza-Borrego Desert,** east of Julian. South of San Diego, just across the border, lies **Baja California** and a taste of Mexico. Whichever direction you choose, you're in for a treat.

The following excursions are arranged geographically going north from San Diego, up to Disneyland, and then heading southeast toward Julian and south to Mexico.

1 North County Beach Towns: Spots to Surf & Sun

Picturesque beach towns dot the coast of San Diego County from Del Mar to Oceanside. They make great day-trip destinations for sun worshipers and surfers.

GETTING THERE

It's a snap: **Del Mar** is only 18 miles (29km) north of downtown San Diego, **Carlsbad** about 33 miles (53km), and **Oceanside** approximately 36 miles (58km). If you're driving, follow I-5 north; Del Mar, Solana Beach, Cardiff by the Sea, Encinitas, Leucadia, Carlsbad, and Oceanside have freeway exits. The farthest point, Oceanside, will take about 45 minutes. The other choice by car is to wander up the coast road, known along the way as Camino del Mar, Pacific Coast Highway, Old Highway 101, and County Highway S21.

The Coaster commuter train provides service to Carlsbad, Encinitas, Solana Beach, and Oceanside, and Amtrak stops in Solana Beach—just a few minutes north of Del Mar—and Oceanside. Check with Amtrak (© **800/USA-RAIL;** www.amtrak.com) or call © **619/685-4900** for transit information. United Airlines and American Airlines fly into Palomar Airport in Carlsbad. The San Diego North Convention and Visitors Bureau, 720 N. Broadway, Escondido, CA 92025 (© **800/848-3336** or 760/745-4741; www.sandiegonorth.com), is also a good information source.

DEL MAR

Less than 20 miles (32km) up the coast lies Del Mar, a small community with just over 5,000 inhabitants in a 2-square-mile municipality. The town has adamantly maintained its independence, eschewing incorporation into the city of San Diego. Sometimes known as "the people's republic of Del Mar," this community was one of the first in the nation to ban smoking. Come summer, the town explodes as visitors flock in for the Thoroughbred horse-racing season and the county's Del Mar Fair (see "Calendar of Events," in chapter 2).

The history and popularity of Del Mar are inextricably linked to the **Del Mar Racetrack & Fairgrounds,** 2260 Jimmy Durante Blvd. (© **858/753-5555;** www.delmarfair.com), which still glows with the aura of Hollywood celebrity. In 1933, crooner and actor Bing Crosby owned 44 acres in Del Mar, and added a stud barn for his Thoroughbreds; he quickly turned the operation into the Del Mar Turf Club, enlisting the help of Pat O'Brien and other celebrity friends (like Jimmy Durante, whose eponymous street borders the racetrack grounds). Soon, Hollywood stars like Lucille Ball, Desi Arnaz, Harry James, Betty Grable, and Bob Hope were constantly seen around Del Mar, and the town experienced a resurgence in popularity. During World War II, racing was suspended. The club housed paratroopers in the horse stalls as well as marines taking amphibious training on the beach; aircraft assembly lines were even set up in the grandstand and clubhouse. Crosby sold his interest and moved out of the area just after the war, but the image of the racetrack—and the town—was set. You'll still hear the song Bing wrote and recorded to commemorate the track's opening day— "Where the Surf Meets the Turf"—played each season before the first race.

ESSENTIALS

For more information about Del Mar, contact or visit the **Greater Del Mar Chamber of Commerce Visitor Information Center,** 1104 Camino del Mar #1, Del Mar, CA 92014 (© **858/755-4844**), which also distributes a detailed folding map of the area. Open hours vary according to volunteer staffing, but usually approximate weekday business hours. Call for a seasonal weekend schedule. There's also a city-run website (www.delmar.ca.us).

FUN ON & OFF THE BEACH

Del Mar City Beach is a wide, well-patrolled beach popular for sunbathing, swimming, and bodysurfing. Take 15th Street west to Seagrove Park, where college kids can always be found playing volleyball and other lawn games while older folks snooze in the shade. There are **free concerts** in the park during July and August; for information, contact the City of Del Mar (© **858/755-9313**). The earlier you go to the beach, the more likely it is that you'll snag a parking space in metered lots or on the street. Del Mar's beach is extra popular between June and September, during the Del Mar Fair and Thoroughbred racing season. The sand stretches north to the mouth of the San Dieguito Lagoon. There are restrooms and showers near the park.

Every evening near dusk, brightly colored hot-air balloons punctuate the skies above Del Mar; they're easily enjoyed from the racetrack area (and by traffic-jammed drivers on I-5). If you find a balloon ride intriguing, this is the place to do it, because flights are, on average, $25 to $35 cheaper than at other California ballooning sites. **Skysurfer Balloon Company,** 1221 Camino del Mar (© **800/660-6809** or 858/481-6800), has been soaring here since 1976. It offers daily 1-hour sunset flights into the San Dieguito Valley. The balloons carry 6 to 12 passengers. The weekday rate is $130 per person, weekend and holiday rates $155 per person. During December, Skysurfer runs a Christmas special, selling advance-purchase rides for only $110. They're good between January and Thanksgiving, anytime but holidays and holiday weekends.

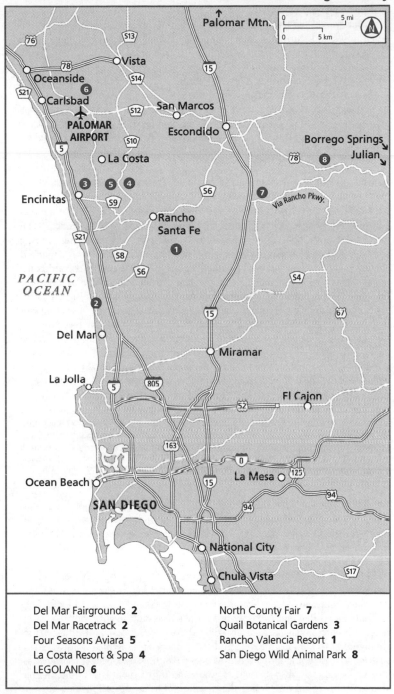

Palomar Mtn.

0   5 mi
0   5 km

Vista

Oceanside

Carlsbad

PALOMAR
AIRPORT

San Marcos

Escondido

Borrego Springs

Julian

La Costa

Encinitas

Rancho
Santa Fe

PACIFIC
OCEAN

Del Mar

La Jolla

Miramar

El Cajon

Ocean Beach

SAN DIEGO

La Mesa

National City

Chula Vista

Del Mar Fairgrounds **2**
Del Mar Racetrack **2**
Four Seasons Aviara **5**
La Costa Resort & Spa **4**
LEGOLAND **6**

North County Fair **7**
Quail Botanical Gardens **3**
Rancho Valencia Resort **1**
San Diego Wild Animal Park **8**

211

WHERE TO STAY

Del Mar Motel on the Beach The only property in Del Mar right on the beach, this simply furnished little white-stucco motel has been here since 1946. Upstairs rooms have one king-size bed; downstairs units have two double beds. Half are reserved for nonsmokers, and only ocean view rooms have bathtubs. This is a good choice for beach lovers, because you can walk along the shore for miles, and the popular seaside restaurants Poseidon and Jake's are right next door. The motel has a barbecue and picnic table for guests' use.

1702 Coast Blvd. (at 17th St.), Del Mar, CA 92014. © 800/223-8449 for reservations, or 858/755-1534. www.delmarmotelonthebeach.com. 45 units (some with shower only). $139–$199 double. Substantial off-season discounts available. AE, DC, DISC, MC, V. Take I-5 to Via de la Valle exit. Go west, then south on Hwy. 101 (Pacific Coast Hwy.); veer west onto Coast Blvd. *In room:* A/C, TV, fridge, coffeemaker.

L'Auberge Del Mar Resort and Spa 🜂🜂🜂 Because Del Mar strives to keep a low profile, most lodgings here feel like an afterthought . . . except for prominent L'Auberge, the town's centerpiece. Sitting on the site of the historic Hotel Del Mar (1909–69), this luxurious yet intimate inn manages to attract casual weekenders as easily as the rich-and-famous horse set, who flock here during summer racing season. Always improving itself, the resort has recently enhanced the lower-level full-service spa, polished up the poolside ambience, and completely revamped the dining room. The result is an atmosphere of complete relaxation and welcome. Guest rooms exude the elegance of a European country house, complete with marble bathrooms, architectural accents, well-placed casual seating, and the finest bed linens and appointments. Many boast romantic fireplaces; all have a private balcony or terrace (several with an unadvertised view to the ocean). The hotel is across the street from Del Mar's main shopping and dining scene, and a short jog from the sand. Redesigned in 2000, the hotel's Mediterranean dining room easily stands alone as one of Del Mar's fine restaurants; at the very least, don't miss its legendary breakfast huevos rancheros.

1540 Camino del Mar (at 15th St.), Del Mar, CA 92014. © 800/553-1336 or 858/259-1515. Fax 858/755-4940. www.laubergedelmar.com. 120 units. $225–$380 double; from $650 suite. Ask about off-season and midweek discounts; spa, romance, and other packages available. AE, DC, MC, V. Valet parking $12. Take I-5 to Del Mar Heights Rd. west, then turn right onto Camino del Mar Rd. **Amenities:** Restaurant; lounge; 2 swimming pools; tennis courts; indoor/outdoor fitness center; full-service spa; whirlpool; concierge; courtesy van; room service (6:30am–10pm); laundry/dry-cleaning service. *In room:* A/C, TV w/pay movies, dataport, minibar, coffeemaker, hair dryer, iron.

Les Artistes *(Finds* What do you get when you take a 1940s motel, put it in the hands of a Thai architect with a penchant for prominent painters, and wait while she transforms each room, one at a time? The answer is an intriguingly funky hotel, just a few blocks from downtown Del Mar, that's an art primer with European and Asian touches.

Although none of the rooms have an ocean view, and an ugly strip of land sits awkwardly between the hotel and busy Camino del Mar, there are still so many charming touches—like a lily and koi pond, Asian chimes, and climbing bougainvillea—that you feel only privacy. At last count, eight rooms had been redone, leaving about a dozen tastefully decorated but standard units. Artists spotlighted include Diego Rivera and (next door) Frida Kahlo—both give you the feeling of stepping into a warm Mexican painting. The Monet room has an almost distractingly abstract swirl of color; and Furo's room is so authentic that a stone-lined stream runs inside the threshold. Other subjects include Georgia O'Keeffe, Erté, Remington, and Gauguin. Though the inn is not for everyone, you really must see it to believe it. Downstairs rooms in the two-story structure have tiny private garden decks.

944 Camino del Mar, Del Mar, CA 92014. © 858/755-4646. 20 units. $50–$85 standard double; $95–$145 designer double. Rates include continental breakfast. DISC, MC, V. Free parking. Pets accepted with $50 cash deposit plus $10 cleaning fee. In room: TV.

Wave Crest 🏖🏖   On a bluff overlooking the Pacific, these gray-shingled bungalow condominiums are beautifully maintained and wonderfully private . . . from the street it looks nothing like a hotel, because a good portion of these condos are owner-occupied year-round. The studios and suites surround a landscaped courtyard; each has a queen-size bed, sofa bed, artwork by local artists, VCR, stereo, full bathroom, and fully equipped kitchen with dishwasher. The studios sleep one or two people; the one-bedroom accommodates up to four. It's a 5-minute walk to the beach, and shopping and dining spots are a few blocks away. There is an extra fee for maid service.

1400 Ocean Ave., Del Mar, CA 92014. © 858/755-0100. 31 units. $216–$246 studio summer (mid-June to mid-Sept), $174–$198 winter; $280–$396 suite summer, $204–$270 winter. Weekly rates available. MC, V. Take I-5 to Del Mar Heights Rd. west, turn right onto Camino del Mar, and drive to 15th St. Turn left and drive to Ocean Ave., and turn left. **Amenities:** Outdoor pool; whirlpool; self-service laundry. In room: TV/VCR, kitchen.

WHERE TO DINE

Head to the upper level of the centrally located Del Mar Plaza, at Camino del Mar and 15th Street. You'll find **Il Fornaio Cucina Italiana** (© 858/755-8876), for excellent Italian cuisine; **Epazote** (© 858/259-9966), for Mexican, Tex-Mex, and Southwestern fare; and **Pacifica Del Mar** (© 858/792-0476), which serves outstanding seafood. Kids like **Johnny Rockets** (© 858/755-1954), an old-fashioned diner on the lower level. On the beach, **Jake's Del Mar,** 1660 Coast Blvd. (© 858/755-2002), and **Poseidon Restaurant on the Beach,** 1670 Coast Blvd. (© 858/755-9345), are both good for California cuisine and sunset views. If you want to eat at either of these popular spots, reserve early. The racetrack crowd congregates at **Bully's Restaurant,** 1404 Camino del Mar (© 858/755-1660), for burgers, prime rib, and crab legs; the gold-card crowd heads for special occasion meals at acclaimed **Pamplemousse Grill,** 514 Via de la Valle (© 858/792-9090). And if you're looking for fresh seafood—and lots of it—head to the Del Mar branch of San Diego's popular **Fish Market,** 640 Via de la Valle (© 858/755-2277), near the racetrack.

CARLSBAD & ENCINITAS

Fifteen miles (24km) north of Del Mar and around 30 miles (48km) from downtown San Diego (a 45-min. drive), the pretty communities of Carlsbad and Encinitas provide many reasons to linger on the California coast. They have good swimming and surfing beaches; a mile-long, two-tiered beach walk that is accessible for travelers with disabilities; three lagoons perfect for walks or bird-watching; small-town atmosphere; an abundance of antique and gift shops; and a seasonal display of the region's most beautiful flowers.

The arrival of the railroad in the 1880s heralded the arrival of Carlsbad as a destination, and the historic depot, built around 1887, still stands in the heart of town. Having seen service as a Wells Fargo stagecoach station, telegraph station, post office, and general store, the depot closed in 1960; it's been reincarnated as the Visitor Information Center (see below).

The town's name was Frazier's Station until the mineral content of its water was found to be almost identical to that of a popular resort, Karlsbad, in

Czechoslovakia. During the early part of the century, the Carlsbad Mineral Springs Hotel capitalized on the water's curative properties, and Carlsbad drew many health-minded visitors. One memorable sales pitch, employing all the hyperbole typical of that era, asked, "What more powerful inducements can be offered than Mineral Wells of Wonderful Medicinal Virtues; Magnificent Marine and Mountain Scenery; a Climate of Perpetual Summer; and Balmy Breezes from the Calm Pacific?" The European connection evoked an old-world sentiment in town, and many parts of Carlsbad still resemble a quaint village. In fact, the Danish toy-maker LEGO recently opened a gigantic theme park; it's since become nearly as popular as the San Diego animal parks. For full information, see below.

ESSENTIALS

GETTING THERE   United Express and America West Express fly into Palomar Airport, which serves Carlsbad and nearby communities. See above for driving directions from San Diego.

VISITOR INFORMATION   The **Carlsbad Visitor Information Center,** 400 Carlsbad Village Drive (in the old Santa Fe Depot), Carlsbad, CA 92008 (℃ **800/227-5722** or 760/434-6093; www.carlsbadca.org), has lots of additional information on flower fields and nursery touring. It's open Monday through Friday 9am to 5pm, Saturday 10am to 4pm, and Sunday 10am to 3pm.

The **Encinitas Visitors Center,** 138 Encinitas Blvd., Encinitas, CA 92024-3799 (℃ **800/953-6041** or 760/753-6041; www.encinitasca.org), is open Monday through Friday 9am to 5pm, Saturday and Sunday 10am to 2pm.

FAMILY FUN

On the way to LEGOLAND is a perfect diversion for music lovers of all ages: the **Museum of Making Music,** 5790 Armada Dr. (℃ **877/551-9976;** www.museumofmakingmusic.org). It takes the visitor about an hour to journey from Tin Pan Alley to MTV, stopping along the way to learn historic anecdotes about the American music industry or to try playing drums, guitars, or a digital keyboard.

LEGOLAND 🎯🎯 *(Kids)*   The ultimate monument to the world's most famous plastic building blocks, LEGOLAND (opened in 1999) is the third such theme park; the branches in Denmark and Britain have proven enormously successful. Attractions include hands-on interactive displays; a life-size menagerie of tigers, giraffes, and other animals; scale models of international landmarks (the Eiffel Tower, Sydney Opera House, and so on)—all constructed of real LEGO bricks! "MiniLand" is a 1:20 scale representation of American achievement, from a New England Pilgrim village to Mount Rushmore. There's a gravity coaster ride (don't worry, it's built from steel) through a LEGO castle, a DUPLO building area to keep smaller children occupied, and a high-tech ride where older kids can compete in LEGO TECHNIC car races.

While the park's official guidelines imply its attraction is geared toward children of all ages, we think the average MTV- and PlayStation-seasoned kid over 10 will find it kind of a snooze. Don't be afraid your toddler is too young, though . . . there'll be plenty for them to do. One last note on age—it may be "a country just for kids," but the sheer artistry of construction (especially Mini-Land) can be enthralling for adults, too.

1 Legoland Dr. ℃ 877/534-6526 or 760/918-LEGO. www.legoland.com. $39.95 adults, $33.95 seniors and kids 3–16, free to children under 3. AE, DISC, MC, V. Summer (Memorial Day–Labor Day) daily 10am–8pm;

off-season Thurs–Mon 10am–5 or 6pm; open daily during Christmas and Easter vacation periods. Parking $7. From I-5 take the Cannon Rd. exit east, following signs for Legoland Dr.

FLOWER POWER

Carlsbad and its neighbor Encinitas make up a noted commercial flower-growing region. The most colorful display can be seen each spring at **Carlsbad Ranch,** east of I-5 on Palomar Airport Road (© **760/431-0352**). Its 45 acres of solid ranunculus fields, planted in wide stripes of contrasting hues, bloom into a breathtaking rainbow visible even from the freeway. Visitors are invited to stroll between the rows and admire the flowers, which are primarily grown for their bulbs. Admission is $1 per person, and the fields are open to the public daily from 9am to dusk. Flowers, bulbs, and garden gifts are for sale.

Even if you don't visit during the spring bloom—or during December, when the nurseries are alive with holiday poinsettias—there's plenty for the avid gardener to enjoy throughout the year. North County is such a destination for horticultural pursuits, in fact, there's a **North County Nursery Hoppers Association** (© **800/488-6742**) in Encinitas. They publish a comprehensive leaflet describing all the area growers and nurseries, including a map; it's available at local visitors centers, or by mail from the Association. Second to Carlsbad Ranch in popularity is **Weidners' Gardens,** 695 Normandy Rd., Encinitas (© **760/436-2194**). Its field of tuberous begonias blooms June through August, fuchsias and impatiens are colorful between March and September, and the holiday season (Nov 1–Dec 22) brings an explosion of poinsettias and the opportunity to dig your own pansies.

Those of us with thumbs of a slightly more somber shade than vibrant green would be satisfied with an afternoon at **Quail Botanical Gardens,** 230 Quail Gardens Rd., off Encinitas Boulevard east of I-5, Encinitas (© **760/436-3036;** www.qbgardens.com). Boasting the country's largest bamboo collection, plus 30 acres of California natives, exotic tropicals, palms, cacti, and other unusual collections, this serene compound is crisscrossed with scenic walkways, trails, and benches. Guided tours are given Saturdays at 10am, and there's a gift shop and nursery. The gardens are open daily from 9am to 5pm, the gift shop and nursery daily from 10am to 4pm. Admission is $3 for adults, $1.50 children 5 to 12, and free for children under 5. The gardens are free to everyone on the first Tuesday of the month.

MORE FUN THINGS TO SEE & DO

Carlsbad is a great place for **antiquing.** Whether you're a serious shopper or seriously window-shopping, park the car and stroll the 3 blocks of **State Street**

Carlsbad's Outlet Mall & Auto Row

Whether you're in the market for a new-model convertible or a bargain on bed linens, Carlsbad's Paseo del Norte is for you. On one side lies the retail magnet **Carlsbad Company Stores,** Paseo del Norte via Palomar Airport Rd. (© **760/804-9000;** www.carlsbadcompanystores.com), a smart, upscale outlet mall featuring close to 100 stores, including Crate & Barrel, Barney's New York, Nine West, and Harry & David. Bellefleur Winery restaurant anchors one end (see listing below). Across the street is Carlsbad's unofficial avenue of cars, a parade of car dealers from Acura to Plymouth—it's a test-driver's dream, or just plain fun for browsing the latest models and features.

between Oak and Beech Streets. There are about 2 dozen shops in this part of town, where diagonal street parking and welcoming merchants lend a village atmosphere. Wares range from estate jewelry to country quilts, from inlaid sideboards to Depression glass. You never know what you'll find, but—at least for me—there's always something. A good place to start is the large **Aanteek Avenue Mall,** 2832 State St. (© **760/434-8742**), where there isn't a loser among the several dozen dealers. A couple have exceptional vintage linen, one a collection of Jadite glass, and there's even a selection of furniture restoration and maintenance products near the register. They're open (as are most area shops) Monday through Friday from 11am to 5pm, Saturday 10am to 5pm, Sunday noon to 5pm.

What about those therapeutic waters that put Carlsbad on the map? They're still bubbling at the **Carlsbad Mineral Water Spa,** 2802 Carlsbad Blvd. (© **760/434-1887;** www.carlsbadmineralspa.com), an ornate European-style building on the site of the original well. Step inside for mineral baths, massages, or body treatments in the spa's exotic theme rooms—or just pick up a refreshing bottle of this "Most Healthful Water" to drink on the go.

Carlsbad has two beaches, each with pros and cons. **Carlsbad State Beach** parallels downtown and is a great place to stroll along a wide concrete walkway. It attracts outdoors types for walking, jogging, and in-line skating, even at night (thanks to good lighting). Although the sandy strand is narrow, the beach is popular with bodysurfers, Boogie Boarders, and fishermen—surfers tend to stay away. Enter on Ocean Boulevard at Tamarack Avenue; there's a $4 fee per vehicle.

Four miles (6.5km) south of town is **South Carlsbad State Beach,** almost 3 miles (5km) of cobblestone-strewn sand. A state-run campground at the north end is immensely popular year-round, and area surfers favor the southern portion. Like many of the beaches along the county's shores, Carlsbad suffers from a high incidence of tar on the beach—you're likely to find packages of "Tar-Off" in your hotel room—but that doesn't seem to discourage many beachgoers. There's a $4 per vehicle fee at the beach entrance, along Carlsbad Boulevard at Poinsettia Lane.

In **Encinitas,** everyone flocks to **Moonlight Beach,** the city's long-suffering sandy playground. After overcoming a nasty sewage problem caused by a nearby treatment plant (don't ask), and receiving a much-needed replacement of eroded sand, Moonlight is back to its old, laid-back self. It offers plenty of facilities, including free parking, volleyball nets, restrooms, showers, picnic tables and fire grates, and the company of fellow sunbathers. The beach entrance is at the end of B Street (at Encinitas Blvd.).

Also in Encinitas is the appropriately serene **Swami's Beach.** It's named for the adjacent Self Realization Fellowship, whose lotus-shaped towers are emulated in the pointed wooden stairway leading to the sand from First Street. This lovely little beach is surfer central in the winter. It adjoins little-known **Boneyard Beach,** directly to the north. Here, low-tide coves provide shelter for romantics and nudists; this isolated stretch can be reached only from Swami's Beach. There's a free parking lot at Swami's, plus restrooms and a picnic area.

Remember the hair-raising aerial escapades in *The Great Waldo Pepper?* You can enjoy everything but wing-walking on a vintage **biplane** from **Air Combat & Biplane Adventures** (© **800/SKY-LOOP** or 760/438-7680; www.barn storming.com). One aircraft even has an open cockpit. Flights leave from Palomar

Airport in Carlsbad, taking up to two passengers per plane on scenic flights down the coast. Prices start at $108 for biplane rides, $68 for Piper Cub rides. Air Combat flights are $249 per person for a 1-hour "dogfight" with another biplane "opponent"—expect 360° loops to be part of your combat strategy!

Bargain-hunter's tip: Discount cards are available at most hotel and visitor center activities displays, or ask when you call.

If you're ready to try **kayaking,** but a little instruction is in order, call Dan Carey's **Carlsbad Paddle Sports,** 2780 Carlsbad Blvd. (© **888/434-8686**). In addition to selling kayaks, paddling accessories, and gear, Dan conducts weekend kayak classes in Oceanside Harbor (introductory course) and at the beach in Carlsbad (surf kayaking). The 2-hour classes cost $40, including equipment. Straight rentals are available for $12 to $15 per hour.

WHERE TO STAY

Beach Terrace Inn   At Carlsbad's only beachside hostelry (others are across the road or a little farther away), the rooms and the swimming pool/whirlpool all have ocean views. This downtown Best Western property is tucked between rows of high-rent beach cottages and proffers its scenic location as its best quality. The rooms are extra-large, and although they suffer from generic "furnished bachelor pad"–style interiors, some have balconies, fireplaces, and kitchenettes. Suites are affordable and have separate living rooms and bedrooms, making this a good choice for families. VCRs and films are available at the front desk. You can walk everywhere from here—except LEGOLAND, which is a 5-minute drive away.

2775 Ocean St., Carlsbad, CA 92003. © **800/433-5415** outside Calif., 800/622-3224 in Calif., or 760/729-5951. Fax 760/729-1078. www.beachterraceinn.com. 49 units. $140–$215 double summer, from $189 suite; $134–$174 double, from $154 suite off-season. Extra person $20. Rates include continental breakfast. AE, DC, DISC, MC, V. Free parking. **Amenities:** Outdoor pool; whirlpool; dry-cleaning service; self-service laundry. *In room:* A/C, TV w/pay movies, dataport, fridge, coffeemaker, hair dryer, iron, safe.

Four Seasons Resort Aviara 🐟🐟🐟   In 1997, the elite Four Seasons chain opened their first ocean-view golf and tennis resort in the continental United States, and Aviara has quickly overtaken nearby La Costa in the battle for chic movers-and-shakers—not to mention winning over the local residents, who head here for summer jazz concerts and a superlative Friday night seafood buffet. The resort offers every over-the-top comfort with the never-off-putting ease that sets Four Seasons apart; when not wielding club or racquet, guests can lie by the pool serenaded by Peruvian pipes, relax in a series of delightfully landscaped gardens, or luxuriate in the recently expanded spa where treatments incorporate regional flowers and herbs. The ambience here is one of both privilege and comfort; rooms are decorated with soothing neutrals and nature prints that evoke the many birds in the surrounding Batiquitos Lagoon. In fact, the name Aviara is a nod to the egrets, herons, and cranes that are among the 130 bird species nesting in the protected coastal wetlands. The hotel's Arnold Palmer–designed golf course was carefully designed to keep the wetlands intact, and incorporates native marshlike plants throughout its 18 holes to help blend with the surroundings. The once-barren hills around the Four Seasons have since been built up with multimillion-dollar homes, but you can quickly escape to the wildness of the lagoon on a nature trail with several different access points; the hotel's staff will gladly point you in the right direction.

7100 Four Seasons Point, Carlsbad, CA 92009. ℭ **800/332-3442** or 760/603-6800. Fax 760/603-6801. www.fourseasons.com/aviara. 329 units. $395–$505 double; from $615 suite. Golf, spa, and attraction packages available. Kids 17 and under stay free in parents' room. AE, DISC, MC, V. Valet parking $16. From I-5, take Poinsettia Lane east to Aviara Pkwy. S. **Amenities:** 4 restaurants; 3 lounges; 2 outdoor pools; golf course (see above); tennis courts; health club; 15,000-sq.-ft. spa; whirlpool; bike rental; concierge; business center; José Eber salon; 24-hr. room service; in-room massage; babysitting; laundry/dry-cleaning service. *In room:* A/C, TV w/pay movies, dataport, minibar, coffeemaker, hair dryer, iron, safe.

La Costa Resort and Spa

At press time the buzz around here was all about La Costa's brand-new owners, the prestigious KSL Resorts, whose world-class properties include Maui's Grand Wailea Resort and the historic Arizona Biltmore in Phoenix. KSL specializes in sunny golf-and-tennis meccas, so they're a perfect fit for La Costa, which has built its reputation on these sports of the idle rich. They boast two championship 18-hole golf courses (home of the annual Mercedes Championships), and a 21-court racquet club (home of the WTA Toshiba Tennis Classic) with 2 grass, 4 clay, and 15 composite courts. In recent years, though, there has been grumbling that this tired property—and especially the cranky old spa—needed a big-time face-lift, particularly after new neighbor Four Seasons Aviara raised the bar on luxury. The ink was still wet on KSL's deal when we went to press in 2002, but we have high hopes for a total makeover. Give a call to check on the status, and let us know how it turns out, OK?

Costa del Mar Rd., Carlsbad, CA 92009. ℭ **800/854-5000** or 760/438-9111. Fax 760/931-7585. www.lacosta.com. 479 units. $345–$520 double; from $570 suite. $35 extra adult. Kids under 18 free in parents' room. Golf, spa, and tennis packages available. AE, DC, DISC, MC, V. Valet parking $16 overnight; self-parking $8. **Amenities:** 5 restaurants; lounge; 4 outdoor pools; golf course (see above); tennis courts (see above); La Costa Spa; 3 whirlpools; complimentary bikes; croquet; concierge; business center; salon; 24-hr. room service; laundry/dry-cleaning service. *In room:* A/C, TV w/pay movies, dataport, minibar, coffeemaker, hair dryer, iron.

Pelican Cove Inn ﹠

Located 2 blocks from the beach, this Cape Cod–style hideaway combines romance with luxury. Hosts Kris and Nancy Nayudu see to your every need, from furnishing guest rooms with soft feather beds and down comforters to providing beach chairs and towels or preparing a picnic basket (with 24 hr. notice). Each room features a fireplace and private entrance; some have private spa tubs. The airy, spacious La Jolla room is loveliest, with bay windows and a cupola ceiling. Breakfast can be enjoyed in the garden if weather permits. Courtesy transportation from the Oceanside train station is available.

320 Walnut Ave., Carlsbad, CA 92008. ℭ **888/PEL-COVE** or 760/434-5995. www.pelican-cove.com. 8 units. $90–$180 double. Rates include full breakfast. Extra person $15. Midweek and seasonal discounts available. AE, MC, V. Free parking. From downtown Carlsbad, follow Carlsbad Blvd. south to Walnut Ave.; turn left and drive 2½ blocks. *In room:* TV, no phone.

Tamarack Beach Resort ﹠

This resort property's rooms, in the village across the street from the beach, are restfully decorated with beachy wicker furniture. Fully equipped suites—similar to Maui-style vacation condos—have stereos, full kitchens, washers, and dryers. The pretty Tamarack has a pleasant lobby and a sunny pool courtyard with barbecue grills. Dini's by the Sea is a good restaurant that is popular with locals.

3200 Carlsbad Blvd., Carlsbad, CA 92008. ℭ **800/334-2199** or 760/729-3500. Fax 760/434-5942. www.tamarackresort.com. 77 units. $140–$215 double; $210–$340 suite. Children 12 and under stay free in parents' room. Off season discounts and weekly rates available. Rates include continental breakfast. AE, MC, V. Free underground parking. **Amenities:** Restaurant; outdoor pool; 2 whirlpools; exercise room. *In room:* A/C, TV/VCR w/complimentary movie library, fridge, coffeemaker, hair dryer, iron.

WHERE TO DINE

The architectural centerpiece of Carlsbad is **Neiman's,** 2978 Carlsbad Blvd. (*©* **760/729-4131**), a restored Victorian mansion complete with turrets, cupolas, and waving flags. Inside, there's a casual cafe and bar where LeRoy Neiman lithographs hang on the walls. The menu includes rack of lamb, chicken Dijon, and smoked chicken with cheese quesadillas. There are also burgers, pastas, and salads. Sunday brunch is a tremendous buffet of breakfast and lunch items. An always-crowded local favorite is **Fidel's Norte,** 3003 Carlsbad Blvd. (*©* **760/ 729-0903**), a branch of the Solana Beach mainstay, known for reliably delicious Mexican food and kickin' margaritas.

Some of our favorites in Encinitas include **Vigilucci's,** 505 S. Highway 101 (at D St.; *©* **760/942-7332**), where the wafting fragrance of garlic always draws a crowd in for authentic southern Italy *trattoria* fare served in a lively atmosphere accented with old-world touches like stained glass and a grand mahogany bar; and the nearby **Siamese Basil,** 527 S. Coast Highway 101 (*©* **760/753-3940**), whose innocuous facade and bland interior belie a well-deserved reputation for fresh zesty Thai food and a friendly attitude—you can even choose your spice quotient, from toddler-safe 1 to fire-alarm 10.

Bellefleur Winery & Restaurant *©©* CALIFORNIAN/MEDITER-RANEAN   This popular restaurant boasts the "complete wine country experience," although there's no wine country evident among the surrounding outlet mall and car dealerships. But its cavernous, semi-industrial dining room, coupled with the wood-fired and wine-enhanced aromas emanating from Bellefleur's clanging open kitchen, do somehow evoke the casual yet sophisticated ambience of California wine-producing regions like Santa Barbara and Napa. This multifunctional space includes a stylish tasting bar and open-air dining patio in addition to the main seating area and a glassed-in barrel aging room. The place can be noisy and spirited, drawing both exhausted shoppers and savvy San Diegans for a cuisine that incorporates North County's abundant produce with fresh fish and meats. Lunchtime sandwiches and salads surpass the shopping-mall standard, while dinner choices feature oak-grilled beef tenderloin or Colorado rack of lamb; mashed potatoes enhanced with garlic, horseradish, or olive tapenade; and rich reduction sauces of premium balsamic vinegar, wild mushroom demi-glace, or sweet-tart tamarind.

5610 Paseo del Norte, Carlsbad. *©* **760/603-1919.** www.bellefleur.com. Reservations recommended for Fri–Sat dinner. Lunch $7–$15; dinner $14–$23. AE, DISC, MC, V. Daily 11am–3pm and 5–9pm (until 10pm Fri–Sat).

OCEANSIDE

The northernmost community in San Diego County (actually, it's a city of 150,000), Oceanside is 36 miles (58km) from San Diego. It claims almost 4 miles (6.5km) of beaches and has one of the West Coast's longest over-the-water wooden piers, where a tram does nothing but transport people from the street to the end of the 1,954-foot (586m) structure and back for 25¢ each way. The 1950s-style diner at the end of the pier, **Ruby's,** is a great place for a quick and inexpensive lunch over the ocean. The wide, sandy beach, pier, and well-tended recreational area with playground equipment and an outdoor amphitheater are within easy walking distance of the train station.

ESSENTIALS

For an information packet about Oceanside and its attractions, send a check for $3 to the **Oceanside Visitor & Tourism Center,** 928 North Coast Hwy.,

Oceanside, CA 92054 (© **800/350-7873** or 760/721-1101; fax 760/722-8336; www.oceansidechamber.com).

EXPLORING OCEANSIDE

One of the nicest things to do in Oceanside is to stroll around the city's upscale **harbor.** Bustling with pleasure craft, it's lined with condominiums and boasts a Cape Cod–themed shopping village. A launch ramp, visitor boat slips, and charter fishing are here. The **Harbor Days Festival** in mid-September typically attracts 100,000 visitors for a crafts fair, entertainment, and food booths.

The area's biggest attraction is **Mission San Luis Rey** (© **760/757-3651**), a few miles inland. Founded in 1798, it's the largest of California's 21 missions. There is a small charge to tour the mission, its impressive church, exhibits, grounds, and cemetery. You might recognize it as the backdrop for one of the Zorro movies.

For a wide selection of rental watercraft, head to **Boat Rentals of America** (© **760/722-0028**), on Harbor Drive South. It rents everything from kayaks, WaveRunners, and electric boats for relaxed harbor touring, to 14- and 22-foot (4m and 6.5m) sailboats, fishing skiffs, and Runabout cruisers. Even if you have no experience, there's plenty of room for exploration in the harbor. Sample rates: single kayak, $10 per hour; 15-foot (4.5km) fishing skiff, $60 half day, $90 full day; and, WaveRunner, $75 per hour. Substantial winter discounts are available; Boat Rentals keeps seasonal hours, so call for specific information.

Behind the harbor lurks the U.S. Marine Corps's **Camp Pendleton,** one of a few clues that Oceanside is primarily a military town—the city hides that fact better than most.

Its other main identification is with surfers and surf lore, and there's no better place to learn all about it than the **California Surf Museum,** 223 North Coast Hwy. (© **760/721-6876;** www.surfmuseum.org). At the final (we hope) headquarters of this peripatetic institution—founded in 1985, the museum was first housed at a restaurant in Encinitas, then temporary digs in Pacific Beach and Oceanside, before moving to its current location—both surf devotees and curious onlookers will delight in the museum's unbelievably extensive collection. Boards and other relics chronicle the development of the sport. Many belonged to surfers whose names are revered by local surfers, including Hawaiian Duke Kahanamoku and local daredevil Bob Simmons. Vintage photographs, beach attire, 1960s beach graffiti, and surf music all lovingly bring the sport to life—there's even a photo display of the real-life Gidget. A gift shop offers unique items, including memorabilia of famous surfers and surf flicks, plus novelty items like a surf-lingo dictionary. The museum is open Thursday through Monday from noon to 4pm; admission is free, but donations are requested.

The **Oceanside Beach** starts just outside Oceanside Harbor, where routine harbor dredging makes for a substantial amount of fluffy, clean white sand. It runs almost 4 miles (6.5km) south to the Carlsbad border. Along the way you can enjoy the **Strand,** a grassy park that stretches along the beach between Fifth Street and Wisconsin Avenue. Benches with scenic vistas abound, and the Strand also borders on the Oceanside Pier, which in turn is usually flanked by legions of bobbing surfers. Parking is at metered street spaces or in lots, which can fill up on nice summer days. Harbor Beach, which is separated from the rest by the San Luis River, charges $5 admission per vehicle. Farther south, there is no regulated admission, and after Witherby Street or so, parking is free (but in demand) along residential streets. Around the pier are rest rooms, showers, picnic areas, and volleyball nets.

Oceanside's world-famous surfing spots attract numerous competitions, including the Longboard Surf Contest and World Bodysurfing Championships, both in August.

Gamblers—and fans of the swingin' Rat Pack movies—can be found at Oceanside's unique gaming house, **Ocean's Eleven Casino,** 121 Brooks St. (© **760/439-6988;** www.oceans11.com). The inside is more contemporary banquet hall than vintage Vegas, but Ocean's Eleven does its best to evoke Sin City. It has murals of Frank Sinatra; Sammy Davis, Jr.; Dean Martin; Joey Bishop; and Peter Lawford at the height of their hijinks, and retro-style Continental fare (veal Oscar, surf-and-turf) served up in the Rat Pack Lounge. There's nightly entertainment in the lounge, and, of course, games: blackjack, poker (Hold-Em, 7-Card Stud, Omaha Hi-Lo, Pot Limit), Pai Gow, and Pan. It's open 24 hours a day, 7 days a week.

WHERE TO STAY & DINE

The inexpensive to moderate **Oceanside Marina Inn,** 2008 Harbor Dr. N., Oceanside, CA 92054 (© **800/252-2033** or 760/722-1561; www.omihotel. com), boasts a scenic perch way at the mouth of the harbor, and offers a quiet, nautical setting for those who want to stay overnight. Despite dingy hallways, we found their rooms spacious, light, and newly refurnished in an attractive, vaguely Colonial-tropical (think Bombay Company) style. An ocean-view pool and spa, complimentary breakfast, and romantic gas fireplace in every room make the deal even sweeter.

Several surf-and-turf harbor-side restaurant stalwarts are close by, including the **Chart House** (© **760/722-1345**), the **Jolly Roger** (© **760/722-1831**), and the **Monterey Bay Canners** (© **760/722-3474**).

Elsewhere in Oceanside, you can get a side helping of history with your burger-and-fries at the original **101 Cafe,** 631 S. Coast Highway (© **760/ 722-5220**). This humble diner dates from the earliest days of the old coast highway that was the only route between Los Angeles and San Diego until 1953 brought the interstate.

2 North County Inland: From Rancho Santa Fe to Palomar Mountain

The coastal and inland sections of North County are as different as night and day. Beaches and laid-back villages where work seems to be the curse of the surfing class characterize the coast. Inland you'll find beautiful barren hills, citrus groves, and conservative communities where agriculture plays an important role.

Rancho Santa Fe is about 27 miles (43km) north of downtown San Diego; from there the Del Dios Highway (S6) leads to Escondido, almost 32 miles (52km) from the city. Nearly 70 miles (113km) away is Palomar Mountain in the Cleveland National Forest, which spills over the border into Riverside County. The **San Diego North Convention and Visitors Bureau,** 720 N. Broadway, Escondido, CA 92025 (© **800/848-3336** or 760/745-4741; www.sandiegonorth.com), can answer your questions.

RANCHO SANTA FE

Exclusive Rancho Santa Fe was once the property of the Santa Fe Railroad, and the eucalyptus trees the railroad grew create a stately atmosphere. After just a few minutes in town, it becomes apparent that Rancho Santa Fe is a playground for the überwealthy, but not in the usual, pretentious sense. Proving the adage that true breeding makes everyone feel at ease, and that it's gauche to flaunt your money, this upscale slice of North County is a friendly town that's enjoyed by everyone. Primarily residential Rancho Santa Fe has two large resort hotels that blend into the eucalyptus groves surrounding the town. The **Rancho Valencia Resort** is a premier destination and choice of the First Family; the more modestly priced **Inn at Rancho Santa Fe** is closer to town (see "Where to Stay," below). Shopping and dining—both quite limited—in Rancho Santa Fe revolve around a couple of understated blocks known locally as "the Village," whose curbs are usually filled with late-model Mercedes, Lexuses, and Land Rovers.

ESSENTIALS

GETTING THERE   From San Diego, take I-5 north to Lomas Santa Fe (County Hwy. S8) east; it turns into Linea del Cielo and leads directly into the center of Rancho Santa Fe. If you continue through town on Paseo Delicias, you'll pick up the Del Dios Highway (County Hwy. S6), the scenic route to Escondido and the **Wild Animal Park.** This road affords views of Lake Hodges, as well as glimpses of expansive estates, some of the most expensive in the country.

SPECIAL EVENTS   If you're looking for Fourth of July festivities with a small-town yet sophisticated flavor, come for the annual **Independence Day Parade.** Residents come out in droves as a marching band, equestrians, and the local fire engines wind through the tiny town center. Anyone with a vintage, classic, or just luxury car gets into the act—you might see vintage Packards, restored Model Ts, classic roadsters, or just shiny new Land Rovers strutting their stuff. Festivities continue with a barbecue and concert in the park. For more information, call © **800/848-3336** or 760/745-4741.

WHERE TO STAY

The Inn at Rancho Santa Fe ⚜⚜   Indulge your inner gentry with a surprisingly affordable stay here, where casual surroundings belie the international clientele. Like the town itself, the Inn is the epitome of genteel, proving that those born to money needn't flaunt it, or pay unnecessarily exorbitant rates. Early-California-style cottages are nestled throughout the resort's 20 acres; the decor is English country-flavored and sturdy, and many rooms have fireplaces, kitchenettes, and secluded patios. A fascinating collection of antique, hand-carved model sailing ships is on display in the lobby. Beautifully landscaped grounds contain towering eucalyptus, colorful flowers, and expansive rolling lawns (a favorite, I'm told, among the canine guests welcomed at the inn). Nifty extras include guest membership at Rancho Santa Fe Golf Club and use of the Inn's private Del Mar beach cottage, complete with showers and elevated deck.

5951 Linea del Cielo (P.O. Box 869), Rancho Santa Fe, CA 92067. © **800/843-4661** or 858/756-1131. Fax 858/759-1604. www.theinnatranchosantafe.com. 89 units. $130–$230 double; from $350 suite. AE, DC, MC, V. Free parking. From I-5, take the Lomas Santa Fe exit, following signs to Rancho Santa Fe. The Inn is on the right just before town. Pets accepted. **Amenities:** Restaurant; bar; outdoor pool; tennis courts; room service (7:30am–9:30pm); in-room massage; babysitting; laundry/dry-cleaning service; coin-op laundry. *In room:* A/C, TV, dataport, safe.

Rancho Valencia Resort ⚜⚜⚜   If you are in need of pampering and relaxation—or a seriously romantic getaway, read on. A member of Relais & Châteaux and Preferred Hotels, this sun-baked Spanish- and Mediterranean-style resort sits on 40 acres overlooking the San Dieguito Valley and the rolling hills of Rancho Santa Fe. Imagine having your own *casita* with cathedral ceilings, wood-burning fireplace, ceiling fans, oversize tiled bathroom, walk-in closet, and private terrace. Fresh-squeezed juice and a newspaper are left outside your door in the morning. Those who venture outside discover grounds filled with 2,000 citrus trees, bougainvillea, and air sweetened by flowers and birdsong. Friday and Saturday nights find a guitarist or cellist entertaining, and there's dancing under the stars on Thursday nights in July and August. Tea and cocktails are served in the La Sala lounge, from which there is a great view of the hot-air balloons at sunset.

5921 Valencia Circle (Box 9126), Rancho Santa Fe, CA 92067. © 800/548-3664 or 858/756-1123. Fax 858/756-0165. www.ranchovalencia.com. 43 units. $450–$875 suite. Sports, spa, dining, romance packages available. AE, DC, MC, V. Free valet and self-parking. Take I-5 to Del Mar Heights Rd. and go east to El Camino Real. Turn left to San Dieguito Rd., turn right, and follow signs to resort. Pets accepted; $75 per night. **Amenities:** Acclaimed restaurant; lounge; 2 outdoor pools; nearby golf; croquet lawn; tennis courts and clinics; health club; spa; 3 whirlpools; complimentary bikes; concierge; 24-hr. room service; in-room massage; babysitting; laundry/dry-cleaning service; self-service laundry. *In room:* A/C, TV/VCR, dataport, minibar, coffeemaker, hair dryer, iron, safe.

WHERE TO DINE

If you're looking for a casual lunch, breakfast, or snack, seek out **Thyme In The Ranch,** 16905 Avenida de Acacias (© 858/759-0747), a bakery/cafe that's only open Tuesday through Saturday from 7am to 3pm. Though hidden on a small plaza behind chic Mille Fleurs on Paseo Delicias, this tiny treasure is well known (as evidenced by constant lines at the counter). Salads, sandwiches, soup, and quiche are the menu mainstays—all delicious—but the baked treats are what keep me coming back!

Delicias ✶✶✶ CALIFORNIAN   Decorated in a mix of antiques and wicker, accented by flowers, woven tapestries, and floor-to-ceiling French doors, this comfortable restaurant is equally appropriate for a casual meal or special occasion. Service is attentive and personable, and the food is delicious. Intriguing—but not overly complex—flavor blends are the hallmark of a menu that ranges from the zesty Pacific Rim to the sunny Mediterranean, interpreted with a subtle French accent. Chinese duckling is slow-roasted with ginger and soy, then served with a spicy mushroom sauce; coriander-crusted salmon is sautéed with miso and ponzu, accented by papaya salsa; and rack of lamb is bathed in tamarind-plum sauce and served with cucumber-mango-mint relish. At meals like these it's not easy to leave room for dessert; but, take my word for it, you'll kick yourself if you don't. Giant umbrellas shade a street-side outdoor patio. Delicias is also a great (and affordable) lunch choice.

6109 Paseo Delicias. © 858/756-8000. Reservations recommended on weekends. Lunch $9–$16; dinner $15–$29. AE, DC, MC, V. Tues–Sun noon–2pm and 6–10pm; extended summer hours.

ESCONDIDO

Best known as the home of the Wild Animal Park (described in chapter 7), Escondido is also the site of the **California Center for the Performing Arts,** an attractive 12-acre campus that includes two theaters, an art museum, a conference center, and a cafe. It's worth the 45-minute to 1-hour drive to Escondido (along I-15 north to the Escondido exits) just to see the appealing postmodern architecture of this facility, which opened in 1994. (To find out what's playing and for ticket information, call © 760/738-4100.)

This city of 125,000 is in the heart of a major agricultural area, so it's not surprising that the farmers' market on Tuesday afternoons is one of the county's best. In total, North County is home to 36 golf courses (some are described in chapter 7). Orfila Vineyards is near the Wild Animal Park; for details, refer to "For Wine Lovers" in chapter 7. Grand Avenue, old Escondido's downtown main drag, is experiencing a pleasant renewal. Classy antique stores and new restaurants, like 150 Grand Cafe (see below), are filling historic storefronts.

WHERE TO STAY & DINE

The **Welk Resort Center,** 8860 Lawrence Welk Dr. (© **800/932-9355**), is a moderate-to-expensive lodging near downtown Escondido. It offers golf, tennis, and live theatrical entertainment.

150 Grand Café 🏵🏵 MODERN/MULTIETHNIC English expatriates Cyril and Vicki Lucas run this delightful cafe on a charming stretch of historic Grand Avenue. Although Escondido is not usually associated with fine dining, this restaurant's reputation stretches to San Diego; it's definitely worth a detour. The bright, attractive decor feels like a cross between a conservatory and a library. Lunchtime favorites include grilled poblano chili (with Havarti cheese, roasted-tomato vinaigrette, tomatillos, cilantro, and red and blue tortilla strips) and flash-grilled tuna salad (Hawaiian ahi, orange basmati, mixed greens, rice noodles, and sesame-ginger vinaigrette). Dinners include grilled filet mignon, forest-mushroom pasta, sautéed salmon, and roast game hen. There's indoor and outdoor seating.

150 West Grand Ave. © 760/738-6868. www.150grand.com. Reservations recommended, especially for weekend nights. Lunch $10–$11; dinner $17–$31. AE, DC, MC, V. Mon–Fri 11:30am–3pm and 5–9pm; Sat 11:30am–2pm and 5–9pm.

PALOMAR MOUNTAIN

Palomar Observatory (© **760/742-2119**) and its mammoth telescope have kept a silent vigil over the heavens since 1949. From San Diego, take I-15 north to Highway 76 east, and turn left onto County Highway S6. Even if you don't want to inch your way to the top, drive the 3 miles (5km) to the lookout or just beyond it to the campground, grocery store, restaurant, and post office. Palomar Observatory's impressive dome is 135 feet (41m) high and 137 feet (41m) in diameter. The telescope has a single 200-inch mirror and weighs 530 tons. Now completely computerized, it has an approximate light range of more than 1 billion light years.

Start your visit in the museum, which is open daily from 9am to 4pm (except Dec 24–25) and has a continuously running informative video that makes a walk up the hill to the observatory more meaningful. Palomar is primarily a research facility, and you'll only be able to look at (not through) the mammoth telescope. The museum and the observatory both have rest rooms. Try to visit the observatory in the morning; late in the day, you'll have the sun in your eyes as you travel back down the mountain. The observatory closes at 4pm.

For a downhill thrill, take the **Palomar Plunge** on a 21-speed mountain bike. From the top of Palomar Mountain to its base, you'll experience a 5,000-foot (1,500m) vertical drop stretched out over 16 miles (26km). **Gravity Activated Sports,** P.O. Box 683, Pauma Valley, CA 92061 (© **800/985-4427** or 760/742-2294; fax 760/742-2293; www.gasports.com), supplies the mountain bike, helmet, gloves, lunch, souvenir photo, and T-shirt. This experience costs $80.

3 Temecula: Touring the Wineries

60 miles (97km) N of San Diego; 60 miles (97km) NW of Julian; 90 miles (145km) SE of Los Angeles

Located over the line in Riverside County, Temecula is known for its wineries and the excellent vintages they produce. The town's very name (pronounced "ta-*meck*-you-la") provides the first clue to this valley's success in the volatile wine-making business/art. It translates (from a Native American language) as "where the sun shines through the mist," which identifies two of the three climatological factors necessary for viticulture. The third is Rainbow Gap, an opening to the south through the Agua Tibia Mountains, which allows cool afternoon sea breezes to enter the 1,500-foot (450m) elevation. It's also one of the few California towns that still goes by its Native American names—Cholame, Lompoc, and Pismo (Beach) are three others. Helen Hunt Jackson used the region as the setting for her 1884 novel *Ramona*.

Temecula has a couple of claims to fame. Granite from its quarries (most of which closed down in 1915, when reinforced concrete became popular) constitutes most of San Francisco's street curbs. The last person sentenced to death by hanging in California was Temecula's blacksmith, John McNeil, who killed his wife in 1936.

Temecula is not as well known for its wines as Napa or Sonoma, because those wine-producing regions have been at it for 100 years longer. Franciscan missionaries planted the first grapevines here in the early 1800s, but the land ended up being used primarily for raising cattle. The 87,000-acre Vail Ranch operated from 1904 until being sold in 1964. Grapevines began to take root in the receptive soil again in 1968, and the first Temecula wines were produced in 1971.

ESSENTIALS

GETTING THERE   Drive north from San Diego on I-15 for 50 miles (81km); when the Temecula Valley comes into view, it'll take your breath away. To reach the vineyards, head east on Rancho California Road.

VISITOR INFORMATION   The **Temecula Valley Chamber of Commerce,** 27450 Ynez Rd., Ste. 124, Temecula, CA 92591 (© **909/676-5090;** fax 909/694-0201; www.temecula.org), in an office complex sharing space with a megamall, is a little hard to find. If you can, call and have the staff mail you the *Visitors Guide,* or stop by Monday to Friday between 9am and 5pm.

For detailed information on Temecula wine touring, call the **Temecula Valley Vintners Association** (© **800/801-WINE** or 909/699-2353; www.temeculawines.org) and request the *Wine Country* pamphlet, a comprehensive guide with winery locations, hours, and a brief description of each.

TOURING THE WINERIES

You can almost hear the murmur, audible from the twisted, grape-laden vines, "If you build a winery, they will come." With apologies to *Field of Dreams,* there was only a nanosecond's lag time between successful vintages coming out of California's southernmost appellation (the official government recognition of a wine-producing region) and the full-blown marketing of this area for wine touring. There has been a development explosion in Temecula during the last decade or so, with new housing developments and the expanding wine-grape industry competing for space. Back in 1968, one vintner recalls, "If you heard a car come down Rancho California Road, you'd go to the window to see who could possibly be lost way out here." Well, Rancho California is now clogged with traffic during rush hour and on pretty weekends—most of the area's 16 wineries are strung along this major thoroughfare—and vintners are way too busy to listen for anything unusual.

Harvest time is usually mid-August through September, and visitors are welcome year-round to tour, taste, and stock up. Most wineries in the area are closed January 1, Easter, Thanksgiving Day, and December 25.

If bicycling is your thing, **Gravity Activated Sports,** P.O. Box 683, Pauma Valley, CA 92061 (© **800/985-4427** or 760/742-2294; fax 760/742-2293; www.gasports.com), offers a wine-country tour that includes a 10-mile (16km) ride around the area followed by a bus tour around the wineries for tasting. The tour costs $90 per person.

Callaway Vineyard & Winery ⊛   The first winery established in the region is also the best known; Callaway's moderately priced chardonnays and other whites show up frequently on California wine lists. This winery offers in-depth tours of its facilities throughout the day—every hour between 11am and 4pm on weekends, and thrice daily Monday through Friday. One of the best parts of the tours is the tasting room; the tasting fee of $4 also buys a souvenir glass. The casual bistro, **Allie's at Callaway** (© **909/694-0560**), overlooks fields of Callaway vines; they serve lunch daily (11am–3pm) and dinner Thursday through Saturday (5–9pm) only.

32720 Rancho California Rd. © **800/472-2377** or 909/676-4001. www.callawaywine.com. Daily 10:30am–5pm.

Thornton Winery ⊛   Across the street from Callaway stands another old-timer, which makes a good choice if you only visit one winery. Thornton provides an all-in-one taste of the Temecula wine country. It has a striking setting, fragrant herb garden, extensive gift shop, award-winning restaurant (Cafe Champagne, discussed below under "Where to Dine"), and Sunday afternoon jazz concerts. Thornton specializes in sparkling wine, a *méthode champenoise* released under the Culbertson label, and also offers free hourly tours on weekends. Tastings are $6 and include a souvenir glass.

32575 Rancho California Rd. © **909/699-0099**. Daily 11am–5pm.

Mount Palomar Winery   They're doing things a little differently at Mount Palomar, and you might see unfamiliar names on some labels. Take the informative tour to learn about the process of handcrafting Mediterranean varietals like sangiovese, cortese, and Rhone-style blends of French grapes; this is also the only Temecula winery producing cream sherry. The tasting fee of $3 gets you a pouring of five wines plus a souvenir glass; the tour is free. An army of picnic tables is scattered throughout the property, and on weekends there's a full-service deli.

33820 Rancho California Rd. © **800/854-5177** or 909/676-5047. www.mountpalomar.com. Daily 10am–5pm.

Cilurzo Vineyard & Winery   Celebrity photos on the wall hint that the proprietor has an alternative persona. In fact, vintner Vince Cilurzo is equally known for his work as a Hollywood lighting director (*Jeopardy!* is most prominent among his credits) as for the petite sirah he claims can be served with anything "from tomato sauce to curry." Tasting is often a friendly affair, sitting around with Vince or his wife, Audrey, pouring their latest vintage; there's a $1 tasting fee. Bring lunch if you'd like to picnic overlooking the small lake on the property.

41220 Calle Contento (off Rancho California Rd.). © **909/676-5250**. www.cilurzowine.com. Daily 10am–5pm.

Temecula

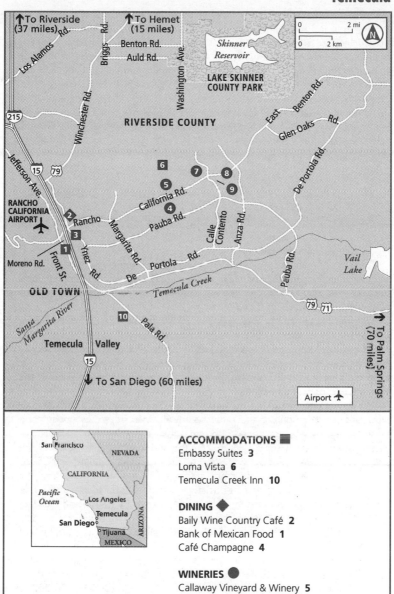

To Riverside (37 miles) Rd.
Los Alamos Rd.
Briggs Rd.
To Hemet (15 miles)
Benton Rd.
Auld Rd.
Washington Ave.
Skinner Reservoir
LAKE SKINNER COUNTY PARK

0   2 mi
0   2 km

215

Winchester Rd.

RIVERSIDE COUNTY

East Benton Rd.
Glen Oaks Rd.

Jefferson Ave.
15   79

RANCHO CALIFORNIA AIRPORT

De Portola Rd.

6
5   7   8
9
California Rd.
4

2
Rancho
3
1

Margarita Rd.

Pauba Rd.

Calle Contento
Anza Rd.

Pauba Rd.

Moreno Rd.

Ynez Rd.

De Portola Rd.

Vail Lake

OLD TOWN

Santa Margarita River

Temecula Creek

79   71

10
Pala Rd.

Temecula Valley

To Palm Springs (70 miles)

15

To San Diego (60 miles)

Airport ✈

San Francisco
NEVADA
CALIFORNIA
Pacific Ocean
Los Angeles
Temecula
San Diego
Tijuana
ARIZONA
MEXICO

ACCOMMODATIONS ■
Embassy Suites **3**
Loma Vista **6**
Temecula Creek Inn **10**

DINING ◆
Baily Wine Country Café **2**
Bank of Mexican Food **1**
Café Champagne **4**

WINERIES ●
Callaway Vineyard & Winery **5**
Cilurzo Vineyard & Winery **9**
Maurice Car'rie/Van Roekel
    Vineyards **8**
Mount Palomar Winery **7**
Thornton Winery **4**

Maurice Car'rie Winery/Van Roekel Vineyards   Perhaps the most welcoming tasting room is the nouvelle yellow farmhouse of Maurice Car'rie. Started by Dutch Minnesotan Budd Van Roekel in 1984, and named for his wife, Maurice, the vineyard produces 14 varietals, the most popular of which is Cabernet. Farther up the road (at 34567 Rancho California Rd.) is the couple's latest venture, Van Roekel Vineyards (© **909/699-6961**), which opened in 1994. The souvenir-minded will love Van Roekel's gift shop, filled with logo items and wine-related gifts. Each winery also has a gourmet deli for composing a picnic to enjoy in Maurice Car'rie's rose-filled front garden and patio. There is no fee for tasting at either winery.

34225 Rancho California Rd. © 909/676-1711. Daily 10am–5pm.

HISTORIC OLD TOWN TEMECULA

An eccentric counterpoint to this area's vineyards, gated housing developments, and shopping centers is the old part of the city of Temecula, preserved as it was in the 1890s—Western storefronts and all. It lies 4 miles (6.5km) west of the vineyards off Rancho California Road, stretches along 6 short blocks, and has a reputation as an antique-hunter's haven.

The best way to explore Old Town is on foot—it's quite easy to see it all in an afternoon. Park anywhere you can find a space. Be forewarned that Temecula has become a traffic-clogged town, and you will hear the drone of cars almost everywhere, even on the golf course.

Beginning in the 1850s, Temecula was a Butterfield Overland Stage stop for pioneers and tradesmen; traffic only increased once the railroad arrived in 1882, and downtown's appearance has remained virtually unchanged since the 1890s. Western souvenir shops, restaurants, and particularly collectibles stores have kept the area alive, with antique hounds and tourists tromping along the wooden sidewalks of Front Street.

The city is renovating and expanding Old Town. Good ideas include old-fashioned street lampposts and more boardwalk-style sidewalks; not-so-good ideas are large parking lots intended to lure would-be developers to the area. For many visitors, the Old Town area's rough edges add to whatever frontier realism and appeal remain, although customers of the dozens of contemporary businesses are generally oblivious to most buildings' origins. Take time to read the bronze plaques on storefronts that intrigue you, and pick up a copy of the *Old Town Temecula Walking Tour Map*. The brief leaflet, with a business index and historic building guide, is free and available at some local shops and restaurants.

At Front Street and Moreno Road is **Sam Hicks Park,** site of the *They Passed This Way* monument ("they" being famous visitors over the years, including mountain man Jedediah Smith, explorer Kit Carson, and *Ramona* author Helen Hunt Jackson). The clapboard St. Catherine's Church, built around 1922, moved to this site to house the **Temecula Valley Museum** (© **909/676-0021**). The museum has Native American artifacts from the Shoshone, who named the town more than 1,000 years ago. There's a collection of household and farm items from the 19th to mid–20th century, a diorama of Temecula as it appeared around 1914, and memorabilia of Temecula's favorite son, mystery novelist Erle Stanley Gardner. It's open Wednesday to Sunday 11am to 4pm; admission is free but donations are appreciated.

HISTORIC BUILDINGS   Other buildings of historical interest include the **First National Bank,** at Front and Main streets. Built in 1914, it managed to remain open during the Great Depression, gaining it the nickname "the pawn shop." It closed in 1941. The main floor now houses an eatery cleverly named the **Bank of Mexican Food** (see complete listing below). On Main Street west of Front is the **Welty Hotel/Temecula Hotel** building; originally built in 1882 with the arrival of the railroad, it burned and was rebuilt in 1891. Restored to its turn-of-the-century decor in 1960, it was then a hotel but is now a private home. The same family was responsible for the **Welty Building** three doors down at the corner of Main and Front streets. It was built as a store and saloon, and later housed a gymnasium that played host to prizefighter Jack Dempsey. Today, an antique store and deli occupy the building. The 1891 **Temecula Mercantile** building, 42049 Main St., was the lifeblood of local ranchers well into the 1950s. Today it houses—you guessed it—an antique store. At **Morgan's Antiques** (© 909/676-2722), the upstairs gallery holds special-interest collectibles.

ANTIQUES STORES   More antiques stores worth seeking out are **Temecula Trading Post,** 42081 Main St. (© 909/676-5759), which boasts that it's the town's "finest antique mall." **The Loft,** 28480 Front St. (© 909/676-5179), has been open for more than 25 years. It specializes in clocks—grandfather, wall, cuckoo, mantle—and other timepieces. If your eye is drawn to all that glitters and shimmers, step into **Nana's Antiques,** 28677 Front St. (© 909/699-3839). While I wouldn't want to dust the place, I simply love browsing Nana's Victorian-era glass and crystal, looking at anachronistically elegant tableware (knife rests, condiment caddies, pickle jars, and such) that might have jumped from a meticulously set Edith Wharton banquet table.

OUTDOOR PURSUITS IN TEMECULA

Besides wine tasting, area activities include hot-air balloon rides over the vineyards, an unforgettable sight. One company, which has been around for about 20 years, is **Sunrise Balloons** (© 800/548-9912). Proprietor Dan Glick also offers horse-drawn carriage rides through the vineyards.

For an outing in more than 7,000 acres of unspoiled terrain, take I-15 north to Clinton Keith Road and drive west for about 5 miles (8km). The **Santa Rosa Plateau Ecological Reserve,** 22115 Tenaja Rd., Murrieta (© 909/677-6951 or 909/699-1856), is owned and maintained by the Nature Conservancy. Walking trails, coyotes, hawks, migrating birds, and maybe even an eagle or two await you.

GOLF   You can't get more countrified than at the **Temecula Creek Inn** (see below), whose 27-hole, 10,014-yard championship golf course features rolling hills and fairways lined with 100-year-old live oaks; wild pheasants and bobcats put in occasional appearances. Lessons and golf packages are available. Greens fees for 18 holes are $55 Monday through Thursday, $65 on Friday, and $85 on Saturday and Sunday, including a cart.

WHERE TO STAY

Embassy Suites   This brand-new all-suite hotel delivers in reliability, convenience, and economy all it lacks in originality. With squeaky clean (if uninspired) furnishings, each two-room suite sleeps between four to six people in comfort, and features a well-lit working/eating area, wet bar, microwave oven, and two TVs. Everyone enjoys a cooked-to-order full breakfast each morning (no chintzy muffin buffet here), making this a favorite for long-term business guests as well as budget-minded families. Situated freeway-side, the property is successfully designed to minimize noise and maximize visual appeal in the other direction; the same holds true for the nicely landscaped outdoor heated pool and whirlpool.

29345 Rancho California Rd. (at Ynez Rd.), Temecula, CA 92591. (℃ 800-EMBASSY or 909/676-5656. Fax 909/699-3928. www.embassysuites.com/es/temecula. 176 units. $109–$159 double. Extra person $10. Kids 18 and under stay free in parents' room. Rates include full breakfast and evening reception. AAA and senior discounts available. AE, DC, DISC, MC, V. Free parking. Take I-5 to Rancho California Rd. east, turn right on Ynez Rd. to hotel entrance. **Amenities:** Restaurant; lounge; outdoor pool; fitness center; whirlpool; concierge; business services; 24-hr. room service; laundry/dry-cleaning service. *In room:* A/C, TV/VCR w/pay movies, dataport, kitchenette, coffeemaker, hair dryer, iron.

Loma Vista 🐟   This tiled-roof, Mission-style contemporary house was built in 1988 as a bed-and-breakfast inn. Perfectly named, it sits on a hill (*loma* in Spanish) overlooking the best vista around. From the living room, you can see the Callaway Vineyard and the Santa Ana Mountains; most of Temecula's wineries lie along the same main road. All guest rooms are named for wines; four have private wisteria-covered balconies.

Besides complimentary fruit and a decanter of sherry in each room, wine and cheese are served by the fire at 6pm. A spa bubbles on the back patio; the front patio, a great place to wile away the hours, has a fire pit. The property is a real oasis, with 85 rose bushes, ranunculuses, daisies, Australian tea bushes, and 325 grapefruit trees. The new owners, Walt and Sheila Kurczynski, took over in 1998. Old Town Temecula is 5 miles (8km) away.

33350 La Serena Way, Temecula, CA 92591. (℃ 909/676-7047. Fax 909/676-0077. 6 units. $115–$195 double. Midweek rates $10 lower. Rates include full champagne breakfast and evening wine and cheese. MC, V. Take I-15 to Rancho California Rd. east; inn is on left just beyond Callaway Vineyard. **Amenities:** Whirlpool. *In room:* A/C, no phone.

Temecula Creek Inn 🐟🐟   This small resort is more a country lodge than an inn, with a casual summer-camp ambience in a wooded setting. The inviting lobby is replete with adobe walls, Native American artifacts, and a fireplace. Rooms in the five two-story buildings have restful views and custom-designed Native American–inspired furnishings. Junior suites are oversized corner rooms with sitting areas, two balconies, and floor-to-ceiling windows. The TV is cleverly hidden away under a piece of sculpture.

Magnolia trees line the walkway from the lobby to the resort's restaurant, the Temet Grill. There is live music nightly in the lounge adjoining the restaurant. Food and cocktail service is available poolside. Amenities include a barbecue under live oaks, 27 holes of golf, driving range, volleyball, croquet, and a golf and tennis pro shop.

44501 Rainbow Canyon Rd., Temecula, CA 92592. (℃ 800/962-7335 or 909/694-1000. Fax 909/676-3422. www.temeculacreekinn.com. 81 units. $125–$185 double Sun–Thurs, $165–$205 Fri–Sat. Golf and wine-country packages available. AE, DC, DISC, MC, V. From San Diego, take I-15 north to exit 79 (Indio); turn right off the exit ramp. At Pala Rd., turn right, go over a little bridge, then take an immediate right onto Rainbow Canyon Rd. Entrance to inn is ½ mile (1km) away. **Amenities:** Restaurant; lounge; outdoor pool; golf course; 2 tennis courts; whirlpool; bike rental; in-room massage; babysitting; laundry/dry cleaning service. *In room:* A/C, TV, dataport, minibar, coffeemaker, hair dryer, iron, safe.

WHERE TO DINE
Baily Wine Country Cafe 🐟🐟 CALIFORNIAN/CONTINENTAL   Baily
has the largest selection of Temecula Valley wines anywhere, including those from the Baily family's winery on Rancho California Road. To show them off to best advantage, the chef concocts some mouthwatering dishes, which change

every few months. At lunch, consider the penne with roasted garlic, fresh vegetables, and tomato sauce made chunky with Italian sausage; Southwestern-style grilled cheese sandwich with cilantro (a regional prizewinner); or, grilled chicken piccata salad with mixed greens and lemon-caper vinaigrette. Dinner favorites include Southwestern pork tenderloin with garlic mashed potatoes; salmon Wellington with cucumber-and-papaya relish and fresh vegetables; and, chicken ravioli in basil pesto. Finish with Carol Baily's white-chocolate cheesecake, a top choice with local diners.

If you're in luck, your visit will coincide with one of the celebrated "Dinners in the Wine Cellar." Members of the Baily family, who choose wines to accompany each course, host the fixed-price, set-menu meal at the Temecula Crest Winery. Picnics can be provided to go with 24 hours' notice.

27644 Ynez Rd. (at Rancho California Rd., in shopping center). ℂ 909/676-9567. www.baily.com. Reservations recommended, especially on weekends. Lunch $8–$11; dinner $13–$22. AE, DC, MC, V. Fri 11:30am–2:30pm; Mon–Sun 5–9pm.

The Bank of Mexican Food *(Value* MEXICAN   From the outside, this casual restaurant in the heart of Old Town looks just the same as when it opened in 1914 as a bank (hence the unusual name). Actually, it looks the same inside, too, right down to the heavy-doored safe (now propped open with one dining table inside). Booths and plain dinette tables have replaced teller windows, and additional seating was added on an outdoor patio with a prime view of visitors strolling Old Western wooden sidewalks. While the traditional gringo-style Mexican food isn't exceptional, it is good enough to recommend, featuring the usual offerings of enchiladas, burritos, tostadas, and quesadillas delivered on steaming hot platters with plenty of hearty red sauce and melted cheese. Lunch specials (Mon–Fri) are a bargain at $4.95 for complete combo plates.

28645 Front St. (corner of Main). ℂ 909/676-6160. Reservations not accepted. Main courses $6–$9. DC, DISC, MC, V. Daily 11am–9pm.

Cafe Champagne ✦✦✦ CALIFORNIAN   The toast of the Temecula wine country, this bistro and cafe features tasty dishes created to be served with nine Thornton champagnes. The wine list also features other Temecula and California labels. The lunch and dinner menus, California cuisine at its best, feature appetizers like warm brie *en croûte* with honey-walnut sauce, crab-and-shrimp strudel, and smoked salmon carpaccio. Among the entrees are angel-hair pasta primavera, angel-hair seafood pasta, mesquite-grilled tuna, and baked pecan chicken. The list of mesquite-grilled entrees expands at dinner, and at lunch tempting lighter fare includes hearty salads and sandwiches filled with mesquite-grilled hamburger, steak, or chicken. The setting, overlooking the vineyard, is sublime. It's a small place, so do reserve ahead. If you want really good food, you're going to like it here.

Thornton Winery, 32575 Rancho California Rd. ℂ 909/699-0088. Reservations recommended. Lunch $10–$21; dinner $13–$21. AE, DC, MC, V. Daily 11am–9pm.

4 Disneyland & Other Anaheim Area Attractions

160 miles (258km) N of San Diego

The sleepy Orange County town of Anaheim grew up around Disneyland, the most famous theme park in the West. Now, even beyond the "Happiest Place on Earth," the city and its neighboring communities are kid-central. Otherwise unspectacular, sprawling suburbs have become a playground of family oriented hotels, restaurants, and unabashedly tourist-oriented attractions. Among the nearby draws are Knott's Berry Farm, another family oriented theme park, in Buena Park. At the other end of the scale is the Richard Nixon Library and Birthplace, a surprisingly compelling presidential library and museum, just 7 miles (11km) northeast of Disneyland in Yorba Linda.

ESSENTIALS

GETTING THERE   From downtown San Diego, take I-5 north until you see signs for Disneyland; dedicated off ramps from both directions lead into the attractions' parking lots and surrounding streets. The drive from downtown San Diego takes approximately 90 minutes.

Ten **Amtrak** (© 800/USA-RAIL) trains go to Anaheim daily from San Diego. The one-way fare is $17, and the trip takes about 2 hours. Amtrak also offers 1-day and 5-day excursion packages.

VISITOR INFORMATION   The **Anaheim/Orange County Visitor and Convention Bureau,** 800 W. Katella Ave. (© 714/765-8888; www.anaheim oc.org), can fill you in on area activities and shopping shuttles. It's across the street from Disneyland inside the Convention Center, next to the dramatic cantilevered arena. It's open Monday to Friday from 8:30am to 5:30pm. The **Buena Park Convention and Visitors Office,** 6280 Manchester Blvd., Suite 103 (© 800/541-3953 or 714/562-3560; www.buenapark.com/cvo), provides specialized information on the area, including Knott's Berry Farm.

THE DISNEYLAND RESORT 🌟🌟🌟

It's not called "The Happiest Place on Earth" for nothing, you know . . . Disneyland sister parks have sprung up in Florida, Tokyo, and even France, but nothing compares with the original. Smaller than Walt Disney World, Disneyland has always capitalized on being the original—and the world's first family-oriented mega theme park. Nostalgia is a big part of the appeal, and despite many advancements, changes, and expansions over the years, Disneyland remains true to the vision of founder Walt Disney.

In 2001, Disney unveiled a brand-new theme park (California Adventure), a new shopping/dining/entertainment district (Downtown Disney), and a third on-site hotel (Disney's California Adventure). They also changed their own name to "The Disneyland Resort," reflecting a greatly expanded array of entertainment options. What does this all mean for you? Well, first of all, you'll probably want to think seriously about budgeting more time (and yes, more money) for your Disney visit—you'll need at least three full days to see it all. If you have limited time, plan carefully so you don't skip what's important to you; in the pages ahead we'll describe what to expect throughout the new resort. And, most of all, get ready to have fun—there's lots of great new stuff to check out!

ADMISSION, HOURS & INFORMATION   Admission to *either* Disneyland or California Adventure, including unlimited rides and all festivities and entertainment, is $43 for adults and children over 11, $41 for seniors 60 and over, $33 for children 3 to 11, and free for children under 3. Parking is $7. Three- and 4-day "Park-Hopper" passports are available, allowing you unlimited in-and-out privileges at *both* parks every day. Prices for adults and children are $111/$87 (3-day) and $137/$107 (4-day). In addition, some area accommodations offer lodging packages that include admission for one or more days.

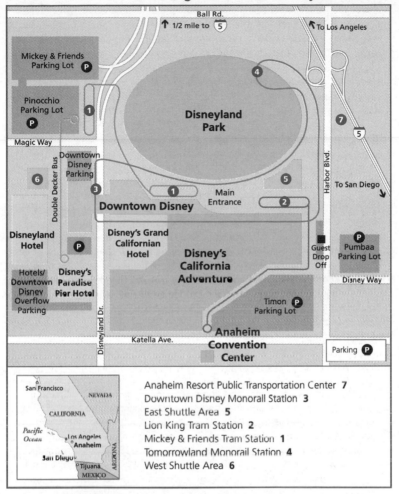

Anaheim Resort Public Transportation Center **7**
Downtown Disney Monorail Station **3**
East Shuttle Area **5**
Lion King Tram Station **2**
Mickey & Friends Tram Station **1**
Tomorrowland Monorail Station **4**
West Shuttle Area **6**

Disneyland and California Adventure are open every day of the year, but operating hours vary, so we recommend that you call for information that applies to the specific day(s) of your visit (© **714/781-4565**). The same information, including ride closures and show schedules, can also be found online at **www.disneyland.com**. Generally speaking, the parks are open from 9 or 10am to 6 or 7pm on weekdays, fall to spring; and from 8 or 9am to midnight or 1am on weekends, holidays, and during winter, spring, or summer vacation periods.

If you plan on arriving during a busy time (when the gates open in the morning, or 11am–2pm), purchase your tickets in advance and get a jump on the crowds at the ticket counters. Advance tickets may be purchased through Disneyland's website (www.disneyland.com), at Disney stores in the United States, or by calling the ticket mail order line (© **714/781-4043**).

DISNEY TIPS Disneyland is busiest from mid-June to mid-September and on weekends and school holidays year-round. Peak hours are from noon to 5pm;

Value The Art of the (Package) Deal

If you intend to spend 2 or more nights in Disney territory, it pays to investigate the bevy of packaged vacation options available. Start by contacting your hotel (even those in Los Angeles or San Diego), to see whether they have Disneyland admission packages. Many vacation packagers include Disneyland and/or California Adventure (and other attractions) with their inclusive packages; see p. 30 for contact information. And put a call in to the official Disney agency, **Walt Disney Travel Co. (© 800/ 225-2024** or 714/520-5050). You can request a glossy catalog by mail, or log onto **www.disneyland.com** and click on "Book Your Vacation" to peruse package details, take a virtual tour of participating hotel properties, and get online price quotes for customized, date-specific packages. Their packages are value-packed time-savers with abundant flexibility. Hotel choices range from the official Disney hotels to one of 35 "neighbor hotel" in every price range (economy to superior) and category (from motel to all-suite); a wide range of available extras includes admission to other Southern California attractions and tours (like Universal Studios, or a Tijuana shopping spree), and behind-the-scenes Disneyland tours, all in limitless combinations. Every time I check, rates are highly competitive, considering each package includes multiday admission, early park entry, free parking (at the Disney hotels), plus keepsake souvenirs and Southern California coupon books.

---

visit the most popular rides before and after these hours, and you'll cut your waiting times substantially.

Many visitors tackle Disneyland (or California Adventure) systematically, beginning at the entrance and working their way clockwise around the park. But a better plan of attack is to arrive early and run to the most popular rides—Rocket Rods, the Indiana Jones Adventure, Star Tours, Space Mountain, Big Thunder Mountain Railroad, Splash Mountain, the Haunted Mansion, and Pirates of the Caribbean in Disneyland; and, Soarin' Over California, Grizzly River Run, and It's Tough to be a Bug in California Adventure. Lines for these rides can last an hour or more in the middle of the day. However, this time-honored plan of attack may eventually become obsolete thanks to the new **Fast-Pass** system. Here's how it works: Say you want to ride Space Mountain, but the line is long—*so* long the wait sign indicates a 75-minute standstill! Now you can head to the Automated FastPass ticket dispensers, which allow you to swipe the magnetic strip of your Disneyland entrance ticket, get a FastPass for later that day, and return to use the reduced-wait FastPass entrance. At press time, about a half dozen Disneyland rides were equipped with FastPass; several more will be added by the time you read this. The hottest features at California Adventure had FastPass built in from the start; for a complete list for each park, check your official map/guide when you enter.

If you're going to spend the night in Anaheim, you might want to consider staying at the **Disneyland Hotel, Paradise Pier Hotel,** or **Disney's Grand Californian.** Hotel guests get to enter the park early almost every day and enjoy the major rides before the lines form. The amount of time varies from day to day, but usually you can enter 1½ hours early. Call ahead to check the schedule.

Attendance falls dramatically during the winter, and sometimes the park offers discounted (about 25% off) admission to Southern California residents, who may buy up to six tickets per ZIP code verification. If you'll be visiting the park with someone who lives here, be sure to check in advance whether the special prices are in effect.

TOURING DISNEYLAND

The Disneyland complex is divided into several theme "lands," each of which has a number of rides and attractions that are, more or less, related to that land's theme.

MAIN STREET U.S.A.   At the park's entrance, Main Street U.S.A. is a cinematic version of turn-of-the-century small-town America. The whitewashed Rockwellian fantasy is lined with gift shops, candy stores, a soda fountain, and a silent theater that continuously runs early Mickey Mouse films. Here you'll find the practical things you might need, such as stroller rentals and storage lockers.

Because there are no rides, it's best to tour Main Street during the middle of the afternoon, when lines for rides are longest, and in the evening, when you can rest your feet in the theater that features "Great Moments with Mr. Lincoln," a patriotic (and audioanimatronic) look at America's 16th president. There's always something happening on Main Street; stop in at the information booth to the left of the main entrance for a schedule of the day's events.

ADVENTURELAND   Inspired by the most exotic regions of Asia, Africa, India, and the South Pacific, Adventureland is home to several popular rides. Here's where you can cavort inside **Tarzan's Treehouse,** a climb-around attraction based on the animated film. Its African-themed neighbor is the **Jungle Cruise,** where passengers board a large authentic-looking Mississippi River paddleboat and float along an Amazon-like river; a spear's throw away is the **Enchanted Tiki Room,** one of the most sedate attractions in Adventureland. Inside, you can sit down and watch a 20-minute musical comedy featuring electronically animated tropical birds, flowers, and "tiki gods."

The **Indiana Jones Adventure** is Adventureland's star ride. Based on the Steven Spielberg films, this ride takes adventurers into the Temple of the Forbidden Eye, in joltingly realistic all-terrain vehicles. Riders follow Indy and experience the perils of bubbling lava pits, whizzing arrows, fire-breathing serpents, collapsing bridges, and the familiar cinematic tumbling boulder (an effect that's very realistic in the front seats!).

NEW ORLEANS SQUARE   A large, grassy green dotted with gas lamps, New Orleans Square is home to the **Haunted Mansion,** the most high-tech ghost house we've ever seen; the clever events inside are as funny as they are scary.

Even more fanciful is **Pirates of the Caribbean,** one of Disneyland's most popular rides. Visitors float on boats through mock underground caves, entering an enchanting world of swashbuckling, rum-running, and buried treasure. Even in the middle of the afternoon you can dine by the cool moonlight and to the sound of crickets in the **Blue Bayou** restaurant, situated in the middle of the ride itself.

CRITTER COUNTRY   An ode to the backwoods, Critter Country is a sort of Frontierland without those pesky settlers. Little kids like to sing along with the audioanimatronic critters in the musical **Country Bear Jamboree** show. Older kids and grown-ups head straight for **Splash Mountain,** one of the largest water flume rides in the world. Loosely based on the Disney movie *Song of the South,* the ride is lined with about 100 characters that won't stop singing "Zip-A-Dee-Doo-Dah." Be prepared to get wet, especially if someone sizable is in the front seat of your log-shaped boat.

FRONTIERLAND   Inspired by 19th-century America, Frontierland features a raft to **Tom Sawyer's Island,** a do-it-yourself play area with balancing rocks, caves, and a rope bridge, and the **Big Thunder Mountain Railroad,** a runaway roller coaster that races through a deserted 1870s gold mine. You'll also find a petting zoo and an Abe Lincoln–style log cabin here; both are great for exploring with the little ones.

On Saturdays, Sundays, and holidays, and during vacation periods, head to Frontierland's **Rivers of America** after dark to see the FANTASMIC! show. It mixes magic, music, live performers, and sensational special effects. Just as he did in *The Sorcerer's Apprentice,* Mickey Mouse appears and uses his magical powers to create giant water fountains, enormous flowers, and fantasy creatures. There are plenty of pyrotechnics, lasers, and fog, as well as a 45-foot-tall (14m) dragon that breathes fire and sets the water of the Rivers of America aflame.

MICKEY'S TOONTOWN   This is a colorful, whimsical world inspired by the film *Who Framed Roger Rabbit?*—a wacky, gag-filled land populated by 'toons. There are several rides, including **Roger Rabbit's CarToonSpin,** but they take a back seat to Toontown itself—a trippy, smile-inducing world without a straight line or right angle in sight.

FANTASYLAND   With a storybook theme, this is the catchall "land" for stuff that doesn't quite fit anywhere else. Most of the rides are geared to the under-6 set, including the **King Arthur Carousel,** the **Dumbo the Flying Elephant ride,** and the **Casey Jr. Circus Train.** Some, like **Mr. Toad's Wild Ride** and **Peter Pan's Flight,** appeal to grown-ups as well. You'll also find Alice in Wonderland, Snow White's Scary Adventures, Pinocchio's Daring Journey, and more.

The most lauded attraction is **It's a Small World,** a slow-moving indoor river ride through a saccharine nightmare of all the world's children singing the song everybody loves to hate. For a different kind of thrill, try the **Matterhorn Bobsleds,** a zippy roller coaster through chilled caverns and drifting fog banks. It's one of the park's most popular rides.

TOMORROWLAND   Conceived as an optimistic look at the future, Tomorrowland employs an angular, metallic look popularized by futurists like Jules Verne.

The jet-propelled ride **Rocket Rods** joins long-time Tomorrowland favorites **Space Mountain** (a pitch-black indoor roller coaster that assaults your equilibrium and ears), and **Star Tours** (the original Disney–George Lucas joint venture; it's a 40-passenger StarSpeeder that encounters a space-load of misadventures on the way to the Moon of Endor, achieved with wired seats and video effects—not for the queasy).

TOURING CALIFORNIA ADVENTURE 🐾🐾

With a grand entrance designed to resemble one of those "Wish you were here" scenic postcards, California Adventure starts out with a bang. Beneath a scale model of the Golden Gate Bridge (watch carefully for the monorail passing overhead), handmade tiles of across-the-state scenes glimmer on either side. Just inside, an enormous gold titanium "sun" shines all day, illuminated by computerized heliostats that follow the real sun's path. From this point, visitors can head into three distinct themed areas, each containing rides, interactive attractions, live-action shows, and plenty of dining, snacking, and shopping opportunities.

THE GOLDEN STATE   This multidimensional area represents California's history, heritage, and physical attributes. Sound boring? Actually, the park's splashiest attractions are here. "Condor Flats" is a tribute to daring aviators; inside a weathered corrugated test-pilots' hangar is **Soarin' Over California,** the ride that immediately rose to the top on everyone's run-to-get-in-line-first list (it's equipped with FastPass, but often sells out by midday anyway). It uses cool cutting-edge technology to combine suspended seats with a spectacular IMAX-style surround-movie—so riders literally "soar" over California's scenic wonders.

Nearby, California Adventure's iconic "Grizzly Peak" towers over the **Grizzly River Run,** a splashy gold-country ride through caverns, mine shafts, and water slides; it culminates with a wet plunge into a spouting geyser. Kids can cavort nearby on the **Redwood Creek Challenge Trail,** a forest playground with smoke-jumper cable slides, net climbing, and swaying bridges.

Pacific Wharf was inspired by Monterey's Cannery Row, and features mouth-watering demonstrations (reminiscent of grammar-school field trips to local factories) by **Boudin Sourdough Bakery, Mission Tortillas,** and **Lucky Fortune Cookies.** If you get hungry, each has a food counter where you can enjoy soup-in-a-sourdough-bowl; tacos, burritos, and enchiladas; and teriyaki bowls, egg rolls, and wonton soup.

Straight from the imagination of Disney CEO Michael Eisner comes the "Bountiful Farm," constructed to pay tribute to California's rich agriculture. The Robert Mondavi **Golden Vine Winery** boasts a demonstration vineyard, Mission-style "aging room" (with a back-to-basics presentation on the art of winemaking), wine bars, and the park's most upscale eatery, **Vineyard Room** (see "Where to Dine in the Disneyland Area," later in this section). Next to a demonstration produce garden lies another California Adventure "E ticket," the interactive film **"It's Tough To Be A Bug."** Using next-generation 3-D technology, *A Bug's Life* characters Flik and Hopper lead the audience on a slap-happy underground romp with bees, termites, grasshoppers, stink bugs, spiders, and a few surprises that keep everyone hopping, ducking, and laughing along.

PARADISE PIER   Journey back into the glory days of California's beachfront amusement piers—remember Santa Monica, Santa Cruz, Belmont Park?—on this fantasy boardwalk. Highlights include **California Screamin',** a classic roller coaster that replicates the whitewashed wooden white-knucklers of the past—but with state-of-the-art steel construction and a smooth, computerized ride. There's also the **Maliboomer,** a trio of towers (giant strongman sledgehammer tests) that catapult riders to the tip-top bell, then lets them down bungee-style with dangling feet; the **Orange Stinger,** a whooshing swing ride inside an enormous orange, complete with orange scent piped in; **Mulholland Madness,** a wacky wild trip along L.A.'s precarious hilltop street; and, the **Sun Wheel Carousel,** featuring unique zigzagging cars that bring new meaning to the familiar ride.

There are all the familiar boardwalk games (complete with stuffed prizes), guilty-pleasure fast foods like pizza, corn dogs, and burritos.

HOLLYWOOD PICTURES BACKLOT   If you've visited Disney in Florida, you'll recognize many elements of this *tromp l'oeil* re-creation of a Hollywood movie studio lot. Pass through a classic studio archway flanked by gigantic golden elephants, and you'll find yourself on a surprisingly realistic "Hollywood Boulevard." In the **Disney Animation** building, visitors can participate in six different interactive galleries: Learn how stories become animated features; watch Robin Williams become an animated character; listen to a Disney illustrator invent "Mushu" from *Mulan;* and even take a computerized personality test to see which Disney character you resemble most.

At the end of the street, the replica movie palace **Hyperion Theater** presents the live-action musical show **Blast!,** and the **"Get A Grip"** stunt show pays tribute to stagehands and reveals some of the simple tricks behind movie illusion. Across the way, step aboard the **Superstar Limo,** where you're cast as a hot new star being chauffeured around Hollywood to sign a big movie deal; the wacky but tame ride winds through Malibu, Rodeo Drive, Beverly Hills, and the Sunset Strip.

The Backlot's main attraction is **Jim Henson's MuppetVision 3D,** an onscreen blast from the past featuring Kermit, Miss Piggy, Gonzo, Fozzie Bear— and even hecklers Waldorf and Statler. Of the bevy of dining options, one of the most fun is the **ABC Soap Opera Bistro,** where you can dine in replica sets from your favorite soap operas.

DOWNTOWN DISNEY 👀

Borrowing a page from Central Florida's successful Disney compound, **Downtown Disney** is a district filled with restaurants, shops, and entertainment for all ages. Whether you want to stroll with kids in tow, have an upscale dinner for two, or party into the night, this colorful and sanitized "street scene" fills the bill.

The promenade begins at the amusement park gates and stretches toward the Disneyland Hotel; there are nearly 20 shops and boutiques, and more than 12 restaurants, live music venues, and entertainment options.

Highlights include **House of Blues,** the blues-jazz restaurant/club that features Delta-inspired cuisine and big-name music; **Ralph Brennan's Jazz Kitchen,** a spicy mix of New Orleans traditional foods and live jazz; **ESPN Zone,** the ultimate sports dining and entertainment experience, including an interactive game room; **Y Arriba! Y Arriba!,** where Latin cuisine combines with spicy entertainment and dancing; and, **World of Disney,** one of the biggest Disney shopping experiences anywhere, with a vast and diverse range of toys, souvenirs, and collectibles. There is also a 12-screen multiplex, LEGO Imagination Center, Sephora cosmetics store, and much more.

Even if you're not staying at one of the Disney hotels, Downtown Disney is worth a visit. Locals and day-shoppers take advantage of the no-gate free entry and validated Downtown Disney parking lots (3 hr. free, 5 hr. with restaurant or theater validation).

KNOTT'S BERRY FARM 👀

Cynics say that Knott's Berry Farm is for people who aren't smart enough to find Disneyland. The reality is that Knott's simply can't compete with the Disney allure, and focuses on newer and faster thrill rides that target Southern California youths and families instead.

Like Disneyland, Knott's Berry Farm is not without historical merit. Rudolph Boysen crossed a loganberry with a raspberry, calling the resulting hybrid the boysenberry. In 1933, Buena Park farmer Walter Knott planted the boysenberry and launched Knott's Berry Farm on 10 acres of leased land. When things got tough during the Depression, Mrs. Knott set up a roadside stand, selling pies, preserves, and home-cooked chicken dinners. Within a year she was selling 90 meals a day. Lines became so long that Walter decided to create an Old West Ghost Town as a diversion for waiting customers.

Locals flock to Knott's Berry Farm in the second half of October, when the entire park is revamped as "Knott's Scary Farm." The ordinary attractions are made spooky and haunted, every grassy area is transformed into a graveyard or gallows, and even the already-scary rides get special surprise extras, like costumed ghouls who grab your arm in the middle of a roller-coaster ride!

GETTING THERE   Knott's Berry Farm is at 8039 Beach Blvd. in Buena Park. It's about a 5-minute ride north on I-5 from Disneyland. From I-5 or Calif. 91, exit south onto Beach Boulevard. The park is about half a mile south of Calif. 91.

ADMISSION, HOURS & INFORMATION   Admission to the park, including unlimited access to all rides, shows, and attractions, is $40 for adults and children 12 and over; $30 for seniors 60 and over, kids 3 to 11, nonambulatory visitors, and expectant mothers; and, children under 3 are admitted free. Admission is $16.95 for everyone after 4pm. Parking is $7. Like Disneyland, Knott's offers discounted admission for Southern California residents during the off-season, so if you're bringing local friends or family members along, be sure to take advantage of the bargain. Also like Disneyland, Knott's Berry Farm's hours vary from week to week, so call ahead. The park generally is open during the summer daily from 9am to midnight. The rest of the year, it opens at 10am and closes at 6 or 8pm, except Saturday, when it stays open until 10pm. Knott's is closed December 25. Special hours and prices are in effect during Knott's Scary Farm in late October. Stage shows and special activities are scheduled throughout the day. Pick up a schedule at the ticket booth.

For more information, call © 714/220-5200 or log onto **www.knotts.com.**

TOURING THE PARK

Knott's Berry Farm maintains much of its original Old West motif, and is divided into seven "Old Time Adventures" areas. The newest attraction—the one you'll see pictured on those freeway billboards—is the Perilous Plunge. True to the name, it's the world's tallest, steepest, wettest water ride. If that sounds good to you, climb aboard!

GHOST TOWN   The park's original attraction is a collection of refurbished 19th-century buildings that have been relocated from deserted Old West towns. You can pan for gold, ride an authentic stagecoach, take rickety train cars through the Calico Mine, get held up aboard the Denver and Rio Grande Calico Railroad, and hiss at the villain during a melodrama in the Birdcage Theater.

FIESTA VILLAGE   Here you'll find a south-of-the-border theme. That means festive markets, strolling mariachis, and wild rides like Montezooma's Revenge and Jaguar!, a roller coaster that includes two heart-in-the-mouth drops and a loop that turns you upside down.

THE BOARDWALK   The park's newest theme area is a salute to Southern California's beach culture, where palm trees are a backdrop for a trio of thrill rides: Boomerang, Perilous Plunge, and Supreme Scream.

CAMP SNOOPY   This will probably be the youngsters' favorite area. It's meant to re-create a wilderness camp in the picturesque High Sierra. Its 6 rustic acres are the playgrounds of Charles Schulz's beagle and his pals, Charlie Brown and Lucy, who greet guests and pose for pictures. There are about a dozen rides in the Camp; several scaled-down rides (including a kid-size version of Supreme Scream) are made for the younger set, while the whole family can enjoy others.

WILD WATER WILDERNESS   This is $10 million, 3½-acre attraction styled like a turn-of-the-century California wilderness park with a raging whitewater river adventure called Bigfoot Rapids, along with cascading waterfalls, soaring geysers, and old-style ranger stations. Mystery Lodge is worth seeing here as well: This truly amazing high-tech, trick-of-the-eye attraction is based on the legends of local Native Americans.

INDIAN TRAILS   The entire family can explore the ride-free Indian Trails cultural area, which offers daily demonstrations of native dance and music by authentically costumed Native American and Aztec dancers, singers and musicians performing in the round. While exploring, you can also enjoy Navajo tacos, Indian fry bread, and fresh roasted ears of corn.

A NEARBY PRESIDENTIAL LIBRARY

Richard Nixon Library and Birthplace   Although he was the most vilified U.S. president in modern history, there has always been a warm place in the hearts of Orange County locals for Richard Nixon. This presidential library, located in Nixon's boyhood town, celebrates the roots, life, and legacy of America's 37th president. The 9-acre site contains the modest farmhouse where Nixon was born, manicured flower gardens, a modern museum housing presidential archives, and the final resting place of Mr. Nixon and his wife, Pat.

Displays include videos of the famous Nixon-Kennedy TV debates, an impressive life-size statuary summit of world leaders, gifts of state (including a gun from Elvis), and exhibits on China and Russia. There's also a display of Pat Nixon's sparkling First Lady gowns and a 12-foot-high (3.5m) graffiti-covered chunk of the Berlin Wall, symbolizing the defeat of Communism, but hardly a mention is made of Nixon's leading role in the anti-Communist witch hunts of the 1950s. Similarly, there are exhibits on Vietnam, yet no mention of Nixon's illegal expansion of that war into neighboring Cambodia. Only the Watergate Gallery is relatively forthright, allowing visitors to listen to actual White House tapes and view a montage of the president's last day in the White House.

18001 Yorba Linda Blvd., Yorba Linda. (C) 714/993-5075. Fax 714/993-3569. www.nixonlibrary.org. Admission $5.95 adults, $3.95 seniors, $2 children 8–11, free for children under 7. Mon–Sat 10am–5pm; Sun 11am–5pm.

WHERE TO STAY IN THE DISNEYLAND AREA
EXPENSIVE

The Anabella Hotel 🞲   Uniting several formerly independent low-rise hotels across the street from California Adventure, the brand-new (in 2001) Anabella started from scratch, gutting each building to create carefully planned rooms for park-bound families and business travelers alike. The new complex features a vaguely Mission-style facade of whitewashed walls and red-tiled roofs, though guest room interiors are strictly contemporary in style and modern in appointments. Bathrooms are generously sized and outfitted in honey-toned granite; most have a tub-shower combo—just a few are shower-only. Though parking areas dot the grounds, you'll also find a pleasant garden around the central swimming pool and whirlpool; a separate adult pool hides out next to the street-side fitness room. Business travelers will appreciate the in-room executive desks with high-speed Internet access, while families can take advantage of "kids suites" complete with bunk beds and separate bedrooms. There's a pleasant indoor-outdoor all-day restaurant, and the hotel is a stop on both the Disney and Convention Center shuttle routes. *Note:* Rooms and rates vary wildly in terms of room size, layout, and occupancy limits; extra time spent with the reservationist will pay off in the most comfortable room for your needs.

1030 W. Katella Ave., Anaheim, CA 92802. ℂ **800/863-4888** or 714/905-1050. Fax 714/905-1054. www.anabellahotel.com. 358 units. $159–$299 double. AE, DC, DISC, MC, V. Free parking. **Amenities:** Restaurant; lounge; 2 outdoor heated pools; whirlpool; exercise room; small nail salon; concierge; activities desk; business center; room service (7am–11pm); laundry/dry-cleaning service; self-service laundry. *In room:* A/C, TV w/pay movies, dataport, fridge, coffeemaker, hair dryer, iron, safe.

The Disneyland Hotel ⭐⭐ *(Kids)*   The holy grail for Disney-goers has always been this, the "Official Hotel of the Magic Kingdom." A direct monorail connection to Disneyland (and California Adventure) means you'll be able to return to your room anytime, whether to take a much-needed nap or to change your soaked shorts after your Splash Mountain or Grizzly Peak adventure. The theme hotel is a wild attraction unto itself, and the very best choice for families with small children. The rooms aren't fancy, but they're comfortably and attractively furnished, like a good-quality business hotel, and all have balconies. In-room amenities include movie channels (with free Disney Channel, naturally) and cute-as-a-button Disney-themed toiletries and accessories. This all-inclusive resort offers more than 10 combined restaurants, snack bars, and cocktail lounges; every kind of service desk imaginable; a fantasy swimming lagoon with white-sand beach; and, video game center. The complex includes the adjoining Paradise Pier Hotel, a tower that once was an independent hotel—but has now been revamped to match the Paradise Pier theme.

Best of all, hotel guests get to enter the park early almost every day and enjoy the major rides before the lines form. The amount of time varies from day to day, but usually you can enter 1½ hours early. Call ahead to check the schedule.

When you're planning your trip, inquire about multiple-day packages that allow you to take on the park at your own pace and usually include free parking.

1150 Magic Way, Anaheim, CA 92802. ℂ **714/956-MICKEY** (central reservations), 714/778-6600 (Disneyland Hotel), or 714/999-0990 (Paradise Pier Hotel). Reservations Fax 714/956-6582 (reservations). 1,198 units. $170–$285 double; from $275 suite. AE, MC, V. Parking $10. **Amenities:** 10 restaurants; 3 lounges; 3 outdoor pools; health club; whirlpool; children's programs; game room; concierge; shopping arcade; salon; 24-hr. room service; babysitting; laundry/dry-cleaning service. *In room:* A/C, TV w/pay movies, dataport, minibar, coffeemaker, hair dryer, safe.

Disney's Grand Californian Hotel ⭐⭐ *(Kids)*   Disney spared no details when constructing this enormous version of an Arts and Crafts–era lodge (think Yosemite's Ahwahnee, Pasadena's Gamble House), hiring craftspeople throughout the state to contribute one-of-a-kind tiles, furniture, sculptures, and artwork. Taking inspiration from California's redwood forests, mission pioneers, and plein-air painters, designers managed to create a nostalgic yet state-of-the-art high-rise hotel.

Enter through subtle (where's the door?) stained-glass sliding panels to the hotel's centerpiece, a six-story "living room" with a William Morris–designed marble "carpet," angled skylight seen through exposed support beams, display cases of Craftsman treasures, and a three-story walk-in "hearth" whose fire warms Stickley-style rockers and plush leather armchairs.

Guest rooms are spacious and smartly designed, carrying through the Arts and Crafts theme surprisingly well considering the hotel's grand scale. The best ones overlook the park (but you'll pay for that view). Despite the sophisticated, luxurious air of the Grand Californian, this hotel truly caters to families, with a bevy of room configurations including one with a double bed plus bunk beds with a trundle. Since the hotel provides sleeping bags (rather than rollaways) for kids, this standard-size room will sleep a family of six—but you have to share the bathroom.

1600 So. Disneyland Dr., Anaheim, CA 92802. (℃ **714/956-MICKEY** (central reservations) or 714/635-2300. Fax 714/956-6099. www.disneyland.com. 751 units. $205–$335 double; from $345 suite. AE, DC, DISC, MC, V. Free self-parking; valet parking $6. **Amenities:** 3 restaurants; lounge; 2 outdoor pools; health club and spa; whirlpool; children's center; game room/arcade; concierge; business center; 24-hr. room service; laundry/dry-cleaning service; concierge level rooms. *In room:* A/C, TV w/pay movies, dataport, minibar, coffeemaker, hair dryer, iron, safe.

WestCoast Anaheim Hotel 🏆
Although this hotel, in the Anaheim Convention Center complex (across the street from Disneyland), draws primarily a business crowd, it has much to appeal to the leisure traveler. The contemporary, comfortable rooms in the 12-story tower all have balconies overlooking either Disneyland or the hotel's luxurious pool area, which includes an attractive sun deck, and snack and cocktail-bar gazebo. The front desk can provide fax machines and refrigerators upon request. The Old West frontier-themed restaurant serves steak and seafood along with a few colorful game selections.

1855 S. Harbor Blvd. (south of Katella Ave.), Anaheim, CA 92802. (℃ **800/426-0670** or 714/750-1811. Fax 714/971-2485. www.westcoastanaheimhotel.com. 500 units. $195 double. Disneyland package available. AE, DC, DISC, MC, V. Self-parking $10, valet parking $13; free Disneyland shuttle. **Amenities:** 2 restaurants; 2 lounges; outdoor pool; fitness center; deluxe whirlpool; activities desk; car-rental desk; 24-hr. business center; room service (6am–11pm); laundry/dry-cleaning service. *In room:* A/C, TV w/pay movies, dataport, coffeemaker, hair dryer, iron.

MODERATE

Portofino Inn & Suites 🏆 *Kids*
Emerging from the multiyear rubble of the former Jolly Roger Hotel renovation, this brand-spanking-new complex of low- and high-rise, all-suite buildings ports a cheery yellow exterior and family friendly interior—just in time for the expanded Disneyland Resort. The location couldn't be better: It's directly across the street from California Adventure's back side, and they'll even shuttle you straight to the front gate. Designed to work as well for business travelers from the nearby Convention Center as for Disney-bound families, the Portofino offers contemporary, stylish furnishings as well as vacation-friendly rates and suites for any family configuration. We especially love the "Kid's Suite," which features bunk beds *and* sofa sleeper, plus TV, fridge, and microwave—and that's just in the kids' room; Mom and Dad have a separate bedroom with grown-up comforts like double vanity, shower massage, and their own TV.

1831 S. Harbor Blvd. (at Katella), Anaheim, CA 92802. (℃ **888/297-7143** or 714/782-7600. Fax 714/782-7619. 190 units. $94–$159 double; $109–$219 Suite. Midweek, off-season, and other discounts available. AE, DC, DISC, MC, V. Free parking and Disneyland shuttle. **Amenities:** Restaurant; outdoor pool; fitness center; whirlpool; game room; tour desk; laundry/dry-cleaning service; coin-op laundry. *In room:* A/C, TV w/pay movies, dataport, coffeemaker, hair dryer, iron.

Radisson Resort Knott's Berry Farm 🏆 *Kids*
Within easy walking distance of Knott's Berry Farm, this spit-shined Radisson (the former Buena Park Hotel) also offers a free shuttle to Disneyland, 7 miles (11km) away. The pristine lobby has the look of a business-oriented hotel, and that it is. But vacationers can also benefit from the elevated level of service. Be sure to ask about "Super Saver" rates (as low as $99 with breakfast at press time), plus Knott's or Disneyland package deals. The rooms in the nine-story tower were tastefully redecorated when Radisson took over. Doting parents can even treat their kids to a Snoopy-themed room!

7675 Crescent Ave. (at Grand), Buena Park, CA 90620. ℭ **800/333-3333** or 714/995-1111. Fax 714/828-8590. www.radisson.com/buenaparkca. 320 units. $129–$169 double; $179–$299 suite. Discounts and packages available. AE, DC, DISC, MC, V. Free parking and Disneyland shuttle. **Amenities:** 2 restaurants; lounge; outdoor pool; night-lit tennis courts; fitness center; whirlpool; video arcade; concierge; 24-hr. room service; laundry/dry-cleaning service; self-service laundry. *In room:* A/C, TV w/pay movies, fax machine, dataport, coffeemaker, hair dryer, iron, safe.

Sheraton Anaheim Hotel ⭐ This hotel rises to the festive theme-park occasion with its fanciful English Tudor architecture; it's a castle that lures business conventions, Disney-bound families, and local high school proms. The public areas are quiet and elegant—intimate gardens with fountains and koi ponds, plush lobby and lounges—which can be a pleasing touch after a frantic day at the amusement park. The rooms are modern and unusually spacious, but otherwise not distinctive. A large swimming pool sits in the center of the complex, surrounded by attractive landscaping. Don't be put off by the high rack rates; rooms commonly go for $100 to $130, even on busy summer weekends.

900 Disneyland Dr. (at I-5), Anaheim, CA 92802. ℭ **800/325-3535** or 714/778-1700. Fax 714/535-3889. www.sheratonanaheim.com. 489 units. $110–$250 double; $290–$360 suite. AE, DC, MC, V. Parking $8; free Disneyland shuttle. **Amenities:** 2 restaurants; lounge; outdoor pool; fitness center; whirlpool; concierge; 24-hr. room service; laundry/dry-cleaning service; coin-op laundry. *In room:* A/C, TV w/pay movies, dataport, minibar, coffeemaker, hair dryer, iron.

INEXPENSIVE

Anaheim Vagabond Plaza Hotel ⭐ *(Value* You can easily cross the street to Disneyland's main gate, or take the Anaheim Plaza's free shuttle. Once you return, you'll appreciate the way this 32-year-old hotel's clever design shuts out the noisy world. In fact, the seven two-story garden buildings remind me more of 1960s Waikiki than busy Anaheim. Astroturf unfortunately surrounds the Olympic-size heated outdoor pool and whirlpool, and the plain motel-style furnishings are beginning to look a little tired. On the plus side, nothing's changed about the light-filled modern lobby, nor the friendly rates, which often drop as low as $49.

1700 S. Harbor Blvd., Anaheim, CA 92802. ℭ **800/228-1357** or 714/772-5900. Fax 714/772-8386. 300 units. $79–$150 double; from $125 suite. Rates include continental breakfast. AE, DC, DISC, MC, V. Free parking and Disneyland shuttle. **Amenities:** Restaurant; lounge; outdoor pool; whirlpool; room service (6:30am–10pm); laundry/dry-cleaning service; coin-op laundry. *In room:* A/C, TV, coffeemaker, hair dryer.

Candy Cane Inn ⭐⭐ *(Value* Take your standard U-shaped motel court with outdoor corridors, spruce it up with cobblestone drives and walkways, old-time street lamps, and flowering vines engulfing the balconies of attractively painted rooms, and you have the Candy Cane. The face-lift worked, making this gem near Disneyland's main gate a treat for the stylish bargain hunter. The guest rooms are decorated in bright floral motifs with comfortable furnishings, including queen beds and a separate dressing and vanity area. Breakfast is served in the courtyard, where you can also splash around in a heated pool, spa, or kids' wading pool.

1747 S. Harbor Blvd., Anaheim, CA 92802. ℭ **800/345-7057** or 714/774-5284. Fax 714/772-5462. 173 units. $84–$129 double. Rates include expanded continental breakfast. AAA discount available. AE, DC, DISC, MC, V. Free parking and Disneyland shuttle. **Amenities:** Outdoor pool; whirlpool; laundry/dry-cleaning service; coin-op laundry. *In room:* A/C, TV, coffeemaker, hair dryer.

Howard Johnson Hotel ⭐ This hotel occupies an enviable location, directly opposite Disneyland, and a cute San Francisco trolley car runs to and from the park every 30 minutes. The guest rooms, which were renovated in 1999, are divided among several low-profile buildings, all with balconies opening onto a central garden with two heated pools for adults and one for children. Garden paths lead under eucalyptus and olive trees to a splashing circular fountain. During the summer you can see the nightly fireworks display at Disneyland from the upper balconies of the park-side rooms. Try to avoid the rooms in the back buildings, which get some freeway noise. Services and facilities include room service from the attached Coco's Restaurant, airport shuttle, and family lodging/Disney admission packages. We think it's pretty classy for a HoJo's.

1380 S. Harbor Blvd., Anaheim, CA 92802. © 800/422-4228 or 714/776-6120. Fax 714/533-3578. www.hojoanaheim.com. 320 units. $74–$109 double. AE, DC, DISC, MC, V. Free parking and Disneyland trolley. **Amenities:** Restaurant; 2 outdoor pools; whirlpool; game room; concierge; room service (7am–11pm); laundry/dry-cleaning service; coin-op laundry. *In room:* A/C, TV w/pay movies, dataport, fridge, coffeemaker.

Ramada Maingate Saga Inn *(Value)* Though recent Disney construction has obscured the formerly imposing "main gate," this motel's name still indicates how enticingly close it is to the theme park. It's a large property, with a vaguely Tudoresque castle exterior undoubtedly borrowed from Fantasyland. If you've still got energy after a day playing at the Disneyland Resort, the Ramada offers minigolf, game arcades, and a branch of reliable Tony Roma's rib joint adjacent to the motel.

1650 S. Harbor Blvd., Anaheim, CA 92802. © 800/854-6097 or 714/772-0440. Fax 714/991-8219. www.ramada.com. 185 units. $71–$108 double. Rates include continental breakfast. Kids 18 and under stay free. AAA discounts available; check website for "Super Saver" rates, often as low as $58. AE, DC, DISC, MC, V. Free parking and Disney shuttle. **Amenities:** Restaurant; lounge; outdoor heated pool; whirlpool; laundry/dry-cleaning service. *In room:* A/C, TV, dataport, iron.

WHERE TO DINE IN THE DISNEYLAND AREA

If you're visiting the Disneyland Resort, chances are you'll probably eat at one of the many choices either inside the theme parks or at Downtown Disney; there are plenty of restaurants to choose from for all tastes and budgets. At Disneyland, in the Creole-themed **Blue Bayou,** you can sit under the stars inside the Pirates of the Caribbean ride—no matter what time of day it is. California Adventure features two actual sit-down options: **Soap Opera Bistro,** on the Hollywood Pictures Backlot, is built of actual sets from ABC daytime dramas like *All My Children* and others, so you can sit in a replica Llanview Country Club noshing on "Erica's Chicken Salad." The Robert Mondavi–backed **Vineyard Room** offers upscale prix-fixe wine country cuisine matched to Mondavi wines. (The more casual Golden Vine Terrace is downstairs.) Make reservations early in the day for dinner, as this one fills up pretty quickly.

And at Knott's Berry Farm, try the fried-chicken dinners and boysenberry pies at Mrs. Knott's historic **Chicken Dinner Restaurant** (see below for full review). We've also listed some of the best bets in the surrounding area, including nearby **Orange,** whose charming historic downtown is home to several of the region's best dining options, if you're willing to drive 10 to 15 minutes.

Catal Restaurant/Uva Bar *(★★)* MEDITERRANEAN/TAPAS Branching out from acclaimed Patina restaurant in Los Angeles, high-priest-of-cuisine Joachim Splichal brings us this Spanish-inspired Mediterranean concept duo at the heart of Downtown Disney. The main restaurant, Catal, features a series of quiet, intimate second-floor rooms that combine rustic Mediterranean charm with fine dining style. Complemented by an excellent international wine list, the menu is a collage of flavors that borrow from France, Spain, Italy, Greece, Morocco, and the Middle East—all united in selections that manage to be intriguing but not overwhelming. Though the menu will vary seasonally, expect to find selections that range from seared sea scallops over saffron risotto or chorizo-spiked Spanish paella to herb-marinated rotisserie chicken or Sicilian rigatoni with creamy ricotta cheese.

Downstairs, the Uva Bar (*uva* means "grape" in Spanish) is a casual tapas bar offering 40 different wines by the glass in an outdoor pavilion setting. The affordable menu features the same pan-Mediterranean influence, even offering many items from the Catal menu; standouts include Cabernet-braised short ribs atop horseradish mashed potatoes, marinated olives and cured Spanish ham, and Andalusian gazpacho with rock shrimp.

1580 Disneyland Dr. (at Downtown Disney). ✆ 714/774-4442. Reservations recommended Sun–Thurs, not accepted Fri–Sat (Catal); not accepted for Uva Bar. Main courses $14–$24, tapas $5–$8. AE, DC, DISC, MC, V. Mon–Thurs 11am–11pm; Fri–Sun 11am–midnight.

Mrs. Knott's Chicken Dinner Restaurant ✿ *Kids* AMERICAN Knott's
Berry Farm got its start as a down-home diner, and you can still get a hearty all-American meal without even entering the theme park. The restaurant that started it all, descended from Cordelia Knott's humble Depression-era farmland tea room, stands just outside the park's entrance, with plenty of free parking for patrons. Looking just as you'd expect—country cute, with window shutters and paisley a'plenty—the restaurant's featured attraction is the original fried chicken dinner, complete with soup, salad, buttermilk biscuits, mashed potatoes and gravy, and a slice of famous pie. Country fried steak, pot roast, roast turkey, and pork ribs are options, as well as sandwiches, salads, and a terrific chicken pot pie. Boysenberries abound (of course!), from breakfast jam to traditional double-crust pies, and there's even an adjacent take-out shop that's always crowded.

8039 Beach Blvd. (near La Palma), Buena Park. ✆ 714/220-5080. Reservations not accepted. Main courses $5–$7, complete dinners $10.95. AE, DC, DISC, MC, V. Sun–Thurs 7am–8:30pm; Fri 7am–9pm; Sat 7am–9:30pm.

Napa Rose ✿✿✿ CALIFORNIA Situated inside the upscale Grand Cali-
fornian Hotel, Napa Rose is the first really serious (read: on "foodie" radar) restaurant at the Disneyland Resort. Its warm and light dining room mirrors the Arts and Crafts style of the hotel, down to Frank Lloyd Wright stained-glass windows and Craftsman-inspired seating throughout the restaurant and adjoining lounge. Executive chef Andrew Sutton was lured away from the Napa Valley's chic Auberge du Soleil, bringing with him a wine-country sensibility and passion for fresh California ingredients and inventive preparations. You can see him busy in the impressive open exhibition kitchen, showcasing specialty items like Sierra golden trout, artisan cheeses from Humboldt County and the Gold Country, and the Sonoma rabbit in Sutton's signature braised mushroom-rabbit tart. The tantalizing "Seven Sparkling Sins" starter platter (for two) features jewel-like portions of foie gras, caviar, oysters, lobster, and other exotic delicacies; the same attention to detail is evident in seasonally composed main course standouts like grilled yellowtail with tangerine-basil fruit salsa atop savory couscous, or free-range veal osso buco in rich bacon-forest mushroom ragout. Leave room for dessert, to at least share one of pastry chef Jorge Sotello's creative treats—our favorites are Sonoma goat cheese flan with Riesling-soaked tropical fruit, and gooey chocolate crepes with house-made caramelized banana ice cream. Napa Rose boasts an impressive and balanced wine list, including 45 by-the-glass choices; and outdoor seating is arranged around a rustic fire pit, gazing out across a landscaped arroyo toward California Adventure's distinctive Grizzly Peak.

1600 S. Disneyland Dr. (in Disney's Grand Californian Hotel). ☎ 714/300-7170. www.disneyland.com.
Reservations strongly recommended. Main courses $12–$16 lunch, $19–$30 dinner. AE, DC, DISC, MC, V.
Daily 11:30am–2pm and 5:30–10pm.

Rainforest Cafe *Kids* INTERNATIONAL   Designed to suggest ancient temple ruins in an overgrown Central American jungle, this national chain favorite successfully combines entertainment, retail, and family friendly dining in one fantasy setting. There are cascading waterfalls inside and out, a canopy of lush vegetation, simulated tropical mists, and even a troupe of colorful parrots beckoning shoppers into the "Retail Village." Once seated, diners choose from an amalgam of wildly flavored dishes inspired by Caribbean, Polynesian, Latin, Asian, and Mediterranean cuisines. Masquerading under exotic-sounding names like "Jungle Safari Soup" (a meaty version of minestrone) and "Mojo Bones" (barbecue pork ribs), the food is really fairly familiar: A translated sampling includes Cobb salad, pita sandwiches, pot stickers, shrimp-studded pasta, and charbroiled chicken. Fresh fruit smoothies and tropical specialty cocktails are offered, as well as a best-shared dessert called "Giant Chocolate Volcano." After your meal, you can browse through logo items, environmentally educational toys and games, stuffed jungle animals and puppets, straw safari hats, and other themed souvenirs in the lobby store. There's a complete children's menu, and the Rainforest Cafe is one of the few Downtown Disney eateries to have full breakfast service.

1515 S. Disneyland Dr. (at Downtown Disney). ☎ 714/772-0413. www.rainforestcafe.com. Reservations recommended for peak mealtimes. Main courses $9–$21. AE, DC, DISC, MC, V. Sun–Thurs 7am–11pm; Fri–Sat 7am–midnight.

Ralph Brennan's Jazz Kitchen ✿ CAJUN/CREOLE   If you always thought Disneyland's New Orleans Square was just like the real thing, wait until you see this authentically Southern concept restaurant at Downtown Disney. Ralph Brennan, of the New Orleans food dynasty responsible for NOLA landmarks like Commander's Palace and a trio of Big Easy hot spots, commissioned a handful of New Orleans artists to create the handcrafted furnishings that give the Jazz Kitchen its believable French Quarter ambience. Lacy wrought-iron grillwork, cascading ferns, and trickling stone fountains enhance three separate dining choices: The upstairs Carnival Club is an elegant dining salon with silk-draped chandeliers and terrace dining that overlooks the "street scene" below; casual Flambeaux is downstairs, where a bead-encrusted grand piano hints at the nightly live jazz that sizzles in this room; and the Creole Cafe is a quick stop for necessities like muffaletta or beignets. Expect traditional Cajun/Creole fare with heavy-handed seasonings and rich, heart-stopping sauces—now *that's* authentically New Orleans.

1590 S. Disneyland Dr. (at Downtown Disney). ☎ 714/776-5200. www.rbjazzkitchen.com. Reservations strongly recommended. Main courses $16–$25 (cafe items $4–$8). AE, DC, DISC, MC, V. Daily 11am–3pm and 5–11pm.

5 Julian: Apple Pies & More

60 miles (97km) NE of San Diego; 60 miles (97km) SE of Temecula; 35 miles (56km) W of Anza-Borrego Desert State Park

A trip to Julian (pop. 1,500) is a trip back in time. The old gold-mining town, now best known for its apples, has some good eateries and a handful of cute B&Bs, but its popularity is based on the fact that it provides a chance for city-weary folks to get away from it all.

People first ventured into these fertile hills in search of gold in the late 1860s; they discovered it in 1870 near where the Julian Hotel stands today, and 18 mines sprang up like mushrooms. During all the excitement, four cousins—all former Confederate soldiers from Georgia, two with the last name Julian—founded the town of Julian. The mines produced up to an estimated $13 million worth of gold in their day.

Before you leave, try Julian's apple pies; whether the best pies come from Mom's Pies or the Julian Pie Company is always a toss-up. Sample all of them and decide for yourself.

ESSENTIALS

GETTING THERE   You can make the 90-minute trip on Highway 78 or I-8 to Highway 79. I suggest taking one route going and the other coming back. Highway 79 winds through scenic Rancho Cuyamaca State Park, while Highway 78 traverses open country and farmland.

VISITOR INFORMATION   For a brochure on what to see and do in Julian, contact the **Julian Chamber of Commerce,** corner of Main and Washington streets, P.O. Box 413, Julian, CA 92036 (© **760/765-1857;** www.julianca. com), where staffers always have enthusiastic suggestions for local activities. The office is open daily 10am to 4pm.

SOME HELPFUL TIPS   Once in Julian, you'll need a car if you want to stay at a B&B outside town. However, Main Street is only 6 blocks long, and some lodgings, shops, and cafes are on it or a block away. Town maps and accommodations flyers are available from Town Hall, on Main Street at Washington Street. Public restrooms are behind the Town Hall. There's no self-service laundry (so come prepared), but you'll find a post office, a liquor store, and a few grocery stores. Shops are often closed on Monday and Tuesday. The town has a 24-hour hot line (© **760/765-0707)** that provides information on lodging, dining, shops, activities, upcoming events, weather, and road conditions.

SPECIAL EVENTS   Julian's popular **Arts and Crafts Show** is held every weekend between mid-September and the end of November. Local artisans display their wares; there's also plenty of cider and apple pie, plus entertainment and brilliant fall foliage.

The **Wildflower Show** is a weeklong event sponsored by the local Women's Club. Held in Julian's historic Town Hall, the event was initiated in 1926, and features displays of native plants; it takes place in early May.

One event that's better than its name is the **Julian Weed Show,** which takes place over the second half of August. Artwork and arrangements culled from the area's myriad wildflowers and indigenous plants (OK, weeds) are displayed and sold during the festival.

If you arrive on the **Fourth of July,** count on participating in a community barbecue and seeing a quilt exhibition and parade.

It's also fun to visit in **December,** when activities include caroling and a living nativity pageant, and the town takes on a winter-wonderland appearance. Over the first two weekends in December, the members of the Julian Bed and Breakfast Guild hold open houses with complimentary refreshments.

The chamber of commerce has further details on these and other local events.

TOURING THE TOWN

If you've never heard of Julian, then you're in for a treat. While Wal-Mart (no offense) and McDonald's (no offense) have permeated formerly unspoiled mountain resorts like Big Bear and Mammoth, this 1880s gold-mining town has managed to retain a rustic, woodsy sense of its historic origins. Radiating the dusty aura of the Old West, Julian offers an abundance of early California history, quaint Victorian streets filled with apple pie shops and antiques stores, crisp fresh air, and friendly people.

Be forewarned, however, that Julian's charming downtown can become exceedingly crowded during the fall harvest season. Consider making your trip another time to enjoy this unspoiled relic with a little privacy. (Rest assured, apple pies are baking around town year-round.) At around 4,500 feet (1,350m) elevation, the autumn air is crisp and bracing, and Julian sees a dusting (and often more) of snow during the winter.

The best way to experience tiny Julian is on foot. Two or 3 blocks of Main Street offer plenty of diversion for an afternoon or longer, depending on how much pie you stop to eat. And don't worry, you'll grow accustomed to constant apple references very quickly here—the humble fruit has proven to be more of an economic boom than gold ever was.

After stopping in at the chamber of commerce in the old Town Hall—check out the vintage photos of Julian's yesteryear—cross the street to the **Julian Drug Store & Miner's Diner,** 2134 Main St. (© 760/765-3753), an old-style soda fountain serving sparkling sarsaparilla—plus burgers and sandwiches—and conjuring images of boys in buckskin and girls in bonnets. Built in 1886, the brick structure is on the National Historic Register—like many other well-preserved buildings in town—and is jam-packed with local memorabilia. Open hours are Monday through Thursday 9am to 6pm, Friday and Saturday 9am to 8pm, Sunday 10am to 5pm.

The **Eagle and High Peak Mines,** built around 1870, at the end of C Street (© 760/765-0036), although seeming to be a tourist trap, offer an interesting and educational look at the town's one-time economic mainstay. Tours take you underground to the 1,000-foot (300m) hard-rock tunnel to see the mining and milling process; antique engines and authentic tools are on display. Tours are given between 10am and 3pm daily; admission is $7 for adults, $3 for children 6 and over, $1 for children under 6.

You'll certainly see one of Suzanne Porter's horse-drawn carriages clip-clopping around town. Some might think it touristy, while others will wax nostalgic for New York's Central Park, but a ride from **Country Carriages** (© 760/765-1471) is a quintessential Julian experience. Even the locals get into the act, snuggling under a blanket on romantic evening rides to celebrate anniversaries and birthdays. The carriages are always booked solid on Christmas Eve. A rambling drive down country roads and through town is $20 per couple; an abbreviated spin around town costs $5 per adult, $2 per child. Call for reservations, or stop by when one of the carriages is parked in front of the drugstore.

APPLE PIES

You won't be able to resist partaking of the apple pie so beloved in these parts. We recommend the aptly named **Mom's Pies,** 2119 Main St. (© 760/765-2472). Its special attraction is a sidewalk plate-glass window through which you can observe the Mom-on-duty rolling crust, filling pies, and crimping edges. The shop routinely bakes several varieties of apple pie and will, with a day's notice, whip up apple-rhubarb, peach-apple crumb, or any one of a number of specialties. There's a country cafe in the store—in case a cup of coffee and a slice of fresh pie prove irresistible. (They always do to me!) Mom's is open daily from 9am to 5pm.

Another great bakery is the **Julian Pie Company,** 2225 Main St. (© **760/ 765-2449**). This blue-and-white cottage boasts a small front patio with umbrella tables, a frilly indoor parlor, and a large patio deck in back where over- hanging apple trees are literally up for grabs. The shop serves original, Dutch, apple-mountain berry, and no-sugar-added pies as well as cinnamon rolls, wal- nut apple muffins, and cinnamon cookies made from pie-crust dough. Light lunches (soups and sandwiches) are offered as well. Open daily 9am to 5pm.

SHOPPING

One of the simple pleasures of any weekend getaway is window- or souvenir- shopping in unfamiliar little shops like those lining both sides of Main Street. Keep an eye open for the old barn housing the **Warm Hearth,** 2125 Main St. (© **760/765-1022**). Country crafts, candles, and woven throws sit among the wood stoves, fireplaces, and barbecues that make up the shop's main business.

Nearby is the **Julian Cider Mill,** 2103 Main St. (© **760/765-1430**), where you can see cider presses at work from October through March. It offers free tastes of the fresh nectar, and jugs to take home. Throughout the year, the mill also carries the area's widest selection of food products, from apple butters and jams to berry preserves, several varieties of local honey, candies, and other goodies.

A terrific browsing store is the **Bell, Book and Candle Shoppe,** 2007 Main St. (© **760/765-1377**), which specializes in only one of the above—candles, candles, and more candles. It sells pillars, tapers, hand-carved representational candles, custom personalized candles, candlesticks, and holders—plus incense, essential oils, and a few other gift items.

You'll have to step uphill one block to find the charming **Julian Tea & Cot- tage Arts,** 2124 Third St. (© **760/765-0832;** www.juliantea.com), where after- noon tea is served amid a treasure-trove of tea-brewing tools and other tea-themed paraphernalia. If that sounds too frilly for you, step next door, where a recent expansion spawned the **Culinary Cottage,** 2116 Third St. (© **760/ 765-0842**), home to stylish housewares, fine cookbooks, and gourmet foods (often available for tastings).

Book lovers will enjoy stopping into the **Old Julian Book House,** 2230 Main St. (© **760/765-1989**). Run by P. J. Phillips, a dedicated purveyor of new and antiquarian volumes alike, it carries a smattering of maps, sheet music, CDs, and ephemera, too. This small shop also has a comprehensive, computerized book search to help track down out-of-print or scarce material throughout the coun- try. Most of the Main Street merchants are open daily from 10am to 5pm.

There are dozens of **roadside fruit stands and orchards** in the Julian hills; during autumn they're open all day, every day, but in the off-season some might open only on weekends or close entirely. Most stands sell, depending on the sea- son, apples, pears, peaches, cider, jams, jellies, and other homemade foodstuffs. Many are along Highway 78 between Julian and Wynola (3 miles/5km away); there are also stands along Farmers Road, a scenic country lane leading north from downtown Julian. Happy hunting!

Ask any of the San Diegans who regularly make excursions to Julian; no trip would be complete without a stop at **Dudley's Bakery,** Highway 78, Santa Ysabel (© **800/225-3348** or 760/765-0488), for a loaf or three of bread. Loaves are stacked high, and folks are often three deep at the counter clamoring for the 20 (yes, 20!) varieties of bread baked fresh daily. Varieties range from raisin-date- nut to jalapeño, with some garden-variety sourdough and multigrain in between. Dudley's is a local tradition; built in 1963, it has expanded several times to accommodate its ever-growing business. The bakery is open Wednesday through Sunday from 8am to 5pm (and may close early on Sun).

HISTORIC CEMETERIES

Finally, what's a visit to any historic hamlet without a peek at the headstones in the local cemetery? If this activity appeals to you—as it does to me—then Julian's **Pioneer Cemetery** is a must-see. Contemporary graves belie the haphazard, overgrown look of this hilly burial ground, and the eroded older tombstones tell the intriguing story of Julian's rough pioneer history and ardent patriotism. You can drive in from A Street, but I prefer climbing the steep stairway leading up from Main Street around the corner; until 1924 this ascent was the only point of entry, even for processions. As you climb, imagine carrying a coffin up these steps in the snow.

OUTDOOR PURSUITS IN & AROUND JULIAN

Within 10 miles (16km) of Julian are numerous hiking trails that traverse rolling meadows, high chaparral, and thick pine forests. The most spectacular hike is at **Volcan Mountain Preserve,** north of town along Farmers Road; the trail to the top is a moderately challenging hike of around 3½ miles (5.5km) round-trip, with a 1,400-foot (420m) elevation gain. From the top, hikers have a panoramic view of the desert, mountains, and sea. Free docent-led hikes are offered year-round (on Sat, about one per month). For a hike schedule, call ✆ **760/765-0650.**

In **William Heise County Park,** off Frisius Drive outside Pine Hills, the whole family can enjoy hikes ranging from a self-guided nature trail and a cedar-scented forest trail to moderate to vigorous trails into the mountains. A ranger kiosk at the entrance dispenses trail maps.

Cuyamaca Rancho State Park covers 30,000 acres along Highway 79 southeast of Julian, the centerpiece of which is Cuyamaca Lake. In addition to lake recreation (for boat rental and fishing information, call ✆ **760/765-0515** or 760/447-8123; www.lakecuyamaca.org), there are several sylvan picnic areas, three campgrounds, and 110 miles (177km) of hiking trails through the Cleveland National Forest. Activities at the lake include fishing for trout, bass, catfish, bluegill, and crappie, and boating. There's a general store and restaurant at the lake's edge. The fishing fee is $4.75 per day for adults, $2.50 per day for children 8 to 15, free for children under 8. A license is required. Rowboats are $12 per day, and outboard motors an additional $13. Canoes and paddleboats can be rented by the hour for $4 to $7. For a trail map and further information about park recreation, stop in at **park headquarters** on Highway 79 (✆ **760/765-0755**) between 8am and 5pm Monday through Friday. An adjacent park museum is open Monday through Friday from 10am to 5pm, Saturday and Sunday 10am to 4pm.

The **Julian Bicycle Company,** 1897 Porter Lane, off Main Street (✆ **760/765-2200**), is involved in the Julian Flat Tire Festival, held in mid- or late April, as well as several other biking-related events. Contact the company for specific information and dates, or drop by Wednesday through Saturday from 10am to 5pm.

For a different way to tour, try **Llama Trek,** P.O. Box 2363, Julian (✆ **800/LAMAPAK** or 760/765-1890; www.wikiupbnb.com). You'll lead the llama, which carries packs, for hikes to see rural neighborhoods, a historic gold mine, mountain and lake views, and apple orchards. Rates run $75 to $85 per person and include lunch. Overnight wilderness trips are available.

WHERE TO STAY

Julian is B&B country. At last count, there were almost 20 bed-and-breakfasts—and they fill up quickly for the fall apple harvest season. Many (though not all) are affiliated with the **Julian Bed & Breakfast Guild** (© 760/765-1555; www.julianbnbguild.com), a terrific resource for personal assistance in locating accommodations. The 23 members include private cabins and other accommodations, but the agency specializes in B&Bs.

Three noteworthy choices are the **Artists' Loft** (© 760/765-0765), a peaceful hilltop retreat with two artistically decorated rooms and a cozy cabin with a wood-burning stove; the **Julian White House** (© 800/WHT-HOUS or 760/765-1764), a lovely faux-antebellum mansion 4 miles (6.5km) from Julian in Pine Hills, with four frilly Victorian-style guest rooms; and the romantic **Random Oaks Ranch** (© 800/BNB-4344 or 760/765-1094), which features two themed cottages, each with a wood-burning fireplace and outdoor whirlpool. To find out more about these and other member properties, call the guild between 9am and 9pm daily, or visit its website, which has links to the above-mentioned B&Bs.

A word of advice: Some people make their fall reservations as much as a year in advance; if you haven't booked by mid- to late August, you'll probably be shut out.

Julian Hotel ℛ   Built in 1897 by freed slave Albert Robinson, this frontier-style hotel is a living monument to the area's gold boom days. Centrally located at the crossroads of downtown, the Julian Hotel isn't as secluded or plush as the many B&Bs in town, but if you seek historically accurate lodgings to complete your weekend time warp, this is the place. The 13 rooms and 2 cottages have been authentically restored (with nicely designed private bathrooms added where necessary) and boast antique furnishings; some rooms are also authentically tiny so claustrophobics should inquire when reserving! An inviting private lobby is stocked with books, games, literature on local activities, and a wood-burning stove.

Main and B sts. (P.O. Box 1856), Julian, CA 92036. © 800/734-5854 or 760/765-0201. Fax 760/765-0327. www.julianhotel.com. 16 units. $82–$130 double; $120–$190 cottage. Rates include full breakfast and afternoon tea. AE, MC, V. *In room:* No phone.

Orchard Hill Country Inn ℛℛ   Hosts Darrell and Pat Straube offer the most upscale lodging in Julian, a two-story lodge and four Craftsman cottages on a hill overlooking the town. Ten guest rooms, a guests-only dining room, and a great room with a massive stone fireplace are in the lodge. Twelve suites are in cottages spread over 3 acres of grounds. All units feature contemporary, nonfrilly country furnishings and snacks. While rooms in the main lodge feel somewhat hotel-ish, the cottage suites are secluded and luxurious, with private porches, fireplaces, whirlpool tubs, and robes. Several hiking trails lead from the lodge into adjacent woods.

2502 Washington St., at Second St. (P.O. Box 2410), Julian, CA 92036. © 800/71-ORCHARD or 760/765-1700. Fax 760/765-0290. www.orchardhill.com. 22 units. $185–$285 double. Extra person $25. 2-night minimum stay if including Sat. Rates include breakfast and hors d'oeuvres. AE, MC, V. From Calif. 79, turn left on Main St., then right on Washington St. *In room:* A/C, TV/VCR.

WHERE TO DINE

Also consider one of Julian's many pie shops, two of which are discussed in "Touring the Town," above.

Julian Grille ☞ AMERICAN   Set in a cozy cottage festooned with lacy draperies, flickering candles, and a warm hearth, the Grille is the nicest eatery in town. Lunch here is an anything-goes affair, ranging from soups, sandwiches, and large salads to charbroiled burgers and hearty omelets. Dinner features grilled and broiled meats, seafood, and prime rib. I'm partial to delectable appetizers like baked brie with apples and mustard sauce, Baja-style shrimp cocktail, and "Prime tickler" (chunks of prime rib served cocktail-style *au jus* with horseradish sauce). Dinners include soup or salad, hot rolls, potatoes, and a vegetable.

2224 Main St. (at A St.). ℂ 760/765-0173. Reservations required Fri–Sun. Main courses $13–$21. AE, MC, V. Daily 11am–3pm; Tues–Sun 5–9pm.

Romano's Dodge House ☞ ITALIAN   Occupying a historic home just off Main Street (vintage photos illustrate the little farmhouse's past), Romano's is proudly the only restaurant in town not serving apple pie. It's a home-style Italian spot, with red-checked tablecloths and straw-clad Chianti bottles. Romano's offers individual lunch pizzas, pastas bathed in rich marinara sauce, veal parmigiana, chicken cacciatore, and the signature dish, pork Juliana (loin chops in a whisky-apple cider sauce). There's seating on a narrow shaded porch, in the wood-plank dining room, and in a little saloon in back.

2718 B St. (just off Main). ℂ 760/765-1003. www.romanosjulian.com. Reservations required for dinner Fri–Sat, recommended other nights. Main courses $8–$16. No credit cards. Wed–Mon 11am–8:30pm.

JULIAN AFTER DARK

Fans of old-style dinner theater will feel right at home at **Pine Hills Dinner Theater** (ℂ 760/765-1100), one of North County's more unusual entertainment options for a Friday or Saturday night. Located at the **Pine Hills Lodge,** 2960 La Posada Way (about 2 miles/3km from Julian off Pine Hills Rd.), the theater has staged more than 80 productions since opening in 1980 in this rustic 1912 building. Theater is usually light and comedic—past productions include *I'm Not Rappaport* and *Last of the Red Hot Lovers*—but in contrast, dinner is a filling buffet of barbecued baby-back pork ribs, baked chicken, baked beans, salads, veggies, and thick sheepherder's bread. With advance notice, the kitchen will prepare a vegetarian meal or accommodate other dietary restrictions. Dinner is at 7pm, curtain is 8pm, and the combined ticket costs $28.50 (show only is $14.50).

6 Anza-Borrego Desert State Park

90 miles (145km) NE of San Diego; 35 miles (56km) E of Julian

The sweeping 600,000-acre Anza-Borrego Desert State Park, the nation's largest contiguous state park, lies mostly within San Diego County, and getting there is as much fun as being there. From Julian, the first 20 minutes of the winding hour-long drive feel as if you're going straight downhill; in fact, it's a 7-mile-long (11km) drop called Banner Grade. A famous scene from the 1954 movie *The Long, Long Trailer* with Lucille Ball and Desi Arnaz was shot on the Banner Grade, and countless Westerns have been filmed in the Anza-Borrego Desert.

The desert is home to fossils and rocks dating from 540 million years ago; human beings arrived only 10,000 years ago. The terrain ranges in elevation from 15 feet (4.5m) to more than 6,000 feet (1,800m) above sea level. It incorporates dry lake beds, sandstone canyons, granite mountains, palm groves fed by year-round springs, and more than 600 kinds of desert plants. After the spring rains, thousands of wildflowers burst into bloom, transforming the desert into a brilliant palette of pink, lavender, red, orange, and yellow. The rare bighorn sheep can often be spotted navigating rocky hillsides, and an occasional migratory bird stops off on the way to the Salton Sea. A sense of timelessness pervades this landscape; travelers tend to slow down and take a long look around.

Many people also visit the park without caring a bit for desert flora and fauna. They're here to relax and sun themselves in tiny Borrego Springs, a city surrounded by the state park but exempt from regulations limiting commercial development. It is, however, somewhat remote, and its supporters proudly proclaim that Borrego Springs is and will remain what Palm Springs used to be—a small, charming resort town, with more empty lots than built ones. Yes, there are a couple country clubs, some chic fairway-view homes, a luxurious resort, and a regular influx of celebrity vacationers, but it's still plenty funky. One of the valley's unusual sights is scattered patches of tall, lush palm tree groves, perfectly square in shape: Borrego Springs' tree farms are a major source of landscaping trees for San Diego and surrounding counties.

When planning a trip here, keep in mind that temperatures rise to as high as 115° in summer.

ESSENTIALS

GETTING THERE   Anza-Borrego Desert State Park is about a 2-hour drive from San Diego. The fastest route is I-15 north to the Poway exit, then Highway 78 east at Ramona, continuing to Julian and on to the desert. Highway 79 to county roads S2 and S22 will also get you there. Another option is to take I-8 to Ocotillo, then Highway S2 north. Follow the Southern Overland Stage Route of 1849 (be sure to stop and notice the view at the Carrizo Badlands Overlook) to S3 east into Borrego Springs.

GETTING AROUND   You don't need a four-wheel-drive vehicle to tour the desert, but you'll probably want to get off the main highways and onto the Jeep trails. The Anza-Borrego Desert State Park Visitor Center staff (see below) can tell you which Jeep trails are in condition for two-wheel-drive vehicles. You can also call © 760/767-ROAD for information on Borrego Springs road conditions. There's a $5 fee per vehicle per day for a Back Country Permit, which is required to camp or use the Jeep trails in the park. You can also explore with Desert Jeep Tours (see below). The Ocotillo Wells area of the park has been set aside for off-road vehicles such as dune buggies and dirt bikes. To use the Jeep trails, a vehicle has to be licensed for highway use.

Another good way to see the desert is to tour on a bicycle. Call **Carrizo Bikes** (© 760/767-3872) and talk with Dan Cain (a true desert rat) about bike rentals and tours in the area.

ORIENTATION & VISITOR INFORMATION   In Borrego Springs, the Mall is on Palm Canyon Drive, the main drag. Christmas Circle surrounds a grassy park at the entry to town. The **Anza-Borrego Desert State Park Visitor Center** (© 760/767-4205 or 760/767-4684 for recorded wildflower information in season; www.anzaborrego.statepark.org) lies just west of the town of Borrego Springs. It supplies information, maps, and two 15-minute audiovisual presentations, one on the desert's changing faces and the other on wildflowers.

Fun Fact The Desert in Bloom

From mid-March to the beginning of April, the desert wildflowers and cacti are usually in bloom—a hands-down, all-out natural special event that's not to be missed. It's so incredible, there's a hot line to let you know exactly when the blossoms burst forth: © 760/767-4684.

The Visitor Center is open October through May daily from 9am to 5pm, June through September weekends from 10am to 5pm. You should also stop into the brand-new **Desert Natural History Association,** 652 Palm Canyon Dr. (© 760/767-3098; www.abdnha.org), whose sleek Desert Discovery Store features an impressive selection of guidebooks, historical resources, educational materials for kids, native plants and regional crafts, and a minimuseum display that includes a frighteningly real taxidermied bobcat. This is also your best source for information on the nearby Salton Sea.

For information on lodging, dining, and activities, contact the **Borrego Springs Chamber of Commerce,** 786 Palm Canyon Dr., Borrego Springs, CA 92004 (© **800/559-5524** or 760/767-5555; www.borregosprings.org).

EXPLORING THE DESERT

Remember that when you're touring in this area, hydration is of paramount importance. Whether you're walking, cycling, or driving, always have a bottle of water at your side.

You can explore the desert's stark terrain on one of its trails or on a self-guided driving tour; the Visitor Center can supply maps. For starters, the **Borrego Palm Canyon self-guided hike** (1½ miles/2.5km each way) starts at the campgrounds near the Visitor Center. It is beautiful, easy to get to, and easy to do, leading to a waterfall and massive fan palms in about half an hour. It's grand for photos early in the morning.

You can also take a guided off-road tour of the desert with **Desert Jeep Tours** (© **888/BY-JEEPS;** www.desertjeeptours.com). View spectacular canyons, fossil beds, ancient Native American sites, caves, and more in excursions by desert denizen Paul Ford ("Borrego Paul"). Tours go to the awesome view point at Font's Point, where you can look out on the Badlands—named by the early settlers because it was an impossible area for moving or grazing cattle. Along the way, you'll learn about the history and geology of the area. Tours include drinks, snacks, and pickup at any Borrego Springs lodgings; prices range from $59 to $99 per person.

Note: Whether you tour with Desert Jeep Tours or on your own, don't miss the sunset view from Font's Point. Savvy travelers plan ahead and bring champagne and beach chairs for the nightly ritual.

If you have only one day, a good day trip from San Diego would include driving over on one route, going to the Visitor Center, hiking to Palm Canyon, having a picnic, and driving back to San Diego using another route.

GOLF & HIKING

Golfers will be content on the 18-hole, par-72 championship golf course at **Ram's Hill Country Club** (© **760/767-5124;** www.ramshill.com), on Yaqui Pass Road just south of La Casa del Zorro. The 6,886-yard course has seven artificial lakes, and the weekend greens fee is $105. For a thrilling 12-mile (19km) bicycle ride down Montezuma Valley Grade, try the Desert Descent offered by **Gravity Activated Sports,** P.O. Box 683, Pauma Valley, CA 92061 (© 800/ 985-4427 or 760/742-2294; fax 760/742-2293; www.gasports.com). See "Biking" in chapter 7.

WHERE TO STAY

Borrego Springs is small, but there are enough accommodations to suit all travel styles and budgets. Other decent options include **Palm Canyon Resort,** 221 Palm Canyon Dr. (© **800/242-0044** or 760/767-5341), a large complex that includes a moderately priced hotel, RV park, restaurant, and recreational facilities; and, **Borrego Valley Inn,** 405 Palm Canyon Dr. (© **800/333-5810** or 760/767-0311; www.borregovalleyinn.com), a newly built Southwestern complex featuring sand-colored pueblo-style rooms and upscale bed-and-breakfast amenities. Camping in the desert is a meditative experience, to be sure; but, if you truly want to splurge, you can do that too.

La Casa del Zorro Desert Resort ⭐⭐   This pocket of heaven on earth was built in 1937, and the tamarisk trees that were planted then have grown up around it. So have the many charming tile-roofed *casitas,* originally neighboring homes bought by the resort's longtime owners, San Diego's Copley newspaper family. Over time the property has grown into a cohesive blend of discreetly private cottages and luxurious two-story hotel buildings—each blessed with personalized service and unwavering standards—that make La Casa del Zorro unequaled in Borrego Springs. Courtesy carts ferry you around the lushly planted grounds, and to the resort's stunning new pool area by the resurfaced tennis courts. It's easy to understand why repeat guests book their favorite *casita* year after year; some have a fireplace or pool, every bedroom has a separate bathroom, and they all have minifridges and microwaves (though a lack of dishes and utensils is calculated to get you into the Spanish-style main lodge's fine dining room). Outdoor diversions include horseshoes, Ping-Pong, volleyball, jogging trails, basketball, shuffleboard, and a life-size chess set. By the way, *zorro* means fox, and you'll find subtle fox motifs throughout the property.

3845 Yaqui Pass Rd., Borrego Springs, CA 92004. © 800/824-1884 or 760/767-5323. Fax 760/767-5963. www.lacasadelzorro.com. 77 units. $225–$380 double, *casitas* from $250 peak season (mid-Jan to mid-May); $175–$300 double, casitas from $200 off-peak. Extra person $10. Off-season and midweek discounts based on occupancy. Tennis, jazz, holiday, and other packages available. AE, DC, DISC, MC, V. **Amenities:** Restaurant (men are required to wear a jacket and a collared shirt at dinner Oct–May); lounge; 5 outdoor pools; 9-hole putting green; 6 tennis courts; health club and spa; 2 whirlpools; bike rental; activities desk; courtesy car to golf; business center; salon; room service (7am–11pm); in-room massage; babysitting. *In room:* A/C, TV/VCR w/pay movies, dataport, minibar, coffeemaker, hair dryer, iron.

The Palms at Indian Head ⭐⭐ *(Finds)*   It takes a sense of nostalgia and an active imagination for most visitors to truly appreciate Borrego Springs' only bed-and-breakfast. Its fervent owners, David and Cynthia Leibert, are slowly renovating the once-chic resort. Originally opened in 1947, then rebuilt after a fire in 1958, the Art Deco–style hilltop lodge was a favorite hideaway for San Diego's and Hollywood's elite. It played host to movie stars like Bing Crosby, Clark Gable, and Marilyn Monroe. The Leiberts rescued it from extreme disrepair in 1993, clearing away some dilapidated guest bungalows and uncovering original wallpaper, light fixtures, and priceless memorabilia. As soon as they'd restored several rooms in luxurious Southwestern style, they began taking in guests to help finance the ongoing restoration.

Now up to 10 rooms, the inn also boasts a restaurant, the Krazy Coyote (see "Where to Dine," below), that's a culinary breath of fresh air in town. Also completely restored is the 42-by-109-foot (13m-by-33m) pool, soon to be joined by the original subterranean grotto bar behind viewing windows at the deep end. The inn occupies the most envied site in the valley—shaded by palms, adjacent to the state park, with a panoramic view across the entire Anza-Borrego region. A hiking trail begins just steps from the hotel. If you don't mind getting an insider's view of this work-in-progress, the Palms at Indian Head rewards you with charm, comfort, and convenience.

2220 Hoberg Rd. (P.O. Box 525), Borrego Springs, CA 92004. ✆ **800/519-2624** or 760/767-7788. Fax 760/767-9717. www.thepalmsatindianhead.com. 10 units. $105–$159 double Nov–May, $95 June–Oct. Extra person $20. Midweek discounts available. DC, DISC, MC, V. Take S22 into Borrego Springs; at Palm Canyon Dr., S22 becomes Hoberg Rd. Continue north ½ mile (1km). **Amenities:** Restaurant; bar; fantastic outdoor pool; room service (8am–8pm); in-room massage; laundry service. *In room:* A/C, TV, fridge, coffeemaker.

CAMPING

The park has two developed campgrounds. **Borrego Palm Canyon,** with 117 sites, is 2½ miles (4km) west of Borrego Springs, near the Visitor Center. Full hookups are available, and there's an easy hiking trail. **Tamarisk Grove,** at Highway 78 and county road S3, has 27 sites. The overnight rate at both is $10 to $15. Both have restrooms with showers and a campfire program; reservations are a good idea. The park allows open camping along all trail routes. For more information, check with the Visitor Center (✆ **760/767-4205**).

WHERE TO DINE

Pickings are slim in Borrego Springs, but we're happy to report an influx of younger, city-savvy residents (OK, maybe just two or three) has helped round things out. Your best bet—if you're not willing to break the bank at La Casa del Zorro's classy but pricey dining room—is still the surprisingly good **Krazy Coyote,** which presents trendy ingredients and gourmet preparations previously unheard of in this small town. One welcome newcomer is the **Badlands Market & Cafe,** 561 Palm Canyon Dr. (in the Mall; ✆ 760/767-4058), which offers a daily board of gourmet light meals, plus a prepared foods deli and store that features imported mustards, marinated sun-dried tomatoes, delicate desserts, and other sophisticated treats. Or you could follow legions of locals into the downtown mainstay **Carlee's Place,** 670 Palm Canyon Dr. (✆ 760/767-3262), a casual bar and grill with plenty of neon beer signs, well-worn pool table, and fuzzy-sounding jukebox. It's easy to understand why Carlee's is the watering hole of choice for motorcycle brigades that pass through town on recreational rides—and the food is tasty, hearty, and priced just right.

Kendall's Cafe COFFEE SHOP   Here's an economical little spot to grab a quick bite. Emu burgers from the local emu and ostrich farm are the specialty of the house. Buffalo burgers and Mexican dishes are also popular. Dinner choices include pork chops and chicken-fried steak. The cafe claims its apple pies are better than Julian's. Anything can be packed to go if you'd rather dine overlooking the desert.

In the Mall, Borrego Springs. ✆ 760/767-3491. Lunch $3.50–$7.95; dinner $5.95–$10.95. MC, V. Sept–May daily 6am–8pm; June–Aug Thurs–Mon 6am–8pm.

Krazy Coyote Saloon & Grille ⚘ ECLECTIC MENU   The same style and perfectionism that pervades David and Cynthia Leibert's bed-and-breakfast is evident in this casual restaurant, which overlooks the inn's swimming pool and the vast desert beyond. An eclectic menu encompasses quesadillas, club sandwiches, burgers, grilled meats and fish, and individual gourmet pizzas. The Krazy Coyote also offers breakfast (rich and hearty for an active day, or light and healthy for diet-watchers). The evening ambience is welcoming and romantic, as the sparse lights of tiny Borrego Springs twinkle on the desert floor below.

In the Palms at Indian Head, 2220 Hoberg Rd. © **760/767-7788.** Lunch $7.50–$12; dinner $10–$22. AE, MC, V. Open daily; call for seasonal hours.

7 Tijuana: Going South of the Border

16 miles (26km) S of San Diego

Like many large cities in developing nations, Tijuana is a mixture of new and old, rich and poor, modern and traditional. With almost 1.8 million people, it's the second-largest city on the west coast of North America; only Los Angeles is larger. The Mexico you may be expecting—charming town squares and churches, women in colorful embroidered skirts and blouses, bougainvillea spilling out of every orifice—can be found in southern Baja California and even more so in the interior, in places such as San Miguel de Allende and Guanajuato. But that's another trip, and a different guidebook.

What you'll find in Tijuana is poverty—begging in the streets is common—sanitary conditions that may make you nervous, and, surprisingly, a local populace that seems no more or less happy than its north-of-the-border counterparts.

If you're spending a few days or more in Baja, refer to "Baja California: Exploring More of Mexico," later in this chapter.

ESSENTIALS

GETTING THERE   If you plan to visit only Tijuana, I recommend leaving the car behind, because the traffic can be challenging. However, bus tours only give you several hours in Tijuana in the afternoon, so you miss evening activities. Another alternative is walking across the border; you can park in one of the safe long-term parking lots on the San Diego side for about $8 a day, or take the San Diego Trolley to the border. Once you're in Tijuana, it's easier to get around by taxi than to fight the local drivers. Cab fares from the border to downtown Tijuana run about $5.

If you plan to visit the Baja Peninsula south of Tijuana, I suggest driving. Take I-5 south to the Mexican border at San Ysidro. The drive takes about half an hour.

Many car-rental companies in San Diego now allow their cars to be driven into Baja California, at least as far as Ensenada. **Avis** (© **619/231-7155**) and **Courtesy** (© **619/497-4800**) cars may be driven as far as the 28th parallel and Guerrero Negro, which separates Baja into two states, North and South. **Bob Baker Ford** (© **619/297-5001**) and **Colonial Ford** (© **619/477-9344**) allow their cars to be driven the entire 1,000-mile (1,610km) stretch of the Baja Peninsula.

Keep in mind that if you drive in, you'll need Mexican auto insurance in addition to your own. You can get it in San Ysidro, just north of the border at the San Ysidro exit; from your car-rental agency in San Diego; or from a AAA office if you're a member.

Another easy way to get to Tijuana from downtown San Diego is to hop aboard the bright-red **trolley** headed for San Ysidro and get off at the last, or San Ysidro, stop (it's nicknamed the Tijuana Trolley for good reason). From there, just follow the signs to walk across the border. It's simple, quick, and inexpensive; the one-way trolley fare is $2.50. The last trolley to San Ysidro departs downtown around midnight; the last returning trolley from San Ysidro is at 1am. On Saturday, the trolley runs 24 hours.

Mexicoach/Five Star Tours (© 619/232-5049; fax 619/4575-3075) offers a $2 round-trip fare (children under 5 free) between the border parking lots and trolley stop and downtown Tijuana, with departures every 15 minutes. The Mexicoach stop is at the Tijuana Tourist Terminal, 1025 Av. Revolución (between calles 6 and 7).

Gray Line (© 619/491-0011) offers a tour to Tijuana for $26, $36 with lunch, with a drop-off in the middle of town; you can spend a few hours or all day. **Contact Tours** (© 800/235-5393 or 619/477-8687; www.contactours. com) also offers a tour to Tijuana for $26.

GETTING AROUND   If you've come to Tijuana on the San Diego Trolley or if you leave a car on the U.S. side of the border, you will walk through the border crossing. The first structure you'll see on your left is a Visitor Information Center, open daily from 9am to 7pm; ask for a copy of the *Baja Visitor* magazine and the *Baja Times*. From here, you can easily walk into the center of town or take a taxi.

Taxicabs are easy to find; they queue up around most of the visitor hot spots, and drivers often solicit passengers. It's customary to agree upon the rate before stepping into the cab, whether you're going a few blocks or hiring a cab for the afternoon. One-way rides within the city cost $4 to $8, and tipping is optional. Some cabs are "local" taxis, frequently stopping to take on or let off other passengers during your ride; they are less expensive than private cabs.

VISITOR INFORMATION   Before your visit, you can request information, brochures, and maps from **Baja California Tourism Information,** 7860 Mission Center Court #202, San Diego, CA 92108 (© 800/522-1516 in California, Arizona, or Nevada; 800/225-2786 in the rest of the U.S. and Canada; or 619/299-8518). Its office—in Mission Valley—is open Monday through Friday.

Once in Tijuana, you can pick up visitor information at the **Mexican Tourism Office** (© 011-52-664/688-0555), which opens daily at 9am, and the **National Chamber of Commerce** (© 011-52-664/685-8472), open weekdays only. Both have offices at the corner of Avenida Revolución and Calle 1 (*calle* is "street" in Spanish), and are extremely helpful with maps and orientation, local events of interest, and accommodations.

The Mexican Tourism Office provides legal assistance for visitors who encounter problems while in Tijuana. The following countries have consulate offices in Tijuana: the **United States** (© 011-52-664/681-7400), **Canada** (© 011-52-664/684-0461), and the **United Kingdom** (© 011-52-664/681-7323 or 6-5320).

You can also get a preview of events, restaurants, and more online at **www.seetijuana.com** and **www.bajatouristguide.com**.

SOME HELPFUL TIPS   The city does not take time for an afternoon siesta; you'll always find shops and restaurants open, as well as people in the streets, which are safe for walking. (Observe the same precautions you would in any large city.) Most people who deal with the traveling public speak English, often very well. To maneuver around someone on a crowded street or in a shop, say *con permiso* ("with permission").

Tijuana

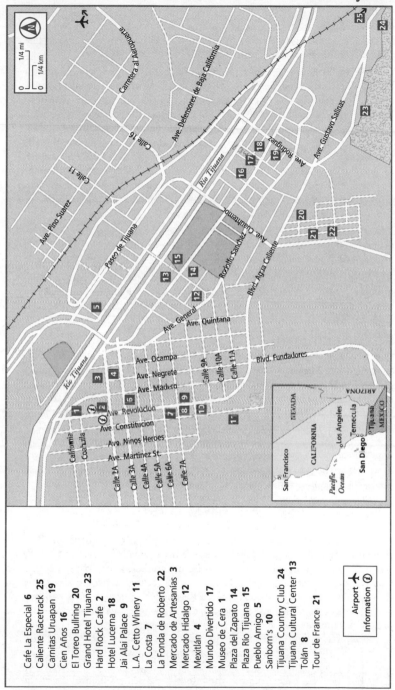

Cafe La Especial 6
Caliente Racetrack 25
Carnitas Uruapan 19
Cien Años 16
El Toreo Bullring 20
Grand Hotel Tijuana 23
Hard Rock Cafe 2
Hotel Lucerna 18
Jai Alai Palace 9
L.A. Cetto Winery 11
La Costa 7
La Fonda de Roberto 22
Mercado de Artesanías 3
Mercado Hidalgo 12
Mexitlán 4
Mundo Divertido 17
Museo de Cera 1
Plaza del Zapato 14
Plaza Río Tijuana 15
Pueblo Amigo 5
Sanborn's 10
Tijuana Country Club 24
Tijuana Cultural Center 13
Tolán 8
Tour de France 21

Airport ✈
Information ⓘ

259

CLIMATE & WEATHER   Tijuana's climate is similar to San Diego's. Don't expect sweltering heat just because you're south of the border, and remember that the Pacific waters won't be much warmer than those off San Diego. The first beaches you'll find are about 15 miles (24km) south of Tijuana.

CURRENCY   The Mexican currency is the peso, but you can easily visit Tijuana (or Rosarito and Ensenada, for that matter) without changing money— dollars are accepted just about everywhere. Many prices are posted in American (indicated with the abbreviation "dlls.") and Mexican ("m.n." *moneda nacional*) currencies—both use the "$" sign. Bring a supply of smaller-denomination ($1, $5, and $10) bills; although change is readily given in American dollars, many merchants are reluctant to break a $20 bill for small purchases. Visa is accepted in many places, but some places will only grudgingly take your card; don't be surprised if the clerk scrutinizes your signature and photo ID. When using credit cards at restaurants, it's a nice gesture to leave the tip in cash. At press time, the dollar was strong, worth between 9 and 10 pesos.

TAXES & TIPPING   A sales tax of 10%, called an IVA, is added to most bills, including those in restaurants. This does not represent the tip; the bill will read *IVA incluído,* but you should add about 15% for the tip if the service warrants.

TELEPHONES   To call Mexico from the United States, after dialing "011" for an international line, dial "52" (the country code), then the three-digit city code (indicated in the listings in front of the slash), followed by the five-digit local number.

EXPLORING TIJUANA

One of the first major tourist attractions below the border is also one of the strangest—the **Museo de Cera** ("Wax Museum"), Calle 1 between avenidas Revolución and Madero (℃ **011-52-664/688-2478**). Come to think of it, what wax museum isn't strange? But that doesn't explain the presence of Whoopi Goldberg, Laurel and Hardy, and Bill Clinton in an exhibit otherwise dominated by figures from Mexican history. If you aren't spooked by the not-so-life-like figures of Aztec warriors, brown-robed friars, Spanish princes, and 20th-century military leaders (all posed in period dioramas), step into the Chamber of Horrors, where wax werewolves and sinister sadists lurk in the shadows. When the museum is mostly empty, which is most of the time, the dramatically lit Chamber of Horrors can be a little creepy. This side-street freak show is open daily from 10am to 8pm; admission is $1.

For many visitors, Tijuana's main event is bustling **Avenida Revolución,** the street whose reputation precedes it. Beginning in the 1920s, American college students, servicemen, and hedonistic tourists discovered this street as a bawdy center for illicit fun. Some of the original attraction has fallen by the wayside: Gambling was outlawed in the 1930s, back-alley cockfights are also illegal, and the same civic improvements that repaved Revolución to provide trees, benches, and wider sidewalks vanquished the girlie shows whose barkers once accosted passersby. Drinking and shopping are the main order of business these days. While youngsters from across the border knock back tequila shooters and dangle precariously at the upstairs railings of glaring neon discos, bargain hunters peruse the never-ending array of goods (and not-so-goods) for sale. You'll find the action between calles 1 and 9; the information centers (above) are at the north end, and the landmark Jai Alai Palace anchors the southern portion. To help make sense of the tchotchkes, see "Shopping in Tijuana," below.

Visitors can be easily seduced, then quickly repulsed, by tourist-trap areas like Avenida Revolución, but it's important to remember there's more to Tijuana than American tourism. Tijuana's population, currently around 1.8 million, makes it the fourth-largest city in Mexico. While many residents live in poverty-ridden shantytowns (you can see these *colonias* spread across the low hills surrounding the city), Tijuana has a lower unemployment rate than neighboring San Diego County, thanks to the rise in *maquiladoras*. They are foreign-owned manufacturing operations that continue to proliferate under NAFTA (the North American Free Trade Agreement). High-rise office buildings testify to increased prosperity and the rise of a white-collar middle class, whose members shop at modern shopping centers away from the tourist zone. And there's tourism from elsewhere in northern Mexico; visitors are drawn by the availability of imported goods and the lure of the big city experience.

If you're looking to see a different side of Tijuana, the best place to start is the **Centro Cultural Tijuana,** Paseo de los Héroes, at Avenida Independencia (✆ 011-52-664/684-1111). You'll easily spot the ultramodern Tijuana Cultural Center complex, designed by irrepressible modern architect Pedro Ramírez Vásquez. Its centerpiece is a gigantic sand-colored dome that houses an OMNI-MAX theater, which screens two different 45-minute films (subjects range from science to space travel). Each has one English-language show per day. Inside, the center houses the museum's permanent collection of Mexican artifacts from pre-Hispanic times through the modern political era, plus a gallery for visiting exhibits. They have included everything from the works of Diego Rivera to a disturbing, well-curated exhibit chronicling torture and human-rights violations through the ages. Music, theater, and dance performances are held in the center's concert hall and courtyard, and there's a cafe and an excellent museum bookshop. The center is open daily from 9am to 8:30pm; admission to the museum's permanent exhibits is free, there's a $2 charge for the special event gallery, and tickets for OMNIMAX films are $4 for adults and $2.50 for children.

Don't be discouraged if the Tijuana Cultural Center sounds like a field trip for schoolchildren; it's a must-see on my list, if only to drag you away from tourist kitsch and into the more sophisticated Zona Río (river area). While there, stop to admire the wide, European-style **Paseo de los Héroes**. The boulevard's intersections are marked by gigantic traffic circles (*glorietas*), at the center of which stand statuesque monuments to leaders ranging from Aztec Emperor Cuauhtémoc to Abraham Lincoln. Navigating the congested *glorietas* will require your undivided attention, so it's best to pull over to admire the monuments. In the Zona Río you'll find some classier shopping and a colorful local marketplace, plus the ultimate kid destination, **Mundo Divertido,** Paseo de los Héroes at Calle José Maria Velasco (✆ 011-52-664/634-3213). Literally translated, it means "world of amusement," and one parent described it as the Mexican equivalent of "a Chuck E. Cheese restaurant built inside a Malibu Grand Prix." You get the idea—noisy and frenetic, it's the kind of place kids dream about. Let them choose from miniature golf, batting cages, a roller coaster, a kid-size train, a video game parlor, and go-carts. There's a food court with tacos and hamburgers; if you're in luck, the picnic area will be festooned with streamers and piñatas for some happy tyke's birthday party. The park is open daily, from around 11am to 10pm. Admission is free, and several booths inside sell tickets for the rides.

Tijuana's most unusual attraction is **Mexitlán,** Calle 2 at Avenida Ocampo (✆ 011-52-664/638-4101). Built on the roof of a parking structure, it's an open-air museum with 200 scaled-down replicas of Mexico's most famous buildings throughout history. The exhibit represents, in exacting detail, everything from pre-Columbian pyramids to Mexico City's opulent 19th-century cathedrals and grand plazas, from the 1968 Olympic Stadium (complete down to the Diego Rivera mosaic on one side) to a topographically correct representation of coastal landmarks. Opened in 1990 to great fanfare, the complex originally included restaurants and gift shops, but hasn't been drawing the crowds envisioned by its ambitious designers (including contemporary architect Pedro Ramírez Vásquez, whose work is amply represented). As a result, some of the exhibit is looking a little worn; still, this "Mexico-land" is awfully fun to see, especially for kids (and former kids) fascinated by miniatures. Mexitlán is open Tuesday through Sunday, and admission is $1.25 per person. Because it faces an uncertain future, including the possibility of being moved to Mexico City, I recommend you call to verify schedule information.

The fertile valleys of Northern Baja produce most of Mexico's wine, and export many high-quality vintages to Europe; they're unavailable in the United States. For an introduction to Mexican wines, stop into **Cava de Vinos L. A. Cetto** (L. A. Cetto Winery), Av. Cañón Johnson 2108, at Avenida Constitución Sur (© **011-52-664/685-3031**). Shaped like a wine barrel, the building's striking facade is made from old oak aging barrels in an inspired bit of recycling. In the entrance stand a couple of wine presses (dating from 1928) that Don Angel Cetto used in the early days of production. His family still runs the winery, which opened this impressive visitor center in 1993. L. A. Cetto bottles both red and white wines, some of them award winners, including petite sirah, nebbiolo, and Cabernet Sauvignon. Most bottles cost about $5; the special reserves are a little more than $10. The company also produces tequila, brandy, and olive oil, all for sale here. Admission is $2 for tour and tastings (for those 18 and over only; kids under 18 are admitted free with an adult but cannot taste the wines), $3 with souvenir wine glass. Open Monday through Saturday, 9:30am to 6:30pm.

SHOPPING IN TIJUANA

Tijuana's biggest attraction is shopping—ask any of the 44 million people who cross the border each year to do it. They come to take advantage of reasonable prices on a variety of merchandise: terra-cotta and colorfully glazed pottery, woven blankets and serapes, embroidered dresses and sequined sombreros, onyx chess sets, beaded necklaces and bracelets, silver jewelry, leather bags and *huarache* sandals, "rain sticks" (bamboo branches filled with pebbles that simulate the patter of raindrops), hammered tin picture frames, thick drinking glasses, novelty swizzle sticks, Cuban cigars, and Mexican liquors like Kahlúa

---

Fun Fact **First Crush: The Annual Harvest Festival**

If you enjoyed a visit to Tijuana's winery (or Ensenada's Bodegas de Santo Tomás), you might want to come back for the festive harvest celebration held each year in late August or early September. In the endless vineyards of the fertile Guadalupe Valley, the day's events include the traditional blessing of the grapes, wine tastings, live music and dancing, riding exhibitions, and a country-style Mexican meal. **L. A. Cetto** offers a group excursion from Tijuana (about an hour's drive); San Diego's **Baja California Tours** (© **619/454-7166**) also organizes a day-long trip from San Diego.

and tequila. You're permitted to bring $400 worth of purchases back across the border (sorry, no Cuban cigars allowed), including 1 liter of alcohol per person (for adults 21 and older).

When most people think of Tijuana, they picture **Avenida Revolución,** which appears to exist solely for the extraction of dollars from American visitors. Dedicated shoppers quickly discover most of the curios spilling out onto the sidewalk look alike, despite the determined sellers' assurances that their wares are the best in town. Browse for comparison's sake, but duck into one of the many *pasajes,* or passageway arcades, for the best souvenir shopping. There, you'll find items of a slightly better quality and merchants willing to bargain. Some of the most enjoyable *pasajes* are on the east side of the street between calles 2 and 5; they also provide a pleasant respite from the quickly irritating tumult of Avenida Revolución.

An alternative is to visit **Sanborn's,** Avenida Revolución between calles 8 and 9 (© 011-52-663/688-1462), a branch of the Mexico City department store long favored by American travelers. It sells an array of regional folk art and souvenirs, books about Mexico in Spanish and English, and candies and bakery treats. You can have breakfast in the sunny cafe.

One of the few places in Tijuana to find better-quality crafts from a variety of Mexican states is **Tolán,** Avenida Revolución between calles 7 and 8 (© 011-52-664/688-3637). In addition to the obligatory selection of standard souvenirs, you'll find blue glassware from Guadalajara, glazed pottery from Tlaquepaque, crafts from the Oaxaca countryside, and distinctive tile work from Puebla. Prices at Tolán are fixed, so you shouldn't try to bargain the way you can in some of the smaller shops and stands.

If a marketplace atmosphere and spirited bargaining are what you're looking for, head to **Mercado de Artesanías (Crafts Market),** Calle 2 and Avenida Negrete. Vendors of pottery, clayware, clothing, and other crafts fill an entire city block.

Shopping malls are as common in Tijuana as in any big American city; you shouldn't expect to find typical souvenirs, but shopping alongside residents and other intrepid visitors is often more fun than feeling like a sitting-duck tourist. One of the biggest, and most convenient, is **Plaza Río Tijuana** (on Paseo de los Héroes at Av. Independencia). It's an outdoor plaza, anchored by several department stores, that features dozens of specialty shops and casual restaurants.

If you have a sweet tooth, seek out **Suzett** bakery, tucked in a corner behind **Comercial Mexicana,** which is kind of a Mexican Target with a full grocery store. At Suzett, grab a tray and a pair of tongs, and stroll through aisles of industrial bakery carts stacked high with fresh-baked breads, pastries, and other sweet treats. All the different shapes and patterns are irresistible; just pluck the ones you want and carry them to the register—a couple of bucks will buy enough for the whole family. *Helpful hint:* Plaza Río Tijuana has ample free parking, and is across the street from the Cultural Center, where private lots charge $5 to $8 to park.

On the other side of Paseo de los Héroes from Plaza Río Tijuana is **Plaza del Zapato,** a two-story indoor mall filled with only shoe (*zapato*) stores. Though most are made with quality leather rather than synthetics, inferior workmanship ensures they'll likely last only a season or two. But with prices as low as $30, why not indulge? Men's styles include dress and casual oxfords and loafers, while women's tend toward casual sandals or traditional pumps. In general, styles tend to mimic current European trends rather than American fashion, and there are almost no athletic shoes.

For a taste of everyday Mexico, visit **Mercado Hidalgo** (1 block west at Av. Sánchez Taboada and Av. Independencia), a busy indoor-outdoor marketplace where vendors display fresh flowers and produce, sacks of dried beans and chilies by the kilo, and a few souvenir crafts, including some excellent piñatas. Morning is the best time to visit the market, and you'll be more comfortable paying with pesos, because most sellers are accustomed to a local crowd.

SPECTATOR SPORTS

If the thrill of athletic prowess and contests lure you, Tijuana is a spectator's (and bettor's) paradise.

BULLFIGHTING While some maintain that this spectacle employs the same cruel disregard for animal rights as the now-illegal cockfights once popular in Tijuana, bullfighting does occupy a prominent place in Mexican heritage. A matador's skill and bravery is closely linked with cultural ideals regarding machismo, and some of the world's best competitors perform at Tijuana's two stadiums. The season runs from May through September, with events held Sunday at 4:30pm. Ticket prices range from $17 to $35 (the premium seats are on the shaded side of the arena). Tickets are for sale at the bullring or in advance from **Five Star Tours** (*©* 619/232-5049). **El Toreo** (*©* 011-52-664/686-1510) is 2 miles (3km) east of downtown on Bulevar Agua Caliente at Avenida Diego Rivera. **Plaza de Toros Monumental,** or Bullring-by-the-Sea (*©* 011-52-664/680-1808), is 6 miles (9.5km) west of downtown on Highway 1-D, before the first toll station. It's perched at the edge of the ocean and the California border.

If you want to catch the bullfights but don't want to drive, **Five Star Tours** (*©* 619/232-5049), based in the San Diego train station, offers bus trips organized around attending the bullfights. It charges $14 round-trip, plus the cost of your bullfight ticket (prices vary). You can easily take a taxi to El Toreo—fares are negotiable, and around $10 one-way should be fair. You can also negotiate a fare to Bullring-by-the-Sea, but fares are unpredictable.

JAI ALAI A lightning-paced ball game played on a slick indoor court, jai alai (pronounced "*high*-ah-lye") is an ancient Basque tradition that incorporates elements of tennis, hockey, and basketball. You can't miss the **Frontón Palacio,** Avenida Revolución at Calle 7; it's a huge, boxlike, arena with baroque adornments in the center of town. Games are held Monday through Saturday at 8pm, with matinees Monday and Friday at noon. General admission is $2, and there are betting windows inside the arena.

GOLF Once the favorite of golfing celebrities and socialites (and a very young Arnold Palmer), staying at the now-defunct Agua Caliente Resort, the **Tijuana Country Club,** Bulevar Agua Caliente at Avenida Gustavo Salinas (*©* 011-52-664/681-7855), is near the Caliente Racetrack and behind the Grand Hotel Tijuana. It's about a 10-minute drive from downtown. The well-maintained course attracts mostly business travelers staying at nearby hotels, many of which offer golf packages (see Grand Hotel Tijuana in "Where to Stay," below). Weekend greens fees are $40, and optional cart rental is $20; if you register a foursome, the group plays for $105, not including carts. Stop by the pro shop for balls, tees, and a limited number of other accessories; the clubhouse also has two restaurants with cocktail lounges.

WHERE TO STAY

When calculating room rates, remember that hotel rates in Tijuana are subject to a 12% tax.

Grand Hotel Tijuana ⭐ You can see the unusually high (32-story) mirrored twin towers of this hotel from all over the city. Modern and sleek, it opened in 1982—the height of Tijuana's prosperity—under the name "Fiesta Americana," a name locals (and many cab drivers) still use. Popular for business travelers, visiting celebrities, and society events, the hotel has the best-maintained public and guest rooms in Tijuana, which helps make up for what it lacks in regional warmth. Rooms have spectacular views of the city from the top floors.

The lobby has dark carpeting and 1980s mirrors and neon accents that feel like a Vegas hotel-casino. It gives way to several ballrooms and an airy atrium that serves elegant international cuisine at dinner and weekend brunch. Next to it is a casual Mexican restaurant; beyond there, the Vegas resemblance resumes with an indoor shopping arcade. Often available is a golf package for around $90 per person—it includes 1 night's lodging with a welcome cocktail and a round of 18 holes (including cart) at the adjacent Tijuana Country Club.

Agua Caliente 4500, Tijuana; (P.O. Box BC), Chula Vista, CA 92012. ✆ 800/GRAND-TJ, or 011-52-664/ 681-7000 in Tijuana. Fax 011-52-664/681-7016. www.grandhoteltijuana.com. 422 units. $90–$150 double; from $180 suite. AE, DC, MC, V. Covered parking $2. **Amenities:** 3 restaurants; 3 bars; outdoor heated pool; tennis courts; whirlpool; sauna; car-rental desk; business center; shopping arcade; 24-hr. room service; in-room massage; babysitting; laundry/dry-cleaning service. *In room:* A/C, TV w/pay movies, minibar.

Hotel Lucerna Once the most chic hotels in Tijuana, the neoclassical Lucerna now offers extremely reliable accommodations with lots of personality. The hotel is in the Zona Río, away from the noise and congestion of downtown, so a quiet night's sleep is easy. It's kept in great shape for the international visitors who enjoy Lucerna's proximity to the financial district, and the staff's friendly and attentive service reflects this clientele. The five-story hotel's rooms all have balconies or patios, but are otherwise unremarkable. Sunday brunch is served outdoors by the swimming pool.

Av. Paseo de los Héroes 10902, Zona Río, Tijuana. ✆ 800/LUCERNA or 011-52-664/634-2000. www.hotel-lucerna.com.mx. 179 units. $80–$140 double; from $145 suite. Extra person $15. AE, DC, MC, V. **Amenities:** 2 restaurants; lounge; outdoor pool; health club; car-rental desk; tour desk; business center; 24-hr. room service; 24-hr. babysitting. *In room:* A/C, TV, dataport, hair dryer.

WHERE TO DINE
EXPENSIVE

If you're interested in haute cuisine, the buzz around Tijuana is all about **Cien Años,** José María Velazco 1407 (✆ **011-52-664/634-3039**). The elegant Zona Río eatery offers artfully blended Mexican flavors (tamarind, poblano chilies, and mango) stylishly presented. It's open daily, and serves lunch beginning at 1pm.

La Costa ⭐ MEXICAN-STYLE SEAFOOD Fish gets top billing here, starting with the hearty seafood soup. There are combination platters of half a grilled lobster, stuffed shrimp, and baked shrimp; fish fillet stuffed with seafood and

---

Tips **Planning Pointer**

This guide uses the term "double" when listing rates, referring to the American concept of "double occupancy." However, in Mexico a single or double room rate refers to beds: A single room has one bed, a double has two, and you pay accordingly. Keep this in mind when making your reservations.

cheese; and, several abalone dishes. La Costa is very popular with San Diegans, and the food lives up to its reputation.

Calle 7, no. 8131 (just off Av. Revolución), Zona Centro. ℂ **011-52-664/685-8494**. fpedrin@telnor.net. Main courses $8–$20. AE, MC, V. Daily 10am–midnight.

Tour de France 𝔊𝔊 FRENCH Martín San Román, Tour de France's chef and co-owner, was sous chef at San Diego's famous Westgate Hotel, then went on to open the top-notch Marius restaurant in the former Le Meridien resort in Coronado. His loyal clientele has followed him from San Diego, and he has acquired new devotees in Tijuana. It's worth a trip to Tijuana just to sample Martín's patés or escargots; the vegetables, prepared and presented with the flair of an artist, all come fresh from local farms. Entree prices include soup and salad. You might try beef tournedos in peppercorn sauce, quail flambéed with cognac, or shrimp in Pernod and garlic sauce. The wine list is extensive and international, and the atmosphere is as fine as the food.

Gobernador Ibarra 252 (on the old road to Ensenada between the Palacio Azteca Hotel and La Sierra Motel). ℂ **011-52-664/681-7542**. Reservations recommended. Main courses $18–$21. AE, MC, V. Mon–Thurs 8am–10:30pm; Fri–Sat 8am–11:30pm.

MODERATE
Hard Rock Cafe AMERICAN/MEXICAN Had an overload of Mexican culture? Looking for a place with all the comforts of home? Head for the Tijuana branch of this ubiquitous watering hole, which promises nothing exotic. It serves the standard Hard Rock chain menu, which admittedly features an outstanding hamburger, in the regulation Hard Rock setting (dark, clubby, walls filled with rock-and-roll memorabilia). While the restaurant's street presence is more subdued than that of most Hard Rock locations, you'll still be able to spot the trademark Caddy emerging from above the door. The restaurant and all its trimmings may have migrated south of the border, but prices are more in line with what you'd see in the United States—and therefore no bargain in competitive Tijuana.

520 Av. Revolución (near Calle 1), Zona Centro. ℂ **011-52-664/685-0206**. Menu items $5–$10. MC, V. Daily 11am–2am.

INEXPENSIVE
Cafe La Especial 𝔊 MEXICAN Tucked away in a shopping *pasaje* at the bottom of some stairs (turn in at the taco stand of the same name), this restaurant is a well-known shopper's refuge. It offers home-style Mexican cooking at reasonable (though not dirt-cheap) prices. The gruff, efficient wait staff carries out platter after platter of *carne asada,* grilled marinated beef served with fresh tortillas, beans, and rice—it's La Especial's most popular item. Traditional dishes like tacos, enchiladas, and burritos round out the menu, augmented by frosty cold Mexican beers.

Av. Revolución 718 (between calles 3 and 4), Zona Centro. ℂ **011-52-664/685-6654**. Menu items $3–$12. Daily 9am–10pm.

Carnitas Uruapan 𝔊 MEXICAN *Carnitas,* a beloved dish in Mexico, consists of marinated pork roasted on a spit until it's falling-apart tender, then served in chunks with tortillas, salsa, cilantro, guacamole, and onions. It's the main attraction at Carnitas Uruapan, where the meat is served by the kilo (or portion thereof) at long, communal wooden tables to a mostly local crowd. The original is a little hard to find, but now there's a branch in the fashionable Zona Río. A half kilo of *carnitas* is plenty for two people, and costs around $12, including beans and that impressive array of condiments. It's a casual feast without compare, but vegetarians need not apply. Another location is on Paseo de los Héroes at Av. Rodríguez (no phone).

Bulevar Díaz Ordáz 550 (across from Plaza Pacífica), La Mesa. (C) 011-52-664/681-6181. Menu items $2.50–$8. No credit cards. Daily 7am–3am. Follow Bulevar Agua Caliente south toward Tecate. It turns into Bulevar Díaz Ordáz, also known as Carretera Tecate and Hwy. 2.

La Fonda de Roberto ★★ MEXICAN Though its location may appear out of the way, this modest restaurant's regular appearances on San Diego "Best Of" lists attest to its appeal. A short drive (or taxi ride) from downtown Tijuana, La Fonda's colorful dining room opens onto the courtyard of a kitschy 1960s motel, complete with retro kidney-shaped swimming pool. The festive atmosphere is perfect for enjoying a variety of regional Mexican dishes, including a decent chicken *mole* and generous portions of *milanesa* (beef, chicken, or pork pounded paper thin, then breaded and fried). A house specialty is *queso fundido*, deep-fried cheese with chilies and mushrooms served with a basket of freshly made corn tortillas.

In the La Sierra Motel, Cuauhtémoc Sur Oeste 2800 (on the old road to Ensenada). (C) 011-52-664/686-4687. Most dishes $5–$11. MC, V. Daily 10am–10pm.

TIJUANA AFTER DARK

Tijuana has several lively discos, and perhaps the most popular is **Baby Rock Discoteca,** 1482 Diego Rivera, Zona Río (© 011-52-664/634-2404). A cousin to Acapulco's lively Baby O, it features everything from jungle rock to hard rock. It's close to the Guadalajara Grill restaurant.

A recent addition to Tijuana's nightlife is "sports bars," cheerful watering holes that feature satellite wagering from all over the United States, as well as from Tijuana's Caliente Racetrack. The most popular bars cluster in **Pueblo Amigo,** Via Oriente and Paseo Tijuana in the Zona Río, a new center designed to resemble a colonial Mexican village. Even if you don't bet on the horses, you can soak up the atmosphere. Two of the town's hottest discos, **Rodeo de Media Noche** (© 011-52-664/682-4967) and **Señor Frogs** (© 011-52-664/682-4962), are also in Pueblo Amigo, as is **La Tablita de Tony** (© 011-52-664/682-8111), an Argentine restaurant. Pueblo Amigo is conveniently located less than 2 miles (3km) from the border, a short taxi ride or—during daylight hours—a pleasant walk.

8 Baja California: Exploring More of Mexico

If you have a car, you can easily venture into Baja California for a getaway of a few days. Since 1991, American car-rental companies have allowed their cars to be driven into Baja. **Avis** (© 619/231-7155), **Courtesy** (© 619/497-4800), and many other rental companies let their cars go as far south as the 28th parallel, the dividing line between the Baja North and Baja South states. **Bob Baker Ford** (© 619/297-5001) and **Colonial Ford** (© 619/477-9344) allow their cars to be driven the entire 1,000-mile (1,610km) stretch of the Baja Peninsula. Whether you drive your own car or a rented one, you'll need Mexican auto insurance in addition to your own; it's available at the border in San Ysidro or through the car-rental companies.

It takes relatively little time to cross the border in Tijuana, but be prepared for a delay of an hour or more on your return to San Diego. If you take local buses down the Baja coast, the delays come en route rather than at the border.

You can also visit Rosarito and Ensenada through a tour. **San Diego Mini Tours** (© **619/477-8687**) makes daily trips.

BAJA ESSENTIALS

See "Essentials" in "Tijuana," earlier in this chapter, for currency and transportation information.

VISITOR INFORMATION   The best source of information is **Baja California Tourism Information** (© **800/522-1516** in California, Arizona, or Nevada; 800/225-2786 in the rest of the U.S. and Canada; or 619/298-4105). This office provides advice and makes hotel reservations throughout Baja California. You can also contact the **Secretaria de Turismo of Baja California,** P.O. Box 2448, Chula Vista, CA 91912 (© **011-52-664/681-9492;** fax 681-9579).

A SUGGESTED ITINERARY   Begin your trip in Tijuana with an afternoon and maybe an overnight stay that includes watching some fast-paced jai alai (see "Spectator Sports," in "Tijuana," above). Then head down the coast to the seaside town of Rosarito Beach, and on to Puerto Nuevo and Ensenada, the third-largest city in Baja.

Two well-maintained roads run between Tijuana and Ensenada: the scenic, coast-hugging toll road (marked *cuota* or 1-D) and the free but slower public road (marked *libre* or 1). I strongly recommend starting out on the toll road, but use the free road along Rosarito Beach—where to exit is readily apparent—so that you can pull on and off easily to shop and look at the view.

Rosarito Beach is 18 miles (29km) from Tijuana; Ensenada is 68 miles (109km) from Tijuana, and 84 miles (135km) from San Diego.

ROSARITO BEACH

Once a tiny resort town that remained a best-kept secret despite its proximity to Tijuana, Rosarito Beach saw an explosion of development in the prosperous 1980s; it's now garish and congested beyond recognition. Why does its popularity persist? Location is one reason—it's the first beach resort town south of the border, and party-minded young people aren't always too discriminating. That should give you an idea of the crowd to expect on holiday weekends and during school breaks.

Reputation is another draw: For years the **Rosarito Beach Hotel** (see "Where to Stay," below) was the preferred hideaway of celebrities and other fashionable Angelinos. Movie star Rita Hayworth and her husband, Prince Aly Khan, vacationed here; Paulette Goddard and Burgess Meredith were married at the resort. Although the hotel's entry still features the gallant inscription *Por esta puerta pasan las mujeres más hermosas del mundo* ("Through this doorway pass the most beautiful women in the world"), today's vacationing starlets are more often found at resorts on Baja's southern tip. While the glimmer (as well as the glamour) has worn off, the Rosarito Beach Hotel is still the most interesting place in town. Nostalgia buffs will want to stop in for a look at some expert tile and woodwork, as well as the panoramic murals throughout the lobby. Check out the colorful Aztec images in the main dining room, the magnificently tiled rest rooms, and the glassed-in bar overlooking the sparkling pool and beach. Or peek into the original owner's mansion, now home to a spa and gourmet restaurant.

Sleepy Rosarito Beach has caught Hollywood's attention for years. Most recently, the megahit *Titanic* was filmed here in Fox Studios' state-of-the-art production facility, boosting the local economy and spearheading an effort to

Upper Baja California

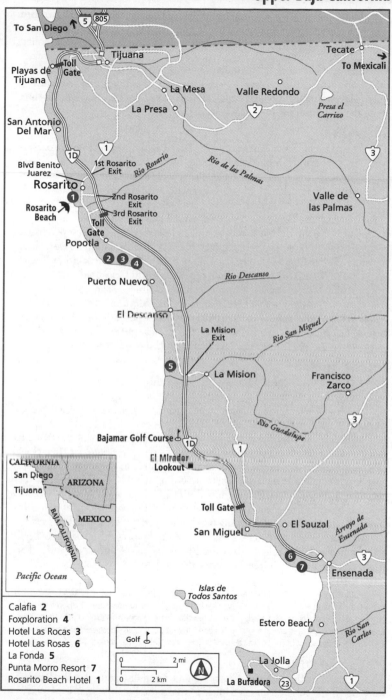

To San Diego
5 805
Tijuana
Playas de
Tijuana
Toll Gate
La Mesa
Valle Redondo
La Presa
2
Presa el Carrizo
San Antonio
Del Mar
1
Tecate
To Mexicali
3
1D
1st Rosarito Exit
Rio Rosario
Rio de las Palmas
Blvd Benito Juarez
Rosarito
1
2nd Rosarito Exit
Valle de las Palmas
Rosarito Beach
3rd Rosarito Exit
Toll Gate
Popotla
2 3 4
Puerto Nuevo
Rio Descanso
El Descanso
La Mision Exit
Rio San Miguel
5
La Mision
Francisco Zarco
3
Rio Guadalupe
Bajamar Golf Course
1D
El Mirador Lookout
1
Toll Gate
San Miguel
El Sauzal
Arroyo de Ensenada
6
7
3
Ensenada
Islas de Todos Santos
Estero Beach
Rio San Carlos
La Jolla
La Bufadora
23
1

CALIFORNIA
San Diego
Tijuana
ARIZONA
MEXICO
BAJA CALIFORNIA
Pacific Ocean

Calafia **2**
Foxploration **4**
Hotel Las Rocas **3**
Hotel Las Rosas **6**
La Fonda **5**
Punta Morro Resort **7**
Rosarito Beach Hotel **1**

Golf

0   2 mi
0   2 km

bring more high-profile (and high-profit) productions across the border. See below for information on Foxploration.

If it's not too crowded, Rosarito is a good place to while away a few hours. Swim or take a horseback ride at the beach, then munch on fish tacos or tamales from any one of a number of family-run stands along **Bulevar Benito Juárez,** the town's main (and only) drag. You can wet your whistle at the local branch of Ensenada's enormously popular **Papas & Beer** (see below), or shop for souvenirs along the Old Ensenada Highway, south of town.

SHOPPING

The dozen or so blocks of Rosarito north of the Rosarito Beach Hotel are packed with the stores typical in Mexican border towns: **curio shops, cigar** and *licores* **(liquor) stores,** and *farmacias* (where drugs like Retin-A, Prozac, Viagra, and Zithromax—all available at low cost and without a prescription—share shelf space with unguents, liniments, and yes, even snake oil).

Rosarito has also become a center for **carved furnishings,** which are plentiful downtown along Bulevar Benito Juárez, and **pottery,** which is best purchased at stands along the old highway south of town. A reliable, but more expensive, furniture shop is **Casa la Carreta,** at Km 29.5 on the old road south of Rosarito (© **011-52-661/612-0502**). You can see plentiful examples of the best workmanship—chests, tables, chairs, headboards, cabinets, and cradles.

For quality **silver jewelry** from Taxco, in the Mexican state of Guerrero, follow the stream of Amex-bearing *Americanos* to **Enrico Sterling,** 890 Bulevar Benito Juárez (© **011-52-661/612-2418**). Enrico carries the cream of the crop—exceptionally artistic creations whose bargain prices belie their quality.

WHERE TO STAY

Rosarito Beach Hotel & Spa 👹   Although this once-glamorous resort has held steady since its heyday, the vestiges of vacationing movie stars and 1930s elegance have been all but eclipsed by the glaring nighttime neon and party-mania that currently define Rosarito. Despite the resort's changed personality, unique features of artistic construction and lavish decoration remain, setting it apart from the rest. You'll pay more for an ocean view, and more for the newer, air-conditioned rooms in the tower (about two-thirds of the units). The older rooms in the poolside building have only ceiling fans, but they prevail in the character department, with hand-painted trim and original tile. The hotel's own pier was recently renovated; it overlooks the beach and has cocktail service. In addition to the wide, family-friendly beach, the hotel has racquetball and tennis courts, and a playground. The stately home of the original owners has been transformed into the full-service Casa Playa Spa, where massages and other treatments are only a smidgen less costly than at home.

Bulevar Benito Juárez, Rosarito, BC, Mexico; P.O. Box 430145, San Diego, CA 92143. © **866/ROSARITO** or 011-52-661/612-0144. Fax 011-52-661/612-1125. www.rosaritobeachhotel.com. 275 units. Sept–June $49–$129 double, July–Aug and U.S. holidays $89–$159 double. Rates include dinner; 2 children under 12 stay free in parents' room, with 3 meals a day for the kids. Spa packages available. MC, V. Free parking. **Amenities:** 2 restaurants; 4 bars; outdoor heated pool; health club; spa; whirlpool; children's summer programs; game room; activities desk; room service (7:30am–10pm); babysitting. *In room:* TV.

WHERE TO DINE

The elegant French restaurant **Chabert's** and the more casual **Azteca Restaurant** are in the Rosarito Beach Hotel. Outside the hotel, a branch of Puerto Nuevo's **Ortega's** on the main drag is the place for lobster. Early risers out for a stroll can munch on fresh, hot tamales, a traditional Mexican breakfast treat sold from sidewalk carts for about 50¢ each.

El Nido 🎭🎭 MEXICAN/STEAKS   One of the first restaurants in Rosarito, El Nido remains popular with visitors unimpressed by the flashier, neon-lit joints that court the college-age set. The setting is Western frontier, complete with candles and rusting wagon wheels; sit outside in the lush enclosed patio, or opt for the dark, cozy interior warmed by a large fireplace and grill. The mesquite fire flavors the grilled steaks and seafood that are El Nido's specialty; the menu also includes free-range (and superfresh) quail and venison from the owner's ranch in the nearby wine country. The generous meals include hearty bean soup, American-style green salad, baked potatoes, and all the fresh tortillas and zesty salsa you can eat.

Bulevar Benito Juárez 67. © 011-52-661/612-1430. Main courses $5.50–$20. No credit cards. Daily 8am–midnight.

ROSARITA BEACH AFTER DARK

Because the legal drinking age in Baja is 18, the under-21 crowd from Southern California flocks across the border on Friday and Saturday nights. The most popular spot in town is **Papas & Beer,** a relaxed, come-as-you-are club on the beach, a block north of the Rosarito Beach Hotel. Even for those young in spirit only, it's great fun, with open-air tables and a bar surrounding a sand volleyball court. Several other adjacent clubs offer thunderous music, spirited dancing, and all-night-long energy. Cover charges vary depending on the season, the crowd, and the mood of the staff. The **Salón Méxican** in the Rosarito Beach Hotel attracts a slightly more mature crowd, with live music on Friday, Saturday, and Sunday nights.

EN ROUTE FROM ROSARITO TO ENSENADA

A few miles south of Rosarito proper, at Km 32.8 on the free road, lies the seaside production site of 1997's mega blockbuster *Titanic.* An 800-foot-long (240m) replica was constructed for filming, and many local residents served as extras in the movie. Rosarito officials are eager to attract more films to the state-of-the-art facility left behind by the *Titanic* staff, and a back lot has even sprung up since its filming; some scenes from *Pearl Harbor* were also filmed here. In May 2001, Fox Studios opened the lot to the public as a sort of theme park on cinematography called **Foxploration,** including a makeshift *Titanic* "museum" with partial sets (like a first-class hallway) and numerous props, including lifeboats, furnishings, and crates from dockside scenes. Admission fees are $12 for adults and $8 for children; Foxploration is generally open weekends and often also on Fridays, holidays, and during busy seasons. For more information, call © **619/661-7178** or 011-52-661/614-9000, or log onto www.foxbaja.com.

Leaving Rosarito, drive south on the toll highway or the local-access road that parallels it. It offers a look at the curious juxtaposition of ramshackle villages and luxurious vacation homes. You'll also pass a variety of restaurants and resorts— this stretch of coastline has surpassed Rosarito in drawing the discriminating visitor. Many places are so Americanized that you feel as if you never left home. My favorites are the funkier, more colorfully Mexican places, like **Calafia** restaurant, **Puerto Nuevo** lobster village, and **La Fonda** resort (see "Where to Stay" and "Where to Dine," below).

After La Fonda, be sure to get back on the toll highway, because the old road veers inland and you don't want to miss what's coming next. Development falls

---

Fun Fact **Surfing, Northern Baja Style**

Surfers from California and beyond come to the northern Baja coastline for perpetual right-breaking waves, cheap digs and eats, and an "Endless Summer" atmosphere. If you're a surfer looking to get your bearings, or a spectator wanting to get your feet wet, stop by **Inner Reef** (Km 34½; no phone). Opened in 1998 by a friendly Southern California expatriate named Roger, this tiny shack offers all the essentials: wax, leashes, patch kits, surfboard sales and rentals, and even expert repairs at bargain prices. Roger's there from noon every day in summer, Wednesday through Sunday in winter.

---

off somewhat for the next 15 miles (24km), and the coastline's natural beauty picks up. You'll see green meadows running down to meet white-sand beaches and wild sand dunes, all skirting rocky cliffs reminiscent of the coast at Big Sur.

The ideal place to take it all in is **El Mirador** lookout, about 11 miles (18km) south of La Fonda. The drama builds as you climb the stairs and gasp at the breathtaking view. It sweeps from the deep-blue open sea past steep cliffs and down the curved coastline to Salsipuedes Point. (Ensenada lies on the other side.) If vertigo doesn't trouble you, look straight down from the railing and you'll see piles of automobiles lying where they were driven off before El Mirador was built. Whether the promontory was a popular suicide spot or merely a junkyard with an enticing twist is best left to urban legend–makers; it nevertheless reinforces your sense of a different culture—nowhere in image-conscious California would the twisted pile of metal be left on the rocks.

A few miles farther south on the toll road, you'll come to a sign for **Salsipuedes Bay** (the name means "leave if you can"). The dramatic scenery ends here, so you can take the exit if you want to turn around and head north again. If you plan to do some camping, head down the rutted road, nearly a mile long, to **Salsipuedes Campground,** set under olive trees on a cliff. Each campsite has a fire ring and costs $5 a day (day use is also $5). The campground has a natural rock tub with hot-spring water, and some basic cottages that rent for $30 a day. There is no easy access to the beach, known for its good surfing, from the campground.

Ensenada, with its shops, restaurants, and winery, is another 15 miles (24km) away.

NEARBY GOLFING

Located 20 miles (32km) north of Ensenada, **Bajamar** (© **888/311-6067** or 011-52-646/155-0151; www.baja-web.com/bajamar) is a self-contained resort with 27 spectacular holes of golf. It's the place to go if you want to feel as though you're in the United States. It was conceived as a vacation home and planned community with a country club, before the bottom dropped out of the market after 1980s speculation. The main attraction is now the golf club and hotel, which play host to high-level retreats, conventions, and Asian tourists attracted by the great golf deals. With oceanfront, Scottish-style links reminiscent of the courses on the Monterey Peninsula, Bajamar lets you combine any two of its three nine-hole courses. Public greens fees for 18 holes (including mandatory cart) are $50 Sunday through Thursday, $60 Friday or Saturday. Hotel guests pay $5 less, and the lavish Hacienda las Glorias offers a bevy of golf packages (see "Where to Stay," below). There are putting and chipping greens, a pro shop, a driving range, and an elegant bar and restaurant.

WHERE TO STAY

Hacienda Bajamar Hotel 🌴🌴 Situated 20 miles (32km) north of Ensenada, this hotel is tucked away in the Bajamar golf resort and community. Popular with business conventions and family gatherings, Bajamar is as Americanized as it gets, and so is this luxury hotel near the clubhouse. Signs for phases of the surrounding vacation-home development, which never really got off the ground, line the long road from the highway. Architecture buffs will note that the hotel is built like an early Spanish mission, with an interior outdoor plaza and garden surrounded by long arcades shading guest-room doorways. Rooms and suites are very spacious and comfortable, with vaguely colonial furnishings and luxurious bathrooms.

The hotel has 27 holes of golf, which are the main draw (see "Nearby Golfing," above); a variety of golf packages, including deals for couples with only one golfer, are available.

At Bajamar Golf Resort, Hwy. 1-D, Km 77. Mailing address 416 W. San Ysidro Blvd., Ste. #732, San Ysidro, CA 92173. ℂ **888/311-6067** or 011-52-646/155-0151. Fax 011-52-646/155-0150. www.baja-web.com/bajamar. 81 units. $95–$125 double; $145–$175 suite. Children under 12 stay free in parents' room. Golf packages available. AE, MC, V. **Amenities:** Restaurant; lounge; heated outdoor pool; golf course; tennis courts; whirlpool. *In room:* A/C, TV, hair dryer.

Hotel Las Rocas 🌴🌴 This polished hotel is run by an American, for Americans, and it shows. English is spoken fluently everywhere, and there are only as many signs in Spanish as you'd expect to see in Los Angeles. Built in Mediterranean style, with gleaming white stucco, cobalt blue accents, and brightly painted tiles everywhere, Las Rocas is in a lovely setting perched above the sea. *Tip:* Try to stay in the main building, and don't rule out a suite—even the $115 junior suite is spacious and includes a romantic fireplace and kitchenette.

There's no beach below the rocky edge, but the hotel's oceanfront swimming pool and secluded whirlpool lagoons more than make up for it. The thatched-roof *palapa* in the poolside garden dispenses tropical drinks and snacks, and swaying palms rustle throughout the property.

Like most Baja resorts, Las Rocas is oriented toward the sea; all rooms have an oceanfront private terrace. The rooms and suites are nicely furnished in Mexican-Colonial style, and bathrooms are well equipped and beautifully tiled. Deluxe rooms and suites feature microwave, fridge, wet bar, and coffeemaker.

The hotel's restaurant, Café Carnaval, attempts to offer both Mexican cuisine and Continental fare. It doesn't really succeed at either, but does make outstanding soups—and guacamole, which you can order by the bowl for chip-dipping at the indoor or poolside bar.

Km 38.5 Free Rd. Mailing address P.O. Box 189003 HLR, Coronado, CA 92178-9003. ℂ **888/LAS-ROCAS**, 011-52-661/614-0354, or 619/234-9810 in San Diego. www.lasrocas.com. 74 units. $89 standard double, $119 deluxe double; $134–$279 suite. Midweek rates available Oct–Apr represent 15–20% savings. Packages and senior discounts available. AE, MC, V. Take the second Rosarito exit off the toll road and drive 6 miles (9.5km) south, or follow the free road south from Rosarito; hotel is on the right. **Amenities:** 2 restaurants; 2 bars; 2 heated outdoor pools; tennis court; sand volleyball; fitness center and spa; 3 whirlpools. *In room:* TV.

La Fonda 🌴🌴 *Finds* Just as American-style Las Rocas has its staunch devotees, many are loyal to La Fonda, a place for people who truly want to get away from it all. The rustic rooms don't come with minibars, state-of-the-art TVs, or phones. What they do have is an adventuresome appeal unlike that of any other northern Baja coast resort. Relaxation and romance are the key words at this small hotel and restaurant, which opened in the 1950s and hasn't changed a whole lot since. Perched cliff side above a wide, sandy beach, all of La Fonda's rooms have wide-open views of the breaking surf below. Although there are some newer motel-style rooms, there's more charm to the older apartments with fireplaces (some with kitchenettes), which are reached by narrow winding staircases much like the pathway down to the sand. The best rooms are numbers 18 to 22, closest to the sand and isolated from the main building. During particularly cold winter months, unheated La Fonda can get chilly—an important consideration. At least be sure you're in a room with a fireplace.

Bamboo and palm fronds decorate the bar next to the acclaimed casual restaurant (see "Where to Dine," below). Ensenada is a scenic 45-minute drive south, and Puerto Nuevo a mere 8 miles (13km) up the road—if you decide you need to leave this hideaway at all.

Hwy. 1-D, Km 59, La Misión exit. Mailing address P.O. Box 430268, San Ysidro, CA 92143. ℭ and fax 011-52-646/155-0307. lafonda@telnor.net. 25 units. $75 double. No credit cards. **Amenities:** Restaurant; lounge; spa; beach access. *In room:* TV, no phone.

WHERE TO DINE

Three miles (5km) south of Rosarito Beach, elaborate stucco portals beckon drivers to pull over for **Calafia** (ℭ **011-52-661/612-1581**), a restaurant and trailer park that isn't visible from the highway. We don't recommend the dismal accommodations, but Calafia's restaurant is worth a stop, if only to admire the impressive setting above the crashing surf. Tables sit on terraces, balconies, and ledges wedged into the rocks all the way down to the bottom, where an outdoor dance floor and wrecked Spanish galleon sit on the beach. At night, when the outdoor landings are softly lit, and the mariachis complement the sound of crashing waves, romance is definitely in the air. The menu is standard Mexican fare, with some Americanized dishes like fajitas, all prepared well and served with fresh, warm tortillas and good, strong margaritas. Calafia serves breakfast, lunch, and dinner daily.

A trip down the coast just wouldn't be complete without stopping at **Puerto Nuevo,** a tiny fishing town with nearly 30 restaurants—all serving exactly the same thing! Some 40 years ago the fishermen's wives started serving local lobsters from the kitchens of their simple shacks; many eventually built small dining rooms onto their homes or constructed restaurants. The result is a lobster lover's paradise, where a feast of lobster, beans, rice, salsa, limes, and fresh tortillas costs around $15.

Puerto Nuevo is 12 miles (19km) south of Rosarito on the Old Ensenada Highway (parallel to the toll Hwy. 1). Drive through the arched entryway, park, and stroll the town's 3 or 4 blocks for a restaurant that suits your fancy. Some have names and some don't; **Ortega's** is one of the originals, and has expanded to five locations in the village. There's also **La Casa de la Langosta** ("House of Lobster"), which has a branch in Rosarito Beach. Regulars prefer the smaller, family run spots, where mismatched dinette sets and chipped plates underscore the earnest service and personally prepared dinners.

About 10 miles (16km) farther south, roughly halfway between Rosarito and Ensenada, is the **La Fonda** hotel and restaurant (see "Where to Stay," above). Plenty of San Diegans make the drive on Sunday morning for La Fonda's outstanding buffet brunch, an orgy of meats, traditional Mexican stews, *chilaquiles* (a saucy egg-and-tortilla scramble), fresh fruit, and pastries. Breakfast, lunch, and dinner are always accompanied by a basket of Baja's best flour tortillas (try rolling them with some butter and jam at breakfast). The best seating is under thatched umbrellas on La Fonda's tiled terrace overlooking the breaking surf. There's a bar, and live music keeps the joint jumping on Friday and Saturday nights (strolling mariachis entertain the rest of the time). House specialties include banana pancakes, pork chops with *salsa verde,* succulent glazed ribs, and a variety of seafood; plan to walk off your heavy meal along the sandy beach below, accessible by a stone stairway. Relaxing ambience coupled with exceptionally good food and service make La Fonda a must-see along the coast. Sunday brunch is around $12 a person; main courses otherwise are $4 to $15. The restaurant is open daily from around 9am to 10pm; Sunday's buffet brunch runs from 10am to 3:30pm.

ENSENADA

Ensenada, 84 miles (135km) south of San Diego and 68 miles (109km) south of Tijuana, is a pretty town surrounded by sheltering mountains. It's about 40 minutes from Rosarito. This is the kind of place that loves a celebration, and at almost any time you visit, the city is festive, be it for a bicycle race or a seafood festival.

ESSENTIALS

The **Tourist and Convention Bureau** booth (© 011-52-646/178-2411) is at the western entrance to town, where the waterfront-hugging Bulevar Lázaro Cárdenas—also known as Bulevar Costero—curves to the right. The booth is open daily from 9am until dusk, and the staff can provide a downtown map, directions to major nearby sites, and information on special events. As in most of the commonly visited areas of Baja, one or more employees speak English fluently.

Eight blocks south, you'll find the **State Secretary of Tourism,** Bulevar Lázaro Cárdenas 1477, Government Building (© **011-52-646/172-3022;** fax 011-52-646/172-30-81). It's open Monday through Friday from 9am to 7pm, Saturday 10am to 3pm, Sunday 10am to 2pm. Both offices have extended hours on U.S. holidays. Taxis park along López Mateos.

EXPLORING ENSENADA

Although Ensenada technically is a border town, one of its appeals is its multifaceted vitality—it's concerned with much more than tourism. The bustling port consumes the entire waterfront (the only beach access is north or south of town), and the economy is dominated by the Pacific fishing trade and agriculture in the fertile valleys surrounding the city.

Try not to leave Ensenada without getting a taste of its true personality; for example, stop by the indoor-outdoor **fish market** at the northernmost corner of the harbor. Each day, from early morning to midday, merchants and housewives gather to assess the day's catch—tuna, marlin, snapper, and many other varieties, plus piles of shrimp. Outside the market are several stalls—the perfect place to sample the culinary craze sweeping *Alta* (upper) California, the Baja fish taco. Strips of freshly caught fish are battered and deep-fried, then wrapped in corn tortillas and topped with shredded cabbage, cilantro, salsa, and various other condiments. They're delicious, cheap, and filling, and it's easy to see why surf bums and collegiate vacationers consider them a Baja staple.

A WINERY Elsewhere in town, visit the **Bodegas de Santo Tomás Winery,** Av. Miramar 666, at Calle 7 (© **011-52-646/178-2509;** www.santotomas.com. mx). While most visitors to Mexico are quite content to quaff endless quantities of cheap *cerveza* (beer), even part-time oenophiles should pay a visit to this historic winery. The oldest in Mexico, and the largest in Baja, it uses old-fashioned methods of processing grapes grown in the lush Santo Tomás Valley, first cultivated by Dominican monks in 1791.

A 45-minute tour introduces you to low-tech processing machinery, hand-hammered wood casks, and cool, damp, stone aging rooms. It culminates in an invitation to sample several vintages, including an international medal-winning Cabernet and delightfully crisp sparkling blanc de blanc. The wood-paneled, church-like tasting room is adorned with paintings of mischievous altar boys being scolded by stern friars for pilfering wine or ruining precious grapes. Anyone used to the pretentious, assembly line ambience of trendier wine regions will relish the friendly welcome and informative tour here. Tours in English are conducted daily at 11am, 1, and 3pm. Admission is $2 (including tastings; $3 more gets you a souvenir wineglass), and wines for sale range from $3.50 to $10 a bottle. *Note:* Most of the winery's product is exported for the European market; none is available in the United States. The website is in Spanish.

Be sure to poke around a bit after your tour concludes, because Santo Tomás has more treasures to give up. The little modern machinery installed here freed up a cavernous space now used for monthly jazz concerts, and a former aging room has been transformed into **La Embotelladora Vieja** ("the old aging room") restaurant (see "Where to Dine," below). Across the street stands **La Esquina de Bodegas** ("the corner of wine cellars"), former aging rooms for Santo Tomás. One of Ensenada's many pleasant cultural treats, the industrial-style building now functions as a gallery that shows local art. There's a skylit bookstore on the second level, and a small cafe (punctuated by giant copper distillation vats) in the rear.

POLITICAL MONUMENTS   Spend just a few hours in Ensenada, and you will begin to see evidence that helps elevate the city beyond mere border town status and underscore its national pride. Lending a European air to the city—not to mention a sense of poignancy when you consider Mexico's bloody and still tumultuous political history—are several larger-than-life political monuments concentrated in the downtown area.

The most visible is **Plaza Cívica** (along Bulevar Lázaro Cárdenas, also known as Costero, at Av. Riveroll), where a wide stone platform dramatically displays 12-foot (3.5m) copper busts of former Mexican presidents Benito Juárez, Miguel Hidalgo, and Venustiano Carranza. A full-figure, mounted representation of Juárez is nearby, in a traffic-stopping monument along the street bearing his name (Av. Juárez at Av. Reforma). Contemporary hero **General Lázaro Cárdenas** is honored at the corner of avenidas Reforma and López Mateos, and a statue of **Miguel Hidalgo,** the priest revered as the "father of Mexican independence," stands tall on Avenida Juárez 1 block north of Avenida Ruiz.

A CULTURAL CENTER   Ensenada's primary cultural center is another must-see in my book: the **Centro Cívico, Social y Cultural** (Bulevar Lázaro Cárdenas at Av. Club Rotario). The impressive Mediterranean building was formerly **Riviera del Pacífico,** a glamorous 1930s bay-front casino and resort frequented by Hollywood's elite. Tiles in the lobby commemorate "Visitantes Distinguidos 1930–1940," including Marion Davies, William Randolph Hearst, Lana Turner, Myrna Loy, and Jack Dempsey. Now used by the Rotary Club as offices and for cultural and social events, the main building is open to the public. Go on, take a peek: Elegant hallways and ballrooms evoke a bygone elegance, and every wall and alcove glows with original murals depicting Mexico's colorful history. Lush formal gardens span the front of the building, and there's a small art gallery tucked away to one side. Through the lobby, facing an inner courtyard filled with the ghosts of parties past, is Bar Andaluz, which is sporadically open to the public. It's an intimate, dark-wood place where you can just imagine someone like "Papa" Hemingway holding cocktail-hour court beneath a colorful toreador mural.

A NEARBY ATTRACTION South of the city, 45 minutes away along the rural Punta Banda Peninsula, is one of Ensenada's major attractions: **La Bufadora,** a natural sea spout in the rocks. With each incoming wave, water is forced upward through the rock, creating a geyser whose loud grunt gave the phenomenon its name (*la bufadora* means "buffalo snort"). From downtown Ensenada, take Avenida Reforma (Hwy. 1) south to Highway 23 west. It's a long, meandering drive through a swamplike area untouched by development; look for grazing animals, bait shops, and fishermen's shacks along the way. La Bufadora is at the end of the road. You park ($1 per car) in crude dirt lots, then walk downhill to the viewing platform, at the end of a 600-yard pathway lined with souvenir stands. In addition to running a gauntlet of determined vendors (hawking the usual wares: woven blankets and fanny packs, painted wooden masks, leather shoes and wallets, carved soapstone animals, cheap sunglasses, silver chains, and earrings), visitors can avail themselves of plentiful, inexpensive snacks, including freshly made *churros*, grilled corn, and tasty fish tacos. While some sightseers proclaim the display spectacular, I think you need to have a real thing for geysers to make the drive when there's so much else to see and do. Nevertheless, visitation is enormous, and there are plans to pave the dirt parking lots and build permanent restaurants and shops. If you do go, stop and sample the wares along Highway 1 south of the city before you reach the La Bufadora cutoff. I was impressed by the hard-working ladies on the side of the road selling homemade tamales with a variety of fillings, including the sweet-spicy *piña* (pineapple). They also have colorful, eye-catching rows of pickled olives, vegetables, and chili peppers in reclaimed mayonnaise and applesauce jars.

SHOPPING
Ensenada's equivalent of Avenida Revolución is crowded **Avenida López Mateos,** which runs roughly parallel to Bulevar Lázaro Cárdenas (Costero); the highest concentration of shops and restaurants is between avenidas Ruiz and Castillo. Beggars fill the street, but the sellers are less likely to bargain—I think they're used to the gullible cruise-ship buyers. Compared to Tijuana, there is more authentic Mexican **art- and craft work** in Ensenada—pieces imported from rural states and villages, where different skills are traditionally practiced.

Curiosidades La Joya, 725 Av. López Mateos (© **011-52-646/178-3191**), is a treasure trove of stained-glass lamps, hangings, and other handcrafted curios. The resident craftsman can be found in the shop most days, executing intricate custom designs for private clients. If you're interested in made-to-order pieces, they charge about $40 per square foot. The shopkeepers are stubborn about bargaining, perhaps because they know the value of their unusual wares.

You'll see colorfully painted glazed **pottery** wherever you go in northern Baja. Quality can range from sloppy pieces quickly painted with a limited palette to intricately designed, painstakingly painted works evocative of Tuscan urns and pitchers. You'll get the best prices at the abundant roadside stands lining the old road south of Rosarito; but if you're willing to pay extra for quality, head to

Mexican Art Bazaar, Calle 1 at Alvarado (© **011-52-646/178-2901**). You can learn about the origins of this "Talavera" style—how invading Moors set up terra-cotta factories in the Spanish city of Talavera, and subsequent migration brought the art to the Mexican state of Puebla.

SPORTFISHING

Ensenada, which bills itself as "the yellowtail capital of the world," draws sport-fishers eager to venture out from the beautiful *Bahía de Todos Santos* (Bay of All Saints) in search of albacore, halibut, marlin, rockfish, and sea bass.

A wooden boardwalk parallel to Bulevar Lázaro Cárdenas (Costero) near the northern entrance to town provides access to the sportfishing piers and their many charter boat operators. Open-party boats leave early, often by 7am, and charge around $35 per person, plus an additional fee (about $9) for the mandatory fishing license. Nonfishing passengers must, by law, also be licensed. Two reliable companies are **Gordo's Sportfishing** (© **011-52-646/178-3515;** www.gordos.8m.com) and **Sergio's Sportfishing Center** (© **011-52-646/ 178-2185;** www.sergios-sportfishing.com)—look for their distinctive banners on the boardwalk. Those disinclined to comparison shop can make advance arrangements with San Diego–based **Baja California Tours** (© **619/454-7166**). In addition to daily fishing excursions, the company offers 1- to 3-night packages that include hotel, fishing, some meals, and transportation from San Diego.

WHERE TO STAY

Remember, in Mexico, a single room has one bed, and a double has two.

Estero Beach Resort 🏖 About 6 miles (9.5km) south of downtown Ensenada, this sprawling complex of rooms, cottages, and mobile-home hookups is popular with families and active vacationers. The bay and protected lagoon at the edge of the lushly planted property are perfect for swimming and launching sailboards; there's also tennis, horseback riding, volleyball, and a game room with Ping-Pong and billiards. The guest rooms were recently refurbished. The casual beachfront restaurant serves a mix of seafood and other Mexican fare mingled with hamburgers, fried chicken, and omelets. Some suites and cottages have kitchenettes, and some can easily accommodate a whole family.

Mailing address Apartado Postal 86, Ensenada, BC, Mexico. © 011-52-646/176-6225. www.hotelestero beach.com. 94 units. $75–$130 double high season (Apr–Sept) and holidays; $65–$110 low season. MC, V. From Ensenada, take Hwy. 1 south; turn right at Estero Beach sign. **Amenities:** Restaurant; 2 bars; outdoor pool; 3 tennis courts; whirlpool; volleyball; playground; bike and WaveRunner rentals (summer only); room service (7:30am–11pm); self-service laundry facilities. *In room:* TV.

Hotel Las Rosas 🏖🏖 Modern and luxurious, this pink oceanfront hotel outside Ensenada is the favorite of many Baja aficionados. It offers all the comforts of an upscale American hotel—which doesn't leave room for much Mexican personality. The atrium lobby is awash with pale pink and sea-foam green, the color scheme throughout—including the guest rooms, which are furnished with quasi-tropical hotel furniture. No luxury is unheard of here. Many rooms have fireplaces, whirlpools, or both; some have kitchenettes or fridges.

One of the resort's main photo ops is the spectacular outdoor swimming pool—it overlooks the Pacific and features a vanishing edge that appears to merge with the ocean beyond; nearby is a clifftop hot tub. If you're looking to maintain the highest comfort level possible, this would indeed be your hotel of choice.

Km 105½, Tijuana-Ensenada Hwy. (2 miles/3km north of Ensenada). Mailing address 374 E. H St. #A-455, Chula Vista, CA 91910-7484. ℂ 011-52-646/174-4310. www.lasrosas.com. 48 units. $132–$190 double. Extra adult is $23; children under 12 are $17. Terrific off-season packages available. MC, V. **Amenities:** Restaurant; lounge; outdoor heated pool; night-lit tennis courts; fitness center and spa; room service (7am–10pm); in-room massage; babysitting; laundry/dry-cleaning service. *In room:* TV, hair dryer, iron.

Punta Morro Resort 𝕏𝕏   There's no better example of how affordable Mexico can be than this upscale, contemporary, small hotel just outside Ensenada. Situated 600 yards away from the highway, Punta Morro exchanges highway noise for the sound of waves lapping at its rocky edge; a wooden observation platform shows the view off perfectly. Every room faces the ocean (winter sunset position) and each features a gas fireplace and private terrace; most are suites. They're decorated in a simple, untrendy manner with clean tile floors and new furniture; bathrooms are spick-and-span, and room heaters are available for chilly nights.

While the hotel tends to attract mainly American tourists, the hotel's exceptionally good dining room is usually packed with Ensenada's well-heeled middle class (who always dress nicer than the *Americanos,* and *always* smoke!) Perched atop wave-crashing rocks, the restaurant presents refined international cuisine, with ultrafresh seafood and imported meats sharing a French-Mexican-Continental treatment that usually hits the mark.

Km 106, Tijuana-Ensenada Hwy. (2 miles/3km north of Ensenada). Mailing address P.O. Box 434263, San Diego, CA 92143-4263. ℂ 800/526-6676 or 011-52-646/178-3507. www.punta-morro.com. 24 units. $98 double; $120–$260 suite. Rates include continental breakfast. Packages available. AE, DC, MC, V. **Amenities:** Restaurant; lounge; heated outdoor pool; whirlpool; room service; in-room massage. *In room:* TV, dataport, fridge, coffeemaker, hair dryer.

San Nicolás Resort Hotel   Most rooms at this modern motor inn face the courtyard or have balconies overlooking an Olympic-size swimming pool. The place is surprisingly quiet, considering it's right on the main drag. The San Nicolás also boasts the city's only indoor swimming pool, and has a casual restaurant, cocktail lounge, and disco. There's a branch of Caliente Sports Book, where you can gamble on games and races throughout the United States.

Av. López Mateos and Av. Guadalupe, Ensenada. Mailing address P.O. Box 437060, San Ysidro, CA 92143-7060. ℂ 011-52-646/176-1901. Fax 011-52-617/6-4930. www.sannicolas.com.mx. 150 units. $88–$108 double; from $130 suite. Extra person $10. Midweek rates $20 lower. MC, V. **Amenities:** Restaurant; 2 bars (1 disco); outdoor heated pool; whirlpool; tour desk; salon; room service (7am–2am); babysitting; laundry/dry-cleaning service. *In room:* A/C, TV, coffeemaker.

WHERE TO DINE

El Charro 𝕏 *Value* MEXICAN   You'll recognize El Charro by its front windows: Whole chickens rotate slowly on the rotisserie in one, while a woman makes tortillas in the other. This little place has been here since 1956 and looks it, with charred walls and a ceiling made of split logs. The simple fare consists of such dishes as half a roasted chicken with fries and tortillas, and *carne asada* with soup, guacamole, and tortillas. Giant piñatas hang from the walls above the concrete floor. Kids are welcome; they'll think they're on a picnic. Wine and beer are served, and beer is cheaper than soda.

Av. López Mateos 475 (between Ruiz and Gastellum). ℂ 011-52-646/178-3881. Menu items $5–$12; lobster $20. No credit cards. Daily 11am–2am.

El Rey Sol 𝕏𝕏 FRENCH/MEXICAN   Opened by French expatriates in 1947, the family run El Rey Sol has long been considered Ensenada's finest restaurant. Decked out like the French flag, the red-white-and-blue building is a beacon on busy López Mateos. It has wrought-iron chandeliers and heavy oak farm tables, but the menu's prices and sophistication belie the casual decor.

House specialties include seafood puff pastry; baby clams steamed in butter, white wine, and cilantro; chicken in brandy and chipotle chili cream sauce; tender grilled steaks; and, homemade French desserts. Portions are generous, and always feature fresh vegetables from the nearby family farm. Every table receives a complimentary platter of appetizers at dinnertime; lunch is a hearty three-course meal.

Av. López Mateos 1000 (at Blancarte). © 011-52-646/178-1733. Reservations recommended on weekends. Main courses $9–$19. AE, MC, V. Daily 7:30am–10:30pm.

La Embotelladora Vieja ✪✪✪ FRENCH/MEXICAN   If you're planning to splurge on one fine meal in Ensenada (or all of northern Baja, for that matter), this insider's find is the place. Hidden on an industrial side street, from the outside it looks more like a chapel than the elegant restaurant it is. Sophisticated foodies will feel right at home in the stylish dining room. It's a former aging room for the attached Bodegas de Santo Tomás winery, resplendent with red oak furniture (constructed from old wine casks), high brick walls, and crystal goblets and candlesticks on linen tablecloths.

It goes without saying that the wine list is exemplary, featuring bottles from Santo Tomás and other Baja vintners, and the "Baja French" menu features dishes carefully crafted to include or complement wine. Look for appetizers like abalone ceviche or cream of garlic soup, followed by grilled swordfish in cilantro sauce, filet mignon in port wine–Gorgonzola sauce, or quail with tart sauvignon blanc sauce.

Av. Miramar 666 (at Calle 7). © 011-52-646/174-0807. Reservations recommended on weekends. Main courses $8–$20. MC, V. Lunch and dinner; call for seasonal hours.

ENSENADA AFTER DARK

No discussion of Ensenada would be complete without mentioning **Hussong's Cantina,** Av. Ruiz 113, near Avenida López Mateos (© **011-52-646/178-3210**). The bar opened in 1892, and nothing much has changed—the place still sports Wild West–style swinging saloon doors, a long bar to slide beers along, and strolling mariachis bellowing to rise above the din of revelers. There's definitely a minimalist appeal to Hussong's, which looks as if it sprang from a south-of-the-border episode of *Gunsmoke.* Beer and tequilas at astonishingly low prices are the main order of business, but good luck when you need the rest rooms, where hygiene and privacy are a low priority.

While the crowd (a pleasant mix of tourists and locals) at Hussong's can really whoop it up, you ain't seen nothing until you stop into **Papas & Beer,** Avenida Ruiz near Avenida López Mateos (© **011-52-646/178-4231**), across the street. A tiny entrance leads to the upstairs bar and disco, where the music is loud and the youthful crowd is definitely here to party. Happy patrons hang out of the second-story windows hollering at their friends, stopping occasionally to munch on *papas* (french fries) washed down with local beers. Papas & Beer has quite a reputation with the Southern California college crowd, and has opened a branch in Rosarito Beach (see earlier in this chapter). You might notice bumper stickers from these two quintessential Baja watering holes, but they don't just give them away. In fact, each bar has not one, but several, souvenir shops along Avenida Ruiz. They carry shirts, duffel bags, sport sippers, pennants, hats, and innumerable other items decorated with the familiar logos.

Appendix:
Useful Toll-Free Numbers
& Websites

MAJOR HOTEL & MOTEL CHAINS

Best Western
✆ 800/780-7234
www.bestwestern.com

Clarion Hotels
✆ 800/CLARION
www.hotelchoice.com

Comfort Inns
✆ 800/228-5150
www.hotelchoice.com

Courtyard by Marriott
✆ 800/321-2211
www.courtyard.com

Days Inn
✆ 800/325-2525
www.daysinn.com

Doubletree Hotels
✆ 800/222-TREE
www.doubletree.com

Econo Lodges
✆ 800/55-ECONO
www.hotelchoice.com

Embassy Suites
✆ 800/EMBASSY
www.embassy-suites.com

Fairfield Inns by Marriott
✆ 800/228-2800
www.fairfieldinn.com

Hampton Inns
✆ 800/HAMPTON
www.hampton-inn.com

Hilton Hotels
✆ 800/774-1500
www.hilton.com

Holiday Inn
✆ 800/HOLIDAY
www.holiday-inn.com

Howard Johnson
✆ 800/I-GO-HOJO
www.hojo.com

Hyatt Hotels & Resorts
✆ 888/591-1234
www.hyatt.com

La Quinta Motor Inns
✆ 800/531-5900
www.laquinta.com

Marriott Hotels
✆ 888/236-2427
www.marriott.com

Motel 6
✆ 800/4-MOTEL6
www.motel6.com

Omni Hotels
✆ 800/THE-OMNI
www.omnihotels.com

Quality Inns
✆ 800/228-5151
www.hotelchoice.com

Radisson Hotels
✆ 888/201-1718
www.radisson.com

Ramada Inns
✆ 888/298-2054
www.ramada.com

Red Roof Inns
✆ 800/RED-ROOF
www.redroof.com

Residence Inn by Marriott
✆ 800/331-3131
www.residenceinn.com

Rodeway Inns
✆ 800/228-2000
www.hotelchoice.com

Sheraton
© 888/625-5144
www.sheraton.com

Super 8 Motels
© 800/800-8000
www.super8.com

Travelodge
© 800/578-7878
www.travelodge.com

Vagabond Inns
© 800/522-1555
www.vagabondinns.com

Westin Hotels & Resorts
© 888/625-5144
www.westin.com

Wyndham Hotels & Resorts
© 800/WYNDHAM
www.wyndham.com

CAR-RENTAL AGENCIES

Advantage Rent-A-Car
© 800/777-5500
ww.arac.com

Alamo
© 800/GO-ALAMO
www.goalamo.com

Avis
© 800/230-4898
www.avis.com

Budget
© 800/527-0700
www.budget.com

Dollar
© 800/800-3665
www.dollarcar.com

Enterprise
© 800/325-8007
www.enterprise.com

Hertz
© 800/654-3131
www.hertz.com

National Car Rental
© 800/CAR-RENT
www.nationalcar.com

Payless
© 800/PAYLESS
www.paylesscar.com

Rent-A-Wreck
© 800/944-7501
www.rent-a-wreck.com

Thrifty
© 800/THRIFTY
www.thrifty.com

AIRLINES

Aer Lingus
© 800/IRISH-AIR
© 0818-0818/365-000 in Ireland
www.aerlingus.com

Aeroméxico
© 800/237-6639
www.aeromexico.com

Air Canada
© 888/247-2262 in Canada
and the U.S.
www.aircanada.ca

Air New Zealand
© 800/262-1234
© 0800/737-000 in New Zealand
www.airnewzealand.com

Alaska Airlines
© 800/252-7522
www.alaskaair.com

America West
© 800/235-9292
www.americawest.com

American Airlines/American Eagle
© 800/433-7300
www.aa.com

American Trans Air (ATA)
© 800/I-FLY-ATA
www.ata.com

British Airways
© 800/AIRWAYS
© 0845/77-333-77 in Britain
www.british-airways.com

Continental Airlines
℃ 800/525-0280
www.continental.com

Delta Air Lines/Delta Connection
℃ 800/221-1212
www.delta.com

Frontier Airlines
℃ 800/4321-FLY
www.frontierairlines.com

Hawaiian Airlines
℃ 800/367-5320 in the continental
U.S. and Canada
℃ 800/882-8811 in Hawaii
www.hawaiianair.com

Japan Airlines
℃ 800/JAL-FONE
℃ 0120/25-5971 in Japan
www.japanair.com (in the U.S.
and Canada)
www.jal.co.jp (in Japan)

Midwest Express
℃ 800/452-2022
www.midwestexpress.com

**Northwest Airlines/Northwest
Airlink**
℃ 800/225-2525
www.nwa.com

Qantas
℃ 800/227-4500
℃ 13-13-13 in Australia
www.qantas.com.au

Southwest Airlines
℃ 800/435-9792
www.southwest.com

United Airlines/United Express
℃ 800/241-6522
www.united.com

US Airways/US Airways Express
℃ 800/428-4322
www.usairways.com

Virgin Atlantic Airways
℃ 800/862-8621
℃ 01293/747-747 in Britain
www.virgin-atlantic.com

Index

See also Accommodations and Restaurant indexes, below.

GENERAL INDEX

A AA (American Automobile Association), 30, 43
Aanteek Avenue Mall (Carlsbad), 216
AARP, 24
Access America, 21
Accessible San Diego hot line, 22
Accommodations, 65–93.
  See also Accommodations Index
  Anaheim, 240–244
  best bets, 6
  Borrego Springs, 255–256
  Carlsbad, 217–218
  Coronado, 89–93
  Del Mar, 212–213
  downtown, 67–73
  Ensenada (Mexico), 278–279
  getting the best room, 66
  Hillcrest/Uptown, 73–76
  Julian, 251
  La Jolla, 84–89
  Mission Bay and the Beaches, 79–83
  Old Town and Mission Valley, 76–79
  price categories, 65
  Rancho Santa Fe, 222–223
  reservation services, 66
  Rosarito Beach (Mexico), 270
  Temecula, 229–230
  Tijuana (Mexico), 264–265
  tipping, 47
  websites, 281–282
  what's new in, 1–2
Accommodations Express, 66
Adams Avenue Business Association, 189
Advance Tickets, 203
Adventure Bike Tours, 158
Adventureland (Disneyland), 235

Aer Lingus, 42
Aeroméxico, 25
Aerospace Museum, San Diego, 139, 184
Afternoon tea, 4
Ah Quinn, former home of, 172
Air Canada, 25, 42
Air Combat & Biplane Adventures (Carlsbad), 216–217
Airfares, 26–27
Airlines, 25–26
  websites, 282–283
Air New Zealand, 42
Airport
  accommodations near, 93
  getting into town from the, 48–49
Airport shuttles, 49
Air travel
  carry-on baggage restrictions, 26, 27
  first-class experience in coach, 28–29
  to San Diego, 25–29
  security measures, 26
Alaska Airlines, 25
Alcazar Garden, 182
Alcoholics Anonymous, 63
Allright Parking, 57
American Airlines, 25
American Airlines Vacations, 30
American Automobile Association (AAA), 30, 43
American Express
  credit cards, 40
  full-service office, 62
  traveler's checks, 12, 40
American Foundation for the Blind, 23
America's Finest City Half Marathon, 167
America's Schooner Cup, 166
America West, 26
Amtrak, 23, 30, 61

Anaheim. *See* Disneyland and environs
Annual San Diego Crew Classic, 166
Annual San Diego Lesbian and Gay Pride Parade, Rally, and Festival, 17, 23
Antique Row, 189
Antiques, 192, 194
  Carlsbad, 215–216
  Temecula, 229
Anza-Borrego Desert State Park, 15, 252–257
APEX (Advance Purchase Excursion) tickets, 42
Arch (Balboa Park), 182
Architecture, sightseeing highlights, 152
ARCO Training Center (Chula Vista), 151
Area codes, 62
Arriving in San Diego, 48–49
Art Festival in the Village of La Jolla, 18
Art galleries, 195
Artists Gallery, The, 195
Art museums
  Mingei International Museum, 138
  Museum of Contemporary Art, Downtown (MCA), 142
  Museum of Contemporary Art (MCA), San Diego (La Jolla), 146, 148
  San Diego Museum of Art, 140
  Stuart Collection (La Jolla), 148
  Timken Museum of Art, 140–141
Arts and crafts
  Ensenada (Mexico), 277–278
  Indian Fair, 17
  Julian's Arts and Crafts Show, 19
  Tijuana (Mexico), 263

ARTS TIX booth, 200
Ascot Shop, 192
Association of British
    Insurers, 39–40
ATMs (automated-teller
    machines), 12, 40–41
Auction airline tickets, 33
Australia, embassy of, 44
Australian citizens
    customs regulations for, 39
    passport and visa informa-
        tion for, 36, 38
Automobile Club of South-
    ern California, 51
Automotive Museum, San
    Diego, 140, 184
Auto racing, 165
Avenida Revolución
    (Tijuana), 260, 263
Avis, 23, 56
    Tijuana, 257

B abette Schwartz, 189
Baby Rock Discoteca
    (Tijuana), 267
Babysitters, 62
Backesto Building, 171
Bahia Belle, 154
Baja California (Mexico),
    267–280
    Rosarito Beach, 268
    suggested itinerary, 268
    visitor information, 268
Baja California Information
    Office, 18
Baja California Tours, 18, 278
Bajamar (near Ensenada),
    272–273
Balboa Park, 4, 50
    attractions in, 135–141,
        151
        Botanical Building and
            Lily Pond, 136
        free, 150
        Hall of Champions,
            136
        House of Pacific Rela-
            tions International
            Cottages, 136
        Japanese Friendship
            Garden, 136, 138,
            184
        for kids, 152
        Maritime Museum,
            142
        Marston House
            Museum, 138
        Mingei International
            Museum, 138

Model Railroad
    Museum, 138
Museum of Man, 139,
    182
Museum of Photo-
    graphic Arts, 139
Reuben H. Fleet
    Science Center, 139
San Diego Aerospace
    Museum, 139
San Diego Automotive
    Museum, 140
San Diego Historical
    Society Museum,
    140
San Diego Museum of
    Art, 140
San Diego Natural His-
    tory Museum, 140
Spreckels Organ
    Pavilion, 140, 184
Timken Museum of
    Art, 140–141
Christmas on the Prado, 20
map, 137
safety suggestions, 41
transportation within, 136
Twilight in the Park
    Concerts, 17
walking tours, 181–186
Balboa Park Municipal Golf
    Course, 161
Balboa Park Visitors Center,
    11, 50, 136, 184
Balboa Tennis Club, 165
Balboa Theatre, 170
Ballooning, 6, 157
    Del Mar, 210
    Temecula, 16–17, 229
Bank of America, 12
Bank of Mexican Food
    (Temecula), 229
Barbers, tipping, 47
Barnes & Noble, 195
Barnes Tennis Center, 165
Barona Casino, 207
Bars and cocktail lounges,
    204–206
Bartenders, tipping, 47
Baseball, 166
Baum, L. Frank, 34, 92, 149
Bay Books, 193
Bayside Trail, 163
Bazaar del Mundo, 150, 178,
    190
Beaches, 131–135. *See also*
    Mission Bay and the
    Beaches; Surfing
    accommodations, 79–83
    Black's Beach, 135

Boneyards Beach, 135
Bonita Cove, 132
brief description of, 54
Children's Pool, 134–135
Coronado Beach, 132
Del Mar, 135
Imperial Beach, 131
La Jolla Cove, 135
La Jolla Shores Beach, 135
map, 133
Mariner's Point, 132
Mission Bay Park, 132
Mission Beach, 132
Mission Point, 132
Moonlight Beach, 135
North County, 210, 216,
    219, 220
northern San Diego County,
    135
nude, 135
Ocean Beach, 132
Oceanside, 135
Oceanside Beach, 220
Pacific Beach, 132
Swami's Beach, 135
U.S. Open Sandcastle
    Competition, 18
for walking, 163
Windansea Beach, 134
Bed & breakfasts (B&Bs),
    67, 73, 74, 76, 82, 86, 251.
    See also Accommodations;
    Accommodations Index
Bell, Book and Candle
    Shoppe (Julian), 249
Bellhops, tipping, 47
Belly Up Tavern, 202
Berkeley, 174
Bicycling West, 158
Bike-N-Ride program, 62
Bikes and Beyond, 158, 164
Bike Tours San Diego, 157
Biking, 4, 61–62, 157–158
    Anza-Borrego Desert State
        Park, 253, 255
    Julian, 250
    rentals, 62
    Rosarito-Ensenada 50-Mile
        Fun Bicycle Ride
        (Mexico), 16, 19, 158
    Temecula, 226
Binoculars, 28
Birch Aquarium at Scripps
    Institution of Oceanogra-
    phy (La Jolla), 146–148,
    152
    WhaleFest, 156
Bishop's School (La Jolla),
    146
Bitter End, The, 204

Black's Beach, 135
Blast!, 3
Blockbuster Music, 189
Blue Cross Blue Shield, 21
Boardwalk (San Diego), 54
Boardwalk, The (Knott's
  Berry Farm), 239
Boating, 158, 160
  events, 166
  Mission Bay Boat Parade of
    Lights, 20
  San Diego Crew Classic, 16
  San Diego Harbor Parade
    of Lights, 20
Boat rentals, 158, 160
Boat Rentals of America
  (Oceanside), 220
Boat tours and cruises, 61
  bay excursions, 154–155
  with entertainment, 204
  gondola cruises, 92, 154
  harbor cruises, 176
  Sea and Land Adventures
    (SEAL), 155
  whale-watching, 156
Bob Baker Ford (Tijuana), 257
Bob Davis' Camera Shop, 62
Bodegas de Santo Tomás
  Winery (Ensenada),
  275–276
Bodysurfing Championships,
  18
Boneyard Beach (Encinitas),
  135, 216
Bonita Cove, 132
Book of Deals, The, 24
Books, recommended, 34–35
Bookstores, 195–196
Borders Books & Music, 195
Borrego Palm Canyon, 256
  self-guided hike, 254
Borrego Springs Chamber of
  Commerce, 254
Botanical Building and Lily
  Pond (Balboa Park), 136,
  182
Boudin Sourdough Bakery
  and Cafe, 124
Bourbon Street, 206
Brass Rail, The, 206
Bread & Cie. Bakery and
  Cafe, 124
British Airways, 25, 42
British citizens
  customs regulations for, 39
  insurance for, 39–40
  passport and visa informa-
    tion for, 36, 38
Brockton Villa, 153

Browning, E. W. and Ellen, 35
Bucket shops, 27
Buick Invitational, 15, 166
Bullfighting (Tijuana), 264
Business hours, 43, 62
Bus Tour Hot Line, 128
Bus tours, 155
Bus travel
  from the airport, 48–49
  within San Diego, 58–59
  around the United States,
    43

Cab drivers, tipping, 47
Cabrillo Bridge, 181–182
Cabrillo National Monument,
  141, 156
Cabs
  to/from the airport, 49
  within San Diego, 60–61
  Tijuana (Mexico), 258
  tipping, 47
Cafes, La Jolla, 118
Calendar of events, 14–20
California Adventure (Dis-
  neyland), 3, 236–237
California Ballet, 202
California Center for the
  Performing Arts (Escon-
  dido), 200, 223
California Coastal Access
  Handbook, The, 131
California Department of
  Fish and Game, 160
California Dreamin', 157
California Surf Museum
  (Oceanside), 220
Callaway Vineyard & Winery
  (Temecula), 226
Calling cards, prepaid, 46
Camcorders, 29
Camera repair, 62
Camping
  Borrego Springs, 256
  Salsipuedes Campground
    (Mexico), 272
Camp Pendleton (Ocean-
  side), 220
Camp Snoopy (Knott's Berry
  Farm), 239
Campus Travel, 40
Canada, embassy of, 44
Canadian citizens
  customs regulations for, 38
  insurance for, 40
  passport information for,
    37–38
Cannibal Bar, 204

Carlsbad, 209, 213–219
Carlsbad Company Stores,
  194, 215
Carlsbad Company Stores
  Factory Outlet Center, 198
Carlsbad Mineral Water Spa,
  216
Carlsbad Paddle Sports, 217
Carlsbad Ranch, 215
  Flower Fields in Bloom at,
    16
Carlsbad State Beach, 216
Carlsbad Village Faire, 19
Car rentals, 56
  for disabled travelers, 23
  insurance, 22, 57
  websites of car-rental
    agencies, 282
Car travel
  to/from the airport, 49
  driving rules, 58
  driving safety, 41–42
  for foreign visitors, 43
  parking, 57–58
  to San Diego, 29–30, 49
  within San Diego, 55–58
Casa de Balboa Building,
  185
Casa del Prado, 185
Casa la Carreta (Rosarito
  Beach), 270
Casbah, The, 202
Casinos, 207–208
  Oceanside, 221
Cathedral, 189
Cava de Vinos L. A. Cetto
  (Tijuana), 262
Cave Store, 192
CDW (Collision Damage
  Waiver), 57
Cemetery, Pioneer (Julian),
  250
Centre City Development
  Corporation's Downtown
  Information Center, 154
Centro Cívico, Social y
  Cultural (Ensenada),
  276–277
Centro Cultural Tijuana, 261
Chandler, Raymond, 34, 56
Charles B. Ledgerwood
  Seeds, 194
Charlotte Bird, 195
Cheap Seats, 27
Cheap Tickets, 27
Cheese Shop, 10, 124
Children's Museum of San
  Diego, 141, 152
Children's Park, 150, 152

Children's Pool Beach
  (La Jolla), 4, 6, 134–135
Children's Zoo, 128
Christmas
  Coronado Christmas Cele-
    bration and Parade, 20
  Dr. Seuss Christmas
    Readings, 19
  Mission Bay Boat Parade of
    Lights, 20
  on the Prado, 20, 208
Christmas on the Prado, 208
Cilurzo Vineyard & Winery
  (Temecula), 226
Cinco de Mayo Celebration,
  17
Circa a.d., 189
Cirrus system, 12
City Fish Line, 160
Classic Sailing Adventures,
  156
Cloud 9 Shuttle, 22, 49
Club and music scene,
  202–204
Club Bombay, 206
Club Montage, 207
Club Nautico, 158
Coaster, the, 61
Coast Walk (La Jolla), 146
Coffeehouses with
  performances, 206
Collect calls, 46
Collision Damage Waiver
  (CDW), 22, 57
Colonial Ford (Tijuana), 257
Colorado House, 178
Columbus Direct, 40
Comedy Store, 203
Concerts, 4, 150
  Del Mar, 210
  Twilight in the Park
    Concerts, 17
Concierges, tipping, 47
Concours d'Elegance, 19
Condor Ridge, 2
Consolidators, 27
Consulates, 44
Contact Tours, 155, 258
Contemporary Art, Museum
  of, Downtown (MCA), 142
Contemporary Art, Museum
  of (MCA), San Diego
  (La Jolla), 146, 148
Continental Airlines, 26
Continental Airlines
  Vacations, 30
Convention Center, 177
Coronado
  accommodations, 89–93
  bridge to, 4

brief description of, 54–55
ferries, 4
main streets of, 51
restaurants, 120–123
shopping, 192–194, 197
sights and attractions, 149,
  151
Coronado Bay Bridge, 50,
  149
Coronado Beach, 132
Coronado Boat Rental, 158,
  160
Coronado Cab Company, 61
Coronado Christmas Cele-
  bration and Parade, 20
Coronado Ferry, 176
Coronado Historical
  Museum, 149
Coronado Hospital, 63
Coronado Livery, 49
Coronado Municipal Golf
  Course, 161
Coronado Shuttle (bus
  Route 904), 59
Coronado Touring, 156
Coronado Visitors Bureau,
  website, 9
Coronado Visitors Center,
  11, 50
Council on International
  Educational Exchange, 24
Council Travel, 24
Country Carriages (Julian),
  248
County Administration
  Center, 174
Courtesy (Tijuana), 257
Cove, 207
Cracker Factory Antiques
  Shopping Center, 194
Credit cards, 13, 40–41
  car-rental insurance and,
    57
Crescent Cafe, 192
Critter Country (Disneyland),
  235–236
Croce's Nightclubs, 6, 202
Cruise-Ship Terminal, San
  Diego, 174, 176
Culinary Cottage (Julian),
  249
Curbside check-in, 26
Curiosidades La Joya
  (Ensenada), 277
Currency, 40
  Mexican, 260
Customs clearance, 42
Customs regulations,
  38–39

Cuyamaca, Lake, 160
Cuyamaca Rancho State Park
  (near Julian), 250
Cybercafes.com, 33

D ale's Swim Shop, 194
Dana, Richard Henry, 34
Dance, 202
  Indian Fair, 17
  Nations of San Diego Inter-
    national Dance Festival,
    15
Dance clubs and cabarets,
  203–204
David Zapf Gallery, 195
Davis, William Heath, House
  Museum, 142, 172
Day at the Docks, 16, 166
Day Tripper pass, 58
Debtors Anonymous, 63
Del Mar, 135, 209–213
  accommodations, 212–213
  restaurants, 213
Del Mar City Beach, 210
Del Mar Fair, 17
Del Mar National Horse
  Show, 16, 167
Del Mar Racetrack & Fair-
  grounds, 166–167, 207,
  210
  Thoroughbred Racing
    Season, 17
Del Mar Satellite Wagering,
  207
Delta Airlines, 26
Delta Vacations, 30
Dentists, 63
Department stores, 196
Desert Descent, 158
Desert Jeep Tours (Anza-
  Borrego Desert State
  Park), 254
Desert Natural History Asso-
  ciation (Anza-Borrego
  Desert State Park), 254
Design Center, 190
Diners Club cathedrals, 40
Dining. See Restaurant
  Index; Restaurants
Directory assistance, 46
Disabilities, travelers with,
  22–23
Discover credit cards, 40
Disneyland and environs
  (Anaheim), 231–238
  accommodations, 240–244
  admission, hours and infor-
    mation, 232–233

Disneyland and environs (Anaheim) *(cont.)*
　downtown, 238
　Knott's Berry Farm, 238–240
　restaurants, 244–246
　Richard Nixon Library and Birthplace (Yorba Linda), 240
　tips on, 233–235
　traveling to, 232
　visitor information, 232
Disneyland Resort, 3
Doctors, 63
Documentation, 26
Dolphin Interaction Program (SeaWorld), 131
Doormen, tipping, 47
Downtown
　accommodations, 67–73
　brief description of, 51
　major thoroughfares of, 51
　restaurants, 97–102, 208
　shopping, 187–189
　sights and attractions, 141–150
Downtown Disney, 238
Downtown Sam, 24
Drinking laws, 44
Driver's licenses, foreign, 37
Driving rules, 58
Driving safety, 41–42
Dr. Seuss Christmas Readings, 19
Drugstores, 64
Dudley's Bakery (Julian), 249–250

Eagle and High Peak Mines (Julian), 248
East County Performing Arts Center, 200
Eddie Bauer, 198
Edward, Prince of Wales (later Edward VIII, then duke of Windsor), 92
Edward Willis and Ellen Browning Scripps: An Unmatched Pair (Preece), 35
El Cid Campeador (sculpture), 184
Elderhostel, 24
Electricity, 44
Ellen Browning Scripps Park (La Jolla), 135, 146
El Mirador lookout (Mexico), 272

Embarcadero Marina Park, 203
Embarcadero walking tour, 174–177
Embassies and consulates, 44
Emerald City Surf & Sport, 131
Emerald-Shapery Center, 152
Emerald Surf & Sport, 165
Emergencies, 44, 63
Encinitas, 20, 213–219
Encinitas Visitors Center, 20
Enrico Sterling (Rosarito Beach), 270
Ensenada (Mexico), 272, 275–280
Entry requirements, 36–39
E-Savers, 27, 32
Escondido, 223–224
Espresso Net, 206
Euphoria, 206
Europ Assistance, 39
Euterpe, 174
Expedia, 32
Eyeglass repair, 63

Fall Flower Tours, 20
Families with children
　air travel, 29
　information and resources, 24
　restaurants, 109
　sights and attractions, 151–152
Family Travel, 24
Family Travel Times, 24
Fantasyland (Disneyland), 236
Farmer's Market (Horton Plaza), 124
Farmers' markets, 6, 197, 249
Fashion Valley Center, 198
Fax machines, 46
Ferrari, Marianne, 23
Ferries, 61
　Coronado, 4
Ferry Landing Marketplace, 194
Festival of the Bells, 17
Festivals and special events, 14–20
Festival Stage, 208
Fiesta Village (Knott's Berry Farm), 239
Fifth Avenue, 50

52-mile San Diego Scenic Drive, 150
Film, flying with, 29
Film Safety for Traveling on Planes, 29
Fingerhut Gallery, 195
Finnegan's Week (Wambaugh), 34
Firehouse Museum, 141
Fireworks, 208
First National Bank (Temecula), 228–229
Fishing, 160
　Day at the Docks, 16
　Ensenada (Mexico), 278
　tournaments, 166
Fish market, 275
Fish tacos, 124
Flame, The, 207
Flea markets, 197
Fleet, Reuben H., Science Center, 139
Floaters (Wambaugh), 34
Flower Fields in Bloom at Carlsbad Ranch, 16
FLY-CHEAP, 27
Foods, New & Nouveau Wine & Food Tasting (Temecula), 19
Football, 166
Foreign visitors, 36–47
　entry requirements, 36–39
　immigration and customs clearance, 42
　medical insurance for, 39–40
　money matters, 40–41
　safety suggestions, 41–42
　traveling around the United States, 42–43
　traveling to the United States, 42
Four Seasons Resort Aviara Golf Club, 161
4th & B, 202–203
Fourth of July (Julian), 247
Foxploration (near Rosarito Beach), 271
Freddy's Teddies & Toys, 198
Free sights and activities, 149–151
Frey Block Building, 172
Frommers.com, 32
Frontierland (Disneyland), 236
Frontón Palacio (Tijuana), 264
F. W. Woolworth Building, 170

Gardeners, sights of
interest to, 153
Gardens, 182
  Japanese Friendship Gar-
    den, 136, 138, 184
  Quail Botanical Gardens
    (Encinitas), 215
Gaslamp Quarter, 4, 152
  accommodations, 67–73
  brief description of, 51
  safety suggestions, 41
  shopping, 187–189
  sights and attractions, 141
  Street Scene, 18
  walking tour, 168–173
Gaslamp Quarter Association
  website, 9
Gaslamp Quarter Historical
  Foundation, 157, 168
Gasoline, 45
Gay and lesbian travelers
  Annual San Diego Lesbian
    and Gay Pride Parade,
    Rally, and Festival, 17, 23
  information and resources,
    23
  nightlife, 206–207
Gay Men's Health Crisis, 37
Gay Travel A to Z: The World
  of Gay & Lesbian Travel
  Options at Your Finger-
  tips, (Ferrari), 23
GEM Publishing Group, 24
George's Camera & Video,
  62
Ghost Town (Knott's Berry
  Farm), 239
Giant Dipper Roller Coaster,
  145
Gill, Irving, 34, 86, 138, 146,
  148, 153, 170, 173
Girard Gourmet, 10, 124
Globe Theatres, 201
Golden Hill, 55
Golden State (Disneyland),
  237
Golden Vine Winery
  (Disneyland), 237
Golf, 160–163
  Buick Invitational, 15
  near Ensenada, 272–273
  Ram's Hill Country Club
    (Anza-Borrego Desert
    State Park), 254
  Temecula, 229
  Tijuana (Mexico), 264
  tournaments, 166
Gondola Company, 92, 154

Gordo's Sportfishing
  (Ensenada), 278
GO 25 card, 25
Grand Circle Travel, 24
Gravity Activated Sports,
  158, 224, 226, 255
Gray Line, Tijuana tour, 258
Gray Line San Diego, 155
Greyhound racing, 207
Grunion Run, 6, 148
Guadalupe Valley (Mexico),
  Harvest Festival, 18
Guatemala Store, 190

Hairdressers, tipping, 47
Hall of Champions, 136
Hamel's Action Sports
  Center, 157, 164
Hand inspections of film,
  videotape, and
  camcorders, 29
H & M Landing, 160
Harbor Days Festival
  (Oceanside), 220
Harbor Drive, 50, 51
Hard Rock Cafe, 3
Harmony on Fifth, 203
Harvest festivals, 18, 262
Health Canada, 40
Health concerns, 20
Health insurance, 20, 21
  for foreign visitors, 39–40
Heart of Africa (San Diego
  Wild Animal Park), 130
Heritage Park, 143–144,
  180–181
Hertz, 23
HGH Pro-Am Golf Classic,
  166
Hiking and walking, 163.
  See also Walking tours
  Mission Trails Regional
    Park, 150
Hillcrest Cinema, 207
Hillcrest Street Fair, 17–18
Hillcrest/Uptown, 23
  brief description of, 51, 54
  main streets of, 51
  restaurants, 102–106, 208
  shopping, 189, 197
Hilton San Diego Resort,
  157
Hines, Thomas S., 34
Historical Society Museum,
  San Diego, 140
Historic houses
  La Casa de Estudillo, 178
  McCoy House, 177

  Robinson-Rose House, 178
  Villa Montezuma, 142
  Whaley House, 144
  William Heath Davis House
    Museum, 142, 172
HIV Hot Line, 63
HIV-positive visitors, 37
HM Customs & Excise, 39
Holiday Bowl, 166
Holidays, 45
Holidays on Horseback, 164
Hollywood Pictures Backlot
  (Disneyland), 237–238
Hornblower Cruises &
  Events, 154, 156, 204
Horseback riding, 164
Horse-drawn carriages
  (Julian), 248
Horse racing, 166–167
  Thoroughbred Racing
    Season, 17
Horse Show, Del Mar
  National, 16
Horse shows, 167
Horton Grand Hotel, 172
Horton Plaza, 141, 168, 170,
  187–188
  garage at, 57
Horton Plaza Park, 170
Hospitals, 63
Hot-air ballooning, 6, 157
  Del Mar, 210
  Temecula, 16–17, 229
Hotel Circle, 76
Hotel del Coronado, 149.
  See also Accommodations
  Index
  famous people associated
    with, 92
Hotel Discounts, 66
Hotel Docs, 63
Hotel Locators, 66
Hotels. See Accommodations;
  Accommodations Index
Hot lines, 63
House of Charm, 182
House of Pacific Relations
  International Cottages,
  136, 184
How to Take Great Trips
  with Your Kids, 24
Humphrey's, 203
Hussong's Cantina
  (Ensenada), 280
Hustler Hollywood San
  Diego, 3
Hyatt Regency La Jolla, 153

Ice Capades Chalet, 164
Ice hockey, 167
Ice skating, 164
Immaculate Conception Catholic Church, 180
Immigration and customs clearance, 42
Immigration and Naturalization Service (INS), HIV-positive noncitizens and, 37
Imperial Beach, 131
    U.S. Open Sandcastle Competition, 18
Independence Day Parade (Rancho Santa Fe), 222
Indiana Jones Adventure (Disneyland), 235
Indian Fair, 17, 139
Indian Trails (Knott's Berry Farm), 240
Information sources, 11, 50
In Good Taste, 193
In-line skating, 164
In Motion, 167
Inspiration Point, 144
Insurance
    for British travelers, 39–40
    for Canadian travelers, 40
    car-rental, 22
    lost-luggage, 21–22
    medical, 20, 21
    travel, 20–22
    trip-cancellation (TCI), 21
Intellicast, 33
International Ameripass, 43
International Dance Festival, 202
International Gay & Lesbian Travel Association, 23
International student ID card, 24
International Visitor Information Center, 11, 14, 50, 51, 151
International visitors, 36–47
    entry requirements, 36–39
    immigration and customs clearance, 42
    medical insurance for, 39–40
    money matters, 40–41
    safety suggestions, 41–42
    traveling around the United States, 42–43
    traveling to the United States, 42
Internet, the. See Websites
Internet cafes, 206
Internet Coffee, 206

InTouch USA, 41–42
Ireland, embassy of, 44
Irish citizens, passport and visa information for, 36, 38
Irish Festival, 16
Irving Gill and the Architecture of Reform: A Study in Modernist Architectural Culture (Hines), 34
Island Hoppers, 192
Islandia Sportfishing, 160

Jackson, Helen Hunt, 34
Jai alai (Tijuana), 207, 264
Japan, embassy of, 44
Japan Airlines, 42
Japanese Friendship Garden, 136, 138, 184
Java Joe's, 206
Jazz, 6
Jewelry, Rosarito Beach (Mexico), 270
Jewish Community Center, 165
Jogging, 164
John Cole's Book Shop, 192, 196
John's Fifth Avenue Luggage, 198
Julian, 246–252
Julian Bed & Breakfast Guild, 251
Julian Bicycle Company, 250
Julian Chamber of Commerce, 18
Julian Cider Mill, 249
Julian Drug Store & Miner's Diner, 248
Julian Pie Company, 249
Julian's Arts and Crafts Show, 19
Julian Tea & Cottage Arts, 249
Julian Weed Show, 18, 247
Junior Theatre, San Diego, 152

Kahuna Bob's Surf School, 165
Kangaroo Bus Tour, 128
Karl Strauss Brewery Gardens, 205
Karl Strauss Brewery & Grill, Downtown, 205
Karl Strauss Brewery & Grill, La Jolla, 205
Kayaking, 4
    Carlsbad, 217

Kearns Memorial Swimming Pool, 165
Keating Building, 171
Ken Cinema, 207
Kensington, 54
Kickers, 207
Kilimanjaro safari walk (San Diego Wild Animal Park), 130
Kite Festival, Ocean Beach, 16
Knott's Berry Farm, 238–240
Kobey's Swap Meet, 197

La Bufadora (near Ensenada), 277
La Casa de Estudillo, 178
La Jolla
    accommodations, 84–89
    Art Festival in the Village of La Jolla, 18
    brief description of, 54
    Buick Invitational, 15
    cafes, 118
    main avenues of, 51
    nightlife and entertainment, 201, 203, 205–208
    restaurants, 114–120
    shopping, 192
    sidewalk cafes, 6
    sights and attractions, 146–148, 150–151
    Underwater Pumpkin Carving Contest (La Jolla), 19
    visitor information, 50
    walking tours, 157
La Jolla Arts Festival, 195
La Jolla Brewing Company, 205
La Jolla Cab, 61
La Jolla Cove, 135, 146
La Jolla Half Marathon, 167
La Jolla Playhouse, 201
La Jolla Recreation Center, 146
La Jolla Rough Water Swim, 18, 165
La Jolla Shoe Gallery, 192
La Jolla Shores Beach, 135
La Jolla Sports and Photo, 157
La Jolla Surf Systems, 165
La Jolla Tennis Club, 165
La Jolla Walking Tours, 157
La Jolla Woman's Club, 146
Lake Miramar Reservoir, 163
Lamb's Players Theatre, 201
La Provençale, 193
La Tablita de Tony (Tijuana), 267

La Valencia Hotel (La Jolla), 146
Layout of San Diego, 50–51
LDW (Loss/Damage Waiver), 57
Lee Palm Sportfishers, 160
Legal aid, 45
LEGOLAND (Carlsbad), 3, 126, 152, 214
Lesbian and Gay Men's Community Center, 23
Le Travel Store, 51, 199
Liberty Travel, 31
Libros, 190
Lincoln Hotel, 172
Lindbergh, Charles, 92
Liquor laws, 63
Little Italy, brief description of, 51
Llama Trek (Julian), 250–251
Llewelyn Building, 171
Loft, The (Temecula), 229
Longboard Surf Club Competition, 18
Long's Drug Store, 64
Loss/Damage Waiver (LDW), 22, 57
Lost-luggage insurance, 21–22
Louganis, Greg, 35
Louis Bank of Commerce, 170
Luggage, carry-on baggage restrictions, 26, 27
Lyceum Theatre, 202

MacPhail, Elizabeth C., 35
Macy's, 196
Mail, 45
Main arteries and streets, 50–51
Main Street U.S.A. (Disneyland), 235
Malls, 198
Manatee Rescue exhibit (SeaWorld), 131
Manchester Grand Hyatt San Diego, 152
Many Hands, 195
Map Centre, 199
Mapquest, 33
Maps
  bike, 61
  street, 51
Marathon, America's Finest City Half, 167
Marathon, La Jolla Half, 167
Marathon, San Diego, 15, 167
Marian Bear Memorial Park, 163

Marie Hitchcock Puppet Theatre, 152
Mariner's Point, 132
Marion's Childcare, 62
Maritime Museum, 142, 174
Market Street, open-air parking lot on, 58
Marston Building, 170
Marston House Museum, 138, 152
Martini Ranch, 204
Mary Star of the Sea (La Jolla), 146
Mason Street School, 180
MasterCard, 13
  ATM Locator, 33
  credit cards, 40
Matheson, Richard, 34
Mature Traveler, The (newsletter), 24
Maurice Car'rie Winery/Van Roekel Vineyards (Temecula), 228
MCA (Museum of Contemporary Art), San Diego (La Jolla), 146, 148
MCA Downtown (Museum of Contemporary Art, Downtown), 142
McCoy House, 177
Medea, 174
Medic Alert Identification Tag, 20
Medical insurance, 20, 21
  for foreign visitors, 39–40
Medical requirements for entry, 36–37
Medications
  prescription, 20
  syringe-administered, 37
Mental Health Access & Crisis Line, 63
Mercado de Artesanías (Crafts Market) (Tijuana), 263
Mercado Hidalgo (Tijuana), 264
Metropolitan Hotel, 172
Metropolitan Transit System (MTS), 48
Mexican Americans
  Cinco de Mayo Celebration, 17
  Serra Museum, 144
Mexican Art Bazaar (Ensenada), 278
Mexican Department of Fisheries, 160
Mexico, 257. See also Baja California; Tijuana

new national phone numbering plan, 3
  San Diego Trolley to, 6
Mexicoach/Five Star Tours, 258
Mexitlán (Tijuana), 261–262
Mickey's Toontown (Disneyland), 236
Microbreweries, 205
Midwest Express, 25
Mike's Bikes, 164
Military buffs, sightseeing for, 153
Mingei International Museum, 138
Mission Basilica San Diego de Alcala, 144
Mission Bay and the Beaches, 4, 132
  accommodations, 79–83
  brief description of, 54
  restaurants, 110–114
  shopping, 190–192
  sights and attractions, 145, 150
  World Championship Over-the-Line Tournament, 17
Mission Bay Boat Parade of Lights, 20
Mission Bay Park, 132
Mission Bay Sportcenter, 158
Mission Bay Visitor Information Center, 11, 50
Mission Hills Nursery, 153
Mission Point, 132
Mission San Diego de Alcala, 17
Mission San Luis Rey (Oceanside), 34, 220
Mission Trails Regional Park, 150, 163
Mission Valley, 54
  accommodations, 76–79
  shopping, 189–190
Mission Valley Center, 198
Model Railroad Museum, 138
Modern Maturity (magazine), 24
Mom's Pies (Julian), 248
Money matters, 11–14
  for foreign visitors, 40–41
Money-saving tips
  on accommodations, 65–66
  Balboa Park, 136
  bus and trolley passes, 58
  on car rentals, 56
Monorail, San Diego Wild Animal Park, 128
Moonlight Beach (Encinitas), 135, 216

Morgan's Antiques (Temecula), 229
Mount Palomar Winery (Temecula), 226
Mount Woodson Country Club, 161–162
Movies, 207
Movies Before the Mast, 208
Mundo Divertido (Tijuana), 261
Murray, Lake, 163
Museo de Cera (Tijuana), 260
Museum of Contemporary Art, Downtown (MCA), 142
Museum of Contemporary Art (MCA), San Diego (La Jolla), 146, 148
Museum of Making Music (Carlsbad), 214
Museum of Man, 139, 182
Museum of Photographic Arts, 139
Museums, 174
    Children's Museum of San Diego, 141, 152
    Coronado Historical Museum, 149
    Firehouse Museum, 141
    free days, 150
    Maritime Museum, 142
    Marston House Museum, 138
    Mingei International Museum, 138
    Model Railroad Museum, 138
    Museum of Contemporary Art, Downtown (MCA), 142
    Museum of Contemporary Art (MCA), San Diego (La Jolla), 146, 148
    Museum of Making Music (Carlsbad), 214
    Museum of Man, 139, 182
    Museum of Photographic Arts, 139
    San Diego Aerospace Museum, 139
    San Diego Automotive Museum, 140
    San Diego Historical Society Museum, 140
    San Diego Museum of Art, 140
    Serra Museum, 144
    Stuart Collection (La Jolla), 148
    William Heath Davis House Museum, 142

N airobi Village, 129–130
Nana's Antiques (Temecula), 229
Narcotics, 37
National Center for HIV, 37
Nations of San Diego International Dance Festival, 15
Native Americans
    casinos, 207
    Indian Fair, 17
    Serra Museum, 144
Natural History Museum, San Diego, 140, 156, 157, 163
Neighborhoods, map of, 52–53
Nelson Photo Supply, 62
Net Café Guide, 33
New & Nouveau Wine & Food Tasting (Temecula), 19
New Orleans Square (Disneyland), 235
Newport Ave. Antique Center, 192
Newport Avenue, 192
Newport Avenue Antiques, 192
Newport-Ensenada Regatta, 16
Newspapers and magazines, 63
New Zealand, embassy of, 44
New Zealand citizens
    customs regulations for, 39
    passport and visa information for, 36, 38
Nightlife and entertainment, 200–208
    bars and cocktail lounges, 204–206
    coffeehouses with performances, 206
    Ensenada (Mexico), 280
    gay and lesbian, 206–207
    movies, 207
    performing arts, 200–202
    Rosarito Beach (Mexico), 271
    Tijuana (Mexico), 267
    what's new in, 3
Nixon, Richard, Library and Birthplace (Yorba Linda), 240
Nordstrom, 196, 198
North County
    beaches and beach towns, 135, 209–231. See also specific towns
    nurseries, 194

North County Nursery Hoppers Association (Encinitas), 215
North Park, 54
Northwest Airlines, 25
Nude beach, 135

O belisk Bookstore, 23, 196
O.B. Emporium, 192
Ocean Beach, 132
    farmers' market, 197
Ocean Beach Kite Festival, 16
Ocean Front Walk, 132
Ocean's Eleven Casino (Oceanside), 221
Oceanside, 135, 209, 219–221
Oceanside Beach, 220
Oceanside Rough Water Swim, 165
Off the Record, 189
Old City Hall, 171
Old Globe Theatre, 182
Old Julian Book House, 249
Old Town, 54
    accommodations, 76–79
    restaurants, 106–110
    shopping, 189–190
    sights and attractions, 142–144, 150
    walking tour, 177–181
Old Town Liquor and Deli, 124
Old Town State Historic Park, 152
Old Town Temecula Rod Run, 15–16
Old Town Trolley Tours, 60, 155
Olé Madrid, 203–204
OMNIMAX, 207
One America Plaza, 152
101 Tips for the Mature Traveler, 24
Online Vacation Mall, 30–31
Open World (magazine), 22
Opera, 201
Optometric Expressions, 63
Optometry on the Plaza, 63
Orange Cab, 61
Orbitz, 33
Orfila Vineyards, 153–154
Organ Pavilion, Spreckels, 140, 184
Organ recitals, in Balboa Park, 4
Ould Sod, 204
Out and About, 23

Outdoor activities, 157–165
  ballooning, 157
  biking, 157–158
  boating, 158, 160
  fishing, 160
  golf, 160–163
  hiking and walking, 163
  horseback riding, 164
  jogging and running, 164
  in and around Julian,
    250–251
  scuba diving and snorkel-
    ing, 164
  skating, 164
  surfing, 164–165
  swimming, 165

Pacific Beach, 132
  farmers' market, 197
  main streets of, 51
Pacific Beach Sun and Sea,
  164
Pacific Classic, 167
Pacific Queen, 156
Package tour operators,
  30–31
Package tours, 30–31
  Disneyland, 234
Packing for your trip, 28
Padres Express bus, 166
Palace Bar, 204
Palm Arboretum, 184
Palomar Mountain, 224
Palomar Observatory, 224
Palomar Plunge, 158, 224
Pandas (San Diego Zoo), 129
Papas & Beer (Ensenada),
  280
Papas & Beer (Rosarito
  Beach), 271
Parades
  Annual San Diego Lesbian
    and Gay Pride Parade,
    Rally, and Festival, 17
  Coronado Christmas Cele-
    bration and Parade, 20
  Mission Bay Boat Parade of
    Lights, 20
  Ocean Beach Kite Festival,
    16
  St. Patrick's Day Parade, 16
  San Diego Harbor Parade
    of Lights, 20
Paradise Pier (Disneyland),
  237
Parking, 57–58
  near restaurants, 95
Parking meters, 58

Parks
  Balboa Park. See Balboa
    Park
  Children's Park, 150, 152
  Ellen Browning Scripps
    Park, 135, 146
  Heritage Park, 143–144,
    180–181
  Horton Plaza Park, 170
  Marian Bear Memorial
    Park, 163
  Mission Trails Regional
    Park, 163
Paseo de los Héroes
  (Tijuana), 261
Passport information, 37–38
Passport to Balboa Park, 136
Pedroreña House, 180
Peerless Shuttle, 49
Performing arts, 200–202
Petrol, 45
Pets, travelers with, 25
Pets-R-Permitted Hotel,
  Motel & Kennel Directory,
  25
Pets Rule! (animal show), 2
Pharmacies, 64
Photo caravan tour (San
  Diego Wild Animal Park),
  130
Photographic Arts, Museum
  of, 139
Picnic fare, 10, 124
Pilar's, 192
Pine Hills Dinner Theater
  (Julian), 252
Pine Hills Lodge (Julian), 252
Pioneer Cemetery (Julian),
  250
Pirates (SeaWorld), 130–131
Pirates of the Caribbean
  (Disneyland), 235
Pizza restaurants, 123–124
Playback (Chandler), 34
Plaza Cívica (Ensenada), 276
Plaza del Zapato (Tijuana),
  263
Plaza Río Tijuana, 263
Plunge, 165
PLUS ATMs, 12
Poinsettia Street Festival, 20
Point Loma Camera Store,
  62
Point Loma Seafoods, 124
Point Loma Sportfishing,
  160
Police, 64
Polo, 167
Portable Petswelcome.com,
  The, 25

Post offices, 64
Pratt Gallery, 195
Prepaid calling cards, 46
Prescription medications, 20
Priceline, 33
Primavera Pastry Caffé, 124
Princess Pub & Grille, 205
Professional Photographic
  Repair, 62
Promote La Jolla, 11, 50
Pueblo Amigo (Tijuana), 267
Puerto Nuevo (Mexico), 274
  lobster village in, 6
Pump House Gang, The
  (Wolfe), 34, 134
Putnam, Arthur, 144

Qantas, 42
Qixo, 33
Quail Botanical Gardens
  (Encinitas), 153, 215
Qualcomm Stadium, 166, 203
QuickAid's Guide to the San
  Diego Airport, 49
Quikbook, 66

Rainfall, average, 14
Ramona: A Story (Jackson),
  34
Rancho Bernardo Inn, 162
Rancho Santa Fe, 221–223
Rancho Santa Fe Polo Club,
  167
Random Oaks Ranch, 251
Reader, 50, 63, 200, 203
Red alert checklist, 12
Regatta, Newport-Ensenada,
  16
Reservation services, for
  accommodations, 66
Restaurants, 94–124. See
  also Restaurant Index
  best, 8–10
  Borrego Springs, 256–257
  Carlsbad, 219
  Coronado, 120–123
  by cuisine, 95–97
  Del Mar, 213
  Disneyland and environs,
    244–246
  downtown, 97–102, 208
  Ensenada (Mexico),
    279–280
  family-friendly, 109
  Hillcrest/Uptown, 208
  Julian, 252
  La Jolla, 114–120
  late-night, 208

Restaurants *(cont.)*
Mission Bay and the Beaches, 110–114
with ocean views, 119
Old Town, 106–110
pizza, 123–124
Rancho Santa Fe, 223
Rosarito Beach (Mexico), 270–271
Tijuana (Mexico), 265–267
tipping at, 47
what's new in, 2
Restrooms, 47, 64
Reuben H. Fleet Science Center, 139
Reversed-charge calls, 46
Richard Nixon Library and Birthplace (Yorba Linda), 240
Rich's, 207
Ride Link Bicycle Information, 157
Rite-Aid, 64
Rivers of America (Disneyland), 236
Riverwalk Golf Club, 162
Roar and Snore program (San Diego Wild Animal Park), 130
Robinson-Rose House, 178
Rodeo de Media Noche (Tijuana), 267
Rosarito Beach (Mexico), 268–271
Rosarito-Ensenada 50-Mile Fun Bicycle Ride (Mexico), 16, 19, 158
Royal Pie Bakery Building, 172
Running, 164
Running with Grunion, 6, 148

S afety, 41–42
Sailing (yachting). *See also* Boating
Newport-Ensenada Regatta, 16
Sail USA, 160
St. Patrick's Day Parade, 16
Salk Institute for Biological Studies (La Jolla), 146, 153
Salón Méxican (Rosarito Beach), 271
Salsipuedes Bay (Mexico), 272
Salsipuedes Campground (Mexico), 272

Sam Hicks Park (Temecula), 228
Sanborn's (Tijuana), 263
Sandcastle Competition, U.S. Open, 18
San Diego Aerospace Museum, 139, 184
San Diego Area Dance Alliance Calendar, 202
San Diego Automotive Museum, 140, 184
San Diego Bed & Breakfast Guild, 67
San Diego Bicycle Coalition, 157
San Diego Cab, 61
San Diego Chargers, 166
San Diego Convention & Visitors Bureau, website, 9
San Diego County Dental Society, 63
San Diego Court House and City Hall, 180
San Diego Crew Classic, 16
San Diego Cruise-Ship Terminal, 174, 176
San Diego Divers Supply, 131, 164
San Diego Factory Outlet Center, 198
San Diego Family Press, 151
San Diego Floral Association, 153
San Diego Gay and Lesbian Times, 23, 200
San Diego Gay & Lesbian Chamber of Commerce, 23
San Diego Golf Reservations, 161
San Diego Gulls, 167
San Diego Harbor Excursions, 154–156, 204
San Diego Harbor Parade of Lights, 20
San Diego Hardware, 170
San Diego Historical Society Museum, 140
San Diego Home-Garden Lifestyles magazine, 63
San Diego Hotel Reservations, 66
San Diego International Airport (Lindbergh Field), 25
accommodations near, 93
arriving at, 48
San Diego International Triathlon, 167
San Diego Junior Theatre, 152, 200–201

San Diego–La Jolla Underwater Park (La Jolla), 146, 164
San Diego magazine, 63
website, 9
San Diego Marathon, 15, 167
San Diego Marriott Marina, 177
San Diego Museum of Art, 140
San Diego Natural History Museum, 140, 156
San Diego North County Convention & Visitors Bureau, 11
San Diego Opera, 201
San Diego Padres, 166
San Diego Performing Arts League, 11, 200
San Diego Reader, website, 9
San Diego Region Bike Map, 61
San Diego Repertory Theatre, 200
San Diego Ridelink, 61
San Diego Sailing Club, 158
San Diego's Historic Gaslamp Quarter: Then and Now, 168
San Diego Sockers, 167
San Diego Sports Arena, 203
San Diego Surfing Academy, 165
San Diego Track Club, 167
San Diego Trolley, 59
San Diego Union Building, 180
San Diego Union-Tribune, 50, 63, 200
website, 9
San Diego Visitors Planning Guide, 50, 51
San Diego Wild Animal Park, 2, 128–130, 151
San Diego Yacht & Breakfast Club, 158
San Diego Zoo, 2, 35, 126, 128, 150, 151
pandas, 129
Zoo Founders Day, 19
Santa Fe Railroad Station, 176
Santa Fe Station, 49
Santa Rosa Plateau Ecological Reserve (Temecula), 229
Sav-On Drugs, 64
Scale model of San Diego, 152–153

SciTours, 139
Score Baja 500, 165
Score Baja 1,000, 165
Scripps Park (La Jolla), 135, 146
Scuba diving, 164
    Underwater Pumpkin Carving Contest (La Jolla), 19
SDSU Open Air Amphitheater, 203
Sea and Land Adventure Tours (SEAL), 2–3, 155
Seafood, 94
Seaforth Boat Rental, 158, 160
Sea lions, 126, 130, 131, 135, 156
Seals, 4, 6
Seaport Village, 141, 152, 176, 188–189
Seasons, 14
SeaWorld, 2, 128, 130–131, 151
Security measures, air travel, 26
Seeley Stables Visitor Center, 143
Senior travelers, 23–24
Señor Frogs (Tijuana), 267
Sergio's Sportfishing Center (Ensenada), 278
Serra, Junípero, 8, 144, 170, 178
Serra Museum, 144
Sevilla, 204
Shamu's Happy Harbor (SeaWorld), 130
Shipwreck Rapids (SeaWorld), 130
Shopping, 187–199
    Ensenada (Mexico), 277–278
    Julian, 249–250
    Rosarito Beach (Mexico), 270
    Tijuana (Mexico), 262–264
    top streets and neighborhoods for, 187–194
    what's new in, 3
Sierra Club, 163
Sights and attractions, 125–157
    Balboa Park. See Balboa Park, attractions in
    Coronado, 149, 151
    downtown, 141–150
    Ensenada (Mexico), 275
    free, 149–151
    for kids, 151–152
    La Jolla, 146–148, 150–151

Mission Bay and the Beaches, 145, 150
    Old Town, 150
    organized tours, 154–157
    special-interest, 152–154
    suggested itineraries, 125–126
    Tijuana (Mexico), 260–262
    what's new in, 2
Simpson, Wallis, 92
Singing Hills Resort, 162
Skates Plus, 164
Skating, 164
Skycaps, tipping, 47
Skyfari, 128
Skysurfer Balloon Company, 157, 210
Smarter Living, 32
Smoking, 64, 202
Snorkeling, 164
Soccer, 167
Society for Accessible Travel and Hospitality, 22–23
Softball, World Championship Over-the-Line Tournament, 17, 167
Soledad, Mount, 146
SOMA and Quint, 195
Some Like It Hot (movie), 92
Somewhere In Time (Matheson), 34
South Carlsbad State Beach, 216
Southwest Airlines, 25
Southwest Airlines Vacations, 30
Spanish Village Art Center, 185
Spas, 1
Special events and festivals, 14–20
Spectator sports, 165–167
    Super Bowl XXXVII (2003), 1, 15
    Tijuana (Mexico), 264
Spencer-Ogden Building, 171
Spirit of St. Louis, 139
Spreckels Organ Pavilion, 140, 184
Stadium Golf Center, 161
Starlight Theater, 208
Star of India, 174
State Department, U.S., 36
STA Travel, 25
Steve McClelland, 195
Stolen wallet, 13–14
Story of New San Diego and of its Founder, Alonzo E. Horton, The (MacPhail), 35

Strand, the (Oceanside), 220–221
Street maps, 51
Streets, 50–51
Street Scene, Gaslamp Quarter, 18
Stuart Collection (La Jolla), 148
Students, 24–25
Studio Arts Complex, 195
Summer Nights, 208
Sunglasses, 28
Sunny Jim Cave (La Jolla), 146, 192
Sunrise Balloons (Temecula), 229
Sunset watching, 6
Super Bowl XXXVII (2003), 1, 15
Super Savings Coupon Book, 50
Surfing, 164–165
    California Surf Museum (Oceanside), 220
    competitions, 18
    Tourmaline Surfing Park, 132
Suzett bakery (Tijuana), 263
Swami's Beach (Encinitas), 135, 216
Swimming, 28, 165
    La Jolla Rough Water Swim, 18, 165
Sycuan Gaming Center, 207
Syringe-administered medications, 37

T aboo Studio, 195
Taco stands, at the beaches, 134
Tamarisk Grove, 256
Taxes, 46
    Tijuana (Mexico), 260
Taxis
    to/from the airport, 49
    within San Diego, 60–61
    Tijuana (Mexico), 258
    tipping, 47
Telephone numbers, useful, 64
Telephones, 46
    Tijuana (Mexico), 260
Temecula, 154, 225–231
    New & Nouveau Wine & Food Tasting, 19
Temecula Balloon and Wine Festival, 157
Temecula Mercantile building, 229

Temecula Town Association, 16
Temecula Trading Post, 229
Temecula Valley Balloon & Wine Festival, 16–17
Temecula Valley Museum, 228
Temecula Valley Vintners Association, 19
Temperatures, average, 14
Tennis, 165
    tournaments, 167
Theater, 200–201
Thomas Bros. Guide, 51
Thomas Cook traveler's checks, 40
Thornton Hospital, 63
Thornton Winery (Temecula), 226
Thoroughbred Racing Season, 17
Thousand Mile Outdoor Wear, 194
Ticketmaster, 203
Tide pools, 131
Tijuana (Mexico), 257–267
    climate and weather, 260
    currency, 260
    helpful tips, 258
    nightlife, 267
    restaurants, 265–267
    shopping, 262–264
    sights and attractions, 260–262
    taxes, 260
    telephones, 260
    tipping, 260
    transportation, 258
    traveling to, 257–258
    visitor information, 258
Tijuana Country Club, 264
Time zones, 46–47, 64
Timken Museum of Art, 140–141
Tipping, 47
    Tijuana (Mexico), 260
Titanic (movie), 271
Toilets, 47
Tolán (Tijuana), 263
Tomorrowland (Disneyland), 236
Top O' The Cove, 206
Torrey Pines Golf Course, 162–163
    Buick Invitational, 15
    Concours d'Elegance, 19
Torrey Pines State Reserve, 157, 163
Toshiba Tennis Classic, 167
Tourist information, 11, 50

Tourmaline Surfing Park, 132
Tours
    Balboa Park, 136
    organized, 154–157
    package, 30–31
        Disneyland, 234
    walking. *See* Walking tours
Toys, 198
Train travel
    to North County beach towns, 209
    to San Diego, 30, 49
    within San Diego, 61
    around the United States, 43
Transit Store, 49, 51, 58, 62
Transportation, 55–62
    within Balboa Park, 136
    bus, 58–59
    car, 55–58
    for disabled travelers, 22
    rail, 61
    taxis
        to/from the airport, 49
        within San Diego, 60–61
        Tijuana (Mexico), 258
        tipping, 47
    transit information, 59, 62, 64
    trolleys, 59–60
    to Mexico, 6
Transportation Safety Administration (TSA), 27
Travel accessories, 198
Travel CUTS, 25
Traveler's Aid Society, 44–45, 63
Traveler's checks, 12, 40
Traveler's Depot, 196
Travelex Insurance Services, 21
Travel 50 & Beyond, 24
Travel Guard International, 21
Traveling
    to San Diego, 25–30
        by car, 29–30
        distances to other California cities, 30
        by plane, 25–29
        by train, 30
    around the United States, 42–43
    to the United States, 42
Travel insurance, 20–22
Travel Insured International, 21
Travel medical insurance, 20, 21

Travelocity, 32
Triathlon, San Diego International, 167
Trip-cancellation insurance (TCI), 21
Trolleys, 59–60
    to Mexico, 6
Trolley tours, 155
Tuna Harbor, 176
Turf Supper Club, 206
Twiggs Tea and Coffee Co, 206
Twilight in the Park Concerts, 17, 208
Two Years Before the Mast (Dana), 34

U CSD Medical Center, 63
U.K. citizens
    customs regulations for, 39
    insurance for, 39–40
    passport and visa information for, 36, 38
Underwater Pumpkin Carving Contest (La Jolla), 19
Unicorn Antique Mall, 194
United Airlines, 25
United Kingdom, embassy of, 44
United Nations Building, 184
United States Tour Operators Association, 31
United Vacations, 30
University of California, San Diego (UCSD) (La Jolla), 146, 150
University Towne Center (UTC), 198
Unofficial Guide to California with Kids, The, 24
U.S. Air Carrier Memorial, 176
US Airways, 25
USA Railpass, 43
U.S. Open Sandcastle Competition, 18

V alet-parking attendants, tipping, 47
Video, flying with, 29
Viejas Casino and Turf Club, 207
Village Hat Shop, 189
Villa Montezuma, 142, 152
Visa
    ATM Locator, 33
    credit cards, 13, 40
    traveler's checks, 40
Visa Information Line, 36

Visas, 36
Visa Waiver Program, 36
Visitor information, 11, 50
Visit USA, 42
Volcan Mountain Preserve, 250

Walkabout International, 24
Walking tours, 156–157
  Balboa Park, 181–186
  Embarcadero, 174–177
  Gaslamp Quarter, 168–173
  Old Town, 177–181
Wallet, stolen, 13–14
Walt Disney Travel Co., 234
Walter Andersen's Nursery, 153
Wambaugh, Joseph, 34
Warm Hearth (Julian), 249
Warwick's Books, 196
Water taxis, 61
Watts-Robinson Building, 170
Wear It Again Sam, 189
Weather, 14
  forecasts, 64
  weather.com, 33
WebFlyer, 32
Websites
  accommodations, 281–282
  airlines, 282–283
  travel-planning and booking, 31–33
Wegeforth, Harry M., 35
Weidners' Gardens (Encinitas), 215
Wells Fargo Historical Museum, 178
Welty Hotel/Temecula Hotel building, 229
Western Union, 14
Whale-watching, 15, 20, 155–156
Whaley House, 144, 180
What's Playing?, 200
Wheelchair Getaways, 23
Wild Animal Park (WAP), 2, 128–130, 151
Wild Arctic (SeaWorld), 130
Wildflowers, 15
  Julian Weed Show, 18, 247
  Wildflower Show (Julian), 247
Wild Water Wilderness (Knott's Berry Farm), 240
William Heath Davis House Museum, 142, 172
William Heise County Park (Julian), 250

William Penn Hotel, 171
Windansea Beach, 134
Windsor, duke of, 92
Wineries
  Disneyland, 237
  Ensenada (Mexico), 275–276
  Temecula, 225–226, 228
Wines
  Cava de Vinos L. A. Cetto (Tijuana), 262
  Harvest Festival (Guadalupe Valley, Mexico), 18
  New & Nouveau Wine & Food Tasting (Temecula), 19
  sightseeing for wine lovers, 153
  Temecula Valley Balloon & Wine Festival, 16–17
Wizard of Oz, The (Baum), 34
Wolfe, Tom, 34, 134
Wooden Boat Festival, 166
Woolworth Building, 170
World Bodysurfing Championships, 18
World Championship Over-the-Line Tournament, 17, 167
Worldwide Assistance Services, 39

X-rays, film, videotape, and camcorders, and, 29

Yacht Club, 177
Yellow Cab, 61
YMCA, 165
Your Open Door to San Diego, 58
Yuma Building, 171

Zagat Survey, 94
Zoo, San Diego, 2, 35, 126, 128, 150, 151
  pandas, 129
  Zoo Founders Day, 19
Zoo Founders Day, 19

ACCOMMODATIONS
The Anabella Hotel (Anaheim), 240–241
Anaheim Vagabond Plaza Hotel, 243

Artists' Loft (Julian), 251
Balboa Park Inn, 73–74
Bay Club Hotel, 93
The Beach Cottages, 78, 80, 82
Beach Haven Inn, 83
Beach Terrace Inn (Carlsbad), 217
The Bed & Breakfast Inn at La Jolla, 86
Best Western Bayside Inn, 70
Best Western Blue Sea Lodge, 82
Best Western Inn by the Sea, 88
Best Western Seven Seas, 78
Borrego Valley Inn (Anza-Borrego Desert State Park), 255
Bristol Hotel, 71
Candy Cane Inn (Anaheim), 243
Catamaran Resort Hotel, 78, 79–80
Comfort Inn & Suites, 78-79
Comfort Inn–Downtown, 72–73
Coronado Inn, 93
Coronado Island Marriott Resort, 89
The Cottage, 75–76
Crone's Cobblestone Cottage Bed & Breakfast, 74
Crystal Pier Hotel, 82
Dana Inn and Marina, 83
Days Inn Suites, 72
Del Mar Motel on the Beach, 212
The Disneyland Hotel (Anaheim), 241
Disney's Grand Californian Hotel (Anaheim), 241–242
El Cordova Hotel, 90–91
Elsbree House, 82–83
Embassy Suites, 68–69
Embassy Suites (Temecula), 229–230
Empress Hotel of La Jolla, 88
Estero Beach Resort (Ensenada), 278
Four Seasons Resort Aviara (Carlsbad), 217–218
Gaslamp Plaza Suites, 7, 71
Glorietta Bay Inn, 89
The Grande Colonial, 86
Grand Hotel Tijuana, 265
Hacienda Bajamar Hotel (Mexico), 273
Heritage Park Bed & Breakfast Inn, 7, 76

Hilton San Diego Airport/ Harbor Island, 93
Holiday Inn on the Bay, 69, 78
Horton Grand, 71–72
Hotel del Coronado, 6, 55, 90
Hotel Las Rocas (Mexico), 273
Hotel Las Rosas (Ensenada), 278–279
Hotel Lucerna (Tijuana), 265
Hotel Parisi, 2, 84
Howard Johnson Hotel (Anaheim), 243–244
Hyatt Regency, 84
The Inn at Rancho Santa Fe, 222
Julian Hotel, 251
Julian White House, 251
Keating House, 73
La Casa del Zorro Desert Resort (Anza-Borrego Desert State Park), 255
La Costa Resort and Spa (Carlsbad), 218
La Fonda (Mexico), 273–274
La Jolla Beach & Tennis Club, 8, 86, 119
La Jolla Cove Suites, 88–89
La Jolla Village Lodge, 89
La Pensione Hotel, 7, 73
L'Auberge Del Mar Resort and Spa (Del Mar), 212
La Valencia Hotel, 8, 84–86
Les Artistes (Del Mar), 212–213
Lodge at Torrey Pines, 1
Loews Coronado Bay Resort, 1, 7, 19, 78, 91–92
Loma Vista (Temecula), 230
Manchester Grand Hyatt San Diego, 1, 8, 67
Marriott Residence Inn, 84
Mission Valley Center Travelodge, 78
Ocean Park Inn, 83
Oceanside Marina Inn (Oceanside), 221
Orchard Hill Country Inn (Julian), 251
Pacific Terrace Hotel, 79
Palm Canyon Resort, 255
The Palms at Indian Head (Anza-Borrego Desert State Park), 255–256
Paradise Point Resort & Spa, 1–2, 7, 78, 80

Park Manor Suites, 74
Pelican Cove Inn (Carlsbad), 218
Portofino Inn & Suites (Anaheim), 242
Punta Morro Resort (Ensenada), 279
Radisson Resort Knott's Berry Farm (Anaheim), 242–243
Ramada Inn, 78
Ramada Maingate Saga Inn (Anaheim), 244
Rancho Valencia Resort (Rancho Santa Fe), 222–223
Red Lion Hanalei Hotel, 76–77
Rosarito Beach Hotel & Spa (Mexico), 268, 270
San Diego Marriott Marina, 7, 67–68
San Diego Yacht & Breakfast Company, 7, 72
San Nicolás Resort Hotel (Ensenada), 279
Scripps Inn, 87
The Sea Lodge, 78, 87–88
Sheraton Anaheim Hotel, 243
Sheraton San Diego Hotel and Marina, 93
Sommerset Suites Hotel, 75
Tamarack Beach Resort (Carlsbad), 218
Temecula Creek Inn, 230
U.S. Grant Hotel, 7–8, 70
Vacation Inn, 77–78
Vagabond Inn, 78
The Village Inn, 93
Wave Crest (Del Mar), 213
Welk Resort Center (Escondido), 224
WestCoast Anaheim Hotel, 242
The Westgate Hotel, 68
W Hotel, 1

RESTAURANTS

Allie's at Callaway (Temecula), 226
Anthony's Fishette, 174, 176
Atoll, 119
Azzura Point, 119, 120
Badlands Market & Cafe (Borrego Springs), 256

Baily Wine Country Cafe (Temecula), 230–231
Baleen, 110
The Bank of Mexican Food (Temecula), 231
Bay Beach Cafe, 119, 122
Bellefleur Winery & Restaurant (Carlsbad), 219
Berta's Latin American Restaurant, 108
Bread & Cie. Bakery and Cafe, 105
Brigantine Seafood Grill, 107–108, 120
Brockton Villa, 8, 117–119
Bully's Restaurant (Del Mar), 213
Cafe Champagne (Temecula), 231
Cafe Japengo, 116
Cafe La Especial (Tijuana), 266
Café Lulu, 10, 101, 208
Cafe Pacifica, 108
Cafe W, 102
Caffe Bella Italia, 9, 112
Calafia (near Rosarito Beach), 274
California Cuisine, 102–103
Carlee's Place (Borrego Springs), 256
Carnitas Uruapan (Tijuana), 266–267
Casa de Bandini, 109, 178
Casa de Pico, 109, 178
Catal Restaurant/Uva Bar (Downtown Disney), 244–245
The Chart House (Coronado), 120–121
The Chart House (La Jolla), 114, 177
The Chart House (Oceanside), 221
Cheese Shop, 10
Chez Loma, 121
Chive, 2, 98
Cien Años (Tijuana), 265
Clayton's Coffee Shop, 122–123
Corvette Diner, 105, 109, 208
The Cottage, 120
County Administration Center cafeteria, 174
Croce's Restaurant & Nightclubs, 10, 98, 171

Dakota Grill and Spirits, 8, 100

Delicias (Rancho Santa Fe), 223

El Agave Tequilaria, 2, 10, 108

El Charro (Ensenada), 279

El Nido (Rosarito Beach), 271

El Rey Sol (Ensenada), 279–280

Epazote (Del Mar), 213

Extraordinary Desserts, 10, 105–106, 208

Fidel's Norte (Carlsbad), 219

Filippi's Pizza Grotto, 8, 10, 101, 109

Fio's, 9, 99, 171

Fish Market (Del Mar), 213

Fish Market (San Diego), 9–10, 100, 119, 176

George's at the Cove, 114, 119

George's Ocean Terrace and Cafe/Bar, 118–119

Girard Gourmet, 10

The Green Flash, 113, 119

Hard Rock Cafe (Tijuana), 266

Hash House a Go Go, 102

High Tide Cafe, 113, 119

Hob Nob Hill, 104

Il Fornaio Cucina Italiana (Del Mar), 213

Jake's Del Mar (Del Mar), 213

Johnny Rockets (Del Mar), 213

Jolly Roger (Oceanside), 221

Julian Grille, 252

Kansas City Barbecue, 101

Karl Strauss Brewery & Grill, 114

Karl Strauss Downtown Brewery & Grill, 100

Kendall's Cafe (Borrego Springs), 256

Kono's Surf Club Cafe, 110

Krazy Coyote Saloon & Grille (Borrego Springs), 256–257

La Costa (Tijuana), 265–266

La Embotelladora Vieja (Ensenada), 280

La Fonda de Roberto (Tijuana), 267

Laurel, 103

Liaison, 104

Living Room, 118

Los Dos Pedros #1, 134

Los Dos Pedros #2, 134

Marine Room, 119

Miguel's Cocina, 120

The Mission, 113–114

Mixx, 104

Monterey Bay Canners (Oceanside), 221

Mrs. Knott's Chicken Dinner Restaurant (Buena Park), 245

Napa Rose (Disneyland), 245–246

Neiman's, 219

Nine-Ten, 2, 117

Old Spaghetti Factory, 8, 101–102, 109

Old Town Mexican Cafe, 109–110, 181

101 Cafe, 221

150 Grand Café (Escondido), 224

Pacifica Del Mar (Del Mar), 213

Palace Bar, 172

Pamplemousse Grill (Del Mar), 213

Panda Inn, 8–9, 100–101

Pannikin, 118

Paquito's Mexican Food, 134

Parallel 33, 104–105

Peohe's, 119, 122

Pizza Nova, 123

Poseidon Restaurant on the Beach (Del Mar), 213

Prado Restaurant, 186

Primavera Pastry Caffé, 123

Prince of Wales, 120

Princess Pub & Grille, 102, 208

Qwiig's, 110, 112

Rainforest Cafe (Downtown Disney), 246

Ralph Brennan's Jazz Kitchen (Downtown Disney), 246

Ramiro's, 134

Rancho El Nopal, 178

Rhinoceros Cafe & Grill, 122

Roberto's Taco Shop, 134

Romano's Dodge House (Julian), 252

Roppongi, 116–117

Rubio's Baja Grill, 10, 124

Ruby's (Oceanside), 219

Sammy's California Woodfired Pizza, 10, 123

San Diego Chicken Pie Shop, 106

Siamese Basil (Carlsbad), 219

Spice & Rice Thai Kitchen, 119

Star of the Sea, 97–98, 174

Sushi Ota, 113

Taco Surf, 134

Tea Pavilion, 185

Thee Bungalow, 112

Thyme In The Ranch, 223

Top of the Market, 9–10, 100, 119, 176

Top O' the Cove, 115–116, 119

Tour de France (Tijuana), 266

Trattoria Acqua, 117

Upstart Crow, 176

The Vegetarian Zone, 10, 106

Vigilucci's (Carlsbad), 219

Wolfgang Puck Cafe, 123–124

Yacht Club, 177

Hit the Road with Frommer's Driving Tours!

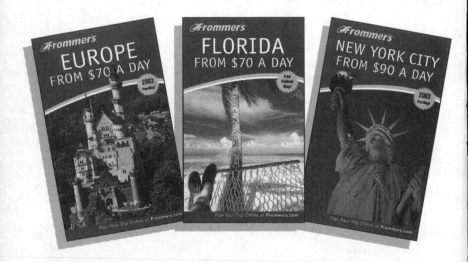

Wickedly honest guides for sophisticated travelers—and those who want to be.

TRAVEL LIKE AN EXPERT
WITH THE
UNOFFICIAL GUIDES

For Travelers Who Want More Than the Official Line!

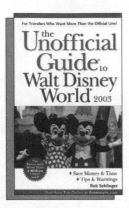

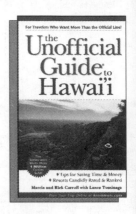

The Unofficial Guides®

Beyond Disney
Branson, Missouri
California with Kids
Chicago
Central Italy
Cruises
Disneyland®
Florida with Kids
Golf Vacations in the
    Eastern U.S.
The Great Smoky &
    Blue Ridge Region
Inside Disney
Hawaii
Las Vegas
London
Mid-Atlantic with Kids
Mini Las Vegas
Mini-Mickey
New England & New York
    with Kids
New Orleans
New York City

Paris
San Francisco
Skiing in the West
Southeast with Kids
Walt Disney World®
Walt Disney World®
    for Grown-Ups
Walt Disney World®
    with Kids
Washington, D.C.
World's Best Diving
    Vacations

Bed & Breakfasts and Country Inns in:
California
Great Lakes States
Mid-Atlantic
New England
Northwest
Rockies
Southeast
Southwest

The Best RV & Tent Campgrounds in:
California & the West
Florida & the
    Southeast
Great Lakes States
Mid-Atlantic States
Northeast
Northwest &
    Central Plains
Southwest & South
    Central Plains
U.S.A.

FROMMER'S® COMPLETE TRAVEL GUIDES

Alaska
Alaska Cruises & Ports of Call
Amsterdam
Argentina & Chile
Arizona
Atlanta
Australia
Austria
Bahamas
Barcelona, Madrid & Seville
Beijing
Belgium, Holland & Luxembourg
Bermuda
Boston
Brazil
British Columbia & the Canadian
    Rockies
Budapest & the Best of Hungary
California
Canada
Cancún, Cozumel & the Yucatán
Cape Cod, Nantucket & Martha's
    Vineyard
Caribbean
Caribbean Cruises & Ports of Call
Caribbean Ports of Call
Carolinas & Georgia
Chicago
China
Colorado
Costa Rica
Denmark
Denver, Boulder & Colorado
    Springs
England
Europe
European Cruises & Ports of Call
Florida

France
Germany
Great Britain
Greece
Greek Islands
Hawaii
Hong Kong
Honolulu, Waikiki & Oahu
Ireland
Israel
Italy
Jamaica
Japan
Las Vegas
London
Los Angeles
Maryland & Delaware
Maui
Mexico
Montana & Wyoming
Montréal & Québec City
Munich & the Bavarian Alps
Nashville & Memphis
Nepal
New England
New Mexico
New Orleans
New York City
New Zealand
Northern Italy
Nova Scotia, New Brunswick &
    Prince Edward Island
Oregon
Paris
Philadelphia & the Amish Country
Portugal
Prague & the Best of the Czech
    Republic

Provence & the Riviera
Puerto Rico
Rome
San Antonio & Austin
San Diego
San Francisco
Santa Fe, Taos & Albuquerque
Scandinavia
Scotland
Seattle & Portland
Shanghai
Singapore & Malaysia
South Africa
South America
South Florida
South Pacific
Southeast Asia
Spain
Sweden
Switzerland
Texas
Thailand
Tokyo
Toronto
Tuscany & Umbria
USA
Utah
Vancouver & Victoria
Vermont, New Hampshire &
    Maine
Vienna & the Danube Valley
Virgin Islands
Virginia
Walt Disney World® & Orlando
Washington, D.C.
Washington State

FROMMER'S® DOLLAR-A-DAY GUIDES

Australia from $50 a Day
California from $70 a Day
Caribbean from $70 a Day
England from $75 a Day
Europe from $70 a Day

Florida from $70 a Day
Hawaii from $80 a Day
Ireland from $60 a Day
Italy from $70 a Day
London from $85 a Day

New York from $90 a Day
Paris from $80 a Day
San Francisco from $70 a Day
Washington, D.C. from $80 a Day

FROMMER'S® PORTABLE GUIDES

Acapulco, Ixtapa & Zihuatanejo
Amsterdam
Aruba
Australia's Great Barrier Reef
Bahamas
Berlin
Big Island of Hawaii
Boston
California Wine Country
Cancún
Charleston & Savannah
Chicago
Disneyland®
Dublin
Florence

Frankfurt
Hong Kong
Houston
Las Vegas
London
Los Angeles
Los Cabos & Baja
Maine Coast
Maui
Miami
New Orleans
New York City
Paris
Phoenix & Scottsdale

Portland
Puerto Rico
Puerto Vallarta, Manzanillo &
    Guadalajara
Rio de Janeiro
San Diego
San Francisco
Seattle
Sydney
Tampa & St. Petersburg
Vancouver
Venice
Virgin Islands
Washington, D.C.

FROMMER'S® NATIONAL PARK GUIDES

Banff & Jasper
Family Vacations in the National
    Parks
Grand Canyon

National Parks of the American
    West
Rocky Mountain

Yellowstone & Grand Teton
Yosemite & Sequoia/ Kings Canyon
Zion & Bryce Canyon

FROMMER'S® MEMORABLE WALKS

Chicago	New York	San Francisco
London	Paris	Washington, D.C.

FROMMER'S® GREAT OUTDOOR GUIDES

Arizona & New Mexico	Northern California	Vermont & New Hampshire
New England	Southern New England	

SUZY GERSHMAN'S BORN TO SHOP GUIDES

Born to Shop: France	Born to Shop: Italy	Born to Shop: New York
Born to Shop: Hong Kong,	Born to Shop: London	Born to Shop: Paris
Shanghai & Beijing		

FROMMER'S® IRREVERENT GUIDES

Amsterdam	Los Angeles	San Francisco
Boston	Manhattan	Seattle & Portland
Chicago	New Orleans	Vancouver
Las Vegas	Paris	Walt Disney World
London	Rome	Washington, D.C.

FROMMER'S® BEST-LOVED DRIVING TOURS

Britain	Germany	Northern Italy
California	Ireland	Scotland
Florida	Italy	Spain
France	New England	Tuscany & Umbria

HANGING OUT™ GUIDES

Hanging Out in England	Hanging Out in France	Hanging Out in Italy
Hanging Out in Europe	Hanging Out in Ireland	Hanging Out in Spain

THE UNOFFICIAL GUIDES®

Bed & Breakfasts and Country	Southwest & South Central	Mid-Atlantic with Kids
Inns in:	Plains	Mini Las Vegas
California	U.S.A.	Mini-Mickey
Great Lakes States	Beyond Disney	New England and New York with
Mid-Atlantic	Branson, Missouri	Kids
New England	California with Kids	New Orleans
Northwest	Chicago	New York City
Rockies	Cruises	Paris
Southeast	Disneyland®	San Francisco
Southwest	Florida with Kids	Skiing in the West
Best RV & Tent Campgrounds in:	Golf Vacations in the Eastern U.S.	Southeast with Kids
California & the West	Great Smoky & Blue Ridge Region	Walt Disney World®
Florida & the Southeast	Inside Disney	Walt Disney World® for Grown-ups
Great Lakes States	Hawaii	Walt Disney World® with Kids
Mid-Atlantic	Las Vegas	Washington, D.C.
Northeast	London	World's Best Diving Vacations
Northwest & Central Plains		

SPECIAL-INTEREST TITLES

Frommer's Adventure Guide to Australia &
New Zealand
Frommer's Adventure Guide to Central America
Frommer's Adventure Guide to India & Pakistan
Frommer's Adventure Guide to South America
Frommer's Adventure Guide to Southeast Asia
Frommer's Adventure Guide to Southern Africa
Frommer's Britain's Best Bed & Breakfasts and
Country Inns
Frommer's Caribbean Hideaways
Frommer's Exploring America by RV
Frommer's Fly Safe, Fly Smart
Frommer's France's Best Bed & Breakfasts and
Country Inns
Frommer's Gay & Lesbian Europe

Frommer's Italy's Best Bed & Breakfasts and
Country Inns
Frommer's New York City with Kids
Frommer's Ottawa with Kids
Frommer's Road Atlas Britain
Frommer's Road Atlas Europe
Frommer's Road Atlas France
Frommer's Toronto with Kids
Frommer's Vancouver with Kids
Frommer's Washington, D.C., with Kids
Israel Past & Present
The New York Times' Guide to Unforgettable
Weekends
Places Rated Almanac
Retirement Places Rated

Booked seat 6A, open return.

Rented red 4-wheel drive.

Reserved cabin, no running water.

Discovered space.

With over 700 airlines, 50,000 hotels, 50 rental car companies and 5,000 cruise and vacation packages, you can create the perfect getaway for you. Choose the car, the room, even the ground you walk on.

Travelocity.com
A Sabre Company
Go Virtually Anywhere.

You Need A Vacation.

700 Airlines, 50,000 Hotels, 50 Rental Car
Companies, And A Million Ways To Save Money.

Travelocity.com
A Sabre Company
Go Virtually Anywhere.